ONE MONTH IN TOHOKU

Advance Praise for
One Month in Tohoku

"A deeply personal story with a universal theme: what can one person do in the face of unthinkable death and despair? *One Month in Tohoku* provides an unexpected but welcome answer: whatever we set our mind to.

In the case of Caroline Pover, the question is whether there is any limit to the acts of courage and compassion this intrepid author, serial entrepreneur, and philanthropist can achieve, and her stirring account provides glimpse after glimpse into the mind of a real-life superhero at work. Each compelling chapter elevates the reader to hope and inspiration from the depths of Japan's crushing triple disasters — an earthquake, a tsunami, and a nuclear meltdown — all related with the unflinching kindness of a woman who overcame strokes and adversity to become a beacon of succour for others.

One Month in Tohoku is a heartwarming tale of thoughtfulness, dedication, and creative generosity, in which the author lifts up a forgotten community and changes the fates of countless people with the help of her extensive personal and professional networks — and her own hands-on tenacity. In this age of overwhelm, Caroline Pover stands out as a brilliant example of what is possible if we discard our jaded apathy and rediscover the joy of helping. A delight and a privilege to read."

— **John Munroe**

"This book is an insightful read into the long-term results of disaster and displacement, not simply a story of a one-person crusade; it is about compassion and uncertainty and perseverance in the face of staggering odds. It is about a group of survivors and those who felt compelled to offer a hand. Having spent considerable time there myself, I found written between the lines an interesting timeline of post-disaster life and recovery. As mentioned in the book, once the mud and debris are all swabbed up and carted off, the real struggle against time, depopulation, and abandonment gets underway, and the bitter battle between hope and despair begins."

— **Robert Mangold**

"This is an important record of the recovery in the peninsula, with its focus on the people who live there. Anyone interested in volunteering or donating to recovery work in areas affected by a disaster will gain so much from this book."
— **Ginny Tapley Takemori**

"This book is such an effortlessly exquisite account of personal and incredibly human accounts of just what long-lasting effects the earthquake and tsunami wrought on the people of Tohoku. I found myself increasingly invested in the lives of the individuals who came into Caroline's life as she did what she could to provide help. I think there are lessons to learn from how Caroline approached her vocation to help this remote region of Japan by listening to people in order to help them in a way that suited them best, rather than deciding what they needed, and it just seemed to be the most perfect way to help the people rebuild their lives in the face of the adversity they had faced.

I must confess I shed more than a few tears at the losses experienced by the people Caroline met and befriended; their tsunami stories were simply unimaginable, but in perfect balance to that aspect of this book, the humour and love shared between Caroline and the people of Oshika was so heart-warming and, in parts, hysterically funny, that there were a fair few tears of laughter, too! I even learned a few useful words in Japanese while reading this book!

This book was such a moving account of Caroline Pover's experiences in helping a large group of people who needed help. It made me face up to the fact that when aid is provided for a natural disaster, and the majority of charities eventually pull out of the area, help may still be vitally important, and without someone as tenacious as Caroline fighting in their corner, it is hard to imagine how the people on the Oshika peninsula would have fared over the years. This book is a tribute, not only to the lives lost, but also to the lives lived, and how love and friendship can make all the difference in the most difficult of circumstances."
— **Jo Shaw**

"Having lived in Tokyo for eight years, including the year after the Tohoku earthquake, I found this book jaw-dropping. It is an account of events there that has largely escaped mainstream media — even in Japan. We all remember the devastating images of the raw destruction caused by the tsunami, which were plastered all over the global media. This memoir transports the reader into the lives of the people most directly affected by this destruction, long after the cameras have gone."

— **Heath Rose**

"Reading the book took me straight back to the time after the earthquake and tsunami, when I visited Oshika-hanto and other parts of Tohoku. Both the beauty of the experiences I had there and the sadness and terror of being there came back to me through the vivid memories that Caroline recounts in the book. Thank you, Caroline, for documenting so much detail from your own personal experiences and for hoping that those who read it will be motivated and inspired to visit the area … it is truly breathtaking to visit."

— **Shelley Sacks**

"A great read — full of great takeaways for anyone who wants to get involved in any kind of disaster relief, aid, or volunteering activities. Apart from the incredibly moving individual stories, I think the biggest takeaway for me was the concept of throwing away preconceptions of any kind and just listening to people speak, hearing their needs, and responding accordingly. So true — not only in relief situations but also in any kind of relationship, I feel. Lots of life lessons for everyone."

— **Tim Burland**

"This is a captivating account of one woman's experience of the Tohoku tsunami and her commitment then, and still today, to support the people of a little-known Japanese town called Oshika whose lives were so devastatingly affected. We learn that this was an incredibly close community, entrenched in traditional beliefs, values, and livelihoods, that was so brutally wiped out on that historic day. Caroline's writing is honest, heart-warming, and humorous, and her outstanding dedication and compassion is obviously evident to the reader. Beautifully written, *One Month in Tohoku* provides us, in our materialistic world, with food for thought about what actually really matters — love, compassion, and friendship — which go a long way in healing the aftermath of such destruction."

— Sarah Laine

"I was totally enthralled — my attention was grabbed right from *that* opening! *One Month in Tohoku* took me back to that fateful day and I welled up quite a bit at certain points; I felt like I was right there with the author. The interactions and buildup of relationships in the book reflect very moving and emotional moments, but alongside that, there is the laughter, the joking and the 'naughtiness' that vividly highlights the endurance and strength of the human spirit against quite tragic circumstances. Caroline has given names and personalities to the people affected and that has made it all the more real."

— S. Z. Cairney

Other books by Caroline Pover

Being A Broad in Japan:
Everything a Western woman needs to survive and thrive

Guide to International Schools in Japan
(English and Japanese editions)

Ask Caroline
(student and teacher editions)

Love with a Western woman: A guide for Japanese men
(English and Japanese editions)

ONE MONTH IN TOHOKU

AN ENGLISHWOMAN'S MEMOIR
ON LIFE AFTER THE JAPANESE TSUNAMI

CAROLINE POVER

One Month in Tohoku: An Englishwoman's memoir on life after the Japanese tsunami

Author, designer, typesetter: Caroline Pover
Proofreader and editor: Cindy Fujimoto
Cover design: Chris May
Maps: Chris May and Caroline Pover
Photos: Cover, author, and inside images ©Caroline Pover unless otherwise indicated. Photo editing by Dexter Fry.

Cover photo: The author took this sunset photo on Oshika, from the village of Oharahama. The sunset was one of the reasons that samurai warlord Date Masamune fell in love with the area. The silhouettes in the foreground are the huge black sandbags that lined the entire Oshika coastline after the tsunami. They were put there to prevent tides from flooding what was left of the villages; the land had permanently sunk by over a metre after the earthquake. The author was fascinated by the images presented by these sandbags, and to her they came to represent the strength and resilience of the local people. The sandbags in Oharahama remained for six years after the disaster, when they were replaced by a six-metre-high seawall that blocked any view of the sea and sunset.

Copyright ©2020 by Caroline Pover. All rights reserved. No part of this book may be reproduced in any form or by any electronic or mechanical means, including information storage and retrieval systems, without permission in writing from the publisher, except by a reviewer who may quote brief passages in a review. For information, please contact the author at caroline@carolinepover.com.

First edition.

ISBN 978-1-8380727-0-4

All events in this book are factual, but some names have been changed to protect privacy.

Although the author and publisher have made every effort to ensure the accuracy and completeness of the information contained in this book, they assume no responsibility for errors, inaccuracies, omissions, or any other inconsistency herein. Caroline Pover and Alexandra Press shall not be liable in the event of incidental or consequential damages in connection with the use of information contained in this book.

For Mabel, Freddie, Zachary, and Hattie

Foreword

On March 11, 2011, a massive earthquake — 9.0 on the Richter scale, the strongest in Japanese history and the fifth most powerful ever recorded in the world — erupted in the sea off the northeast of Japan, near the Tohoku region. Although the earthquake itself resulted in comparatively few fatalities, the tsunami that followed an hour later did devastating damage to many towns and villages along the Tohoku coast — and went on to destroy the Fukushima Daiichi nuclear reactor, a hundred kilometres to the south, causing the most serious nuclear accident since Chernobyl in 1986. The final death toll from the tsunami is still unclear — nearly 16,000 people are known to have died and 2,500 are still missing.

I was the British Ambassador to Japan at that time. In the Embassy's emergency response, we liaised with the Japanese authorities in providing assistance on the ground; I travelled with the first Embassy consular team to the affected region that weekend to help find British residents and travellers in the area who were caught up in the disaster. And over the next two years I made a number of visits to the area as part of the reconstruction process, in which the British government and so many British people and organizations in the UK and Japan were involved. The extraordinary fortitude of the Japanese people as they dealt with the immediate aftermath of this terrible natural catastrophe is etched on my mind.

Caroline Pover had lived in Japan for fifteen years as a businesswoman, entrepreneur, teacher, publisher, and editor when the earthquake happened. Back in the UK, she raised people's awareness about what was happening in

Japan and collected donations to help with the immediate needs of the communities that had been torn apart by the disaster. She had delivered this assistance to a remote region, the Oshika peninsula, and moved by the way she saw the people there beginning to rebuild their lives, she devoted more and more of her time in Tokyo and Britain to raising funds for them. She returned to Oshika, and particularly the village of Ohara, again and again, living and working in the community, helping her new friends there with reconstruction projects, mobilizing support for them elsewhere, and making a real contribution to their economic and, more importantly, psychological recovery.

One Month in Tohoku is the story of that work. It is an engaging and very personal story of one woman's journey, and of the energy and dedication she brought to the task of helping to rebuild a shattered community. In the almost ten years since the tsunami, her efforts have funded more than thirty projects in Oshika, and Caroline has spent some time there each year — except during the recent pandemic, which has so cruelly disrupted everyone's lives. As she says in this record of her work: "One friend [named] me as someone who had 'adopted a village.' But in all honesty, I think Ohara adopted me." The book introduces us to many people who live in a remote region of Japan, and whose courage and resilience in the face of great suffering — and earthy good humour as East meets West in a common endeavour to recover from adversity — are an example to us all.

— Sir David Warren, KCMG
British Ambassador to Japan, 2008–2012
June 2020

Acknowledgments

I must first thank the bilingual Japanese volunteers I met in my early days on Oshika, when my Japanese language skills left a lot to be desired. Seiji Yoshimura, Hiroyuki Okuda, Tsukasa Kurosawa, Hanako Yokota, and Chise Horikoshi — you showed kindness and patience to this strange Englishwoman who appeared from nowhere, telling me many of the stories of the little villages and their people that appear in this book. I'm sure it would otherwise have taken me forever to find out those stories for myself. You introduced me to so many people, and facilitated so many discussions, doing this when you already had enough of your own work to do. I am incredibly grateful.

Thank you to all the people who helped jog my memory or assist with factual details as I reflected on the past ten years: Andrew Abbey, Gillian Ashcroft, Jamie El-Banna, Sarah Gould, Megan Jones, Robert Mangold, Robin Maynard, April McBride, Justin McCurry, Duane Parnell, Shelley Sacks, and Ginny Tapley Takemori. And thank you also to those who answered questions when I couldn't be on Oshika myself due to coronavirus's impact on global travel: Joseph Calandria, Kolby Imai, Takashi Matsumoto, Kit Nagamura, Yuki Onodera, Shigenori and Miyoko Sasaki, Tadashi Takemori, and Mika Yanagibashi.

Thanks again to Robert, Shelley, and Ginny; along with Emily Downey, Sarah Laine, Jim McKinley, and Heath Rose, for reading my first drafts, and for being so encouraging. Heath in particular — you spent so much time reading everything so carefully and your feedback was invaluable.

Chris May, thank you for working your magic on the cover, and Cindy Fujimoto, thank you for all the attention you pay to ensure my words are the best they can be. What an absolute pleasure to be working with you both again after all these years. And my sincere thanks goes to Sir David Warren for taking the time to write the Foreword to the book.

I want to thank the people involved in my pickling business, Auntie Caroline's, for making it possible for me to take a whole month off the business in order to write this book. Thank you to Matthew and Jack Smith for working so incredibly hard in the months leading up to my writing break to ensure that I had plenty of stock and all shop orders were filled. Thank you to all the shops and individuals that support my pickle business, and gave me the time and — let's be honest — the income to write. And thank you to my fellow traders at Cirencester Charter Market for watching my unstaffed stall and taking care of any customers.

Matthew — thank you also for your patience when I turned the living room completely upside down, and your understanding when I had to rearrange the room "just so" in order to feel able to write. And thank you for all the loving hugs when memories of the past ten years triggered overwhelming emotions and tears in me.

Thank you to everyone who has been part of everything I have done to support the people of Oshika during the past ten years — people who have donated time, supplies, or money; people who have invited me to give talks; people who have made the effort to visit and see the beauty of the peninsula for themselves; and people who have spread the word and so kept the lives of the tsunami survivors in other people's minds.

And finally, thank you to the people of Oshika, for sharing your lives with me during your most vulnerable time. For allowing me to share your lives with others. For welcoming me into your homes. And for welcoming me into your hearts.

You will forever be in mine.

Caroline Pover
August 2020

Oshika Project Sponsors

My most sincere thanks goes to the following individuals and organizations that have donated money toward projects that have helped the people of Oshika as they have taken steps toward rebuilding their lives. There are countless others who have donated items such as clothing to the free shop, or cat food to the Sasakis, as well as space in their homes to host Oshika visitors. If I unintentionally left anybody out, please, please let me know and I will amend this list for future editions, and ask you to accept my apologies.

None of this would have been possible without your generosity. Much love to you.

Group Sponsors

3rd Tokyo Rainbows
Amity Yokohama
Association of Women in Finance
Azabu Music Together
Bolham Community Primary School
Bratton Fleming Community
  Primary School
Farmor's School
Foreign Executive Women
Foreign Wives of Japanese Men
Furla Yoga
Happy Days International Preschool
  and Kindergarten
Helping Hands for Japan
HOPE International
India International School
International Women's Network in
  Tsukuba
Jambo
Japan Intercultural Consulting
Kendal Choral Society
Kids World
King Henry VII School
Kspace International School
Married in Japan
Meikei High School

Group Sponsors (cont.)

Microscooters Japan
Miyabi Arashi Taiko Group
Nagoya Expat Help
Northowram Primary School
Notre Dame Roman Catholic School
Ohana International School
Oxford Japan community
Peace by Piece
Planet Depos
Riken BSI PDFA
Rotary Club of Plympton
Sainsbury's Leamington
Shizen Yoga Studio
St Alban's Nursery
Summerhill International School
Sun and Moon Yoga
Thomas Keble School
Tokyo International Kindercare
Tokyo Mothers' Group
Tokyo Photowalkers
Waseda International School
Waterbeach Community Primary School

Individual Sponsors

Mike Alfant
Narmina Aslanova
Samantha Aso
Peter Bacon
Aya Bird
Stephen Bird
Claire Brown
Vanessa Buswell
Lara Chho
Philippe and Myriam Cols
Nuala Connolly
Jackie Cumming
Katherine Delp
Nora Dessing
Katie Dingley
Kevin Dodd
Emily Downey
Sabine Dume
Cathy Eburst
Carole Faucher
Chris Foskett
Ken Fujioka
Naoko Fukai
Stephen Gill
Maria Godebska
Mathew and Marian Godebska
Marian Hara
Roslyn Hayman
William Hill and Kellie Fitzmaurice
Jacinta Hin
Debbie Howard
Moko Igarashi
Ruthie Iida
Minoru Iketani
May Ishikawa
Angela Jeffs
Nick Johnston
Akira Kagawa
Kathleen Kano
Lucie Kapner
George Karger
Erin Kennedy
Maria Kikillos
Marian Kinoshita
Rochelle Kopp

Miyuki Kurihara
Bonson Lam
Masumi Le
Alison Lester
Mikiko Lethbridge
Natsuko Lobo
Veronica Lonsdale
Tom Lovell and Meha Thind
Leza Lowitz
Julian Lusardi
Annette Macandrew
Barbara Manning
Nick Masee
Michiyo Matsumoto
Robin Maynard
Jane McDonald
Tara McNulty
Anna Mertens
Rika Meynell
Yuriko Miyazaki and Andrew Robinson
Sarah Mulvey
Allan Murphy
Jeorge Nadia
Lorna Nagamine
Erin Levine Nakamura
Iwao Nishiumi
Patricia Nyiri
John O'Brien
Catherine O'Connell
Sue O'Regan
Kirk Patterson
Tricia Perhirin
Lorelle Phoenix
Carolyn Pieroway
Nick Plummer

Alison Pockett
Jay Ponazecki
Cindy Price
Dan Raines
Jean-Guy Rioux
Mayoko Rutledge
Angela Saeki
Noriko Saji
Jeremy Sanderson
Eri Sato
Grace Sekimitsu
Ai Shimohama
Kenzo Shiomi
Satoshi and Shina Shiraki
Matthew Smith
Nadia Sobert
David Stetson
Soness Stevens
Kit Stock
Monique Strauss
Lucy Sturman
Anita Symonds
Junichi Taguchi
Alastair Taylor
Tracey and Ashley Thredgold
Martin Urban
Euft van der Berg
Liane Wakabayashi
Bill Ward
Rick Weisburd
John and Emi Whetsel
Maureen Wipf and Aziz Besalely
Samantha Woodgate
Victoria Yardley
Mariko Yasuda
Marcus Yeung

Preface

I wrote this book in a month — 29 days to be exact. But it had been writing itself in my head for almost nine years before the urge to get it all out became overwhelming. I had been blogging throughout those years, but blogging didn't feel like enough. The people of Oshika deserve more.

At 2:46 p.m. on March 11, 2011, a massive earthquake of magnitude 9.0 occurred off the northeastern coast of Japan, shaking the entire country for six minutes. It was quickly followed by a tsunami that in some places reached as high as 40 metres, and travelled up to 10 km inland, triggering a cooling system failure at Fukushima Daiichi Nuclear Power Plant. The tsunami completely destroyed 120,000 buildings and partially destroyed over a million. It took five million tons of debris back out to sea with it. Almost 16,000 people died, and 2,500 are still missing. Half a million people were displaced.

During the almost ten years since the disaster known as the Great Tohoku Earthquake (referred to as "March 11" and "311" in the text of this book), I have spent an average of one month per year living alongside the fishermen and women of a tiny village of just seventy people, on a very remote peninsula called Oshika. Oshika, as the closest part of Japan to the earthquake's epicentre, was the first part of Japan to be hit by the tsunami. And it has been one of the last places to recover — at the time of writing, reconstruction is still ongoing.

I am not a relief worker, or a disaster expert, and I have never been to any other disaster zones before or since — I just felt compelled to help here. I couldn't *not* help.

I first visited Oshika in the weeks soon after March 11, when the peninsula looked like something you only ever see in a disaster movie. Despite that, I fell in love with the place. Over the years I have witnessed both the physical and emotional recovery first-hand, documenting everything along the way. I never planned to write a book about Oshika — but the desire to share Oshika's story just grew stronger and stronger.

I am sharing Oshika's story because I want to encourage people to look beyond the images we see in the media whenever and wherever disasters occur; to know that when the images disappear from the media, people are left to pick up the pieces of their lives and they have to try to rebuild. Rebuilding — both practically and emotionally — after a disaster is an arduous and extremely complicated process that goes on much, much longer than any of us would like to believe. And it never really ends.

These are *real* people — people who were living full and complete lives before disaster struck. Time stops at the moment of any trauma, and nothing is ever the same again. The people affected are faced with the challenge of determining a new normal. And the rest of their lives will be focused on accepting that new normal.

I also want to share Oshika's story because the humour and laughter I found in this beautiful place are certainly not *at all* what I expected to find in the aftermath of such a massive tragedy. I hope that readers find moments in this book that make them shed tears of laughter as well as sadness.

Another reason for writing this book is that I hope to perhaps inspire people to dedicate part of their lives to the service of others — to volunteer either within their own communities or elsewhere. To always look around them and think, how can I affect this person or place in a positive way? How can I leave this person or place better than the way I found it?

And there are seven much-adored nieces and nephews that I especially want to inspire. This book is not just a story about the impact of a natural disaster in a remote part of Japan; it's also a story about what a crazy auntie gets up to when she takes those long trips back "home."

I cleared my entire schedule for the whole month of March 2020 in order to write this book — I wrote one chapter a day and did not stop until each chapter was done. While I had written four books before, I had never written a memoir, and I hadn't expected the process to be so all-consuming. I woke up way before my alarm went off, when that day's chapter immediately started writing itself in my head. I'd get it all out by writing all day, then go for a run, only to find the next chapter racing through my head as I raced through the streets of Cirencester. It felt like I was reliving every single moment, and the emotional rollercoaster I found myself on was challenging at times. But I found something beautiful in that challenge, too.

I wrote this book when the whole world was dealing with coronavirus. When I started writing, China was already in lockdown, but life in the UK was relatively normal. When I was halfway through writing, the UK also went into lockdown, but because I was hidden away and so focused, I barely noticed. When I did come up for air, I was deeply saddened by the actions of the people who'd stripped the supermarkets bare while I was reliving a time where I remembered having to beg people who'd lost everything in a natural disaster to take more than just one free tube of toothpaste.

I did not write this book because I want to share a story of disaster; I want to share a story of love, kindness, compassion, and resilience. I want to share the story of a very special community of people, and the way in which they live — everybody takes care of everybody else: they trust each other, put the needs of their community above an individual's needs, listen more than they talk, find ways to laugh even when they want to cry, look for similarities rather than differences, don't care which country you're from nor the colour of your skin, and share *everything*, even when they have nothing.

It is a beautiful way to live, and I feel like we need to be reminded of this in today's world.

Introduction

This book will mean different things to different people — if you're looking for a story that tells you about the long-term *human* impact of a disaster, you'll find it. If you want to learn about volunteering, then you'll find that, too. It will appeal to anyone interested in Japanese culture, or anyone who's ever thought about visiting or living in Japan. It would be a useful tool for any teacher with students interested in learning about natural disasters or about a significant period in Japan's history — I tried with all my might to keep my swearing to a minimum!

Despite the timeline of this memoir spanning a decade, I decided to call it *One Month in Tohoku* because the first month I spent there unexpectedly became a truly life-changing experience for me; an experience that led to a lifelong bond and commitment. It was during that month that the seeds of deep love and friendship were sown, and I discovered such strength and patience not just in the people of Oshika, but in myself — I never knew I had it in me. And it was a month during which my Oshika friends became utterly baffled by this strange Englishwoman — on my subsequent visits they were used to me, but that first time ... it was a month full of surprises for all of us. I had no idea what to expect during that time, and I was surprised to find myself emotionally investing so very deeply in this beautiful place and its beautiful people.

In writing this book I also wanted to plant the idea that any of us can take one month out of our life and dedicate it entirely to others. What would that month look like? Where would you go? What would you do? It's exciting to think about!

I really recommend that you read the whole book and then reread Chapter 6: Oshika-hanto — it will feel completely different to you on a second reading.

And if you'd like to specifically know more about volunteering, there's a "warts and all" blog entry on my website www.carolinepover.info that outlines what, in my opinion, makes a good volunteer (and what makes a bad one). You'll also find details about how to get to Oshika and where to stay, if you're thinking of visiting.

In this book I have deliberately been inconsistent in the ways I have referred to people, referring to them in the same way that I refer to them in real life. For some people I have used first names only; for others I have used their full names. I have referred to some Japanese people by surname with *san*, such as Onodera-san; but for some I have used the gender-specific English titles, such as Mr Sasaki and Mrs Sasaki — this generally has been determined by how I spend time with them. For example, I usually spend time with Onodera-san without his wife, whereas I usually spend time with the Sasakis together, so if I wanted to distinguish between the Sasakis, it was easier to use Mr or Mrs rather than san. And despite san (or *chan/kun* for a child or to show familiarity) being the appropriate way to address or refer to people in Japan, there are times on Oshika where I don't use either, but instead use a nickname — I have done the same in this book. For example, Yachan should really be referred to as Yasuhiro Naganuma (Naganuma Yasuhiro in the traditional Japanese way of putting the surname first), or Naganuma-san, but he is known by everybody as Yachan, so I've stuck with that.

I've also referred to the villages in different ways — most of the villages have "*hama*" (seashore) at the end of their formal names, such as Oharahama or Kugunarihama, but are locally referred to as simply Ohara or Kugunari. I have used both. The map of the peninsula on page 142 may be useful.

All of my conversations with Japanese people, unless otherwise indicated, were in Japanese, but I have reported them in English, and acknowledge that some things may have been lost in translation!

I've used different currencies (mainly British pounds or Japanese yen depending on where a specific fundraising effort or project expense occurred), but I haven't given the equivalent in another currency. This book spans an entire decade, and exchange rates fluctuate all the time. In general though, it might be helpful for readers to think of ¥1000 as being about £7 or $10.

It felt more natural to me to use Japanese words for certain things throughout this book, which I have attempted to translate on first mention. However, the following may be helpful if you need a quick reference as you read.

bento	packed lunch/dinner meals
danwashitsu	communal room in temporary housing communities
dashi	some may know this word as meaning "soup base," but in this book it means "festival float"
gaijin	foreigner
ganbatte	don't give up (also commonly means "do your best")
gareki	debris
genkan	entrance space after a front door where shoes are left before entering
genpatsu	nuclear power plant
giri-choco	obligatory gift of chocolate on Valentine's Day given by women to men
hama	seashore
hanto	peninsula
Igirisu	UK/England (the Japanese word sometimes doesn't distinguish)
ishigaki	stone wall
ishiku	stone mason
jin	person (usually a suffix for a compound word)
juku	cram school
kamisama	god
kanetsukido	bell tower
kanji	Chinese-derived Japanese characters
kanpai	cheers
kappa	PVC raincoat (on Oshika, specifically used in reference to the brightly coloured thick PVC overalls worn by people working in the fishing industry)
kasetsu jutaku	temporary housing unit/units/community (referred to on Oshika as "kasetsu")
koban	police box/mini police station
konbini	convenience store

kotatsu	low table with heated blanket to sit under
kucho	head of a village ("head of a ward" in some contexts, depending on how the municipality is referred to or the way it's named)
mandara	mandala (sacred Shinto art)
mikoshi	portable shrine
Nihon	Japan
onsen	hot spring
pachinko	Japanese gambling arcade game
sake	rice wine
shinden	the part of a shrine that houses the god
shinsai-go	after the disaster
shinsai-mae	before the disaster
shishi	lion mask
shishimai	lion dance
shotengai	shopping street
sutobu	a kerosene heater that is also used as a stove
tanuki	Japanese racoon dog
tarento	Japanese media celebrities
torii	gateway to a sacred place (usually, but not always, related to a Shinto shrine)
wakame	type of seaweed
yukata	cotton summer kimono
zuzuhoido	a local insult that literally means "an impudent or greedy person" but is a bit like calling someone a "wanker" in the UK

Contents

Foreword v

Acknowledgments vii

Oshika Project Sponsors ix

Preface xiii

Introduction xvii

Contents xxii

Prologue 1

ONE DAY IN TOHOKU 3

   1: Saipan 5

   2: England 16

   3: The Schools 26

   4: Heathrow 40

   5: Tokyo 48

   6: Oshika-hanto 59

ONE MONTH IN TOHOKU 91

   7: Preparation 93

   8: Back to Oshika 103

9: My Routine 111

10: Oharahama 119

11: The Ohara Boys..130

12: The Peninsula...143

13: Valentine's Day..155

14: The Sasakis 163

15: The Donations...172

16: Farewells and the Future 181

ONE DECADE IN TOHOKU 197

17: Gardens...199

18: Ohara Summer Festival 212

19: Creating Beautiful Spaces 223

20: Creating Beautiful Memories 236

21: What to Wear 247

22: Remembrance 258

23: Settling..268

24: Shrines and Wines 278

25: A Princess 288

26: A Prince 299

27: New Homes 316

28: New Year's 330

29: New Normal 345

30: The Tenth Year 353

BEHIND THE STORY 373

Prologue

January 2012: I squatted under the elevated highway, holding onto my knickers and the jeans that I'd pushed to just above my knees, trying desperately to keep my balance as I went for what felt like the longest wee in the world. The noise of the traffic above me masked my tinkling on the metal walkway just a few feet below the Tohoku Expressway. I'd held on for as long as I could, but when the traffic had come to a virtual standstill with no end in sight, and I hadn't yet got out of Tokyo, I knew I wasn't going to make it. Spotting a neon emergency exit sign, I had pulled over, thinking that Japan, with all its elegant efficiency and love of luxurious toilets, would surely have put a public toilet somewhere under the highway. It would probably be soundproofed and play relaxing music to give stressed drivers a few moments' escape from their journey. It might even be combined with a shoulder massage machine …

Of course there wasn't a toilet below the highway. Just a walkway, and the way my bladder was feeling, I wouldn't even make it to the end of it. I had no choice but to whip my jeans down and pray that the salarymen in the office immediately opposite wouldn't look out the window and see my wobbly white bum looking back at them. The mobile phones would come out. I'd be on YouTube before I'd done my zip up. My backside would become a *tarento* (Japanese media celebrity) in its own right. Or maybe my big white bum would be mistaken for the sun, equally blinding in its brightness on this beautiful winter morning, so typical to Tokyo.

Luckily, none of the salarymen saw me (although honestly, to this day, I'm not 100 percent sure), so it was back up the metal stairs to the highway, keeping my head down in the hope that nobody would notice me.

Who was I kidding? How could people not notice me? Just the fact that you are a foreign woman in Japan is enough for people to notice you. Drivers in stationary vehicles stuck in traffic with nothing to look at would *all* notice a Toyota jeep pulled over on the highway. I mean, who pulls over on a highway in Japan? And my entire vehicle was covered in Union Jack flags, which I had put on so that the people of Tohoku would know that the people of England were sending them lots of love. Instead, the people of Tokyo would think that the women of England weren't ladies at all, but just urinated wherever and whenever they felt like it.

What did I think I was doing?!!!!!

It was a question that, in the month that followed, I was to ask myself again many, many times. That, and "How did I get myself into this?" So let me back up a little and explain just how I got into this; let me explain how I found myself weeing under a highway in broad daylight, just feet away from the window to an office full of Japanese salarymen, as I set off to spend *One Month in Tohoku*.

ONE DAY IN TOHOKU

1: Saipan

After that one day in Tohoku, life would never be the same again for anyone who called Japan home.

I wasn't even in Japan on March 11, 2011. I was on an island in the middle of the Pacific Ocean. I'd decided to go to Saipan at the beginning of March for a week to be on my own for a while. I wanted to get away and immerse myself in writing a book for Japanese men on the topic of their dating foreign women. I didn't have a lot of personal experience with this, despite having lived in Japan for almost fifteen years. But during that time, I had learned a *lot* about foreign women in Japan — I'd published a magazine and written a book (both with "Being A Broad" in their titles!), given speeches, provided consulting services, and organized events, all with the intention of helping foreign women make the most of their lives in Japan. All of this made me well aware of the frustrations that many foreign women experienced in romantic relationships (or lack of them) with Japanese men. I wanted to write a book to help Japanese men in their relationships with Western women. I'd interviewed 150 women about their experiences with Japanese men, had all my research ready to go, and had set myself a target of 5,000 words per day. I was making great progress and meeting my daily targets.

I was staying at the Pacific Islands Club (PIC) Saipan — they were a client of mine that advertised in a Tokyo magazine I owned called the *Weekender*. They'd wanted to do a part-cash, part-room-nights deal, which I'd agreed to. Clients occasionally offered services in exchange for promotion, and in previous years when I'd had a bigger office and twenty employees it made me really happy to be able to give those perks to the staff. Having intentionally scaled down following a series of strokes I'd had a few years earlier, I now worked from a home-based office and had only a few staff, none of whom were able to go to Saipan. The room nights had to be used before the end of March and I wasn't interested in taking a holiday but preferred to use the time more productively — a week on Saipan would be the perfect opportunity for me to get this book done.

I loved my routine during that week on Saipan. Every morning I went for a 4 km run on the island before breakfast. I was 39 and had done very little exercise since I was a teenager, but in January I decided that I was going to start running. It had nothing to do with turning 40 that year, which I was looking forward to, and it had nothing to do with weight loss, which I'd never been interested in. Instead, I decided to start running because on New Year's Day I realized that some aspects of my personal life needed to change, and I was overwhelmed with a strong sense that 2011 would require incredible emotional strength. Running was the only thing I could think of doing that would get me that strength.

Within two months I went from shuffling along Tokyo backstreets in my Diesel trainers and slobby bottoms and sweatshirt (without a bra, much to the amusement of my "proper" running friends and more than a few Japanese construction workers) to maintaining a fairly respectable pace for 4 km every day (and by this time I had a decent pair of trainers and a sports bra).

After my 4 km run, I'd have breakfast in the massive dining hall, full of the families that generally comprise most of the guests at PIC resorts. I was the only person staying alone, and the staff always made a special effort to chat with me. I know that some people (especially women) hate eating alone and probably would never imagine going on holiday alone, but I loved it. Japan had taught me so many things, one of which was being able to eat alone, and I saw this as a bit of a badge of honour. I was very happy with my own company and had no problem doing things on my own.

I'd shower, then take my computer down to the open-air beachside restaurant. It was closed during the day, so I'd set up my laptop and look forward to hours and hours of uninterrupted work while facing the beautiful ocean just a few metres away from me. I'd spend the morning going through all my research, organizing themes that ran through interviewees' comments, and planning that day's chapter. I'd go back to the main restaurant for lunch, return to the beachside to write, and go for a 30-minute swim in the gorgeously clear sea, swimming out to the reef that surrounded Saipan. When I got back from the reef, I'd finish off the day's chapter. On the other side of that reef is the Marianas Trench, which is the deepest part of the ocean in the world. I found the idea of swimming out to it every day really exciting. Saipan was an amazing place to write and the words were pouring out of me.

I didn't interact with many people, which was fine by me. I did a lot of people-watching that, although fun, was very difficult on the day I wrote the chapter on what Western women find attractive about Japanese men. On that day I was immersed in all these women's comments about Japanese men's beautiful skin, lean bodies, and thick, glossy hair, and just a few feet away from my table was a large group of young Japanese men playing volleyball wearing just their beach shorts. *All day*. They weren't the only ones who got hot and bothered!

And the day I wrote the chapter on sex — well, I felt like a dirty old perv who shouldn't be allowed in a resort like this. Japanese families would walk past me, parents smiling and nodding politely, no doubt thinking, "Ah, there's that poor English girl who says she's writing a book, but that's probably because she feels badly about eating alone" — they'd likely be horrified if they knew that I'd just finished writing a section on penis size and was about to give instructions on how to be really good in bed.

By the Friday of that week I got to the final chapter on schedule and planned to leave the weekend for tweaking and perhaps a little bit of free time before I flew home to Tokyo that Monday. I got up from my table and was about to wade into the sea for my afternoon swim when I noticed a security guy with a walkie-talkie, going up and down the beach and looking out to sea. I heard the words "Tokyo" and "not pretty," so watched him for a while, trying to catch the rest of what he was saying. I had a very odd feeling and, remembering that we had had an earthquake in Tokyo just a couple of days earlier, asked the guy if anything was up. He said that there had been an earthquake in Japan, so Saipan was now on a tsunami alert. He seemed very calm but continued pacing and looking out to sea.

Suddenly, one of the staff from the bar next door came out looking for me and said, "Hey! You live in Tokyo, don't you? You've got to see this." I followed him in to find all the staff that were supposed to be preparing for that evening's shift instead standing around the bar, staring at the huge TV screen fixed above it. Nobody said a word.

The sea was destroying the country I loved.

Helicopters were showing footage of waves — no, not waves — huge *walls* formed by the ocean. Walls of sea water that grew bigger and bigger as they got closer to land, then crashed through buildings, buses, bridges, and boats — *anything* that got in their way. The walls of water grew dark and dirty as they surged on, dragging everything in their path along with them, causing even more destruction. Over and over again.

I'm not Japanese, but a little piece of my heart broke as I watched that footage.

It couldn't be real! All of us were transfixed by the television, which showed the tsunami over and over again. We couldn't stop watching it. Nobody could work out what part of Japan it was. I couldn't think straight at all. I'd look at the screen to my left, then look out to the beautiful ocean to my right … that same ocean. And, still out there, was the same security guy, walking up and down the beach, and staring out to sea.

Eventually I went back to my table. I didn't have an Internet connection, so couldn't get online to check what was happening in Tokyo. I just stared at my laptop, numb, not really knowing what to do or think. The security guy was heading my way.

"There's been a big earthquake and tsunami in Japan," he said.

"Yes, I've just seen it on TV."

"The tsunami's heading this way."

"What?" At that point I knew nothing about tsunamis and how they travelled across oceans, "Should we be concerned?"

"I don't think so. But if you see the water recede, let me know," he said as he laughed and walked off to the main building.

If you see the water recede, let me know? What the fuck? If the water recedes I won't have any time to let you know!

Maybe the security guy was joking. Maybe not. I looked around me … the beach was empty except for me. Do I just sit here and see what happens? I looked at my bikini, sarong, and flip-flops. Images of people running from the beaches in the 2004 Indian Ocean tsunami flashed through my head. If the water did recede, I'd have no chance. I packed up my computer and walked calmly to my room, changed into my running gear, picked up my passport, and headed for the lobby.

The lobby was in chaos. While I'd been sitting at the beach, Saipan had officially issued a tsunami warning and everyone on the island had been instructed to go to high ground. Most people had access to vehicles, so were driving off with their families. A bunch of triathletes who'd arrived a couple of days earlier for a competition were at the entrance getting their fancy bikes ready before heading off to an evacuation point together. There was no way I'd be able to keep up with them. I was on my own, and really not sure what to do. So I picked what looked like the nearest hill and started running toward it.

I laughed at the realization that I was literally "running for the hills." I wasn't panicking … just very calmly running as if I were going for a morning jog. No adrenaline or heart-pumping or any of those feelings that you'd expect to have — just very calm and collected running.

After a few kilometres a police car stopped and told me to get in so they could take me to high ground. They were driving around making sure everyone was making their way to evacuation sites and gave me a lift to the nearest one. On top of the hill they dropped me off on were a small fire station and an evacuation space. Nobody seemed to know what was happening in Japan because they were all focused on the tsunami warning for Saipan.

More and more locals turned up in their cars and the place got busier — my Japanese phone wasn't working and I had no way of finding out what was happening in Japan or to let anyone know I was OK. I'd travelled to Saipan alone and I knew my Mum would be frantic. One lovely local lady, Nora, had a small computer with an external Internet connection, so she let me borrow that to get on Facebook. Being a local, her phone was working so she said she had no problem contacting her loved ones with that, and was more than happy to lend her computer to me. Because of Nora I was able to contact friends in Tokyo, all of whom were very much shaken by the massive six-minute earthquake that had preceded the tsunami, and were dealing with the city coming to an abrupt halt as all transportation had shut down. I posted an open invitation to my Ebisu home, announcing that anybody was welcome to stay if they couldn't get to their own home that night.

I then reassured the UK people who were worried about me by explaining that I wasn't even in Japan, but then got them even more worried when I said I was on an island in the Pacific Ocean, whose inhabitants had been evacuated to high ground because the tsunami was on its way.

Nora, the firefighters, and I sat back and watched horrific images being broadcast on the Internet, as we wondered whether this giant wave would soon be with us. Villages, towns, and cities were engulfed in sea water. Houses were destroyed. Buildings were on fire. An airport had been flooded. To have access to information brought an odd sense of comfort, but also eliminated my until-then calm mood and instead, given where I was at that moment, sparked anxiety in me — perhaps something similar would happen in Saipan! I found myself constantly jumping at the sound of the trees behind us. Their swishing in the breeze sounded like water to me, and my sense of direction is appalling at the best of times — I had no idea where the sea was or just how high up we were. The fire brigade got called out, leaving only one firefighter behind to staff the office inside.

It was pitch black by now and you couldn't see a thing beyond the little clearing where the fire station was. Everybody was on edge.

Suddenly, some cars raced past the fire station, with the occupants sticking their heads out of the windows and shouting, "It's coming!" They sped past, shouting all the way, and all the drivers around me got in their vehicles and drove off in a panic, following the other cars as fast as they could go, before I could really work out what was happening. The car park around the fire station was suddenly empty. *Where the bloody hell do I go?!* The firefighter emerged from inside the station, asking where everyone had gone, and was met by me repeating his own question to him over and over again. He insisted that it wasn't safe to leave the site, so I had to stay there.

I sat down on the dusty floor again. I waited. And waited. Jumping at every sound those bloody trees made, not knowing what was on the other side. And fighting images in my head of giant waves crashing through them.

Red flashing lights suddenly appeared in the distance, coming toward to the fire station. Some huge buses pulled into the car park. And out of the buses stepped over a hundred men wearing orange jumpsuits, chained to each other, and accompanied by armed guards. I was in the evacuation area for the Northern Marianas Department of Corrections. And I was now surrounded by high security prison inmates.

It was all becoming very surreal.

At 11 p.m., the tsunami warning was lifted from Saipan. The inmates went back to prison, and I went back to the hotel, catching a lift in another police car. All hotel guests who weren't able to evacuate had been moved to the second-floor lobby, although a bunch of Russians had been found even higher up, hiding on the seventh floor and wearing all the hotel's lifejackets. The hotel staff reassured everyone that it was safe to stay at the resort now, although some of us were too spooked to feel reassured, myself included.

Even though I'd been on high ground, I'd felt very much on edge there, and couldn't get the images of Japan that I'd seen on TV out of my head. It genuinely felt like, at any moment, a huge wall of water would appear to swallow us all up.

I felt claustrophobic. The idea of sleeping in my room with the door locked made me feel very uncomfortable, so I sat in the hotel lobby watching the news, trying to absorb what was happening in Japan, while constantly jumping at the sounds of the water chutes in the swimming pool that sounded like water was about to crash through the hotel. By 4 a.m. I couldn't stand the sound anymore and reluctantly went up to my room, sleeping fully clothed and with my trainers on and the doorway clear in case I had to make a run for it.

In the first few days after March 11 I was confused by what had happened in Saipan — why the entire island had been evacuated so dramatically, yet we'd all been safe? It was a really scary experience, and I continued to sleep in my trainers for a few nights afterward. It was later explained to me that the tsunami *had* hit Saipan. The security guard had stood right where I was writing, and watched 15-foot high waves as they surged toward land. But the Marianas Trench blocked the waves, and they broke over the reef around the island. By the time the tsunami reached the shore it only went up the beach a matter of metres. It turned out that Saipan had had a very lucky escape, yet I was still consumed by a constant feeling of fear.

Years later (through very different means), I unfortunately learned about PTSD and the effects that trauma can have on a person. While what happened to me on March 11, 2011 is in no way comparable to what the people who actually experienced the tsunami and the earthquake that caused it went through, what happened that night in Saipan was terrifying *to me*. I was in shock for a week. I later heard from a non-Japanese friend, also a Japan resident who was out of the country at the time visiting a Pacific island, that she too was terrified at finding herself evacuated to high ground. Waiting for what you genuinely think will be "the end" results in great psychological impact.

I was consumed with fear after my own experience, which then moved into despair when I saw what happened to people in Japan. I then became consumed by a strong desire to help the survivors. I'd always been easily moved by people who didn't have the same advantages or opportunities that I did. Even as a child I remember raising money for Downham — a school for developmentally challenged children in my hometown of Plymstock — and volunteering there to help feed the pupils. This desire to raise money for charities or help those less fortunate continued throughout my life, from when I was in charge of Exeter University's student union charity fundraising committee in 1993 and came up with the idea for the now infamous Safer Sex Ball, which was initially instituted to raise money to prevent the closure of an AIDs centre, to hosting art and photography exhibitions attended by the Tokyo expat community to benefit numerous charitable endeavours. Volunteering, fundraising, and helping in general had always come naturally to me, but in the days immediately after the tsunami, I felt utterly useless.

I felt useless because, despite having lived in Japan for almost fifteen years, my ability to speak Japanese was appalling. I had always been too busy to study Japanese. When I first moved to Japan in the mid '90s I was teaching English in order to pay off student debts. With a full-time job in a school, an evening job teaching company classes, and private students on the weekends, I quickly paid off my student debts, but all that activity left me very little time for anything else. Nine months after moving there, I started my first business. I taught during the day and published a magazine by night, leaving myself about four hours' sleep a night. When I became self-employed full-time, that didn't save me any time at all because I was constantly working on developing my business. And after having strokes in 2006 and 2007, I spent the following years trying to decrease my responsibilities and activities, not add to them. I'm ashamed to say that learning Japanese, while living in internationalized Tokyo, with English-speaking employees and clients, was not a priority. At this point, I really regretted that. I felt that my lack of Japanese skills would prevent me from being any help whatsoever.

So I spent the week immediately after March 11 trying to get my head around my own fear and feelings regarding what had happened in Saipan, and at the same time desperately wondering what on earth I could do to help in Japan, given my pathetic Japanese language skills.

I wasn't glad *at all* to be 1500 miles away from Japan. I couldn't wait to get back home to Tokyo, and was due to fly back on the Monday. However, concerns were arising around the Fukushima Daiichi Nuclear Power Plant. Residents in that area were being evacuated and the first explosion had already occurred, sending many residents of Japan (Japanese and international) out of the country. I wanted to get back in, but was in a real dilemma regarding whether I should. After talking to Tokyo friends I decided to stay in Saipan a little longer, at least until my mind had cleared and I could work out what to do to help.

The triathletes took me under their wing in the week after the tsunami. They'd heard that Japan was my home, and wanted to check whether I was OK. I just sat around the hotel in tears most of the time. They were a kind, caring bunch, many of whom had taken up triathlons later in life, which I found very inspiring given my own late interest in running. Their triathlon had gone ahead on March 12, and they talked of how they had never swum in a sea like the one around Saipan that day. They had to swim out to the Marianas Trench for part of the triathlon, and they said when they got there the sea looked fine on the surface, but was pulling in all different directions underneath. It took a long time for the tsunami to calm down.

Triathlete Duane was still healing from an old injury, so couldn't join his mostly Australian mates in the various activities that are part of a triathlon event. He invited me to explore the island with him on the back of a scooter, and I was eventually persuaded to move away from the news and have my mind taken off things a little. He was incredibly kind, taking care of me when I was such a mess. Although I was supposed to check out on the Monday, I instead moved into one of the triathlete's rooms, which had a spare bed. It was a relief to not be sleeping alone actually, and I was very much in awe of my new roommate, Daz Parker, who was a Hollywood stunt double. I felt *very* safe in her company.

The triathletes invited me to joined them on a night run through the Saipan jungle. I explained that I wouldn't be able to keep up with them, but they assured me that I could — they'd seen me go off running in the mornings — and they were right, I could keep up! It was an amazing experience that finished as we sat around a fire and took a moment to think about the disasters that had affected Christchurch, Brisbane, and Japan in recent months.

But I felt guilty the whole time. I felt guilty that I was off exploring the island, and guilty to be sitting around a fire in the jungle after running with new friends. I felt guilty that I had a suitcase full of clothes, enough MAC makeup to open a mini-shop, crazy pink highlights in my hair, and my stupid special pink shampoo I had to use to keep it that way. I felt guilty about everything I had when there were people who had lost everything in the tsunami. People from a country I love so deeply.

My love for my adopted home runs deep. Japan hadn't always been an easy place for me to live, but after the first few years of adjustment, I fell in love with the country. I never planned on staying there as long as I did, but it started to feel like home in a way I could never have imagined. I love how polite people generally are, and how safe it generally is (especially for a woman). I love the seasons — spring with its beautiful cherry blossoms, being able to sit outside late on warm summer evenings, the beautiful trees and their changing colours in the autumn, and the freezing cold winters with their bright blue skies and glorious sunshine. I love the New Year's holiday in Japan — visiting the shrines, seeing the first sunrise, and enjoying how fresh, bright, and shiny everything seems. It is impossible to get the winter blues.

I love the juxtaposition of ancient shrines and modern architecture. I love how, in Tokyo, you really can do anything anytime of the day or night. I love it when someone simply raises their hand in front of them and bows their head as they slide in front of you, as an apology for cutting you off. I love bowing in general. I love phrases that don't exist in English but that show such thoughtfulness for others, my favourite one being "*otsukaresama deshita*," which acknowledges the effort someone has put into something. And I love the feeling I get when I arrive in Japan and walk through Narita Airport. That feeling of arriving home.

I sometimes wonder whether when you adopt a country, the love you have for it is deeper than what you have for the country you are born to.

And so, as the days went by, I thought less about my scary night on high ground, and less about how useless I felt. Instead I thought more and more about how much I loved Japan, and why; I became more determined and confident in my own ability to help. Just because I couldn't speak Japanese very well didn't mean that I didn't have other skills that could be helpful. I am determined and organized, and I have a "can-do" attitude to life in general. I hate being told "no." My huge network of contacts not only in Japan but also in the UK, despite my having not lived there for fifteen years, would prove indispensable! I had credibility … I'd received a number of awards for my business and philanthropic endeavours in Japan over the years. And I was a known public speaker, having even given a TED talk a few months earlier. I might not be very good at speaking Japanese, but I am bloody good at speaking English.

So instead of heading back to Japan, I decided to go in a different direction. I went to England. I had a plan.

2: England

I wasn't a big fan of England. I hadn't visited much during my years in Tokyo, and I had never been "homesick." The only thing I really missed was pickled onions, and when I'd eaten the entire stash I'd brought with me from England, I started making my own. When I did have to visit the UK, I just found myself frustrated with how impolite I felt everyone was, and how poor the service was. I found people to be racist, and winced whenever I heard someone use the word "Jap," even though they didn't mean to be unkind at all. It drove me nuts to hear everybody talking at the tops of their voices on mobile phones in public places. I found public transport to be unreliable, the streets were littered, and I was bewildered to discover that the whole country seemed to be developing an obsession with something called "reality television." I remember being picked up from Heathrow by an old friend, who greeted me with, "We've got to get back, it's the Big Brother finale tonight," and I had no understanding of what she was talking about, nor when reality TV had become more important than friendship. For a lot of my time in Japan, I didn't even have a television. I felt like I didn't belong in England. And every trip back was a reminder that I shouldn't be there.

But as I was tossing and turning in bed in Saipan, on the seventh night after the tsunami, it occurred to me that England was *exactly* where I needed to be. Because it was where I could be of the best use to the country I loved.

I decided that I was going to drive a van around the UK, giving talks to schools and community organizations. I was going to give talks on all the wonderful things about Japan and, in doing so, share my love for the country that I called home. The country whose disaster was currently being splashed all over the UK media. I was very aware that the images of the tsunami's destruction, including what was going on in Fukushima, were selling newspapers in England. I felt that these very powerful images might well be a lot of children's first impressions of Japan, and that they would likely stay with them. It upset me to think that this was how young English kids might feel about Japan, and I thought that perhaps I could do something about that. At a time when interest in Japan was at a high, I could counteract the horrifying and negative images being portrayed in the media by showing some beautiful images of Japan and talking about all the reasons why I loved it.

The talks were to be free of charge, but in exchange for the talks, I would ask schools and community groups to bring emergency supplies or whatever else was needed by tsunami survivors. And they'd have to keep the van topped up with fuel. That would be the deal. I'd then load the donations into the van, and get them back to Japan and to the people who needed them.

This felt like the *only* way I could possibly help, and absolutely the right thing to do. I had no idea what I could do from *within* Japan at that time … you couldn't get up to Tohoku to help, and I didn't speak good enough Japanese anyway. I didn't want to draw upon resources within the country when people were already panic buying, and at that point nobody cared whether that month's issue of my magazine didn't come out or my book wasn't finished yet. I felt I could be more useful in England.

The next day, exactly one week since the tsunami, I raced around Saipan, getting myself organized for the trip, with Duane helping me along the way. I managed to book flights from Saipan to the UK, via first Seoul, then Shanghai; get some contact lenses as I was on my last day of those; and get a heparin prescription. Since I had my strokes I have to inject myself with heparin — a blood thinner — when I fly long distance. And because the flight from Tokyo to Saipan is only three and a half hours long, I wouldn't have needed to inject any heparin, so didn't have any with me. Nor did I have any documentation proving that I needed it, but miraculously I still managed to find a doctor who would prescribe me an injection for the twelve-and-a-half-hour flight from Shanghai to London. Getting someone to prescribe the contact lenses was much more difficult, to my surprise, but I got them in the end.

I also got Virgin to agree in advance to fly any donated items I managed to collect from the UK to Japan. Iain Raymond was head of Virgin Atlantic in

Japan at the time. Iain and I were friends ... we went to the same networking events and shared a similar sense of humour, strong work and play ethic, "can-do" attitude, and love of dogs. He was also very direct and always said it as it is, which I love. We had frequently hung out in Tokyo, and he was a good, kind man — I knew that he'd do anything he could to support what I was trying to do, so I felt comfortable asking him for help. He understood immediately what I wanted to do, and agreed to assist, along with helping me organize the Shanghai–London flight. Given all the requests for help he was dealing with, the disruption to his airline, possible evacuation of British citizens to manage if Fukushima got worse, and his own family to take care of, Iain was incredible.

Once I got confirmation from Iain, I put a message out on my blog and Facebook page, telling people what I was doing and why. I asked for assistance in getting hold of a van, a satnav (mobile phones didn't have them back then), and some publicity, as well as welcoming schools in the UK to contact me about arranging talks. I cleared my diary — I still used a paper one (still do now, actually). I love a good list, so my diaries are always full of them, although instead of crossing things off, I highlight them in bright pink — I feel it's a more positive action that allows you to reflect on what you've achieved. But in light of my new plans, I needed to cross off everything that had been scheduled for what was supposed to be my return to life in Tokyo — lunch meetings, speeches, publishing deadlines, consulting sessions, intern interviews, beauty salon appointments — everything was frantically scribbled out to make space for a new focus. I didn't know it then, but I would never return to my pre-311 Tokyo life again.

I packed my suitcase and sat with the triathletes in the PIC lobby until late into the night. My flight wasn't until 3:30 a.m., so there was plenty of time. They were their usual chirpy selves and I was sad to say goodbye to them. Renata had given me her triathlon flower crown the day after her win, Allan and Julia had offered me their home in Australia if I couldn't get back to Japan, and dear Duane had not only made it his personal mission to keep me sane that week, but insisted on giving me some money to use as I saw fit. They had all been so kind to me when I'd felt so lost, alone, confused, and grieving for a country I loved so much. I wasn't aware of what an "empath" was at that point in my life, but having learned about them since, I now have a better understanding of why so many people were so deeply affected, the way

I was, by the loss suffered by so many people in Tohoku. Not to mention that it also felt like I was facing the possibility of losing everything I loved in Japan myself, because of Fukushima. The nuclear power plant situation had made all of us with a life in Japan completely uncertain of what the future held, or for how long that future might last. It was a very odd time and the uncertainty was just getting worse.

I was sad to leave my new friends, and I was sad to leave Saipan in general. Everyone on the island was genuinely upset about what Japan was facing. During my rushing around town that day, I'd been touched to see donation boxes for Japan in all the stores. The Hard Rock Cafe staff were all wearing special stickers on their T-shirts. And the Pacific Islands Club staff had been wonderful, some of them offered me their homes to stay in, too. I wanted to absorb all the love and kindness I saw expressed toward Japan, and toward me, and somehow keep it inside so that I'd be able to share it with others when they needed it.

But I was struggling with my own state of mind — I'm never very good when I'm faced with a difficulty and can't see a solution. I don't mind the difficulty per se, I just hate not knowing what to do, and the uncertainty of not knowing what to do during the past week had taken a toll on me. Along with constantly thinking about what the poor people in Tohoku must be dealing with, I found myself alternating between feeling numb and feeling terribly emotional when I saw images of the people in Japan and what they were coping with. And then I'd be uplifted by stories of babies being born by flashlight, old men being rescued at sea, and dogs staying beside injured friends.

The media coverage coming out of Japan was appalling, and was not helping anyone, least of all anyone with loved ones in Japan. My mother was getting herself in such a state and I wasn't even in Japan! It wasn't so much the footage of the destruction caused by the tsunami, but more the fear that the media seemed to be encouraging by discussing a number of potentially disastrous scenarios should the Fukushima situation get worse. I remember CNN's coverage by Anderson Cooper being the worst — I told worried friends and family to just stop watching it. I knew I couldn't watch it anymore, and I was glad to be able to escape the television coverage during my long journey to the UK.

My 24 hours in Shanghai provided plenty of reminders about why I loved Japan — not that I needed any more of them! I was initially refused entry to

China for lack of a visitor's visa, even though I had a flight out of there the following day, and when I eventually persuaded immigration to let me in, I asked a taxi driver to take me to the nearest hotel, thinking there should be one just a few minutes away. Instead he drove me about half an hour away from the airport, while I grew increasingly nervous, and he eventually dropped me off in some back streets of a residential area, and directed me into what looked like a normal residential building and not a hotel at all. I took one look inside the room I was supposed to stay in, felt that it was entirely possible that I'd end up dead in it, and walked the streets until I could find another taxi straight back to the airport, where I was harassed non-stop by people trying to get me to go and stay in their hotels. I resorted to swearing loudly at anyone that approached me — I don't care what anyone says, swearing *always* makes you feel better, and as long as you pronounce those swear words correctly it doesn't need to make you sound less intelligent. After foul-mouthing my way through the airport, I came across an actual airport hotel *within the airport*, checked in, and slept for 16 hours straight.

    I landed at Heathrow at 4:30 p.m. on March 20, and went to stay with family in Newbury. My little niece and nephews, so used to seeing bubbly Auntie Caroline on visits, were silenced by the tears I couldn't keep myself from bursting into as soon as I walked in the door. It had been a long, emotional journey.

    I hadn't had any Internet connection during the journey, so a couple of young British women who used to work for me — Marie and Erika — had been doing their best to coordinate things in the UK in the meantime. Marie was working in the media in England at the time, and had a lot of media contacts there. She was letting them know what I was planning. Between them, the girls had done a great job, with some talks already booked, and a few cars offered, but no van.

    Some of my friends had contacted the Japanese embassy and a few relief agencies to tell them about my plans to collect items and bring them to Japan — I think my friends secretly were of the opinion that I had given myself an unrealistic task, and thought that if I could work with an organization it would at least save me worrying about distributing everything. Everyone they spoke to was polite and extremely encouraging, but had absolutely no idea of how to distribute items either.

    On my first day in England, I hit the ground running. I got GazKaz, a clothing printing company in Newbury, to print three free T-shirts for me with the Japanese flag and the words "Help Japan" on them. I planned to wear them at every talk I gave and when I went running every morning — I liked road-running and didn't want to miss any opportunity to keep Japan in people's minds, even if they were sitting in traffic. I ended up wearing those T-shirts every day until I was to return to Japan. I also got some vehicle signs printed, and received a £100 donation. Not bad for a first day!

Collecting money wasn't in the front of my mind, and I was surprised when people insisted on giving me money. I wasn't a registered charity or any kind of organization. I didn't know what to do with the money that people wanted to donate. All I could do was just promise that I would get their money to Tohoku, keep a record of it, and deal with the financial details later.

I was in touch with a number of other foreigners in Japan who, like me, had been moved to do something to help but, unlike me, were actually in Japan and spoke really good Japanese. A Facebook group called Foreign Volunteers Japan had been set up and was the go-to place for information for anyone who wanted to help. Some people were already doing a lot of work to get donated items directly to where they were needed, and seemed to be having even more success than the relief agencies. I suspect that relief agencies have to wade through lots of red tape, of which there is *a lot* in Japan, even during a disaster. However, the foreigners I knew who lived in Japan at that time — especially the entrepreneurs, who formed a large part of my social circle and seemed to be doing a lot to help — generally had the kind of personalities that meant they just went ahead with their vision and worried about details or obstacles later, and then only if those obstacles occurred or the Japanese authorities alerted them to something they should have been paying attention to. This way of working is simply part of an entrepreneur's psyche, and how we all functioned when running our companies in Japan — you'd never start a business there if you worried about the rules. It was an extremely valuable attitude to have in these circumstances.

So I created a list of items I'd be willing to accept in return for giving my talks, based on the information I was gathering from foreigners who were on the ground and distributing donations. I would only accept items that had been clearly identified as needed, and I had to be strict with that. There was no point in just collecting anything well-meaning donors wanted to give — they had to be things that were actually needed. I sent the list to the schools that had already booked me, and asked them to circulate it among their communities.

I wanted not only to collect donated items that could offer practical support to tsunami survivors, but also to offer emotional support to other people who had been affected by the disaster. It was becoming apparent that people throughout Japan had been deeply affected by what damage the tsunami had wrought. Japanese male friends were telling me stories of depressions their wives had entered during the week since the disaster — people in other parts of Japan also needed encouragement to be able to help their struggling fellow Japanese. This gave me the idea, during my school visits, to ask the younger children to draw pictures of love and good wishes to give encouragement and provide support. And with older children, I would film them saying messages of support in Japanese. These messages of hope and love would be very easy to send to Japan, and would let the Japanese know that people from all over the world were thinking of them. Again, that idea of absorbing or gathering up love and passing it on to those who need it kept growing in my mind. People wanted to know how to help, and I kept trying to think of ways for my trip to generate support for Japan — both practically and emotionally.

So many schools around the country were asking me to visit them, and were willing to donate items that were very badly needed, but until I had that van, I was stuck in Newbury. I was keenly aware that the disaster could disappear from the media at any moment, and therefore from people's minds. Hundreds of thousands of people were desperately in need of help — I didn't know much about disasters, but I knew that help would be needed not just now but long term, into the future. I didn't want the people of Tohoku to be forgotten when the media changed their focus to the next "story."

I started preparing for the talks, focusing on putting together images that would counteract what was in the media. I went through my computer and put together lots of happy images of Japan to share — modern technology, Disneyland, sumo wrestlers, cherry blossoms, ancient shrines, women in kimono — anything that children and teenagers might find interesting — images through which I could teach people about Japanese culture, traditions, history, and life in general.

But still no van. I spent a day on the phone, calling about twenty van hire and removal companies to ask whether they would lend a van for a couple of weeks, but no luck. I was getting frustrated in not being able to get moving yet. I was becoming disheartened, and it wasn't helped by the nastiness that was developing on social media. Fellow foreigners judging each other for leaving Japan, as some had done in the days immediately after the earthquake because of concerns over the severe damage to the Fukushima nuclear power plant. Judging each other for *not* leaving Japan ... for putting their families in danger by staying there. Judging each other for overreacting or even for *reacting at all* — "stop making a fuss, everything's normal." Judging each other for not doing enough. My Facebook feed was filling up with people making unpleasant comments toward each other. Somebody designed a T-shirt for sale that said "I stayed," with the date of the earthquake; somebody else went to the effort of writing a poem directed at all the foreigners who flew out of Japan, ending with a desire for their planes to crash on the way out. I wondered what on earth was happening to the community I thought I knew.

I'd started to receive negative comments about my efforts, and my efforts hadn't even really started yet. When I posted the list of items I'd accept for tsunami survivors, and received this snide comment: "Japan doesn't need any more socks," I burst into tears. I was trying so hard to do what I thought would be the right thing, in the right way — giving people a way to help that I'd researched beforehand — but maybe I was wrong. I started to question myself. What was I doing? Why was I doing this? Was this a crazy idea? Who was I to think I could do *anything* of value to help in a disaster this size? What do I know about disasters? Maybe I'm not the right kind of person to do this! People think I'm tough, but I'm not. I'm too fragile. I'm sensitive. I get upset so easily. And I take things so personally. I'm not strong enough to do this. I don't know what I was thinking. I just wanted to help. And I couldn't even get that right — and still no van!

The next day, I got that van.

Hitachi Capital were thrilled to be approached to lend a vehicle for this mission — they had donated more than £2.5 million to fund relief efforts immediately after March 11 and were actually having a meeting about other practical ways they could help when they heard from a family member I had roped into making some calls. I really couldn't have hoped for a better result — they were offering a fully insured van for three months, fully signwritten by them, and the use of their PR team. I couldn't believe it.

That afternoon I gave my first talk. It was to a class of seven-year-olds at St John the Evangelist School in Newbury. I started by asking them what they already knew about Japan, and it was all earthquakes and tsunamis, as I'd suspected, so I showed them my photos — they were all fascinated by Mount Fuji and asked me lots of questions. This was wonderful — I had changed my first group of people's ideas about Japan. The teachers took the list of items needed; I planned on collecting them at the end of the trip, when I'd have the van. In the meantime, the children drew pictures of love and encouragement (lots of hearts and volcanoes) and wrote lovely messages to Japanese people. And they were thrilled to learn some Japanese words and be featured in a video I was making of English kids saying Japanese words of encouragement. I was overwhelmed with all the cuddles the little ones gave me, and I really wasn't expecting it at all. Again I got that sense of wanting to absorb all the love I received and somehow transport it back to Japan. I wished that everyone in Japan could feel all the love and kindness that came from these seven-year-olds in a little English town very far away.

The next day I headed off to Hitachi Capital in Trowbridge to collect the van — I couldn't have met a nicer bunch of people. They were so keen to have the van spotless, filled up with petrol, and with countless emergency numbers in case I needed them, and then insisted that when I returned it, I do so with an empty tank. They promised to collect donations between themselves for me to pick up when I came back. Nothing was too much trouble for them.

And then it was off to Plymouth, where I grew up, and where my mum still lived. I had six schools booked in for talks there, including my old comprehensive school in Plymstock. I was driving down on a Saturday and didn't have anything booked for that weekend, but I'd waited long enough to get started on this — I decided to just pull up in busy parts of Plymouth and simply ask passers-by to donate items. And I had a bit of backup waiting there in the form of my second niece, Emily, and my best friend Sarah from school, along with her teenage daughters, who I'd persuaded to join me.

My mother was convinced that I was going to get arrested if I just randomly stopped people on the street to collect donations. We had developed an understanding over the years while I lived in Japan that, in order not to worry each other, anything upsetting or stressful going on in our lives was better off not shared. And it had worked for us. She'd even had no idea how sick I'd been during the stroke years. However, there was no way to keep things from her during the past couple of weeks, during which I had become a constant source of worry for her. First of all for being in Saipan on my own, then being stuck on high ground with convicts during a tsunami warning, and then long-distance flying with all my heparin issues. Watching media coverage had got her absolutely beside herself, and it was the last straw for her to know that I'd be driving around England on my own in a van. To be fair, I couldn't blame her for that … the last time she'd seen me drive I'd forgotten that almost all British cars are manuals, so went half a mile in first gear, and narrowly missed knocking down one of her neighbours.

She had nothing to worry about though — I felt very comfortable and confident driving the little van from Hitachi Capital, which actually started my preference for driving vans, which I still have today. I posted some pictures of the van online, as well as some videos I'd made around Newbury and at the school. The response to the videos was quick, with Japanese friends saying that it brought tears to their eyes to see little English children wishing them well.

And a Japanese woman wrote that they were the first "happy" tears she had cried in two weeks.

3: The Schools

My old school, Plymstock School, had done a great job of alerting its community about my visit. It felt like everywhere I went people were collecting items to bring to the school for my talk. On my first morning in Plymouth, I popped into the corner shop after my run, to see whether the owners might be interested in helping. This was the same shop that gave thirteen-year-old me my first job, delivering papers. A couple of lads from the school were picking up their own paper rounds and one of them said he had spent the day before with his mum collecting on Plymstock's small shopping street — the Broadway — for Japan. I was so touched that I had to give him a huge hug despite being all hot and sweaty after my run, then hoped I hadn't traumatized the poor boy and resolved to make a special effort to be sweet-smelling and presentable by Tuesday when I was to visit the school.

Since March 11, I'd actually been having an odd reaction to anything that would make me "presentable." I was experiencing a massive rejection of things like perfume, makeup, hairstyling, and "smart" clothing. They all seemed hugely unimportant and things I didn't want in my life anymore. I had never been obsessed with my appearance, I'd never bought into media pressure to look a certain way, and I didn't have any negative body image issues (in fact the TED Talk I'd given in the December before the earthquake was about exactly that topic). *But*, the Tokyo lifestyle had gradually led to me wearing a full face of makeup every day, not leaving the house without styling my hair, and instead of in a wardrobe or closet, my clothes hung in a small room. The crazy colours on my face and in my hair, perfectly manicured funky nails, big fluffy coats, animal print skin tight jeans, and four-inch heels were all my way of rebelling against the conservative, male-dominated business world I'd found myself in as an entrepreneur. I'd more than embraced all the dressing up.

Not any more.

I had no time or patience for superficial affectation. How could I possibly look myself in the eye while putting on that shimmery eyeshadow when so many people had lost so much? How could I get any joy from those fancy clothes when there were people who now had only the clothes they were wearing when the tsunami swept their homes away? I wanted to spend every moment helping Japan, and any time I spent doing my hair, or thinking about what to wear, was time taken away from my mission. So I gave my MAC makeup collection to Sarah's eldest daughter, threw out the pink hair shampoo, took clothes to a charity shop (although I only had my Saipan clothes, so there wasn't much … the rest would be dealt with later), and was amazed at how light and free this made me feel. Every morning I threw on my running clothes (including one of the Help Japan T-shirts of course), went for a run, showered, tied my hair back in a ponytail, applied an absolute minimum of makeup, and put on the same clothes I wore every day — some borrowed jeans and a Help Japan T-shirt — and got straight on with my day.

Everybody seemed to want to do something to help on that first day in Plymouth. A long-lost cousin and his wife, Phil and Linda, turned up at my mother's house with lots of cardboard boxes, because they thought they might be useful. Yes! I hadn't even thought what I was going to put all the donations in. I drew the flag of Japan all over the boxes and planned to use them to put on the floor in front of me while I asked people for donations. Emily, my 17-year-old niece, joined me in the Guildhall car park where I picked a parking spot and opened up the back of the van, put the cardboard boxes on the floor, and handed out shopping lists of items we were requesting for Japan. The traffic warden turned a blind eye to me not paying for parking, and the police officers — instead of arresting me as my mum was convinced they would — took the shopping list and said they'd get the station on the case, too.

When the city centre started getting quiet we headed back to Plymstock and noticed that the big Morrison's supermarket was packed, so I asked the store manager, Ian Matthews, if he'd let us hang around the entrance for the rest of the day, which he kindly agreed to. I was amazed at the reception we got — lots of people already knew I was coming to the school, and one woman had actually brought a printed copy of the list from my website so she could shop with it in mind — this brought tears to my eyes. Some people had been to Japan or had had relatives living there at some point, and everyone loved the chance to wave the Japanese flag and say an encouraging Japanese word for my video. This was not the England I remembered, and I found myself overwhelmed by how much the hearts of the people of a country I had rejected many years ago were really going out to the people of a country I adored.

We ended up filling our boxes with sanitary products, toothpaste, toothbrushes, cotton buds, nappies, babywipes, pet items, underwear, toys, food, and yes, socks, which had stayed on my list despite the online criticism. I started itemizing everything. The Virgin team had already told me that absolutely everything had to be itemized in order to get the boxes accepted by Japanese customs — fine by me, queen of the lists. And people had again insisted on donating money, bringing the total I'd collected on the trip so far to £460. Ian kindly agreed to let me go back to Morrison's the next day.

It had been a great first day in Plymouth, but I ate breakfast the next day with tears pouring down my face. I had been focusing on helping from England, but constantly checking in with Tokyo to see how everyone was doing. My friends in Japan were talking about uprooting their entire lives and leaving Tokyo for a while, people were quitting their jobs, questioning their marriages, and having crises about their futures. Entrepreneur friends felt that their businesses were in serious jeopardy. This had all really upset me — I wanted to be with them so we could go through all this together. Comfort each other. Help each other make these difficult decisions. I felt so alone and I missed my home. And the tsunami-related stories coming out of Japan two weeks after the disaster were heartbreaking — a playground full of children that was swept away, the fields and fields of coffins being set up, thousands of bodies washing up on shores, volunteers in Sendai being told they could only volunteer for four days rather than the usual seven because of the mental health risk, and government organizations and relief agencies simply not being able to get supplies to everyone who needed them.

Every time someone in England told me how much they admired how the Japanese were coping it made me want to cry.

The next day I went back to my old school. I'd always kept in touch with my old Head of Sixth Nick Johns (although it felt really weird to call him Nick instead of Mr Johns), and I'd given speeches at the school whenever I visited Plymouth over the years. I'd loved my time at Plymstock School, and liked the idea of giving back to it. The teachers would ask me to give talks about the books I'd written, about running a business, or about life in Japan, and would always take me to one side, whispering, "Please tell them to leave Plymouth and see the world — the kids don't ever leave here!" This lack of adventurous spirit had become a big concern for the educators in the area. I hoped to perhaps inspire an interest in Japan by showing the students my photos during an assembly Nick had arranged with about 100 year seven students.

Nick had done a great job in spreading the word about my visit — as soon as I pulled up, kids came running across the roundabout area with boxes and bags for me to put in the van. And right after assembly, a huge shopping trolley appeared, full of items the staff had collected. The students got to work sorting and counting everything into boxes — it was a good feeling to parcel up a box of 200 toothbrushes and 200 tubes of toothpaste, knowing that that little box alone could play a part in helping a village feel like their lives were being rebuilt, even just a tiny bit. Ever since I found out about the difficulties that relief agencies were having in reaching everyone, the little villages of Tohoku had been playing on my mind.

By the time I left Plymstock School with their supplies, along with what I'd collected from Morrison's, the van was completely and utterly full, and it was only my second school visit! I was going to need somewhere to store things. In addition to a full van, I had a mobile phone to use — Mo, a former student at Plymstock who had coincidentally come to one of my speeches in Osaka years before, happened to also be in Plymouth and thought I might need a mobile phone to use on my trip. Life saver!

Then it was off to Laira Green Primary School, where I spent an hour with the 11-year-olds. They enjoyed looking at my images of Japan and were especially keen to talk about samurai and Disneyland before drawing pictures and writing lovely letters of encouragement to people in Japan. This visit was a last-minute arrangement and worked out really well because the students and teachers were inspired to plan their own fundraising and item collection (good job, because I had a full van to deal with already). This was so encouraging — if somehow I could inspire each school I visited to start their own initiatives for long-term financial, practical, or emotional support for Japan, then this effort would make such a difference to people. I was already beginning to think of this as a long-term undertaking.

I spent the evening reading a report that Tokyo photographer friends Dee and Tracey had written after volunteering in Sendai. They were beautiful writers and photographers, but I'd been dreading reading it. I took a deep breath and got started, thinking that the healing love and energy that came from all the kids I had spent that morning with would keep my chin up. At the end of each paragraph I had to compose myself before reading on, but it all became too much. The images of upside down cars and boats on houses shook me, but in an oddly detached way, whereas the images of Japanese people smiling as they clambered over the wreckage of their homes broke my heart. I was overcome with feelings of inadequacy and the knowledge that, despite all my efforts, the ways I could help were so tiny.

For now I had to work out what to do with this full van, given that I had three more Plymouth schools to visit the following day. I remembered Clint Pethick who lived in the Staddiscombe area of Plymstock, who'd offered me his storage facility in case I needed it. Problem solved. In true entrepreneurial style, I'd work out the details of getting it all to Heathrow later. I had to build up a pallet's worth of donations before I could get it on a plane there, which I guessed was two or three vans' worth of boxes. I had assumed that there was a lot of support from Plymstock School because it was my old school, but wasn't expecting as much from the other schools. If I could fill half the van the following day, then I'd be happy.

By the end of the next day, I'd filled the van four times over!

I started off at Plymouth College, where my mum used to be the cook before I was born. When I arrived, I found the entrance to one of their buildings half full with items the students and their parents had brought in. And the word was spreading. April McBride, a Tokyo acquaintance who was Plymouth-born and bred, had parents who lived nearby, so her father turned up to donate items, too. I felt the urge to give him a great big hug for his daughter. Parents whose adult children were living in Japan were so terribly worried and it felt nice to offer him a little comfort, too.

I left the students sorting, counting, and packing everything after my speech so that I could run off to Coombe Dean School for another talk. I hadn't factored in the time it would take to organize all the donations, and had left very little time in between school visits. But I also hadn't realized how much students, in every single school I ended up going to as it was to turn out, and regardless of student age or year, simply *loved* organizing all the donations. They'd allocate people to sort, people to count, and people to pack. And this was done without any input from me — again, this was an England I didn't remember. I was moved by their commitment and kindness.

I did my A Level Maths at Coombe Dean, and it was nice to be back. I'd lost touch with so many people when I'd moved to Japan and had been late to join Facebook — the place where everyone seemed to have reconnected with people from their past. I'd only signed up a couple of months earlier, so was surprised to see that I'd been to school with a few members of staff there, who welcomed me with big smiles. It felt like everywhere I went I was so warmly welcomed. Six hundred students piled into the gym for my talk and slideshow of images of Japan. At the end, one girl asked me whether she could give me some money for Japan, which I wasn't expecting. I wasn't going to the schools to collect money. And the catchment of Coombe Dean wasn't exactly wealthy. One of the teachers retrieved the red bucket from my van, which is what I had used when people were giving me money outside Morrison's. Back in the hall, the girl tipped her little wallet upside down and emptied the *entire contents* into the bucket. Suddenly, about half the children jumped up out of their places and ran to the front, throwing money into the bucket ... three hundred teenagers spontaneously giving whatever they had in order to help people on the other side of the world! I just stood there watching them all with a lump in my throat and tears in my eyes, trying to absorb everything. I hoped that I could somehow transport this moment back to Japan. I still get tearful thinking about those Coombe Dean kids.

My third school that day, and my final one in Plymouth, was Downham Special School. This very small school had tables set up with collection boxes they had made themselves, and were excited to see the pictures of Japan during my talk, but the highlight for them was my van with the Japanese flag on the side. The school was so full of excitement and happiness. I was initially surprised when they contacted me and asked me to give a talk there, and that their community wanted to contribute. Downham was the school that had given me my first experience of volunteering all those years ago — I'd raised money for them in primary school and helped to feed the children at lunchtimes during secondary school. At first I felt a bit odd about accepting help for Japan from Downham, when they themselves were a community that so often relied on support from others.

Despite all my years of philanthropy, I think I had yet to learn a very important lesson about the nature of helping others — people that we may perceive to be in need of our sympathy, compassion, and generosity, *must* be given the opportunity to offer *their* sympathy, compassion, and generosity to others. You can't always be the person who helps, nor can you always be the person who receives help. There has to be a healthy flow of help and goodwill. Otherwise, certain people in society will always be seen (and possibly by themselves, too) as life's victims. Whether they are children who suffer with genetic disease or brain injuries like some students at Downham, adults who find themselves homeless or struggling with poverty, or communities that have been destroyed by natural disasters. None of us are without some level of struggle that we need help with at some point in our lives. And regardless of your own challenges, there is always something that you can do to help others. I had thought it unfair of me to accept the Downham community's offer of help, when in fact it would have been unfair of me if I *hadn't* accepted it.

The uncle of a Tokyo friend, Richard Thornley, lived in Plymouth and was waiting outside Downham for me as I left — I was struck by the realization that the world really is a small place and word really spreads around it very quickly! He wanted to give me some money to show his support. With that and the money raised by Coombe Dean, the total was £800. I wasn't set up for handling cash donations and I had no idea what to do with the money — I didn't feel comfortable putting it in my own bank account. I asked my mum to change the coins into notes and tried to work out where to hide them. I didn't want to put them in my suitcase — what if it disappeared?! My camera case, my computer, my own purse — they could all disappear, too. If that money were lost, I would have been devastated. So throughout the whole trip I had hundreds of pounds taped inside my underwear. Now you know.

I dashed back to Plymouth College to collect everything I'd left them organizing, only to find that there was so much that it would never fit in my van. So we filled up one of the Plymouth College vans and dropped everything off at Clint's storage facility. Clint had informed me that his company would pay for everything to be palleted *and* driven up to Heathrow when the time came, and he wanted to fill my van up with fuel so it would be ready for me to head up to Gloucestershire the next day. Such, such kindness.

The next morning I drove three hours to Fairford, where I ran around Farmor's School making videos of the kids who'd been practising their Japanese good wishes. I gave a presentation to the sixth formers, who then helped me sort, count, and pack up enough donations to fill the van again, so I stored them at the school to collect later. They also gave me a huge folder filled with lovely letters the students had written to children in Japan, which I immediately posted to a school I knew in Tohoku — and I wondered whether this would be the beginning of some lovely friendships.

I continued driving up the country that evening, this time heading toward Leamington Spa. It was a stunningly beautiful drive along the Fosse Way through the Cotswolds, an area of England I had never been to before. I drove through little villages with charming names such as Bourton-on-the-Water, Stow-on-the-Wold, and Moreton-in-Marsh. And pretty Bibury — I would later learn that this tiny village was a favourite with Japanese tourists who flock to the area throughout the year, apparently because Emperor Hirohito fell in love with it during a European tour. I would also later learn that this part of the Cotswolds was where my parents had met while they were both in the Royal Air Force — they'd lived here when they were first married and before moving to Plymouth. It was an absolutely beautiful part of the country. I again found my feelings toward England changing a little, and I wondered how I might be able to develop this incredible support that the UK seemed to have for Japan.

The next day I gave a talk to the year sevens at King Henry VIII School in Coventry, and then packed their donations into the van. One of their teachers at the time, Dr Michael Reddish, had lived in Japan, so they had all been practising their Japanese phrases with impeccable accents and couldn't wait to be part of one of my videos. I met one girl there who had been in the Thailand tsunami and was clearly keen to talk about it — the Japan tsunami must have been very triggering for people who were caught up in the one on Boxing Day in 2004.

An old friend, Nick Meynell, had been coordinating things in this area — he was familiar with getting roped into helping me with charitable endeavours from our time at university together. He'd got local pharmacies to donate lots of items, and made it a personal mission to set me up at a supermarket for the day, getting the Sainsbury's in Leamington to support my efforts. We were met at the entrance by one of their friendly staff, who was holding a donation bucket and had a huge grin on her face. Next to her was the fabulous Nicola, who promptly treated me to lunch in their canteen. As we walked to the canteen, we passed walls with photos of all the staff and their charitable activities. I was astounded to see not only the amounts of money this store raises for a variety of good causes, but also to see how the staff really throw themselves into these activities.

Helping Japan was no exception. They had placed 15 donation buckets all over the store, and quite a few of their staff spent time holding them and talking to customers about what I was doing. Announcements were made over the loudspeaker system throughout the day, encouraging customers to support the people of Japan. There were two huge containers near the entrance, with a list of the accepted items stuck on them, and they were already full before I got there! Throughout the day, staff kept on coming over to me and asking what we were short of, and then wandering off and buying it themselves, and customers came to me with bags full of items to put in the van. The outpouring of genuine care and concern was quite overwhelming.

I met quite a few people who had relatives in Japan, and I met one Japanese lady who lived in the UK. She was with her parents, who were from Ibaraki (which is about 180 km south of the damaged nuclear facility), and after March 11 their daughter had insisted that they fly over to the UK because she was so worried about them. We talked for a bit about the earthquake, refugees staying in Ibaraki, and their worries about returning. They said that three weeks on, they still had nightmares about the earthquake every night. I told them about all the love and support the people of England had for Japan, and how everybody wanted to help. Japanese people tend not to hug, and I knew this, but I am a big hugger, and I had to give them all big hugs, which they seemed not to mind. I was so glad they had this opportunity to see how much English people cared about them.

And my goodness, didn't those people in Sainsbury's care?! They filled the van up yet again, and when all the donation buckets were emptied and counted ... it came to almost a thousand pounds! It was a great way to end the first week of talks ... five van loads of donations and £1800!

It may have been a great way to finish off the first week, but physically I didn't feel so great, and I wasn't sure at all what I felt emotionally. I was on my fifth cold in four months, had almost lost my voice, and still hoped to find the strength to resolve a personal situation that needed to be dealt with. I spent that weekend constantly on the verge of tears. Many of my friends had headed out of Tokyo while there was still so much uncertainty around what would happen at the Fukushima nuclear plant. Some would never return. I was unsettled and unsure of what the future would bring. But I had one more week and six more schools to visit, so I knew I had to do something to make myself feel better.

Running had become my newfound medicine for everything, so off I went, at every opportunity. By now I had upped my daily distance to 6 km. I ran along roads, through fields, got covered in mud, soaking wet in the rain, and found myself exploring an England I had never known when I'd lived there. And I liked it.

I stored the current van load with family in Newbury, and headed back to Devon, but North Devon this time, to Southmead Primary School in Braunton, which happened to be just down the road from where I was born in Barnstaple. One of the parents, Monica Carter-Burns, was friends with a woman who was interning with me in Tokyo, Carole Hallett Mobbs, who'd been devoting herself to spreading the word among her UK-based mum friends. Monica was keen to get me into the local school and introduce me to some of her North Devon media contacts. The day started with a whole-school assembly during which I showed the students my pictures and talked about Japan, as I did with the other schools, but in Southmead it was a little less rushed, so I had quite a bit of time to visit the individual classrooms, and spent a lot of time answering children's questions about what it was like to live in Japan.

One class had gone to such efforts before my arrival — they collected money from parents in the playground, and then went shopping to buy items on my shopping list. The local Tesco's also donated vouchers to the students' shopping fund, and filled the van up with fuel before I headed off to Hungerford to speak to some sixth formers at St Johns Marlborough School.

St Johns Marlborough was a really interesting school — very state-of-the-art and dynamic both in terms of its facilities and students. You could sense an unusual energy as soon as you stepped inside the building. Near the main entrance was a space that was used as a dining hall, in the middle of which I saw a tall triangular "wall." On one side was the word "WORRY," and on the other side, "WONDER." Students were encouraged to write about things that made them look at the world in wonder on one side, and things that were worrying to them on the other side. Sure enough, one student had written that they were worried about Japan.

My mum could have filled the "worry" side of that wall on her own — she was still beside herself with worry about me and where I was staying every night. Most nights I was sleeping in strangers' homes, which didn't bother *me* at all. In fact I found it quite amusing to say that I was spending a lot of time sleeping in teenage boys' bedrooms recently — a sentence I never thought I'd say. Most people just responded by asking about the smell. I stayed in a different place almost every night, and was hosted by some truly lovely people and their truly lovely sons who lent me their rooms.

Next stop: Cambridge, where I offered nine-year-old Isaac, the son of the previous night's host, a lift to school in the "Japan van." His little face lit up, and he put some of his pocket money in the donation bucket. I gave an assembly at Waterbeach Primary to about 300 students aged 4 to 11 years old. They were so interested in Japan, and oohed and aahed in all the right places. I was very happy to hear one of the staff announce that she was putting Japan next on her list of places to visit. This was one of my goals everywhere I went — to get more people interested in visiting Japan.

Cressi Downing and Sara Noel, mums at Waterbeach, had done an amazing job of motivating their school community. At the front of the school, people were dropping off one bag of supplies after another, and some extremely helpful year fives helped me sort, count, and pack them all until the van was filled again — the seventh time on this trip. I had started to notice a big difference between year fives and year sixes — the year fives asked what sanitary towels were. Year sixes had already had *that* lesson. Usually I was happy to get stuck right in with a tricky conversation with a ten-year-old, but this one I thought I'd better leave to the parents.

I met Mayumi Geater and her friend Misa at Waterbeach. Mayumi had lived in England for ten years and was a mum at the school — it was lovely to give her a big hug and to speak a bit of Japanese with her. Even though my Japanese wasn't very good, it always made me feel happy to speak what little I knew. Mayumi was the first Japanese person to watch my presentation, so I was a little self-conscious, but I shouldn't have been. Afterward I was so touched to hear her say that even though she taught Japanese at a local college, she could never show her love for Japan the way I did. She said she could see in my eyes how much I loved my adopted country.

Misa's playgroup had made some "Prayers for Japan" posters and she had tried contacting charities to see whether they would accept the posters and get them to the people of Sendai. Nobody would accept them, so when she heard about my visit she had come along to ask me to take them. I added them to my growing collection of beautiful pictures and words about sending love to Japan. Misa then told me that she had been in the Kobe earthquake in 1995, and said that she thought she had recovered from that experience until March 11, more than sixteen years later, when all the images, emotions, and even smells of the dust and burning city all started coming back to her.

Mayumi and Misa made me think about all the people who were out of Japan during the disaster, but considered Japan home. Up to this point, I had tried to dismiss my own feelings of grief, loss, and bewilderment, seeing them as self-indulgent and self-centred when so many people had lost so much and I wasn't even in the country when it happened. But Mayumi and Misa made me realize that many of us who lived overseas but called Japan home, or who chose to go overseas in the aftermath or happened to be overseas on March 11, were feeling terribly isolated. There is so much comfort to be had by physically being with people who form part of your community, and so much healing that comes from a shared grief or concern — I remember when a school friend had died suddenly the year before and even though I hadn't seen that friend for many years, I was surprised to find myself really wanting to be with other school friends as everybody grieved.

After visiting Waterbeach, Mayumi and Cressi, along with a couple of other mums, took me out for lunch. I felt guilty for any time I spent enjoying myself when I could be on the road collecting donations, writing up the day's activities for my blog, or making videos, but my hosts insisted. And I had taken to Cressi — she was a member of the "Bad Mothers Club," of which if I'd chosen to have kids, I'm sure I would have been a very active member. We went to a local pub and Cressi asked the bartender whether we could put the donation bucket on the bar while we had our lunch. Before he'd picked up the phone to ask the boss, a lovely gentleman came over and put a fiver in. He then insisted on buying all our drinks. Such kindness, again! Cressi then fuelled up the van, and it was off to Twickenham for the final talk at Trafalgar Infant School.

The Trafalgar talk was to five- and six-year-olds, who I knew would especially like the pictures of Disneyland, fireworks, puppies in outfits, and sumo wrestlers with their bum cheeks showing, which *always* made little ones giggle. I assumed that this talk would be quite lighthearted given the age of the children, although perhaps a little emotional for me because it was my last talk.

I ended up crying four times by midday.

The first set of tears fell when Tokyo friend Sam Woodgate turned up with a hundred bags she had made *by hand*, containing toys, pencils, notepaper, and a postcard upon which she had drawn the Union Jack — so thoughtful. Immediately afterward, a lady turned up with an envelope full of letters from students at another school in the neighbourhood, and then it was chaos as bags and bags of donated items were handed over to us by smiling children and their parents. Dear Marie, who'd worked so hard to help out behind the scenes throughout the whole trip, turned up in person at Trafalgar.

I hadn't seen anyone from my Japan life for weeks and there was such a comfort to be had in hugging both Sam and Marie. They had both moved away from Japan before the earthquake, but had clearly left their hearts there and were deeply affected by March 11. We talked about how the people who cared about us in the UK seemed so relieved that we hadn't been in Japan when the earthquake happened, but how none of us shared that sentiment at all. We all wished that we'd been there, although appreciated that that probably sounded very odd to anyone who heard it. The three of us just kept sniffling and sobbing as we organized the donations.

Some Japanese people that lived locally came along to lend a hand, and also to hear my talk. One woman, Emi, told me afterward that she was touched to hear me say "we" instead of "they" when I referred to people living in Japan. And Nori, who, along with six other Japanese people, lived in the UK and worked for the Hitachi office near Twickenham, also came along. He wanted to tell me that they appreciated everything I was doing, and gave me £100 that the Hitachi workers had collected among themselves.

Another Japanese woman who was there had lost her London-based friend who was visiting family in Sendai on March 11. She wanted to thank me for what I was doing, but was just too upset to speak when it came to it, so passed on her feelings to my host, Tamsin Burland. We couldn't believe that this dear lady, so deeply grieving her friend and her country, could somehow find it necessary to come along and thank us.

I felt a mixture of emotions when Japanese people thanked me. I was pleased to know that my efforts brought just a little bit of comfort to the Japanese people that lived overseas and felt so isolated. I wanted them to know that many foreigners — not just me — who considered Japan home were doing their best to take care of the country as much as they could. But I also felt really uncomfortable in being thanked. It was the same discomfort that I had with some of the media coverage of my trip. It wasn't that I was uncomfortable with media interviews in general — I couldn't afford to be when I ran my own business and often needed publicity — and I understood that it was important to keep the people of Tohoku in the news. I was just *really* uncomfortable with the attention being on me.

None of this was about *me*. I was just giving people a way to help. Channelling other people's love and care. I felt no personal sense of pride or achievement in doing all these talks — I considered them to be my duty, and I was constantly aware of how little my impact could ever be, and how much more I wished I could do. So when Japanese people thanked me, I simply said, "Please tell your friends in Japan that England cares." And I welled up every time I said it.

By the end of the two weeks of talks, it was very clear how much England cared. We had filled an incredible 92 boxes with over *10,000* items. There were 8 jerry cans, 290 packs of nappies, 26 packs of nappy bags, 120 packs of baby wipes, 33 cans of dry shampoo, 71 nail clippers, 176 medical items, 183 rolls of cling film and garbage bags, 18 Ziploc bags, 225 dust/surgical masks, 294 packs of cotton buds, 305 food items, 531 packs of sanitary towels, 546 packs of underwear, 1252 tubes of toothpaste, 2876 toothbrushes, and 3438 children's toys, games, and books. And for pets: 8 blankets, 1 collar, 27 packs of flea treatment, 675 food items, 9 bottles of shampoo, 8 toilet mats, 140 towels, and 1 toy. Not to mention £2085 in cash donations.

On the final day of talks, I got the go-ahead from Virgin to start dropping boxes off at Heathrow. I had to now retrace my steps and collect everything that was stored in boxes all around the country.

Except for the money. That was still in my knickers.

4: Heathrow

I had taken three planes and travelled 8200 miles from Saipan to England, where I'd slept in ten different people's homes, and driven 1600 miles over two weeks, to visit thirteen schools and two supermarkets. I shouldn't have been surprised when both my body and my van decided enough was enough. Within an hour after my last talk I had a debilitating migraine that paralyzed one side of my body, and the following day the van broke down on the M4.

Hitachi were fantastic — their 24-hour breakdown service rescued me and the van and drove us both to Newbury, where one of Hitachi's mechanics arrived the following day to see what the problem could be. I felt awful. I was imagining all sorts of things that I might have done (or not done) to the van during the past couple of weeks and was feeling pretty bad about the possibility that it was my fault — it had been so long since I'd had a vehicle to look after! I didn't have a car in Japan. While I'd driven friends' and hire cars there, in Japan you rarely even open up your own hood. Everything got checked by service station attendants whenever you refuelled, your windows and wing mirrors got cleaned, ashtrays and rubbish bins got emptied, and this excellent service was completed by traffic being halted for you, so you could exit safely as you were sent off with a bow. The last time I'd maintained my own car was when I lived in England fifteen years earlier.

Since I'd had the van, I'd somehow forgotten every single bit of basic car maintenance knowledge I'd ever had. So when the mechanic told me I had driven the equivalent of five months' of distance in two weeks, I knew I'd done something wrong and should have been checking everything, daily — *especially the water*. Of which there was zero in the radiator. I was mortified.

So the Japan van was taken away just to check that nothing else had caused the water to evaporate, and within minutes another van was delivered — Hitachi were just incredible. And instead of making me feel like he was either annoyed or amused by what I'd done to their van, Hitachi's Glenn was absolutely lovely and gave me all sorts of other reasons for why it could have broken down. At least it was going back to them clean — I'd been obsessed with keeping the van spotless, especially after all the muddy West Country lanes. It had the Japanese flag on the side, which needed to be treated with respect — dirt on it wouldn't do at all!

I'd been on the way back from Heathrow to Newbury when the van had broken down, after having dropped off the first load of boxes at the airport. Virgin had arranged for me to work with Vantec — a logistics company that would sort out all the details necessary to get the pallet on and off the plane, and through customs. Kim was my point of contact there and, right from the beginning, she made the process, which I felt was surely incredibly complicated, so very simple. All I had to do was turn up with the vanloads of boxes, Mike and Paul would be ready with their forklift, and space had been allocated for me inside their huge warehouse. The very helpful Clint in Plymouth now had somewhere to bring the three vanloads he was storing in his garage, and I would spend the next week retrieving the other boxes from their various storage locations around the country, and dropping them off, bit by bit, at Vantec.

The Japan van was fixed within a couple of days, so I drove over to Hitachi to swap vans, and picked up everything they had been collecting in their seven offices around the country. The Hitachi people were, as always, just lovely — and reassured me that it wasn't my neglect at all that had caused the water to evaporate; it was, in fact, a broken water pump. I'm still not convinced they didn't just say that to try to make me feel less guilty. Nonetheless, I had the Japan van back, and got on with collecting the boxes and bringing them to Heathrow.

By the end of the week, every single box was with Vantec, including those Clint had brought up from Plymouth, and Kim was very pleased to receive my extremely detailed list of the contents of those 92 boxes.

I was still being contacted by people who wanted to help. When I'd returned to Newbury after all the talks, there was an envelope from my Tokyo intern's mum waiting for me. Mrs Hallett had made a quilt, initially intended for Japan, but had then found out that I wasn't taking bedding back with me, so she sold the quilt to one of her friends and sent me the £100 she'd received for it. I called her and we had a lovely chat on the phone — the members of her women's group were very upset about what had happened in Japan and had collected various items, which she delicately described as "things ladies wouldn't want to ask for" that she also delivered to me. She and her friends sounded so elegant and sophisticated that I was relieved we were talking on the phone and not in person so she couldn't see exactly how unladylike I was rapidly becoming. Having spent the best part of a month in a van, I was starting to smell like a mechanic. A weird combination of oil, fuel, and sweat. Nice.

I was still being asked to give talks in schools, but I didn't want to take any more bookings while I was trying to get all the boxes to Vantec. I was starting to feel a sense of urgency and hoped that all the items I'd collected would still be needed — it was coming up to a month after the disaster. Maybe everybody would have everything they needed by now? I was so naive.

The UK schools would have to wait, but there was clearly still a strong desire in England to help. Was there somehow a way I could keep gathering support? Could I manage a trip like this again? Some ideas were starting to form in the back of my mind but, for now, my focus was on the next stage of the mission — getting everything to Japan. I was a little anxious about what I'd be going back to — not because of the Fukushima situation, which was still a concern to many, and not because of all the destruction, because that was in an area very far away from Tokyo — I was worried about what was happening within my own social and professional community in Tokyo.

People in Tokyo seemed to have such different responses to the disaster and its aftermath — there were some who, even the day after the earthquake, continued going about their normal lives as if absolutely nothing had happened, "Everything's fine, I'm off to golf and then drinks at the Oak Door." And then there were others who were so deeply affected by the disaster that they found it impossible to return to the life they had before. Some were consumed with a desire to help. To them, "normal" life didn't matter anymore, and things would never be the same again. Through my blog and Facebook posts and activities in England, I'd been very open about how I felt, and it was clear which camp I was in. Like-minded people had been reaching out to me.

One email I received from an acquaintance in Tokyo particularly touched me. We didn't know each other very well, but since March 11, people seemed to be opening up in a way that hadn't felt appropriate before. Her employer had moved her to Osaka for a few weeks just after the earthquake and she had just returned to Tokyo. She felt that people in Tokyo were pretty much going about life as usual, but that somehow felt fake to her and she felt that life had changed forever. I strongly shared the feeling that life would never be quite the same again, and assured her that she wasn't alone in her feelings. I already knew of people who were questioning their jobs, their homes, their life choices. And the people questioning these things were Japanese as well as foreigners.

It's amazing how much life can change in such a short time. On March 10 I was in the middle of a seven-day book-writing frenzy, planning a five-day 40th birthday celebration for that October, and my various business projects were going really well. I was working seven-day weeks and had set a lot of professional goals for 2011, toward which I was making good progress. After March 11 none of those things felt important anymore, and instead I felt a need to redesign my life to incorporate whatever I could do to provide some kind of long-term support to people in the north of Japan.

I wasn't the only one. Many entrepreneur friends were trying to balance their strong sense of wanting to help rebuild Japan both practically and emotionally with the need to make decisions related to their businesses, which were already starting to suffer. Well-known Tokyo entrepreneur and fellow publisher Terrie Lloyd wrote in that week's "Terrie's Take" that while he thought the disaster would actually bring about plenty of business opportunities for certain industries, media and advertising would be the first to get hit — and they were the core of my professional life in Japan. My clients and my projects still looked fine at that point, but for how long?

For all of Japan there were so many questions and so much uncertainty, even for those of us who hadn't lost our homes — and I needed to stay focused on getting these supplies to those who had.

When I first got the idea to collect items and get them to the northeastern part of Japan, I was in touch with a number of organizations in Japan that were facilitating the distribution of supplies. It hadn't occurred to me that I'd be able to take the items there myself. By the end of two weeks' travel around England, being witness to the genuine kindness, compassion, and generosity from everyone I met, I was absolutely determined to take those items up there myself. Every single one of them. I no longer cared about my lack of Japanese ability. I had an obligation to the people who had donated goods and money. People who didn't care that I wasn't a charity and had given me money anyway. People who believed in *me*. Just as I'd driven a van around England, I could drive one to the north of Japan and back. Given how much stuff I had though, it would have to be a much bigger van. And I'd need a co-driver, if for no other reason than to put my mother's mind at ease.

The media were still spouting their scaremongering about Fukushima, and my mother wasn't the only person to ask whether I wasn't *sure* I wanted to stay in England a bit longer. There was a strong feeling in the UK that Japan was very unstable. I dismissed everyone's concerns except for the one about the heart implant I'd had fitted in 2007 to prevent more strokes. I forget I've got it most of the time, and it hadn't occurred to me to check whether it would be OK given the uncertainty that still existed around Fukushima. A quick call to the manufacturer in the US eased our minds — although it was interesting to discover that if my trip were to take place within the first three months after surgery, I would have been advised to not go to Japan because of the radiation concerns. However, I was three and a half years on so it didn't matter.

So I was going to drive up north and deliver the items myself and couldn't wait to get there! It would be good timing — the financial and emotional resources of individuals and corporations who had jumped in to help immediately were starting to run out. People in Japan had heard about what I was doing and were emailing me asking for help. There may well have been some people living "normal" lives in Tokyo, but a lot of others were really struggling. This was another reason why I thought it would be a good idea to continue encouraging support from people outside Japan — in Japan the whole country was being affected financially, practically, and emotionally, with little "escape" from the day-to-day effects of living in a country under so much pressure, not to mention the frequent aftershocks. People living outside Japan could continue to help on a more long-term basis, and at the same time not be completely drained of their own emotional reserves.

My emotional reserves were being maintained by my little niece and nephews. The pace of that last week in England was slower than the past two weeks had been, and there were pockets of free time in between the daily journeys back and forth between Vantec and Newbury. I cherished my opportunities to spend time with the kids, and realized how much I missed them. I had always felt guilty about not being there to see my older Plymouth nieces grow up because I was living in Japan, and here were three more little ones to love. I felt like I'd grown so much closer to them on this trip. And there would soon be a fourth. I wanted to be a bigger part of their lives, and them to be a bigger part of mine.

I was surprised by how *healing* I had found the company of my niece and nephews, and that of all the school children I had spent time with during those weeks. I'd been scanning some of the children's letters and pictures for Japan, and some of them were so touching. They were full of optimism and a desire to comfort that was written so confidently, with notes such as "I know everything will be fine" and "You will be OK." I loved how children seemed to be so in tune with other people's emotions and so free with the very human instinct to comfort others and make other's unhappiness go away.

I took my niece and nephews to the park, and watched them on the climbing frame, thinking about the children in Japan, in playgrounds with their parents, aunties, uncles, and grandparents. There were extended families who'd been living together in coastal homes that had washed away in minutes.

Six-year-old Mabel fell over and was convinced she had twisted her ankle as she lay bawling dramatically on the floor, so I did my funny noisy kissing thing on her (it involves several sets of ten very loud kisses, in rapid succession, repeated until the crying child stops, and sometimes results in another child saying, "Now me!" even though they're not crying). It only took three sets until a laughing Mabel skipped back to the climbing frame. I watched her go and wondered how many children in Japan had lost the people who used to kiss their bumps better. And if only the pain those children had felt during the past month could be made to disappear with the help of a few silly noisy kisses.

My running went up a level that week to a daily 7 km — I needed it more than ever now that I had more free time and was waiting, oh so impatiently, to get back to Japan. One day my terrible sense of direction meant I got totally lost, but I couldn't stop. I just kept running and running, only realizing when I checked Google afterward that I'd run 13 km. Purely by accident. I was better off running with my brother-in-law. We ran along the streets, canals, and fields of Newbury, fast and focused, and just far enough. I loved it. Two months earlier I'd been shuffling along the Tokyo backstreets, and would never have imagined I'd be running every day like this in England — not only that, one of the strokes I'd suffered four years earlier had put me in a wheelchair for a short time. If I'd known then, as I'd looked down at my foot that had turned inward and refused to move, that four years later I'd be running 13 km, I wouldn't have believed it.

My brother-in-law Marc and I had always been close and I loved having some time for just the two of us. He'd always been direct with me — as soon as we stopped, he said, "You know it's going to hit you hard when you get back to Tokyo."

He was probably right. It wasn't just the tsunami, the survivors, the media coverage, the ongoing Fukushima worry, or the fact that the awful situation in Japan was constantly in my mind. Nor was it the stress of my own experience of March 11, worries about my loved ones not just in Japan but also in England (all the stress was really affecting my mother), my business, my personal situation, or my future. It was also the unsettling and confusing feelings I was having about England. I was starting to feel that I was being pulled back to the country of my birth, but I didn't know whether I wanted to be — had this mission unexpectedly brought me closer to England?

I had been so deeply moved by the kindness shown to Japan by English people. I knew why *I* wanted to help — Japan was my home and it was the right thing to do. It was a country that I loved. A country that became part of who I am. A country that had a special place deep in my heart. But why had English people been so moved to help? During those weeks after the Japanese tsunami, the English people I came across showed me the best that humanity could be. They showed an understanding that when one of us suffers, we all suffer. When one of us feels pain, we all feel pain. They demonstrated that there is a deep need in all of us to offer love and compassion to others, regardless of race or nationality — we do actually want to do whatever we can to try to make the world a better place.

I was so overwhelmed. And a little ashamed. There was more to England than I thought. Maybe I was wrong to have written it off! There *was* love, kindness, and compassion here. Perhaps I had to be more open to it myself. Less judgmental. Very unexpectedly, a new love for the country I had left so many years ago was beginning to blossom. It was all so confusing.

I spent six weeks out of Japan — the longest time I had ever spent away since I'd moved there in 1996. I was so excited when I finally got on that flight back to Tokyo ... *I'd done it* ... that crazy idea I came up with during that sleepless night in Saipan — I'd pulled it off! I'd travelled around England, collected supplies, raised money and awareness, promoted the beauty of Japan, and brought comfort to Japanese people both in and out of Japan. My UK mission had succeeded *far* beyond my expectations! I was one step closer to getting some financial, practical, and emotional support to the people who needed them.

I was going home. Wasn't I?

5: Tokyo

I'd been back in Tokyo for a week and, apart from the train stations and convenience stores that were dimly lit in order to save energy, everything looked *exactly* the same as when I'd left. Beautiful. The skies were bright blue, the sunshine was bright and cheerful, and the trees were blooming. The cherry blossoms had just finished, and Golden Week — four days of national holidays at the end of April and beginning of May, which sometimes landed in a way that meant everyone in Japan got a week off, if not more — was just around the corner. While a lot of people got tired of the concrete jungle that was Tokyo, after fifteen years I had never stopped looking up at the buildings and thinking, "I live in Tokyo — what a wonderful place to be." I still, even today, love to stop and just gaze at everything around me, in awe of Tokyo's beauty.

In April 2011, I gazed at the buildings with a different kind of awe, as I was full of admiration at their ability to withstand such a big earthquake. The epicentre had been over 370 km away, and almost 30 km under the sea, but at a 9.0 magnitude, it had been the biggest earthquake on record in Japan (and the fourth biggest in the world) — Tokyo shook for a full six minutes. Yet all the buildings remained, standing tall. I felt secure in the knowledge that I was safe in the Tokyo buildings amid all the talks that Tokyo itself was long overdue for "the big one," and tried not to worry too much about the daily aftershocks.

Tokyoites didn't seem to be too concerned about radiation and the impact Fukushima might be having on the capital city. There weren't especially more people than usual walking around with face masks on, the panic buying had stopped, and people were drinking tap water again. There were people for whom the only way the disaster had impacted their lives was through the breaking of a vase or picture frame. And plenty of people were going about life as before, both emotionally and practically — but I wasn't close to any of them.

The people I was close to were in shock. Either resignedly adjusting to a new normality, or struggling to define what that normality would be for them. I could see small changes in the way my Japanese and non-Japanese friends lived their lives in Tokyo — mums who wouldn't venture far from their kids' schools unless the whole family were together; women who thought twice before putting on those three-inch heels and instead opted for flats; drivers who constantly kept a full tank of fuel in their cars; and the surfing enthusiasts who made a pact not to go into the sea until every one of the missing bodies was found and paid appropriate respect to.

Maybe it was because I had been out of Japan for six weeks that I could see such a big change in everyone, because when I first reconnected with people after returning I was shocked when I looked in their eyes. The eyes of my friends had stopped shining.

My foreign friends' eyes were now hard and cold, steeling themselves for something they couldn't imagine but were afraid might be waiting for them, their families, their homes, their futures. They felt unable to plan too far ahead, and were just getting through, day by day. The rare full night of sleep, uninterrupted by an aftershock, brought a smile in the morning, but only briefly because the need to gather strength to go to work, take care of the kids, do their bit to support a volunteer endeavour, would then take over.

And my Japanese friends' eyes, usually so full of warmth with their beautiful deep dark glow, seemed empty of anything but sadness. They tried to remain "Japanese" and keep their emotions in check, but I could see through it. So I held their hands, stroked their backs, and hugged them with all my strength. Trying to give them every bit of love I had brought with me from England — and then their tears would flow.

People were struggling *hard* with their attempts to put on a brave face, but just couldn't shake off the feeling that life would never be quite the same again — and they needed to cry. Not just to cry for the people in the north of Japan, but to cry for other things that they probably didn't cry enough about at the time — crying for the fights with their father, the mother they never got to say goodbye to, the baby they'd miscarried, the wife who cheated on them, the people who let them down, the end of a marriage. I cried myself for two days, non-stop, then comforted friends while they cried. I remember sitting in my garden, on the lap of a male friend as he sobbed and sobbed while I wrapped my arms around him. He was an artist, and despite his leather-wearing, motorbike-riding exterior, he was an especially sensitive soul, and the past few weeks had been too much for him. He was the first of my friends to start making plans to leave Japan, and had already decided to close down his studio. I had worked with him to promote his business a lot over the years, and we decided to organize a closing sale to benefit Tohoku.

Two of my closest girlfriends were Emily and Sannah. I'd met them years earlier when they started working for me, and we stayed friends when they left to focus on being mothers, religiously meeting every Wednesday morning for coffee. Between us we'd seen each other through a lot, and they were like sisters to me. I had missed them so much during my time away, and made sure to make up for that now that I was back. Australian Emily loved the Royal Family and there was a royal wedding to watch. There was a lot of comfort to be had in spending an evening together watching England celebrate as William and Kate said their vows, and Emily's son paraded up and down the living room dressed as a bridesmaid.

Friendships became stronger as we comforted one another. Or more distant depending on our responses to the disaster. Couples and family units were affected, too. One couple that had separated the year before found themselves reconsidering their decision, and started wearing their wedding rings again. The gap that existed between them before was bridged by this tragedy. But they were in the minority. Most already rocky relationships fell apart in this atmosphere of grief and confusion. Cultural or individual differences meant that some people's responses to the disaster were dramatically different from their partners' reactions, which could be extremely frustrating. It wasn't unusual to hear comments like: "I begged my wife to take the kids south, but she wouldn't"; "My husband wasn't there for me"; and "He/she was hysterical." Some people were questioning whether their relationship would survive. And whether they wanted it to.

People were also questioning their professional lives — whether they would still have a job in the coming months, and whether they even wanted that job anymore. Some had handed in their notice so they could participate in the relief and rebuilding efforts. Some people were making big, life-changing decisions in response to the earthquake, tsunami, and radiation concerns. And they felt the need to justify those decisions, along with a fear that they'd be judged for making them.

Whether people stayed in or left Japan during the days following the earthquake, it seemed that many people had to face hard questions from friends and family, and sometimes from people they hardly knew. Public insults and negative comments related to people's choices were not uncommon, and sadly made the emotional impact of the earthquake more difficult to bear. Instead of feeling supported by their friends in whatever decisions they made, for whatever reasons they had, those friendships were crumbling. I hated watching how this was fragmenting the international community — a community that I'd always loved and felt part of. I wasn't sure how I felt about it anymore — Tokyo had changed. Amid the beauty of those buildings, I now saw an ugliness in how some people were treating each other. I felt there was a little less love in Tokyo.

But a lot of love was on its way from England: 92 boxes full of it, to be precise. Waiting for a space on one of the Virgin Atlantic flights, many of which were being cancelled because of all the upheaval and uncertainty that still surrounded Japan. It would be four weeks until the boxes arrived at Narita, so I had plenty of time to plan my trip up north.

My diary soon filled up again, and I found myself rushing around Tokyo from one meeting to the next. My good friend Mike Alfant was one of the first people I caught up with — he was king of the entrepreneurs in Tokyo and I admired him immensely, not just for his business acumen but his philanthropic nature. It didn't surprise me at all that he'd already been up to Tohoku and was contributing to the relief effort. He wasn't much older than me, yet because he'd been one of my mentors for some years, I'd always felt a desire to make him proud. So it was nice when he told me that he was pleased I was going up there myself. But his words stayed in my mind … "It's not what you think."

I was asked to give a couple of speeches about what I'd been doing in England since the earthquake: one at Tokyo American Club, and another at Amity Yokohama Friendship Group. Amity was an English-speaking group, mostly made up of retired Japanese men, who had invited me pre-311 to give a talk on "A British Woman's Adventures in Japan," intended to be one of their key events for the year. But with recent events and electricity conservation at the venue, they wanted to postpone that talk and instead invited me to a casual lunch where I could tell them about my recent trip around the UK.

So I told the story of my experience on high ground in Saipan (everyone I told found the appearance of the convicts very funny), described my journey to England, and showed photos of British people and their desire to support Japan — the supermarket staff holding buckets to collect money in, passersby stopping to learn some encouraging Japanese words as they waved the Japanese flag, and children with their thoughtful pictures and messages.

The elderly gentlemen were visibly moved and there were more than a few tears. They had no idea that English people were thinking so much about Japan, and were touched and encouraged by everyone's concern. They liked the thought that a disaster like this could somehow turn into an educational opportunity for children in another country so far away, and were thrilled that so many British people I'd spoken to had since decided that they now wanted to visit Japan.

"We need more ambassadors for Japan right now!" one old man declared, not knowing that he was fuelling an idea that was already developing in my mind.

We spent the rest of the afternoon talking about how people can help each other deal with tragedies like this. They felt that they were too old to be able to help, and I could see that they really struggled with accepting that. I tried to reassure them that there were plenty of people helping out, and told them of all the foreigners I knew who were busy fundraising or actually volunteering in Tohoku. I'm not sure many of those volunteers at the time knew just how much of an impact their efforts were having — they weren't just encouraging the people of Tohoku, they were encouraging people all over Japan, just like these elderly Japanese men, who were more than supportive of any fundraising and on-the-ground aid efforts.

That May in Tokyo it felt like you could go to a fundraising event every single day if you wanted to. I helped on the door at one event, but felt terribly out of place. I felt unsettled by all the laughing, partying, eating, and drinking, even though it was for a cause I really believed in — my mind was up north and I was still rejecting anything that involved dressing up or being frivolous in any way. I'd given up alcohol months before the earthquake (something I still like to do now and again, especially if I have something I really want to focus on), so it wasn't like I could have a drink to see whether that would make me feel a little less like an outsider. I just felt as though I didn't belong there, and started longing to return to the solitude of being alone, in a van, driving around the English countryside.

I was still confused by my feelings about England. I had spent a month unintentionally connecting with places that were a key part of my life — some of the schools were in the area where my parents had met, others were in the place where I was born and places I had grown up. And I hadn't settled back into Tokyo at all — from my perspective, everything there had changed. It felt like everyone I knew had a broken heart — from the disaster rather than from a relationship. Most people I knew had people they loved around them to help them heal and from which to gather strength. I looked at the couples around me that were helping each other heal, or the children that were making the adults around them smile through their sadness — I had wonderful friends but I didn't have *that*. For the first time in my fifteen years in Japan, I missed England. I felt deeply alone in a city that was so full of sorrow.

So in conjunction with planning my Tohoku trip, I started to pack up my life in Tokyo. This was, thankfully, quite straightforward from a practical perspective, given that I was still completely uninterested in any material belongings. I either gave things away or put them into storage. I'd be back. I had years left on my resident's visa, so I could come and go as I pleased. I just needed some time to gather my thoughts and make a plan. Take a break from "normal" life. Redesign the new one I'd been thinking about that could somehow incorporate living in both England and Japan during my mum's older years. I could still publish my magazines, as everything was done via the Internet now, and everyone I worked with worked from home or was happy to do so.

The idea of doing more travelling around England, giving talks on Japan, and generating more support was extremely appealing, as was being without "stuff" and living out of a suitcase for a while. I didn't *quite* know what I was doing yet, but in the middle of all this I'd had a call from England, with concerns for my mum's health. Nobody seemed sure what was going on, but I was expected to deal with it, so I provided a list of tests the doctors be asked to arrange (my own complicated medical history had made me quite good at organizing such things), and said they'd have to hold the fort until I got there. I already had a flight booked for the end of May. I thought the timing might work out well — I could be closer to Mum, and perhaps get some fundraising for Japan going while I was there.

The fundraising event I was helping out at in Tokyo did an amazing job that resulted in several millions of yen going to an organization that was getting volunteers up north to clear the debris. Lots of people had been up to Tohoku already, especially during Golden Week when thousands headed up during their time off work. I was picking their brains on their return and doing as much research as I could, desperate to find the *right* place for all these donations from England. A consistent comment people were coming back with was that the survivors and organizations there were worried about being forgotten. I desperately wanted them to know that they hadn't been! There were so many people in England who were keeping them in their thoughts.

Another consistent comment coming back from Tohoku was that people within the big shelters were, for the most part, being taken care of. I didn't want to drive up to a shelter that was already fully stocked and just dump more boxes of stuff off, leaving them with the burden of distribution. It was the people *outside* the shelters and especially in remote areas that still needed a lot of help — many were still eating just one rice ball per day — these were the people I wanted to focus on. The roads to the remote areas were still being cleared, whereas the main roads around Tohoku had been fixed remarkably quickly.

I was especially interested in hearing stories about other people who were doing their own thing in terms of participating in the relief efforts. Like me, not everyone was affiliating themselves with an NGO or official body, because, to be blunt, we could see all the disadvantages to doing so. I loved the stories of trucks making their way north independently, only to be told by officials along the way that they weren't allowed to drive along a certain route, or deliver to a certain shelter, to which the drivers responded by completely ignoring the "rules" and pushing on through to deliver items to neighbourhoods that really, really needed them. Some drivers were turned away by shelter "officials," so they simply left boxes of donated goods at the entrance and waited and watched from afar as the shelter inhabitants or passersby came along and took what they needed. The drivers then took what remained somewhere else.

The official line on the distribution of donations at shelters was that "refugees cannot receive relief without advance notice." It was an understandable attempt to bring some order to chaos — but in those early days, *everything* was needed. The general consensus among the people I knew who were taking donations up north was just to go — *go anywhere*. And you'd find people who needed help. This disaster was that big. *Half a million people had been displaced.*

I was willing to just get in a truck, head north, and see where I ended up, but preferred to have a bit of a plan that ideally would benefit a place that wasn't getting any help at all. It was now almost two months since the disaster — I knew I'd been doing my bit, but I hadn't actually been up north.

Some people had been north several times already, to drive donated supplies or help with the cleanup operation. Shelley Sacks had been up there twice. Shelley was the head of Ohana International School in Tokyo — I'd written about her school in my second book, which was a guide to international schools in Japan, and helped her develop her school website. Ohana was also one of the schools regularly featured in one of my magazines, so we had a close professional relationship. She called me as soon as she got back from Tohoku.

I didn't know it then, but that phone call would turn out to be one of the most influential phone calls of my entire life.

Shelley had just got back from her second volunteering trip to Tohoku. She had been volunteering in Minamisanriku, more than 400 miles away from Tokyo, a town that had lost 95 percent of its buildings and almost half of its population. It was a popular destination for foreign volunteers — there were a number of organizations in the area that welcomed English speakers, and some that were actually run by English-speaking foreigners. Shelley had been volunteering with one of them, helping to clear debris.

Shelley had gone to Tohoku with water, clothing, and other things she'd been told were needed and was looking for somewhere to leave them when she'd finished her volunteering responsibilities in Minamisanriku. A friend invited her to meet a colleague's family an hour and a half away, and the two of them were driven along winding coastal roads by an apologetic chain-smoker, who told them his tsunami story.

He'd ignored the warning siren after the earthquake on March 11 and continued driving — people in these areas were used to earthquakes and the small tsunamis that sometimes followed them. Before he knew it, a wall of water had swallowed his car, with him inside it. He managed to smash a window and get out of his car, eventually hauling himself up onto part of a roof that was floating by. He later helped a pregnant woman and her child climb aboard too, and they huddled together as it started snowing. They stayed there throughout the night, and only got off when the waters had subsided a little the following morning. That day, he started smoking.

As the driver told his terrifying story, Shelley was in awe of the scenery around her. There were little villages scattered along the coastal road, one after the other, some of which had survived the tsunami, others that had not. The beautiful views out to sea, and so much devastation inland. She saw beyond the devastation and found her eyes and heart opening to possibilities and beauty. She sensed she was being taken to a very special place.

They eventually reached their destination — one of the few houses that had survived in one of the villages, purely because it had such a steep driveway. The water had come up to the front door, but no further. The house was now providing shelter to fifteen people who had been living there for nearly two months with very few supplies. And the whole of this remote peninsula was full of people living like this. The peninsula was called Oshika-hanto.

On Shelley's return to Tokyo she felt compelled to tell me about what she had seen, and how people were trying to survive in this isolated part of Japan that nobody seemed to have heard of. She wanted to find a way that her school could support the area. And she urged me to take my supplies there.

This was *exactly* what I was looking for. Somewhere remote. Somewhere that wasn't getting the supplies they needed. Somewhere that wasn't full of volunteers. A place with people who were trying to make it on their own, two months on from the biggest natural disaster that Japan had ever seen. People who felt isolated and needed reminding that they *hadn't* been forgotten. To be reminded that people *were* thinking of them.

I was going to Oshika-hanto.

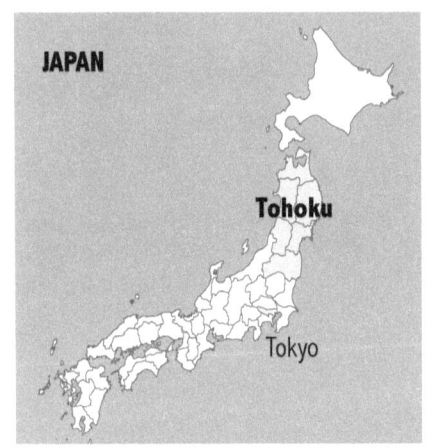

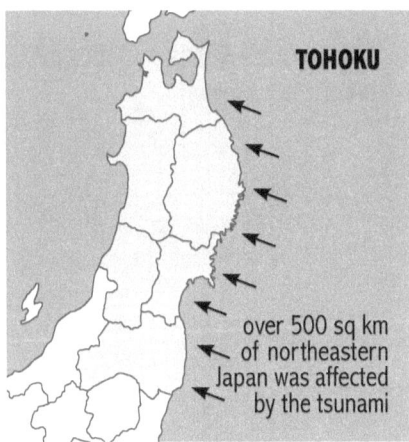

JAPAN
Tohoku
Tokyo

TOHOKU
over 500 sq km
of northeastern
Japan was affected
by the tsunami

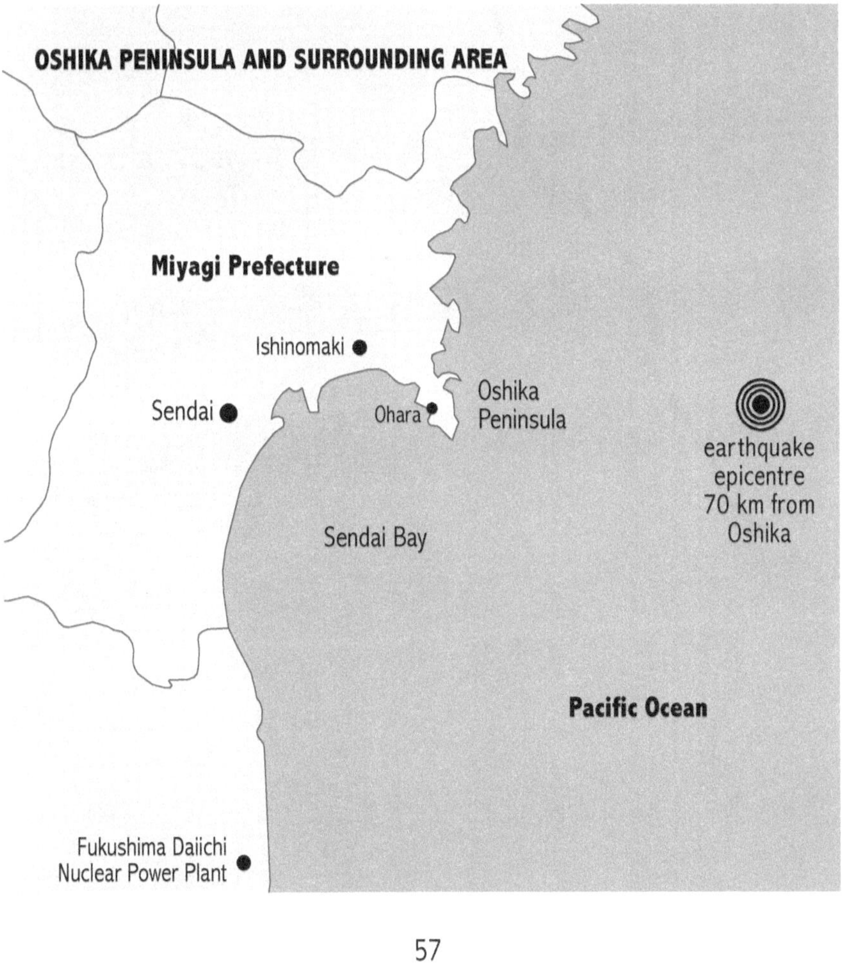

OSHIKA PENINSULA AND SURROUNDING AREA
Miyagi Prefecture
Ishinomaki
Sendai
Ohara
Oshika
Peninsula
earthquake
epicentre
70 km from
Oshika
Sendai Bay
Pacific Ocean
Fukushima Daiichi
Nuclear Power Plant

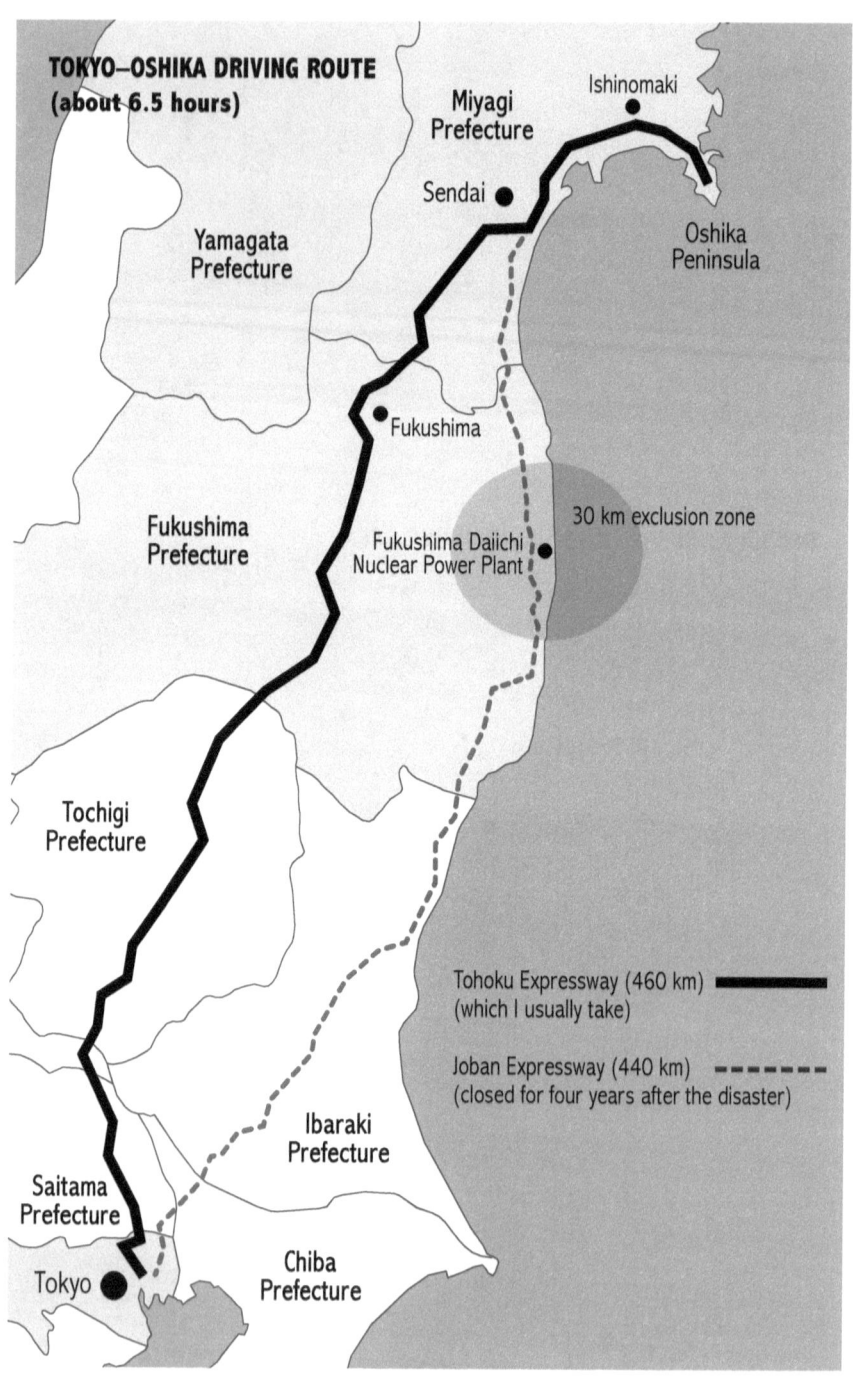

6: Oshika-hanto

Oshika-hanto (Oshika peninsula), the closest part of Japan to the epicentre of the earthquake, was the first part of Japan to be hit by the tsunami. The land there has permanently sunk by a metre, 80 percent of the homes were destroyed, and the peninsula was entirely cut off from the rest of Japan for a week. The tip of the peninsula was about a seven-hour drive from Tokyo, and that was where we were headed.

My companion and co-driver was Andrew Abbey, a fellow Brit who was also a long-term resident of Japan who ran his own business. He'd responded to my Facebook call for someone to drive up with me. He'd already been up to Tohoku a few times on delivery runs, and understood that we were going to a *very* remote area. He was up for the challenge, and was determined to get the contents of these boxes of donated goods to people who needed them.

The boxes were waiting at Narita. Iain from Virgin was disappointed that he couldn't make the trip up north with me, and even though he'd already done so much he was still keen to offer assistance, so drove me to the airport to help load up the truck. We stopped at Shin-Koiwa on the way to meet Andrew at the truck rental company. After the rental agent took a quick glance at our driving licences, we were all off to Narita.

Not long after we arrived at the cargo shed, the truck rental company called. They'd given us a truck that neither of us were legally allowed to drive. The law had recently changed so that anyone with a driving licence issued during the past few years could not drive a 2-ton *long* truck. We could drive a 2-ton *short* truck — it just wouldn't be big enough to fit all the boxes in. So two vehicles arrived one hour later, with huge apologies from the rental company's staff, who we roped into helping us load up all the boxes.

It felt especially good to load up the nappies — I'd been told about a group of young mothers who were not in shelters and not getting the supplies they needed, and they'd be getting first dibs on them. In addition to all the boxes, we also loaded up a bicycle and a bright yellow bicycle trailer I'd been given by Paul Kraft — a friend of a friend who had used it for hauling his kids in when they were little, and thought it might come in handy for the people of Tohoku. I had taken it, thinking it would be helpful when we needed to get items to places where the vehicles couldn't go, and then planned on giving it to someone up there who could put it to good use. The boxes almost reached the roof, so we only just managed to squeeze our sleeping bags into the tiny space at the top.

We decorated the vehicles with Union Jacks so that Japanese people might feel encouraged by the efforts of complete strangers halfway across the world. The rental company staff were themselves very touched, and were full of excitement and encouragement about our trip, saying "ganbatte" to us as we set off. This struck a chord with me — *ganbatte* was the word that I had taught English people to say in the videos I'd made. I hadn't expected to hear Japanese people say it to me.

I also hadn't expected to be driving alone. Neither had Andrew. But now that we had two vehicles instead of one, we had no choice. Andrew hadn't thought to tell me that, while he'd been up north on a number of occasions, he'd never been the actual driver, and in fact hadn't driven in Japan before. And he claimed that his Japanese, while better than mine, wasn't that great. Neither of us could work out how to use the Japanese satnavs in the vehicles, so I was supposed to be navigating with my iPad from within the smaller vehicle, while Andrew followed me. This was going to be entertaining!

We stopped off at a service station and a lovely old man gave me the biggest, brightest smile as I bought a coffee from him. I was wearing my Help Japan T-shirt, which intrigued him, so I pointed out the trucks, telling him what British people had done. Then he beamed even more, bowed several times, and handed me a huge bag of *umeboshi* (pickled plums) as he said possibly the most sincere thank you I had ever heard in my life.

There were two highways that would get you to Tohoku, and both took you through Fukushima prefecture, but only the Tohoku Expressway was open because the other one, the Joban Expressway, went near the coastline — 400 km of which was a disaster area. Toll fees had been waived on the Tohoku Expressway, but you had to have documentation showing that you were part of the relief effort. We had obtained official paperwork, but a new document had just come into existence, which we weren't aware of. So we found ourselves apologizing a lot at the toll booths, as we explained what we were doing and crossed our fingers. Eighty percent of the time they let us through without charging a fee.

It was a time when people who drove the Tohoku Expressway had Geiger counters in their car to measure the radiation, which was known to spike as soon you got to Fukushima prefecture, despite the damaged nuclear power plant being on the other side of it. There were red flashing signs all along the way, some of which showed the radiation levels, but I couldn't read any of them. I really had no idea where we were, or whether we would accidentally enter the exclusion zone, so just hoped that none of the signs were saying we had to turn off or we'd face a massive fine. There were very few vehicles on the road — just a few trucks and small vans, and Japanese army (Self-Defence Force or SDF) vehicles. We drove right through Fukushima prefecture, and the city to the right of the highway looked as lit up as any city would, with no indication of the drama now associated with this area.

In fact, for the entire journey, you would not have known that anything had affected this area. Andrew warned me that the scenery would suddenly change, and that the affected areas were literally a few minutes away from "normality."

Everything was still looking normal when we arrived at Sendai around 11 p.m. Sendai was the closest major city to Oshika-hanto, and the largest city in Tohoku, with a population of over one million. The tsunami had travelled up to ten kilometres inland in the Sendai area, destroying countless residences and businesses, including the airport, which was a busy international travel hub.

It was far too late for us to call the young mums we were delivering to in Sendai, or the pet shelter I'd found out about. Oshika was another two and a half hours away, and all we had done until this point was drive. We hadn't got rid of any boxes, so there was no chance of us sleeping in the truck like we'd planned, and we couldn't see any hotels anywhere. There was only one option. A love hotel.

Love hotels are everywhere in Japan, and easily identified by brightly coloured signs indicating the fee for a "rest" or "stay," more often than not in

English. To be frank, people go to them to have sex. A rest means you're popping in for a few hours, a stay means you're staying overnight. Some are themed, which can range from things like Disneyland or a tropical island, to a classroom or a doctor's office, or a full-on S&M dungeon. But most are just like normal hotels. They're mostly frequented by married couples who want a bit of privacy from the extended family they might live with. There's no stigma or shame associated with them. They're great fun!

But Andrew and I weren't there for fun, and surely had to be one of the few "couples" who have ever stayed in a love hotel for the purpose of actually *trying* to get a good night's sleep. We stayed in the same room, fully clothed, in the same bed. I was relieved to be sharing a room because I was somewhere so unfamiliar, and so close to the coast while the aftershocks kept coming.

However, I was so paranoid about rolling over that I actually didn't get much sleep at all. It was a tiny bed, I was next to someone I didn't know that well, and most certainly didn't want to be giving off any signals to him that might be misinterpreted or deemed inappropriate. Andrew was probably feeling exactly the same. After finally getting a bit of shut-eye, we were shaken awake by a 5:30 a.m. earthquake that gently rocked the building, and we rather sleepily got ready for the day ahead. As we had arrived late the night before we hadn't taken much time to notice anything other than the red lights amusingly lighting the walkways to each hotel room, but in the daylight we could see how the entire set of stairs leading to the second floor had been lifted out of the concrete floor — the first evidence that *something* had happened here.

Our first stop was the Japan Earthquake Animal Rescue and Support (JEARS) Sendai house. As soon as I had announced my mission and headed off for the UK on March 19, my friend Nina Godoy had asked me to collect pet items, of which people in the UK — a nation of animal lovers rivalling that of Japan — had donated almost 900. We finally found a tiny building, which we didn't think could possibly be an animal shelter until Cheri Deatsch opened the door and we saw some pet goods through the doorway. Cheri and the others had travelled all the way from the US to rescue animals that had been abandoned after the tsunami. Cheri was a Field Disaster Response Manager with Kinship Circle — a US-based non-profit organization devoted to helping animals affected by disasters around the world — and had some other volunteers with her. I was surprised at how young these American women were, some looking the same age as my teenage nieces, and I was amazed at their compassion that had led them to fly across the world to help a country with which they had no connection. Four of them were sleeping side by side in a tiny tatami room, with cats all around them.

They were taking care of eleven cats, including two tiny kittens and their mum, who hissed at anyone that came near her. The kittens were really sick, with one of them unable to open one eye, and it was doubtful they would make it. But the volunteers were busy coordinating vet appointments and trying to find the time to organize everything. There were boxes of donated goods stacked up in the entrance, and I wondered whether our items were actually needed and whether we should take them to another one of the JEARS houses, but Cheri assured us they were very much needed — their Fukushima house was closing and they were about to receive a lot more animals from there as well as the many that came in each day. Just the previous day, the girls had rescued five cats that had been living in a tiny office for two months since the earthquake. Their owners had fed them, but not cleaned up after them, so the office was inches thick in faeces and the cats were traumatized — I couldn't imagine what these volunteers had had to deal with.

Cheri was especially pleased to see that we had brought so many towels — 140 to be exact. Towels and crates were things they went through on a regular basis. After a little cuddle with a poorly kitten, I took a list of everything they needed and promised to spread the word.

Then we were off in search of the young mums. I had heard about Miho through Kieron Cashell, another person who'd once worked for me and then become a good friend. Kieron was married to a very impressive Japanese woman who'd been doing everything she could to identify young mothers that needed help. Kieron's wife had been in touch with Miho, a 22-year-old who had climbed to safety from the tsunami, with her tiny baby in her arms.

Miho, along with ten of her girlfriends who were also young mothers, was *really* struggling. Kind parents in the UK had donated almost 300 packs of nappies and I knew that Miho and her friends really needed some. Until recently, Miho had been living in one of the shelters and receiving the basic necessities, but once a small apartment had been found for her, she was on her own. This was happening to a lot of people once they'd been moved out of the shelters, and it made me even more determined to find people who were trying to make it on their own.

I was doing my best trying to find Miho's address with my iPad, as Andrew drove behind me. I ended up down a tiny lane with what looked like very old houses on either side, and called Miho to see if we were in the right place. Nope. I handed over my mobile to an old woman who was watching curiously from the garden of the house I had pulled up in front of, and hoped that somehow between them I would be able to find out where we were and then find Miho. It was eventually decided that the *gaijin* should head to a convenience store, to which the old woman gave directions, and where Miho agreed to meet us. I thanked the old woman and opened the door of my van to get back in, when I felt her hand on my arm.

"What's inside?" she asked, looking me in the eye.

I tried to process the three things that had just happened that were distinctly different to my previous experiences with Japanese people — one, she had touched me; two, she had asked a direct question; and three, she had looked me in the eye. This didn't happen in Tokyo.

"In the truck?" I asked, not quite understanding why she would be asking.

"Yes, what do you have in there?"

"Just some things from England." Suddenly it dawned on me, so I asked, "Do *you* need anything?"

She nodded. I looked in her eyes again and this time stopped thinking about directions and actually *looked* at her. I saw fatigue and deep sadness. And I felt like such an insensitive idiot. I looked around at the tiny houses that ran along this little lane. Who was I to assume that the people living here hadn't been affected? Who was I to come up here thinking I'd be able to tell who needed help? I was embarrassed that my lack of awareness meant that this old woman had to *ask* me for the help I had come here to offer. I was ashamed of the person that had been about to get in the van and drive off *without really seeing a thing*.

I called Miho and told her we would be another thirty minutes. My usually good instincts had kicked back in — amidst the fatigue and sorrow I'd seen in this woman's eyes, there was also hope. And I realized that, sure, I'd come to Tohoku to bring supplies, but I'd also come prepared to be gentle, to listen, and to offer a bit of TLC; however, those skills weren't really needed. Mike Alfant had been right when he'd said, "It's not what you think." They didn't need sad, sympathetic faces, however well-intentioned. They needed to be entertained by bright, happy faces, even if it was just for a few moments.

I slapped on some red lipstick, put on my biggest smile, and started chatting away in my rubbish Japanese, making loads of mistakes but really not caring. I would make this little old woman smile if it was the last thing I did — along with all her little old lady friends who suddenly appeared out of nowhere. They found it funny that this English girl, not much taller than them, could yank open the back of a truck and climb right inside it. They oohed and aahed at all the boxes that were piled up. They giggled when, after they took just one tube of toothpaste, I insisted on giving them four. And when they pointed out their houses they laughed at me as I insisted on running down the lane with a whole box of nappies for their grandchildren, which I put outside their front doors so they wouldn't have to carry anything. Andrew understood what I was doing right away. He was brilliant — loading and unloading the back of the van as quickly as possible and grabbing the camera to take a few pictures — both of us struggling with our reluctance to take photos of what should be completely private, but knowing how important it would be to show the people who gave these goods exactly what happened to them, and what a difference their kindness and generosity was making.

Two energy drinks were presented to us by the old woman who started it all off, and two cans of coffee came from a neighbour. We were late to meet Miho, but both felt we wanted our new friends to see us enjoy our drinks, so we stayed with them as we gulped them down, thanked them for their generosity, and moved to get in our vehicles. I looked around at the old woman as she watched us go, and then I ran back, overcome with the impulse to throw my arms around her and hug her tight before grabbing her hands in mine, which I did. I looked into her eyes, which were now welling up with tears — I tried to tell her to take care, that England was thinking of her, and that she would be OK. The actual sentences I attempted to make were probably full of mistakes, but it didn't matter. She might not have understood my words, but I know she understood my heart.

We pulled into the convenience store car park, and within minutes Miho drove up. On a first glance at the area around the *konbini* you wouldn't have known that anything had happened here, and then just to one side of the car park I saw that giant cracks had ripped the entire walkway apart. People seemed to be going about their business as usual, but after the experience with the old ladies I was now certain that we shouldn't assume anything based on appearances. I asked Andrew to open up the back of the truck and let people take what they needed, while I ran off to the bank with Miho. I still had thousands of pounds tucked in my knickers!

When I'd returned to Japan on April 17, I had immediately gone to a currency exchange office at Narita Airport, where I explained what the money was for and asked them to waive any fees — I was always determined that all of the money I had raised would either be used to transport the items up north or get into the hands of the people there. I didn't want any of it going on administration fees or any other fees that weren't absolutely relevant to the people who had been affected by the tsunami. I understood the need for a charity's administrative costs to be covered, and for staff to be employed and paid — I had worked in that capacity myself during a year off from university — I just didn't want any of the money I'd collected in England to go toward such costs. I had looked people in the eye in England and told them that it would be used to get these items to Tohoku, and as for the rest, I would physically take it up north with me. And I was going to stick to my word.

The Narita currency exchange staff had advised me to wait until I actually got to Sendai to exchange the money, because the banks there would be able to waive the fees, and I had £2085, along with ¥162,000 from the Tokyo fundraiser I'd organized with my artist friend.

On the way to the bank, Miho and I chatted about what had happened to her and her family, and how she and her friends were doing now. Miho had lost everything. The water had come up to her waist as she held on to her baby and climbed to safety. And now she no longer had access to the supplies that had been available at the shelter. Her girlfriends, all also in their early twenties and with young children, were in the same situation. Their husbands no longer had jobs, and they had no way of getting what they and their children needed. Miho had at least been given a car now, but it meant that she was constantly running around trying to support her girlfriends and neighbours as well as attending to her own needs.

After asking her gentle questions about how she was managing, I decided to take the plunge and ask her directly whether she and her friends needed money. As with the old ladies, I was surprised at how forthcoming this young woman was — they did indeed need money and were really struggling. I knew Japanese people well enough to know that they would not answer in this way unless they were *really* struggling. I started to feel annoyed at some of the information that I had read before going to Tohoku — it claimed that the affected people were all being taken care of and they had more than enough of what they needed, that handing out cash would be disrespectful, and it was the government's responsibility to take care of everyone — blah, blah, blah. What I was seeing was very different to that.

I was there to find out what people needed, and do my best to give it to them. Miho and her friends needed money, we had it, and they were more than welcome to it. So I changed the English money into yen, and ended up with more than ¥300,000 to use in response to the needs we saw in the people we would meet throughout our trip.

The bank was packed full of people — Miho explained that because so many people had lost their ID or bank books or cards, the bank was constantly full as the staff tried to replace all the lost documents. I was surprised that the mood was so upbeat among both customers and staff — senior personnel came around the front of the bank and just wandered along the aisles, chatting casually to people. A woman came out from behind the counter and greeted Miho — it turned out to be the first time they had seen each other since March 11. She asked Miho whether she was OK, and Miho told her that her house had been washed away, but she was fine — the woman replied that the same had happened to her. But both of them were smiling and laughing together as they said it. It was touching, humbling, and yet also energizing to see this brief exchange. It reaffirmed the earlier sense I'd had with the old ladies: that feeling "sorry" for everyone wasn't what was needed here — perhaps that had been necessary during the weeks immediately after the earthquake, but now did not seem like the time for it at all. Instead it was more like "shit happens, and granted this is pretty big shit, but let's get on with it."

I told Miho that we were planning to go to Oshika. To my surprise she said that her parents were on Oshika, and that there was absolutely nothing there anymore, and that they needed water. I remembered Shelley taking water there, but that was a few weeks earlier. How could people *still* be in need of water two months on? This just didn't make sense to me. Our drive up had been so easy that anyone could take water up, or buy it from the local shops (which had loads of it), then just go for a drive! There seemed to be no excuse for people not to have water.

I explained to the bank staff where the English money had come from, and about how English people cared so much, and it was clear that this meant a lot to them. They thanked me again and again, and I left Miho to sort out a few of her own affairs. I walked through the busy bank, with rows and rows of people sitting patiently looking in the direction I came from as they watched a huge TV screen. I held my head down as I walked past — I am not a shy person, but suddenly I found it very hard to make eye contact. I was also hyper aware of my "Help Japan" T-shirt and whether it could be interpreted as patronizing or make anyone feel uncomfortable in any way. The very last thing I wanted to do was make anyone feel like they couldn't cope with what nature had thrown at them, and that they *needed* outsiders to "interfere." I didn't consider myself an outsider in Japan, but how were they to know that? The few unkind and insensitive comments that had been made by some people online and directed at my activities popped into my head but didn't stay long — I'd already seen first-hand that people were *very* much in need of support and that's what we were there for.

While Miho finished up in the bank, I opened the back of the van and pulled out ten copies of a book I had written a while before, for Japanese women. I had put a few boxes in the van as I'd heard that people were in need of something to relieve their boredom and knew that my *Ask Caroline* book, with a few slightly saucy sections, would bring about more than a few giggles. I put some money in each of the books, then put the books in some goodie bags that were left over from the book's launch party — one bag each for Miho and all her girlfriends. When Miho came out of the bank, I pointed out what was in the books so she would make sure her friends didn't miss it. Conscious of not offending, I asked her whether it was OK that I had done that. The relief on her face was incredible — I could not understand why people in Tokyo were saying that people in Tohoku didn't need any money.

When we drove back to the konbini to find Andrew, we found him standing in the back of the truck, with unloaded boxes on the floor, surrounded by a huge group of women choosing items they needed. Moving quickly into action, I climbed into the back of the truck to locate specific items, and was again surprised by how willing everyone was to be helped. I started asking them where their cars were parked, how many children they had, how many people lived with them, etc., and then loading up their cars with triple the amount they actually asked for. I had them in stitches as I ran clumsily about the car park with boxes I insisted on giving them. We really could have stayed there for hours and it felt awful to say to people that we had to leave, but we had to get to Miho's place and still head off to the peninsula. We followed Miho to her tiny apartment and unloaded a wide range of supplies for her to distribute to her friends who were coming by that evening.

And those lovely posters that Misa had brought along to Waterbeach Primary in Cambridge — they were perfect to share with Miho and her friends. She was thrilled to read all the Japanese and English messages from parents so many thousands of miles away. I asked her for a list of other items she needed that I could share online and that people could send her directly, we both gave her big hugs, and then she led us to a nearby grocer before we waved her goodbye.

I had been in touch with Damian Penston, another foreigner who was really active in the aftermath. He had heard that I was going to Oshika, and had called me the previous day to tell me of a community centre at the very tip of the peninsula in a little town called Ayukawa. They needed gasoline and fresh fruit and vegetables. We knew it would be difficult to find a grocer on the peninsula, so we stocked up with boxes and boxes of anything that did not require cooking — the store staff took us to the storage room out the back and we just told them to load up our trolleys with everything. Having that cash with us was just brilliant — we were able to respond to immediate needs by buying items locally, therefore supporting their economy, and then delivering them directly to where they were needed.

Until this point, we had seen very little evidence that anything had happened to this part of the country, but knew that the peninsula would be a very different story. And we were getting closer. Despite not being able to see the ocean, it soon became clear that we were driving through a seaside town — wherever you are in the world, they always seem to have a certain feel to them.

Traffic going in both directions along the main road was busy, and we noticed more SDF vehicles. We also noticed that the street was becoming increasingly dusty, tatami mats were piled up next to the road, and entire first floors of some buildings were empty. But the buildings themselves, windows and all, remained intact.

When we drove over the bridge between Ishinomaki Bay and Mangoku Bay, the landscape quickly changed. Officials wearing dust masks filled the streets, waving orange batons to direct traffic. We had those jerry cans still to fill with gasoline — we'd wanted to leave it as late as possible to ensure the money went to a gas station that really needed the income, but I was worried we might be leaving it too late, so pulled over and waited for Andrew to catch up with me. When I got out of my van to speak to him, I was hit by a stench I had never encountered before or since. I'd heard about it — everyone who had visited the disaster area had talked about it. Some said it was the smell of rotting wood or fish. Some said it was other things rotting that nobody wanted to think about. It was strong and pervasive, but it was surprising how quickly you got used to it.

I ran to a police officer to ask him if there was a gas station ahead; it had started to look a bit like we were about to enter a disaster movie so I didn't hold up much hope, but he assured me that there was one right around the corner, so we kept driving. On either side of the road were the remnants of buildings and cars that had been destroyed — Andrew was later to comment on how he had expected to see cars that had been battered about a bit, but not to see them so completely and utterly mangled. Next to one elementary school was a big swimming pool — a couple of cars jutted out from one end, and one car sat right in the middle of the pool. We were to drive past this pool four times in the following 24 hours, and each time there was a bunch of officials standing and staring at the car in the middle of the pool, surely wondering how on earth to deal with it. I had mixed feelings about the idea of taking photos of all this sadness and destruction, but Japanese people were standing around taking photos, so I felt it would be OK to take one of this bizarre sight.

There were plenty more bizarre sights, but we didn't photograph them; I had become tired of seeing all the photos that volunteers had returned to Tokyo with and I didn't want to add to them. It felt a bit like a competition to see who could come back with the most shocking photo. Andrew and I agreed that those weren't the memories we wanted to carry with us nor share with others — we were on the same wavelength with so many different aspects of this trip. As we drove through the town looking at all the broken houses and mangled cars, we knew this was caused by a force of nature, but somehow forgot that it was the sea until we came across a ship right in the middle of it all — random sea vessels were found everywhere inland, and many of them were balancing precariously on the tops of buildings and piles of debris.

We drove through what looked like a massive puddle that covered the entire width of the road — the puddle was about a foot deep and 100 metres long. We soon reached the gas station. It was a small family-run business, so it felt good to leave money with them after filling both vehicles plus the jerry cans we would be delivering further along the peninsula.

The proprietor of the gas station was a woman who explained that she had been celebrating her 60th birthday — a significant birthday in Japan — on the day of the tsunami, and she, along with her husband and son, had escaped to the second floor of the gas station. She pointed to a line just below the ceiling of the first floor, indicating how far up the water had come. I was amazed at how cheerful she seemed as she pointed out all the damage that had been caused, and I was also amazed that she had found the time and made the effort amid all this chaos to have put on the most beautiful false eyelashes: their toilet had to be filled from a hose, tsunami sludge was packed up against the side of the building, and they had no fruit or vegetables, yet she had impeccable eyelashes. I loved her.

We offered her some fruit and vegetables and set up a "free shop" of goods donated from England so that her customers or anybody passing by could help themselves. She urged us to be careful of the tide, indicating water that had suddenly appeared along the road by the gas station, and it was then that I remembered that the land here had sunk after the earthquake. We hadn't driven through a puddle to get here — it had been the tide. Any place that was near the sea now got flooded twice a day. I had read about this but hadn't expected the water to come up out of the concrete before I realized anything was happening. We started moving quickly.

We'd distributed enough supplies that we now needed only one vehicle, so we left my smaller van around the corner, and for the first time Andrew and I were driving together. I was so glad of his company.

Andrew and I had met for a coffee a week before we left for Tohoku. We didn't know each other well, and while I really appreciated his offer to drive north with me and all the supplies from England, I had heard stories of people going up north with companions they didn't know well, only for the whole experience to turn into a nightmare because of differing opinions on what to do. I'd always had the sense that simply getting in a vehicle, driving up north, and responding to what I recognized as immediate needs was the best way to distribute the items and cash I'd collected. I had wanted to travel with someone who was prepared to rough it by sleeping in the truck, didn't care about needing a shower, and would be able to cope with my lifelong tendency to charge full steam ahead on occasion — I am fully aware that this can be irritating for some people around me, but also aware of how handy it can be if you need someone to make a quick decision and act on it. I wanted to be honest with Andrew and forewarn him about what I could be like. I didn't have anything to worry about — we were in complete agreement about everything. He was more than happy to just stop randomly without too much planning, and also wanted to focus on the people who were trying to make it independently. I couldn't have hoped for a better companion.

Oshika took my breath away. Not just because of the destruction that the tsunami had left behind, but because of the fact that despite that, it was *stunningly* beautiful. I had never seen anything quite like it. Incredible views of a clear blue sea, shimmering far out into the distance, and dotted with little islands. The forests sprawling high up into the mountains, with huge trees on the mountainsides, growing right to the top. Little fields scattered around, full of fruit and vegetables grown by the local farmers. I had not expected to find such beauty here.

We drove up and down the hills of Oshika, and I was reminded of driving through the English West Country lanes where I grew up and that I had reconnected with while giving my recent talks. In between the hills we came across what used to be tiny villages, with most of the houses completely destroyed, a random roof perfectly intact but without a building underneath it, boats lying on their sides in the middle of the rubble, and large buoys scattered around the broken wood. Village after village presented us with these scenes of devastation.

As we drove down the windy roads I could feel both Andrew and I tense up as *yet again* we drove through *yet another* village that had been destroyed by the sea, which was now only inches away from the recently cleared roads. We breathed our tension out as we started the drive up the next hill. It was an odd rollercoaster of emotions, but strangely I found a peace that I had been missing since March 11 — something was happening to that bit of my heart that had broken when I'd watched the television footage in the Saipan bar. My heart was being put back together. I felt like I was where I should be, where I could help.

To the left I saw half a house that had been left standing, and some people were walking around outside it. Andrew was driving and I asked him to stop. I was out of the truck door almost before he'd come to a halt. I ran up through the rubble toward the house, remembering stories of how dangerous the wreckage was just in time to miss jumping on a huge nail pointing upward — I had prepared by having a tetanus shot beforehand and bought metal-soled wellies just in case, but didn't want to waste time rummaging around trying to find them, so I was still wearing my trainers.

I cheerily yelled hello, asked how they were doing, and whether they needed anything. I encouraged them to bring their car down to the truck to take whatever they wanted, saying it was all from England and there was plenty of stuff for them and their friends. (I hadn't expected to see cars in such perfect condition amid such wreckage until I remembered that this was probably how a lot of people managed to escape the tsunami and survive.) A woman and two men drove toward us, down a track road I hadn't seen before. I handed them a piece of paper with some Japanese sentences printed on it that I thought might be useful. It read: "I went to England and gave talks to schools about what a wonderful country Japan is, and how much I love living here. I showed the children some photographs of how beautiful Japan is. Their parents donated lots of items that could help you in your daily lives. And many of their teachers now want to visit. Please know that England supports you! Please tell me if you need any of these items: jerry cans, nappies or nappy bags or baby wipes, cans of dry shampoo, nail clippers, any medical items, cling film, garbage bags, dust/surgical masks, cotton buds, food items, sanitary towels, brand new underwear, toothpaste, toothbrushes, or children's toys, games, and books."

They studied our printout, pointed out what they needed, and we loaded up their car. The fruit and vegetables were a huge hit and again we were so pleased to have brought that cash up with us. Two men in overalls soon joined us and also studied our "mission statement." We assumed they were from the neighbourhood until they explained they were JCB (backhoe loader) operators from Yokohama near Tokyo, and had volunteered their time to help clear the area. They were to become the *only* volunteers we came across over the entire 30 km we ended up driving in total on that part of Oshika, but connecting with them was going to turn out to be invaluable when we unexpectedly encountered them again.

And so we continued in the same way along the Oshika coastline — pulling over when we came across anyone attempting to make it independently in the remains of their house. We met a few women who had the most incredible view of the sea and the sun setting right in front of what used to be their home, which was now a makeshift tent made of blue plastic sheeting. We stopped and chatted to them, along with their little poodle, as they accepted the fruit and vegetables. They were especially pleased to also have some children's toys for their own amusement. One young woman asked whether Andrew was my other half, to which he made some joke along the lines of "I wish," which had her in fits of laughter as she then told us she wanted an English boyfriend. She chose a Winnie the Pooh colouring book for herself.

Eventually we made it to our destination at the end of the peninsula — a community centre in Ayukawa, next to Ishinomaki city's Oshika Branch Administrative Offices. Ishinomaki is the nearest city to Oshika and since 2005 it has had governance over the peninsula. Prior to that, Oshika was an independent district.

There were very few people at the community centre, which you could see was once the heart of Ayukawa, again with a beautiful view of the ocean. The tsunami had reached more than three metres high in Ayukawa, and it destroyed 80 percent of the town's buildings. There was what seemed like a never-ending mass of debris, with just a few houses left up in the hills that overlooked what had once been a busy port.

We met Eriko, who was coordinating the relief effort in Ayukawa, and asked her what was needed from our supplies as we handed over the gasoline we had bought for the town earlier in the day. She took us to what looked like a huge gymnasium. It was full of donated supplies that she assured me were going out every day, which was good to hear, because I didn't want to leave anything sitting around anywhere for ages if we knew it would be of immediate use to others we were finding along our route. Eriko took lots of food from England, and the fruit and vegetables, along with some other items, but was most pleased with the yellow bike trailer that Paul Kraft had given me, so we left it there to help her with her delivery efforts.

The stress that Eriko and her team were under was visible in their faces, the way they walked, and the way they communicated — I couldn't imagine how they were managing to be there for everyone else in their community when they were probably grieving their own losses. I felt sad that we couldn't make more of a difference to the Ayukawa community.

It was starting to get dark but, as long as we still came across the odd person, we were both determined to keep stopping and offering help. We flagged down an old man who looked rather bemused at seeing these two foreigners and their truck, and then he called his family to come see what was going on. Our mood, upbeat again, got the adults smiling and the children excited about what was in the truck. One young lad, in his Oshika Junior High School uniform, was fascinated to see me clamber all over the boxes to reach for items they might like and need that were located at the very back. I sensed that he was itching to get in the back of the truck, too, so told him I really needed some help finding things and asked if he would like to help me. Grandpa shone the torch for us both as his grandson climbed over the boxes to take things from me. Dad told us that there was a primary school nearby, so we left a couple of boxes of toys for the school children before heading off into the darkness.

By now it was absolutely pitch black, and of course there weren't any lights on the road. So we drove really carefully, stopping when we saw a light on in a building, to again offer items from England or to find out what was needed. We came across another place that had become a shelter, this time with people staying in it — it was the health and welfare centre in the Seiyukan building. The staff seemed to bear the signs of extreme stress, while a group of children were at the back of the entrance hall, pulling items out of cardboard boxes as their parents wearily looked on. Some boys saw us arrive with our boxes and came charging toward us, ripping open the boxes to grab what was inside. The shelter staff watched as the parents came running after them, trying to tell them off. I'd heard stories of how children in the shelters had been exhibiting "brattish" behaviour, but it was really upsetting to see first hand — I didn't blame them and I sympathized with the parents who, especially given their own trauma, must have been finding it so hard to say no to children who had lost so much.

We didn't go further into the shelter, but remained at the entrance — it was late and everybody there seemed exhausted. We got the feeling that we weren't wanted. It was interesting to see not only how people's needs differed in different places, but also how their *energy* differed — we found the people who were trying to make it on their own were so much more upbeat than the people who took help from or sheltered at centres. I felt ashamed at being glad that we didn't go in. And I was haunted for weeks afterward by a little girl I saw there. She had just stood watching the boys while they ripped open the boxes, with no words, no expression, no movement. I wished I had stayed and talked to her, held her hand, played a game. Given her my time. But I didn't. I just left some letters and pictures from the children at Trafalgar School, and we headed back off into the darkness.

I had friends who had spent time at the shelters playing with children and talking to their parents, and I really admired them for doing so. I didn't feel able to do that — I found the energy at the shelters really affected me. I found it much more difficult to be at a shelter as opposed to driving around the areas that had been completely destroyed.

We were starting to think about where we might park the truck and get some sleep in the back of it now that we had unloaded some boxes and therefore made quite a bit of space to sleep "comfortably." Then we saw a couple of lit windows in the distance, so decided to do a final check to see whether anything was needed. We pulled up in a tiny car park outside a small building and walked up to the full-length clear glass doors, behind which we saw about seven Japanese men sitting around a table. They were drinking cans of beer in front of a huge TV screen — not what we had expected at all!

We peered through the doors and two of the men pointed at us and gestured for us to come in and join them — they were the Yokohama JCB operators we had met earlier in the day. They were getting nicely drunk with a couple of village officials and a few disaster relief workers. They asked us where we were going to sleep, and when we told them "in the back of the truck," they insisted that we sleep there, in the village community centre. There were a few tiny rooms off from the main room they were drinking in, they had futons, and they were extremely insistent with their hospitality, pulling up chairs and offering us cans of beer. There really didn't seem like a more appropriate time to have a beer than this one, so even I took a can and we decided to stay the night. We said *kanpai* ("cheers") along with everyone, and settled down for what was left of the evening.

I did not expect to find so much laughter and silliness amid all the destruction we had seen that day, and for the first time since March 11 I didn't feel guilty for laughing. For two months I had found it really hard to find joy in life; I had found it very difficult to laugh with my usual abandon, and smiles had felt a little half-hearted. As much as I had needed to cry, I also needed to laugh. And the men we met that night made me feel that it was OK to laugh again.

These incredible men, who had either lost their entire communities or had travelled throughout northern Japan to volunteer to help clear rubble that went on for miles and miles, had us in stitches. If they could laugh, I certainly could. When I enquired about any local people who might require nappies, I got the response, "Only if they're for big, old women!" and I didn't expect to hear someone else joke about making his own tsunami when he spilt beer on the floor. The laughter continued as I showed them my *Ask Caroline* book for Japanese women on my iPad. The Yokohama boys instantly went to the underwear chapter and sat giggling about G-strings and then tried to tell me all about "*batoru pantsu*" and "*ekusaitingu pantsu*," with batoru (battle) pants being big, cotton pants that cover everything, and ekusaitingu (exciting) pants being lacy, sexy ones.

When it came to getting the futons out to go to bed, I was amazed to find myself joining in on the "pile ons" amid fits of laughter. One of the locals took a bit of a shine to me, and when I came back after popping outside, he was giggling away to Andrew about something, which Andrew refused to repeat to me at the time. The next day he told me that Takahashi-san had been enamoured with what he had called my "lovely big English bottom," which sent me into hysterics. Mine's not especially big by English standards, but I know that some Japanese consider Western women's behinds to be quite impressive, so I wasn't at all offended.

Of course it wasn't all hilarity — I was interested in finding out more about what this area actually needed and was keen to talk to the men about what was going on. I had been surprised that, over a 30 km drive along the coast, we had found only these volunteers and had not yet seen anything being rebuilt or even cleared away. I knew the destroyed area was extensive, and I knew that rebuilding *had* begun in some places, but why did there seem to be no progress along this stunningly beautiful coastline? While Andrew entertained the pig farmer who liked English bottoms, and the Yokohama boys giggled away over my iPad, I started chatting to a quieter man who spoke excellent English and was to give me the final piece of the puzzle I needed to add to the plans I was making for my next "Help Japan" trip around the UK.

In 1995, Seiji Yoshimura was the youngest-ever city councillor in Japan. Four days after the Great Hanshin earthquake that year, he was compelled to visit Kobe and offer assistance. Frustrated with the limitations placed on him as a politician, he soon realized how ineffective he would actually be as a government official and became disillusioned with the career in which he had been making such impressive progress. He resigned from his position and followed the strong desire he had to be with the people of Kobe to help them — he moved to Kobe and dedicated his life to helping the city recover. He lived there for twelve years. Since leaving Kobe in 2007, Seiji has visited disaster-struck areas throughout the world, dedicating his life to a very people-focused recovery strategy. In March 2011 he'd ended up on Oshika.

Seiji worked independently — he didn't want to work for the government because they worked so slowly, yet he was very well-respected by government officials and corporations alike — the huge TV screen in the community centre had been sent by NHK so that Seiji and others could have constant access to the news, much of which of course centred on the tsunami. Seiji was spending much of his time talking to the Oshika Fishermen's Association, finding out what they felt they needed, and working directly with them. He explained that city people and fishermen had completely different needs in response to the tsunami's destruction, and talked about respecting what the local people actually wanted as they rebuilt their lives. He felt that the government tended to impose ideas based on what politicians believed the local people *should* have. At that point, the Oshika residents were being told that if they wanted government assistance, they'd have to move to the cities.

But these people wanted to stay. They had lived *with* the sea for their entire lives. For some people, their ancestors on Oshika could be traced back hundreds of years. They weren't afraid of the sea. When the tsunami came they had known what to do — go to high ground or further out to sea in their boats. They understood the risks that living with the ocean brought, they respected the sea for its strength, and they were grateful for the life the sea had given them. They wanted their lives back, and those lives were lived directly in harmony with the ocean. They wanted to stay on Oshika.

Seiji saw hope on Oshika, as opposed to Rikuzentakata, a city further north that had also lost about 80 percent of its houses. The tsunami had been double the height of the town's sea wall, all the town's evacuation centres had been flooded, and many young men of the town had been killed trying to close the harbour gates. About 1900 people were either missing or dead. Within two months of the earthquake, over 200 people had committed suicide there. Seiji felt that the people of Rikuzentakata had lost all hope and couldn't see any way to recover and resume any relationship with the sea. But the people of Oshika had hope, and Seiji felt that the key to the peninsula's future was helping the fishermen and women to live with the sea again.

The government recognized the importance of the fishing industry on Oshika, and it was paying local people who'd lost their jobs ¥12,000 per day to collect rope, nets, and other fishermen's goods. We'd seen the massive buoys stacked up all along the coast; they could be found *everywhere* the tsunami had been, and the government was also paying a fee per buoy that was collected. But there weren't any plans for people's homes. Seiji was trying to find ways to rebuild the communities on Oshika, right back by the sea where they felt they belonged.

Seiji got up and headed off to the kitchen, as I sat jotting down ideas for what I could do to help on my return to England. He soon returned with a big pot of curry that he dished out over rice to everyone and we all sat around, laughing at the man who liked "lovely big English bottoms," as he had fallen into a *sake*-induced sleep in his chair. He eventually woke up and the locals returned to wherever they were sleeping that night. The two Yokohama boys were sleeping in their truck — we were a futon short for all of us, so one of them insisted on sleeping in the truck, and the other went to keep him company.

So I found myself sleeping on the floor in a tiny room alongside Andrew and three Japanese men, only metres away from the sea, and *surrounded* by evidence of what that sea could do. The community centre we were sleeping in had been completely submerged in the tsunami, but miraculously stayed standing. Parts of the room's walls had been ripped away and cold air blew through, out of one window a mangled car lay on its side, out of another the roof of a house lay intact but on the ground, and in between was the rubble of broken buildings that seemed to go on forever. And as if we needed another reminder, the ground gently shook as we drifted off to sleep.

Yet I felt so safe. These men were amazing — strong, kind, capable, self-sufficient, and gentlemanly. Men who threw together a meal at the drop of a hat *and* cleared it up afterward; men who were physically fit and would clear rubble and rebuild houses so that complete strangers could have their homes back; men who talked intelligently about their own emotions as well as those of others, yet could be childish and silly and really make you laugh. These men were fighting for their country in the way it needed to be fought for at that moment: a way that required love and patience instead of fear and violence — they were the modern day samurai that all those foreign women I'd interviewed for my guidebook had fallen in love with.

A little bit of me fell in love with them, too.

We were shaken awake at 5 a.m. by a huge jolt. Another aftershock. Seiji immediately started making coffee for everyone, and soon a village official turned up with instant ramen for our breakfast. We were asked if we'd like to visit the village's shrine — it had been the local people's priority right after March 11. Of course we said yes, so Andrew and I followed Seiji up there. The shrine had been badly damaged by the earthquake and not the tsunami, which didn't quite reach it. As we walked up the steps to the shrine, we paused to see how far the water had come up them — we stopped to turn around and look back. It was *incredible* how far away from the sea we were and how high up this point was. How on earth did *anything* remain between this point and the ocean? It was staggering to think of what had happened.

From the steps I could see a building close to the edge of the sea — the top floor seemed intact but the entire first floor had been destroyed. The sign on the building was clear though: it was a Hitachi building. I thought of the kindness and support that Hitachi Capital gave me on the UK trip that had eventually led us to this point, and hoped that the Hitachi community on Oshika knew that their "colleagues," very, very far away, were doing a lot to help them.

As we walked up the steps to the shrine we saw how each step had been numbered and placed one on top of the other to rebuild the walkway. At the top there was a huge pile of rubble to one side of the main shrine building — the rubble was what remained of the *kanetsukido* (bell tower) and the bell was on the ground. The shrine was over four hundred years old.

To everyone's delight a snake came to join us — apparently this was a sign of good luck.

As we walked back to the community centre, a man in a small pick-up truck with two boxes in the back stopped to chat — it was the father of the boy who'd wanted to climb in the back of our truck with me as we'd distributed items the previous night. He was on his way to the local school to deliver our toys and wondered if we'd like to come along. So we followed him around the corner and met with some of the teachers and students of Ohara Elementary School. The school was now two schools combined, because Yagawa Elementary School, on the northern part of the peninsula, had been completely destroyed by the tsunami. There were now 29 students and nine teachers at Ohara. We chatted to the school administrator and some of the kids for a while, handing over pictures and letters from the Laira Green School students — the samurai drawings were very popular. As with everywhere we were going, before we left I got a list of what was needed, an address, and permission to publicly share the information. Then we headed back to the community centre to say our goodbyes, and find out what was needed there. Seiji just asked for anything that could be used for carpentry or building work to be sent to Kurosawa-san at the Nippon Foundation, a Tokyo-based NGO established in the '60s with the mission of providing humanitarian aid especially relating to maritime development.

We found the two Yokohama boys with no signs of a hangover at all, happily operating their JCBs side by side. They were clearing away rubble, that they were loading onto a small truck, which then took away the debris. When I saw the extent of the destruction it made me wonder how on earth it would ever get cleared away, but it did. And 70 percent of the clearing on Oshika ended up being done by dedicated volunteers just like these.

The JCB operators waved cheerily at us before our departure, and Seiji gave us a couple of special magnetic signs for our vehicles that he thought might make our trip a little easier, especially seeing as we didn't have the correct documentation. With our new Japanese "emergency supplies" and "helping the Oshika fishermen" signs we thought we would be fine on the highway, and began our journey off Oshika, finding it easier to see people in need now that it was daytime.

We came across one house that had much of its frame propped up by beams, and there was a woman alone outside. We stopped at the side of the road and opened up the back of the truck to find what she needed. As had happened the previous day, passing cars stopped to take a look, and neighbours walked down the road to see what was going on. We had a big box of new underwear that we brought out for people to go through, and Andrew nudged me to draw my attention to one woman who had sat down on the step at the back of the truck as she put on a brand new pair of socks. The relief on her face and the happiness in her voice was heartbreaking. Japan *did* still need socks.

One car that stopped had two very young children in the back, so I found a box of toys and put them in the trunk. I opened up the box and handed each of the children a toy. The little boy very politely asked for another, so I gave him a second one. His sister did the same. Then he asked for a third, and when I told him that they were *all* for him, he looked at me wide-eyed. I was overcome with the need to give him a cuddle, so I went round to his side of the car, opened the door, and held my arms out to him. With a big smile he held his arms out to me, toys still firmly in his grip, and I picked him up; his sister soon indicated that she wanted to join in. So the three of us, with all the toys, stood by the side of the road, hugging and smiling at each other.

By this stage of our trip, I was completely and utterly in love with Oshika, and Andrew and I couldn't stop talking about Seiji and what I could do to generate more support from England. Whereas before we had been reluctant to take pictures of the destruction, and had focused on photos that would show people in the UK what had happened to their kind donations, we now realized that we needed to take photos of the land for future reference. One of the most incredible images was of a huge ship right next to the road.

All we had left by now were some toothbrushes, toothpaste, nappies, and children's toys and books. Pretty much everything else had gone. It was incredible to think that everything I had collected in England was so needed two months on, but I was a little concerned about being left with items that people couldn't use. I needn't have worried. We had been told that at around 11 a.m., Watanoha Station, a train station back on the mainland, would be full of people in need, so we headed over there.

We arrived at the station to find a long line of people sitting on the pavement, and a non-profit organization setting up a lunch station of some kind. It turned out that people were queuing for lunch that would be ready at noon. It was awful to see. So many people, all sitting patiently; it was mostly older people, but there were more than a few very young mums with tiny children, and one heavily pregnant woman. I stood there feeling upset, helpless, and intrusive — I wasn't sure that the jolly attitude I had brought to the people who were making a go of it on their own would have any effect here whatsoever.

Andrew came back from talking to the person who seemed to be in charge, who had said that we needed to drive over to the volunteer centre and register before we could offer anything here. Bollocks to that, I thought, possibly not thinking clearly and letting emotion get the better of me at this point, but anyone could see that these people needed stuff! I opened up the back of the truck, pulled out a box, carried it over to the queue, and ripped open the top, asking if any of them needed anything and, if so, to help themselves. I went to and fro again and again, carrying one box at a time, until the people in charge realized that I was going to go ahead and empty the whole truck on my own, regardless of any rules or regulations. Before we knew it there was a gang of officials unloading the truck themselves and placing the boxes in a long, extremely orderly line in front of the station, next to which the people arranged themselves in another long, extremely orderly line.

This would have made an incredibly powerful image for everyone in England: for the Virgin Atlantic team who flew all these boxes over for free, for the Vantec team that loaded and unloaded all the boxes for me, for the school children that counted all those items and packed the boxes, and for the shoppers who put some extra things in with their normal shop. *This is what happened to that toothbrush you bought for some people in a far away country who you will likely never meet. This is what caring for another human being means. Without your love and kindness — all of you, companies and individuals — this would never have happened.* I knew it would be important to show this very powerful moment to everyone involved.

But we couldn't take a photo. Neither Andrew nor I could do it. It was so deeply upsetting to see everyone lined up like that. And it did not feel right to take a photo of them in all their vulnerability. I walked around in a daze, trying to get rid of the lump in my throat that wouldn't go away, and hide the tears that were welling up — who was I to even think about being so emotional?! Nobody here needed that!

To try to both distract myself and connect with the people queuing up, I started chatting with them. They were curious about our truck, and where all our items came from, so I handed one woman our leaflet that explained everything. She read it out loud and they all clapped at the end, but it was too much for me. As I had in England, I felt very uncomfortable with such recognition. I left Andrew talking to some officials, and wandered off to offer the pregnant woman assistance, taking an empty box and filling it up with things for her and then loading it into her car. I focused on the young mums and made sure they had plenty of what they needed, and encouraged the little kids to choose some toys they liked. I was relieved when Andrew came over and suggested that we go to a supermarket and buy them other things that the officials said they needed here, so we headed off in the truck while everyone walked along the long line of boxes, taking out what they needed.

Again, the cash that I had came in handy as we filled our trolleys with shampoo, soap, and ramen, as well as a few bottles of sunscreen — the man in charge had told Andrew that he'd worked in an office his whole life and was now burning his skin every day. Many others now found themselves in the same situation. We drove everything back to the station and were amazed to find that *everything* except the children's books (in English) had gone. Everything.

One of the people in charge indicated for us to follow him on his bicycle. We drove for a few minutes and stopped opposite an elementary school playground. There weren't any people there, so I was a bit confused as to what was going on. We put the ramen and shampoo on the ground and people suddenly appeared, seemingly from nowhere, and took what they needed. Everything was gone within minutes.

It was now early afternoon and we were conscious of the six-hour drive back to Tokyo that we had ahead of us, and knew we had to make a move. But we still had the children's books and wanted to leave them with someone here who could use them. We drove over to the elementary school and Andrew popped in to see whether they could use them while I waited around outside. I spotted three kids playing in a huge pile of debris, clearly not at all safe but obviously the most interesting thing they could find to play with, despite the fact that one of them was holding a football under his arm. I wandered over and said that I wasn't very good but I wanted to play football with him, so we all ran around the empty school playground kicking the ball to each other and attempting to score a few goals until Andrew, who *was* good at football, came to join us. No luck with getting rid of the English books — nobody spoke English in this area. But we had cheered up a few kids for a bit and prevented them from having an accident in the rubble.

As we sat in the truck trying to think of what we should do with the English books, I remembered another school I'd written about in my guidebook, and gave Tohoku International School in Sendai a call. They said that they would be very happy to receive our books, so we picked up my van and set off in our vehicles to the school, losing each other on the highway along the way. The look on Andrew's face was a real picture when a massive SDF lorry cut him off and he realized too late that I had turned off. He had no means of navigating his way to the school (we *still* hadn't worked out our satnavs and I was navigating with my iPad) so we texted frantically and hoped we would manage to find each other.

Eventually we connected and arrived at Tohoku International School, where they were thrilled to receive so many English-language books for their students, many of whom had lost everything. Andrew unloaded the van while I let some of their staff pick my brains about a publishing project they were thinking about doing as a fundraiser and also to raise awareness about the post-disaster situation.

As the Head of School walked us out of the building and back to the vans, I noticed that the walls and beams of the entrance were covered in letters and pictures. I stopped to read one — it was from Farmor's School — one of the schools I had visited in the UK! I remembered that I had mailed an envelope full of letters from Farmor's students while I was actually in the UK, and as I looked around I saw all these letters posted up around the school entrance. It was amazing to see those letters there! They would remind students, staff, and parents on a daily basis that teenagers in England cared about them.

It was already early evening and we knew we had hours and hours ahead of us on our drive back to Tokyo. Neither of us had slept properly for two nights and we were completely exhausted. We stopped several times along the way to reconnect and keep each other going. We stopped at Fukushima Service Station and decided to get something to eat. Sitting down with the local delicacy of beef tongue, I noticed how the entire service station was full of rather fit (in both senses of the word) Japanese men in one kind of uniform or another: construction workers, officials of some kind, and police officers. It did appear to be the case that all the hot Japanese men were hanging out in Tohoku.

One casually clothed police officer in particular caught my eye — he was wearing a T-shirt that said "Aiming at gorgeous achievement," and despite my complete exhaustion, I thought I might try to convince him that if I showered, I could indeed be his gorgeous achievement. I sat myself down next to him and started chatting away as Andrew tried not to laugh. My time on Oshika had already lifted me out of the low mood that had consumed me since March 11.

My fruitless flirting over with, it was back in our vehicles for the rest of the journey to Tokyo. We arrived at the truck rental place at about 1 a.m., and wearily started cleaning out the vehicles and pulling the Union Jacks off the sides. The night-duty staff member realized where we had been and insisted that he would clean out the vehicles, and also refill them without charge. He also said he would take care of all the cardboard boxes we had brought back with us. Before we'd left on our trip, I'd noticed a lot of TV coverage saying that the cardboard boxes used for donations were becoming a big problem up north, and I was determined to not leave any unnecessary trash up there for someone else to have to deal with, so we'd brought all the boxes back with us.

Andrew and I hugged an emotional goodbye — we'd made a great team. He was a wonderful companion and I would miss him. I grabbed a taxi back to my, by now, almost empty home in Ebisu.

I counted 26 bruises all over my legs from climbing around the back of the truck as I thought about my conversation with Seiji, and the incredible impact that Oshika had had on me. I'd found a peace that had eluded me since March 11, and a renewed sense of purpose to my life in general. With no relationship, kids, or mortgage to think about, and an income from a business that was entirely mobile, I realized that I was free to fully pursue the ideas that had been forming in my mind since the earthquake. Maybe it would be possible to split my time between Japan and England, at least for a while. I could do so much more to help Japan if I were based in England. And then I'd be back; not to Tokyo, but to Oshika. And not just for a few days next time. Next time I'd come back for a month.

One month in Tohoku.

Top left and right: Destruction caused by the tsunami in the village of Oharahama. Middle left: The Hitachi building still standing on Oshika after the tsunami. Middle right: Looking down at Oharahama from the shrine steps. Bottom left: The JCB volunteers from Yokohama hard at work clearing debris. Bottom right: A huge boat brought inland by the tsunami.

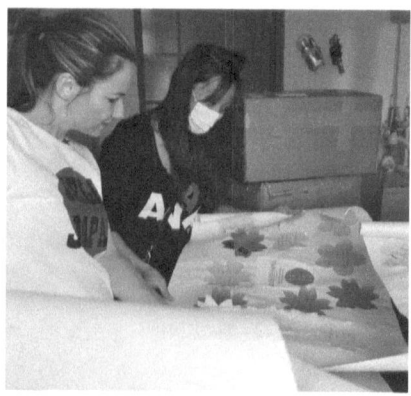 

Top left: Loading up the truck at Narita. Top right: Making sure survivors would know that the UK was thinking of them. Middle left: Cats rescued by JEARS. Middle right: Stopping outside a konbini in Ishinomaki to distribute donations. Bottom left: Looking at Misa's artwork with Miho. Bottom right: Outside Watanoha Station going through the list of donations with a local official.

Top left: Ohara Community Centre driveway, with the ice cream cone that was left by the tsunami. Top right: Unexpected laughter with Ohara village officials and volunteers. Middle left: The centre acting as a distribution centre. Middle right: Walking up to the Ohara shrine. Bottom left: Where I slept on my first night on Oshika — surrounded by debris. Bottom right: Andrew and me with Seiji.

Top left: Featured in the *Plymouth Evening Herald*. Top right: Giving a speech in a British school. Middle left: The "Japan van" loaned by Hitachi. Middle right: An encouraging message from a Laira Green School student. Bottom left: Speaking at Trafalgar Primary. Bottom right: 92 boxes packed with over 10,000 donated items, waiting at Heathrow to be flown to Japan.

ONE MONTH IN TOHOKU

7: Preparation

I had a lot to do before I could spend my one month in Tohoku. First of all, I had to get more support from England. I spread the word among my network that I was coming back, posting on Facebook and my blog, setting up a mailing list, and contacting all the schools I had visited as well as everyone who had helped. I planned to be in England for six months, was willing to go anywhere and talk to anyone about Japan, and wanted people to make the most of me. But instead of spending one day in each place, this time I'd be in each place for a week.

The lovely people at Hitachi Capital had been following my blog, so knew what had happened to those 10,000 items that I'd collected in their wonderful van, but I met up with Hitachi's Nicola in person to fill her in, show my appreciation, and let her know about the branch office I'd seen right there on Oshika. Hitachi was keen to continue their support and very kindly arranged for me to have another van for the duration of this trip. I was thrilled with their generosity — this was a six-month trip around England — not just a few weeks like the previous one. *And* a friend wanted to pay for the insurance to make up for the fact that she couldn't make it to my fortieth birthday celebrations. This support made a world of difference as I was to book talks that would mean travelling hundreds of miles every week.

My first stop was Warwickshire, where old uni friend Nick Meynell had set up a full week of talks at seven schools and one scout pack, as well as a meeting with a supermarket. He'd also signed me up for the Two Castles 10 km run from Warwick to Kenilworth, where I would run wearing my trusty Help Japan T-shirt to boost awareness.

Most of the Warwickshire schools were first-time visits — Kingsway Primary, Clinton Primary, St Patrick's Catholic Primary, St Paul's Church of England, Priors Field Primary, and Moreton Morrell Church of England. But Nick had also booked me to go back to King Henry VIII three times, to different groups of students. First-time visits got a talk similar to the one I had given when I'd originally gone around England collecting items; it focused on Japanese culture and customs, and all the reasons why I loved the country. I was doing my best to be an ambassador for Japan, as one of the gentlemen at my Amity Yokohama talk had hoped. Return visits provided a different slideshow and a different talk, focusing on how all the donated items had got to Japan and from Tokyo up to Tohoku. The teachers especially liked that the children got to see the results of all their efforts, which they said didn't happen very often.

In Gloucestershire I visited Balcarras, Thomas Keble, Kings Stanley, Fairford Primary, High School for Girls (now Denmark Road High School), and Brockworth Enterprise (now Henley Bank High School), all for the first time, and returned to Farmor's School. Farmor's had filled an entire van on their own with the donations I had collected from them a couple of months earlier, so it was wonderful to let the students know what had happened to their boxes afterward, as well as tell them about how I'd seen their letters pinned to the walls at Tohoku International School. Along with the talks I gave to an assembly and a number of classes, I met with the Farmor's Sixth Form Charity Committee, who wanted to do some long-term fundraising for Oshika.

Thomas Keble School in Stroud also committed to do some long-term fundraising — each year the school raised about £12,000 through a sponsored walk. And they ran a "Twenty Pound Challenge" in which each tutor group (homeroom class) was given £20 and had to see how much money they could make for a charity from that £20. The students had been very inspired by my talk and had independently brainstormed all sorts of ways they could help Japan. They were also keen to build links with a school in Japan — not necessarily one in Tohoku — and so I started linking schools in the UK to schools I was connected with in Japan through my guidebook and my monthly newsletter, *Japan School News*. Some of those connections remain active.

Thomas Keble's sponsored walk was held in October, and seeing as Oshika was to be one of the beneficiaries, I decided to join them. This event

— where the 700 students walked along the streets, through the countryside, and beside the canal in Eastcombe — was regularly the highlight of the school year. I joined the class leading the walk, and painted Japanese flags on the kids' faces before they set off, full of excitement. It was an incredible day and they raised over £11,000.

I caught up with the Bad Mothers Club in Cambridge when I returned to Waterbeach, where dear Mayumi told me in tears that everybody there had been moved to care so much about Japan after my talk on the first trip. They'd been inspired to do all sorts of fundraising, and another school mum, Gina Clark, had a cheque for £420 waiting for me. Half of it had come from a "Sing for Japan" event that lots of the mums had participated in, which I initially assumed had been a sensitive and sedate choral event. Not so. They'd convinced a local karaoke booth to lend them the place for free and, in typical Japanese style, got suitably inebriated. It's a shame I wasn't there to join in with *that* particular fundraising event.

In South Devon there were first-time visits to Stoke Damerel, the Dame Hannah Rogers Trust, Notre Dame, and Woodfield Primary schools, and a return visit to Laira Green School, where I thanked the year sixes for their pictures, which were now at Ohara Elementary School. And of course I spent time at my old secondary school, Plymstock — another school that filled an entire van with their donations alone.

I was invited to talk at Saltram Rotary Club — at that point I didn't really know much about rotary clubs and their mission of providing service to others. After hearing about my trip up to Oshika, they were keen to spread the word among their community to see whether other groups were interested in supporting Oshika, and their interest led to long-term support.

I also visited The Castle, Sampford Peverell, Bickleigh, and Bolham primary schools in the middle of Devon; and in North Devon I had first-time visits to Bideford College, Ilfracombe College (now Ilfracombe Academy), Landkey Primary, Instow Community Primary, and Braunton School. Some of the year sevens at Braunton had been year sixes at Southmead back in May, and remembered my talk and collection then, so it was really nice to be able to tell them — as well as the students still at Southmead who I visited later — what had happened to their donations.

I visited Fremington at the invitation of a friend from university, Gillian Ashcroft. She wanted me to talk to the 1st Fremington Guides, and spend some time at Bratton Fleming Community Primary School where she worked, and had organized a full-day of activities for my first visit.

It was an incredibly well-organized and extremely thoughtful day at Bratton Fleming. It started off with the students all perfectly pronouncing "*konnichiwa*" (hello) in response to their names being called during registration, and ended with me doing a talk to the parents while the older students handed out sushi. They'd spent the afternoon actually making the sushi themselves, in the staffroom with Natsuko Lobo, a local Japanese woman. And a number of school-wide, Japan-themed activities had gone on all day. It was a *wonderful* example of how to bring an entire community together, as well as generate support.

It turned out that Natsuko had contacted me during my first trip to North Devon, when I'd been racing around the country and hadn't had time for anything else. I had more time now, however, and I was so glad that we were able to get together. When people ask me, even today, what I miss when I'm not in Japan, it is always the people — I miss *seeing* Japanese people *everywhere*. I miss hearing the Japanese language, and I miss hearing English spoken with a Japanese accent. I miss being able to speak Japanese, and when I do meet someone in England with whom I can speak Japanese, my English friends say that I light up as I yap away with them. During those months in England in 2011, I missed seeing Japanese architecture a little, but I was running and driving through such incredible countryside in the southwest of England that I didn't really miss the concrete of Tokyo too much. I did miss the *smell* of the streets, the sight and sound of the Yamanote Line going past, and the comfort of little *koban* (mini police station) on the corners. And when I met Natsuko and her husband, it wasn't long before I welled up with tears as I explained what I'd been doing since March 11 in a way that wasn't so much focused on the fundraising, but more about being in love with a country and needing to share that love with other people.

Natsuko and I shared stories of life in the countries we'd adopted from each other, but mainly we talked about the effects of the tsunami and the Japanese government's handling of the situation. It was clearly hard for her to watch everything happening from so far away, and I really felt for her and so many other Japanese expats that must have been feeling the same way. As I left, her British husband told me he hadn't expected to discover that I had the same kind of connection to Japan that his Japanese wife did. I teared up again, but this time so did Natsuko. I asked her to make sure that her Japanese friends knew that many people all over the world felt connected to and still cared about Japan, very, very much.

By my second visit to Bratton Fleming a few months later, the school had decided that all their fundraising for that school year would be split between a local charity and Oshika. The children had brainstormed all the different ways they could raise money — they had remembered me telling them that some of the shelters people had to live in after they lost their homes were schools, and we had talked about what it would be like to have to sleep in your school every night. This really stayed in their minds, so they decided to do a sponsored sleepover in the school hall, and were already planning it for the summer of 2012.

I was *deeply* touched by Gillian's efforts and everything she did to inspire her school community to support Japan.

I had trained as a teacher with Gillian at university in Exeter in the early '90s, and fulfilled one of my childhood dreams of becoming a primary school teacher (the other was to become an author). My first job, straight out of university, was actually in a school I had attended, Goosewell Primary in Plymstock, which I had *loved* both as a student and a teacher. But I hadn't loved living back in Plymouth, and it was my desire for adventure that had taken me to Japan after only one year of teaching. These Japan talks were taking me back into the classrooms of England, and I was revelling in it.

My school visits usually consisted of either individual class visits or whole-school assemblies. The children I spent time with were very interested in Japan, had so many questions, and were keen to learn how to say things in Japanese. Away from the classroom, when I visited friends, their younger children had me in stitches as they tried to get me to teach them some Japanese swear words and then thought they'd be able to teach me some English swear words — as if I didn't know any! I loved the way they thought they'd discovered such words.

Children in general were fascinated by what I had done as well as by Japan in general. They wanted to know everything about my getting stuck in Saipan, travelling around England, packing up boxes, getting everything on a plane, and driving it up north, and about all my experiences right there in the middle of a disaster zone. The talks became opportunities to look at all sorts of topics — being community-minded, volunteering, global citizenship, travel and adventure, entrepreneurship, language acquisition, and even speech-making — in one school, some of the students were later reported to have studied my talk as they tried to develop good presentation skills. And I found that quite flattering!

Very few of the school visits focused on disaster relief only — I joined economics classes to talk about the Japanese transport system; business classes to talk about marketing; geography classes to talk about the climate; citizenship classes to talk about volunteering in general; science classes where students created their own tsunami and experimented with the effects of water on sand, paper, plasticine, and Lego; and an after-school Japanese club to answer their questions about life in Japan in general and rate their bowing techniques.

These young people weren't just interested in helping Japan; they were interested in learning about all sorts of things, including their role in helping to make the world a better place. I still get told now that I really inspired those kids to think about what they wanted to do with their lives, which was *never* my goal in visiting the schools. I didn't feel that I had any special skills or knowledge. I wasn't anybody to look up to. I wasn't working for a charity. I was just an ordinary person that cared. But perhaps I made it seem possible that even ordinary people could do something to help — they just had to care enough. That was all that mattered.

What didn't seem to matter was the fact that I wasn't affiliated with any kind of registered organization. I had toyed with the idea, but eventually decided against it. Setting up a charity would mean having yet another entity to manage, and I didn't have the time or inclination. I just wanted to focus on the talks, not on paperwork. And I didn't want one penny of what I was raising to end up on any kind of administrative costs. I wanted everything to go directly to Oshika.

People seemed to like what I was doing and how I was doing it. And they *insisted* on giving me money. I was constantly receiving emails from people saying they wanted to send me money to either fund my trip or buy things for up north. There were news stories circulating about the huge amounts of money that international charities had received immediately after the earthquake, but were yet to distribute, or had allocated to another disaster. People were fed up with what Sara at Waterbeach had called "blind giving," and wanted to contribute to something from which they could see real results, very quickly. What I had done in distributing those 10,000 items on Oshika was exactly the kind of thing that some people were looking to support.

So I accepted money when people offered it to me, knowing that I'd be "on the ground" and able to put it to really good use when I'd completed this second trip around England.

In the meantime, everywhere I went, it felt like odd coincidences kept happening. There was Rob, the South African bartender I came across when I was grabbing lunch in between Warwickshire schools. I recognized his voice instantly but couldn't place him, until he reminded me that he'd worked in Paddy Foleys, a favourite hangout during my wilder days in Tokyo, before I'd had my strokes. Ah, no wonder I didn't remember him very clearly. We pored over an album he'd just been looking at that morning, filled with photos of mutual friends partying, and he promised to connect me with friends of his that taught in England.

And there was Masatoshi, whose Japanese T-shirt I spotted during the warm-up for the Two Castles run, so I'd gone over to say hello. Masatoshi had been living in England for eleven years, working for Deloitte. He was from the northeast of Japan and all his family had been affected; he'd actually lost his aunt and uncle. He was just back from a couple of weeks volunteering to clear debris.

Japan seemed to be with me everywhere I went, but just to make doubly sure, I decided to get a pink Japanese cherry blossom tattoo around my wrist for my fortieth birthday that October. I was still rejecting anything material and enjoying living out of a suitcase, so I'd told friends and family not to give me any gifts but instead to contribute toward the tattoo cost. I celebrated my birthday with them all at a simple garden party, rather than the big five-day bash I was planning pre-311.

I was trying to balance both reconnecting with England and staying connected to Japan. Instead of fighting my feeling of being torn between the two countries, I tried to embrace it. While I desperately missed Japan, all the talks I was giving made me feel constantly connected to my adopted home. It was strange though — my longing to be in Japan somehow did not place me in Tokyo, which had been my home for so long, but instead in the hills and valleys of Oshika.

I made a point of staying with friends or family as I made my way around England, trying to work on the feeling of disconnection that I'd always had when visiting the UK in the years before the earthquake. And I was happy to deepen the relationship that had been growing with my Newbury niece and nephews.

I took my four-year-old nephew to see *Cars 2* — he was so excited that he put on his Dad's aftershave. The film didn't have me quite so excited at first — I sat there thinking how dreadfully boring it was, and how stupid to have all these cars acting like spies, when suddenly the movie relocated to Japan — and that put a smile on my face. They did Japan so well! The racetrack was set throughout Tokyo, going past Tokyo Tower, over Rainbow Bridge, and alongside what looked like the Okura Hotel. Some of the cars were dressed like geisha, and the sushi chef cars were really cute. Mount Fuji looked amazing and the tall buildings with their neon signs were fantastic. It was *really* good fun for someone whose heart was in Japan. And my nephew loved it.

Like me, my six-year-old niece was known for her love of farts. And she was good at them, too. I have a definite rival there in Mabel. So I suggested that we should have a sleepover party with a midnight feast consisting of baked beans, fig rolls, and pickled onions, followed by a "trumping" competition ... it was *all* she could talk about for a week. To anybody who would listen. Including everyone at her school, where I'd given a talk. "Are you talking about that nice lady who writes books and talks about Japan?" "Yes, that's my Auntie Caroline and she likes trumping." She still talks about the sleepover even now! I think most of Newbury has heard about it.

I threw myself into family life wherever I was and whoever I was staying with, and to do that meant changing my pace to match the distinctly different one in the rural and West Country areas I was mostly going to, where people were generally home by five for dinner. This was very different from workaholic Tokyo, but I tried to go with the flow.

I was losing my passion for my work anyway — all I could think about was Oshika and how I just wanted to get back to helping the people there. The hectic Tokyo entrepreneur lifestyle had lost its appeal since the earthquake — in truth, I'd become disillusioned with it even before then. Spending time in England was working out well for me. It turned out to be a good decision.

Other people in Japan were making big decisions too, deciding to take some time out like me; months after the earthquake they were still searching for answers on the next step for their businesses, their careers, their children, their marriages. Some left permanently, with big migrations to Singapore and the UAE. Some were heading back to their home countries. The Tokyo I knew and loved wasn't going to be the same when I returned, and I had trouble accepting that. But I found comfort in England. Talking to school children about Japan made me fulfilled, and I delighted in being able to spend time with friends and family that I'd neglected over the years.

It was weird to me to think that England — the country I'd rejected for so many years — was such a source of strength as I accepted all the changes that had happened in my life since March 11.

I kept in regular contact with Seiji, keeping him posted on the level of support that I was gathering, and finding out how things were progressing on Oshika. They were progressing *very, very* slowly, especially when it came to rebuilding the communities that had been destroyed — the locations had to be planned very carefully because so much of the land had sunk and was now either subject to the tide or too close to the sea. The government wouldn't give permission for any residences to be built anywhere that the tsunami had reached, and there were a lot of complications relating to land ownership. Many people now found themselves owning what used to be very valuable land, with which they could now do absolutely nothing. One convenience store was open on the peninsula, so that was something.

Along with all the meetings and discussions he was having, Seiji was busy with clean-up work, whether it was coordinating hundreds of volunteers to clear piles and piles of debris on the mainland, or going to a small island on his own, where he would navigate his way around the coast by canoe, into which he loaded debris. He was amazing.

But the story Seiji was telling me was different to the one I was getting from people who had been regularly travelling to different areas in the north. They could see that some progress was being made. A lot of land had been cleared in other areas and temporary housing was beginning to go up. Of the original 450,000 people living in shelters immediately after the earthquake, 90,000 remained in emergency housing by the early summer of 2011. Some were put in temporary accommodation, and some had moved in with relatives. Progress was definitely being made in Tohoku, it just didn't seem to be moving very quickly on Oshika.

With the commencement of construction of the temporary housing units (*kasetsu jutaku* — referred to locally as *kasetsu*), I was told that there came a significant decrease in the number of volunteer organizations in that area of Tohoku. Some organizations left because they were for emergency response only, some because their responsibilities were transferred to local people, and some because their funding ran out. The creation of permanent housing was still out of the question — there was still too much debris to deal with. The clearing of that debris had created a lot of temporary job opportunities though, helping some people in the short-term, but understandably there was so much concern about the long-term.

I tried to be a little careful in any possible criticism of the Japanese government — I didn't want to offend any Japanese people during what was a highly sensitive time. But it was the *Japanese* people I knew or was meeting who were frequently expressing their disappointment and frustration in their government for a number of reasons, especially relating to the nuclear power plant.

Nobody seemed to believe anything the Japanese government was saying about Fukushima. YouTube videos of Japanese parents tearfully begging their local government to test their children's urine for radiation poisoning went viral. Professor Tatsuhiko Kodama, head of the University of Tokyo's Radioisotope Centre, showed such raw emotion in an interview he gave — so uncharacteristic of a Japanese man in his position.

I was focusing so much on Oshika that I didn't have the mental capacity to consider other people that needed help.

It was overwhelming for *everyone* in Japan as they tried to work out how best to be part of Japan's financial, practical, and emotional recovery. No wonder some people left, never to return. But for those for whom Japan would remain home, there was a constant dilemma. Should you carry on as normal and contribute to Japan that way? Should you spend time up north clearing debris? Should you raise funds? Should you offer healing in whatever form you could? Should you lobby? I had friends doing each of these things and whenever I read about their activities I was overwhelmed with the enormity of what was necessary for Japan to recover. I had recurring dreams of tsunamis and landslides, houses sliding down hills, people clinging to trees — and I was always unable to help them.

It was impossible to help everyone and no single person or organization could do everything. But as I often said during my school visits: if enough people do enough little things, that combination can result in a large and successful effort!

The little things that *I* could do were centred on Oshika — and after staying in England for what ended up being eight months, I couldn't wait to get back there!

8: Back to Oshika

I landed in Japan on January 10, 2012, beaming at the immigration official as he stamped my passport, and grinning my way through the airport. I sat with my face glued to the window of the limousine bus on the 90-minute journey into Tokyo. *I was home.*

I was home — but without a home. I stayed with my good friend Ali as I made preparations to go up north. Ali was also a long-term resident, and was in the process of packing up her life. She was one of the many who left Japan in the year after the disaster — too heartbroken to see what was happening to the country we all loved. Like many, she'd never return. It was just too hard.

I ended up buying Ali's car from her. It was perfect for what I needed on Oshika. It was a little old Toyota RAV4, and I'd be able to sleep in the back if the need arose. It was a little bit knocked about as Ali had once reversed it into her mailbox, so I didn't mind if it were to get a few more dents while on Oshika. She'd christened it Mavis.

Mavis had an extraordinary amount of space in the back, which I planned on filling with winter coats. A friend had spent New Year's in Tohoku and said that people were in desperate need of warm coats during what was their first winter after the disaster. She had given someone her own coat as she was leaving to return to Tokyo. So I was rushing around Tokyo collecting winter coats from anyone who could spare them.

My diary for those two weeks I spent in Tokyo preparing for my month on Oshika rivals any scheduling I'd ever done in my busy pre-311 life. It is packed full of lists, addresses, and appointments, and *everything* got highlighted in pink, indicating that it had been completed. I was running again, but following a program this time after all the injuries I'd struggled with during my past eight months in England. Not surprising really. Couch to 5 km in nine weeks? At the age of 39 I'd gone from couch to 13 km in 12 weeks. Then suffered for it. So was getting back into it. Slowly.

I loved going running in Tokyo. Having jet lag meant that I was awake just before dawn, so more often than not, I was jogging along the Tokyo streets watching the sunrise reflected in the buildings that towered above me. I felt so at peace.

I caught up with Elise Mori, an old friend I'd met when she wrote for my very first magazine back in 1997. She'd recently started studying tarot, and after lunch she said she wanted to "do my cards." I wasn't especially into it, but I acknowledged that some people found tarot helpful when trying to clarify and organize their thoughts when they might need some help in making decisions or knowing which direction to move in. And I could sit and talk to Elise for hours, so was more than happy to prolong our time together.

Out came the black cloth and some beautifully designed cards were placed on the table. The conversation went a little like this:

Elise: "Anything you want to ask?"
Me: "Er, no. No questions on my mind."
Elise: "Anything you're not sure about at the moment?"
Me: "No. Everything's pretty clear."
Elise: "Anything you want to know about the year ahead?"
Me: "No. I know what I'm doing."
Elise: "Any guidance you need on anything?"
Me: "No. I have never felt more at ease with the world."

So Elise gave up and we had another coffee. I was, indeed, at peace.

I also caught up with Andrew Robinson and Yuriko Miyazaki, a married couple who were my good friends and often found themselves the subject of my writing; I'd written a whole chapter inspired by my friendship with Andrew in my *Ask Caroline* book. Yuriko and I had once owned a company together and we worked on a lot of projects over the years.

I had desperately missed Japanese food while I was away, and Andrew and Yuriko were always the best people to go and eat Japanese food with. Andrew enjoyed sharing his knowledge about and love for Japanese food, and Yuriko had a knack for knowing exactly what I was going to like. I'd been to some amazing Japanese restaurants with them, and that night they took me to a tiny place in Kagurazaka — one of those places where you can only get about ten people in there and the owners make you feel like old friends within minutes. It was run by a famous kabuki actor and his family, and we got to chat with them throughout our meal.

We caught up on what had happened in all our lives since the earthquake. They were fascinated by what I had been doing in England during the past eight months. When we'd entered the restaurant, Yuriko had introduced me (in Japanese) as their friend who had gone back to England to do various things to help with earthquake relief and was visiting Japan again to help. Andrew later brought up how it was actually the other way round — I was coming *back* to Japan after *visiting* England. He knew me so well.

Japan was most definitely still home, and I wasn't sure whether I'd ever feel that England was "home" again, but I was perfectly OK with that uncertainty.

I think old friends from Tokyo were surprised to see how comfortable and at peace I was with being so nomadic. I had spent months free of the stresses brought about by money, relationships, and work, and the time in England had done me good. I was positive, full of energy, and focused on my mission. My life wasn't perfect, but I was at ease with what was going on and the people around me, and felt comfortable about my place in the world. In absorbing all the love and support England was still offering to Japan, with the intention being to then share it on Oshika, perhaps I had absorbed a little of it for myself.

I caught up with people who had been part of the original Oshika mission. Virgin's Iain Raymond, who had gone above and beyond the call of both professional duty and friendship in his support; Nina Godoy, who had coordinated the needs of the animals in the shelter I'd visited; and Richard Thornley, who'd worked so hard to spread the word in England, and whose uncle had turned up outside Downham School, cash donation in hand. I gave another speech to the lovely retired gentlemen at Amity Yokohama, and they insisted on giving me fuel money. And amidst the bureaucratic nightmare that was involved in transferring Ali's car to me, I managed to catch up with my dear friends Emily and Sannah. I had so missed the weekly gatherings with my Tokyo sisters!

I met with a number of other friends — including Debbie Howard, who'd been president of the American Chamber of Commerce in Japan; and Peter Wilson, who ran what was possibly the biggest (definitely the noisiest) online community of foreigners in Japan — Gaijinpot. The support I was receiving from movers and shakers in the Tokyo international community was incredible.

And I was staying with one of the biggest movers and shakers of all! Ali knew *everyone* in Tokyo, and everyone knew her. Especially the foreign women in Tokyo. Not just any foreign women, but the kind of women who you really wanted around you because they got stuff done. They were the old gang from the '90s generation of Foreign Executive Women, of which Ali had been president, and they were a force to be reckoned with. Her house was complete chaos not just from all of her own packing going on, but with all these women constantly coming and going — either saying their goodbyes to her or turning up with something for my trip, which everyone seemed to know about by now.

The night before I left they all fussed around me, making sure I had lots of food and emergency cash, and that my mobile phone and iPad were fully charged and in working order. Conny Jamieson turned up with some construction boots for me to wear, which she insisted on waterproofing before she left. Those boots were to become my *most treasured* possession on Oshika. I still have them now.

Little Mavis was jam-packed to the roof with 91 coats, 20 hats, six pairs of gloves, 14 scarves, two electric blankets, two normal blankets, three pairs of ski pants, 14 fleece zip-up jackets, and one pair of ski boots. I also had seven knitted dolls made by my mother, who had made a wonderful recovery, and I wanted to keep it that way, so I'd told her a *huge* lie about going to Oshika with a massive group of people and staying in a hotel, whereas in fact I was going alone and would be sleeping in the Ohara community centre the entire time. I literally couldn't get anything else in the car and had to leave my futon behind, deciding that I could manage sleeping on a floor for a month. I was glad of the experience of driving a van around England, because I couldn't see a thing out of the car's back window.

I'd decorated the car with Union Jacks, signs with Japanese words of encouragement, and the magnetic stickers that Seiji had given me, one saying that this was an "emergency supply vehicle" and the other one showing support for the Oshika-hanto fishermen. The highway tolls would be free from Fukushima onward, and I had a document that gave me special permission to drive on any other highway in the country without paying a thing. Mavis had had an oil change and a new battery, and I left Tokyo in the early hours of the morning of January 22, keen to avoid the Tokyo traffic.

I failed miserably, and found myself at a standstill on an elevated highway for two hours, still in Tokyo. And I desperately needed a wee …

When I eventually got out of Tokyo, I was amazed to see how beautiful the drive was. There were *breathtaking* views of the mountains in the distance for most of the journey. I hadn't noticed them when Andrew Abbey and I had driven up — it had been getting dark and I'd been too consumed with worrying about losing him on the highway, keeping an eye on my iPad, and wondering what all the flashing red lights that periodically appeared along the side of the road had said. This journey was quite, quite different. Or maybe it was me that was different?

I stopped at Fukushima for my coffee break to show just a bit of support to the area and, yes, possibly to have a little look around the station where all the good-looking men in uniforms had been months earlier. There were a lot fewer of them now. I bought some drinks and snacks to take with me for the rest of the journey.

I had asked beforehand whether I should bring food for myself, or buy locally — supporting the local economy was my preference — and had been told that there were a couple of temporary shops on Oshika now, ten months on. The nearest "proper" shop was a 40-minute drive away from where I'd be based. I knew I was going to a really remote place, but the fact that the nearest shop was that far away surprised me — how had people there been coping?

I really wasn't sure what to expect, and whether I had come with the right things. I knew that people needed coats, but what else might they need that I hadn't brought with me? I reminded myself that I'd be there for a month this time, so there was ample time for me to find out what exactly was needed in the area (every area affected had different needs), and to get things up from Tokyo. Later on this trip my dear sister-friend Emily and her husband would be joining me for a couple of days, and they could fill their car with donations from Tokyo.

I had cash with me as well — ¥34,000 from Bratton Fleming, ¥12,000 from Notre Dame, ¥26,000 from Northowram in West Yorkshire, and ¥76,000 from individuals — all happy for their money to be spent however I saw fit to help with recovery. Including the money I received for my first trip, I'd so far raised £6000 since the disaster happened.

After seven hours of driving, I arrived at Seiji's "base camp" near Ishinomaki Station — he'd asked me to stop off there first so he could drive with me to Ohara, which was forty minutes away. Despite my long drive, Seiji got straight to the point and within minutes we were discussing his activities and the ideas I'd had to try to support the area he was working in. I loved that he seemed to know that I didn't want to waste any time at all.

Seiji explained what had happened to everyone in Ohara — the tiny village where we first met. Before the earthquake there were 150 people in Ohara. Only two people had died, but nearly everybody lost their home. Most of the village was now in temporary housing, even the people who had been living in what was left of their homes in the tsunami's aftermath — nobody had the money to rebuild them. Even if they did, the government wouldn't allow anyone to live anywhere the water had reached. Some people had to walk away from their still-standing homes and move into temporary housing. Those homes were torn down as the land was cleared of debris, and everything had been dumped at Yagawa — the neighbouring town that had been completely wiped out and whose elementary school kids had joined Ohara Elementary School, where I'd left Laira Green's samurai drawings on my first visit.

The government had given ¥2 million to the people whose homes were *completely* destroyed, and that money was expected to be used toward the building of a new home. But if people had lost their homes, those homes would have been on land that the tsunami had reached, and nobody was allowed to build on that land. So people had *some* money to put toward building a home, but nowhere to build one. And if the tsunami had left part of a house standing, the owner received nothing. Paying for a brand new house to be built was a big enough challenge for anyone, let alone people who were without jobs, a position most people on Oshika now found themselves in. And there were a lot of elderly people in Ohara. People couldn't afford to build brand new homes.

Both groups of people were given temporary housing while it was decided where new homes could be built. People were expected to privately fund the building of their new homes, although the government would fund the clearing of the land in preparation for construction. However, the only land that was far enough away from the sea was covered in trees and prone to landslides, so it would have to be levelled before anyone could build on it. Flat spaces needed to be identified or created, and all of this was taking a long time.

Some people were hoping that the government or an enterprising individual would buy their land from them to give them a bit more money to work with (at that time the going rate was ¥5,000 per three square metres), but they weren't holding out for it. The homes or land belonging to people who had died in the tsunami had been inherited by their children, most of whom lived in the nearby cities of Sendai or Ishinomaki, and they'd just handed the homes or land to the government to avoid inheritance tax. There was a lot of uncertainty throughout the peninsula.

Seiji's base camp used to be a medical clinic, and was located just a few minutes away from the sea. The building had been completely submerged by the tsunami, but Seiji and his team had repaired it and were now renting it along with another organization that was coordinating a car-sharing program. This program was proving to be extremely successful and very much needed because so many people had lost their vehicles to the tsunami.

The medical clinic was now a bustling volunteer centre, supporting about 130 temporary housing communities in and around Ishinomaki (not just those on Oshika), each made up of anywhere from ten to 500 homes. At any one time there were usually 15 volunteers working in the centre. On weekends there were up to 50. I met some of them when I arrived that Sunday night.

There was Joji, who spent every day going around the temporary housing communities asking how everyone was, and trying to create a sense of camaraderie in the absence of a little shop, a bus shelter, a playground, a library, a market — all those spaces that we take for granted in our own little communities, spaces that contribute *so much* to our sense of community.

And there was "Mr Tall," a canoeing instructor whose expertise was invaluable and allowed teams of volunteers to reach the most remote parts of Oshika and clear the little beaches there. Mr Tall could also cook for up to 7000 people in one day and had been in Ishinomaki on and off since the first few days after the earthquake.

Then there was Hiroyuki, who was in the Ohara Community Centre the night Andrew and I had turned up. It was good to see him, and I was pleased to know that he was also coming to Oshika, and was actually based in Ohara now. I left a bottle of wine for those remaining, and the rest of us set off in a convoy of four vehicles for the 40-minute drive to Ohara.

By the time we got out of Ishinomaki, it was so dark that I couldn't see much of the hills of Oshika up ahead, at all. I started to recognize some places as we drove through Watanoha, where Andrew and I had come across the lines of desperate people waiting for their lunches. The cars had been removed from the swimming pool, and the debris had mostly been cleared. The buildings that remained seemed mostly empty, although brightly lit convenience stores, gas stations, and *pachinko* parlours were interspersed among them.

Pachinko is a bit like an arcade game or slot machine, and pachinko parlours can be found everywhere in Japan. You exchange the tiny balls you're playing with for money or prizes, rather than winning money outright, thereby taking advantage of a legal loophole in a country where gambling for cash is illegal. I found it odd and a bit of a shame that there were so many pachinko parlours along the otherwise derelict road we drove down, and was later told that pachinko companies had so much money that it was really easy for them to build quickly in these areas.

It was pitch black on Oshika. As we drove up and down the hills and valleys I was so relieved not to be doing that last part of the journey alone — the coastal road still looked incredibly dangerous, with huge drops on the left that meant you were driving on the edge of a cliff, and the threat of falling rocks on the right. And even though I couldn't see much because of how dark it was, I could see that the areas where the fishing villages used to be had been *completely* cleared — there was absolutely nothing there now. Oshika was a wasteland.

We pulled in to Ohara Community Centre to unexpectedly find the man who liked English women's bottoms had been preparing *shabu-shabu* (a kind of hot pot) with meat from his pig farm. Not for the first time in the coming month, I abandoned all codes of behaviour deemed acceptable on either side of the world, and changed into my fluffy bright pink pajamas for dinner.

I had thought of Oshika every single day for eight months, and now that I was actually there, I felt rather emotional. The homes that people were trying to live in when I had been here before were gone, and somehow this upset me *more* than the rubble I came across before. There was no evidence that people had once lived here. No evidence of *hope* for the future. I felt overwhelmed and terribly helpless.

I got hardly any sleep that first night on Oshika; I was tossing and turning all night, full of anxiety. How on earth would I be able to do anything at all that would make the slightest bit of difference here? *What had I been thinking?*

9: My Routine

In the middle of my sleepless first night on Oshika I got my period. Fantastic. Thank God I'd thought to pack something. There wasn't a toilet in the community centre so I dealt with it in my room — the centre was made up of one communal room, one kitchen, a room in which the male volunteers slept, and a room for the female volunteers, which on that night, consisted of just me.

To go to the loo I'd have to walk through the main room, across the car park, and into what used to be a tiny government office building. This was to be my closest toilet for the next month, in which I changed my tampon in the morning, but couldn't see an appropriate bin, and didn't know who to ask. I was yet to meet a woman in Ohara. The only people I'd met were Japanese men, and I didn't know them very well, and my Japanese was still rubbish — I didn't even know the word for period. So I wrapped up my used tampon in some toilet paper, and tied it all up in one of the scented dog poo bags I'd brought with me just in case (of what I'd had no idea), and tucked it into my coat's inner pocket. I'd deal with that later.

Outside, Hiroyuki was dealing with the thick snow that had fallen overnight. Soft, powdery snow, inches thick, that covered everything and hid the wasteland underneath. It was a beautiful sight.

Beautiful, but not especially safe for the school bus that was soon to be making its way up the little hill to drop off the local children outside the centre, just a short walk from Ohara Elementary School. Hiroyuki was shovelling the snow so I started to throw salt all over the car park. Once we were done, and the children had all safely got to school, I made a Western-style snowman to greet the kids at the end of the day — complete with arms, nose, and scarf — very different from a Japanese snowman, which would just have eyes and a mouth. Mine was just like one they'd see in a foreign movie.

I was surprised to see a foreigner show up — Jake Derector was the local English-language teacher, and he rotated among all the schools on the peninsula each week. He was just as surprised to see me — he had been living on Oshika for two years and said that while there were a lot of foreigners there right after the earthquake, he didn't see so many anymore. He thanked me for coming.

Hiroyuki had a routine that usually meant he was based in the centre all day. I didn't want to be a burden to him, and while he was based long-term on Oshika, he wasn't actually local, and my goal was to find ways to directly support the locals. I wasn't there to be Hiroyuki's assistant, nor his burden. And sitting around waiting for someone to tell me what to do was not really my style. So I just went off and did my own thing, soon establishing my own routine.

That routine first involved the distribution of the car-load of winter coats I had with me, which I couldn't do until my tyres had been sorted out. They were the cause of much laughter among the locals — normal tyres may have worked fine in Tokyo, but they wouldn't do me any good on Oshika, so Hiroyuki found me some snow tyres at a bargain price. Even the courier laughed at my normal tyres when he delivered the replacements I needed for driving around the steep hills during winter on the peninsula.

I thought I'd have to be quite sensitive as I drove around handing out donated goods — it wasn't like when I'd first come when everybody I met needed something and I could just ask them directly the minute I met them. Most people had the basics by now, although it was surprising how many people needed things like new socks or a new coat. I employed the same method I had when I'd first come to Oshika, and spent every day driving around, looking for people and stopping to chat, but this time I very casually asked them what they needed. And just as when I'd first visited, it was *incredibly* effective. I spent my days saying "What do you need?" to every single person I met, and my nights saying "How can I help?" to myself.

The winter coats flew out of the back of the car. This was the first winter since the disaster, in which many people had lost everything. During summer the peninsula had been teeming with volunteers as they cleared debris and offered summer clothing donations, but the number of volunteers visiting had already started to dwindle. *And* the donation of clothing to Tohoku had become a rather troublesome topic.

In the immediate aftermath of the disaster, as with any major disaster, thousands if not hundreds of thousands of well-meaning people had sent up items of clothing without knowing (a) who was going to distribute it, and (b) exactly what kinds of clothing were needed. Fancy high heels would have absolutely no place in little fishing communities that might not have the ability to organize the distribution of clothes anyway. The result was that inappropriate and unnecessary clothing had piled up in the shelters. But there was still a need for clothes. I immediately saw a way I could fill a gap — I could find out *exactly* what kind of clothing was needed, manage all the distribution, and collect anything that was left behind.

So as I distributed the winter coats, I'd stop and chat, asking what else people needed. I wrote down as much detail as I could — what sizes were needed? And for how many people? These little communities thought more of the group than they did the individual — it wouldn't have been appropriate to deliver five pairs of trousers when there were 20 women that needed them. Then I'd post a wish list on Facebook or my blog, and, sure enough, within a few days a box of requested clothing would arrive.

People in Tokyo really wanted to help, and I could give them a way to do so. Shelley Sacks was thrilled that I had a found a way for her school community to help the area she had felt compelled to tell me about back in May 2011. And countless others were sending items — the response from Tokyo was incredible. It wasn't long before boxes started to arrive daily, thankfully also including the fuel contributions I'd requested. I was still set on keeping all the cash donations to use on specific projects that presented themselves to me (rather than for general expenses), so had asked people to pop in a bit of cash for the fuel I was using in getting all these clothes around the peninsula. I was constantly busy. I'd sort through every box and take the contents straight to the person or the group that had requested it. As quickly as the back of my car emptied, I filled it right up again. People literally had what they needed *within days* of asking for it.

I was soon taken to the temporary housing communities by Hanako Yokota. Hanako was just nineteen years old, and had been studying technical theatre at a Canadian university before 311, after which she had decided to take a year off to volunteer. She was spending that year working as personal assistant to Kurosawa-san of the Nippon Foundation, where she could also offer her carpentry skills. Hanako was completely bilingual, and became incredibly helpful to me as I was getting to know my way around Oshika.

The temporary housing communities were scattered throughout the peninsula, high up in the hills and often hidden away among trees. They consisted of about ten rows of temporary units, each row made up of five dwellings. A community could consist of up to a hundred units, but most of them were much smaller.

Either Hanako or Hiroyuki provided me with initial introductions to each temporary housing community's leader (usually male). Their wives usually ran the *danwashitsu* (communal room), in which I would set up a little free shop. I'd ask for permission to bring in the coats, or whatever else had been sent up from Tokyo, then arrange everything nicely on the tables so it felt a little less like a second-hand jumble sale and more like a shopping experience. The people living in temporary housing would come in to look at what I'd brought them, at which point I'd step outside.

I was intensely aware of doing anything that might seem insensitive. I didn't want to intrude on any private moments between people that had grown up together, shared a trauma together, and were healing together. I didn't want my presence to be triggering or insulting in any way. I didn't want them to be made uncomfortable by my bringing them secondhand clothing from Tokyo.

I needn't have worried! Whenever I stood outside a danwashitsu, all I ever heard was laughing and chatting as they (usually women in their sixties and over) went through everything, trying things on or pointing out what might suit a friend.

"Shall I try this on?"

"Oh no, you're too fat for that. Does this hat suit me?"

"No, it doesn't cover your face."

I loved the women of Oshika. They talked *a lot*, all the while interrupting each other, telling saucy jokes, and cackling away. It was just like listening to a rather loud and very direct bunch of girlfriends in a communal changing room, anywhere in the world.

Once every item of clothing had been thoroughly examined, I'd ask them what else they needed, and add that to my list. Socks, wellies, and thermal underwear were really popular, but so were things like cup ramen and pasta. And even makeup and face creams. Wherever I went, it was different. I now knew other foreigners who were part of the recovery effort in different areas of Tohoku, so was aware of what people in different parts of the region needed. It was becoming clear that *everybody's needs were different*. It would have been impossible to provide a blanket solution for the whole area. A very specific approach, tailored to each individual community, was required; and in order to work out what that approach would be, I had to ask questions, listen to the answers, and act on them, irrespective of my own opinions.

Whatever was left would get packed into the back of my car (sometimes I'd leave clothes in the danwashitsu for a day or two and return to find the unwanted items neatly folded in a box, ready for me to collect). And then I'd be invited to stay for a drink and a snack. Oshika was *never* short of drinks and snacks. They love their food there, and they enjoy sharing it.

Older people who didn't have a car would give me shopping lists when they heard I'd be going anywhere there was a shop, or would ask me for a lift so they could visit a friend that they hadn't seen for ages. There were buses on Oshika, but the tsunami had destroyed the shelters and it was too cold to be standing around outside in order to meet someone for lunch.

I usually ate at the community centre with Hiroyuki, outside the konbini, or at one of the little temporary restaurants that had popped up. I was constantly being presented with something or other as a thank you for my efforts, and even if it didn't look at all edible, it probably was. Sharing food was how Oshika people showed their appreciation, and I gratefully accepted everything that was offered to me, but decided I'd rather not always know what it was.

There was food everywhere, and huge efforts were being made to ensure that everyone had enough to eat. Trucks full of fish, fruit, and vegetables regularly arrived at the temporary housing communities. Kei-chan with his "live fish truck" was a regular and hugely popular visitor. He had given out all the food he had right after the earthquake, and when that was gone, he'd filled his truck with drinking water and delivered it wherever he could.

Some of the food trucks were local businesses that were trying to rebuild; some were operated by groups of volunteers that would cook delicious meals on the spot for the people that had lost their homes. I had never seen so much fish in my life, and the Oshika people seemed to eat every single bit of it. By the end of that month I could munch on fish bones with the rest of them, and didn't think twice when brushing my teeth over the kitchen sink in Ohara ... next to a bowl full of fish guts.

People were always inviting me to eat with them. It was during all these coffees, snacks, and meals with the men and women of Oshika that I started picking up language skills and truly learning about their lives. Until then I'd *really* been struggling with the local dialect and frequently wondered what on earth I'd been thinking to come here for a whole month without an interpreter. I'd become even more aware of just how poor my Japanese was; I couldn't get away with the weird mixture of Japanese and English I used in Tokyo. I *had* to speak Japanese all the time. So I frantically made notes of all the words I kept repeatedly hearing so that I could look them up later, got on with communicating using whatever words I *did* know, and hoped for the best. It wasn't long before I managed to hang out with my new friends for hours at a time without having too many problems.

Despite my poor Japanese language skills, I'd talk non-stop to anyone on Oshika, asking them about the weather, their car, that tasty snack they'd just offered, that hair style of theirs that I liked. *Anything I could see right there in front of me.* I never asked anybody about anything I couldn't see. And I never asked anybody their tsunami story. If they started to tell me about it, I would go silent, giving them the space to talk. I didn't just learn to speak Japanese on Oshika. I learned to listen. And I listened with my heart, not my ears.

Popping in and out of the temporary housing communities became a regular part of my routine, and it was how I got to know a lot of people on the peninsula. But I also wanted to help people who were living in their own homes — just because they hadn't lost their home didn't mean they weren't struggling. Many had lost jobs, and as with the months immediately after the disaster, those that were living independently were not getting the same support as those in the temporary homes.

So as I drove around Oshika, I'd go with my instincts and if I saw people in their garden, I'd pull over, introduce myself with a huge grin, then casually mention that I had a few things in my car in case they happened to need anything. Afterward, I'd then try to pop in on them every few days just to say hello.

I thought the gas station would be a good place to meet people and make them smile, so I asked the owner, Suda-san, if I could clean car windows when customers pulled up to refuel. Bemused, he agreed, and I spent some of my free time diligently wiping windscreens, all the while yapping away in my childlike Japanese and trying to make the occupants laugh. I met *a lot* of people at that gas station.

I said hello to every single person I met, and greeted them with either a huge smile, a big wave, or, if I was driving, a beep of my horn — regardless of how far away they were. Some people might not have benefitted from a coat, but I figured that everyone would benefit from a smile. And everybody seemed to love my little blue car, which was covered in Union Jacks, with one even taped to the antenna!

I wasn't just exploring the peninsula by car — I was keeping up with my running, which was another thing that bemused my new friends on Oshika. Nobody went jogging there. And after my first run, I understood why — *all those bloody hills*. I'd be going uphill, absolutely dying inside, and a car would come round the corner, so I'd quickly lift my head up with a huge smile and a big wave as if it were no trouble at all, only to drop my head and shuffle along until the next car approached. A woman once shot out of her home, having been waiting for me, and pressed sweets into my hand as she enthusiastically said, "*Ganbatte*!" as if I were in the Tokyo Marathon; and it wasn't unusual for a car to pull over so the driver could ask where I was going and whether I needed a lift. Pouring with sweat, I'd somehow manage to convince them that I was fine.

I only really paid attention to personal hygiene on those running days. I hadn't been sure what access the local people had to showers or baths, so had come expecting to possibly not shower for a month and, as such, was fully stocked with wet wipes and dry shampoo. As it turned out, all the kasetsu had showers and baths, and there was a public bath on the peninsula that provided free access to volunteers. And the Ohara Community Centre had had a shower installed because of all the volunteers that had been staying there. Still, I didn't want to use up local resources, and it was so cold I couldn't bear to put my icy fingers near my own body, so I wore the same clothes for days at a time. The pipes kept freezing, so more often than not there wasn't any hot water for a shower anyway, as I once found out *after* going for a run and standing there shivering in my knickers.

Everybody both on Oshika and in Tokyo seemed to be very concerned with how warm I was — it was indeed *freezing*. I had chilblains on every toe. I had been given an electric blanket to sleep on (which I was mortified about — I felt it was terribly indulgent there), and even a heater next to my futon, with the explanation that the Japanese women volunteers who had stayed there had complained about the cold. I tried to offer some reassurance by saying that us *gaijin* girls had a lot more fat on us, but I obviously did not have enough. Every day I wore layers and layers … tights, thermals, jeans, a sweatshirt, a fleecy zip-up jacket, a thick padded coat, a woolly hat, a scarf, and a pair of thick gloves — sometimes two. And, on the nights I could bear to get undressed, I wore my bright pink fluffy pyjamas, which I'd brought more for the purpose of making people laugh than anything else. It worked — anyone hanging out in the centre in the evenings learned to sing "She'll be wearing pink pyjamas when she comes …"

Pretty soon everyone had heard of the strange girl that had come all the way from England to live on Oshika for a month. And as I got to know more and more people on the peninsula, the days were full of so much more laughter and warmth than I could ever have imagined. But the words "How can I help?" constantly ran through my head. I'd spend each evening answering Facebook messages from people asking me the same thing, or emails from schools in England with their latest fundraising total; then write on my blog and update that day's wish list before saying goodnight to everyone in the main room as they giggled at me in my pink pajamas.

I'd then settle in for what became another in a series of long, difficult nights.

There was a deep grumbling periodically throughout every night. Low, loud, and long. It was a horrible noise. It's a noise that I'm told can only be heard in very remote parts of Japan, just before an earthquake (even a little one). The noise unsettled me, along with the building creaking, and the wind blowing a gale outside. I lay there for hours worrying about everything — my lack of language ability, whether I was unintentionally upsetting anyone, how to really be of help, and whether I was going to gas myself with the heater I'd been kindly given but really wasn't sure how to operate.

More often than not, an aftershock would wake everyone else on the peninsula at 5:30 a.m. And I'd get up with a smile on my face, as though I'd had the best sleep ever.

Ready for another day on Oshika.

10: Oharahama

My home on Oshika was Oharahama, otherwise known as Ohara, meaning "a place where wealth and good luck increase." It is thought to be the oldest village on all of Oshika, with a gravestone dated 1673 being one of the earliest pieces of evidence of people living there. It has a very special history.

Date Masamune, a famous samurai warlord in Tohoku during the early 17th century, founded the nearby city of Sendai. Many of the samurai clans he conquered fled to remote areas throughout the region. Historically, before the coastal road was built, Ohara could only be reached by boat. It was a perfect hideaway for the defeated samurai. Nonetheless, they were still discovered by Date who, moved by the beauty of the location with its stunning sunsets, decided to establish a home there.

Date used Ohara as a hunting base — the area was teeming with wild deer (the "shika" in Oshika means "deer") — and built a shrine up on a hill, filling it with art. He spared the lives of the defeated samurai who had been living in the forests of Ohara, and gave them permission to live in the new village he was building, as long as they protected it. The descendants of those samurai still live in Ohara today, and Date's art still hangs in his shrine at the top of the hill.

During the following two hundred years, Ohara became a famous fishing town, and it certainly lived up to the meaning of its name. Businesses thrived and the local population could not keep up with all the work that was required, so they had to hire people from other places, and even other countries, which was most unusual during a period of time in Japan's history when the country was closed to foreigners. This coastal community grew bigger and busier, and developed a culture of acceptance of everyone, regardless of nationality, race, or origin. Everybody was welcome in Ohara. They still are today.

Traditionally, people's homes needed to be large — big enough to accommodate the vast numbers of people who were brought in to work in the fishing industry. People from all over would settle in the area, also falling in love with its beauty, and this is why the locals say that in Ohara, unlike in other similar villages in Japan, you can find people with lots of different surnames, and lots of different faces.

The population started to decline toward the end of the 19th century as young people moved to the big cities in search of a different life. The tsunami from the Chilean earthquake in May 1960 affected the fishing industry so badly that those who chose to stay in the area had to look for other work, so Ohara became a village of farmers as well as fishermen. And the population continued to dwindle.

At the time of the 2011 earthquake, Ohara had a population of 150. Afterward, it was left with half that.

The Ohara people knew what to do when the ground shook on March 11. Even before the tsunami sirens started they stopped their work at the port or in the fields, and began heading to higher ground, which luckily wasn't too far away. Some congregated outside the community centre, just a little bit raised and overlooking the village — you could get a really good view of what the sea was doing from there. The people of Ohara liked being able to see the sea and know what it was doing — having lived there for generations they respected the sea enough to always keep a watchful eye on it and were glad not to have a sea wall there that would have prevented them from doing so.

And it was from there that they watched the sea swallow their entire village. Not just once, but over and over again.

The first surge reached about 100 metres inland, just up to the path leading to the community centre. The second reached the building itself, at which point the villagers moved further up, to land just a bit higher, by the elementary school entrance. And from there they watched as the third and fourth surges engulfed the entire community centre and all of the area where they had been standing a few moments before. After the fourth surge, some people on other parts of Oshika returned to what was left of their homes or offices. One hour later a fifth surge came. Nobody had expected that fifth surge, so some people who had originally escaped, died.

Only a few buildings remained in Ohara, but because most people had immediately headed for high ground and stayed there, just two people died in the village. Those who survived in Ohara, along with others who happened to be in the area on March 11, spent the month immediately after the earthquake living in Ohara Elementary School. There were 200 people living in a building without electricity or water, although in true Ohara style, people smiled as they retold the stories of what that month spent crammed together was like: "Very friendly!" they would say, and then laugh at the memory of carrying water from the school swimming pool so they could use the toilets.

When the sea had receded, the villagers searched through the piles and piles of debris, hunting for items that could be useful in their living quarters. Whatever was in decent condition was salvaged, dried out, and used in the elementary school. Living in those conditions was just too much for many of them, so some returned to what was left of their homes, or went to stay with friends or family in other parts of Japan. By the middle of April, 100 people were still living there, but decided that they should leave the school to allow the children to start the new school year, keeping things as close to normality as possible for the youngsters. So they also either returned to what was left of their homes, or went to stay in other parts of Japan. It was to be a further four months until temporary housing came to Ohara, during which time more people, unable to cope, left the village. Most never returned.

The disaster reduced this once thriving village's population to only 70 people.

Most of the Ohara residents were living in temporary housing when I arrived to spend my month there, and after I had been to the danwashitsu with coats a few times, people there started to invite me into their homes. I was initially a bit uncomfortable about being invited in — the volunteer leaders I had come across on Oshika always told their teams not to accept invitations into the temporary houses and even though I was there doing my own thing, I didn't want that to be the *wrong* thing. But these lovely people in Ohara were so insistent that I made a decision to take my cues from the locals rather than from those who were not — a decision that was to stand me in good stead throughout my time on Oshika.

Pretty soon I was spending half my time going in and out of these tiny spaces that had become people's homes. Each unit had its own mailbox on the sliding front door, with the name of the family written on it, and each had a recycling box. There was a *genkan* (entrance space) that was about a metre by half a metre that was always filled with shoes because it is unheard of in Japan to enter any living space without first removing one's shoes. After that was another door, which would be the one that I'd knock on to see whether anyone was in, before sliding the door open.

A unit for a single person or a couple was about three metres by three metres, and consisted of a living room in which you ate, relaxed, or slept; a little cooking area to one side; and a small bathroom with a vanity unit, a toilet, and Japanese-style bath (short, so you sat in it with your knees pulled up to your chest, but deep enough to then have the water come up to your shoulders). If you lived with a parent or parents, or your children, you had an extra living room. Each unit was provided with a small cooking stove, a heater that doubled as an air conditioner, and a massive television. These units provided shelter and an element of privacy, but were tatty — not even brand new and not designed for the harsh weather on Oshika. Some even had tape along the join between the wall and the ceiling to keep the rain out. They had cost the government between ¥4 and ¥12 million each.

Inhabitants had initially been told to expect to live in this temporary housing for six months. They had been there for five months when I first started popping in, and there were no signs that anything was being built that they could plan on moving into. There were too many legal complications over the land and too many restrictions from the government. They were later told to expect to live in the kasetsu for two years, but in Ohara they ended up living in them for almost five years.

Except for one person who happened to win ¥6 million on a lottery and bought a trailer home, which arrived during my month there. The owner parked the trailer on the land where they used to live; although they owned the land, they weren't allowed to build on it because the tsunami had reached it. People had already had enough of kasetsu life and were trying to find ways around the restrictions that had been imposed on them. A trailer was technically a temporary building, and so was allowed to be "parked" anywhere.

Only a few Ohara residents had homes that the tsunami had spared, although the earthquake had caused some damage to the older, ancestral homes and to the ground beneath the newer ones, which affected their stability. The people whose houses remained had to deal with the constant nuisance caused by the wild deer that still roamed on Oshika. Whereas prior to the earthquake they stayed in the hills and didn't bother anyone other than the odd motorist driving round a bend at dusk, the earthquake had disturbed the vegetation on the now unstable higher ground. So the deer, no longer deterred by any buildings in the villages, roamed around freely, helping themselves to the flowers and vegetables that were growing in the remaining gardens. I went to sleep every night with the sound of deer calling to each other, right outside my window.

Ohara had mostly been a residential area, with a few little family businesses that related to the fishing industry, and a couple of tiny restaurants. One small family-owned factory remained at the southern end of the village, with construction workers there constantly trying to repair and rebuild it. Nearby was Kanta, a temporary restaurant built inside a shipping container. I went there as often as possible — not just because I wanted to support the owner as he rebuilt his life, but because he served the most delicious fried rice I had ever had. Opposite Kanta was a huge "Land for Sale" sign at the top of a hillside, which as I fell more and more in love with Ohara, I would stare longingly at over my lunch.

I was developing a connection with this village that was difficult to explain. I wondered whether it was because my own ancestors, many years ago, were sailors. My great-grandmother had done some research into our family tree, and when she'd discovered that we were the result of dirty weekends between French sailors and Cornish milkmaids, she'd been horrified. But I loved that story.

I just felt so *at home* in Ohara. Whether I was at the tiny pebbly beach that you had to clamber down a little cliff to reach, hiking through the forests to pick mushrooms, or walking down to the little port from which the young men of the village had, for centuries, raced into the sea during summer festivals while carrying *mikoshi* (portable shrines) on their shoulders.

Mikoshi are only carried around the village during summer festivals. During winter festivals, a wooden float is pulled around the village instead. And there was to be a winter festival in Ohara during the month I spent there! While I'd seen some festival-like activities in Tokyo, until that February on Oshika I'd never actually participated in a festival in Japan before.

Ohara's February festival marked the beginning of the fishing season, and would give everyone in the fishing community the opportunity to pray for a good season — something everybody desperately needed after the disaster. The winter festival was highly anticipated by the little village community that year. It was the first community celebration since the disaster, and it would provide everyone who had been welcomed into the Ohara community the chance to return once more — not to help, but to celebrate. And native Ohara people loved any opportunity to celebrate — they knew how to put on a great party!

Preparations began the day before the festival, when the men of the village met at the bottom of the steps to the shrine to erect two huge white banners in front of the massive *torii*. Torii indicate a "gateway to a sacred place"; specifically, they are built before a walkway that leads to a Shinto shrine. They can be made of stone or wood, and are often painted bright red. I'd always been fascinated by torii when I'd lived in Tokyo — I found their towering strength filled me with awe, whether it was at the incredible Meiji Shrine complex in Tokyo, or at a little neighbourhood shrine I'd unexpectedly come across when wandering the backstreets of Tokyo.

Ohara's torii is huge and made of stone. It has two pole brackets in front of it, and in preparation for a festival, the poles for the festival banners are laid on the ground with the base of each lined up with the base of a bracket. The huge white banners are attached to the poles, along with three pieces of thick rope, several metres long. Three people each take hold of a piece of rope and gradually raise a pole so that its banner stands almost as tall as the torii, then attach the pole to the bracket with an ancient latch. I love watching the village men raise those banners — something they have done together again and again over many years in a way they were probably taught by their fathers, and their fathers before them.

That February, I walked with the villagers up the stone steps to the shrine at the top of the hill, which overlooked all of Ohara. This shrine, which I had first seen in May 2011, looked like it wouldn't remain standing for much longer — it was covered in support beams, brackets, weights, and huge heavy bands that were holding it all together. It was around four hundred years old, and had withstood countless earthquakes and typhoons in its time. While unaffected by the tsunami due to its high location, the 2011 earthquake had severely damaged it. And the kanetsukido had been completely destroyed.

This was the shrine that Date Masamune had built, and was still filled with art and relics that were hundreds of years old. And the men I walked up the steps with had tended to this shrine for their whole lives, as had their ancestors before them. I could only imagine the responsibility they felt to somehow restore this ancient building.

We swept the shrine inside and out, and weeded the cobblestone path leading from the shrine to the top of the steps, along with every single step all the way down to the village. I preferred to use my hands but everybody else had hand sickles, which I couldn't quite get the hang of. They looked so old and rusty that I wondered whether they had been first used by Date himself. But they were very effective. It was exhausting but satisfying work, and the cobblestones looked beautiful when we had finished.

The level of teamwork as the Ohara men bustled about getting everything ready was exceptional. Everybody seemed to know exactly what to do. They did not get in each other's way. They were serious, focused, and professional. With a little bit of playful teasing thrown in.

We returned to the centre, where a huge 400-year-old *mandara* (mandala) was unrolled and placed at the front of the main room. This ancestral mandara belongs to Ishimori-san's family, who have lived in Ohara since Date Masamune's time — the castle that had once stood in the mountains behind Ohara was named Ishimori-jo after Ishimori-san's family. The mandara was a beautiful combination of artwork and embroidery, representing the interconnected relationships between humans, nature, and spiritual deities. It was faded in many places, but it would soon be restored by specialist artists in Japan.

The priest started writing beautiful calligraphy all over a very long, thick block of pale wood that was placed in front of the banner. This wood represented the *kamisama* (god). The original kamisama had been washed away by the tsunami, and despite the Ohara people searching and searching for it among the debris, it was never found. I often heard stories during that month about communities that had been devastated not just by the loss of their homes, but also by the loss of items and precious relics related to their gods, their shrines, and their festivals, which are such an important part of life on Oshika. So, a new kamisama for Ohara was made by the priest, and it was surrounded by food offerings — fresh fish, rice, fruit, and vegetables.

The walls of the centre were covered with huge flags from the fishing boats. They were beautiful, brightly coloured flags with symbolic images on them that expressed the hope that the coming season would result in lots of fish being caught. The bold colours of the flags all over the centre contrasted with the more sedate arrangement of the kamisama and offerings at the front of the room — although I was to learn that this was how Ohara did festivals: solemn when appropriate, but full of life and laughter, too.

When the centre was deemed ready, we returned to the shrine for the ceremonial part of the day to begin. The other Ohara residents arrived one by one, greeting me with an excited wave or showing off the new warm clothes they'd got from the danwashitsu on one of my visits there. We all huddled together inside the shrine, and the priest began his melodic chanting, praying for a good fishing season, as well as for the people of Ohara and those who had helped them since the disaster. I found it very moving to be sitting in such a sacred building, with such a special history, among people who were celebrating for the first time since a particularly horrible disaster had befallen them. I felt truly honoured to be there. And completely mesmerized by the priest's voice.

After the ceremony at the shrine, there was another ceremony at the centre, this time involving praying to the wooden kamisama. As part of the ceremony, people who were considered to be key members of the Ohara community were called to the front of the room where the priest offered symbolic branches to them. Each person knelt in front of the priest, then turned to lay the branch in front of the kamisama, bowing twice, clapping twice, and bowing once more before returning to their seat. I watched from the back of the room, fascinated by the entire ritual, and enjoying every wonderfully calm and peaceful moment. It was beautiful.

Suddenly I heard my name being called out, and my serenity disappeared in an instant as I audibly gasped in shock. *Oh no, do I have to go to the front and do that now?!* The people sitting next to me had picked up on my panic, but smiled and nodded, indicating that I should go up. I got up, but did so unsteadily because I'd been sitting on the floor for so long that my legs had gone numb. It hadn't occurred to me that I'd be expected to get up in front of everyone. I made my way to the front, mortified because everyone was watching me, and desperately trying to remember ... was it bow first or clap first? Clap first or bow first? Two claps separated by bows or three claps with a couple of bows at the end? *What if I get it wrong and it's somehow seen as massively disrespectful and I manage to upset everyone?* Still, to this day, I have no idea whether I did it correctly, but as I walked back to my seat, I caught sight of my Ohara friends smiling proudly at me, delighted at my actions.

I vowed to learn *exactly* what to do during the prayer ritual so that I would never be taken by surprise again.

With the solemn part of the festival over, it was time for lots of eating and drinking, followed by some entertainment. A lot of young adults had come to Ohara for the festival — they were volunteers or relief workers who had come to know of the village in the months after the disaster — and the Ohara residents loved the opportunity to drag their new friends into some rowdy, quite physical indoor games. One game involved sitting in a circle, passing around a long circular string of huge wooden beads, which you had to gather up, wrap around the person next to you, and yank them off balance, symbolizing the catching of a fish. You ended up getting dragged along the floor or piled on by the people closest to you — it was great fun.

The festival ended with all of us sitting together and watching some kind of stand-up comedy routine. I couldn't follow much of it, but I was happy just looking around at the smiling faces of the local people as they forgot about their worries for a while. I *think* I managed to work out that what made them laugh the most were jokes about drunk people, old people, and Japanese people travelling overseas. As well as any jokes that involved farting. No wonder I felt so at home.

The Ohara Community Centre was a hub of activity during the festival, and the centre of the entire village. Thousands of volunteers slept there in the months after the disaster as they worked hard to clear the area. Volunteers also came to run classes for the locals, keeping them busy, entertained, active, and optimistic. I watched some volunteers from Kanagawa giving a CPR course. There were only two portable AED machines in the village, and while the ambulance response time on the mainland was six minutes, it would take an ambulance forty minutes to reach Ohara. So it was important that everybody have CPR knowledge. They were having a brilliant time practising their newly learned skills in the centre — Ohara people didn't need much encouragement to have fun and they were always laughing about something. They found it hilarious that I was staying at the centre for an entire month, and joked that perhaps I was sleeping in the exact same spot where Date Masamune had!

Every morning, kids from the neighbouring villages arrived in the school bus, and ran up the little hill to school. They were always so upbeat, and loved going to school. I wasn't surprised about this after I met the teachers — kind, gentle people who loved their jobs and loved Oshika. At the end of the day, they'd walk the children back to the bus stop, and watch them as they played in what was left of the playground in front of the centre. All that remained after the tsunami was a rusty swing set, yet the kids still raced down the hill to play on it. There was a broken panda seat that the kids still loved, and, randomly, a giant ice cream cone. This giant ice cream cone had been carried by the tsunami from another town and it landed in Ohara. It had been very badly damaged and had huge holes in the side, but it became something that always made people laugh. The original owner had been traced and said they didn't require it back, so it stayed in Ohara. It's still there now.

The school and the community centre were on land that belonged to the local government, but most of Ohara consisted of privately owned land. One of the biggest landowners was Takako-sensei, who had married into a family that had been in Ohara since Date Masamune's time.

I met Takako-sensei one morning as she was waiting for a bus outside the community centre. The bus hadn't turned up, so Hiroyuki asked whether I would give her a lift to Ayukawa, twenty minutes away. I was happy to be of help, so we set off and she talked the whole way there — I wasn't surprised to later be told that everyone referred to her as *mashingan* (machine gun) because she talked so much. She'd been a preschool teacher on Oshika for thirty years, so everybody knew her. She thanked me for the lift and invited me to her home for dinner that night, saying that the nights were long now and she could do with the company.

Takako-sensei used to live in a beautiful big ancestral home just a few metres away from the sea. She'd had a huge garden, which she spent all her time and money on, and had a great deal of pride in. It all disappeared in fifteen minutes.

As soon as the earthquake happened she knew she had to get to high ground, which she did, with only the clothes she was wearing. She yelled at her neighbour to do the same, who reassured her that she was going to, but she wasn't fast enough. Takako-sensei never saw her again. In addition to being a preschool teacher, she was also a highly sought-after teacher for adults who were interested in pressing flowers. She never again saw the student she'd been teaching that day — the student had set off for Ayukawa after the fourth surge, not thinking there could be a fifth on its way.

Takako-sensei moved into one of the kasetsu in September after spending six months with her sister in Fukushima. She was struggling, more from the lack of privacy than the lack of space, and said that her young female neighbours were so noisy. I asked her how old they were — I hadn't seen any young women in Ohara — and she said they were in their sixties. I loved her.

Takako-sensei had nothing left of the ancestral home she had loved so much — just a few photos that a kind man from Tokyo, Toru Konishi, had retrieved from the debris and restored. He ended up restoring 10,000 photos from the debris, and helped to bring back so many wonderful memories for people. He was very fond of Takako-sensei, but then, it was easy to become fond of her. True to her nickname, she really didn't stop talking as she bossed me about because she wanted me to lay the table *just so*. She was not only openly talking about the tsunami, but telling me all about everyone in Ohara … who does what, whose family was samurai, and whose family used to live in the castle all those years ago.

Then she turned her interest on me, firing one question after another. Was I really staying there for a month? Did I really drive all that way from Tokyo on my own? She spent ages trying to work me out and, eventually, grasping at one of the few English words she knows, she pronounced me to be "abnormal," which gave me a fit of the giggles, which then set her off. She had meant "unusual," but for the entire month she referred to me as "Abnormal-san," even entering my number under that moniker in her mobile phone.

I regularly popped in on Takako-sensei, who didn't drive, to see if she needed anything from the shops, or just wanted a bit of company. And I got to know all of the women in the temporary housing community, but they weren't the people I spent most of my time with.

To everyone's amusement, I spent most of my time hanging out with the old fishermen of the village. The Ohara boys.

11: The Ohara Boys

Every evening, just as the sun was setting in front of Ohara, Ishimori-san took his dog for a walk all around where the village used to be. He'd wave cheerily at me, sometimes saying "*Guddo-ibuningu*," thrilled at the English word I had taught him. Ishimori-san was the head of Ohara, or the *kucho*, so everybody called him Kucho-san, or Kucho.

Kucho was shorter than me, and for a man in his sixties, he had an impressive head of thick jet-black hair. He had a big smile, which he employed surprisingly frequently despite his responsibilities. He had become the head of Ohara after the disaster, when the former head couldn't cope anymore and had left the village. Before that, Kucho-san was a postman.

Kucho was married to Fukumi-san, who was just as jolly and always smiling. She was round and seemed to be on a mission to make everyone else the same way as she constantly plied you with plates and plates of delicious food she'd made, or snacks she'd bought from the department stores in Sendai. When I first met her, she worked in a small fishing factory at a nearby port, but before the earthquake she had worked in the local government office based in Ohara. This was the tiny building that was still standing on the other side of the centre's car park but wasn't used anymore except for its toilet — it was the nearest toilet to the centre, which didn't have one. The number of times I traipsed across the car park late at night, through thick snow, in my bright pink pajamas, for a final wee before bedtime ...

Kucho and Fukumi's dog Koro was a Shiba, a type that's very common in Japan. And Koro was a total psychopath. Nobody could go near that dog without losing a finger, except Kucho. Not even Fukumi-san. More often than not, when I slid open the door to their home, Kucho would be sitting in the genkan feeding Koro a delicious treat by hand, as the dog lay there in its bed, ready to turn on anyone else who ventured near.

They lived just behind the community centre, so we were neighbours. Kucho's ancestral home was on high enough ground that it escaped the tsunami, but the earthquake had dislodged some of the ground underneath the newer part of the house, which was slowly collapsing until the Ohara boys rallied round to repair it. You didn't call a builder, plumber, or carpenter for such things in Ohara — you just got your mates to help you get on with it.

Kucho was hugely respected by everyone, not just because of everything he was doing to lead the village through this difficult time, but because his family dated back to samurai times, and were one of the first to live in Ohara. He had relatives all over the peninsula.

Abe-san was Kucho's deputy (the *fukukucho*). He was incredibly slim, whereas most people on Oshika were rather stocky. He had a slightly nervous laugh, and a kind smile. He was a farmer before the earthquake happened, but in his youth he had been an engineer on huge ships, so had travelled the world having adventures and knew just a little bit about a lot of different cultures. He lived with his wife and mother in a huge brand new house that was far enough from the sea that it wasn't affected by the tsunami.

The temporary housing community was located right opposite Abe-san's house and I often wondered how hard it must have been for him to look out every day and see where people he had known his whole life were now living. He seemed to be such a sensitive man, and nothing was too much trouble for him. Before the end of the month I went back to every spot where Andrew and I had taken photographs on the first trip here and took another one from the exact same spot to show the debris-clearing and rebuilding progress (or lack of it), and Abe-san spent a whole afternoon helping me with it, making sure I had the camera in just the right spot.

I once asked Abe-san why the men in Ohara seemed to treat women so differently from the way I noticed men in Tokyo treat women, of course knowing full well that I was generalizing. But it was something I became aware of quite early on. Men and women seemed to have very traditional roles on Oshika — they might both work in the fishing industry, but the domestic responsibilities (such as child raising, cooking, and cleaning) were very much a female domain, and the decision-making responsibilities were very much a male domain (especially regarding village meetings, at which would attend one representative from each household, an extremely efficient way of getting things done in a small village). When entertaining guests, the women prepared all the food, brought in the dishes, and cleared them away again, usually not joining the people who were eating, but instead eating later when the guests had left. However, it wasn't the traditional roles that interested me so much — I didn't want to make judgments about their way of life — it was the men's *attitudes* toward their wives as they both fulfilled these traditional roles; they just seemed so much more respectful and appreciative than a lot of the older Japanese men in Tokyo.

Abe-san wasn't surprised that I had asked this question — he knew that things were different on the peninsula. He explained that this respect that the Ohara men had for their wives was due to the fact that they came from a very long line of fishermen, who historically would go away to sea for months and months on end, during which time their wives took care of everything — the home, the kids, the money, and the family business. Abe-san said you couldn't just come back from being at sea for months and then treat her badly when she'd been working hard doing all that for you! And that respectful attitude toward their wives was passed down through the generations.

Onodera-san not only respected his wife but took very special care of her. About twenty years before the disaster, in her early forties, Mrs Onodera had had two brain haemorrhages, one of which had left her blind. Her husband never left the house in the evening unless one of his adult children was there. The Onoderas lived across from the centre's car park so they were technically my other neighbours.

Onodera-san had first caught my attention when I'd heard him swear. One of the other Ohara boys had poured water on a fire (they were always burning something in Ohara), and the steam had gone into Onodera-san's face, prompting him to say "*konchikusho!*" ("You bastard!"). I learned this word when I'd first moved to Japan, but never, in all my fifteen years there, had I ever heard anyone say it. I instantly fell in love with him and we were to become close friends.

Despite his language, Onodera-san was another respected senior member of the Ohara community, and he played a big role in coordinating everything necessary for the festivals. He had moved from Ishinomaki to

Ohara to marry his wife, who had lived there her whole life. He was a tennis player before injuring his elbow, and after that he was a tree surgeon, which didn't help his arm a lot, but he was *much* stronger than you'd think and would surprise me with a vigorous shiatsu massage when I'd complain about my sore shoulder.

Onodera-san's son Kuni had a couple of jobs — one working in a demolition yard and another working as an HGV driver, both of which were in great demand in the months after the disaster. He was also a volunteer community firefighter, along with some of the other younger Ohara boys — part of Ohara culture was that everybody did their bit for the community. As he got older, Kuni would start to play an important role in the festivals, was the best at leading the *shishimai* (lion dance), and did a fantastic impression of the priest's melodic chanting.

Kuni's younger sister Yuki worked in a restaurant on the mainland, so she took the bus into Watanoha every morning, and back again every evening. She had been living with a friend in Watanoha at the time of the earthquake — they lost their home and Yuki became stuck on the mainland, with no way of contacting her family on Oshika. For a week, the Onoderas had had no idea whether Yuki was dead or alive.

In addition to his colourful language, another reason I loved Onodera-san was that he refused to adhere to any regulations nor did he have any interest in what the authorities said. The tsunami had reached the ceiling of his home, so really he wasn't supposed to be living in it. But after he'd cleaned it up, he insisted on staying. I spent many an evening over there when nights alone in the centre became a little too cold, scary, or lonely, and the Onoderas treated me like family. I'd pop over in my pajamas, say *"tadaima"* ("I'm home") and settle myself under the *kotatsu* (heated table with a thick blanket) between Kuni and his mum to watch that evening's local variety show on TV and listen to Mrs Onodera sing her favourite songs at the top of her voice.

Takahashi-san, in his late seventies, was one of the oldest men in Ohara. Before the earthquake, he and his wife operated a ramen restaurant near the seafront, where everybody said they made the most delicious ramen ever. They had married young, worked together all day, every day, for their whole lives, and were still very much in love. They'd lived above the restaurant.

On the day of the earthquake, the Takahashis were at work, as usual, and headed up to the second floor as the tsunami rushed toward the village.

Despite her husband's protests, Mrs Takahashi ran downstairs to retrieve something. Her body was found a few days later.

After that, Takahashi-san spent each day walking all around the land where the village used to be. His daughter Miyoko lived several hours' away, and called him every day at 10 a.m. to check whether he was eating properly and to see how he was feeling. Even months after the disaster, Miyoko still cried for her mother, every single day.

There was another Takahashi-san in Ohara but they weren't related — and to distinguish between the two Takahashis, the other was jokingly referred to as Takahashi-*buta* (Takahashi pig). He wasn't from the area, but had been sent there by the company he worked for so that he could manage the pig farm just behind the village. He was often laughing and being silly, but then would surprise you sometimes by speaking about something serious, and straight from the heart. I was frequently moved by his emotional honesty. He was always looking for ways to show his appreciation for the volunteers that visited Ohara by giving them little gifts, cooking for them, or giving them lifts so they could access the public transport system. He gave me a beautiful good luck charm bracelet, saying that I was always thinking about Oshika and needed some good thoughts for myself.

Takahashi-buta was in charge of the temporary housing community, but was single, and he really didn't want to be. The other Ohara boys teased him because everywhere they went he tried to chat up women, but there were very few single women on Oshika, so who could blame him? He paid a lot of attention to his kasetsu, keeping it spotless and decorating it inside and out with anything and everything pink. There were pink picture frames, pink plastic flowers, pink table mats, even a pink hairdryer despite the fact that he didn't have any hair. He said that single men's homes were usually so dull and he wanted his to be pretty. He wanted female visitors to feel comfortable there, at which point his mates would roar with laughter and say that no woman had ever been *near* his home.

One of the other single men was Yukio-san, but he wasn't bothered about being single. He had a tendency to be a bit of a loner, which would sometimes worry Kucho, who would ask me to cheer him up. Everybody in the community cared so much about each other. So I worked out a most effective way of lifting Yukio-san out of his moods — it involved me making a nuisance of myself by regularly turning up at his kasetsu unannounced. I'd tell him that I was trying to do x or y, but couldn't quite manage it on my own, so would he help me? He'd always refuse, then ten minutes later his car would turn up at the centre, with the tools necessary for the job, and he'd join in with whatever I was doing, saying he could only help me for a little bit. We'd end up working together for days on end. I loved working with him. On the last day of my month there, I found him washing my car (it had got *filthy* while I was there), so it was immaculate for my drive back to Tokyo.

Yukio-san and I became quite fond of each other, but it would be some time before he told me his tsunami story. A lot of people would end up telling me their stories — sometimes straight away and sometimes after we'd known each other a while. It always felt different when it was someone you had grown close to over some time — when for a long time you had looked at them and seen a friend, rather than a survivor. So when Yukio-san asked me if I wanted to climb up a hill just by the port that would give the most beautiful view of all Ohara, and while we were at the top, he suddenly said, "This is where I watched the tsunami," I was shocked. He had stood up there, alone, and watched as the entire village was destroyed. He even saw the tsunami lift the roof off the ramen restaurant and sweep it inland with the elderly Takahashi-san standing on top of it, desperately clinging to an antenna, beloved wife nowhere to be seen.

Saito-san was the father of the only children in Ohara. Emi-chan, his wife, was from Thailand and had come to live in Ohara with her husband ten years ago — she loved asking me about what it was like to drive to Oshika all the way from Tokyo by myself. She was the youngest woman in the temporary housing community, and aside from Yuki Onodera, the youngest woman in Ohara. Saito-san carried a lot of responsibility on his shoulders as a husband, a father, and an important member of the Ohara community. But he knew how to let loose and he loved the festivals, when he'd do his best to get the priest as drunk as possible.

Saito-san was an oyster and *wakame* (a kind of seaweed) fisherman, and when the tsunami came, he was out at sea. His boat's propeller got caught up in rope and he was stuck out in the ocean until other fishermen came to rescue him. His boat wasn't damaged at all, but everything else he needed to be able to work was washed away — including the couple of million yen in cash that all the fishermen kept hidden in their homes so they could pay the various casual workers that are essential to their industry. Saito-san was desperate to get back to work, aware that the wakame season was only a few weeks away, and wondering how, without the right equipment, he would harvest the wakame that he had managed to plant the previous autumn.

The rest of the Ohara boys included Taira-san, who had been a fruit seller and deep sea diver, was an incredible taiko drummer, and could talk about healthy eating for hours; Ogata-san, the moody carpenter who worked, lived, ate, and slept in a huge, chaotic workshop high in the hills; Ogata-san's younger brother, the one-toothed Take-chan, who must have inherited all the family's happy genes because nothing ever seemed to get him down; Hirota-kun, who lived in a beautiful old house with the best view of the Ohara sunsets; and Kiyotaka-kun, who worked in Yachan's wakame and oyster processing factory and had lived in Tokyo, but said his heart never left Ohara.

Yachan's factory was a building at the south end of the village, and it was still being repaired after the tsunami. After the disaster, when his father couldn't cope anymore, he unexpectedly and rather suddenly had to take over the family business. Yachan was closer to Kuni's age than Onodera-san's, but the two men were buddies. Yachan was born and grew up in Ohara, but had attended university in Tokyo, and we often talked about Tokyo life. He now owned the family wakame and oyster business, which he ran with his mother's support. He also owned the land on which Ohara's kasetsu were built.

Locating land for the temporary housing communities had been a very difficult task. Once a suitable area had been identified (on higher ground, flat, and not reached by the tsunami), if the land didn't belong to the local government then permission had to be requested from the private owners. Everybody was of course willing to do their bit to assist with the recovery, including offering their land, but in many cases, that land had previously been used in some capacity by local business owners, either as storage, or as space in which the harvested wakame would be cut, or shells threaded for the oyster farms. Either way, it was valuable space essential to somebody's business; space they wouldn't be able to access at a time when it was crucial for these businesses to recover quickly — they provided employment.

And there wasn't a lot of that on Oshika after 311.

In the absence of employment, the Ohara boys, so active before the disaster, were totally and utterly bored. And extremely frustrated. Not so much about the lack of income, because any fishermen who were unable to work received ¥12,000 per day from the government. To qualify to continue receiving that money they had to spend three days a week doing "community work," which often involved picking up any debris that still remained, or maintaining woodland. Once a month they had to take photographs of themselves doing the work, while someone held a sign with the date written on it. The photos were sent to Tokyo to prove they had done something to earn their money. To these men, who *proudly* cared for their community anyway, and were desperate to get back to their normal work, the whole process was ridiculous. They didn't want handouts. They just wanted to work again.

During that month on Oshika, I sought out the Ohara boys on the days they were doing community work, and tagged along with them. I felt it was the least I could do, seeing as I was staying in their community centre for a month. Nobody batted an eyelid at my presence.

They'd gather together at the community centre, then set off in a few open-back trucks — someone driving, someone in the passenger seat (they insisted that be me), and two standing up in the back holding on to the driver's cab. This was how you travelled if you were a proper *Ohara-jin* (Ohara person), even if you were going just a few minutes away to the little pebble beach — a popular destination as there was always something washing up on the shore that needed clearing up. The things that got washed up could even provide just a few moments of amusement, as Take-chan and Abe-san proved with an impromptu game of bowls they set up on the beach with a bowling ball that had washed up.

Or we'd collect wood from all around the village, then head back to the centre to load it into an empty oil drum with a hole cut out of the bottom, and sit in a circle warming ourselves as the huge flames shot up into the cold air.

One of my favourite jobs was clearing the bamboo forest. Lots of the bamboo had died partly because of salt water from the tsunami, but also because of the heavy rainstorm that hit this particular area very badly soon after March 11. We dragged the dead bamboo out of the forest, broke it up, and then stacked it so it was ready to later throw onto the back of one of the trucks. I knew they didn't really expect me to do much, but I had no intention of sitting around and this was some physical work I could really get stuck into. They soon noticed my efforts, because I had my own big stack of bamboo, so Kucho-san joined me, passing bigger and bigger pieces in my direction. We made a good team, although I managed to poke my eye four times, rip a contact lens, and give myself a split lip. The dust and dirt got everywhere, even through my gloves, but none of this bothered me at all.

Taira-san said that I now had a red nose and red cheeks and looked like a proper English country girl. And I impressed them all when I had a go on the chainsaw and turned out to be a natural — they couldn't believe that I had never used one before. I wanted to show them that they really could give me anything to do and I'd do it. After these work sessions were over, we'd drive back to the centre in typical Ohara-style — this time with *me* standing in the back of the truck.

They dressed me up in the *kappa* that everybody in the fishing industry wears — thick, waterproof PVC overalls and jackets in bright colours — and took me out on their boats with them. Six of us got into Saito-san's tiny four-seater boat that had an engine that kept dying. I thought "surely he doesn't do any fishing from this thing," and was relieved to find out that that boat was just used to get out to his actual fishing boat, which was much more impressive. I stayed out of the way on the boat because there were ropes everywhere and the side of the boat was so low that it was easy to see how someone could fall overboard.

I was content to observe how they attached new buoys to the oyster ropes, and then actually harvested some oysters then and there. It was a treat to watch. The rope was attached to a pulley and the oysters got dragged into some kind of device, which then detached the oysters from the rope, and they landed with loud crashes in the baskets waiting below. And we ate them straight away, fresh from the ocean. They were constantly eating oysters — raw, boiled, or covered in breadcrumbs and deep fried. They could do a million things with them. I tried to explain that oysters were considered an aphrodisiac in England, and that if they kept feeding them to me I'd end up in big trouble.

While out on the boat, they'd check the wakame they had managed to plant the previous autumn. It would be ready in less than a month, but Saito-san had no idea how they were going to harvest it without the equipment they needed.

And if the weather was just too cold, wet, or windy to work outside, we'd stay inside in the community centre. I taught them a few English words and we played Hangman together. Kucho would worry whether I was too cold, and would lend me his *donbuku* (short, padded winter kimono jacket) to wear over my clothes.

From the moment I arrived, all I'd heard the Ohara boys talk about was a trip to a hot spring resort (*onsen*) that they were planning. And that they'd be taking me with them. I couldn't work out whether they were joking or not. Not, as it turned out. Mortified, I told Hiroyuki that I had no intention of swanning off to an onsen when I'd come to Ohara to help out, but Hiroyuki told me that I *was* helping out because they were all so excited about me going with them. In doing so, I was making them happy.

So a few days later, about ten of us piled into a few cars, and the Ohara boys took me off to Sendai with them, teasing me all the way about it being a mixed onsen. I had heard of mixed onsen in the countryside, and given that I generally had no idea what was going on most of the time, thought it was entirely possible that what they were saying could be true. At least I wasn't the only woman — Chise, a Japanese woman about my age, who was also helping in the area, had been persuaded to come along, too.

Before the earthquake, the Ohara boys would go to Akiu Onsen together three or four times a year. This was their first trip since the disaster. It was a two-hour drive through some beautiful scenery that included a huge hydro dam that was covered in snow on both sides. As soon as we got to the luxurious hotel, the boys headed straight off to the onsen while Chise and I went to our room, with Chise mirroring my thoughts as she mused, "This is *not* volunteering." She spoke really good English and, having been helping at Oshika for some months now, had a huge amount of knowledge about the peninsula, which she kindly shared with me.

Saito-san was known for loving onsen and everybody teased him for going into the baths four times between our arrival and dinner. Our dinner consisted of a massive buffet and the biggest glasses of beer I had ever seen. Everybody got nicely tipsy, so we piled into the little karaoke booth, but all agreed after just the first song that the booth was distinctly lacking in the kind of atmosphere and stage necessary to match our excitable mood, so we took over the hotel bar, which was full of other guests who were also wearing the obligatory slippers and *yukata* (a cotton kimono used as a kind of dressing gown) that all onsen hotel guests change into as soon as they've checked in.

The next thing I knew, I was standing on a huge stage, in slippers and a dressing gown, with about sixty old Japanese men, leading the whole bar in a Beatles medley.

The Ohara boys had been quite a hit in the hotel bar, and at some point Abe-san had introduced our group over the microphone to the other guests, saying that we were from Oshika-hanto, which had been very badly damaged in the tsunami, at which point everybody nodded sympathetically and clapped in admiration as well as solidarity. Some of them were from areas that had also been very badly affected. Then Abe-san explained that they had a friend who'd come all the way from England to help them, and I remember being so touched that even in the early days of our relationship they had referred to me as their friend. Once we left the stage, I noticed the other guests introduce themselves to the members of our party, and they sat talking for some time about the disaster, bringing comfort to one another.

We drove back through the snowy mountains the next day, losing each other on the way. Kucho-san drove straight into a snow drift, where we waited for the others to find us as the snow got heavier and heavier. Dear Kucho, as jolly as always, just laughed as we all pitched in to dig out his car.

With Oshika up ahead, we were nearly home, and the Ohara boys stopped off at an Ichiban Kalbi restaurant in Ishinomaki, thereby introducing me to the closest restaurant to Oshika that served what had always been one of my favourite foods in Japan ... Korean barbecue (*yakiniku*). I was to be eternally grateful for this introduction! Full of delicious grilled meat, fish, and vegetables, Kucho decided that he was too sleepy to make the drive back to Ohara, and to my surprise, handed me the keys and asked me to drive our party back. I had only driven those windy roads onto Oshika myself once before, and I was terrified. But I was also touched that he trusted me enough to drive his lovely car.

By the end of the month I'd gained the trust of all the Ohara boys. And proved myself to them in so many ways. I could drink a beer from a glass as big as my head, I would put my *all* into karaoke if asked, I didn't get sick on a boat, and while on that boat I could eat whatever was caught from it. I could lift heavy stuff, I could use any tool they gave me, and not only could I stand in the back of the trucks alongside them, I could also drive those trucks — they said better than any Japanese young men because they could only drive automatics these days. And to my delight as well as theirs, I had perfected the local swearing.

I had become a true Ohara-jin.

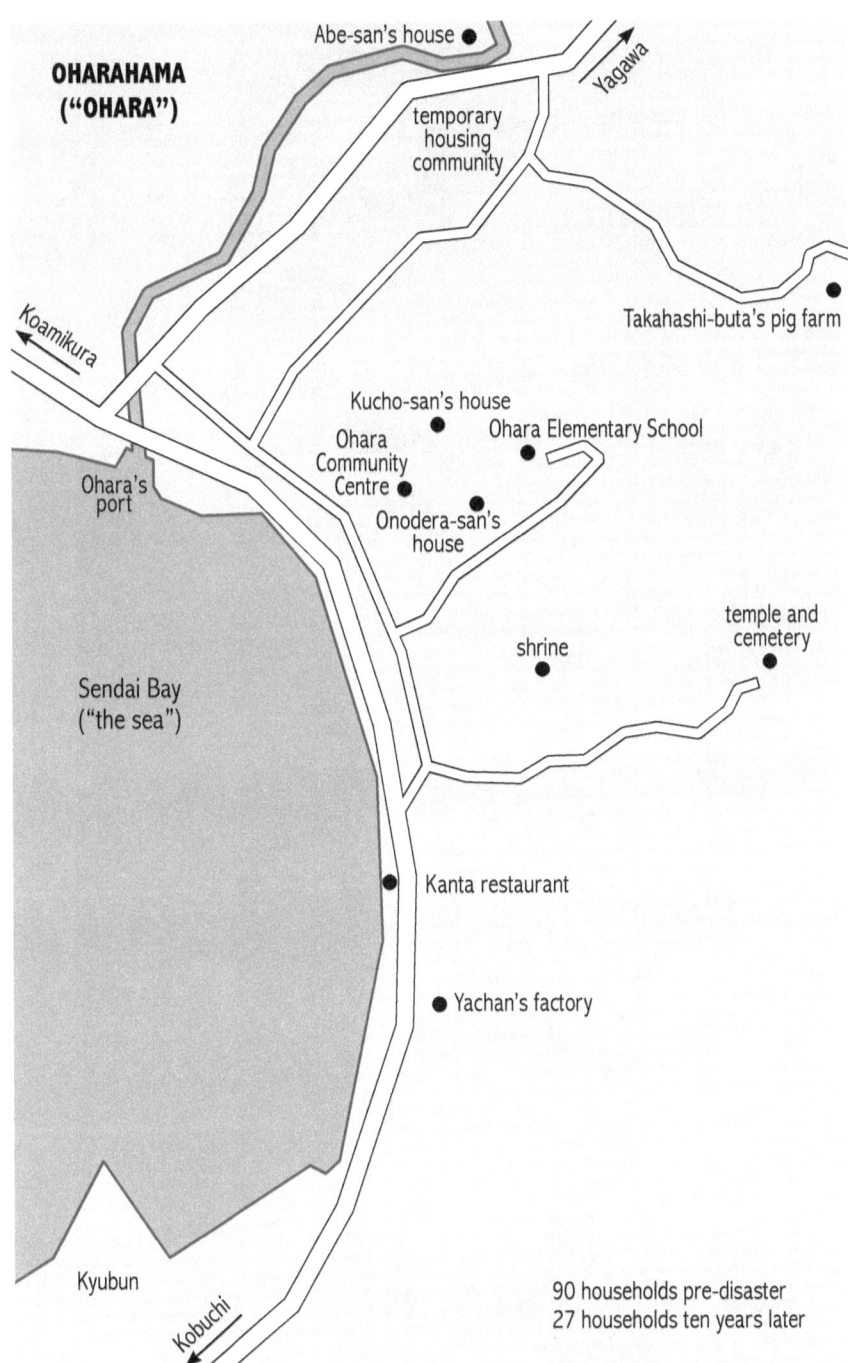

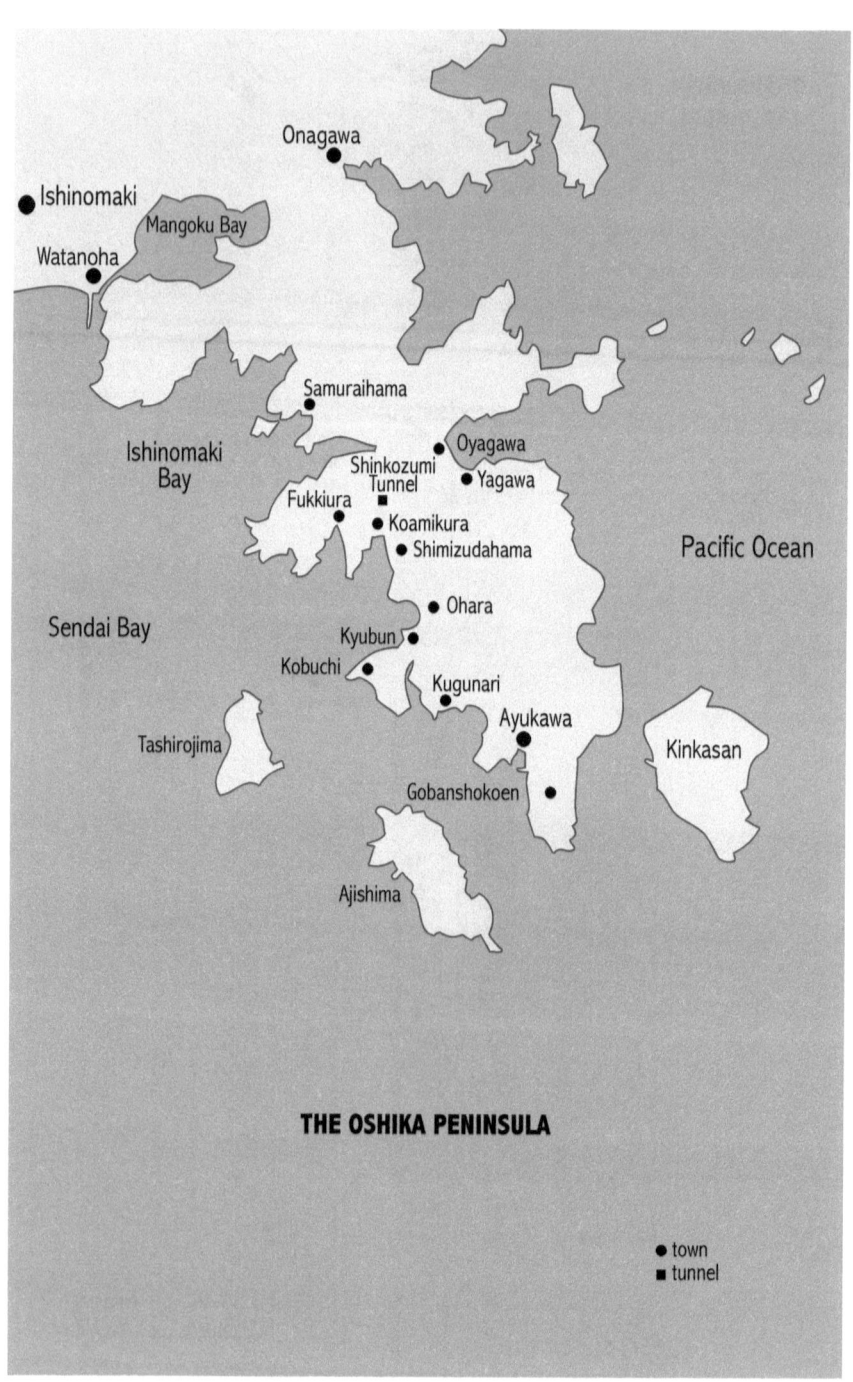

12: The Peninsula

They say you're only a true Oshika-jin if you live after the south side of Shinkozumi Tunnel, which is about halfway down the peninsula, but there is so much to see before that!

Ishinomaki is Oshika's closest city, about three-quarters of an hour's drive from Ohara. It is a busy port on mostly flat land, and during the winter after the tsunami it was a dirty, dusty, noisy hive of activity as cranes, diggers, and lorries set to work moving mounds of debris that included a can the size of a house. Prior to March 11, the can had been fixed on top of a building, advertising a brand of tinned fish, but it now sat in the middle of a busy road while locals worked out how to have it removed, and volunteers and disaster tourists took photographs.

The Oshika district had technically been considered part of Ishinomaki City since 2005, but nobody on Oshika really considered themselves part of Ishinomaki. The assimilation just meant that the Ishinomaki government had, since 2005, been responsible for any public services or maintenance on Oshika, whereas before that, Oshika had its own government office and was in charge of its own pubic services and maintenance. This transfer of decision-making power had resulted in the Oshika people feeling — for quite some time *prior* to 311 — that they were not a priority. And after 311, it provided an explanation for why the Oshika people would feel so forgotten in the recovery process.

I rarely went into Ishinomaki during my month on Oshika, but when I did, I'd get an odd form of culture shock, so comfortable was I with the lifestyle and environment of Oshika. Other than a tiny hand mirror, I didn't have any means of checking my appearance on Oshika, nor did I have any desire to do so, so I'd give myself a shock when I caught sight of a proper country bumpkin staring back at me in the Ishinomaki supermarket restrooms.

You drive through Ishinomaki to reach Watanoha, the little town where Andrew Abbey and I had distributed our last boxes of emergency supplies. By that winter, this particular area was a surreal mix of bare wasteland, piles of rubble, buildings with skeletal first floors, and the odd new shop.

It was also the location of It's Not Just Mud — a wonderfully named non-profit organization set up by Jamie El-Banna, a young British man who was living in Osaka at the time of the disaster. He'd been compelled to give up his self-described meaningless life of drinking and debauchery when he started volunteering in Tohoku, eventually moving there full-time and coordinating teams of volunteers from all over the world as they cleaned out people homes and businesses and helped rebuild communities. In the middle of all his own activities, he was kind enough to become someone who would find time to give me advice and listen to the frustrations I sometimes had with my own pursuits.

From Watanoha you leave the mainland by driving onto the Mangoku Bridge over Mangoku Bay, which flows out into Sendai Bay and then feeds into the Pacific Ocean. Mangoku Bridge was destroyed during the tsunami, so no one could access the coastal road going along the west side of the peninsula. No one could get on or off Oshika for a week after the earthquake, other than by helicopter.

The peninsula greets you with the most beautiful trees; they grow all the way to the top of the mountain ahead. Then there are roads that wind through the forests until you emerge to stunning views of the sea on your right. Dotted all along the coastal road are tiny villages. The names of these little villages on the seashores (*hama*) sound beautiful when you say them — they roll off the tongue like waves rippling along on the sea: Oginohama, Orinohama, Kozumihama, and the village with my favourite name, Samuraihama.

Samuraihama was completely spared by the tsunami. It was right on the coast, but so tucked away that the tsunami hadn't reached it. This was not the case with the other villages — some had been completely destroyed, and residents were now living in the temporary housing communities that were dotted all along the coastal road, interspersed with other temporary buildings.

There was even a temporary temple, Dosenji. The priest, Mr Yamaki, was from the area but had met his wife while at university in Tokyo. Mrs Yamaki had moved to this remote area to work alongside her husband. The peninsula was full of couples who worked together or had small family-owned businesses, and were trying to rebuild by setting up in temporary buildings or huge shipping containers that had been brightly painted by volunteer art groups who were hoping to liven up the area.

About halfway along the peninsula is Shinkozumi Tunnel, south of which lies the "real" Oshika-hanto. And that's where I spent most of my time.

Immediately after the tunnel, to the right, is Koamikura. Or rather it used to be there. The tsunami took all but two buildings in this little fishing village and it was hard to imagine that people had ever lived there. All who survived were living in a temporary housing community in Shimizudahama, which was settled in the hills but directly overlooked the wasteland that used to be their homes.

The women at Shimizudahama had to be some of the naughtiest on Oshika, with their saucy dancing and filthy cackling. I loved visiting them with a car full of clothing, and listening to them tell me about their lives both before and after the tsunami.

The Shimizudahama women I spent time with were mostly in their seventies, and had still been working alongside their husbands before the earthquake, supporting them in the oyster fishing industry. In many cases, their parents had also worked in the industry, and their children were following suit. When I first met them, they told me that since the earthquake, there wasn't any work and they had very little to occupy their time — they just ate and slept and were totally bored. They had no sense of a future and no answers when asked about any hopes or dreams for their later years. And they had years left in them yet.

Unprompted, they'd start talking about what actually happened to them on the day of the tsunami.

I'd been told that for months people here couldn't speak about what happened, and my visit came at an interesting time — people had started to feel able to talk about that day, *and they needed to*. They spent most of their time in their own individual rooms and rarely got together in the communal rooms, so delivering the coats was a nice way to gather everyone in the same place for a while — it gave them some space to talk. Spontaneously. Naturally.

One woman told the story of what had happened to her — she had twelve minutes to get out of her home before the tsunami came, so she had no choice but to escape to high ground with just the clothes she was wearing. She said she stood on top of a small hill just watching her entire house and everything in it get washed away. She said that no tears came — just a strange wailing as she watched. Wailing and wailing.

She wore those same clothes for three weeks. They all did. And as they reflected on that time, all the women started laughing and teasing each other about how badly they had smelled. The woman who had initiated the conversation about the day of the tsunami started cackling away as she said that I should write about her sad story, and make everyone who read it cry. She thought this was a hilarious idea.

I met best friends Masayo and Keiko at Shimizudahama. Masayo lived with her husband, daughter, and two grandsons, all in the same kasetsu. Masayo whispered to me that her daughter was divorced, which was a big taboo on Oshika. But for something so taboo, there seemed to be an awful lot of people whispering to me about couples who had divorced. It wasn't just Tokyo where relationships hadn't survived the disaster.

Masayo's grandsons were pretty typical preteen boys — mooching around on their bikes, developing just a little bit of attitude, and shovelling down their food as we sat to eat dinner together. Despite the mooching and shovelling, like many of the youngsters I would meet on Oshika, they were shy and didn't say a word to anyone, least of all the foreign stranger who said they could practice their English on her if they wanted to.

Keiko had lived next door to Masayo in Koamikura before the tsunami. She was a tiny little old lady, in her seventies like her friend, but absolutely full of beans and incredibly cheerful. She lived alone in her kasetsu, and often joined Masayo's family for dinner. I was told that she lost her husband in the tsunami, although I never asked for details. Keiko laughed *a lot*, but somehow every time she did, it brought a lump to my throat.

Back at Koamikura, where Masayo and Keiko used to live, there's a shrine in the distance, on a little hill like all the shrines in this area, overlooking what used to be the town. The people of Koamikura were especially sad about the fate of their shrine, the steps to which were first badly damaged by the earthquake, and then by the tsunami, and finally by a landslide after a heavy rainstorm blew through soon after the former two forces of nature. You couldn't even walk up to the shrine anymore, and this was a great cause of distress to everyone. The town's community centre was washed away, along with everything important to the shrine and its festival. Unlike the Ohara torii, Koamikura's stone torii had not fared well against the tsunami, and it lay on the ground in the same place where it fell over during the disaster. Nobody really had much of an idea of what to do with Koamikura. There was very little hope for the future here in the time after the tsunami.

With the shrine on your right, if you follow the coastline you come to one little port after another, then the village of Fukkiura, which now had 28 kasetsu with *immaculate* gardens. Katsuzo-san was the Fukkiura gardener. Like many people on Oshika, he was in his seventies. He liked to talk, he liked to keep busy, and he liked the land around the temporary housing community to be pristine. And he liked to smile ... a lot.

Then there was Fukkiura, where I met Mika Yanagibashi, along with a group of other young mums — I was beginning to wonder where all the young people were! Mika worked alongside her husband in the oyster industry, and they had three very young children. Just before the disaster, they had bought a lovely new home, where they hoped to add to their family. The house was on low ground, and while still standing when the tsunami receded, and easily fixable, the government wasn't allowing anyone to live in any buildings that the tsunami had reached. Including theirs. So every day, from her kasetsu up in the hills, Mika could look down at the brand new home she couldn't live in. So that she didn't become too disheartened, Mika had motivated herself to be part of a group of young men and women in the fishing industry who were dedicated to reviving it, calling themselves the "Tough Wave Oysters." There were many old people on Oshika who felt frustrated at being unable to help after the disaster (although many still did, however they could), but the young people who remained were keen to play their part in the peninsula's recovery.

After driving back through Koamikura, you could see a very different kind of house next to the temporary housing community of Shimizudahama. Looking up at the mountain, the temporary housing community and its car park were on the left of a stream that made its way down the mountain and into the sea. From the car park there was a little bridge going over the stream, leading to a house that looked quite different from any of the others standing on Oshika.

This was where Kameyama-san lived.

Like most of the other people of Koamikura, Kameyama-san lost everything on March 11. He had been allocated a kasetsu to live in with his wife, son, and daughter. His daughter ended up leaving her husband after the earthquake because she'd had to live in a kasetsu with her father-in-law while her husband went away for six months. Another relationship casualty, courtesy of the disaster.

Most people who lived in the tiny temporary residences were relieved that they at last had shelter and something to call a home, but they were feeling totally lost. There were no jobs, and there was nothing to do and nowhere to go. It wasn't like you could go for a walk for a bit of physical or mental stimulation — who wanted to walk around a barren wasteland? How could that offer hope at a time when many people on Oshika had no clear sense of what was next for them?

Kameyama-san, who by the October after the tsunami had had enough of sitting around his kasetsu, decided to build his own home. He owned a bit of farmland that the tsunami hadn't quite reached and decided to build a house on it. He'd worked on boats before, and had never done any carpentry, happily admitting that he had no idea what he was doing. On the first day, his neighbours from the kasetsu had all lined up against the fence to watch and laugh, saying he would never be able to do it.

But he did. He collected scrap from the debris, careful to get permission for every single piece, and constructed his entire home all by himself. He used some of the money from the government to buy items he couldn't find in the debris, but was very careful in trying to build the whole house without going over the ¥2 million compensation. He didn't want any help with the construction work because he thought that any carpenter that set foot in the place would say it was a disaster and suggest he tear it all down. He was more than happy to build the whole house on his own.

He was 72 years old.

I couldn't believe it when he told me his age — my eyes stung at the thought of a 72-year-old man building his own home from scratch. It was difficult to process. And anyway, how on earth did he have the energy? He'd waved away my disbelief and said, "If you keep thinking you are young, you will never get old."

I made a point of popping in on Kameyama-san whenever I could, even though his accent was so strong that I could hardly understand what he was saying. He was thrilled when I took him some clothes that I thought might suit him. He'd been wearing the same clothes every day for two months.

Continuing on the coastal road past Shimizudahama, the next village is Ohara, where I stay. Just as you reach Ohara though, there's a turn to the left that takes you all the way to the other side of the peninsula, to Yagawa. The villages on that side of the peninsula were left much worse off than those on the Ohara side. Nobody lived there anymore — everybody was living in the Yagawa kasetsu, just down the road from Ohara.

Yagawa was nestled between hills, which had created a funnel for the tsunami, leaving the water with nowhere to go except higher and higher. The tsunami had reached 30 metres high and went to a point so far inland that the sea was not even visible from it. Just half a house remained when I first visited there, along with Yagawa temple's roof. Just the roof. Along with this comes a fascinating story. The tsunami had ripped the roof off the temple and carried it a kilometre inland, where it landed on the *exact* building in which it had been made. The carpenter who made it did not survive, but his best friend said that he felt that the roof came back to its original home to ensure that the carpenter would be at peace.

Yagawa Elementary School had been built right by the sea, making it the most beautiful setting for children to learn in. The playground and classroom windows overlooked the ocean, without any other buildings nearby. Just behind the school was a little hill, not that much taller than the school itself. To the left of the school were tiny steps that wound up the hill to the shrine. Right after the earthquake had hit, the students and staff went straight up the steps to the shrine, where there really wasn't much space at all, and huddled together as they watched the sea engulf their entire school. Thanks to the teachers, none of the children were lost, and they joined the students at Ohara Elementary School.

If you drive back to the other side of the peninsula, you can take a right turn that will lead you onto the Cobalt Line — a road that goes higher and higher into the mountains, winding around steep roads and along cliff edges. It is a terrifying drive, especially in winter, but it provides the most incredible views, and you can look down upon each of the villages far below, including Ohara.

Back on lower ground, the coastal road takes you past Ohara and then to Kyubunhama, where the konbini had recently reopened — but only during the daytime; not 24 hours a day, as before. With so few people now on Oshika, and no tourists visiting, there wasn't much demand. A new temporary building had just been set up next to the konbini, which had everybody talking — people on Oshika loved to talk and speculate about any new developments on the peninsula. Endo-san, the owner of the konbini, especially liked to know what was going on. She was a powerhouse of a woman in her late seventies, who owned not just this business but also a chicken farm in another part of the peninsula. And she was really interested in England; she loved hearing all about how English people were thinking of the people on Oshika.

In front of the konbini was a huge car park, where the English word "HELP" had been painted in massive letters on the ground. After the earthquake, this car park was the only flat and clear ground on which the residents could paint a message to the helicopters flying above — there had been a heavily pregnant woman in need of assistance.

The konbini became a hive of activity on weekends, which is when busloads of volunteers would descend on Oshika. On one occasion, a group of children from Saitama took over the car park with an incredible taiko drumming performance, while their parents gave away loads of clothing that they'd brought and set up free food stalls. These kinds of social occasions were hugely popular on Oshika, and very effective in providing both practical and moral support. And *everyone* on Oshika loved a bit of taiko drumming!

It was on one of those busy weekends at the konbini that I *literally* bumped into Tokyoites Lowell Sheppard and Erin Sakakibara. They were both on the board of HOPE International Development Agency, along with my old friend Mike Alfant who'd been so supportive of all my activities over the years, including my efforts on Oshika. HOPE was involved in a number of projects in Tohoku, and Lowell showed me a photograph he'd taken from a helicopter in the days immediately after the tsunami. It was a photo of debris floating in the sea, and that debris was in the perfect shape of a heart. Floating just off Oshika. The peninsula had found itself a special place in Lowell's heart, too.

Near the konbini was a shipping container with a blue and white barber's pole out front. The local barber had received ¥600,000 from the government after the tsunami destroyed his business. He bought the container for

¥350,000, but had to spend ¥2 million in total on renovating the building and kitting it out to become a barbershop. He was charging ¥3,000 for a haircut, so I worked out that he had to do about 500 haircuts before he got his money back. I thought what a wonderful way that would be to support these areas — just by getting a haircut.

A little lane that ran beyond the konbini led to Kobuchi, and further along on the coastal road was the lumberyard, run by one of Kameyama-san's relatives, also called Kameyama-san. And then you'd come to Kugunarihama. If I happened to be in a vehicle with *anyone* from Oshika they would proudly tell me what an incredible beach it had been before the tsunami. But because the land had sunk, all that remained was just a tiny bit of sand. No beach at all.

After Kugunarihama you'd head up a steep hill and then turn right to go to "Hot Maru," a huge building that had been paid for by the *genpatsu sangyo* (nuclear power industry) when they'd built the Onagawa Nuclear Power Plant on the northern part of the peninsula. Hot Maru consisted of a gym, a swimming pool, and a public bath and, at that time, it was completely free to all volunteers. I would go there every few days, partly when I needed a wash, and partly because the cold had reached deep into my bones. I would take my bright pink pyjamas with me to put on right after the bath, and not care one bit about being seen out in public with them on as I walked from Hot Maru to the car park.

On the other side of the car park was the health and welfare centre, which people refer to as "the Seiyukan," and which functioned as a shelter after the earthquake. This was the same shelter that Andrew and I had visited, and been deeply upset by. When I returned the following January, the people who had been living there were in temporary housing, and the main hall had been turned into an interim preschool.

There were previously three preschools on Oshika, and all were completely destroyed by the tsunami. So the children had been put together in a newly created preschool, with "rooms" separated by cardboard. The school was managed by Utsumi-sensei, whom I grew close to as I became a regular visitor there, first with winter coats, and then with other items the parents requested. The staff made beautiful displays of the adult clothing, which they encouraged the parents to browse through when they collected their kids.

I started to love visiting the preschool, as the children were always full of smiles. They sometimes asked me to read the English on their clothes, which they thought was hilarious. They were so excited to see me turn up in my little blue car with the Union Jack flags flying in the breeze. They'd insist on bringing the boxes of clothes in with me, even if the boxes were far too big for them to manage, all the while chatting to me non-stop. There was a huge demand for clothes, socks, and coats, and the teachers were great at turning the donated items into prizes for educational games they would make up. I still have every single picture and letter given to me by those kids. After they went to one of the elementary schools on the peninsula, these kids would then end up at Oshika Junior High School, just a few minutes away, and overlooking Ayukawa.

Ayukawa is the main town on Oshika, and the last town you come to — for Andrew and I, it had been our mission's destination, and the point at which we turned and went back the way we had come. It was where we delivered the jerry cans to a huge gymnasium that was being used to store donations. There had been very little else left standing.

Ayukawa was a traditional little fishing port, and one of the few towns in Japan with a whaling licence. Very few people still worked in the whaling industry, which had been in decline for many years, but I came across one old man who had spent his entire life doing carvings in whalebones. He'd learned his craft from his father, who'd learned it from his father before him. Ayukawa had once been quite a popular tourist destination, with a seafront lined with shops selling souvenirs, beach goods, and delicious food. All that was gone.

But a temporary shopping street had been set up by an NGO within the first year after the tsunami. Ayukawa's *shotengai* (market street) consisted of sixteen shop units, each about three metres by three metres, which were free to anyone who wanted to try to rebuild their business. The shopkeepers would have to kit out the unit themselves, but they'd then be able to earn an income and, more importantly, have something to do to occupy their time in a place where people really needed a sense of purpose. These little shops were another great way to support the area, and I ate and shopped there as often as possible, encouraging any visitors to do the same — the Maekawas did a delicious half-ramen/half-chahan (half noodle soup/half fried rice) meal that was legendary. And next to the shotengai were temporary restrooms *with heated toilet seats*. I regularly seriously considered making the 20-minute drive from Ohara to Ayukawa just to sit on a warm seat.

After Ayukawa there's a steep drive up to Gobanshokoen, the highest point on Oshika, from which you can get the most incredible panoramic view.

Just a kilometre away is Kinkasan, a small island inhabited only by the priests and shrine maidens that staff the shrine complex there. It is one of Tohoku's most sacred places, and the reason why so many tourists used to visit Ayukawa, where the boat to Kinkasan was based. It is believed that if you visit Kinkasan in three consecutive years, you'll never have to worry about money again. But in the early years after the earthquake, hardly anybody visited Kinkasan, and the little boat just sat tied up in the port, rarely used.

When you look over at Kinkasan from Gobanshokoen, you can see beautiful trees all over the island, but the greenery doesn't start until far above sea level. Everything below that point is brown. This is a clear indication of how far up the tsunami reached — everything below that point died because it was inundated with salt water. Even more shocking is the fact that the kilometre-wide bay — between the peninsula and Kinkasan — had completely emptied of water just before the tsunami hit. Tourists on the island at the time reported being able to see the bottom of the ocean as the sea had rushed out to the northeast, toward the epicentre, which was just 70 kilometres off the coast of Oshika.

Standing on Gobanshokoen, you can look out toward that epicentre and see exactly where the sea that surged back in came from. You're standing on the first part of Japan to be hit by the tsunami.

2011 wasn't the first time that Oshika had been hit by a tsunami. In 1933, an 8.4 magnitude earthquake with an epicentre again near Oshika caused a tsunami that wiped out parts of the peninsula, including Yagawa. And the 1960 Great Chilean Earthquake, with a magnitude of 9.4, caused a tsunami that travelled all across the Pacific Ocean to Oshika, destroying homes and businesses once more. Oshika wasn't unfamiliar with tsunamis, and tall stones can be found throughout the peninsula marking locations that tsunamis had reached before. There are also memorials to previous disasters — I came across a school satchel in front of a memorial. The memorial had been placed there by a parent who lost a child in the 1933 tsunami. It said: "Even though you are far away, I will always love you."

The peninsula was full of stones that had been engraved with warnings to not build houses beyond that point. But the 2011 tsunami destroyed homes that were far beyond these warning stones.

With the land on Oshika now permanently sunk, the tide had to constantly be prevented from flooding roads and whatever buildings remained, so black sandbags lined the Oshika coastline. These massive plastic bags full of gravel were piled three high in some places, and were a constant reminder of what had happened. I was mesmerized by those sandbags — there was something about them standing there, so tall, strong, and defiant against the ocean. To me, they came to represent the resilience of the Oshika inhabitants. I found them strangely comforting.

Everywhere on the peninsula, huge mountains of debris towered ten metres high above you — when the land was cleared after the tsunami, it had to be put *somewhere*. And on top of these huge mountains were diggers, balancing precariously as they worked on what seemed to be the never-ending task of separating the *gareki* (debris) into wood, plastic, or metal before sending it elsewhere in Japan on ships with the biggest cranes I had ever seen.

The big pieces of gareki had all been cleared and put into these massive piles. The rest of the area was a flat wasteland; everything everywhere was grey with dust. The ground was mostly gravel or broken stones, but with tiny bits of plastic, broken glass, and smashed crockery that was embedded deep in the ground and was almost impossible to get out. You'd never be able to clear the area of everything that the tsunami had brought with it.

However, now that the *big* things had been taken care of, it felt like it was time to pay attention to the little things. To spread a little love around Oshika. So that was what I spent each day trying to do. And the perfect opportunity for this presented itself during the month I spent there.

Valentine's Day.

13: Valentine's Day

Valentine's Day is a much-loved celebration in Japan. Shopping streets are a mass of pink and red decorations, there are love hearts everywhere you look, and high-end chocolatiers in Tokyo have queues going all the way down the street. The Japanese way of celebrating Valentine's Day is all about chocolate. And it's all about women giving chocolate to men.

On February 14, women throughout Japan give chocolates to the men in their lives, but not necessarily to men in whom they are romantically interested. Chocolates are given to fathers, sons, male colleagues, male bosses, and male teachers as a gesture of appreciation — these are called *giri-choco* (obligation chocolate). As with all gifts in Japan, the chocolates are beautifully presented and usually gift wrapped by a store, but the *really* special chocolates are saved for a romantic interest. The chocolates given to a loved one would likely be handmade, and personally wrapped with beautiful accessories.

A month later, on what is known as White Day (March 14), the men return the gesture by giving gifts to the women they received chocolate from. But in Japan, actual Valentine's Day is all about women giving chocolate to men.

Most of the younger men in Ohara were single, which was a constant source of worry to Kucho and the other older people in the village. Whenever I asked them what they needed, more often than not they'd laugh and say "single women." And the young men would sigh and say that yes, it was true, they did indeed struggle to meet women.

And they're such lovely men — hardworking men — thoughtful, respectful, and caring toward their parents, siblings, and community. And when I talked to them on their own, I found out how romantic they were. It wasn't just Takahashi-buta who longed for a partner — with all his efforts to keep his kasetsu spotless and decorated in a way that he hoped would be pleasing to the feminine eye — but the other Ohara boys did, too. Yachan wanted to provide for a wife and children not just financially, but emotionally as well, and he hoped to meet someone who would join the family business so they could work together every day. Kuni dreamed of one day meeting someone, falling instantly in love, and then they'd spend every moment thereafter together. Kiyotaka-kun wanted to sit with someone and watch the sun go down each evening.

I was becoming very fond of the Ohara boys and thought that, on Valentine's Day, I'd like to give them some chocolates to show my appreciation for how much they had welcomed me into their community. Then, as is my way, my idea grew and grew until I decided to go on a mission to give chocolates to every single man, woman, boy, and girl on the whole peninsula. I was there to spread love, after all!

I reached out to my online network. People had been so generous in sending up more coats, warm clothing, and other random items I'd discover a need for. Friends from all over Japan, not just Tokyo, and some people in other countries, were always asking whether there was anything else they could send. So I asked them for chocolates, sweets, or any little gifts with hearts on them, saying that I would deliver them on Valentine's Day. People immediately responded, so in addition to the boxes of clothing that would arrive for me at the centre, boxes and boxes of chocolates started to arrive. Hundreds of them piled up in three massive boxes in the corner of my room. I could just about fit them in the back of my car.

I have often wondered during my Oshika-related activities whether the stars align in order to help things go smoothly, or present me with *exactly* what I'm in need of at the time I need it. This has happened so many times there, and Valentine's Day was not an exception.

When I first had the idea, I thought that I didn't want to just hand out the chocolates, but instead offer a wide selection to people so they could have fun choosing what they liked. I'd thought that an old-fashioned woven basket would be perfect, but had no idea where to get one from in Tokyo, let alone on Oshika. The very next day I was wiping car windows and generally helping out at the gas station, when Mrs Suda, whose husband owned the gas station, invited me in for coffee.

The Sudas lived right behind the gas station, in a house up on a little hill, so their home was not affected by the tsunami. Their home has a conservatory-style entrance, and it was filled with beautiful handmade art and craft items — it turned out that Mrs Suda was an incredibly creative woman. She was showing me the countless dolls, wreaths, and various woven items she'd made herself, when I suddenly spotted a huge, beautifully woven basket, exactly like the one I had in mind for Valentine's Day. I told her my plans and asked if I could borrow it, to which she kindly agreed.

So on Valentine's Day, I spent five hours driving all over the peninsula, jumping in and out of the car with a beautiful basket that I filled over and over again with chocolates from the boxes in the back.

As soon I had the car loaded that morning, I saw the local bus pulling into Ohara, with lots of older people onboard, as usual. I flagged the driver down, jumped on the bus and ran up and down the aisle handing out chocolates to the driver and his passengers. I'd been told that most people on the peninsula had heard of me by now; the ever-helpful Hanako told me that people were always asking her whether she knew there was an English girl on Oshika and asking whether she had spoken to me — which we both found very amusing. The old ladies on the bus were quite happy to have met the English girl at last.

My first stop was, of course, to give chocolates to Kucho and Hiroyuki in the centre. Whitney Houston had just died and Hiroyuki hadn't stopped playing "I Will Always Love You" for two days, which I sang to him at the absolute top of my voice as I offered him some chocolates.

Then I made my way down to the beach where I knew the Ohara boys would be doing their community activities — trying not to fall down the steep slope as I balanced the huge basket full of chocolates. I handed round the basket, wishing them all a Happy Valentine's Day, then went back to the centre, where I was pleased to run into Takako-sensei. I pulled out what looked like an especially posh box of chocolates for her. Her nickname for me had stuck and she would later text me with the message, "Abnormal? Thank you today. *Choco oishii*" (the chocolate was delicious).

Then I went up to Ohara Elementary School and walked in and out of all the classrooms (not forgetting the teachers' room) wishing everyone a Happy Valentine's Day. Children and teachers alike were thrilled, and they featured the special visit on their school website the next day. I saw some of the kids later that day when I was going for my run, and they all waved and yelled at me in the distance.

I stopped off at Yachan's factory and handed out chocolates to all his staff, as well as the out-of-town construction workers who were rebuilding his factory. There wasn't a lot of interaction on the peninsula between the construction workers and the locals, and I always felt a little bit sorry for the workers. Most of the people hired to remove debris or fix buildings had to be brought in from other parts of Japan, and so they were spending months on end away from their families, in areas where there was simply nothing to do because it had all been destroyed. They weren't really part of the community in which they were working. When I'd first arrived, they'd stared at the English girl driving a blue car covered in Union Jack flags just as much as the locals had, so I'd ended up waving cheerily at them, just as I'd done with the locals. Over time, this became a regular occurrence — we'd all wave and smile at each other, which would then make other people in traffic smile, and I thought that more smiling in the middle of the dirty, dusty roads was always a good thing. And, of course, they got some chocolates on Valentine's Day!

As I left the coastal road from Ohara and headed toward Kyubun, I just stopped my car whenever I saw people walking along and handed out Valentine's treats to them. While slowing down over a particularly broken and bumpy part of the road, I even wound down my window to hand out a chocolate heart to the driver of the vehicle next to me who was heading in the opposite direction. The faces of the people in that car were a real picture!

There were two faces I was always looking out for on Oshika, and on Valentine's Day, completely unexpectedly, I found them. When Andrew Abbey and I had gone to Oshika, we had found a lady and her adult daughter just off the road, living under a big plastic sheet attached to half of their home, surrounded by debris. The daughter was totally bored, so had gone right for a box of children's toys and games, pulling out a Winnie the Pooh book, saying she was thrilled to hear that it came from England because she had always wanted to have an English boyfriend. She'd been extremely cheerful, but I remember her mother being expressionless and clearly in shock, as well as exhausted. They had both stayed in my mind for different reasons, and I had told the story of meeting them and showed their photo in every single school I visited in the UK. That very same photo was on the homepage of my website for months.

I'd carried with me a secret hope of coming across them the whole time I had been here; a hope to find out that they were OK. On Valentine's Day I spotted two people huddled around a fire just up a little hill, and ran up to offer them chocolates from my basket. I immediately recognized the woman as the mother. I'd thought of this woman literally every day since I met her, and couldn't believe my luck in coming across her again.

She remembered me, and proudly told me that her daughter now had a job in Ishinomaki, lived in a temporary home, and that they were both doing just fine. I gave her and her companion some chocolates and it felt *wonderful* to give her something not because she needed it this time, but because it would make her smile. And she truly did smile. Just as I was saying goodbye, I tried to explain to her that I had thought about her and her daughter every day since May, but suddenly realized I was about to burst into tears, so I instead rushed off, waving, and kept the tears for the car.

After my little cry, I dropped by Endo-san's konbini and handed chocolates out to all her staff and customers, and then did the same at the barber's around the corner. A little further along I remembered the lady who'd encouraged me with sweets when I'd been running up the hill, and popped in on her, too. Then I drove up to the temporary preschool at which I'd become a regular visitor, and was happy to find that all of the little ones were in the same room, along with all their teachers and a few mums, too. It predictably turned into complete chaos and was great fun.

Then it was off to Ayukawa, where I handed out chocolates in every shop in the little temporary shotengai, and had some fun with one of the guys who tried telling everyone that his wasn't giri-choco, to which all the women told him off for being so flirtatious. It was fun to explain the cultural difference, too — I noticed that the women needed more encouragement to choose some chocolate, so explained that in the UK, Valentine's Day isn't a day for only men to feel special, but for men and women to feel special (and perhaps women even more so). So there was a lot of laughter when I kept telling everyone that Japan had got it all wrong and that women were the special ones on Oshika today.

By the afternoon I'd visited all the main places I'd wanted to, so I decided to go to a couple of the temporary housing communities where I had made friends, and literally knocked on one door after another, dropping some chocolate or sweets in the post-box if there wasn't anybody home — a nice surprise for them that evening! One old man's face was a picture! He just could not comprehend what on earth this foreign woman was doing at the door of his temporary home, miles away from anywhere, grinning so madly, offering him chocolates, and wishing him a "Happy Valentine's Day!" I really think he might have believed that I'd flown all the way from England just to give him some chocolate. And in a way, he'd have been right.

It was a wonderful way to spend the day, and still, to this day, was my best Valentine's Day ever.

I didn't drink very often that month, but at the end of my day delivering Valentine's goodies I decided to get some red wine for myself. So I popped over to the konbini to see what they had — only one kind, and less than a thousand yen. My kind of wine shopping! My neighbour Onodera-san was there, and as I took the wine to the counter to pay he grabbed it off me and insisted on paying. Of course I said he wasn't to, but he said that I had given presents to everyone on Oshika that day, so he was giving me a present. You didn't argue with Onodera-san, so I accepted, but only on the condition that he join me in drinking it.

So I spent the evening in the centre with Hiroyuki and Onodera-san, talking about love, and especially talking about Onodera-san's love for his wife.

It was that night that I learned about Mrs Onodera's brain haemorrhages, one of which had caused her blindness. I couldn't imagine how terrified she must have been during the earthquake and tsunami. Onodera-san told the story of how he was at the port working in a wakame factory when the earthquake happened. He immediately headed back home to his wife because he knew that a tsunami was on its way. When he got inside his house, he found that the earthquake had brought all the furniture crashing down and his wife was nowhere to be seen. Despite his damaged elbow from all those years playing tennis and cutting down trees, he found the strength to pull all the furniture out of the way to find his wife underneath. She was on her knees, gripping on to either side of the kotatsu, with her head tilted downward. She was in such a state of shock that he had to say her name five times before she responded, and finally he managed to lift her up and guide her up the mountain just before the tsunami hit their home and the water came up to the ceiling. They had both had a very, very lucky escape.

Throughout the evening, Onodera-san kept rearranging my jeans, which had got soaking wet during the day and were drying next to the fire. I only had one pair with me, and I needed them for the next day. I didn't want him to make a fuss over me, but I could see that he just wanted to take care of me somehow. He said that he was an expert because he did all the laundry at home, which was very unusual in such a traditional community, but Onodera-san and his children all pitched in to take care of Mrs Onodera and each other in any way necessary. He talked about how much he took care of his wife, and how much he loved doing so, and it wasn't because of any sense of obligation or duty. Instead he said very simply, "She is my wife. I love her. She is my heart."

It was a beautiful conversation, but it triggered a lot of difficult emotions in me. My strokes were still quite fresh in my memory, having only happened four years before the earthquake. I had been very, very sick for two years, at times not knowing whether I'd make it. My partner at that time had found it very hard, partly because he didn't know what to do, but also because he really didn't want any disruption to his life. He admitted to others that he didn't want to take care of me, even telling a close girlfriend of mine, "I didn't sign up for this," and I had felt deeply let down and incredibly hurt. I was still carrying that pain with me, and hearing Onodera-san talk about his wife and how *unthinkable* it was to him that he would do anything other than care for her, really hit home for me.

Pretty soon all three of us were crying.

Later, as he said goodnight, Onodera-san hugged and hugged me, and had tears in his eyes again as he said, "This has been the best Valentine's Day ever." He then handed me my dry jeans and walked off across the car park.

My jeans, along with the rest of my laundry, were soon to become a topic of interest for everyone in Ohara, not just for Onodera-san.

I'd travelled light, so I knew at some point I'd have to find somewhere to do some laundry, but given the living conditions and my desire not to use up local resources, I had a strict rule before an item of clothing was permitted entry into my little laundry bag — it had to fail the sniff test. If it was dirty on the outside but still passed the sniff test, then it would be turned inside out and worn that way. Nobody ever noticed.

One day, when I started getting desperate, I spotted a little washing machine around the side of the community centre that had a pipe attached to an outdoor tap. I threw in all my clothes at once — no separating anything — added a sachet of laundry detergent I'd found lying around, and some hot water from the kettle, then turned on the wall tap and the washing machine. It was a bit like being at university when I used to just throw everything in and hope for the best — my mother still tells the story of how she visited me at uni to find me sitting on top of the washing machine, with a pair of filthy trainers mixed in with beautiful silk underwear. I did eventually learn how to take care of laundry appropriately, but there are times in life when worrying about such things feels very unimportant.

The Ohara Community Centre's washing machine sloshed around for about six minutes, after which I then ran the cold water to rinse everything, and took it all out to put it in the spinner standing next to it. It was a bit like something I remember my grandmother using, but a lot noisier. Hiroyuki told me to hang my clothes in my room in the centre, but I'd been taught never to dry clothes indoors and that clothes needed to blow in the wind. I looked outside the Centre and spotted a length of rope with pegs on it tied between wooden poles. Someone else had obviously hung their laundry outside before. Perfect. So I started to hang my clothes out.

Hiroyuki and Kucho were in the centre, watching me do this, Kucho looking amused and Hiroyuki slightly worried. I may have worn dull, plain coloured jeans, tops, and a jacket on Oshika, but underneath I wore the most colourful, fancy underwear anybody there had ever seen.

Hiroyuki *freaked*! He said that Japanese people *never* hung their underwear outside, and ordered me to take it down immediately. Worried that I'd mortally offended everyone, I looked to Kucho for guidance — he was the boss, Hiroyuki wasn't local, and I'd started following what the locals wanted me to do. Kucho was laughing and laughing — I couldn't tell whether he was laughing at the underwear or at Hiroyuki's ranting. Either way, Kucho thought this was one of the funniest things he'd ever seen.

"Shall I take it down, Kucho?"

"No, no!" He laughed.

"But I don't want to bother anyone."

"No, no it doesn't bother anyone. Please make a beautiful display! It will cheer everyone up."

So to Hiroyuki's horror, I hung my underwear all around the Ohara Community Centre. Soon the centre was adorned with leopard print knickers, a fuchsia pink polka dot bra, black lace thongs, and all sorts of other brightly coloured and patterned undergarments. The little bus turned up and the driver gawped, to Kucho's delight. And Kucho said that there was a meeting that night at the elementary school, which all the Oshika teachers would attend — he loved the thought that they'd all feel happy after seeing the centre's beautiful new decorations.

I was told that at dinner that night, everyone in Ohara was talking about who had seen the English girl's underwear and who hadn't. Nobody seemed to be offended. Instead, Kucho had been right — it did cheer everyone up. It was a bit like bunting. He decided that everyone should treat the display like a shrine, and pray to it in the hope that love would come to Ohara.

14: The Sasakis

Whenever I'd come up with a new slang or swear word, the Ohara boys would ask if I'd been hanging out at the Sasakis again. While they'd started my education in the local insults, Mr Sasaki added the finishing touches — teaching me how to perfect my pronunciation, tone, and facial expressions. I learned some incredible swearing from him — my favourite being *norokusabozu*, which means something like "priest of all who defecate outdoors." It sounds so dramatic in both languages, and I think the English translation belongs in a Shakespeare play. But the one I used the most was *zuzuhoido*, which means something like "you wanker." I've always loved the English word "wanker," and I *really* love the Oshika equivalent. There are so many different ways of saying it … you can whisper it quietly to make your feelings about someone discreetly known, or you can say the "zuzu" part really quickly then put all your effort into "hoi," pushing all the air out of your lungs, and finishing on a short "do." I prefer the latter. It makes me feel like a samurai.

Zuzuhoido became my nickname for Mr Sasaki. I'd turn up at the Sasakis' place, calling up to the second floor where Mr Sasaki might be snoozing, and instead of saying "Hello," I'd call out "Zuzuhoido!" to alert him to my presence. And if I wanted to ask Mrs Sasaki where her husband was, instead of "Danna wa?" I'd say "Zuzuhoido wa?" Not "Where's your husband?" but "Where's that wanker?" Zuzuhoido stuck.

I'd met the Sasakis very early on during that month on Oshika. They didn't live in Ohara, but lived in the second village over, Kobuchi, down a tiny lane off the main road, and I'm sure I would never have met them if it hadn't been for an introduction by Robert Mangold.

I'd emailed Robert for months while I was planning this trip to Oshika, and met him in person within a few days of my arrival. And I was completely in awe of him. He was an American who'd lived in Japan for twenty years, and was based in Kyoto, an 11-hour drive away. He had decided after ten years of living in Japan that he would take a year out to study the language full-time, so his Japanese was fantastic. But unlike some foreigners who are really good at Japanese, he didn't make someone like me, with very poor Japanese language skills (notwithstanding a special aptitude for swearing), feel at all inadequate.

Robert had found himself drawn to Oshika because it reminded him of the place where he grew up. We shared similar attitudes toward helping people on the peninsula, both firmly believing that it was the right thing to do if you had the correct skillset for work in this kind of environment. He had been in the US marines and was also a trained carpenter, so he felt that he was made for this kind of work and therefore had to do it — he felt that modern society meant that everybody was chasing money now, but this kind of voluntary work was actually far more satisfying. He went to Oshika as often as he could and was playing a major part in the clearing and rebuilding. I was very moved after meeting Robert. I think he's a truly special person, a genuinely lovely and caring man who walks his talk.

He had been doing some carpentry work for a couple in their late fifties, and needed to visit them, but said I was welcome to join him. So I tagged along, bombarding him with questions and trying to find out what people needed, taking notes all the way. He was so patient with me.

The Sasakis, like many couples on Oshika, worked together in the fishing industry. They owned a wakame and oyster business. Mr Sasaki was one of five siblings, all of whom ran their own businesses. One sister ran a hotel on Ajishima, a tiny island off Oshika; another sister ran a bar on the mainland; and one brother had had a factory in Ohara before the tsunami took it away. So they were quite literally known from one end of the peninsula to the other. They were an impressive clan.

Mrs Sasaki had moved to the area after marrying her husband. Before that she worked in the beauty section of a department store, and sometimes you'd still find her wearing carefully applied makeup and tending to her nails, massaging cream into hands that had once been perfectly manicured, but were now rough and sore from the harsh weather and demanding work. She was incredibly tall and you could see that she had been very slim in her youth, whereas Mr Sasaki was shorter than me, with a big round belly that had probably been there for quite some time. He had a huge smile that reached every inch of his face, in contrast to his wife's smile, which was betrayed by her incredibly sad eyes.

When Robert introduced me to them, they were living in a storage facility, nestled in a hill at the back of the village. It consisted of a kind of garage, in which they had stored all the things they had retrieved from the debris — they had lost part of their home in the tsunami, but, as with the Koamikura shrine, most of the damage had come from the heavy rainstorm that had blown through in the days that followed. So they now lived in this garage. Robert had made a little living space to one side of it, which meant they now had a tiny kitchen area, and a little shower. Outside was a wooden bath, with a place for a fire underneath it to heat up the water. Next to their living quarters, some men were busy constructing the skeleton of what was intended to be a work space so that they could try to rebuild their business.

Robert and I sat chatting with the Sasakis while the sound of hammers on wood echoed through the forest above us. I instantly warmed to her and her husband — they were both very tactile, as were quite a few people on Oshika, which had been a surprise to me after living in Tokyo for so long, where even Japanese friends I'd known for years would freeze at the sight of me approaching them with a smile and my outstretched arms. Mrs Sasaki was so affectionate, warm, and welcoming, insisting that I come and stay with them while I was on Oshika.

I asked the Sasakis if they needed any coats, which they said they did — Mrs Sasaki showed me all the holes in her coat, so I invited them to go through the coats in my car to see if there was anything suitable. Mrs Sasaki and three of her female neighbours went through the coats, and were thrilled to find so many that actually fit them — the coats, mainly donated by the foreign community, were larger than ones you'd usually find in a Japanese shop, and the women on Oshika aren't like skinny Tokyo women — they're gaijin-size. Mrs Sasaki and her friends put the unclaimed coats back in my car, perfectly folding each one as they did so, while the men carried on with their carpentry — I turned around to see Robert walking over the roof and getting stuck in with them. And I loved him for that.

I popped in on the Sasakis every couple of days the whole time I was on Oshika that month. During that time, the space where the carpenters had been busy working when I'd first met the Sasakis got extended into the area where I had initially parked my car — it was always surprising how quickly things happened when the locals were able to just get on with rebuilding their lives, free of restrictions and authority. The whole area was now covered with a metal frame, which was the first step in creating a little wakame processing facility. Like Saito-san and the rest of the Ohara boys, Mr Sasaki was desperate to get back to work, and looked forward to the upcoming wakame season, but was also very worried because he didn't have everything he needed to make the most of the harvest. He had the frame for the facility, but no walls, and in the meantime was planning on covering the harvested wakame with plastic sheets and praying it wouldn't rain; otherwise the entire wakame harvest would be ruined.

The Sasakis were two of the few people I knew who didn't live in temporary housing — they had a kasetsu in the nearby temporary housing community (built on their land), but they found it more comfortable to live in their storage facility and try to move forward in rebuilding their lives that way, rather than waiting for the local government to make decisions for them. They were the kind of people I always wanted to focus on helping, even when I came to Oshika for the first time in May the previous year — people who were living independently, with the result that they might have been slipping under the radar when it came to receiving support. It was sort of easy to connect with people in the temporary housing communities; it was much more difficult to find people trying to make it on their own — I was incredibly grateful to Robert for his introduction.

Every time I popped over I'd ask whether they needed anything, and Mr Sasaki would always ask me to bring him a new wife some day, so Mrs Sasaki would say that she wanted a new husband. But he had to be tall. And definitely not bald like zuzuhoido over there.

I'd say that I didn't have any husbands or wives for them, and would instead invite them to have a look at the latest batch of clothes that had arrived from Tokyo. They would only ever take what was absolutely needed — nothing more. The one exception to this was that Mrs Sasaki would accept unlimited amounts of cat food.

Not long after the tsunami, a kitten turned up. It was blind, traumatized, and had some kind of neurological condition. Mrs Sasaki christened her Tora-chan, and nursed her back to health, but she never regained her sight. Pretty soon, more cats started showing up, and the Sasakis became a sanctuary for all the neighbourhood cats that had lost their homes or their owners, or stray cats that had found themselves on Oshika after the tsunami. They mainly lived under the Sasakis' garage, and roamed around the area. Tora-chan was the only indoor cat. Cat food was added to my wish list and soon boxes of it started arriving for me at the centre, which I would then deliver to Mrs Sasaki.

While I was delivering a box of cat food one day, Mrs Sasaki reminded me about her invitation to come and stay the night, and while I had no idea where I might sleep and certainly didn't want to inconvenience them, it felt rude not to accept her offer. I had got to know them quite well by then, and Mr Sasaki and I had discovered a mutual love of sexual innuendo and toilet humour — he was always calling me a bad girl because of all the naughty things I talked about.

Mr Sasaki and I could spend hours making each other laugh while his wife rolled her eyes and told us that we were both disgusting. On a regular basis she'd look at him and sigh, commenting woefully on his short legs, to which he'd always reply, "These legs may be little, but my third leg is *huge*!" and I'd be in fits of laughter. Every visit turned into an opportunity to laugh about something (usually something rude and childish), and it was hard to imagine that they'd been through anything more awful than losing part of their home, as if that wasn't awful enough.

One day they told me what actually happened to them on the day of tsunami. And again, even though of course I was aware that dreadful things had happened on Oshika, it was quite different listening to someone I now knew tell me, right there in front of me. Someone who had welcomed me into their home, and seemed to consider me a friend. Someone who gave me a massive hug every time we said hello and goodbye — someone who, as I've always believed about people who come into our lives, felt like they had become a little part of me.

On March 11, the Sasakis were mourning their beloved dog, who had passed away the day before. Mr Sasaki had buried him in the mountain behind where they now lived, and the couple got straight back to work. The wakame season had just begun on Oshika and all the fishermen were out in their boats while their wives were either at their village's little port, ready to process each boatload of wakame as it was brought to shore, or at home preparing that evening's meal for their husbands and the seasonal workers.

Mr Sasaki was out at sea when the earthquake happened, and immediately knew that a tsunami would follow. He knew that he had to save his boats from any possible damage caused by the tsunami, so he tied his four boats together, and *singlehandedly* sailed them further out to sea, riding through waves and troughs, and then through the tsunami on its way to shore. He waited in the middle of the ocean for two days, without telephone or radio contact, and no idea what was happening inland. He eventually returned to the port, and stood there with tears rolling down his face as he looked at the unbelievable destruction in front of him. Everything was gone. Many other fishermen had exactly the same experience.

Mrs Sasaki was on land, in their little house near the seafront, where they lived with Mr Sasaki's elderly and disabled mother. Mrs Sasaki senior was in bed sleeping at the time of the earthquake, and Mrs Sasaki junior, like her husband, immediately knew that this was the kind of earthquake that would be followed by a tsunami. She picked up her mother-in-law and tried to carry her out of the house. Then the tsunami hit.

The water rapidly filled the house and Mrs Sasaki was trapped inside with her mother-in-law in her arms. She tried kicking at a window to smash it open in the hope of escaping, but it was too late. She could no longer hold on to her mother-in-law and the tsunami ripped the elderly lady from her arms. Mrs Sasaki found herself completely submerged in the water. The water briefly subsided and she saw her mother-in-law lying on the ground. She checked for a pulse but couldn't find one. Then another tsunami surge hit and took Mr Sasaki's mother out to sea — her body was never found.

Mrs Sasaki would say that it was always important to talk about these things because if you didn't they would stay in your heart. She said that she talked to some of her friends about it, but mostly she talked to the "heart care" workers who popped in on her from time to time, or she talked to Robert, and now she had me to talk to. The heart care workers were people who belonged to a number of groups that had been set up in and around Ishinomaki or on the peninsula that were dedicated to providing emotional support to the survivors. They did a wonderful job of organizing healing events such as yoga classes or foot massages, or just popped in on people to give them the space to talk. The workers were young and full of happy smiles

— they brought a general sense of hope and optimism with them — and they played a vital role in the recovery process.

But despite her efforts to get all her feelings out, Mrs Sasaki had been on medication since the tsunami — many people on Oshika were. We referred to it as *kurukurupa* medicine. Kurukurupa literally means "going round and round," and is a politically incorrect word used to mean something like "insane," or "bonkers." But it allowed for conversations to be made in a light, jokey manner when it felt right, and it became another word that stuck — we still use it now when referring to a situation that might be tormenting us. Or you can just put one hand to your temple then flick it outward, simply saying "Pa!" to show you've finally had enough of something.

The fact that Mrs Sasaki senior's body was never found would forever torment the Sasaki family. Without a body, there could be no funeral at which to grieve, and no grave to take care of, all of which are an important part of the circle of life in any culture and especially so in Japan. Ancestors are treated very respectfully, as if they are still part of the family, and every home in Japan has a little shrine with pictures of loved ones that have passed. Daily offerings are made at these home shrines, as well as prayers to the deceased. The Sasakis had a huge shrine in the little living room that Robert had built for them, and Mrs Sasaki prayed for her mother-in-law's forgiveness every day.

It was next to that shrine that I found myself during my sleepover at the Sasakis. Mrs Sasaki had prepared an amazing meal, and I'd been invited to have a nice bath before going to bed. When I emerged from the little bathroom, I found a futon laid out ready for me on the floor next to the shrine, with one corner folded back. Next to the futon there was a little tray with strawberries and a drink on it. It was like staying in a hotel. I was completely overwhelmed with the hospitality shown to me by people who were still very much struggling in an environment that was only one step along from being a disaster zone.

I'm not sure whether the Sasakis, or indeed any of my other friends on Oshika, ever realized how healing it was for me to be around them. During the almost twelve months between the disaster and my one month on Oshika, there had been a huge amount of turmoil in my personal life, not to mention my own experience of 311, and the uprooting of my life from Tokyo to England. I didn't once think about my own personal situation while I was on Oshika; first, because it would have felt very odd to be dwelling on my own losses, dramas, or worries when in such an environment and committed to such a mission of healing others; and second, because such thoughts just didn't enter my head. I was so, so happy there. Every day felt meaningful. Every day was full of smiles and laughter. Every day was full of people being kind to each other. Being on Oshika, quite unexpectedly, healed *me*.

There is something very, very special about Oshika, and very, very special about the people who live there.

My dear Tokyo sister-friend Emily experienced its healing energy for herself when she lived up to her promise of coming to see me on this visit to Oshika. Emily and her husband arrived just in time for me to drive them to Gobanshokoen so they could take in the panoramic view of the peninsula, look out to Kinkasan, gaze in the direction of the epicentre, and see a typically beautiful Oshika sunset. Not a lot of hotels survived on Oshika, but those that did were fully booked with various government and construction workers involved in the recovery and redevelopment efforts. Nonetheless, Emily and Hiro had managed to find a place to stay, and I joined them there for dinner.

The next morning I took them straight to meet the Sasakis. I had more cat food to give Mrs Sasaki and a lovely Japanese lady in Tokyo had sent me a homemade cake, so I wanted to share it with my old and new friends over coffee. Mr Sasaki was his usual outrageous self and it was nice to be able to reassure my Tokyo friends that the Oshika people were taking care of me.

I then drove Emily and Hiro to Yagawa on the other side of the peninsula — where absolutely everything was wiped out. I told them the various stories I had learned about the little villages that used to be there, and we headed back to Ohara where we had lunch at Kanta. I pointed out the "Land for Sale" sign that just kept teasing me.

Even though Emily visited for only a very short time, the impact Oshika had on her was huge and I wasn't surprised. Like me, Emily had had a rather tumultuous time since the disaster, and had been dealing with a range of emotions that weren't just about that day. She'd been in need of healing, too.

Since March 11, 2011, I had come across so many people in need of healing — of course there were the people right there on Oshika for whom the impact was unfathomable; their homes, families, lives, jobs, and everything they knew needed healing. But in seeing, first hand, how well these wonderfully warm people were coping there on the peninsula, I wondered whether this was bringing healing to people in other places. It really *was* amazing to see how people on Oshika were literally living among the piles and piles of debris that used to be their lives. This wasteland was now their home. But they laughed and smiled and went about life in their new reality with courage that was also unfathomable.

It was 11 months on, and people outside Tohoku still wanted to help — I came to realize that this was part of their healing, too. I saw Japanese friends who were disappointed in their government, and unsure of the future of a country of which they were once so proud. I received extremely long emails from non-native English speakers who were following what I was doing on Oshika, and were encouraged by the stories I shared. These people wrote in the beautiful way that I always think Japanese people who are not great at English write — they find *pure* ways to express their feelings and they always make me just a little tearful. It hadn't really occurred to me that my month on Oshika and sharing the stories of the friends I was making there would be *healing* for *anyone*, but maybe it was turning out to be … just a little bit; it certainly was for me.

As it was for Emily, who took me to one side as her husband got the car warmed up, ready for their drive back to Tokyo. Within minutes we were both in tears as she pushed money into my hand and asked me to find someone who needed it. She wanted me to do that in the name of her mother, with whom she'd had a complicated relationship, and who had recently passed away.

It was obvious that as it did for me, visiting Oshika had brought about some healing that was necessary for Emily, and also as with me, that healing wasn't just about the earthquake.

15: The Donations

Emily wasn't the only one who'd urged me to accept a cash donation during that month on Oshika. Throughout my whole time there, people from all over Japan, and from overseas as well, not only sent me boxes and boxes of clothes, chocolates, general supplies, and fuel contributions, but they also sent cash without my asking, saying that they wanted me to find someone who needed it. So as the month came to an end, I had unexpectedly accumulated over ¥200,000, and had ¥60,000 more than I needed for fuel, plus the money I had brought from England. It was time to spend it.

    I had spent a lot of my time on Oshika chatting and laughing with people, but I had also spent an awful lot of time listening. Partly because I had to *really* concentrate to understand conversations, because my Japanese still wasn't very good, and partly because I was trying to identify ways in which I might be able to help. Even though it became obvious that I was there to support them, my Oshika friends didn't know me very well at that time, and they wouldn't have dreamt of asking me for anything more than a few warm clothes; and only then when I'd *really* encouraged them to do so. And when I'd asked them what they needed, I don't think they realized just how big a network I had behind me, and just how much the people in it wanted to support Oshika — I certainly didn't entirely realize it myself at that time.

    I'd hoped to financially support any projects related to the rehousing of people on Oshika, but it had become apparent during the trip that there were all sorts of issues that were making the permanent rehousing very complicated. The temporary housing had been tricky enough. I was beginning to understand that it would be *years* before people would have real homes again, unless, like Kameyama-san, they took matters into their own hands. In the meantime, I'd have to find other ways to use the money that had been donated. I didn't want to start accumulating a general "pot" of money — I wanted the schools and individuals that had donated to know that their money had been allocated to a project that would lead to a very quick result. So as I went around the peninsula getting to know everybody, I was quietly looking for ways that would help individuals or businesses, thereby helping with the rebuilding of communities, and bringing both practical and emotional support.

Kameyama-san was an obvious choice. But it was tricky to get information out of him. He had been a little withdrawn when we'd first met, and reluctant to tell me the kinds of things that might help him in his efforts to make a home. But with a lot of persuasion, I had managed to get him to tell me about how he would love a *sutobu* (a kerosene heater that is also used as a stove), Japanese floor cushions, and a kotatsu, so I added those to my call for donations in the hope that some kind people would send them up to me.

During my month there I had visited him quite a few times, each time bringing him something different — some clothes I thought he would like, a sutobu, my toolbox from Tokyo, and some chocolates on Valentine's Day. By the end of the month he wouldn't stop chatting to me when I visited, although I wasn't always entirely sure he was speaking Japanese because I didn't understand most of what he said, but he laughed non-stop and that made me laugh, so somehow we managed to have a lot of fun together.

I decided that I wanted to spend some of the money on Kameyama-san. He had worked so hard, all by himself, and had built a lovely home *without knowing a thing about carpentry*. I found him to be such an inspiration and I always think that people like him deserve a break. I decided to spend ¥100,000 to help him kit out his kitchen, and used donations from three dear Tokyo friends — Andrew and Yuriko, and Emily in memory of her mother. And I asked Kameyama-san if we could go shopping together to get what he needed — we laughed so much when we were together that I thought it would be fun.

So Kameyama-san and I headed off in his little truck to Ishinomaki, where he introduced me to some amazing recycle shops that would prove to be incredibly helpful in the future. We got the biggest fridge I have ever seen (and it was worth it just to see his smile), a gas range, a microwave, a sink and cupboard unit, a kotatsu, and a small home shrine. It all came to ¥85,000, so I gave him the remaining ¥15,000 to pay for an electrician and plumber to help him set it all up.

The recycle shop staff loaded up the back of Kameyama-san's truck, and tied everything down with ropes. I took one look at it — especially the huge fridge, which had been stood upright on the back of this little truck — and knew it would all end up crashing down the side of the Oshika mountains, possibly taking us along with it, and expressed my concern about the stability of the goods to the staff, who didn't look at all bothered themselves. Until I told them we would be driving *on Oshika*, at which point they all became very concerned indeed, and reloaded everything. Even the fairly local people in Ishinomaki worried about driving on Oshika. Kameyama-san just stood there laughing the whole time — he never worried about anything.

He especially didn't worry about any other vehicles on any road, nor indeed did he have any level of road safety whatsoever, which you could kind of get away with on Oshika, but not on the mainland. I wondered why on earth I had suggested I come with him when I found myself desperately holding onto the dashboard shouting "AKA AKA AKA!" as he drove straight through a red (*aka*) light with traffic coming from every direction. That just made him laugh even more.

By some miracle, we made it back to Oshika safely. Kameyama-san could only access his home by walking over a tiny bridge from the temporary housing community. Watching him and his friend unload everything, put it all in a wheelbarrow, which they then pushed down a hill, over the tiny bridge, and down another hill (which happened to be covered in mud) to the house was a sight I will never forget. We all agreed that the fridge wouldn't make it, so I came back the next day with strongmen Seiji and Hiroyuki, except it had snowed in the night, so now the fridge had to make that same journey, but in the snow — watching those four men carrying that massive fridge all the way to the house was hilarious. All done, of course, with Kameyama-san laughing the whole time. I loved the way that Kameyama-san could find fun and laughter in everything he did, and it was such a privilege to be a part of that whole experience.

Next, I decided to give the Sasakis ¥150,000 to help them complete work on the processing facility they'd been building beside their home. It was just the kind of project I was looking for — Mr Sasaki had done as much as he possibly could on his own, was getting worryingly close to the time when he really needed to be able to work, and was a genuinely lovely person with whom I had connected. I felt sure that the people who donated funds would love to support him and his wife as they rebuilt their life.

The ¥150,000 would be a large part of the cost of the walls that were needed to fix to the frame they'd already built. With this work done, Mr Sasaki wouldn't need to cover the wakame with plastic sheeting and hope it wouldn't rain. With this done, there would be no chance of this year's harvest — the first harvest after the disaster — being wasted. The work would be paid for by a combination of individuals and organizations from both the UK and Japan.

The walls were delivered a few days before the end of my trip, just a couple of minutes before I popped in to say hi to them. The Sasakis were standing there with huge grins on their faces, absolutely *thrilled*. Mr Sasaki talked to the delivery guys outside while I went inside with Mrs Sasaki. She showed me the invoice and apologized because it was a little higher than the original ¥140,000 they had quoted me, but I had set aside ¥150,000 for them, which almost covered it all, so gave them that — she was very touched and visibly moved. Mr Sasaki came in and we all sat and had coffee together. I tried to work out whether I'd have a couple of hours on my last day during which I could help hammer in a few nails with Mr Sasaki, but in the meantime, we had a huge hug.

Suddenly, Mrs Sasaki started sobbing — really big sobs that broke my heart. Emotions ran very close to the surface for everyone on Oshika, and the combination of the kindness of all the people that had donated, along with the idea that we would soon be saying goodbye, was too much for her. Her husband stroked her arm, saying "No tears, no tears" in English, and she apologized for being so emotional. Pretty soon I was crying myself, so we ended up laughing at each other's tears. It was truly lovely to be able to help them and I hoped that all the people who paid for those walls would one day get the chance to give Mrs Sasaki a hug, too.

The third need I had identified belonged to the Ohara boys, who were so keen to get back to work and aware that the wakame harvesting season was just about to start. They hadn't been able to work, partly because the tsunami took all their equipment, and partly because the sea had been too dirty for such a long time. But now, at last, the sea was clear, and Seiji had a radiation detection machine on its way so the wakame, fish, and soil could be monitored. People were hopeful that this area, famous for its fishing, was about to reach a turning point. But only if they had the equipment they needed.

The government helped out a little by supplementing the purchase of rope, and volunteers collected thousands of the special buoys (some were even found in the mountains), which was a big help because they would otherwise cost ¥15,000 each to buy brand new. The special shells that are used to grow oysters were also washed away or damaged, but again, volunteers had recovered some. The Ohara boys had done their best to find and collect what they needed to get back to work. But they were still in need of a special water pump.

The pump was an essential part of processing wakame, which is first boiled and then has to be cleaned and cooled. The pump could be shared not only between the Ohara fishermen, but also with the Ohara farmers who needed the very same pump to get water from the river to their storage tanks. I felt that supplying this pump would be the perfect way to support these fishermen and farmers who were so keen to get back to work and be independent again.

Saito-san drove Abe-san and me into Ishinomaki to a special fishing equipment store — they took ages searching for precisely what was required, which I was pleased about; I wanted them to take their time and not feel rushed or pressured at all. They found exactly what they needed, checked with me about the price, which was within my ¥75,000 budget, and we headed off to pay. The pump was paid for by three schools in England — Bratton Fleming, Northowram Primary, and Plymouth's Notre Dame.

I always felt very strongly that the project sponsors should be appropriately recognized — not for *their* benefit necessarily, but so that the beneficiaries could gain encouragement from the reminder that there were people all over the world thinking about them, caring for them, and urging them on as they faced the huge task of rebuilding their lives. And I came up with what I felt was an appropriate way to recognize the sponsors. I remembered my favourite drinking den in Tokyo — the notorious Geronimo on Roppongi Crossing — where if you completed the fifteen-shot challenge you got your name engraved on a plaque and it was put up on the wall (I'd done it and got a plaque myself, many, many years ago). I contacted the owner, Stewart Bailey, to see whether I could order some plaques with the sponsors names on them for each of these three projects. Not only did he order them for me but he paid for them as well, and within a few days, Kameyama-san's house, the Sasakis' building, and Ohara Community Centre had plaques hung in them so that they could remember that people were thinking of them.

Three projects had been completed, each making a big difference to people I'd come to know during that month on Oshika, and I still had ¥60,000 left over from the fuel contributions that people had sent up. I decided to donate it to the Ohara shrine fund. The villagers had already managed to raise ¥2 million and were trying their best to raise a further ¥3 million, hoping to have the shrine repaired before that summer's festival — a hugely symbolic event that everybody looked forward to throughout the year. Holding the festival would be a much-needed celebration and would enable the villagers to feel proud of Ohara again. Looking forward to positive things in the future was now more important than ever.

The Ohara community had been so wonderfully welcoming to me, and I knew how much their 400-year-old shrine meant to them and how hopeful they were as they tried to raise the funds they needed to repair it, so I thought this was a good project to support with this extra money. And it was my way of saying thank you.

I wanted to say thank you to *everyone* that had welcomed me with open arms on Oshika. I thought I could go around the peninsula saying thank you to everyone, or I could invite them all to Ohara. These little villages tended to keep themselves to themselves, rarely interacting with each other, and I'd seen just how much people loved the opportunity to get together during this time of difficulty, stress, and loneliness. So, with Kucho's permission, I decided to invite my new Oshika friends to Ohara Community Centre, and cook them an English-style roast dinner on my last Sunday.

I hadn't quite realized just *how many* new friends I'd made on Oshika, and neither had Kucho. I don't think the Ohara boys had really known what I had been doing on Oshika when I wasn't chopping down bamboo, swearing with them, or hanging my knickers all over the place. Loads of people started turning up — people I wondered whether I'd even met before — word had got around that everyone was welcome. Utsumi-sensei was there, along with her daughter and granddaughter, and some children from the preschool.

Kameyama-san came along, as did the Sudas from the gas station, and the Sasakis of course. Then there were all the Ohara boys, and people I didn't know well but to whom I had given either Valentine's chocolates or some clothing or other donated items.

Takahashi-buta kept saying over and over again how surprised he was to walk into the centre and find so many people there that he didn't know. And they were all from Oshika! He said he just loved the fact that people from different parts of the peninsula were all brought together, and how great it was that they could share ideas and experiences. It made me so happy to know that they were having a wonderful time getting to know each other, and I happily stayed in the kitchen for most of the day, cooking one thing after another. I had mountains of food to prepare.

I'd put a call out to my network the previous week, asking if they'd like to send up any food items for an English-style Sunday dinner, and as always, had been amazed at the response. I'd even been sent some stuffing and OXO cubes. And to go with everything were four boxes of *real* English beer that the Hobgoblin pub had very kindly sent up.

I set to work attempting to make my favourite Sunday roast dishes without the use of an oven — there wasn't an oven in the centre's kitchen, just three huge gas rings. This was going to be interesting. I got hold of vegetables from the mainland — potatoes, carrots, cabbage, peas, broccoli, and onions. As soon as Abe-san and Takako-sensei saw me on my own in the kitchen surrounded by mountains and mountains of food, they insisted on helping, and before I knew it they were right in the middle of it all and somehow knew exactly what needed doing. Saito-san's youngest daughter, Haruka, was fascinated by what English food looked like, so she spent most of the time hanging out in the kitchen, tasting everything and taking photos.

I love making roast dinners, and usually I roast each side dish in its own sauce. But for this Sunday roast, I had to improvise. I steamed the carrots in fresh *mikan* (Japanese orange) juice and ginger; stir-fried the cabbage with onion, peas, and Takahashi-buta's bacon; marinated sliced onions overnight in olive oil and balsamic vinegar to be sautéed instead of roasted whole; and boiled the potatoes before sautéing them in oil and *lots* of salt and pepper. These "roast potatoes" were the highlight of the meal for everyone — 8 kg of potatoes were consumed and the dish has since become a regular addition to Mrs Sasaki's cooking repertoire. The steamed broccoli was covered in cheese sauce and breadcrumbs which, to Abe-san's horror, I finished off with a blowtorch in lieu of a grill.

I fried lemon-marinated chicken breasts and salt-and-pepper-covered steak, then sliced the meat into thin pieces. I made gravy with all the vegetable stock, meat juices, and loads of red wine, and I showed my Oshika friends how to pour the gravy all over everything just like English people do. Although I quite enjoyed watching people dip their vegetables and meat in the "sauce," Japanese-style.

It took six hours of prep and five hours of cooking. Everything had to be chopstick-friendly, as I hadn't once come across a knife or fork for the entire time I'd been there. Haruka and her friends played waitresses for the event and took the dishes out one by one. And I had to go out and tell everyone not to wait but to start eating, and that we would do *kanpai* (cheers) later.

For dessert, I made trifle for the first time in my life, musing on how I might have achieved quite a bit in the past month but, at that moment, I was most proud of making custard from scratch for the first time. The trifle turned out beautifully, but I ended up putting way too much rum in it. I warned everyone that there was rather a lot of alcohol in the dessert, so most of the old women stayed away, although I did spot Takako-sensei sneaking a bowl to one side to take home with her, which really made me giggle.

The kitchen was absolute chaos. Which I love. I like to use every single pan I can get my hands on in any kitchen and then just pile everything up in the sink — and the Ohara centre had the biggest sink I had ever seen, so I was really in my element. I didn't expect anyone to clean up after me, but two of the Ohara boys cleaned *everything* as I went along, including the three pans I burned — it had taken me at least an hour to work out how to control the gas rings. And at the end of the evening I was surprised to find five old ladies cleaning the *entire* kitchen (including the floor). I was so grateful.

When it was time for the kanpai, one of the little girls from the temporary preschool came forward to give me a homemade envelope filled with messages from the children who couldn't make it that evening. I opened the first one and started blubbing, so thought I'd better put the rest away for later. Then Abe-san asked me to say a few words.

It was hard to know what on earth to say about my month on Oshika — there was so much *to* say, and I was so grateful for this incredible experience. I had been welcomed into people's homes and lives during a time of intense vulnerability for them, and they had allowed me to help them in whatever small ways I could. I had had the opportunity to convey the love and care that so many people in other parts of Japan, and indeed the world, had for the people of Tohoku, and I hoped I did them proud with the ways in which I chose to convey that love and care.

I hadn't expected to have gained quite so much for myself personally while being there, and to be leaving with such incredible memories — I had used a chainsaw, driven a digger, cut down bamboo, been out on a fishing boat, opened oysters fresh from the sea, spoken Japanese *almost exclusively* for a month, washed car windows in a gas station, gone without washing myself for four days, hung my underwear out for all to see, munched fish bones along with the best of them, and jogged over earthquake-damaged roads and alongside wild deer. I had seen the most beautiful sunsets in my life, and spent time with beautiful people.

It would have taken forever to explain my feelings about my time on Oshika, so instead (with the help of Hanako's translation) I kept my words simple: "I came here for a month because I wanted to help and give *you* something, but instead, I think *you* gave *me* so much more."

16: Farewells and the Future

I cried all the way to Watanoha when I left Oshika. Saying goodbye to my new friends had been *awful*. I didn't want to leave them. I didn't want to go to Tokyo. And I didn't want to go back to England. I just wanted to stay there with them, in a place that I had completely fallen in love with. I was, again, so torn between countries. That "Land for Sale" had spoken *loudly* to me and I was yet to settle anywhere in England, still enjoying a rather nomadic existence.

But I accepted that it wasn't practical for me to live on Oshika — it was still very much an area in recovery and I didn't want to use up any resources for any longer than necessary. Besides, I didn't feel comfortable with the idea of actually making a home there while so many people were living in temporary homes. That just didn't feel right. And there were some personal issues in England that were pulling me more toward making a base there, as long as I could regularly return to Japan.

So I said goodbye to everyone, with tears streaming down my face.

The Ohara boys loaded my suitcase into the back of my car, which was now sparkling clean thanks to Yukio-san. It wasn't unacceptable to have a dirty vehicle on Oshika, but elsewhere in Japan, cars were spotless. And, just as Oshika drivers seemed to have their own set of "rules of the road," I'd now have to keep a close eye on my driving on the way back to Tokyo, and asked the Ohara boys to remind me of the speed limit on the expressway. They seemed to think that 75 miles per hour was fine.

One final act before setting off — I retrieved my fuchsia pink polka dot bra from my suitcase and hung it up, all on its own, on one of the washing lines outside the centre, catching Hiroyuki's eye as I did so, knowing it would wind him up. A little parting gift. Kucho thought it was hilarious.

Hiroyuki and I hadn't always seen eye to eye during that month — Hiroyuki had initially seen me as someone he was "in charge of," and I didn't take well to being told what to do unless it was by the locals. I'd been determined to do my own thing on Oshika, and that meant following my instincts a lot, which had baffled and frustrated Hiroyuki sometimes, so we'd occasionally knocked heads. But I deeply appreciated how generous he'd been with his time, showing me around and explaining so many things to me in English. And he'd eventually grown to understand and respect my efforts; even if I did make him roll his eyes in despair at times.

Despite my childish behaviour in hanging up the bra to annoy him, Hiroyuki hugged me warmly when I left, saying in English, "One month is very long time. But it is also very short time. You did great job," and I bowed respectfully to him. His approval meant a lot to me.

The Sasakis hadn't come to Ohara to wave me off — Mrs Sasaki said it would be too much for her. We had become so close during that month. So we said our goodbyes the previous day. During our final slightly emotional coffee together, a group of fifteen "heart care" volunteers that Mrs Sasaki often talked to showed up wearing fancy dress costumes. They did a hilarious dance routine that ended with them enveloping her in a huge hug. I looked at the massive smile on her face as she towered above all these wonderful young people who were laughing and laughing, literally surrounding her with love, and felt a huge lump come to my throat and my eyes began to sting. So I hid in the kitchen, bawling, before saying a last goodbye.

My final goodbyes were just to the Ohara boys. They all gathered outside the community centre to wave me off and, to their embarrassment, I hugged each of them, one by one. Abe-san giggled his usual nervous giggle, and Kucho-san laughed his usual laugh, while Onodera-san combined English and Japanese by bidding me "Bye-onara" with a massive slap on my back, then an inability to stop laughing because he found his own multilingual farewell joke so hilarious. I promised I'd be back soon. I meant it.

And I drove off in my little blue car, with the Union Jack flags flying, tears blinding me to the point that I almost drove straight into a car full of government officials making their way up the little driveway to the centre. Worried, I looked back at Kucho to see if I'd finally unintentionally managed to do something that had annoyed him, but no, he was there laughing away along with everyone else. And the Ohara boys ran around to the other side of the community centre so that they could wave to me until I was at the other end of the village, and starting to go up the little hill and round the bend, finally out of sight.

Those government officials I nearly crashed straight into were the only official people I saw during my whole month on Oshika. The closest would have been the two police officers that stopped by the centre one day because they'd heard there was an English girl on the peninsula and they wanted to meet me. When they first showed up asking for a foreign woman, I immediately started worrying whether I'd done something wrong or whether my visa had expired without my realizing it, but no, I had years left on that — these neighbourhood police officers literally just wanted to say hello. So we had a coffee together and one of them asked very politely to take a photo with me for his Facebook page. This was the extent of my interaction with any official people on Oshika. Nobody official seemed to go there. It genuinely felt like a rather forgotten part of the disaster.

While travelling around this forgotten peninsula, I'd just tried to do what I could to help. I'd focused my energies on the human impact of the tsunami on a very individual level, trying to make a tiny difference to the people that I met during my time on Oshika. And I was very, very aware that the help I could offer was minuscule in the grand scheme of things. I had very little power to make any real difference. As I discovered things that just didn't make sense to me, I wondered what the people who *did* have power were doing for Oshika. I tend to be of the opinion that we are all responsible for the wellbeing of the people around us, and Ohara's culture definitely followed that community-driven philosophy, but in our developed countries we put people in government positions where they are supposed to be responsible for the well-being of others. Coming up to the first anniversary, the news was full of stories of how one area or another was being supported and therefore recovering after the tsunami, but not this remote peninsula. I wondered what the politicians were doing for Oshika.

Mr Ohnishi, a self-described "volunteer politician," had also fallen in love with Oshika. I met him in an entirely unofficial capacity about halfway through my month on Oshika. Since the earthquake, he had been trying to bridge the gap between central government in Tokyo and the individuals affected by the disaster.

Based in Yokohama, Mr Ohnishi had played a senior role at JP Morgan until he became disillusioned with what he called a "soulless existence." He'd spent the first twenty years of his life making money, and decided that his industry no longer made sense to him — he wanted to spend the following twenty years creating something of real value. He got involved in a couple of business ventures, one of which was an Italian restaurant in Yokohama. Whereas JP Morgan had taught him to look at the world in terms of huge numbers — billions of dollars and millions of people — the restaurant business taught him about individuals. So at the time of the disaster, Mr Ohnishi had a useful understanding of how "the system" worked, but also appreciated how it affected people on a very personal level.

He could see that the people of Tohoku were not only suffering from the effects of the tsunami, but also from the effects of decisions made in Tokyo by people who didn't fully understand the impact of those decisions. He recognized that there was a major lack of communication between the decision-makers and the people in Tohoku and he wanted to try to help. There were so many things that hadn't made sense to me, and Mr Ohnishi's insight helped explain them — there really was a huge gap between what was going on in Tokyo and what was going on on this little peninsula I'd come to love so much.

Mr Ohnishi had seen that I was falling in love with the area, and that I was keen to help in any way I could. He invited me along for a drive to the mainland one day — he was going to a meeting with the local government officials and wanted to hear about my ideas. At that point I was full of ideas about what *I* thought was necessary but had kept them to myself, partly because I was extremely aware that I didn't want to offend anyone, partly because I was still working to acquire the language skills necessary to communicate my ideas, and partly because I was still building relationships. Despite all that, the local people had started to confide in me and I had a good sense of how *they* felt. Mr Ohnishi was quite Western in his ways, spoke excellent English, and wanted me to speak very directly with him, so I appreciated the chance to speak so openly with someone about the things on Oshika that didn't make sense to me. Or to the people who lived there.

The people living in the temporary housing communities felt that they had no say in their future. They felt entirely dependent on the government to make decisions for them — what their future would hold, where they would live, and what they could do with their land. There appeared to be no timeline set for when new houses would be built — the land still hadn't been found. During the time when the debris was being cleared there had actually been evidence of progress and a sense of moving forward. But now that the debris was gone, people found themselves living in a wasteland. The residents felt they were in a kind of limbo, with the most elderly among them wondering whether they would end their days in their tiny kasetsu. Sadly, some of them would.

To understand why it was taking so long to build the new homes, one first had to understand Japan's construction limitations *without* the impact of a natural disaster. Mr Ohnishi helpfully explained that during any one year, Japan had the capacity for a maximum of 800,000 new builds — and 5 percent of them would be in Tohoku. So under *normal* circumstances, Tohoku had the resources for building 40,000 new homes. Those resources included things like carpenters, electricians, construction workers, and materials. According to data released while I was on Oshika, over one million houses needed attention in Tohoku: 150,000 that were completely wiped out, 250,000 that were half destroyed and were rendered uninhabitable, and 600,000 that were partly damaged. If all of the 400,000 homes that had been lost or uninhabitable were rebuilt, and assuming that Japan was even capable of doubling their house-building efforts, it would still take ten years to create the required number of permanent homes.

On top of that, the ¥19 trillion that the government set aside as a restoration budget had been determined in July 2011, only four months after 311, when the full extent of the disaster and recovery needs weren't even close to being known. Mr Ohnishi felt that the government's handling of everything surrounding March 11 was a mess. However, he also felt that the disaster was an opportunity for Japan to change in many ways — to change how information was shared, to change how budgets were divided, and to change the direction in which Japan was heading. He believed that, in the past, most Japanese people hadn't had the courage to speak up when something wasn't right, but that the disaster may have brought about people who are ready for change; people who were no longer willing to stay quiet.

On Oshika, almost one year after the disaster, I had seen people who were still in shock, but they *were* coming out of it. I had met people who weren't *quite* ready to stand up and speak out, but they were ready for others to hold their hands as they took their first steps toward identifying and expressing their needs — such a vital part of the beginning of recovery. Because this was a situation when all power over their lives was so instantly and violently taken away, I was beginning to develop the firm belief that the decision-making belonged in the hands of those who were directly affected — that giving them a sense of power over their own destiny again was an important part in the *next* stage of recovery. The ideas I'd enthusiastically brought to Oshika — they were irrelevant. The only ideas that mattered were those that came from the communities themselves. It was not my place, not any well-meaning NGO's place, not even the government's place to make decisions — all that the rest of us needed to do was to listen to what the local people said they required, and then do our best to fulfill their needs.

These thoughts were running through my mind during the long drive back to Tokyo, and they filled me with optimism. I *would* return, and I would listen. People on Oshika knew me now, and they trusted me. They didn't look at me as a "volunteer," but as a friend. I would spend my next trip finding out more about what they required, and I would do *everything* I could to fulfill their needs. I may have been there for only one month, but Oshika had affected me in such a way that at the end of that month I left there with a firm commitment to the place and the people.

Full of the memories of such a wonderful month, as well as excited about thoughts of the future, I put on the '80s music I always listen to, turning the volume up high. Driving along and singing at the top of my voice, I suddenly realized there was a police car alongside me, lights flashing, with a very annoyed-looking officer inside who was indicating that I should pull over. I hadn't even heard the sirens because my music was so loud, and clearly hadn't been paying attention to the road, which was usually empty of traffic.

It turned out that 75 miles per hour was *not* fine.

The police officers were furious with me, interrogating me with questions. They'd never come across a foreign woman, on her own, driving in the north of Japan, and speeding, no less! And they'd never heard of a place called Oshika-hanto. Who was I? What was I doing here? Where had I been? Where was I staying? Whose car was this? What was all that stuff in the back of the car (it was leftover clothing I planned on delivering to the Salvation Army)? What did I mean I'd been helping in Tohoku? No, they didn't want a photo for their Facebook pages. Did I have a visa? Could they see my passport? Brilliant … I was about to ruin all my good efforts by ending up detained in a koban!

In my fifteen years in Japan I had learned enough to know that if the police got hold of you it would be a very, very tricky situation to get out of. But I had also learned that, despite what the police may think, they did not have the right to take your passport off you, so when one of them insisted that I give it to him, I refused. When he promised to post it to me after I'd returned to England, I soon realized they weren't especially bright and didn't really know how passports worked, so I apologized over and over again incredibly politely, thanked them profusely for all their help in teaching me about the road laws in Japan and drove off, imagining the Ohara boys laughing their heads off when they heard about this.

Back in Tokyo, I got stopped by the police *again*. Not for speeding, because the traffic in Tokyo was so slow that you could rarely get up enough speed to break the limit there anyway — this time I'd unintentionally made an illegal turn. Realizing that I really shouldn't be trusted to drive anywhere except Oshika, I figured the quicker I could get rid of this car, the better. Richard Thornley, who'd been following my activities since March 11, and whose uncle had turned up in Plymouth, had offered me the spare parking space under his apartment, not far from where my dear sister-friend Emily lived, so I gladly parked the car and wheeled my suitcase to Emily's place. For the first time in a month, I had a shower in a *warm* room, and slept on a mattress in another *warm* room. So different from Oshika.

Everything in Tokyo felt different from Oshika. I experienced a huge sense of culture shock upon my return to the city that had been my home for so many years. It wasn't just the number of people, the amount of traffic, the lack of greenery, the absent sea, the huge buildings, the fancy clothes, or the busy train stations. It was how everybody seemed to be going about their lives, completely oblivious to how other people, not that far away, were living. People who were living in tiny temporary housing units that shook with the wind, and let the rain trickle in. People with holes in their coats. People who'd been wearing the same clothes for months. Children without playgrounds. Parents without jobs. Old people who were resigned to dying in what amounted to tiny boxes instead of their familiar old homes. *A 72-year-old man who was building himself a house with his bare hands.* Surely this wasn't right?

There were people in Tokyo who also felt it wasn't right that they were going about their normal lives while hundreds of thousands of people, only a matter of hours away, were still struggling so much. Word about my month on Oshika had spread, and people had been reading my blog, as well as my Facebook posts, which were both full of photos of *real* people. I had been absolutely transparent not only about where the coats and other clothes and donations had gone, but also about what every single penny or yen had been spent on. Not everybody was comfortable with the numerous charities that had been set up in the year after the disaster; not everybody was comfortable with the idea of donations being used to cover administrative costs in general. I was doing something different. Not intentionally trying to be different, but just going with what felt right, in my heart. People liked it. And they wanted to be a part of it.

I'd gone to Oshika for that month just to do what I could to help, and the way in which I'd gone about it had — completely unintentionally — meant that I'd gained trust and built relationships that would last far beyond that one month in Tohoku.

And not just with the people of Oshika, but with people from all over the world: people who would ultimately fund elements of the recovery during the next decade in Tohoku.

ONE YEAR ON: Top left: Date Masamune's shrine. Top right: Tsunami-ravaged buildings. Upper middle left: Damaged torii resting on a hill. Upper middle right: A temporary housing community. Lower middle left: Mounds of cleared debris piled up along the coast. Lower middle right: Sandbags protecting against tidal floods. Bottom: Looking out to the epicentre from Gobanshokoen.

Top left: The priest sitting in front of the mandara and kamisama he had just painted. Top right: The Ohara boys raising the festival banners at the foot of the steps to Date Masamune's shrine. Middle left: The shishimai at rest. Middle right: My first experience of being called to pray. Bottom: The Ohara community in the Ohara Community Centre, holding their first festival since the disaster.

Top left: Dressed up in kappa with Taira-san and Saito-san. Top right: An oyster farm out in the bay by Oharahama. Middle left: Oshika fishing boats. Middle right: Abe-san pulling in the oysters from the farm. Bottom left: Opening oysters fresh from the sea. Bottom right: The Ohara boys with their new fishing equipment.

Top left: The women of Shimizudahama. Top right: Mr and Mrs Yamaki of Dosenji Temple. Middle left: Furuuchi-san and his son in their temporary sushi restaurant. Middle right: Mr and Mrs Maekawa in their temporary restaurant. Bottom: 72-year-old Kameyama-san outside the house he built from scratch.

Top left: Kei-chan on top of the fish truck he filled with drinking water after the tsunami. Top right: The Sasakis with their new walls, delivered just in time to protect the wakame. Middle right: Endo-san, who ran the konbini. Bottom: Mika and her mother friends with some of their children in Fukkiura's danwashitsu.

Top left: Leaving Tokyo for Oshika in Mavis. Top right: Mrs Sasaki with one of her adopted cats. Middle left: With Taira-san, using a chainsaw in the bamboo forest. Middle right: Seiji teaching me how to use a digger. Bottom left: My bedroom for the month. Bottom right: My underwear hung outside the Ohara Community Centre, to Hiroyuki's horror.

Top left: Organizing donations that were sent for me to distribute. Top right: A mini-shop set up in a danwashitsu. Middle left: Cleaning a windscreen at the local gas station. Middle right: At the onsen with the Ohara boys and Chise. Bottom left: Me and Utsumi-sensei with her grandchildren. Bottom right: Cooking for my new friends in the kitchen at Ohara Community Centre.

Top left: Toru Konishi with a wedding photograph he restored. Top right: Hiroyuki with Takako-sensei sitting on the bench he made her for her birthday. Middle left: Robert Mangold showing how deep the tsunami "sludge" was in a building he cleared. Middle right: Nippon Foundation volunteers. Bottom: "Heart care" volunteers surrounding Mrs Sasaki with love.

ONE DECADE IN TOHOKU

17: Gardens

On March 11, 2012, the first anniversary of the disaster, the Ohara community found comfort in placing beautiful bamboo candle holders all the way up the steps to the shrine, and lighting candles in every one of them. Some Tokyo friends joined large gatherings of people and held moments of silence together, finding comfort in that. Some stayed at home with loved ones. I was in England, and started the day by going running through sea mist on a North Devon beach.

It was a strange day for me, reflecting on the events of the past year — remembering where I was when I'd heard about the earthquake, the hours spent stuck on high ground in Saipan while watching the tsunami footage online, and various "aftershocks" in my personal life that came from that moment onward. I was also thinking about the aftershocks in the lives of my friends — even though the earthquake affected none of us in the same way that the people of Tohoku were affected, we were all still affected one way or another. And then of course thinking about the very real impact on the people of Tohoku, and especially the people on Oshika.

In stark contrast to my previous time in the UK, after spending that month on Oshika I felt unable to watch anything about the earthquake. Family would text me when there was something about it on British TV, but I had no desire to watch any of it. It's not that I wanted to block it out or pretend it hadn't happened, or that I had "disaster fatigue," because I thought about Oshika and the people there every single day. It was just too upsetting to watch what happened on TV now that I knew the people to whom it had happened, and their personal stories. In my mind I could see Kameyama-san, the Ohara fishermen, Saito-san's little daughters, Mrs Sasaki holding her mother-in-law, and Onodera-san saving his wife; it felt like this disaster on television had happened to friends of mine now. I couldn't watch it from a distance, yet I was completely comfortable in the middle of the aftermath when on Oshika.

Maybe it's because I found so much love, laughter, and beauty during my time on Oshika that I now felt that these were the things that bring us strength when dealing with unimaginable loss, pain, and destruction. It's the laughter of little kids asking you to read the English phrases on clothes donated to the temporary preschool, the hugs and smiles from an old fisherman whose mother's body still hasn't been found, and the cackling of the fisherwomen as they tell saucy stories to each other despite having lost their husbands.

When you strip away everything — money, homes, personal belongings, even access to food, all you are left with is the human spirit. How we treat each other, how we talk to each other, how we smile at each other, and how we hold another person in our arms — these are the things that keep us going when all else is gone. And these are the things that the people I met on Oshika were so good at — maybe this is why in the middle of a wasteland with piles of debris all around they were finding the strength to rebuild their lives, and, along the way, give strength to those of us who had the privilege of helping.

I was determined to use that privilege wisely and respectfully, to share everything I had learned during my month on Oshika with as many people as possible, and to continue giving talks around England. I'd freed up some more time to devote to Oshika because, while in Tokyo, I'd finalized a deal to sell one of my magazines, which left me with just one monthly publication to produce — it would only take four days of work a month, but would still earn me enough to renew my visa when the time came.

I continued giving talks in England, and now I had even more photographs to show and stories to tell. I went to Somersham Primary in Cambridge, Orleans Infant School in Twickenham, and returned to Trafalgar Infants, Bolham Primary, and Plymouth College. I also returned to Bratton Fleming, where the students had forged ahead with their plan to have a sponsored sleepover in the school hall. It was one of the many fundraising activities put on by this little school, and I wanted to show my appreciation for their efforts, so I joined them for this particular activity.

Which is how I ended up spending a Friday night sleeping on the floor of a North Devon primary school's hall, literally surrounded by sixty children, all under the age of eleven.

The children queued up to be let in for the second time that day, this time wearing their pyjamas and carrying sleeping bags or duvets and their favourite teddy. Six adults had volunteered to join the sleepover, including Gillian and Natsuko, as well as headteacher Sue Denham. I gave the children a quick talk to remind them of why we were there, and tell them about the special water pump for the Ohara fishermen that they had partly sponsored. Then they split up into four groups to take part in some Japan-related activities that had been set up around the hall and in the kitchen.

One table played a Japanese board game that Natsuko had brought in, to which she had added English instructions. Another table did origami, and another table was for colouring in Japanese cartoon characters. I love colouring and spent a lot of my time just sitting at the colouring table, thoroughly enjoying chatting away to the kids around me. Natsuko and her husband were busy in the kitchen, teaching children how to make *okonomiyaki* (savoury pancakes) — they were all having a great time cooking and eating. Each group rotated so that every child got to do every activity until it was time to get the sleeping bags and duvets out. The children organized themselves around the hall and sat on the edge of their "beds" while we brought round milk and cookies. Then it was time for them to use the toilet and brush their teeth — it was complete chaos!

Once everyone had settled down, the teachers and myself found spaces on the floor and spread ourselves out among the children. I found myself next to a tiny girl who looked so young that I couldn't believe she was there. I asked her how old she was and she replied proudly, "I am four years old," and I was amazed to see that she didn't look one bit nervous about being away from Mummy for the night. We turned all the lights out and Natsuko sat in the middle of the hall with a small torch that she shone into a Japanese children's storybook in her lap, from which she read (entirely in her native language) "Little Red Riding Hood" to us. It was a beautiful, beautiful scene, all the more so when you thought about why this community was doing it.

Very slowly the children started going to sleep, although I don't think any of us adults got much sleep at all, especially my university friend, Gillian. Occasionally through the night you could hear little half-asleep voices say "Mummy," at which point Gillian immediately leapt out of her sleeping bag and somehow found the voice in the middle of everything, offered a soothing hair stroke and reassuring word to the little one in question, then leapt back to her own spot without treading on anyone at all. I have no idea how she did it and still looked like she'd had a good night's sleep the next day.

The children knew they were supposed to wait until others were awake before getting up and about in the morning, so while they were waiting for the all-clear, they thoughtfully whispered to each other. Except that the sound of sixty children whispering is actually *really* loud! I sat up to see that a few of the children had jumped on their headteacher's sleeping bag and were giving her a cuddle, which was really sweet. When I trained as a teacher, you weren't allowed to have any physical contact with the kids at all, which with younger children was actually very difficult and, I always thought, a bit of a shame. So it really brought a smile to my face to see the children so fond of their headteacher (although I'd already assumed Sue had to be a very special person to not only let all this madness go on, but to join in, too).

The teachers had organized breakfast for the parents as well as the kids. Bacon sandwich after bacon sandwich came out of the staffroom and they were handed round to the parents. I gave another talk, slightly more grown-up this time, speaking above all the chaos, showing my photos of Oshika, and thanking the adults for all their efforts to support people in Japan — the sleepover raised almost £400 for Oshika. And to date, it is the only event at which I have given a speech in my pajamas.

In between the school talks I continued spending time with friends and family, and deepening my renewed connection with England. There was number two niece's eighteenth birthday to celebrate, and I was thrilled to be in the country for such a special event. I've never given my nieces and nephews any birthday presents — they have enough and I've always chosen to show my love in other ways. But when it comes to their eighteenth birthdays, I like to give them something special. I'd given my eldest niece, Megan, a trip to Japan for her eighteenth, and she spent a few weeks with me in exciting Tokyo, going to sumo, Disneyland, Tokyo Tower, and attending a launch party for one of my books. Her younger sister Emily would also receive a trip to Japan, but her trip couldn't have been more different from Megan's — she would be joining me on Oshika in two years' time — so we had fun making plans for that.

I finally finished writing the book I'd begun when I was on Saipan, and started becoming very fond of the Cotswolds, spending a lot of time in Cirencester, which I really liked. I connected with David Lee in nearby Oxford — David and his Japanese wife Yuri operated Into Japan Specialist Tours, organizing unique tours of the country that David had also fallen in love with many years earlier. They are part of a large Japanese community in the Oxford area, and had set up a registered charity called Helping Hands for Japan not long after the disaster. Helping Hands added me to their list of projects, so at last I had somewhere to direct people who wanted to donate money specifically in support of my efforts, and a way to get donations from the UK to Japan with minimal fees. I no longer had to carry money around in my knickers! Very handy, because after only a few months in England I'd managed to generate about £4000 for Oshika, where I'd be returning in July.

And so, as planned, on July 2, I found myself in the very familiar Narita Airport. I got the limousine bus to Tokyo, and went straight round to Richard Thornley's building to collect my little car, which was still in the spare parking spot under his building where I'd left it. Full of good intentions and enthusiasm for the ways I might be able to help Oshika on this trip, I suddenly realized that I might be full of something else, too — the airline food hadn't quite agreed with me. I was in the middle of a quiet residential area, Richard wasn't at home, Emily lived a ten-minute walk away, and there wasn't a public toilet anywhere to be seen. I frantically looked around the parking space under Richard's building to see whether I could discreetly deal with the impending situation, but I would be too exposed; anybody could walk past at any time. And time was something I really didn't have. *I had to deal with this now. RIGHT NOW.*

I clambered into the back of my car, thankful that I'd already pushed the backseat forward, and retrieved one of the dog poo bags I'd always kept in my winter jacket on my previous trip to Oshika. If it was good enough for dogs, it was good enough for humans, surely?

My plane poo went on *forever*. Just when I thought I was done, no … there was more. Now done? No. It went on and on and on. But it eventually finished, at which point I started feeling so much better, and congratulated myself on coming up with such an ingenious way of dealing with it so discreetly.

Then I turned around to find poo *everywhere*. All over my clothes. All over my shoes. All over the carpet. All over the inside of the back doors. And when I turned around again I found it all over the folded down back seats. It was literally everywhere. *Even on the steering wheel.*

Absolutely mortified, I got out of the car and changed my clothes behind it, no longer caring about possible passersby, then walked miserably up to Emily's. I always have such good intentions in life, yet somehow always manage to get myself into such messes — and they usually involve some sort of bodily function. If the people who supported my efforts on Oshika could see what had just happened …

I greeted my dear friend with, "Give me all your cleaning products, I've just shit all over my car," shoved some clothes in her washing machine, and returned to clean up the scene of the crime. Alone. Emily and I would do anything for each other, but there are some things in life where, quite understandably, you're on your own.

Thankfully, my first week in Tokyo greatly improved. I had some very good business meetings, Oshika-related meetings, and caught up with friends, all the while managing to keep jet lag at bay and enjoying wonderful runs along the Shinagawa riverbank at dawn. People commented on how much more relaxed I looked, and I was sure that the English countryside had played a part in that. I'd got so used to the little everyday stresses and bureaucracy that were seemingly involved in everything that needed to get done in Tokyo, that I hadn't realized just how much of a toll they'd taken over the years. It was nice to visit, but I knew I didn't want to live there anymore. My heart had moved further north anyway.

I managed to make the seven-hour drive to Oshika without getting pulled over, and I was, for the third time, in awe of the scenery as I drove along the winding coastal roads. But this time it was summer, and the wasteland had disappeared. Everything was green. The mountains of debris were still there, but where the villages once were, all you could see were tiny bits of debris and tall grasses, weeds, and flowers that had grown up through the dirt. It was all wild and completely unkempt, but to me, it felt like I was looking at change, progress, and new life. It was a good feeling, but for some reason it made my question about how I might be able to help rise up in me.

Word had got around that I was coming back that day. Endo-san from the konbini had called me en route, and I popped in to say a quick hello soon after I arrived. She had three *bento* (packed lunch or dinner meals) ready and waiting for me — I don't know how much food she thought I needed! And I briefly caught up with Hiroyuki who, no longer based in Ohara Community Centre, was now living in the village in a tiny house that had survived the tsunami, but whose owners had not returned. He and two others had been employed by the local government and were given ¥105 million to use in the support of businesses, children's mental health care, and community activities such as festivals or the upkeep of shrines on Oshika. This was wonderful news, but I did think it was a shame that local people hadn't been employed for such a task. And, since Hiroyuki and his team had been allocated all this money, I began wondering whether there was anything I could possibly do to help — I didn't want to be in the way as things progressed.

Progress had definitely been made for the youngest Oshika residents, as I found out for myself when I went to see Utsumi-sensei. Right around the corner from the temporary preschool, near Hot Maru and the Seiyukan, was an absolutely stunning brand-new school building that she was about to move everyone into. It was the very first permanent new building to go up on Oshika, financed entirely by UNICEF; no government money went into the preschool. Sixteen months after the disaster, the little children would finally be able to go to a proper school again.

And what a school it was! I marvelled at the smell of the wooden beams throughout the building, the kitchen with a counter at a perfect height for children on one side, the stage that opened out into the hall, the piano already moved in, and what looked like state-of-the-art toilets and urinals perfectly located to assist if any little ones got caught short during class. Outside there was a small pool, and plenty of space for playing. My eyes stung a little at the memory of visiting this area with Andrew in May 2011, just over a year ago, when we saw the despair in the teachers' faces, and now, seeing the difference in the happiness in Utsumi-sensei's face. I noticed stacks and stacks of boxes of books and toys in the new preschool and told Utsumi-sensei that she was to call me if she needed any help at all unpacking. She called me later that day to say that if I was serious about helping, she could really do with an extra pair of hands.

The Sasakis had made great progress with their building during the time that I'd been gone. The walls had been put up and, after having used the building for processing during that first wakame season since the disaster, they were thinking ahead and now planning to convert the building into a place where their seasonal workers could sleep — taking one step at a time to rebuild the business they'd lost. They were upbeat despite some terribly sad news the previous week, news that gave an insight into some of the complications involved with the deaths caused by the 2011 earthquake and tsunami.

One of Mr Sasaki's cousins had been lost in the tsunami. The week before I'd arrived, the police had contacted him to say that his cousin's body had been found. The fact that the body had finally been found brought peace to the family, *but* the body was found on March 20 … not this year but the year before … just nine days after the tsunami, yet it had taken this long to process the DNA results and notify the family. I wondered how on earth that was even possible.

I also wondered how it was still possible, on my first day back, that an elderly lady found it necessary to quietly take me aside and ask me whether there was any chance of getting some large-sized women's underwear from my friends in Tokyo. I knew that my network would still be willing to send items that were needed.

It seemed that, despite the beautiful flowers waving in the breeze, the clear sea, the bright sunshine, and the smiles on everyone's faces, there was still an awful lot of help required, both practically and emotionally. So, I could help, and with some more cash donations that had come in during my time in Tokyo, I now had about half a million yen to spend. I got straight to work.

One of the reasons that the peninsula was so overgrown was because all of the gardening equipment had been taken away by the tsunami, and it understandably hadn't been high on the list of priorities during the first year of the recovery. But the overgrowth was starting to bother people. People on Oshika took great pride in the gardens they had before the tsunami, and taking care of the communal areas was always a group activity — an opportunity for people to come together. Gardening is often an activity that is recommended to help people deal with stress, and it's a great way for people (especially the elderly) to keep active. It turned out to be a great way to support these communities at this stage of the recovery.

The overgrown grasses around the Fukkiura temporary housing community had been driving Katsuzo-san mad for quite a while. He tried his best to keep them under control, but without a weed trimmer, he was fighting a losing battle. I allocated about ¥50,000 to help make the land around Fukkiura more pleasant for the residents. So, Katsuzo-san, young mum and community motivator Mika, her husband, and I drove into Ishinomaki to find a weed trimmer. It didn't cost very much, so I asked Katsuzo-san to get any other little things that would make his life easier. Even after that, there was still money left over, so we started looking at flowers and, before I knew it, I had somehow agreed to make them a Union Jack garden! I had no idea how I was going to do this — I could just about manage to keep a cactus alive, but Mika was especially excited about this idea and I didn't want to disappoint her.

Back on the peninsula, when a woman cycled past me on her way home from work, telling me how much she was looking forward to the following day's "gardening event," I realized that on Oshika, things one might assume would be so simple, such as buying a weed trimmer, had a way of becoming so much more. I also realized that the pressure was on for me to make something vaguely resembling a Union Jack out of plants and flowers!

When Mika introduced me to everyone at Fukkiura the next day, I realized that "gardening event" (which I had assumed involved people from the community working in the garden together) meant that a load of old people stood by a fence bossing me about, which actually was quite funny, and very helpful because I really didn't know what I was doing. Mika, a lady from the Japan-based NGO Peace Boat, and, of course, the resident expert, Katsuzo-san, helped me as I tried to make a Union Jack out of flowers and plants.

In seeing the old people's delight in telling us what to do, then hearing their oohing and aahing as they watched me working on each stage of the flag, I felt really sad that they probably didn't have too many opportunities to boss people about. So many young people had moved away after the earthquake. I wondered how the older people felt about not having much of a chance to pass on knowledge to other generations, as well as simply not being able to experience the joy that comes from watching younger people learn new skills. Passing on knowledge is a lovely part of getting older — in so many ways, the children and young parents here play a big part in people's *emotional* recovery.

It was a privilege to make that Union Jack flower garden with Katsuzo-san and to be able to watch the look on his face as he used the weed trimmer for the first time — he gleefully trimmed everything in sight. It was not such a privilege to discover that by the end of the day I had builder's bum sunburn — I know that everyone on Oshika is pretty relaxed, but surely *someone* could have told me that my backside was hanging out while they bossed me about all day!

I saw a lot of Mika, and to get to Fukkiura I had to drive through what used to be Koamikura, so I ended up driving through this area pretty regularly. One day, best friends Masayo and Keiko, from the Shimizudahama temporary housing community, took me for a walk around the Koamikura wasteland. They showed me the places where their houses used to be, and because they weren't allowed to build on the land, they'd turned it into vegetable and flower gardens — gardening on Oshika wasn't just about keeping active and taking care of shared spaces, it was also about self-sufficiency. Masayo and Keiko tended to their gardens every morning, picking the food that they would eat during the rest of the day. It gave them a routine and a sense of purpose, and kept them active rather than being stuck in their kasetsu. They were creating life, and watching that life grow, and others around them were watching that happen. Who knew who else might be thinking that they could do the same?

I had wanted to do something to help Koamikura, and Masayo and Keiko seemed like good people to start with. They needed sheds — a place to store the tools they worked with, to shelter when taking a break, and to store supplies to perhaps help others start off their own gardens. I allocated ¥70,000 to them, which was made up of donations from ten different people from all over the world, and worked with Kurosawa-san and his team from the Nippon Foundation to build the sheds. We bought the wood from the lumberyard further down the peninsula, keeping the money within Oshika, and set to work.

It was amazing how the construction of something as simple as two sheds could attract so much attention in what appeared to be an utterly deserted area. People on foot, on bicycles, or in cars or trucks would stop by and ask what was going on. There would follow a long conversation about what we were building and why, and word about the garden sheds soon got around. People would sit down and watch us work, all the while making comments that indicated they knew rather a lot about me even though I'd never met them before. If it made them happy, then I didn't mind people on Oshika gossiping about me at all!

A shed doesn't sound vitally important, but when you're putting that shed in the middle of a wasteland, at that stage of disaster recovery, it's surprising how important that shed becomes. I had come on this trip with the intention of just listening to what people needed and trying to make that happen, entirely trusting what the local people said they needed. And I learned that, in a community-driven environment such as this, helping just a few people would often lead to helping a lot more. The sheds were a great example of that as I saw how much they benefitted the wider community when I later heard that Masayo and Keiko were inviting their friends for tea parties next to their gardens.

The equipment needed by the Yagawa fishermen was another great example of this, and I was keen to find a way to support Yagawa — the story of the schoolchildren huddled together at the shrine on top of the hill had stayed with me.

The Oshika fishermen had gone back to work one year after the tsunami, and while the industry was nowhere near what it was before the disaster, these proud men at least had some kind of work that meant they were not dependent on an income from the government. Unlike people in other parts of Japan, and other parts of the world, the people on Oshika weren't too worried about radiation (Yagawa was previously known for its *hoya* — a kind of sea pineapple — which was immensely popular in South Korea until that country banned its import after Fukushima). The prefectural government performed daily tests on the fish from this area, and all but two kinds — sea bass and flat fish — were considered to be completely safe to eat. And there was a mushroom native to the southern part of Miyagi that had been found to be very high in radiation levels. Everybody steered clear of those foods and, in fact, the locals generally considered Tokyo to be more at risk than Oshika. Everybody had seen a national TV program that said the sand along Edogawa River in Tokyo had levels of radiation matching Fukushima's 20 km exclusion zone — far more than the waters around Oshika.

Kurosawa-san told me that the Yagawa fishermen needed a jet-wash and tank used for cleaning their boats, which would cost about ¥120,000. I could allocate funds for that from money raised by the Bolham and Bratton Fleming schools, Microscooters Japan, and the elderly gentlemen from Amity Yokohama, who were still supporting my efforts. I told Kurosawa-san to go ahead and tell the Yagawa fishermen that I'd like to help them by purchasing the jet-wash.

Kurosawa-san and I met at the port with Baba-san, the leader of the Yagawa fishermen, to discuss the details. I didn't know Baba-san or any of the men with him, so I allowed Kurosawa-san to manage all the discussions. This included a request for me to join them while they went to buy the jet-wash. I didn't want the Yagawa fishermen to feel that they couldn't speak openly, and I was very aware that they were proud people — I didn't want my help to make them feel uncomfortable in any way — so I stood politely back while all these discussions were going on.

As a result, the Yagawa fishermen assumed I didn't speak Japanese, but welcomed me on their shopping trip, even though they had aired their concerns to Kurosawa-san about how they should behave around an Englishwoman. He reassured them that I was very laid back and they didn't need to behave any differently around me, but he didn't tell them that my Japanese actually wasn't too bad at all.

So I hopped into Baba-san's car as he drove us and his friend into Ishinomaki, with me sitting quietly in the back. I spent the whole drive admiring the wonderful scenery and listening to their conversation, which mainly consisted of them talking about how pretty they thought I was, and whether I was single or not — unbeknownst to them I understood every word, but I just sat in the back, giggling to myself.

We bought the jet-wash from a small, family-run business, where it became apparent that my Japanese wasn't too bad at all — I often wondered how embarrassed Baba-san and his friend must have been when they realized this. The owner of the business was a lovely, warm man, who told me how this was such a great gift for anyone because it could be used by so many people, but I still hadn't quite grasped the impact of such an item. Back on Oshika, Baba-san thanked me and invited me to join them that afternoon when they would use the equipment for the first time.

When I returned to Yagawa and saw all the fishing boats in a long queue at the port, and the excitement on Baba-san's face, it was then that I realized what a fantastic help this was for their whole community.

Underneath any boat is all sorts of "stuff" from the sea — this gunk is thick, extremely difficult to remove, and can permanently damage the underside of the vessel. Twice a year, every boat needs to undergo a thorough cleaning. The necessary equipment is always stored on land, so it had been washed away by the tsunami. The last time the boats were cleaned was in the October after the disaster. It took all the fishermen working together for five hours to clean just one boat because they had to clean it by hand. With the jet-wash equipment it takes one person half an hour. It was an incredibly powerful piece of equipment, which they invited me to have a go on. I discovered it wasn't just extremely practical but *very* therapeutic to spray off all the chunks of muck and get the underside of a boat really clean.

After the jet-wash demonstration, we stood around drinking coffee as they tried to get the latest Ohara gossip out of me, which I found quite amusing. But every so often they would turn to admire the jet-wash, play with some of the settings, and talk about how great it was that they had this now. It was truly lovely to watch.

It wasn't just the Yagawa fishermen who asked me for the latest news from Ohara — I was now considered an Ohara-jin, so everybody on the peninsula asked me what was going on in the little village where I stayed. Everybody knew that Ohara had recently been in the newspaper — and not just a local one at that.

Against all odds, that summer, almost a year and a half after the disaster, this little village managed to pull off the biggest festival Oshika had seen in a very long time.

18: Ohara Summer Festival

The Ohara summer festival is, without a doubt, the highlight of the year, bringing together all the Ohara-jin, even those who have moved away, and also those non-locals who have been welcomed into the community. From the beginning of the year, Kucho starts making calls to people all over Japan, telling them the date for that year's festival, and inviting them to come for the weekend. All the villages have their own summer festivals, so throughout July, as you drive along the coastal road, you can see huge banners placed at the bottom of any steps that go up into the hills where the shrines are. These banners show that there is a festival about to take place at that shrine, and just the sight of the banners can make me excited, even if I don't know that village very well.

That summer, I had arrived on Oshika the week before Ohara's eagerly anticipated festival. The previous summer's festival hadn't gone ahead for obvious reasons, so this would be the first summer festival since the tsunami. All anybody could talk about was who would carry the mikoshi (portable shrine). With so many young people having moved away from the area after the disaster, there were relatively few people left who were physically able to carry on the more vigorous of the traditions, which were hundreds of years old. The senior Ohara boys spent much of the week on their mobile phones, either borrowing barbecues or gazebos from the government offices because the other villages had lost theirs, too, or calling people from throughout the region and asking them to come along. Kucho had managed to get 70 young people to come — they'd been volunteers in Ohara in the months after the disaster. But everyone was still worried about whether they had enough people to carry the mikoshi, because they'd been given a new mikoshi, and this one was *huge*.

Mikoshi are used to transport the local shrine's god. Wooden poles are placed through the mikoshi's base so that the bearers can heave it up onto their shoulders. Mikoshi vary in size, are elaborately decorated, and are constructed of high-grade lacquered wood with many gold sculptures, fixtures, decorations, and gold leaf on them, so even the small ones are extremely heavy. The bearers lift the mikoshi and move it up and down, over and over again, while walking through the village, trying to get the gold coins and bells that dangle from it to make as much noise as possible — this is considered to bring about good luck. Traditionally in Ohara, despite their gentle manners, the young men would become extremely boisterous while carrying the mikoshi, speeding up to go around corners and even racing it down the dock at the port and into the sea. It's very dangerous, and other members of the village are encouraged to stand back as they watch the mikoshi go by.

Each village on Oshika has its own mikoshi, which is stored in the village's community centre, along with all the other items necessary for a festival. There are taiko drums of different sizes, special clothing to be worn by the young people who carry the mikoshi, banners to go at the bottom of the shrine steps, huge ceramic vessels for *sake*, and the *shishi* — the lion mask and costume worn by three people during the *shishimai* (lion dance). The mikoshi and shishi are unique to each village, and are a big part of their history, culture, and sense of identity. Because most of the community centres were on low ground, many villages lost these items in the tsunami, and because anything to do with shrines — portable or not — is held in reverence, the villagers searched and searched for them in the debris to see if anything could be salvaged. Koamikura lost *everything*. Ohara managed to retrieve its shishi — it had miraculously only suffered a scratch on its nose, which everybody liked to point out and seemed quite proud of.

Ohara's mikoshi had also been retrieved from the debris, but the salt water had damaged it to such an extent that it was ruined and unusable. Sadly, it was now stored away up at the shrine. But a new mikoshi had very generously been donated by Koyo Grand Hotel in Sendai. It had been featured in the regional newspaper, and everybody on Oshika was talking about it. The newspaper photo made it look like it was a very impressive mikoshi.

Seen up close, it was a breathtakingly beautiful piece of art that had been made in the 1960s, and it cost ¥8 million at that time. It was used when the hotel hosted weddings, and it was hoped that it might bring love to the singletons of Ohara as well as general good fortune. Prior to the festival, the new mikoshi was resting on a stage in the community centre where I spent so much of my time, and I couldn't stop looking at it — alternately gazing at the intricate details up close and standing back in awe to admire it from a distance. I took some beautiful photographs of the details, and those photographs still hang in my bedroom today. The gift of this mikoshi had given the people of Ohara a huge boost at this stage of their recovery. Rituals like festivals become even more significant when they are held for the first time after a disaster. And these festivals can't be held without a mikoshi.

The daytimes of my first week on Oshika that summer were busy with my Ohara friends worrying about who would carry the mikoshi, but the evenings were quite different. At 7 p.m. the shrine's bell would ring out over the town and a handful of us would head up the steep steps to practise our performance so we'd be ready for Saturday night. With the kanetsukido destroyed in the earthquake, the bell had been fixed onto some scaffolding, and it hung rather forlornly to one side of the shrine while we practised.

Kuni, the youngest man in Ohara, was learning how to lead the shishimai, and was trying really hard to snap the lion's jaws in just the right way. During the dance, the shishi approaches the audience, who lower their heads so that the shishi can remove any evil spirits by opening then closing its mouth above their heads. Having the shishi snap over your head is a highly anticipated part of the dance, and Kuni was trying his best to make sure he did it right. Every now and again, the older and more experienced Saito-san got up to show Kuni how to do something properly, and everybody cheered in admiration, commenting on how the shishi's eyes came alive with Saito-san's expertise. The perfecting of tiny movements, over and over again, went on all night.

Taira-san was the resident taiko expert, and set the pace on a huge drum while Take-chan encouraged Yachan and me along on the smaller drums, and Kucho and Yuki played flutes. There were just two rhythms to learn, one of which was fairly easy, but the other went at a frantic pace that neither Yachan or I could keep up with for very long. The slower rhythm was to accompany the "waking" of the shishi, and the quicker one would have the shishi moving at such speed that Kuni, and whatever other two people were under the costume with him, emerged at the end pouring with sweat.

This preparation was a big part of what the festival was all about. Instead of sitting in their kasetsu watching pointless television night after night, the town was preparing for a huge celebration — sitting out in the open air, playing music together, dancing around, and entertaining each other. Creating something that would bring even more of their community together and bring new memories of laughter and fun.

Those rehearsals for Ohara's summer festival are one of my favourite things to do in the world, even today. There is nothing quite like sitting at twilight on the floor of a 400-year-old shrine that might be falling apart, but is still so, so beautiful; being high up on a hill overlooking the ocean; watching Kuni lead the shishimai; listening to the drumming and flute-playing; and drinking beer with people I love, who have welcomed me into their lives with open arms. The feeling of serenity that never fails to wash over me every time I do this with them is indescribable. Although ... to be fair ... my thoughts about some of the snacks they suggest might go with my beer — boiled squid mouth, anyone? — are also indescribable.

With all the rehearsals completed, the morning of the festival weekend started with the sound of the shrine's bell ringing out across the village. Its 5:30 a.m. call to the villagers got a prompt response, as everybody sleepily made their way up the steps, picked a job without needing to be told, and got on with it. This was my second festival with Ohara, and I no longer worried about doing the wrong thing, so I just threw myself into it alongside everyone else, laughing at the playful screams and big fusses made when somebody found a leech on themselves.

At 7 a.m. a siren rang out throughout the peninsula, followed by an announcement that there would be a tsunami drill that would urge everyone to get to high ground. These drills were now going to be held annually, and that day's drill was the first since the earthquake. Ohara's designated evacuation zones were the local elementary school, the temporary housing community, and the shrine, so we were all fine where we were and just carried on with our work. Even that early in the morning, and despite the tsunami siren triggering so many memories, there was still such an air of excitement among us all.

With the shrine cleaned inside and out, and the steps leading to it swept clean of every speck of dirt, huge banners were erected in front of the torii at the bottom, and metres and metres of lanterns were taken from the store room next to the shrine. These red lanterns had the names of the people and businesses that had supported the shrine over the years written on them in beautiful calligraphy. They were attached to the shrine's entrance, and hung all the way down either side of the steps, all the way to the road, far below. The celebrations could begin!

Many of the older women in Ohara had yukata, the cotton summer type typically worn at festivals, ready for the occasion. Whereas in Tokyo people tended to buy commercially made yukata (foreigners and Japanese alike), on Oshika it seemed to be the done thing to make your own, which of course, having lost all their clothes in the tsunami, many of the women had found themselves doing that year. Takako-sensei was one of those women.

Soon after my arrival, I surprised Takako-sensei. Her nickname for me had stuck, and when I phoned her, she exclaimed, "Abnormal-san?!" I asked, "Where are you?" to which she replied, "In my kasetsu. Are you in England?" and when I replied, "No, I'm outside your kasetsu!" she rushed to the door to find me standing there grinning away, and we had a huge hug.

She was so excited to show me the yukata she had just finished making especially for the festival. She'd made it by hand, all by herself, with some lovely fabric from Ishinomaki, and wanted me to take lots of photos of her wearing it, insisting that the edge of the sleeve was positioned *just so*. And then we sat down to coffee and biscuits as she pulled out the flowers she had started pressing last month — her pressed flowers have been featured in several books in Japan. Her special equipment was all washed away by the tsunami — all the things she had collected over years and years of this very elaborate labour of love were gone.

Only a few months earlier, Takako-sensei had talked and talked about the tsunami every time I saw her, but this time she didn't speak of it once, nor did she speak of the ancestral home and beautiful garden she had spoken so wistfully of before. Instead, she was full of life, talking about what she was creating *now* and would create in the future, pointing out every detail and unique part of each individual flower she had pressed since last month. They were all painstakingly folded into tissue paper with the date of pressing written on the top fold. The flowers could only be handled by special tweezers, and were sealed carefully in a homemade version of vacuum packing that she showed me. She'd hurt her wrist, so I did the awkward manoeuvres for her. One of the things I loved about Takako-sensei was her bossiness, and usually it's a trait I really don't like in people. But Takako-sensei's bossiness made me feel safe and cared about and that she somehow knew what I was feeling and needing, even though I still struggled to find the right vocabulary. I suppose this is how she made generations of children feel as she guided them through preschool.

The Takako-sensei I'd first met hated the time spent alone cooped up in her kasetsu. The long hours that passed with her just sitting in the little room by herself made her feel very depressed. She dreaded the evenings, saying that the nights were worst of all, and I would frequently get a call asking whether I wanted to pop over for dinner. Now, however, as I watched Takako-sensei sit and create these beautiful works of art, carefully placing one petal after another and arching a few grasses delicately over the top "like a mountain," she said that the time just flew by.

Takako-sensei, along with the other Ohara residents, made their way up to the shrine for that evening's ceremony and entertainment. The women wore yukata for the first time in a long time, and even the Ohara boys scrubbed up nicely. The boys commented on how nice I looked in my yukata, like a proper Japanese woman, then laughed as they said that they hadn't even realized I was a woman until then.

I had brought my yukata with me especially for the occasion, but forgot the instructions for how to put it on, so had rushed over to Kucho's house just before the festival to ask Fukumi-san to help me. A call was made to Katsumi-san, the village's kimono expert, and she arrived to dress me properly. Then the two women gave me a stern talking to, asking me to try my best to behave like a lady for the evening and not to go throwing my legs and arms all over the place like I usually do.

Up at the shrine, the festival began with a small ceremony followed by a beautiful dance by the maidens from a shrine based at Mount Fuji, which Ohara is twinned with. This was followed by the taiko and shishimai performance, which went brilliantly. Kuni later told me how he was so nervous that he was shaking all over; I told him he did a fantastic job. Once the main performance was over, it was time for eating and drinking, after which the Mount Fuji guests departed, and the locals could relax. As the drinks flowed, the taiko drumming got louder and louder, with one young man after another jumping up to get under the shishimai and give it a go.

Behaving "like a lady" was killing me, and it wasn't long before I'd leapt up and got under the shishimai with the local men, emerging covered in sweat with my hair all over the place and yukata skew-whiff, as Fukumi-san rolled her eyes, not especially surprised. Legs and arms very much thrown about.

The celebrations went on into the early hours of the morning, but there was a sudden moment of silence when Toshiyuki Suzuki (known as Tochi) appeared. Tochi was from the Sendai mountains, and had been drawn to Ohara after the disaster. He still helped out whenever he could. He was a *yamabushi*, a hermetic "warrior monk." Yamabushi are considered to have magical powers in Japan, and they are deeply respected by others. Despite his gravitas, he was very laid back and good fun, and immediately joined in with the partying — he had rather a lot of catching up to do. Tochi and Kuni actually slept at the shrine, which really made me giggle — I couldn't imagine people in England spending all night partying in a church and crashing there. They were made of strong stuff, however, as there was no mooching about with a hangover the next day — it was all hands on deck first thing in the morning for the all-day celebration, which included the much-anticipated carrying of the mikoshi around Ohara.

The mikoshi was first carried to the bottom of the shrine steps, where we left it while we all went to the shrine at the top of the stairs for a small ceremony. Afterward, back down at the mikoshi, there was another ceremony in which Kucho expressed his gratitude to the chairperson of the Koyo Grand Hotel, who had made the effort to come along and join the festival. Tochi was there in full yamabushi regalia, wearing his white robes and carrying his conch shell, which he blew into to signal the start of the mikoshi procession. It was a beautiful sound that echoed throughout the village.

About 30 of us arranged ourselves around the poles at the base of the mikoshi; young men and just a few women of all nationalities led by the younger Ohara boys — a *most* unusual sight anywhere in Japan, where mikoshi would usually be carried by local Japanese men only. Together we lifted the mikoshi and carried it over the land where the village used to be, all the way to the little pebble beach, with Kuni loudly leading a chant to wish everyone good luck. It was hard work.

Onodera-san went out in front of the mikoshi in his little truck, making sure no traffic or pedestrians were in the way, followed by Kucho and Taira-san in another truck, playing instruments. Other senior villagers threw salt on the ground as we went along (to ward off evil spirits), followed by the priest, then the hotel chairperson, and all the people who were taking it in turns to carry the mikoshi. For a while I walked with the hotel chairperson, who spoke excellent English and said that he had visited the UK many times to play golf. I warmed to him immediately. I wasn't surprised to find him to be a very lovely man; after all, he had organized the generous gift of the mikoshi.

After a little break we carried the mikoshi to the port, where traditionally it would then be carried into the sea, but the new mikoshi was considered too expensive and elaborate to do that with, so it was set down while the priest prayed to the god in it, to us, and to the sea — a quiet, emotional moment in the midst of such excitement. Then it was off with it to the temporary housing community, where the old people came out to cheer, and then on to the two businesses that were left in the village ... Yachan's factory and the temporary ramen restaurant. We paused outside each of them and shouted extra loud as we lifted the mikoshi up as high as we could before bringing it low down to the ground, hoping to bring the businesses good fortune.

We had breaks at every place we stopped — it was such hard work that these breaks were very much needed. At each break, cans of juice and beer would appear seemingly from nowhere, and we would be offered snacks and ice cream from the residents or factory workers. Even though there wasn't very much left of Ohara at all, we paraded the mikoshi around the village for about three hours, working off the effects of the rapidly consumed alcohol before the next stop.

You could see that the Ohara boys *loved* the opportunity to show off and generally be really rowdy, because they were boisterous in a way I had never seen before. When we arrived at our last stop — the community centre, which sits on a little hill — people from all over were standing on the hill to take photos, and there was a sudden surge of energy as we raced the mikoshi up the sloping driveway, then turned it around and around, shouting and shouting, as the older ladies looked on, worried that someone would get hurt. It was honestly a miracle that nobody got injured. I had never been part of something like this before, and quite enjoyed the look of surprise on the old ladies' faces when they saw me in the middle of all this madness. It was an incredible experience.

Despite the rowdiness and all the heaving up and down of the mikoshi over and over again during the festival, I could see that it was treated with great pride and respect. In between all the shouting and bravado, during every break the Ohara boys carefully wiped down the mikoshi. Young and old alike stood admiring the details everywhere we took it. Leaving a beautiful treasure of such cultural significance sitting in the centre without any protection was something that Kucho-san and the other senior members of the village had already started to be concerned about.

I'd started to sit Kucho down during this trip to ask him what people needed at this stage of the recovery, to see whether there were any gaps I might be able to fill. It had been difficult for him to answer at first — people had temporary homes now, but pretty much *everything* else was still needed. Where do you start? And he wasn't used to people just asking him what was needed. So I would gently guide him, perhaps telling him a little bit about a sponsor who was interested in donating some money toward something that matched their interests or industry, or giving Kucho a budget to prompt some ideas.

It was when I was telling him about Tokyo Photowalkers, who'd asked me to find something their ¥20,000 could support, that Kucho told me that the new mikoshi needed to be protected from gathering dust in between festivals. It sounded like such a small thing, but it was the perfect match for a group of photographers who would appreciate the need to protect something so beautiful, so Kucho ordered a custom-made cover for the mikoshi, and it's still used today. It's completely transparent, so the mikoshi can be admired in the centre, all year round.

I also had about ¥70,000 from those "Bad Mothers" at Waterbeach Primary — the mums who, among other events, had held a wild karaoke night in order to raise money for Oshika. I knew that those party girls would have *loved* everything about the festival and wanted to find a good match for their donation. Kucho said that the special white clothing worn by all the mikoshi-bearers needed paying for, which was perfect. The outfits would be used every single year, and would be a big part of bringing this community together in the passing on of cultural traditions as they rebuilt their lives, as well as giving them a LOT of fun and laughter.

In the years to come, there were other festival-related items that Ohara would need assistance with, and I was always able to find someone within my network who was happy to help — people understood the importance of supporting community rituals after such a disaster. Tokyo Mothers' Group paid for a barbecue set, and the lovely gentlemen at Amity Yokohama paid for a gazebo, so Ohara would no longer need to worry about borrowing such items from others. They were able to plan their festivals and other social events, knowing that they had everything they needed. But those "things" that were donated weren't just about the festivals, they were about the great sense of pride and joy that the whole town had again, and the knowledge that people still cared about them.

By the end of my third visit to Oshika, sixteen months after the disaster, I had developed a good system for channelling the care that people had for my new friends. When sponsors contacted me expressing a desire to donate, I would ask them what kind of project they would like to support, and how much they would like to contribute. At the same time, the local people had started to open up to me when I asked them what they needed. Granted, at this stage it took a *lot* of pushing on my part, but I was starting to compile a list of projects that needed financial support, so I was able to look down my list, and more often than not, I'd find something that was a good match. Or I would share that list to my network, and something would speak to someone who had been looking for an opportunity to help in Tohoku.

I was always transparent about what I was doing and how I was doing it, including any financial interactions (which never included any administrative costs or general expenses involved for me to be there because I covered those myself). I developed a system of managing those donations that was to become incredibly effective, and that involved keeping sponsors fully informed along the way. People outside Oshika liked what I was doing there.

And the Oshika people seemed to like me being there. Talk about what I was doing each day would spread throughout the peninsula, and I liked to think that if they were talking about what I was doing, then they were at least talking about progress or the future … not dwelling on the past. If my clumsy, unladylike ways gave them something to laugh about together, then I didn't mind — there were so many ways to spread love and happiness in the world!

Unlike the official volunteers, I went in and out of people's homes, kasetsu or not, just as I would with any other friends. People started to see me as a friend or part of their community.

Our relationship changed into one where my Oshika friends helped me, too, which initially I felt rather uncomfortable about because I didn't want to burden anyone. But I realized that in order to have a truly equal relationship, I sometimes had to let them in when I felt vulnerable, just as they were allowing me in while they were vulnerable. And they liked the chance to take care of me — if I got sick, they brought me bowls of soup and packets of medicine.

I started to feel like part of the Oshika community and to look at my friends there a little differently, too — they were just people, and as I'd discovered on the very first day of that trip, shit happens in life! Granted, an unbelievably large amount of shit had happened to them, but they were getting on with it, as best they could. In many cases, with huge smiles and lots of laughter.

On my previous trip, there had been something about those huge sandbags along the water's edge that had stuck in my mind — that they somehow represented the resilience of the people on Oshika. The sandbags were still there, but on this trip it was the flowers that were growing everywhere amid the grasses that struck me — despite everything, they were growing wild in places where the tsunami had hit. Flowers were growing in unexpected places, where nobody lived, where no soil or fertilizer had been placed, and no care or attention had been paid. They were growing in places that were once covered in sea water and debris; places from which trucks and diggers had lifted out tons and tons of metal and wood; places that had been trampled over by thousands of feet as volunteers worked to clear away debris.

This time, the flowers on Oshika represented the people. They were blossoming, regardless of what had happened to the ground beneath them.

19: Creating Beautiful Spaces

"When you came here last year, you were full of ideas. But we were still in shock and not ready to think about the future. But you haven't given up. You just keep coming back. And we can't really believe it. But now, we're ready."

These were Abe-san's heartfelt words to me in March 2013, two years after the disaster, during my fourth trip to Oshika. By this time, the locals were starting to realize that they'd have to start moving forward on their own, and that the level of support they could expect from the government was limited. They were living in a kind of limbo — the fishing industry was recovering very, very slowly and many people were still out of work; people still didn't know what they were allowed to do with land they owned that the tsunami had reached; very few new buildings were going up, so visual signs of progress were limited; and while people had been allocated temporary housing units, any permanent housing seemed a very, very long way off. The second year post-disaster was a very difficult one for Oshika.

The local government had at least decided that a little hill area in Ohara was suitable to build houses on, and was prepared to build a limited number of houses there. The houses would be available to rent at 10 percent of the usual rate for 20 years, after which normal rent prices would be charged. If more people wanted houses than the government were prepared to support, then individuals would have to pay for them. It had taken two years for this decision to be made, and the government officials arrived on Valentine's Day to inform everyone, just as I was heading out with a car full of chocolates to deliver again like the previous year. I could tell they were government people: not by their nice cars but instead by the miserable looks on their faces — Oshika people didn't look like that.

Takako-sensei hadn't waited around for the local government to tell her where she could live. A few months earlier, she'd found a way around the building regulations that said you couldn't build anywhere that the tsunami had hit: she decided to raise some land she owned further inland from her previous home, and built a new house on it. Takako-sensei's house was the first permanent building to go up in Ohara.

She was thrilled to show me around her new house and, quite unexpectedly, tears began to sting my eyes. I remembered how she had talked with such sadness about her ancestral home as she shared the stress of living in the temporary housing community. I knew how much having her own home meant to her. She cheerfully showed me how she prepared vegetables while looking out her kitchen window, keeping an eye out for the Union Jack flags flying from my car as I drove by in the distance. She was like a different person.

The emotional impact of living in the temporary housing communities could not be overestimated. Yes there had been the relief when they had first been built, but after that, it was almost as though the people living in them had been ignored. There was a lack of communication between the decision-makers and the locals, and the locals were frustrated because they felt that they weren't involved in making decisions that would seriously affect their lives. The living conditions created a huge amount of stress for people, and at that time it seemed as though there would be no end to it. The elderly truly believed they would die in those little units.

One of Ohara's younger residents — Saito-san — had actually passed away the previous September, of heart failure ... *way* too young. He was such a lovely man and he played a major part in uplifting the spirits of everyone in the community, partly because of his role in the passing on of traditions, partly because of his leadership, and also simply because he was the father of the only two children left in Ohara. The other children at Ohara Elementary School came from neighbouring villages. Ohara would not be the same without the sound of Saito-san's laugh, and I remember the kindness he always showed me. His Thai wife, Emi, found it impossible to stay on Oshika — her job was on the mainland and the stress of living in the temporary houses was just too much for her. So Ohara lost its only children.

At times it seemed like things were moving backward rather than forward. Kucho and I watched as one of the few buildings left standing in Ohara was pulled down despite the fact that residents wanted to keep it and it was safe to use. It was the little government building just across from the centre's car park, right by the playground. It was the building I had walked through the snow to during my first month on Oshika because it had a toilet when the centre didn't have one. It had a reception area, a large main room, two smaller rooms, a kitchen, and the bathroom. It would have made a perfect tourist information centre, tsunami museum, or cafe. It was perfectly usable, and Kucho had asked whether Ohara could have the building, but it was to be torn down "because the budget has been set to do so." Kucho and I worked out that it had probably cost about ¥2 million to demolish a perfectly good building — money that could have been used for other, more positive actions. Even the demolition team were full of apologies, saying what a waste it was, and we all agreed that it had been a stupid decision by the local government. The demolition led Kucho and I to come up with the phrase "Big Baka Basho Hito," which literally means "Big Stupid Place People," and we used it to refer to the local government. We still use it today, especially when a decision has clearly been made by them that makes absolutely no sense to the locals.

Destroying that building did absolutely nothing to encourage people to take positive steps forward. Two years after the disaster, when the locals were emerging from their state of shock, was the time to be creating new out of the old; the time to look for opportunities where local residents could create something they could look upon with pride.

As per my previous trips, I asked Kucho what he needed, but unlike my previous trips, this time he didn't hesitate to respond, although it wasn't quite what I was expecting …

"We need a bus shelter."

I was bringing a *lot* of support with me on this trip, which would be my longest as I was staying on Oshika for two whole months. People had become inspired by my efforts the previous summer, and the time between this trip and the last had been filled with more talks and lots of fundraising, both in the UK and Japan.

Before I left for Japan, I'd updated Bratton Fleming on what was achieved with the money they'd raised at the sleepover. The children were very excited at being reminded of that fun night they'd spent in the hall, although the teachers still looked slightly traumatized. As the children filed out of the hall after one of my talks, a little boy asked me when they could do the sleepover again!

I visited St Joseph's Catholic Primary School, Devonport High School for Girls, Devonport High School for Boys, Woodfield Primary, and City College in Plymouth. I gave assemblies; joined geography, and travel and tourism classes; and talked not just about Japan, but also about the importance of helping others. I also met with Kagemusha Taiko in Newton Abbot (a taiko drumming school), and gave a speech to Plympton Rotary Club at the invitation of my old school friend Darren Hands — this was my second experience of speaking at a rotary club, which had previously been unfamiliar to me. I decided that I really liked rotary clubs. I loved the way that they promoted the idea of service, and not only talked a good talk but walked a good walk, too, raising huge amounts of money for local, national, and international beneficiaries. At the end of the talk, they asked me to come up with a project that they could support, so I added them to my list of interested sponsors and hoped to find a project that matched them.

During that time I also established a base in Cirencester — a relatively small town in Gloucestershire that was *worlds* apart from busy Tokyo. In my Tokyo days, I could never have imagined living somewhere like Cirencester, but I liked it there. The old stone buildings are beautiful and the people so friendly. I'd been completely in awe of the lovely Christmas market they'd had in front of the huge 12th-century church. There were rows and rows of beautiful stalls selling lovely handmade goods in such a festive atmosphere — it was my first time to see a Christmas market and it had a big impact on me.

I was still working four days a month, publishing my one magazine, but had established a base for my talks and was focusing on them being held only in Gloucestershire, where Cirencester is, or Devon, where mum still lived in Plymouth, so I had some spare time to catch up on some of my other publishing projects. And I started working remotely with Nick Johnston, an entrepreneur friend from Tokyo, now in Singapore. Nick was writing a book on building a business in Japan and asked me to edit and help him publish it, so we started regular contact and correspondence.

Before heading up to Oshika, I'd given some talks in and around Tokyo, at Kspace International School, the International Women's Network of Tsukuba, Meikei High School, Summerhill International School, and, of course, at Ohana International School, run by Shelley Sacks. These school communities were busy raising money any way they could.

By this time, two years after 311, I'd managed to generate ¥3.4 million, and there was much more to come. *Of course* we'd be able to get Ohara a bus shelter.

But it wouldn't be just any old bus shelter. I was overwhelmed with the desire that *anything* new built on Oshika *must* be beautiful. It would have to somehow compensate for the fact that this area was still a wasteland, especially at this time of year when the grasses and flowers were nowhere to be seen. It would have to make up for the mountains and mountains of debris that still lined the coast; the dump trucks noisily making their way through the peninsula, leaving dust and dirt in their wake; and the senseless demolition of perfectly good buildings. And it would have to be made with *love*. My feelings about this became even stronger when I found out that Kucho-san had repeatedly asked the local government for a little bus shelter and had been repeatedly told that there wasn't any money available with which to build one, yet they could spend ¥2 million on demolishing a perfectly good building! I decided that if Ohara needed a bus shelter, I'd build them one that was *unlike any shelter anyone had ever seen!*

The peninsula's bus service had become a lifeline for many people — it connected Oshika to Watanoha and central Ishinomaki, where many jobs, supermarkets, and even friends and family were located. The public transport system was relied upon not just for practical support, but also for emotional support. However, these little coastal villages are very much exposed to the elements, and the winters can be harsh, with biting cold wind, and massive sprays of sea water that shoot high in the air and drench everyone within their reach. For the two years since the disaster, all Ohara had had in the form of a bus stop was a little bench just a few feet away from the open waters of Sendai Bay.

In my mind I could see a beautiful little building made of wood that was warm and cosy, with a sofa and cushions, framed photographs on the walls, and a little coffee table in the middle. The kind of place you would just *love* to spend time in, a place that would always make people smile. A little haven where people could wait, completely protected from the wind, rain, and spray from the bay outside. A beautiful little living room in the middle of bare, empty land, in a town where very few people even had a living room anymore.

During my Tokyo talks, the Summerhill mums had asked me to find a project they could support, and the bus shelter seemed to be a good match for their ¥200,000 budget. Also, while I was at Meikei High School, I'd been invited to join a teacher and his family at their Tsukuba home for dinner. The second I stepped inside Stephen Bird's beautiful wood cabin home, I was overwhelmed — I had already envisioned his home in my mind! And in my mind that building was on Oshika — on that patch of land for sale that I was always looking at. It was such an incredible coincidence that I'd asked for an introduction to the architect, Tsukasa-san at Kigumi, a small construction company just outside of Tokyo. Tsukasa-san and I emailed one another a few times and attempted to speak on the phone, really just saying hello rather than planning anything, but when the idea for the bus shelter arose, I immediately thought of him.

I asked Tsukasa-san what he'd be able to do with that kind of budget. His English was great on email, so I tried calling him to discuss ideas, but we were completely unable to communicate on the phone. He was later to tell people that he never really understood who I was, what I was doing, or what I really wanted from him, but he was overcome with a sense that he simply *had* to go to Oshika and meet me. It was all very odd because from the second we met in person, we greeted each other with a huge hug like we were long-lost friends. And we were instantly on the same wavelength.

Tsukasa-san designed the bus shelter using remnants of materials from other projects, which is why he was able to keep the costs so low. During the planning stages it became apparent that the location of the previous bus stop would be problematic — the land belonged to the local government and it would take about a month to get permission to build from them, and even then there was no guarantee that they would give that permission. The sponsorship money was there, the architect had been found, the materials had been sourced — but we didn't have the land.

That is, we didn't have permission until Kucho-san suggested that we put the shelter on the opposite side of the road, which was privately owned, so permission would only be required from the owner — there would be no need to involve the local government at all. Takahashi-san, who had once owned the ramen restaurant, owned the land all around that area. In recent months, Takahashi-san's friend had built a big storage shed there, into which the old man had put any belongings he'd managed to retrieve from the debris. I had seen the shed before, and something about it had always made me feel so sad, but I didn't know why at the time — but when I learned that it belonged to Takahashi-san, who had lost his beloved wife so tragically on 311 at that very spot, I understood why the building had such sad energy around it.

Takahashi-san immediately gave permission for us to build a bus shelter on his land. He didn't use the space for anything other than storing memorabilia, because he wasn't allowed to build a personal residence on it. He wasn't going to do anything with it — he spent every day walking around the wasteland, trying to keep his spirits up so he could assure Miyoko, his daughter, that he was OK when she made her daily call to him.

As we stood next to the storage shed, talking about the bus shelter, I asked Takahashi-san whether he would like me to brighten up his building with some paint. He said he *would* like that, so I asked what colours he thought would be good — he told me to go ahead and do whatever I wanted — so I did just that! I started by painting the whole building bright blue, then I painted a red heart on it, then a white heart, then another heart, then more and more hearts. I couldn't stop painting hearts on Takahashi-san's building — I was consumed with the urge to give this dear man, who was mourning his wife, as much love as I possibly could. People stopped and asked me what I was doing, then got out of their vehicles to join me. I accosted volunteers who were sitting around the centre and persuaded them to join in — there was never much sitting around in Ohara when I was there. Yukio-san was roped in. Pretty soon, the whole building was absolutely covered in hearts, with a special one by the door inside of which I painted the first names of Takahashi-san and his wife in English: MITSUKO + KIYOSHI FOREVER. He loved it.

Now that we had the land, it was time to tackle the bus shelter itself — Tsukasa-san first laid the concrete foundation, locally sourced, and a group of us started work. It was terrible timing — a very heavy rainstorm descended on the peninsula on our first day. We worked under a tarpaulin that we attached to the heart-covered storage shed and the crane that Tsukasa-san had brought with him. Despite the tarpaulin and my "waterproof" puffy jacket, I was soaked to the skin by 11:30 a.m. and worked another five hours while wearing it. The following day was the same. Tsukasa-san and his team worked so incredibly hard and did not follow the "Ohara working rules" at all — rules that I would soon learn from Ogata-san, Ohara's grumpy carpenter. Tsukasa-san and his team took only very short breaks and lunches, and worked until it was too dark to work anymore.

On one of the construction days, Stephen Bird brought his family up to Oshika — coincidentally, he was very familiar with the peninsula and had rather a soft spot for it; it had been a favourite family vacation spot prior to the disaster. There was quite an amusing moment when Stephen, to Kucho-san's horror, ran off in the pouring rain to get coffees from a vending machine for us all: "Is the *guest* going to get the coffee?!" to which Stephen's Japanese wife replied that they weren't guests, but friends. I enjoyed explaining to Kucho-san how we were all the kind of people who appreciated being allowed to feel at home, and going to grab coffees for everyone made it feel like you were immediately welcomed. After explaining this little cultural difference, I worked with Stephen's son on the wall insulation, and the others went over to Kobuchi to help the Sasakis with the wakame harvest — they were having such difficulty finding seasonal staff who were prepared to come and work in the former disaster zone, and I'd been doing my best to spread the word and encourage people to come and work on Oshika. The Sasakis had completed their building work and now had an annex consisting of three rooms filled with bunk beds where the seasonal workers could stay — if only they could get people to come.

Every day, whether I was painting hearts on the building, or working on the bus shelter, Takahashi-san insisted on joining me, even if it was just to hang around. I was happy that he wasn't wandering about the village, deep in his own thoughts, and that we were giving him things to laugh and smile about. I started sending Facebook messages to his daughter, telling her how her Dad was doing each day, and telling her not to worry — and when the weather was really awful I would threaten him with calling Miyoko to tell her that he wasn't staying warm and dry at home. There was a lot of laughter throughout the construction.

When I was eventually to meet Miyoko in person, I cried when she told me that after I covered the storage shed with hearts, her father smiled again for the first time since losing his wife.

Finally the rain stopped, and Tsukasa-san and his team happily threw off the tarpaulin and finished the bus shelter. Kucho and I drove a truck to the Sendai branch of IKEA. I'd contacted them just to see whether they might be able to offer a discount on anything. They'd immediately understood what I was trying to do and very kindly offered a couple of two-seater sofas completely free of charge. Kucho and I went to collect the sofas, and he left some fresh wakame in the store for the staff to enjoy. He had never been to an IKEA before and loved the whole experience.

The next day, when the paint inside the bus stop had dried, it was time to put all the finishing touches together. In addition to the IKEA sofas, there was a garden furniture set that had been donated by Amanda Jane Jones from Tokyo, so we made an outdoor terrace, and there were ornaments, cushions, and plants to organize. I'd printed out photos I'd taken of the locals laughing together to put in frames and hang on the walls — photos of new, happy memories to treasure. And there was a piece of artwork that the Summerhill kids had made.

The completed bus shelter, and everything around it, turned out perfectly. The shelter not only made everyone in Ohara smile, but also made everyone who saw it smile. I lost count of the number of people who pulled over to find out what we were doing, to take pictures, and who went inside to try out the sofas. It made the Ohara people so *proud* of their town and became the talk of the peninsula — I was told that where people would once have stood looking out to sea to take photographs, they would now stand with their backs to the sea and take photographs of the famous bus shelter and the big blue building covered in red and white hearts.

The bus shelter was a beautiful space that happened to be mainly used by adults — and I was keen to create a beautiful space for the children, too. Gloucestershire-based school Thomas Keble had raised just over £1800 for Oshika during their annual sponsored walk. I managed to find the perfect use for a donation that was generated by children being active outdoors — a playground.

One of the reasons I wanted to build the playground was so that parents had somewhere safe to take their children to play, but also provided a place where the kids could be noisy, as kids naturally are. I'd already heard mothers tell me how hard it was to keep their children quiet in the kasetsu with their incredibly thin walls. And 60 percent of the children lived in temporary housing communities. I hoped that the playground would support the parents as much as the kids. Children are more resilient than we think — I always felt like I wanted to look out for the parents.

Outside the Ohara Community Centre was a rusty old swing set on a small piece of dusty land — the tsunami had destroyed everything else. Despite that, the children from the school still rushed to the swings while they waited for the school bus. Along with the school's vice-principal, I searched through a catalogue, looking for an all-in-one outdoor playset that would be small enough to fit on the land, but discovered that it wasn't possible to get hold of such sets in Japan.

Good friend and fellow Tokyo entrepreneur Michael Anop had set up Playground of Hope in the aftermath of the disaster, building huge playgrounds for children all over Tohoku. Michael's knowledge about the types of play equipment that were needed in the Tohoku area was amazing — he could talk forever about the kind of wood needed given the climate, transportation issues to be aware of, and how to construct the playsets. I would have loved to work with him, but Playground of Hope's playgrounds were way above the Thomas Keble budget and were designed for huge spaces — Ohara needed something fairly simple that you could probably get from Toys"R"Us, so I contacted them.

Toys"R"Us not only had the right kind of playset, but could ship it directly to Ohara, and when the invoice arrived, the company had very kindly only charged me shipping cost, so in effect the playset was free, leaving me with a bigger budget to work with to kit out the rest of the space. During my previous visit, I'd noticed that there was a huge shipping container at the back of the playground — very practical, but not an attractive backdrop to a playground — and I thought how lovely it would look if it were covered in smiling faces. And when I arrived this time, I was delighted to see that a kind and creative soul had somehow thought to do *just* that!

As soon as we had some decent weather, Kucho-san, Onodera-san, and I set to work on building the playset. As the set had come from Australia, the instructions were all in English, so I was designated as the *toryo* (supervisor). I *love* building things like this — I love following the instructions, seeing all the pieces come together, and using drills and hammers. Kucho and Onodera-san just wanted to guess what fitted where, yet couldn't picture what the playset was supposed to look like, whereas I obsessively stuck to the instructions.

Needless to say, I learned a lot of interesting new words from Onodera-san as we put it together.

I also learned a lot about how Ohara's grumpy carpenter, Ogata-san, liked to work. He was supervising a team working on the construction of the "*dashi* house" next to the playground, where we were working. The dashi house was to store the new wooden float (dashi) Ogata-san had made for the February festival, which is held to bring good luck and success to the fishermen at the start of the season.

Kucho-san found it hilarious to refer to Ogata-san as *Nihon no toryo* (the Japanese supervisor), and me as *Igirisu no toryo* (the English supervisor). At 10 a.m. on the dot, Ogata-san insisted everybody stop and have a break. At midday he did the same, and sent everyone off for lunch. They would be back at 1 p.m. on the dot. He also stopped everyone for a break at 3 p.m. If I wanted to carry on working just a few minutes into the breaks, he would start grumbling about the Igirisu no toryo and I'd later be asked whether people took breaks in England. So, even though we were working on different projects, I stopped whenever Ogata-san wanted to and learned to rest now and again — something that didn't come very naturally to me.

I also learned a lot just watching how Ogata-san worked. In building the dashi house, he worked *with* the wood — he didn't measure everything and then cut it; instead, he cut it roughly, put it together, and then cut off the extra wood so that it fit together perfectly. There is a real beauty and creativity to his method — it's like he works with all the lumps and bumps presented to him and creates something in harmony with its environment.

The playset was already cut and ready to be fitted together. The wood smelled absolutely beautiful — it was lovely to work with and to watch it all come together. And it was great to work together with some of the Ohara boys (along with random volunteers who happened to be around) on something representing a new start, rather than clearing up something from a tragic past. It was a good example of a project that the locals were very much involved with that was supported by non-locals.

Every day the kids would run down the hill from the elementary school and wait for their buses, always curious about what we were doing, and as soon as part of the playset was actually in the playground, they started to throw themselves all over it. In the UK there would have been a huge health and safety issue, but there is quite a different attitude to things like that on Oshika, where common sense prevails. So we continued building around them. And actually, it was lovely to build it like that. Every day I looked forward to when the kids would come tearing down the hill, throw their bags to the ground, and then throw themselves all over the playground as it was being created around them.

Once the playset was made, it was time to think about the other elements of the playground; the elements that would make it a beautiful space. We put plants and bushes all around the playground, all the while aware of the harsh weather and the deer searching for food. I repainted some wooden flower boxes I'd found and planted bright flowers in them, while Kucho made protective nets for them.

I wanted to incorporate two things that had been damaged during the tsunami. First, the panda — he was battered and scratched, and had a few holes in his side. He had lost a couple of the concrete bases that used to be attached to his feet, and he'd also lost his nose, along with his smile. So I repaired the holes, and set to work repainting him, giving him a lovely new smile again. My other attempt at repairing something that had been damaged was the ice cream cone. This was the giant ice cream cone that had been carried by the tsunami from another town and had landed at Ohara — it had been very badly damaged and had huge holes in its side, but had become something that always made people laugh — they thought it was funny that the cone had ended up in Ohara. I patched it up using old beer cans, duct tape, and filler, and gave it a couple of coats of paint.

Second, the playground needed a fence — I visited Homac (a chain of hardware stores in Japan), where Kucho's son worked. I immediately recognized him … he was like a mini-Kucho. I found some fencing in Homac that was a similar colour to the wood used in the playset, and Yukio-san and I put the fencing up all around the playground area. The fencing really did finish everything off beautifully. Then I made a large toy box to go in the playground — there was enough money to buy some outdoor toys, but I wanted them to be stored at the playground, not in a separate building. I felt confident enough to have a go at making the toy box all by myself, so, using some of the tricks I had learned by observing Ohara's grumpy carpenter, I did it. Then I visited the nearest Toys"R"Us, and bought roller-skates, pogo sticks, hoops, and all sorts of other outdoor toys and games. It was nice to be able to give a little back to the company that had helped make the playground happen. And Microscooters Japan very kindly sent up some scooters to go in the toy box, too.

In preparation for the playground's official opening ceremony, I borrowed Endo-san's ice cream machine from the konbini, and tied a big red bow around the toy box. When the children pulled the ribbon to open the lid of the toy box, they were amazed at what they saw in there! The playground and the area around it, usually used for parking, was filled with children playing on the swings, skating and scooting around, and throwing Frisbees to one another. It was wonderful to see!

I felt incredibly emotional when I finished the playground — it had a really big impact on me, perhaps because it triggered a memory from when I was about six years old. I was living in Saudi Arabia then, in a compound for British and American families, because of my father's job with the Saudi air force. In between each set of about ten villas on the compound, there was a small communal garden, and one morning we had woken up to find that in each of those communal gardens, a playset had been installed overnight. I remember being incredibly excited about it, but even more so, very touched that somebody would do such a kind thing. In finishing the playground for the Ohara children, I suddenly realized that I had perhaps made some other children feel the same way I had when I was so young, and it made me quite emotional.

Even today, when I hear the children race down the little hill from Ohara Elementary School, I get a lump in my throat at seeing the happiness they get from the playground. I remember looking at it quietly one evening, and thinking that if I never did anything else with my life, then it wouldn't matter, because I had done this.

Like the bus shelter, the playground became a hot topic of conversation on the peninsula and people soon began to stop by Ohara just to let their children play in it. The playground not only allowed the local children to have fun, but it also sent a very important message: the village was rebuilding, young people were valued, and people were looking to the future.

20: Creating Beautiful Memories

I believe that an important part of looking to the future on Oshika is to create memories that aren't necessarily about the disaster — events that people can look back on with a smile rather than with sorrow, that they can laugh about with their friends, and take photographs of to share. Things to look forward to as well as reflect upon.

Kucho, Yukio-san, and I went on a crazy road trip to Ibaraki Prefecture that spring that we still talk about even now. I'd been told about thousands of cherry tree saplings that were available for free for Tohoku, and asked whether Kucho wanted any for Ohara. The three of us had set off at 5:30 a.m. for a five-hour drive to dig up 60 saplings — 50 for Ohara and 10 for the Sasakis. The saplings were free, but the journey generated some cost, which was paid for by a donation from Anna Mertens, who had happened to visit Oshika just a week before the disaster and had been deeply moved by its beauty. Bringing beauty back to Oshika was a perfect match for her donation.

While we'd all been too tired to talk on the long drive there, digging up the saplings woke us up for the drive back. Kucho had never forgotten my karaoke performance at Akiu Onsen, so he bombarded me with requests for Beatles songs the whole way back to Oshika. I'd sing them, and Kucho and Yukio-san joined in with what they thought the choruses were. None of us will ever forget that road trip. We planted one of the cherry tree saplings in the middle of the playground, and it blooms every single year, providing the beautiful cherry blossoms that are so beloved by the Japanese.

Then there are the knitting clubs I set up — one in the Ohara centre and another in the temporary housing community. The wool and needles were sent up from Tokyo, and we'd sit around knitting and chatting. The temporary housing community sessions were full of hardcore female knitters, and would go on all day, with people popping back to their kasetsu to bring snacks to share. Elderly Mr Nagashima didn't knit and wouldn't let me teach him, but insisted on joining because he liked hanging out with us. I loved seeing him and his wife together — they both had what my friend Zoe calls "a naughty twinkle," and were always teasing each other. He once asked about one of my tattoos, and then his wife piped up that he had one, too (tattoos are very taboo in Japan, and traditionally associated with the mafia). Mr Nagashima sat there grinning as his wife went on about how it was nothing to do with her, he'd done it before they got married, and how shocking it was. Their interactions always made me smile.

One day the karaoke machine was switched on, at which point I thought I'd better leave them to it before the *sake* appeared and I ended up dancing on a table on a Monday afternoon — we just had so much fun together.

I was always thinking of ways my Oshika friends could have fun, and issued an open invitation to anyone in Japan who had any special skillset that they'd like to share on the peninsula and therefore provide opportunities for people to come together, have fun, and create more memories. Liane Wakabayashi and Kristin Ormiston visited together from Tokyo, with Liane teaching an art class while Kristin played her guitar and sang.

Music was always a very healing way to bring people together on Oshika, which is why it had become so important to support the villagers in their efforts to put on festivals at this stage of their recovery. The Ohara summer festival the previous year had been the talk of the peninsula, but had also sadly reminded neighbouring Koamikura of their own situation. All but two buildings in their village had been destroyed, all of their festival gear had been washed away, and they had no idea how to replace such expensive items. They couldn't even walk up to their shrine because its steps had been so badly damaged. They had no idea how they would ever be able to hold a festival again.

The previous summer, after Kurosawa-san, his team from the Nippon Foundation, and I had finished building Masayo's and Keiko's sheds, they'd invited me back to the temporary housing community to join them and their friends for coffee. After the usual catch-up, one of the more outspoken women said that I was developing a reputation for being someone who somehow "made things happen," and she asked for my help so that Koamikura could have some kind of festival again. She said they could do it even if all they had was a taiko drum, a flute, and a shishi, and it would be OK if they couldn't get to their shrine. They would just have a simple, small festival. Anything to be able to celebrate together again.

I had no idea how I would be able to help them because of how much these things cost. Even just a couple of musical instruments and a shishi and the rest of the costume would cost millions of yen. I left the ladies of Koamikura saying that I would see what I could do, but I truly didn't expect I'd be able to help them at all. I know it's not possible to help everyone, but I try to live by the philosophy that if someone asks for help, I have to at least try to offer it to them. I really didn't have much hope though, and I felt a little out of my depth.

I emailed Shelley Sacks, who runs Ohana International School. She was not only the person who had introduced me to Oshika, but happened to be the only person I knew in Japan who knew anything about taiko, just in case there was the slightest chance she might know of a spare drum somebody might be willing to donate. At least that would be a good place to start.

Shelley had held countless fundraising events while I'd been in the UK between trips to Oshika, and she responded above and beyond *anything* I had expected. She motivated her whole school community as well as her partner's Miyabi Arashi Taiko Group and the British School in Tokyo to sponsor an entire festival for the town of Koamikura. Many members of the Tokyo-based school community were willing to travel up to Oshika to join in the festival, at which Miyabi Arashi Taiko were going to put on a very special performance for the people of Koamikura. It was all incredibly exciting!

The festival date was set for that spring, so I was busy coordinating details with Abe-san, the kucho of Koamikura. People don't use email on Oshika — they don't often use the phone for detailed discussions either. Instead, you meet in person to talk through planning details, which actually is how I prefer to communicate on Oshika anyway — my Japanese language skills, while improved, seem to fall apart when I speak on the phone, and as for reading *kanji* (Chinese-derived Japanese characters), that's never going to happen.

Abe-san and I discussed the allocation of the ¥1.5 million that Shelley had so far managed to raise. It was decided that most of it would go to repair the shrine's steps just in time for the festival. The next step would be to repair the roof, and finally the stone torii still lying broken at the bottom of the steps.

Abe-san said over and over again that when he'd watched the tsunami envelop his village, he couldn't believe his own eyes. For almost two years, the people of Koamikura, which was completely destroyed by the tsunami, had felt very little hope. Not being able to get to their shrine, having very little reason to celebrate anything, and having almost the whole village living in these tiny temporary buildings had all taken a heavy toll. They felt that few people had bothered to truly help them rebuild or develop a vision for the future. Volunteers were helping them little by little to cope with everyday life, but the lack of *hope* was tough to deal with.

I met Abe-san more than a few times to discuss the festival, and each time I noticed his energy change. Just a little. His eyes became a bit brighter and the words he spoke were a bit more hopeful. He smiled more often than before, and both he and his wife, who was very quiet when we first met, talked about how the kind of support that was being offered to them was making such a difference.

I encouraged them to invite former residents, now in Ishinomaki and Sendai, to return for the festival and join in the celebrations, at which point Mrs Abe became quite animated, saying how lovely it would be to see their old friends again, and to have something *exciting* to call them about! Her friends were not going to believe it when she told them that fifty people would be coming all the way from Tokyo to join this little village's festival! Even children were coming!

When I had originally mentioned that the Tokyo group would include some quite young children, Abe-san worried that, even though the steps would be fixed, having young children up at the shrine would be too dangerous. Over time I managed to reassure him, and he eventually got more and more excited at the thought of them coming. Just before I left our last meeting, Abe-san told me that having children visit Koamikura would be a wonderful thing for a village that had so many elderly people who had lost so much hope. He expressed deep emotion and gratitude, and his eyes glistened with joy, and I began to tear up, too.

The festival weekend arrived, and I greeted the Tokyo bus in Watanoha so I could talk the visitors through the sights on their 45-minute journey along the peninsula to where they were staying at the other end — the recently reopened Hotel New Sakai, which faces Kinkasan. While a very nervous bus driver focused on navigating the winding road, I introduced the tiny fishing villages and explained what had happened both on and after March 11, 2011. My intention was to give people the chance to ask questions they would inevitably have but might not feel were appropriate to ask the local friends they were about to make, and I wanted to explain more about Koamikura itself. I also wanted to remind people that they shouldn't feel sad, but should instead plan on descending upon the village and its residents with huge smiles and a desire to party. I later discovered how unnecessary my words were.

I had dinner with Shelley and the others at the New Sakai, filling them in on how things were going in general on Oshika. The next morning I arrived at Koamikura very early, and had my breakfast alone at the foot of the shrine. It was nice to have a quiet moment to look at the steps that had been repaired in recent weeks and think about how happy the local people were to be able to walk up to their shrine for the first time in two years. The area around the shrine had been cleared, the steps at the actual shrine had also been repaired, and the banners were standing tall and proud, announcing to everyone that Koamikura had reason to celebrate again!

I told the Tokyo visitors that I would be helping the Koamikura people prepare for the festival, so needed them to organize themselves when they arrived at the village. As it happened, they arrived a little early, and the Koamikura people were all running a little late, so with Abe-san's permission, I encouraged the guests to go and explore the shrine on their own. The shrine was about a 15-minute walk from the temporary housing community where we were preparing, so I watched the visitors make their way over to the shrine in the distance, and saw them walk up the steps. It made me so happy to watch Shelley and her team walk up the very steps they had worked so hard to raise money to repair — what a unique opportunity to see and *feel* the impact of all their efforts. I was so glad that the morning had worked out so that they had that private time to themselves at the hillside shrine, and felt perhaps more than a little emotion as they stood overlooking the land where the village used to be. It was so right that it happened this way for them — I was learning that things seemed to work out just as they should on Oshika.

Some of the village members remained in the temporary housing community to prepare for the celebrations that would take place a little later, and I made my way over to the shrine with the rest of the village. We walked up to the top of the steps, and the visitors stood back a little, as we had discussed beforehand. I hadn't been entirely sure how much they could be a part of the actual activities at the shrine — I had to be prepared to go with the flow a little and expect the unexpected.

But it couldn't have worked out more perfectly — Abe-san asked whether my Tokyo friends would like to actually enter the shrine for the ceremony, which of course would be such an incredible experience for them. So we all piled into this tiny shrine on the side of a hill, tightly squashed up together, emotions running high and very intense but kept in check by the mesmerizing sound of the priest's chanting. Recalling the ceremony itself brings tears to my eyes so very easily — kneeling next to Shelley, who was the first person I thought of when this town asked me to help them, who spearheaded the fundraising, and happened to be the person who first told me about this forgotten peninsula in the spring of 2011. I felt so very grateful for her kindness and that of her caring community.

After the ceremony we went outside to listen to and watch the playing of the taiko drums and flute and see the shishimai. The drums, flute, and dragon dance mask and costume had all been donated by the Nippon Foundation, thus leaving Shelley's donation for the shrine's benefit. As this was the first time the instruments were to be played and the dance performed, it all had to be done at the shrine itself. Nippon Foundation's Kurosawa-san, with whom I had built Masayo and Keiko's sheds, had appeared by that time, and greeted me with a huge hug that said so much more than words possibly could.

I remembered meeting Kurosawa-san for the first time a year earlier, when he had been very distant — he'd seen so many people go to Tohoku full of good intentions and ideas, only to leave and never return. At that time he couldn't know that I wouldn't do that — I'm sure he just saw this weird Englishwoman who couldn't even communicate properly — he had no idea what I was doing there. Over the past year his attitude toward me had really changed and he had become someone who would do anything to support my activities on Oshika. He said that hardly anybody had helped Koamikura, and he was so happy to see all these people from Tokyo showing their support. It was a very emotional moment as we hugged, each feeling proud of what the other was doing for people who we both now cared so much about.

Then it was back to the temporary housing community to get the party started. The Miyabi Arashi Taiko Group set up their instruments on asphalt-covered ground just below the housing units — everyone had been worried about the rain because there really was *nothing* in Koamikura, and nowhere to play in bad weather. But the rain was holding off and once everyone got settled down to watch, the group brought this little village *alive* with their drumming, their energy, and their huge smiles. I'm sure the whole experience must have been incredibly emotional for the drummers — but all the audience could see was their wonderfully happy faces, whereas from where the musicians were playing they could see the land where the village used to be. If the drummers had even one teary moment, you couldn't tell — I've never seen a bunch of people happier to perform. They were truly incredible.

There were, however, lots of teary moments in the audience. I was sitting on the floor linking arms with and snuggling up to Okabe-san and Keiko, both of whom I always found myself seeking out when I visited Koamikura. They both lost their husbands in the tsunami and Okabe-san also lost her son, so they lived alone and I liked to cuddle with them whenever I could — they always made me giggle because they said they liked cuddling up to my boobs. We were jigging about together where we sat, along with their friends, one of whom grabbed my attention and said she couldn't stop crying because the taiko was so moving. Then the others pointed out their red eyes and that made me cry, too. So we were all sitting on the floor together crying. But they were good tears.

I wanted to make sure every single person from Koamikura had a wonderful time, so I rushed about doing one thing or another: helping them with handing out the amazing bento they made for all their out-of-town guests to eat, bringing the old ladies at the back to sit at the front so they would get a fantastic view of the performance, and cuddling or holding hands when the desire arose. It was one of the occasions on Oshika where I took no photos — I was too focused on the actual creation of that beautiful memory to be worried about images of it.

One memory that was to forever stay in all our minds was the image of the woman who spontaneously got up out of her seat, threw on a *happi* coat (a loose jacket traditionally worn at festivals), and performed her own slightly saucy dance right in front of the whole village and everyone from Tokyo — it became the talk of the peninsula in the days to follow. She later told me that her husband, adult children, and a grandchild were all there and she had totally embarrassed them. But she didn't care at all and was happy to have got so utterly carried away with the music, the moment, and the love that everyone had brought with them. She was the *very same woman* who had sat me down the previous summer and said she wanted my help to give Koamikura a festival again. I bet she never imagined that conversation could have led to such an incredible event, or that it would be etched in everyone's memories forever.

The Koamikura festival brought Tokyo people to Oshika for the purpose of creating a beautiful memory, and that spring I also brought Oshika to Tokyo for the very same purpose. I'd had the crazy idea of taking a busload of Oshika children and their parents all the way to Tokyo Disneyland for a weekend, including an overnight stay with a host family.

It turned out to be a logistical nightmare and definitely one of the most challenging of all the projects I've done on Oshika — but any stress I had was replaced by a huge lump in my throat as soon as the first child turned up one Saturday morning in spring 2013, pushing his family's suitcase through the car park to the bus waiting next to the Fukkiura temporary housing community.

I worked on this project for months while I was in both the UK and Japan — putting calls out to my network in search of host families with children of similar ages, coordinating sponsorship from individuals who weren't able to host but still wanted to help, booking the bus and the tickets, and reassuring the Oshika families that they didn't have to worry about not being able to speak English. Enough host families and sponsors came forward to allow 19 children aged 2 to 12 and their mums to visit Tokyo. There was actually 28 of us altogether, including me and Mika from Fukkiura and her friends.

The bus driver was lovely — with my foreign name written on a sign stuck high up on the bus window he thought he would be picking up a bunch of volunteers and taking them back to Tokyo. But when he saw all the children get on the bus and I explained what we were doing, he couldn't stop grinning. *For the entire journey.*

The kids were also in very high spirits throughout, and the mums sensibly stuck together at the back of the bus, letting their kids get on with it in the middle section. I joined the mums and went through the details about their host families again — I had done this a couple of weeks earlier but just wanted to confirm what we had talked about before. They also wanted to check that they were pronouncing "please" and "thank you" correctly and also to find out how to say "I need a wee/poo," which then led to lots of hilarious gestures they could use in case they forgot. Those Fukkiura girls were quite a naughty bunch and had me in fits of laughter.

Most of the host families had made contact with their guests either by phone or on Facebook during the past week, so they were already feeling very welcomed. I called each of the host families from the bus and passed the phone over to anyone who hadn't had a chance to say hello to their hosts yet.

As we got closer to Tokyo, everyone started staring out the windows at the sprawling city — for quite a few of the children it was their first trip to Tokyo and they were glued to the windows. It was lovely to point out Tokyo Tower and the clusters of cherry trees still in bloom.

Finally, after nine and a half hours of travelling, we arrived at Tokyo Station where we were greeted by the host families, who had very patiently been waiting because we'd had a 90-minute delay. There was 15 minutes of chaos as I tried to introduce everyone, and suddenly everyone was gone. I made my wobbly way to Emily's house — I always feel unsettled and a bit shaky when returning to Tokyo after Oshika. Later that night, photos started to appear on Facebook, showing what fun everyone was having together, and each one got me a little teary — the trip wasn't only about Disneyland, it was also about the time spent with the host families, and I could see from the way the children were having so much fun together that friendships were definitely forming.

The next morning the hosts handed off their guests to me at either Tokyo Station or Disneyland, and some decided to stay at the theme park for the day, too. I handed out the tickets, maps, and some spending money in envelopes to everyone (I'd been given more money than the trip required), then waved them off, found somewhere with Wi-Fi, and settled down to work on my visa applications — I was conscious of the fact that my visa would expire the following year, so was applying for a new working visa, along with something I should have applied for years earlier: permanent residency. Having lived in Japan for fifteen years full-time, I still paid taxes there despite all my to-ing and fro-ing between countries, so I'd decided to finally go for it. Japan was still my home. I couldn't even bring myself to say the words "I live in England."

As I worked on my applications, my eyes kept welling up as I saw the photos my Disneyland guests were posting on Facebook throughout the day.

Then I suddenly remembered that one of the hosts had stuffed something in my pocket that morning outside Disneyland, before he'd disappeared. I put my hand in my pocket and pulled out ¥40,000. It was from William Hill.

Will, his wife Kellie Fitzmaurice, and their three children had hosted and sponsored Mika and her family. To make up for their lack of Japanese language ability, Will and Kellie had gone to the effort of hiring an interpreter to ensure their Oshika guests felt comfortable. So they'd actually managed to have some lovely conversations together during the homestay. Will and Kellie had been so moved by Mika's stories about Oshika and the tsunami that they wanted to do more than just host a family. Will had stood there watching everyone gather together outside Disneyland, and started thinking about what he *really* needed to spend that day, worked out that it was probably only a couple of thousand yen, and decided to empty his wallet of whatever else was in there.

With that, and some other unexpected donations, I bought lightweight Disney jackets for all the children, and some fun underwear for the mums and dads. Zip-up hoodies and underwear were always needed on Oshika, so this seemed like the right thing to do — these were extremely practical souvenirs that I would hand out on the bus on the way home.

After they'd stayed another night with their host families, I met the Oshika families at the designated bus pick-up point, where they were dropped off by their hosts. Kellie had remained with the Oshika families to wait for the bus and immediately offered me their place to stay in during the final week of my trip, for which I'd be back in Tokyo. This was something I knew I'd be doing, but I hadn't got even close to sorting out. I usually stayed with people I'd known for a long time, who I knew wouldn't be offended by me basically using their home as a base with Internet, and wouldn't mind that I wasn't very sociable. But I had been moved by Will's generosity the previous day, as well as the kindness of both of them in opening their home to strangers. In just the few minutes I spoke with Kellie I discovered that we had very similar ways of looking at the world. I wanted to get to know her and Will better, so I gratefully accepted.

We headed back to Oshika as the children and mums excitedly opened the gift-wrapped souvenir clothing. They were all full of stories that would one day turn into beautiful memories, and I was rather overcome by their happiness, as well as the warmheartedness of the host families and sponsors.

I am naturally very easily moved to tears anyway, and especially about anything to do with Oshika — but in my efforts to help people create beautiful memories I was finding myself moved more often by happiness and kindness than sadness. Seeing my new friends laughing and smiling and enjoying themselves deeply touched me. There was something about seeing the pure joy on their faces that *really* made my eyes sting. And thoughts of the generosity of those who had helped to create that joy were sometimes overwhelming.

The weekend was originally about giving families a break, letting the kids run about and just be kids, and creating new, happy memories for people who had lost so much. Of course it was still about that, but it actually became something quite different as well. It became a celebration of the joy that can spring from the kindness of people who open up their hearts, homes, and wallets(!) to complete strangers.

21: What to Wear

In the middle of all my efforts to create beautiful spaces and beautiful memories, there were still, two years on, some very practical needs on Oshika. And that included clothes.

During my third trip, in the summer of 2012, I hadn't done a clothing drive; instead, I focused on projects that I had raised money for. I had mistakenly assumed that people wouldn't need clothes over a year after the disaster. But from my very first day on that trip, I was asked for clothing. There were so many people on Oshika who had lost their income and had no idea when or how they would have a permanent home again, so they didn't want to spend what little money they had on clothes (or on the fuel needed to drive an hour to Ishinomaki, which was the closest place you could go shopping anyway).

So for my fourth trip, in the spring of 2013, I'd wanted to find a way to try to meet that clothing need, while still being sensitive to the fact that it was two years after the disaster — people weren't in the same desperate situation they'd been in, but many of them still had to choose between food and a new pair of socks. I didn't want the distribution of clothing to be done in a way that reminded people of what they had lost or didn't have, but instead I wanted it to be something that made them feel happy — I wondered if I could build on that "fun" shopping experience I'd inadvertently created in some of the temporary housing communities during my first month on Oshika.

Endo-san came up with the perfect solution. She'd pointed out the shipping container that was standing empty next to her konbini, and asked if

I wanted to make a little shop there, which I thought was a wonderful idea. Everybody used the konbini, so it was a very convenient spot for people to have a quick look for any clothes or household items or even knickknacks they might fancy — little things that would make those grey kasetsu feel a bit more cozy.

So I'd put a call out before my fourth trip, asking people to start collecting items that I knew I'd always be able to find a home for; this way, they'd be ready to send up when I'd next be there — I never let anybody send items to Oshika unless I was there to receive them. They'd end up becoming a burden to the people who lived there, and who already had enough to think about. And I didn't want people just emptying their wardrobes and sending up inappropriate items — clothing distribution during disaster recovery is a very complicated issue.

On Oshika, the things I knew I'd *always* be able to find homes for were wellington boots, "granny pants" for want of a better phrase, incontinence pants, slippers, any of UNIQLO's HEATTECH items, thermal underwear, Crocs, and lightweight waterproof windbreaker jackets. So Claire Blandford, who ran Kids Talk Children's English School, took it upon herself to be the wellie lady and motivated her school community to collect hundreds of pairs of wellies. And my tarot-reading friend Elise decided to be the granny pants lady. By the time I'd arrived on Oshika, there were lots of items on their way.

Also, I'd hosted a clothing swap in Tokyo the day before driving up, and my car was packed full of all the leftover items that I thought would be appropriate. The clothing swaps had been regular events that I'd hosted during my pre-311 days, when I ran Being A Broad — a support network for foreign women living in Japan. It was a constant struggle for foreign women to be able to find clothes that fit, so clothing swap events were a great way of dealing with that challenge. I'd always end up with leftover clothes, and given that the Oshika women were more gaijin-sized, I thought a clothing swap was a good way to gather up some items to stock the shop.

Keeping in mind my desire to create an enjoyable shopping experience, I covered boxes with gift wrap from Endo-san's konbini, and made "shelves" all around the edge of the shipping container, then hung all the clothes attractively around the room. Eventually I got clothes rails up from Tokyo, so everything was hung nicely, or was folded on the shelves, and everything was organized in appropriate sections. On the front of the shipping container I spelled out in black tape the words "Caroline's free market, 8 a.m. to 6 p.m., everything ¥0, open every day" and made it big enough to be seen from the road — and I triple-checked to make sure that I hadn't made any mistakes in my Japanese writing.

I went to the shop first thing every morning to open up and unpack any new boxes that had arrived, making sure to thank via Facebook or email anyone who had sent things up — the thanking was completely genuine on my part and not expected by these kind contributors, but I discovered that it was also a wonderful way to encourage others to send up items. Often there would be a lovely written message included in a box, which I would then stick up on the wall for everyone to see, even if they couldn't read it. I left the shop open all day so people could come and go as they liked, then would end my day by going back to see what had been taken, and tidy up before closing. It was incredibly satisfying when items that had been delivered that very morning were all gone by the end of the day — it was an extremely efficient way of distributing clothes *and* monitoring what was really needed at this stage of recovery.

People could see my blue car with the Union Jack flags fluttering atop it parked outside, so they knew when I was there, which resulted in my having a lot of visitors. Some were driving through from the mainland and wanted to meet the strange Englishwoman they'd heard about, some were Oshika friends just saying hello, and others were people who made requests for certain items that I would then put out a call for. Hundreds, if not thousands, of items were given away for free during that two-month stay.

Having someone able to manage donated goods seemed to be key not just at this later stage of recovery, but in the immediate aftermath as well. I learned that when items were first donated to what was left of each village, necessary items were bagged up and handed out so that every survivor had the same items. If there weren't enough of the same items to go round to everyone, then those items weren't distributed and nobody would get them. Anything left over was put away and people moved on to meeting the next immediate need. For example, clothing became less of a necessity after basic needs had been met, and anybody capable of organizing anything then directed their time toward the next level of need. People who were not involved in the clothing distribution decision-making process then assumed that the "leaders" were keeping items for themselves, and the whole issue of clothing donation became a source of conflict.

During February 2013 I came across boxes and boxes of brand new items, still in their packaging, dated December 2011 — this is when they were donated to Tohoku. I was completely shocked. I had met people, on every visit, who had really needed these items. I asked if I could take care of these items and my suggestion was met with a look of relief — I took everything to the free shop and every single item was taken. And thereafter I always kept an eye out and asked sensitively if there was anything that I could unburden people of. So the shop also became a solution for something that had been causing other people stress and which nobody had had time to manage.

I learned to manage post-disaster clothing distribution with three things in mind: 1) to listen very carefully to what people on the ground say they need as opposed to what non-locals think might be needed; 2) to promote the idea that people should only send items to those who are directly getting them into the hands of people who need them; and 3) to have a backup plan if items ended up not being distributed. For me, number three was the Salvation Army in Tokyo. Otherwise, donated items, even though given with kind hearts and good intentions, *would* become a burden to someone.

When it came to clothing donations in Tohoku, or even other donations, there was always a debate concerning how good it really was for people's spirits when they accepted free items, along with the concern that it could lead to people expecting everything to be handed to them on a plate — but I never saw that attitude on Oshika. I will never forget one woman who came into the shop two years on — she had lost everything in the tsunami. She was living in a temporary housing community and had just lost her husband, mother, and sister in a car crash. She took just one babygro suit for her two-week old daughter. I wanted her to take the whole shop.

While the shop fulfilled most of the clothing needs at that time on Oshika, I was made aware of a special clothing need during one of my meetings the previous summer with Oshika Junior High School — school uniforms.

There was only one junior high school on Oshika, and it served all the children on the peninsula, as well as children living on nearby islands — there is even a boat timetable alongside the bus timetable posted up in the school staffroom. As the local population declined, so did the number of students at the school, with just 102 students *before* the earthquake. After the earthquake, there remained exactly half that number. Thankfully, no students were lost to the tsunami itself — the school is on one of the peninsula's highest points

— but instead, half the students moved inland to cities because there was nowhere to live and no way for their parents to make a living. On Oshika, it was a struggle to support even half the number of people that used to live in this beautiful part of Tohoku.

The school itself was just about managing, although it was no longer able to participate in events such as festivals and sports tournaments, which used to be held at a junior high school that was completely destroyed by the tsunami. District events had been moved to Sendai, but for Oshika students to get to Sendai they needed a bus, a driver, and accommodation, all of which were very expensive. All of the schools affected by the tsunami faced similar problems. Despite such problems, when I asked the principal what the school needed, he was quick to say that the school itself didn't need anything, but explained that the parents *really* needed help.

The biggest worry for any parent in Japan whose child is about to enter junior high school is how to pay for the school uniform. On Oshika, where 86 percent of the families had lost their income source, parents were taking out loans they could not afford to repay in order for their children to feel "normal" on their first day of "big school." The cost of all the items that each student needed to go to Oshika Junior High School was about ¥65,000 — this included all uniform items, sportswear, and textbooks for one child. It did not include any trips. There were 14 children due to start at the junior high school on April 8, 2013 and their parents had been worrying about how to pay for the uniforms for months.

It would have been easy to respond by suggesting that they use second-hand clothes, find a cheaper supplier, or even abandon uniforms completely for a while, and in fact I did receive a few suggestions like this when I wrote about the need on my blog. But I'd learned that if you truly want to help, you have to do it with a completely open heart and mind. You have to leave your own opinions and judgments behind and help with what the local people — the ones you say you are there to help — tell you they need. Helping shouldn't be about you and your own needs or opinions. If they say they need money for uniforms, then I will try to get them money for uniforms.

Juliet Rogove, the founder of Kspace International School, had asked me to look out for a project that would benefit a community of children, and I had tentatively mentioned the school uniforms to her, even though at that time it was one of my more costly projects, so I wasn't feeling very confident.

But she responded to me with a commitment to pay for every single uniform for the 2013 intake, and pulled her whole school community together as she embarked on a huge fundraising effort. I couldn't believe it, but it was happening!

There were other things the students needed, too — simple things like stationery and, perhaps more important, to be reminded that other people were thinking of them during what was such a difficult time. I came up with a way to combine those two things by connecting the Oshika students with some of Stephen's students at Meikei High School, who put together a stationery bag for each Oshika student, complete with a little letter to help start some beautiful old-fashioned penpal friendships.

Everyone in the Oshika school community was incredibly grateful, and keen to take advantage of the opportunity to teach the students the importance of helping other people — right now they needed help, but one day they wouldn't, and they should always look to offer support to others whenever they could.

I happened to be at the school when the uniform supplier was there with samples to choose from and to do the measuring. As I watched what the whole process involved, I understood why the uniforms had to be brand new, why they had to be from this specific supplier, and why everything had to be *the same as it always was*. Because in the midst of a world where nothing was normal anymore, as a parent, wouldn't you want this one day, an occasion that the entire family had probably looked forward to since the day the child was born, to be as normal as possible? You'd want your child to look just the same as all the other children; you'd want them to participate in the very important rituals associated with entering a junior high school in Japan in the same way that you had yourself. You'd want to see your child walk down the centre of that huge school auditorium in a new uniform, and maybe *you'd* need that day for your own healing as much as for your child's.

I was invited to the entrance ceremony, so I got to watch those students walk down the centre of the Oshika Junior High School auditorium. I'd never been to a junior high school's entrance ceremony in Japan before, and it was such a treat to watch all the children walk into the hall, wearing the new uniforms that were made to last the next three years, so were just a little bit too big for them. I found it terribly emotional though, and couldn't imagine how the parents must have been feeling. I was also a little overwhelmed because a few days before the entrance ceremony I'd been Skyping Nick Johnston, whose book I was still editing, and the conversation had resulted in a very unexpected outcome. We'd had our editorial meeting and I'd been ready to sign off when Nick had asked me what I was doing in Tohoku. I explained a few of the projects I was working on, and right then and there, he shocked me by saying that he would pay for the uniforms for the 2014 incoming students.

I continued to be surprised and pleased by the generosity of my friends, acquaintances, business associates, and complete strangers throughout that two-month trip, by the end of which my fundraising total had reached ¥8 million!

Some of that fundraising was directed toward parents who were struggling to return to work, including young mum Mika from Fukkiura and her naughty girlfriends whose company I had enjoyed on that bus to Disneyland. There was a very specific item of clothing that was desperately needed by people in these tiny fishing villages, and it was surprisingly easy to arrange to get it. Introducing ... the Oshika Pink Ladies!

In the months soon after the disaster, Mika, as a key member of the Tough Wave Oysters (the group of young people in the fishing industry who were determined to motivate others as they rebuilt their lives), was working especially closely with a lot of women in the area, looking for any ways she could elevate their spirits and help them not give up hope for the future. Nippon Foundation's Kurosawa-san wondered whether there was anything I could do to support them, and we'd come up the idea of sponsoring the working outfits called kappa for these women.

Kappa are the thick PVC overalls and jacket I mentioned earlier that are worn by everyone in the fishing industry, whether they work on a boat or on land. They are brightly coloured and can be seen hanging everywhere — in people's homes as well as at the ports. Kappa are the Oshika uniform. Unfortunately, most of them were washed away by the tsunami, along with much of the equipment so vital to the peninsula's main industry.

Having been so active in the women's community in Tokyo, I was delighted to find something that could support a group of women on Oshika — and given my many contacts in foreign women's groups all around Japan, I was sure I'd be able to find some sponsors. I was introduced to Oota in Hokkaido, a company making specialist workwear, and they had lots of different kappa, including some in bright pink. Not wanting to promote gender stereotypes, I wasn't too keen on the bright pink ones, but Mika and Kurosawa-san *loved* the idea — kappa were usually blue or yellow — nobody had had a bright pink one before! So pink it was.

I contacted every women's organization I knew of in Japan, asking whether they would like to sponsor a Pink Lady — a kappa set (overalls and jacket) cost ¥20,000. Nearly every organization responded immediately with a promise to sponsor an outfit, in some cases more than one outfit. It was such a wonderful way to support a community practically as well as emotionally — those bright pink outfits would make everybody who saw them smile!

Oota sent the outfits directly to Oshika, where I loaded them into my car before driving over to Fukkiura to meet Mika and deliver them. I was also going there for a group photo shoot. One by one, the women — ranging in age from their twenties to their seventies — turned up where the little port used to be. I explained that the outfits were a gift from the international women's community and told them a bit about each of the organizations that had sponsored them. I told the women that everybody was thinking about them and hoped that the outfits would bring them a bit of encouragement.

We then opened up the boxes of kappa and there were lots of comments about how cute they were. Fishermen working nearby walked over to see what all the fuss was about, and when it was discovered that two of the women couldn't make it that morning, we roped in a couple of the men for the photos. They thoroughly enjoyed themselves while trying on the outfits and posing with the women.

The kappa looked enormous to me, but they came with belts, and Mika explained that they cut off the bottoms to make them the perfect length. Over time, I found sponsors for many more kappa for the peninsula — for men and women in all sorts of colours — and the outfits I sourced gained a reputation for being *very* hardwearing. And they really did make people smile — whether you were the person wearing one, or someone catching a glimpse of a Pink Lady hard at work. Over the years, people have been quite delighted when they open up the kappa packages — they are proud to put them on, and keen to get to work. We all need a little boost at work sometimes, especially when working under challenging circumstances, and the kappa really do give people that boost.

The Pink Ladies project became one of the most effective ways of supporting the fishing communities in Tohoku that I have been involved with. I still find sponsors for those much-loved outfits today.

Kurosawa-san took me into Ishinomaki one day, and sat me down over lunch because he wanted to talk to me about something important. He had noticed that for every project I worked on, I would find a way to acknowledge the sponsor. I had put plaques on buildings like Kameyama-san's home, and the Pink Ladies' outfits all had big square patches on the front with the name of that outfit's sponsor. I felt that it was important to recognize the individuals and organizations that had made these projects financially possible, and always enjoyed the opportunity to tell the beneficiary a little bit about their sponsor, so in an area where people felt very much forgotten, they would know that people *were* thinking of them.

Kurosawa-san pointed out that I was working on all sorts of projects all over the peninsula, my work wasn't limited to just one area, and people on Oshika had no idea that it was the same person doing everything. A flower garden in Fukkiura, gardening sheds in Koamikura, a bus shelter in Ohara … all these things were happening that were bringing so much hope. He suggested that I start finding a way to put my name as well as the sponsors' names on these projects so that people knew who was behind it all.

I was horrified at this idea. It had absolutely no place or purpose in anything I was trying to do on Oshika. Nobody needed to know who I was or that I was behind any of it. I could see the importance in associating the sponsor's name with a project, but not in associating my own name with anything. The whole idea went against everything I was there for. I didn't want or need attention or recognition.

"It's not for you. It's for the children. It's for the future."

I had no idea what Kurosawa-san meant until he explained that, one day, the children of Oshika would be adults out in the world. They wouldn't always need help — one day they would be in a position to offer help to others. They needed to know that in their time of need, a woman travelled halfway around the world to help them. Not just once, but many times. And with her she brought all this help and love from others in the world. But it was just her — one person — that kept all that love and support coming. If the young people of Oshika knew that, they might be inspired to do such a thing themselves one day.

Kurosawa-san somehow knew my sensitive spot — the idea of inspiring young people to contribute to the world around them. It had been an ongoing theme in so many of the speeches I had given to all those schools in the UK. I had tried so hard to inspire the children of England, but it never occurred to me that I could inspire the children of *Oshika*.

I finally understood what Kurosawa-san was urging me to do and, remembering the junior high school principal's similar words, I knew he was right. So, together we came up with a logo that I could feel comfortable with. It would incorporate the sponsor's name in English, and my name in Japanese so I could disassociate myself from it and therefore deal with my own discomfort at having attention drawn to me personally. And to acknowledge the vast network of people behind me, I would not use my name on its own, but instead use "*Kyarorain no nakamatachi*," which kind of means, "Caroline's buddies." This was all brought together by a heart-shaped Union Jack — not because I am especially patriotic, but because everybody on Oshika had come to really love the little flags that always fluttered above my car.

The Union Jack hearts took off. I had no idea how much my friends on Oshika would love this idea. If I'd known it was going to make them so happy I would have been more enthusiastic at Kurosawa-san's initial suggestion.

Every Pink Lady outfit from then onward was ordered with a heart flag on the front. I returned to previous projects to see if they wanted me to paint a heart by the plaque — everybody wanted one. After painting Union Jack hearts on Masayo's and Keiko's sheds, I told Katsuzo-san, the Fukkiura gardener, that I would make him a little Union Jack for the garden. But when he saw Keiko's shed, he took me to a temporary building by the sea that he slept in sometimes and said he wanted a big heart on the side facing out to sea so the boats could see it. It had to be big like Keiko's ... no ... even bigger. So one evening I snuck down to paint him one as a surprise for the morning, watched by a Pink Lady on a bicycle who was on her way home from work.

When Kameyama-san heard about it, he dragged me up to the house he'd built all by himself, saying that he wanted a heart on the side of it, but it had to be so big that it could be seen from the temporary housing community. He even wanted people to be able to see it from the road down below. So I spent one boiling hot day painting a huge heart on the side of his house while the temporary housing residents all leaned on the fence, watching and commenting on how a Union Jack was made … main red cross first, then outlined with white, then a diagonal red cross, outlined with white, then the gaps filled in with blue.

Everybody heard about the Union Jack hearts — random strangers would pop into the free shop by the konbini and talk about how much they loved the heart on Kameyama-san's house. And Mrs Sasaki greeted me one day with a huge stepladder in hand, saying that she wanted a massive heart on the side of her building. She planned on saying good morning and goodnight to me via it every day after I returned to England.

And that is why, still today, on a very remote peninsula in northeastern Japan, you find Union Jack hearts *everywhere*.

22: Remembrance

Two years after the disaster turned out to be a great time to visit Oshika to help — at this point, people had been in their temporary housing long enough to be feeling anxious about what the next steps were. There was progress being made in other, less remote, more industrialized parts of Tohoku that, of course, generated a lot of hope in some people, but for those on Oshika, it made them feel even more forgotten. The peninsula's scenery was a wasteland interspersed with black sandbags and mountains of debris, with truck after truck driving through what used to be family homes and businesses. People were fed up and didn't really know how to move forward, but as Ohara's Abe-san had said when I'd first arrived, they were *ready* to move forward. Which is why it was possible to achieve so much on my February through April 2013 trip — eleven different projects in all.

It would not have been possible to get so much done had I not been there for two whole months — the longest time I have ever spent on Oshika in one go. It wasn't just because of the length of time I stayed though; it was also because of the way in which the locals had begun to see me, and also how I had begun to see myself.

From my point of view, my confidence in my Japanese ability had increased, and my worrying about upsetting people had decreased. When you don't speak a language fluently, you listen. A lot. You listen with your ears, but you also listen with your heart. And I spent so much time *listening* and concentrating on what local people were saying and feeling that I ended that trip with a much better understanding of Oshika than I had on previous trips.

From the local people's point of view, they knew me now, and they trusted me. They liked the things I was doing and they let me get on with them. They knew I couldn't be there all year round, but when I *was* there, I was part of their lives.

My life on Oshika filled me with a sense of it being the place where I should be, with the people I should be with, and doing the things I should be doing. It wasn't always about building a shed, or painting a heart; sometimes it was just about having a coffee with the police who popped in to say hello again because they'd heard I was back. On one visit they'd looked surprised to see my knickers swaying in the wind, and Onodera-san explained that in England it was normal to stick your undies outside — people had got used to some of my ways, just as I'd got used to theirs.

I was rarely treated like a "foreigner" on Oshika. It was when Hiroyuki roped me into joining him and a bunch of Tokyo volunteers on a trip to Kinkasan, to clean and repair the shrines hidden away in the mountain, that I was reminded of being a foreigner by the Tokyo volunteers who threw me a few odd looks and then practised their English on me. I hadn't realized when I was in Tokyo, just how much I'd been treated differently — I only realized it when I went to Oshika because the people there treated me so *equally*. I rarely got asked anything about England, and we didn't often talk about cultural differences — we talked about *Oshika* life and the work we were doing. They didn't even care that I couldn't understand them half the time — they just yapped away at me in the local dialect.

Although I must admit that it was on Oshika that I got asked what still remains the funniest cultural question I have *ever* been asked since I first set foot in Japan in 1996: "Are farts in England the same as farts in Japan?"

I loved how everyone was so open about everything on Oshika. On the subject of farts, the Sasakis and I became so close during those two months that we really were like family, and in my family, that means being comfortable enough to let rip if the need arises. One afternoon, Mr Sasaki was farting away and, always confident in my own abilities, I just couldn't resist the urge to join in. Mrs Sasaki looked genuinely shocked. Not because of the fact that I'd farted, because she didn't care about that, but because she said she'd expected mine to be little, cute, high-pitched ones, not massive ones to rival Mr Sasaki's. As far as I was concerned, that was a huge compliment.

I had discovered that Mr Sasaki actually spoke a little bit of English (apart from the rough translation of zuzuhoido, that I had cheekily taught him). I discovered this quite by accident when I was driving him along the coastal road and he suddenly said, in perfect English, "Caroline, please slow down." Despite that, we only ever spoke in Japanese together, except for one phrase he would regularly use: "Good job, good job."

When I would tell him about some project I'd been working on, he'd respond by putting one thumb up and saying "Good job, good job." I also felt comfortable sharing my frustrations with the Sasakis, especially when they concerned the actions of non-local decision-makers, media coverage, or people I felt were taking advantage of Oshika people's wonderful hospitality (it happened more often than you'd think). Mr Sasaki would more often than not respond with "Good job, good job" to show that he agreed with my opinion on something, or to show his approval at my understanding of life for them after the disaster. The phrase wasn't always in reference to my actions; it was also used in reference to my thoughts.

I was still running, and also sometimes went swimming at the pool up at Hot Maru, keen to keep myself fit and healthy, although I wasn't on one of my occasional no-drinking phases, which Onodera-san took full advantage of one night and gave me a brutal mid-week hangover. I managed to get a cold *twice* during that trip, and word quickly spread around the village — I kept finding bowls of hot miso soup in the centre's genkan with little notes on them. I could only read my name in Japanese, so I never knew who they were from until someone would ask me days later if I'd enjoyed the soup they'd left for me. Sometimes soup would arrive just because somebody had seen me working outside all day in cold weather.

The centre was such a hub of activity and such a big part of Ohara's recovery — it provided a place for emergency supplies to be distributed in the weeks immediately after the disaster, and even for other supplies that would be shared further down the line. Often, gifts of fresh fruit would arrive at the centre, and someone would then share all the fruit equally between the residents of the village, and the little bags would sit on tables in the middle of the main room, waiting to be collected. The first time this happened, I didn't pay a huge amount of attention to it, but after a while I noticed that there was one bag left. Upon closer inspection, I realized that it had my name on it. My Ohara friends really did think of me as part of their community.

The centre was also a place where decisions got made. Kucho started inviting me to the village meetings, which were attended by people who each represented about five Ohara households. These meetings were incredibly difficult for me to follow, but very good practice for my Japanese listening skills. I loved them — I loved the way in which everybody communicated with each other, which was so unlike meetings I had participated in elsewhere. There was more listening than talking. Each person was given the opportunity to speak, while everyone else listened respectfully. Nobody interrupted, and there was silence after each comment so that people had time to process. There were no egos in play.

I felt honoured to be invited to these meetings, but always felt a little out of my depth. I felt more comfortable working outside. Someone would always turn up to join me — more often than not it was Yukio-san. It wasn't the done thing to work alone in Ohara, which was handy because they all had fantastic tools, whereas my collection was very limited. I'd spend most of any day with a drill in my hand, but I was also let loose with a pick-axe, was constantly hammering *something*, and the bigger the truck I could drive, the happier I was. My much-loved work jeans were covered in paint, woodstain, and a bit of curry rice, and they had a huge rip in the backside, which Mr Sasaki said was caused by my impressive farts. He may have been right.

When Utsumi-sensei invited me to the preschool's graduation ceremony, she looked me up and down, and then very delicately asked whether I had any other clothes I could wear. Unfortunately not, but after raiding the free shop, putting on some Tokyo makeup, and washing but *not* braiding my long hair, I managed to scrabble together a fairly decent *clean* look for the ceremony. Utsumi-sensei was very pleased.

I cooked for everyone again on this trip — this time making an English brunch. People might not have been that interested in the fact that I was from the UK, but they were certainly interested in English food. It was again my way of thanking everyone for welcoming me into their homes, but more importantly, it was a lovely way to bring together people from all over the peninsula, from the different villages, who would otherwise not be interacting. This time, people came and went over a six-hour period, and enjoyed bacon, sausages, beans, mushrooms, tomatoes, fried bread, potatoes, and lots and lots of poached eggs. All served up with Bucks Fizz (very similar to Mimosa, with orange juice and sparkling wine) and proper English tea.

Throughout my time on Oshika I was coordinating fundraising efforts in Tokyo, liaising with sponsors, compiling my huge permanent visa application, finishing off my Japanese tax return, and encouraging people to come and visit Oshika to support the hotels that were gradually reopening, the little temporary restaurants that were popping up, as well as the temporary shopping street in Ayukawa. I was also inundated with emails from people who wanted to volunteer with me.

I wasn't set up to manage volunteers, nor did I have any inclination whatsoever to start. Jamie was doing a fantastic job in Watanoha with It's Not Just Mud, so I would direct people to him if they wanted to volunteer. He doesn't have the people-pleasing issues that I have, so could be strict with people and tell them what to do, and he had way more patience. I had unlimited patience when it came to the Oshika people, but very little for anyone who came from outside Oshika if they didn't have what I considered to be the right attitude. Having to deal with employees who didn't know how to treat people kindly, couldn't work conscientiously, would inconvenience others, or had no sensitivity to their environment had been an element of my entrepreneur life that I had absolutely *loathed*. It had caused me a huge amount of stress and I didn't want to put myself in a position where I had to manage anyone ever again — I still actively avoid it today.

Besides my own reluctance to manage people, and despite having always had such a strong belief that we have a responsibility to help others if we can, I was seeing a "volunteering in Tohoku movement" that was making me very uncomfortable, and really question whether some people should be volunteering at all.

I *know* that a huge number of hardworking, kindhearted volunteers played a massive and important role in the recovery effort in Tohoku — I'll never forget the young man I once sat next to who, along with a hundred other people, had spent the previous day clearing human and animal bones from a ten kilometre beach in Sendai, two years after the disaster. The bones were all sent to the police for DNA testing so that families, still waiting for answers, could be informed and finally start to heal.

But there were more than a few volunteers I encountered who seemed to have gone to Oshika for a weekend of eating and drinking with maybe a little bit of work thrown in, completely oblivious to the fact that they were inconveniencing everyone more than they were helping. And I wasn't the only one who encountered this — I remember hearing from one poor woman who was trying to deal with a teacher who *insisted* on bringing her students to Tohoku to "help," yet expected to be fed, put up, and driven around everywhere. I found such behaviour really disappointing and frustrating.

Staying on Oshika for two whole months was incredibly rewarding, but it was also incredibly challenging. The wind that spring seemed to shake the whole centre all through the night, and little wild animals would scurry around under the building, so I'd lie awake for hours with the walls banging away or the sound of rats or *tanuki* (Japanese racoon dogs) coming through the floorboards. I'd put my music on really loud just to drown out the sound of the wind and animals, and finally get to sleep only to be woken an hour later by an exceptionally loud gust of wind. Fleetwood Mac's *Rumours* album can still take me right back to those nights. People who asked to join me admired what I was doing, and wanted to do it, too, not realizing just how challenging it actually was.

If it wasn't the wind and the animals stopping me from sleeping, it was the groups of university students who volunteered so they could improve their resumés, and who mostly stayed awake all night at this exciting opportunity to have such a big sleepover. Or the groups of adults who volunteered, and would then stay up noisily drinking until the early hours of the morning. I got more sleep surrounded by sixty primary school kids in North Devon!

Two months of interrupted sleep (especially as a survivor of multiple strokes) made me even less patient with volunteers who, in my opinion, weren't making the most of every single moment where they had such a great opportunity to help others. So when I received an email from Sophie Middleton, a British woman living just outside Tokyo, asking whether she could join me on Oshika for a week or so, I was initially very reluctant about the idea. I eventually agreed to a week, telling her she'd be working with the wakame processors and not with me. I sent her instructions on how to get all the way to this remote little village purely by public transport, not entirely sure she'd even make it.

Sophie arrived in Ohara in complete darkness, the only passenger on the Ayukawa bus. I thought that anyone who didn't emerge traumatized by the journey and being dropped off in the middle of nowhere had some balls, and would probably be fine on Oshika. And work out fine she did, not *once* inconveniencing me or anyone else in any way.

Sophie got herself around the peninsula using an old bike she found next to the community centre. She spoke very little Japanese, and just got on with things, not letting it bother her, and developed a really lovely friendship with the 84-year-old woman with whom she processed wakame every day. Onodera-san became very fond of her, too, inviting us both over in the evenings, and being most amused at how different his two female friends from England were. Sophie was incredibly tall and slim, with blond hair and a gentle, ladylike manner. I was short and curvy, with dark hair and a penchant for swearing (in Japanese or English, I didn't mind which). Onodera-san would put a rice bowl and a *sake* bottle in the middle of the table, saying that I was the rice bowl and Sophie was the *sake* bottle, then laugh hysterically for hours at his own joke.

Once Sophie finished her wakame work she'd often find me and get stuck in with whatever I was doing — a short-arse like me who doesn't like ladders couldn't have painted the top of Takahashi-san's heart building, and it would have taken me days to cook the English brunch if it weren't for her. She gave herself enough private time to process some of the emotions that were inevitable in that environment, but she did it without imposing on anyone else. And she took care of me, too, actually — I'd walk back from painting something to find her emptying my car of the mountains of rubbish I'd pile up in the passenger footwell.

Sophie's one week volunteering on Oshika turned into four. She was a pleasure to have around and I was happy for her to stay. She, quite simply, *got it*. She didn't burden anyone at all; in fact, quite the opposite. It was only in her last few days that I discovered that she was, in fact, a vegetarian.

"But I've seen you eat meat when we've been invited to people's homes!" I said.

"It's *my* choice to be a vegetarian, not theirs. If people are feeding me, I don't see why my choices should inconvenience them."

Sophie Middleton was an incredible volunteer, and became a really lovely friend — a person who shows Ohara that much love and respect is sure to find a special place in my heart.

It was all the love surrounding Oshika that made it possible to do what I did there, despite the lack of sleep, and despite my frustrations with some things. There was so much love coming from other parts of Japan, every day, when boxes arrived for the free shop. I stuck the more personal notes that came in the boxes up above my futon where I could see the kind words on them every day. The love I got from all the people who wanted to help Oshika or support my activities was overwhelming on that trip — and often came from complete strangers. As with my UK school visits, I felt like I wanted to channel all that love onto Oshika.

And there was all the love coming my way from people on Oshika, too — thoughtful gifts that would be dropped off, the doors that were always open to me, the friendly waves as people saw me go by in my car with its Union Jacks fluttering, the cans of drink that would be tucked into my pockets. There was so much love and happiness on Oshika, and so much focusing on the present, that sometimes it was easy to almost forget that such a horrific tragedy had taken place there. Just for a moment.

The second anniversary coincided with my two-month trip. I didn't expect March 11 to be much different from any other day on Oshika — even if you did find yourself momentarily caught up in all the love on Oshika, there was never any *real* escape from the tsunami, no matter what the day was. Even the temporary location of the bank in Ayukawa had its old clock — salvaged from the debris — taped to the wall, and still showing 2:46, the moment the earthquake started.

Every day was a day for remembrance. As Takahashi-san had said when we started work on the bus shelter, when you wake up on Oshika, the tsunami is the first thing you think about. It is simply everywhere — when you look at the surrounding wasteland, piles of debris, houses falling apart; when you look at the temporary housing communities, when you see the small efforts at rebuilding, when you look into the eyes of the people who live there. It's just *always* there and people live with it *every day*. In many ways, March 11 is a day for *others* to remember.

I was so naïve to think that it was going to be like any other day.

At first, it *seemed* like any other day. I spent most of it planting flowers for the playground, which felt like an appropriate thing to do. Yukio-san worked alongside me, constructing extra stabilizers for the playset. We were quieter than usual, but I think that was because we were working on separate tasks, whereas usually we worked on the same task at the same time and chatted away throughout. I really enjoyed working with Yukio-san — he did most of the playground fencing with me. Each day he would say, "I'll just do one day's work with you and that's it," then the next morning he would turn up again saying he'd been thinking about how to get a tricky bit of the fence *just right*, and then get on with it, again saying, "I'll just do one day." At 56, he was one of the youngest people in Ohara, and I think that's why he generally made the coffee for everyone at break time, so I'd enjoyed doing that for him during my stay.

We had lunch together in the free shop that day, while a volunteer group, just outside, made the most delicious ramen for people who were part of the Oshika community, which included construction workers and volunteers as well as the locals. Then it was back to work on the playground for the afternoon. Not long after 2 p.m. the children from the primary school came tearing down the little hill to the playground, as they had done on a daily basis since the playset went up. They came screaming down, arms waving, threw their bags on the ground, and raced on to the swings, monkey bars, climbing wall, and slide. The more curious ones always came over to see what I was making or doing before dashing over to the playset to be with their friends. It was always lovely to see them all running around, and to hear them laughing.

As it got close to 2:30 p.m., the adults started to arrive. A lady I didn't know, along with her daughter, shyly came over to me to say thank you for helping Ohara, and it turned out that her father lived in Ohara, and she had come from out of town to spend the afternoon with him.

It was past 2:30 and the earthquake had started at 2:46 — I wasn't entirely sure what was going to happen, but the children had all jumped off the playset and were now sitting on a big rock together, facing out to the ocean. I wasn't sure what I should do and Yukio-san had disappeared. He was driving to and from the temporary houses, giving lifts to the older people so they could be at the community centre.

I was always so aware of not intruding, but really should have known not to worry — I was always treated like I belonged there. I was beckoned over to join everyone, so I put down my tools and stood with the others, all facing the ocean. Yukio-san and the last of the old ladies arrived. Two small bunches of carnations were balanced upright amid a pile of small rocks — no grand gestures. It was so simple. And so heartfelt. A loudspeaker announced throughout the peninsula that it was coming up to 2:46. We bowed our heads toward the ocean and suddenly the peninsula's tsunami warning siren blared out as we stood in silence. I have no words at all for how it felt to be standing there, facing the ocean, in what used to be a busy village, and hearing that sound. In fact, there were no words or thoughts going through my mind at all — just emotions. Raw emotions. Anger. Sadness. Shock. And disbelief. Two years on, all those emotions. They took me by surprise.

When the siren stopped, we exchanged looks but few words, then took deep breaths and headed into the community centre for coffee. Hearts became lighter very quickly, as is the way with people in Ohara, who always seem so quick to smile and laugh at anything. After an hour or so, people left one by one, and eventually there was just me left at the community centre, saying goodbye and thank you to Yukio-san for his hard work. As soon as his car turned the corner I burst into tears.

This wasn't like the odd sting behind the eyelids that often happened to me on Oshika but was easy to hide; I could feel this was going to turn into those massive uncontrollable sobs that just have to come out no matter what. It had happened just once before to me on Oshika, and it took me by surprise then, too — it was in February 2012, in my last couple of days at the end of my one-month stay. I was watching Mrs Sasaki laughing and laughing at a group of volunteers who had dressed up and performed a silly song and dance just for her. Something about watching her being so happy had touched something so deep in me that I'd had to hide in her kitchen area so no one could see me crying.

I was annoyed with myself back then and I was annoyed with myself now. This wasn't *my* tragedy. I hadn't had to live through what people there had lived through. I always told people who were interested in coming to Oshika to only come if they could leave their own emotions behind, and I meant it — I told them to bring laughter and smiles and silliness, but not to bring tears. There was no place for them on Oshika. And there was I on the verge of losing it.

At least nobody could see me.

I didn't realize that I wasn't alone until I spotted Onodera-san, to whom I had ended up dedicating my "love" book for Japanese men, and with whom I'd always felt I shared a similar kind of heart. He was on the other side of the car park, watching me. I wiped away my tears but they wouldn't stop, so I just walked over to him and apologized, feeling so uncomfortable that he had seen me without my usual smile and instead caught me so emotional on this day. *Their* day. It was a struggle to speak through the tears, but I tried to explain, "This day … all of you … my friends."

Onodera-san replied, "It's OK. I understand," and gestured to show that our hearts were one.

23: Settling

At the end of spring 2013, it was more difficult than ever before to leave Oshika because I'd spent such a long time there, and I was again in tears saying goodbye, as were many of the Ohara women. It had been an incredible two months. When I arrived in Tokyo to spend some time before returning to the UK, I had the same feelings of discomfort I'd had before, perhaps even stronger. It was more than two years after the disaster, and in Tokyo there was no evidence at all of the trauma that the whole country had suffered, whereas just a matter of hours away, people were living in temporary housing, with no sign of permanent housing anytime soon. It was very unsettling and I felt in a bit of a daze a lot of the time — I would try to "run" that sensation away.

I was out running one morning when an old man, also jogging, just stopped me on the street. He said how much he loved my wrist tattoo — the pink Japanese cherry blossom I'd had done for my fortieth birthday. He said that I should cover my whole torso in them and gently ran his hands all over my arm and my back as he said it — most unusual in non-tactile Tokyo. Suddenly I felt OK again. Settled. Soothed. It had felt like something my Oshika friends would say or do.

My car was now parked outside Andrew Abbey's home, and it made me happy to think that while I was in the UK, it would be of some use to the good man who had accompanied me on that first trip to Oshika to hand out emergency supplies. I went back and forth to my storage unit, gradually emptying it, as I had accepted that I would not live in Tokyo again. I felt mentally able to deal with some of the belongings that I'd become very fond of during my Tokyo years but had rejected in the months immediately after the earthquake — I had a base in Cirencester that I wanted to make more homely, so packed up some huge suitcases with my eclectic furnishings: bright purple curtains with leopard print tabs, Missoni cushions, blue Chinese bookends, and much-loved artwork, along with as many books as possible. I would deal with the rest of the stuff later. While I still couldn't say the words, "I live in England," I was at least taking a little step in that direction.

I gave talks in Tokyo to the Foreign Women's Lawyers Association, Tokyo Mothers' Group, Foreign Executive Women (FEW), and of course the lovely old gentlemen at Amity Yokohama. I had plenty of photographs of Oshika, which now included a collection of "then and now" photos — photos of the exact same spots on each of my trips, showing the progress, or lack of it.

Dana Levy attended the FEW talk, and was inspired to help through her yoga school, Furla Yoga. One of Furla Yoga's key members of staff had a connection with Oshika, having gone on many happy camping trips there as a newlywed when she'd lived in Sendai. Dana wanted to support the spiritual healing of the area that carried so many happy memories for her coworker, and pledged to raise ¥100,000 before my next trip — she ended up raising ¥120,000!

I was staying at Will and Kellie's lovely apartment, and right from my first night, Will had been full of questions about Oshika and what I'd been doing there. His family had loved having Mika and her children stay during the Disneyland trip, and wanted to find out if there was anything else they could do to help. His friend Tom Lovell, and Tom's wife Meha Thind, also wanted to help, so a few days later we had dinner together and I showed them photographs of my latest trip. I told them about some of the things on Oshika that needed support, one of which was the 400-year-old Date Masamune shrine in Ohara, which was now looking worse than it did right after the disaster.

Ten days later, when I was back in the UK, I received an email from Will pledging millions of yen for the shrine. Will and Kellie, and their friends, understood how important it was to continue giving support *long-term* after major disasters. Yes, their donations would help repair buildings, but they would also help repair hearts so that people would know that they'd not been forgotten.

Bratton Fleming Community Primary School in North Devon certainly hadn't forgotten Oshika, and a few months after I returned to the UK, I'd gone there to support their "Japan Day," through which they were hoping to add to the money they'd already raised since the disaster.

I heard the children before I saw them — loud shouting and the banging of drums could be heard from outside the school gates. I walked into the hall to find my old university friend Gillian surrounded by kids in a huge circle, shouting Japanese words at the tops of their voices as they struck the huge taiko drums in front of them. They spent the entire day immersed in Japanese culture, rotating among different activities. They made sushi, origami, and koi-themed lanterns. All the children had come to school that day wearing clothes that were somehow inspired by Japan — some were wearing Japanese football kit, some were wearing kimono-like dressing gowns, and some simply wore the red of the Japanese flag. Many of the children had their names written on their clothing in katakana (which unlike kanji, I can read, for the most part), and one boy was delighted when I said to him, "Well, I think you must be Jake."

I gave a whole-school assembly, which included a quick recap of my previous talks, before letting everyone know about the current situation in Tohoku. My recaps weren't really necessary — I was amazed at how so many of them remembered things I had told them before. Then they all headed off to their classrooms and the parents arrived. Bratton Fleming had always been really good at keeping the parents informed about what was happening to the money their children raised, and I had spoken to them several times before. This was a larger group than usual, all of whom seemed very moved by the situation two years on. I felt very touched by their support. Including all their previous fundraising efforts, Bratton Fleming had raised over £850 for Oshika, which was quite amazing for a little village school in England.

And Bratton Fleming's "Japan Day" in July 2013 had been raising money for a very specific project — futons.

After the disaster, 200 people had sheltered in Ohara Elementary School, salvaging what they could from the debris, including futons. There weren't enough futons for everyone, but somehow they managed. A month later, when everybody decided to find shelter elsewhere so that the local children could go back to school, the futons were stored in Ohara Community Centre, and used by people who came to help with the recovery effort. Thousands and thousands of people from all over the world, who brought vital supplies and helped clear away the rubble during the first year, slept in the centre and on these futons. After the first year, when the "masses" of volunteers stopped coming, there were still smaller groups and individuals that continued to support the area, and the centre, with all its futons, was a vital part of facilitating this support.

It was almost two and a half years after the disaster, and these futons were in a terrible state — they smelt awful, were ripped and covered in stains, and many of them were mouldy, as I had discovered the one I slept on was, halfway through my previous trip. I'd even had a respiratory infection upon my return to the UK. I knew, first-hand, what a state they were in. But I also knew that I really didn't mind sleeping on them. During my conversations with Kucho, about what the village needed, he'd mentioned futons, and given that neither I nor the other volunteers really cared what we slept on, I couldn't understand why he'd mentioned futons not just once, but on a number of occasions. I, as sensitively as I could, said as much to Kucho, and he patiently explained why replacing those futons was an incredibly good way to support the village.

What I didn't realize was that the former residents of Ohara also used the futons when they visited — suddenly the need for new ones made more sense to me. I could understand that these shabby futons with such a sad history would absolutely not be the kind of thing that the current residents would want their old friends to sleep on. I didn't want them sleeping on them either. These were friends they were hoping would return permanently to Ohara one day. Kucho wanted them to see how the town was progressing, how they were getting back on their feet, how things of beauty were returning to a place that held such terribly ugly memories for so many. I had seen the impact that little gestures could have on Oshika, and I had seen how news traveled fast — I could suddenly imagine how people would be excited to tell their old friends about the lovely new futons awaiting them in the community centre.

It was another good reminder to me that if I was there to help, I had to do so by listening to the local people, and not impose any of my own judgments or opinions on them. I wasn't quite at that point when Kucho had first told me about the futons, but by the end of the two months, it was all very simple to me — get the locals to tell me what they needed and do my very best to make that happen. No judgments. And my opinion on what *they* said they needed didn't matter. It wasn't about me.

So, while in the UK, I set about researching futon sets and, in doing so, discovered another story. Ginny Tapley Takemori, a like-minded British woman living in Japan who had been volunteering in Ishinomaki, and It's Not Just Mud's Masae Ishikawa both introduced me to Murakami-san.

Murakami-san had run Minato Futon Shop in Ishinomaki for 53 years. He was incredibly well-respected — a true artist in his field — and one of only two people in Ishinomaki with the highest qualification a futon-maker in Japan can possibly get. The shop was also his home, and the entire building was destroyed by the tsunami. Murakami-san lost many of his neighbours and friends, and his days after the tsunami were spent removing bodies from the rice fields. And soon after that he helped turn the local school into a shelter for those who had lost their homes. As with in many towns in Tohoku, it was people like Murakami-san who, in the midst of dealing with their own trauma, emerged as real heroes.

Murakami-san decided to set up his business again, in the exact same place it had stood for over fifty years, despite there being absolutely nothing around it. He was living in temporary housing, and he got a small prefab building from which he could run his business. He worked with a factory on the other side of Ishinomaki that had survived the tsunami. All business that came his way directly supported the local area. I couldn't think of anyone more perfect to provide the futons needed for the centre.

In the two days after I alerted my network to Kucho's request for twenty futon sets, sponsors for every single set had come forward — the response was incredible! So I ordered twenty sets from Murakami-san — each set included a mattress, a duvet quilt, a sheet, a pillow, and a pillow case and each set had a patch with the sponsor's name on it. Murakami-san was thrilled to receive such a large order — it made a big difference to his business as he was starting up again. They were delivered to Ohara that September, and Kucho was delighted.

I was busy coordinating other projects from the UK, too — kappa for the Pink Ladies were an ongoing need and had really captured the attention of those still keen to support Tohoku. People were sponsoring outfits in their own name, their organization's name, or even in the name of a loved one, with one man sponsoring one for each of his daughters.

I was also coordinating preparation for the construction of another playground. The shop owners in Ayukawa's temporary shopping street had heard about the Ohara playground and asked whether it would be possible for them to have one, too. And when Stephen Bird had visited while we were building the bus shelter, he had been inspired to help, as had his students at Meikei High School following my talk there. They had raised ¥430,000, which we decided would go toward paying for the Ayukawa playground. This time, because we had the budget for it, I ordered the equipment from my old friend

Michael Anop, who was still running Playground of Hope — the organization that had developed into building playgrounds for at-risk children in communities all over Japan, not just Tohoku.

In the middle of coordinating everything remotely from the UK, I was still working on a couple of publishing projects, one of which was a Japanese edition of my "love" book for Japanese men. But I didn't miss the entrepreneur life at all — I'd grown so tired of it and was relieved to no longer be a "business owner." It was nice to finally have some time to spend with family and friends.

I'd given family and friends a special gift that autumn — I made some of the pickled onions I used to make in Tokyo and stuck a label on them that said "Auntie Caroline's." They didn't last long, and people started asking me for more — my neighbour became a big fan and asked for some for a charity event he was organizing; my best friend from school ordered fifteen jars to give to her friends at a party in her home, at which they consumed two whole jars before I'd even left the room. And Jesse Smith's Butchers in Cirencester had ordered 24 jars for resale, unwittingly introducing a new path into my life — there had been something about the look in the eyes of those lads in Jesse's when they'd tasted the pickled onions that ignited a spark in the entrepreneur in me. A spark that I'd assumed was long gone.

With my publishing work, and making a few jars of pickles to sell to the local shops, I was feeling more comfortable in Cirencester, just as long as I always had the next trip to Japan booked. I always needed to know when I'd be going "home."

It was never long between trips. My second trip of 2013 was from October through December, starting off with the usual week or so in Tokyo to host another clothing swap so I could get the free shop going again, empty my storage container of things that would be useful in the free shop, and of course, give more talks. I went back to school uniform sponsors Kspace, who, to my delight, the Oshika students were planning on visiting during their final year of junior high. I also visited Amity Yokohama again; the retired Japanese gentlemen members were, in addition to Oshika, also interested in the Japanese edition of my "love" book for Japanese men, which had recently come out, and were raising all sorts of interesting intimate questions.

When I arrived on Oshika, I discovered that the Japanese edition of my love book was also of great interest to my friends there, when a little old lady ran up to me and said, "Your book for men is a GREAT read. Can I get another copy?!" and Endo-san insisted that she stock it in her konbini's book section. I was so touched when one lovely woman said that her son had recently got married and she wanted to give him a copy so that he would be sure to know how to make his wife happy.

Kucho-san urged any visiting volunteers to buy a copy, and given that I often spoke English to visitors, they didn't always realize just how good my Japanese was by that point. I remember watching one man reading aloud the section on penis size, and his friend asking whether English men were different in that respect, to which he'd replied, "Yes, that's why they all wear knee socks. They need something to tuck their big penises into." They were mortified when they realized I'd understood everything they'd said.

Mr Sasaki, needless to say, *loved* my slightly saucy book, saying, "Good job, good job," at every chapter. The Sasakis were still working incredibly hard to rebuild their business — their insurance had only compensated them for 25 percent of what they had lost. And they were still struggling to find enough people who were willing to work as the casual staff who are so necessary to the fishing industry. So many people had left the area, and other people didn't want to visit. A Christian missionary group had set up a camp in the area, and made the offer to supply people who would work for free to those who would attend their sermons, which put some Oshika people in an impossible position. Mrs Sasaki explained that she had her own religion and didn't feel comfortable attending another church — besides, they didn't want free help, they wanted to pay people fair wages — so they were making do without the missionary group's assistance. But it had got to the point where Mrs Sasaki, who usually worked on land, would have to go out to sea, too.

Two and a half years on from the disaster, Mrs Sasaki *still* had not set foot in a boat. She was still too traumatized after what had happened and still felt terribly guilty for not being able to save her mother-in-law. I cancelled everything I'd had planned for that day and told her I'd go with her for moral support.

So we went out in Mr Sasaki's boat, and worked on the wakame farm out in the bay together. It was actually quite enjoyable work, pulling up the frames that had been previously planted with wakame, and snipping off pieces of rope that had little wakame leaves growing out of them — these would be the wakame "seeds." And then we sailed along the farm, stopping periodically to haul out metres and metres of rope attached to metal weights and buoys. Two of us sat opposite each other, with one person holding the thick, heavy rope and pulling it over them, untwisting it about every 50 cm so the other person could pop in a "seed." Then we'd unload all the rope, metal, and buoys back into the sea, and move further along the farm.

The boat was tiny, and we worked very quickly — we had to be aware of everything around us at all times because there was rope everywhere and it wouldn't take much for someone to end up overboard. I resisted the urge to help with anything other than the actual seed planting — better to let the experts handle everything else and for them to know where I was (that is, I stayed in one place rather then wandering about to get a better vantage point and satisfy my own curiosity).

Aside from getting a little seasick after lunch, Mrs Sasaki managed very well — she said as long as she kept her mind on the work at hand, she felt fine. So she focused on the work, grumbling about the poor quality of the rope, which they now had to get from China because the usual supplier, based in Sendai, had lost their whole business in the tsunami. They were used to rope that lasted ten years and Mrs Sasaki said they'd be lucky if this stuff lasted three.

The Sasakis had been worried about me getting seasick and were surprised that I didn't — I explained that my ancestors were French sailors and we agreed that that was probably why I was good on a boat, fitted in with Oshika, liked swearing, and had a bit of a dirty mind. I did think that the easily offended probably wouldn't do too well at sea for a number of reasons — if you're in the way, you quickly get shoved aside; if you're not acting quick enough, then you get yelled at; and if you need the loo, you either hold it in or stick your private parts over the side of the boat or in a bucket (assuming you'd thought to bring one), announcing what you're about to do at the top of your voice so that everybody turns away.

It was hard work, in conditions that, granted, weren't for everyone, but I put a call out to my network nonetheless, asking for people to come up to Oshika and work for the Sasakis. The bunk beds in the Sasakis' completed annex were really comfortable, so there was a lovely place to stay, and the Sasakis were wonderful hosts — you never went short of food or drink. Meals were huge, always freshly made, and very healthy, with plenty of fruit and vegetables, as well as fish, of course. They were really hoping that they'd be able to attract workers for the next spring's wakame season, so in preparation they were constructing a proper kitchen-diner. Making huge meals in the tiny room that Robert Mangold had built for them just wasn't practical anymore.

When the Sasakis started telling me about their plans for the next stage of rebuilding their business, I immediately thought of Furla Yoga's donation pledge — they had been keen for their donation to help with the "spiritual healing" of people on Oshika in some way. I kept seeing a bright, cheerful dining area in my mind — not a plain, ordinary, functional room, but a room put together with love and care, in just the way the Sasakis put together every meal for everyone around them. I shared my vision with Dana at Furla Yoga and she agreed that this was something that they would love to support — a kind of retreat from the wasteland that still existed on much of Oshika.

The Sasakis were delighted that Furla Yoga wanted to support them in this way, and they were both rather tearful when I told them. The three-year anniversary was only a few months away and outside help and aid had naturally dramatically decreased, so it meant so much to them to discover that people were still thinking about them and wanted to help them in their efforts to put their lives back together.

We sketched out a plan for the dining room, and decided on a yellow colour theme — both Mrs Sasaki and I had this colour in our minds — then made a plan to go shopping. Thanks to Kameyama-san, I knew where all the recycle shops were and could make money go a *very* long way. The Sasakis didn't even know that such shops existed and were really excited about exploring them.

I was in Mrs Sasaki's car with her, and Mr Sasaki followed us in his truck. Mrs Sasaki pointed out the place where she grew up, and said that there was nothing there anymore. When we got off the peninsula we grabbed a sandwich, which we ate in the car park in front of a newly built supermarket. As we were eating, she told me that a lot of people died in this area and when the construction workers came to build this new supermarket they all complained of constant headaches. She said there were a lot of ghosts in this area and even though this brand new supermarket had been built, nobody wanted to shop there, so it stood empty most of the time. Stories of taxi drivers picking up passengers only to later find there was nobody in the back seat were well known there, and taxis had started refusing to drive past it at night.

We found everything the Sasakis wanted in just two shops — a couple of washing machines, a huge fridge-freezer, an industrial-sized sink, a gas stove, a microwave, two lovely yellow ceiling lampshades, two dining tables with benches that could seat sixteen people, a brand new canteen-sized rice-cooker, and plenty of crockery. And there was still money left over, so we decided to use that on some finishing touches that would make the room feel like a home.

On the way home, Mrs Sasaki talked a lot about the tsunami, saying that she thought about her mother-in-law every day. But then happily said that she wasn't on the kurukurupa medication anymore; she knew that the healing came little by little. It was days like this, days that were focused on building new things and moving forward, that helped with healing.

Over in Ohara they'd heard some news that made them feel like they were moving backward rather than forward: their beloved community centre was going to be torn down! They'd be given the money to build a new one, but still, the existing centre remained standing despite having been submerged in the tsunami, and had subsequently played such a huge part in the recovery effort — surely it could be used for something? But no, the Big Baka Basho Hito had decided that the centre was to be demolished. At the same time, the junior high school's principal told me that he was very concerned about the deterioration of the children's education because of a lack of space for doing homework — most of the children lived in temporary housing, which didn't offer much space to study. Kucho and I started working on a plan to save the centre and turn it into a youth club with study facilities.

My Ohara friends were reluctant to tell me what they needed on this trip — perhaps because they were a little despondent about the news of the centre's demolition, perhaps because they thought I'd already done so much on my previous trip — but I trusted that at some point those conversations would come. I noticed there had been progress since my last trip — the little port in Ohara (as well as ports in other villages) had been raised to compensate for the land having sunk, which now made it easier for people to work; the konbini was closing much later than before in response to an increase in demand; a few new permanent buildings had gone up; and the roads on my jogging routes had finally been fixed.

But parts of the Ohara shrine were about to cave in unless something was done about it, and quickly.

24: Shrines and Wines

One of the reasons that rebuilding work took so long after the disaster (and is still ongoing) is that some of the ancient buildings couldn't be repaired by just any old carpenters and builders — a 400-year-old shrine such as the one in Ohara needed to be repaired by craftspeople with very specific skills. And finding those skilled people was extremely difficult — Kucho-san had no idea where to find an *ishiku* (stone mason) who could rebuild the *ishigaki* (stone wall) at the back of the shrine to save the *shinden* (room that houses the god) from collapse. By now, however, I not only had a network in Tokyo, I also had one on Oshika, so I put the word out that we were in need of an ishiku. Thanks to Koamikura's Abe-san, a father and son team were found and began work in Ohara — these fairly local men were able to construct just the right kind of wall to support an ancient shrine. And thanks to David Lee's Helping Hands for Japan in Oxford, we were able to find the money to pay for it.

Luckily, Ohara did have one person skilled enough to work on the shrine itself — Ogata-san, the grumpy carpenter. One of my favourite running routes would take me past his workshop, high on one of the hills and at the edge of a forest. It would always make me smile to see him at the back of his workshop, with one little spotlight hanging from the ceiling, poring over designs that were stuck to the wall. He never saw me, and if he had, he would never have smiled — he was always too grumpy for that.

So I was shocked when one day he walked into the community centre with a huge grin on his face, and handed me a rolled up sheet of paper. It was his design for Ohara's new kanetsukido — the old one had been completely destroyed by the earthquake, and Will and Kellie from Tokyo, along with their family and friends, were busy raising money for a new one.

Ogata-san presented his design to the shrine "council" meeting, to which I was invited. He also brought along some of the bits and pieces that were rescued from the debris of the original kanetsukido. All four of the corner pieces that held the roof in place had been rescued, as well as all four pieces from the middle that did the same thing. These would all be used in the new design. One of eight decorative corner pieces had been salvaged — it was thought to be over a hundred years old, and everyone oohed and aahed over it. Ogata-san was going to try to replicate the original corner piece in order to make the other seven that were needed. All eight were to be used together in the new design. I thought it was wonderful that parts of the original kanetsukido were to be incorporated in the new one.

It was decided that work would start immediately, so six of us went to Ogata-san's storage facility the next morning and loaded tons of wood onto a truck to take up to his workshop. I loved the way the Ohara boys worked together — everyone got involved, everyone pulled their weight, and everyone enjoyed working together for the benefit of their community. I think there's a lot to be learned from the way of life on Oshika.

With all the wood ready at Ogata-san's workshop, two very important rituals needed to take place before the work could begin — one was a purification ceremony at the space in front of the shrine where the kanetsukido would be erected, and the other was in front of a tree that would be cut down and used during construction. The latter was held early in the morning, and involved drinking *sake*. On a Monday.

The goal was to complete the kanetsukido before the following summer's festival, giving Ogata-san more than enough time to finish this huge job, and enough time to enjoy talking about the project — it often seemed on Oshika that the excitement generated by creating something new could be just as important as the actual completed project.

The Koamikura shrine was receiving ongoing support from Shelley and the Ohana school community, who were arranging for other parts of the shrine to be repaired, and planning another taiko visit for the following summer. And Keiko's shed had been destroyed in a recent heavy rainstorm, so I'd retrieved whatever wood I could and made her a new one with stronger foundations.

The rainstorm had also given Takahashi-san's heart-covered building a bit of a battering, so I decided to give it a fresh coat of paint, roping in Yukio-san, who Kucho told me had been feeling rather down for a while. Nobody seemed to have any luck in getting him to leave his kasetsu unless it was for a very special occasion, and Kucho thought I might be able to manage it. So when I spotted Yukio-san at a barbecue that the Ohara boys threw for twenty high school kids visiting from Nagoya, I jumped at the chance to chat with him, and asked whether he could give me a hand in repainting Takahashi-san's building.

"Tomorrow's Sunday. I'm not working. And I have to go to Ishinomaki."

"It doesn't have to be tomorrow — any time you're free would be fine."

"I'll think about it."

Later that evening he sat next to me and asked me to sing the Beatles songs I had sung when we were on our long drive to get cherry tree saplings. So I sat around the fire with him and the students, singing the songs he requested as one of the teachers played along on a guitar.

The next morning, after washing all the new futon bedding that the students had used, I had just sat down at 9:30 to get on with some of my computer-based work when, suddenly, Yukio-san's face appeared between the sheets hanging outside the community centre.

"Are you ready to go painting?"

"You said you were busy today!"

"I'll go to Ishinomaki later. Let's paint."

And we spent the whole day together, painting, having our lunch on the terrace outside the bus shelter, and looking out to sea. That was the day he took me to the top of the really steep hill that overlooked all of Ohara and told me how he had stood there, alone, and watched the whole village get swallowed by the sea. He talked and talked, and I listened in silence. It was two and a half years on, but to him it was like yesterday.

Mrs Nagashima (I usually referred to her and her cheeky husband as Mr and Mrs Naughty Twinkle) was one of Yukio-san's neighbours in the temporary housing community, where I still regularly popped in to see whether anybody needed anything from the free shop, or just to say hello. One day I sat down in the danwashitsu with my lunch — all the women were there singing karaoke. I looked at Mrs Nagashima and was overcome with a feeling that her husband was no longer with us. It was a very strange sensation. When I was halfway through my lunch, she came over and sat next to me and whispered in my ear that her husband had died three months earlier. So many of these elderly people dreaded the thought of dying in the temporary houses, and my heart really went out to her. Mrs Nagashima said she still couldn't believe it and was still crying every night. We sat there hugging each other and shedding a few tears together. She pointed to the sky and was obviously saying something about him being up there, but I couldn't completely understand. From that moment onward, to this day, whenever I look up at the beautiful stars on Oshika I think of Mr Nagashima and the twinkle in his eyes when he looked at his wife with such devotion.

You can see some incredible stars from Oshika — it's not unusual to catch a beautiful night sky full of shooting stars, coming one after the other. The peninsula's beauty has never failed to amaze me, and I love any opportunity to go out on the sea or up into the forests, but my days on this trip were becoming fuller with meetings, coordinating projects, talking to sponsors, or reporting back to my network of supporters. Abe-san could now tend part of his farmland, the fishermen were planting wakame seeds for the following spring, and Onodera-san seemed to be doing lots of random jobs here and there. There was less opportunity for us to work together, so when one of my favourite people told me he was going off to the forest to pick mushrooms, I jumped at the chance to go with him.

Despite the fact that I was running 4 km most days, and Onodera-san smoked and drank a lot, took heart medicine, and was twenty years older than me, I was out of breath within *minutes* while he happily carried on ahead, up the steep hill. We didn't follow any paths because there weren't any — we were literally wandering about in a completely wild forest.

Onodera-san kept saying how there were hardly any mushrooms there anymore, and that three years ago the forest was full of them and they were really easy to find. The tsunami hadn't reached the forest, so that wasn't the reason the mushrooms were gone, and he couldn't figure out why there hadn't been any for the past two years. The few that we could find were growing in different places than they were before. It was like the ones that were there had shifted position.

When we did come across some mushrooms, we would stop to get our knives out and then slice the mushroom stalks as close to the ground as possible. Onodera-san knew which ones were edible and which ones weren't, and I quickly learned the difference, too. I was fascinated by the thick, white, spongy mould they grew out of, and by the fact that they grew in a long line. Once you found one mushroom, if you moved some of the branches and leaves a little, you'd find clusters of them. Then if you looked around, you'd see them all following the same line. Some of them were huge — bigger than my hand. I found the whole thing fascinating, and I just loved being with Onodera-san.

We filled the bamboo rucksack, which Onodera-san insisted on carrying, but he needed my help to get it on his back because of his damaged right arm. It was always a bit of a weak spot for him because he'd played a lot of tennis when he was young, and after the tsunami he spent every day clearing debris alongside the young volunteers, lifting heavy things he shouldn't have been lifting, so he ended up doing permanent damage to his arm — these are the kinds of long-term effects of the tsunami that aren't readily apparent. When he told me about his injury, we both said at the same time that as long as he could lift a drink with his left arm, it wasn't a big problem — but of course it was.

We only took what Onodera-san felt was enough to share with everyone else in the village — I liked that he didn't just keep taking more and more even when we'd come across a really big patch on our way back. And I liked that he didn't want us to take the small, baby ones, instead covering them up with leaves and branches so they could continue to grow.

Onodera-san knew that I liked red wine, and would often have a bottle ready for us when I'd pop over to spend the evening under the kotatsu with him and his family. He once asked me what kind of snacks are eaten with red wine (it would have been unheard of to drink Asahi beer without some kind of dried fish or nut snack), and I told him cheese and biscuits. I was so touched when, on our next evening together, he presented me with some "Baby Cheese" — rectangles of processed cheese that are a bit like Dairylea, which I loved as a child in England, and some salty American-style crackers.

One evening there was a bottle of rather murky liquid placed on the table. Upon closer inspection I realized that there was a snake in the bottom of the bottle. I learned that if Onodera-san came across a snake during his forest wanderings, he would capture it and put it, live, into a bottle of *sake* to make *mamushi sake*, believed to have medicinal properties. I tried pretty much everything they put in front of me on Oshika, but I drew the line at snake wine.

This trip was far less exhausting than the previous one had been — the autumn weather on Oshika tends to be mild and far less windy than in the spring, so I'd managed to get a lot of sleep. Apart, that is, from the night when I made the mistake of letting a kitten sleep in my room — this kitten appeared from nowhere one day, and to everyone's amusement it started to follow me everywhere. I don't know why it did that: I'm much more a dog person than a cat person. We laughed about how the kitten's parents had probably been among the animals under the centre that had kept me awake during my previous trip.

I seemed to be a bit of a magnet for little creatures on this trip — I would come across tiny rats and the weirdest looking bugs everywhere I went in the centre. Some of the bugs were *huge*! They joined me in the shower, ran around the kitchen when I went to get water to make a cup of tea, and crawled across the tatami just as I was about to turn the light out at night. I made the decision to try to live alongside them and not to stress too much — after all, it was their space that I was invading.

I said farewell to my Oshika friends by hosting a Christmas party — this time setting up little gas stoves all along the tables in the centre, and teaching everyone how to make mulled wine. Because Japan is not rooted in Christianity, December 25 is a normal working day, and Christmas itself isn't really celebrated. Christmas trees and decorations, however, are another matter entirely, and most cities in Japan have incredible light displays throughout December and January. And learning about new kinds of drinks is always popular in Ohara!

It had been another productive trip, but I came away feeling sad — many of my Oshika friends just felt so forgotten. Tokyo's successful bid for the 2020 Olympics had been such a shock to many of them, and there was a feeling that this cause for celebration was distracting attention away from the realities of life for people in Tohoku. And they were right — as I continued my talks in Tokyo, I discovered that many Japanese and non-Japanese alike *living in Japan* were shocked when they saw my photographs and heard my stories of what life was like in Tohoku. The very few news stories they had seen always portrayed the recovery process as being hugely successful — they had no idea that hundreds of thousands of people still lived in temporary housing. It made sense when an employee of Dentsu (Japan's largest advertising agency) admitted to a friend of mine that they had specifically been told to "sweep Tohoku and Fukushima under the carpet" when Tokyo won the bid that September. The tsunami survivors hadn't been forgotten — *they were being ignored.*

I was so touched by the continuing efforts of people within my network who refused to ignore Oshika. People had been inspired to raise money within their own networks — Tokyo Mothers' Group had a whip-round at a lunch I attended and, in that very short space of time and with a relatively small number of people, they collected enough to sponsor a Pink Lady kappa; Kspace pledged to raise enough money to sponsor another year of incoming students' school uniforms; and Will and Kellie and friends had managed to raise over ¥2 million through direct donations and a big event at What The Dickens!, a popular Tokyo bar. Even individuals had been inspired to do whatever they could — Lorna Nagamine in Hawaii was putting aside what she would normally spend at Starbucks in her attempt to save some money for Oshika. By the time I returned to the UK, my fundraising had reached over ¥14 million!

Before leaving Japan, I finally submitted my permanent residency application — it was 10 cm thick! As a self-employed person who is not married to a Japanese national, I felt that I couldn't give the officials *any* excuse to not grant me a permanent residency visa, so I'd gone totally overboard with all sorts of supportive documentation that would prove that I somehow contributed to Japan. I handed over my application and waited while the immigration officer went through everything. Eventually he called my name out, handed me a postcard confirming my application, and waved the Japanese edition of the Love book at me with a huge smile, saying, "Your book is wonderful!" I took it as a good sign and crossed my fingers that I'd have a positive result by the time I returned to Japan.

Christmas was in full swing when I arrived back in England, and I'd decided to take the pickled onions to the Cirencester Charter Market, where I discovered that they'd already acquired a bit of a reputation thanks to Jesse Smith's Butchers. I also took some runners and cushions that I had made out of *obi* — the long piece of thick fabric that winds around the waist over a kimono. Opposite one of the recycle shops in Ishinomaki I had spotted a second-hand kimono shop, and a bit of a shopping addiction had developed. While ordinarily I hate clothes shopping, I could spend hours in that shop (and still can). I decided to bring lots of obi back to England and make runners and cushions out of them — another way to share my love for Japan with people in England, while supporting a small business near Oshika at the same time.

I missed Japan every day, but New Year's always felt the hardest. I loved the tradition of going to a shrine for midnight so that I could hear the bell ring in the new year. When in Tokyo, I'd also loved being able to go to the Kamakura seaside in time to see the first sunrise, another popular New Year's activity in Japan. I researched any Shinto shrines in the Cotswolds but found none, and Cirencester was about as far away from the sea as you could get, so I settled for walking alone up Broad Ride — the tree-lined path through Bathurst Estate — on New Year's Day to welcome 2014 in. It was beautiful, but not the same.

Inspired by the success of my pickled onions over Christmas, I started adding some new lines and supplying more shops — my little Auntie Caroline's business was really taking off! While managing that, I was also supporting a fundraising event at Farmor's School — one of the schools I had given talks to in the past.

Kenzo Shiomi, who ran Amity Yokohama, had introduced me to his old school friend Hiroyuki Takashima, head of Takashima Artists Management, and the man responsible for bringing the Beatles to Japan in 1966. In 2013, he was managing a string quartet of four dynamic young women who covered Beatles songs. They were called 1966 Quartet and were scheduled to visit the UK for a recording session at Abbey Road. Takashima-san had been very impressed by my efforts in Tohoku, and said that he would make the musicians available to perform at a fundraising event in the UK. So together with the Farmor's School music department, we put on a very special event.

I'd reached out to all my contacts from Japan who were pretty high up in British businesses, as well as to any of my Japanese contacts in the UK, asking them to support the event's raffle. The prizes I received in response were incredible, and included one from an old client of mine, Aston Martin, who donated an Experience Day for two. Japan was a big market for Aston Martin, and the company was very keen to support Tohoku's recovery efforts. They donated an Experience Day unlike any of the usual ones you could purchase — it included a tour of the factory, access to areas that even journalists didn't get to see, a get-together with design staff, lunch, and an hour-long drive of one of their cars, which to the Farmor's students' delight, appeared outside the music department on the evening of the event.

It was a hugely successful evening. The performances by 1966 Quartet and the school's own music students were incredible. The audience's generosity greatly surpassed what I'd anticipated — the event raised almost £2000.

A couple of months later I supported another fundraising event in England, this time organized by the Japanese community in Oxford; it was a Japan-themed day for children and adults alike. The day included people playing traditional Japanese music, kimono to try on, prizes to win in Japanese games, and lot of delicious Japanese food. I gave a presentation about my work on Oshika, during which I made quite a few people cry, including Helping Hands for Japan's David Lee, who compered the whole event, and star volunteer Sophie, who was now based in Bristol, and with whom I enjoyed an emotional reunion. The event raised £1000. This turned into an annual fundraiser and awareness event to support Oshika and other Japan-related projects, and it still goes on today.

Before I knew it, it was June, and I was heading back to Japan for the summer, soon to be joined by my second niece Emily, who would be using the flight I'd given her for her eighteenth birthday a couple of years earlier. I had a busy summer planned, and Emily's presence for the first couple of weeks was very much appreciated. She fit right in on the peninsula, threw herself into anything that was asked of her, and ate everything put in front of her. She didn't care that she didn't understand what was being said, and didn't expect me to constantly translate for her. She was happy just to be there, and I loved her so much for that, truly treasuring the opportunity to spend time with her as well as introduce her to a place that meant so much to me.

Showing Emily around Oshika was a good way not just to say hello to everyone, but also to see what progress had been made. Temporary "stations" for little fire trucks had been set up all over the peninsula because an actual fire station was yet to be built. One of the little stations was right outside the centre where we slept. It housed a tiny fire truck — on Oshika trucks had to be small in order to get down the narrow streets. On Sunday mornings the local volunteer firefighters could be seen doing their exercises all over the peninsula, prompting me to recall what I'd learned a few years earlier: that the only thing better than a man in uniform was a Japanese man in uniform.

Koamikura had just had their summer festival, attended again by Shelley and her taiko friends all the way from Tokyo. They had continued to financially support the village — thanks to them the stone torii had been repaired and re-erected just in time for the festival, more than three years since it had been battered to the ground. At its base there now stood a beautiful monumental sign, engraved (in Japanese) with the names of all those who had sponsored its repair: Ohana International School, Miyabi Arashi Taiko Group, and the British School in Tokyo. And to my surprise, my name was there, too!

The Ohara shrine wall was finished and the two buildings that made up the shrine at least had secure foundations, even if their roofs were still in need of work. The kanetsukido was just about finished, and it was truly breathtaking — I got my first glimpse of it through the trees as Emily and I walked up the shrine steps, and my heart really did leap. I couldn't wait for Will to visit Oshika the following month and join in with the Ohara summer festival, when the bell would be rung from the kanetsukido for the first time.

I had known that Ogata-san would do a fantastic job on the bell tower, but his work totally surpassed my expectations — the amount of detail he had put into it was amazing. The fact that he incorporated wood from the previous kanetsukido really impressed me, but I was told that he also incorporated wood that was carried to Ohara by the tsunami. It was absolutely beautiful — a true work of art.

And — in a gesture that deeply touched me and still does when I look at the bell tower even now — Ogata-san incorporated heart shapes into his kanetsukido, which he said represented my heart.

25: A Princess

I noticed two major differences that summer in 2014, three years after the disaster: the first concerned the ports and the second concerned a brand new road. Completely funded by the government, the working areas, paths, and roads that made up the little ports on Oshika had (for the most part) been raised and rebuilt over the months that had passed (the land needed to be raised because it sank a metre after the earthquake). The fishing industry was functioning again to some extent, but people were accepting that it would never fully support this area economically again. Tourism was Oshika's main hope for the future.

The second thing I noticed was that seemingly random bits of land were being raised throughout the peninsula. A new elevated road was to be built inland, far away from the current coastal road. Most people I spoke to seemed to think it was a waste of time, effort, and money; and I wondered why that time and money weren't being spent on getting people out of temporary housing — people had been living in those little boxes for almost three years.

On the surface though, people seemed quite jolly — the weather on Oshika during the summer is wonderful and the sea is calm. It's a quiet season for the fishing industry, so nobody's in a rush to be anywhere or do anything. The Sasakis were remarkably relaxed when my niece Emily and I visited to put the finishing touches to their dining room to make it more homely, which included metres and metres of beautiful old-English-style bunting that my mother had made to match their colour scheme — it still hangs there now.

Mr Sasaki took us over to Ajishima Island, where two of his sisters lived, and we enjoyed a wonderful meal at the hotel run by one of the sisters. Emily even ate *uni* (sea urchin) straight from the shell, and so fresh that its spikes were still moving, thoroughly impressing Mr Sasaki, who said, "Good job, good job." He turned away and walked along the beautiful beach when Emily and I stripped off to our underwear and threw ourselves into the stunning blue water. Ajishima was like an island paradise.

Everybody seemed so relaxed that summer — old married couples who usually worked hard were instead relaxing together, and it was lovely to see. These were couples who had lived and worked together for most of their lives, and their love and respect for each other never failed to touch me. In the summer months, grass now grows wild over the land where people's houses used to stand, and it would have been understandable for strangers to assume that nothing tragic had ever happened on Oshika. Yet amid the relaxed and loving atmosphere that summer, there was still such unexpected fallout from what happened in 2011 — situations that you'd never imagine people would have to deal with three years later, when they'd already dealt with so much. For example, there was the man who had just found out that the ashes he buried three years ago, which he *thought* were those of the wife he lost to the tsunami, weren't actually her ashes at all.

There *had* been progress on Oshika — practically, emotionally, and spiritually — but for some people it had been three years of very, *very* tiny steps forward, followed by a *huge* step back. How do you comfort someone in that situation? There are no words that can provide any kind of relief. He had so many questions that nobody seemed able to answer, so he became determined to educate himself, as shown when he asked if I could get hold of a book about DNA for him.

I had been asking everyone I knew on Oshika about which books they wanted. And I did that because that summer I'd invited Tsukasa-san up to Oshika again. I wanted him to create another very special building. Not a bus shelter this time, but a community library that would be funded not just by the money raised at the 1966 Quartet event, but also by appeals to a number of different organizations and individuals in both the UK and Japan. A total of ¥2.25 million was raised!

The library was to be built next to the playground, on higher land than the rest of Ohara, and with an incredible view out to sea. A group of us — me,

Seiji Yoshimura, and a few of the Ohara boys — got started early one morning. We moved a campervan, a shipping container, pallets, and various bits of debris that had accumulated on the land that Kucho-san had chosen for the library. Mr Sasaki wasn't from Ohara, so it wasn't quite the usual thing for him to be involved, but he turned up in his forklift anyway, and he moved those massive objects with impressive skill. It was hugely entertaining, with Seiji clambering all over a roof, the forklift getting stuck and needing towing, and the whole container being moved without anybody bothering to disconnect it from the electricity!

We were left with a much bigger space than I had imagined, and with the wonderful view of the sea that Ohara has been famous for since Date Masamune first set foot in it over four hundred years ago. My mind went into overdrive, thinking about how this space could be transformed. At one point, my niece Emily and I had come across a couple of men sitting in the bus shelter with the door open, drinking canned coffees and catching up with the latest gossip. I asked them where they were taking the bus to, and they said that they weren't waiting for a bus but were just relaxing in the shelter because it was such a beautiful space — it was then that I realized just how much people on Oshika benefitted from having a cosy, welcoming place in which to spend time with their friends. I wanted the library to be just that.

The land Kucho had chosen actually belonged to the local government, and before the tsunami it was the location of the koban, and it used to have a little garage next to it for the patrol car. One of the local police officers had been to school with Mr Sasaki, and the latter confessed that during their wild younger days, a bunch of them had a crazy drinking night together, at the end of which they realized that none of them was safe to drive home. It was impossible to get a taxi on Oshika, so they decided that the best thing to do would be to take the patrol car and drive along the winding roads at just five miles an hour, with the lights flashing the whole time.

The police no longer had a base on Oshika, and there were no plans to do anything with that piece of land, so Kucho-san, with an attitude I had seen become increasingly bold and decisive since I'd first met him in May 2011, decided that the library would be built there.

Construction regulations meant that anything over ten metres square required planning permission, so in order to avoid months and months of meetings and the sucking of teeth that Japanese bureaucrats were so fond of, we decided to make the library itself *exactly* ten metres square, and create an outdoor terrace of the same size extending out in front of the library, thus in effect creating double the amount of communal space. In addition, there was an old parking space next to the library, just lower down, and full of small bits of debris and dried mud that the tsunami had left behind. Once the parking space was cleaned that up, it would be used for another outdoor seating space. There was also some bamboo that we could use — it had originally been bought to make candle holders for the first-year anniversary, but the surplus had not been taken away afterward. I decided to create a fence around the lower terrace with it.

When it was time for building to begin, the ground was prepared and space was cleared by some Ohara-jin, my niece Emily, and some of the people who had raised money for the library who were able to visit as the project started — including enthusiastic teenager Lucie Kapner and her father. Lucie had managed to raise ¥100,000 all by herself and was keen to be hands-on, too. It was great to collaborate on preparing the ground, and we had fun working together. One day, Kucho-san drove past on his way to a meeting on the mainland. He turned his car around, changed out of his suit and into his casual clothes, and set to work clearing the land with us. He did it, he said, because it was a much more enjoyable thing to do. I always loved it when he joined in!

On the day construction started, I was actually at the other end of the peninsula, building the Ayukawa playground. Stephen from Meikei High School, the playground sponsor, was joining me to build it, and the timing meant that I had the two projects going on simultaneously. But I trusted Tsukasa-san with the library and knew that I could leave him to it. He later told me that I had missed a very entertaining interaction between Kucho-san and some local government officials. The suit-wearing officials had turned up on the day construction began, to try to put a stop to it. They spent some time asking questions and objecting to the library being built when Kucho-san simply asked them what they were planning to do with the land, to which they replied, "nothing." So Kucho-san said, "Well we're going to build a library on it," so the suits left. And the construction continued.

I returned to the library construction on a break from the Ayukawa playground construction, and as Tsukasa-san and his team did the actual construction, Mr Sasaki helped me with building the framework for the bamboo fencing. Using the bamboo for a fence around the lower outdoor seating area was a great use of materials we had found lying around. I loved making that fence with Mr Sasaki — learning so much about scaffolding and how to wind wire around and in between each bamboo strip, and becoming quite good at it, with Mr Sasaki frequently saying, "Good job, good job." IKEA had again been fantastic — they totally supported the library and had given me a very generous budget to spend on furnishings to make the space comfortable and appealing.

In my efforts to make the library a very special place, one that would be truly useful for the local people, I had decided to ask *them* what books they wanted. I could have just put a call out to my network for them to send up any books they didn't want anymore, and knowing how big-hearted my network was, I would have received hundreds of books, if not thousands. But most of them would have been in English (which nobody speaks on Oshika), and many others may not have been of interest. I had to find out what books were actually needed and wanted by my Oshika friends.

So I set up a wish list on Amazon, and carted my computer around, asking people to look through Amazon with me and add books to the wish list. I asked them to think about the books that were special to them when they were children, and books they had lost in the tsunami. Books can be comforting, they can be decorative, and, in my opinion, they really make a place "home." I wanted the people on Oshika to feel literally *at home* in the library.

It was quite a challenging process. With very few people using computers on Oshika, it often took a while to explain the actual process to them — this is where I realized that I did truly have unlimited patience when it came to my friends on Oshika. But once they got into it, it was really fun to do this together — it was sad to see them think back to the books that were washed away from their homes, but I loved seeing them get excited when they spotted a book they were so fond of. And I really enjoyed seeing Yuki, Onodera-san's daughter and the youngest person in Ohara, sit down with some of the elderly ladies from the temporary housing and gently coax the titles of their favourite books out of them.

It was interesting to see the kinds of books people chose; I learned a lot about people's interests. I would never have guessed that Takahashi-buta, the pig farmer, wanted to learn all about the history of Israel. And I was really surprised to discover that the vast majority of books people added to the wish list were non-fiction — very few novels.

Kucho-san really made me giggle when I sat down with him. The first books he requested were books on fishing; when I pushed him for more ideas, he responded with, "fishing in Miyagi-ken," and when I pushed him for other things he was interested in, he came up with "boat maintenance." It turned out that what he really wanted to see in the library were some Chinese books — not for himself, but for the Chinese seasonal staff that had recently joined Yachan's factory as his business was finally able to hire again after the disaster. Kucho was worried about the Chinese workers feeling homesick, and he thought they might like to read something in their own language. I thought this was such a sweet thing to think of, but this was really typical of the people on Oshika — many of them, when asked about books *they* liked, often had some ideas of books that other people living on Oshika might like. And when I sat down with the Chinese ladies that evening, they said that they wanted to read books that would teach them about Japanese conversation, so that they would be able to speak appropriately to Kucho-san, for whom they had a lot of respect.

So I created a small wish list on Amazon China, and the main list on Amazon Japan. Tsukasa-san and I had been excited to work out that the library would have space for a thousand books — I put the word out to my network to start their online book shopping! The response was, as always, incredible. Amazon's wish list service was perfect for a project like this — people from anywhere in the world could support this project by just clicking a button, and the books would be delivered directly to Ohara. Boxes of books arrived every single day, and the pile in my little "bedroom" in the centre got bigger and bigger. When the library was completed, they were all carried over and organized into categories. I made bilingual hearts with information about each of the sponsors to decorate the walls, bought wooden toys and games for both children and adults alike that would be stored inside the IKEA stools, and had a special stamp made for the inside front cover of all the books.

The finished library was beautiful; it was everything I had hoped for! It was warm and welcoming, with comfy cushions for both inside and outside seating. It had a wide range of books that were curated to suit everyone's interests. And the three spaces — the indoor library, the outdoor decking in front of the library, and the lower "beer garden" (the Ohara boys christened it that) — all provided much-needed spaces away from the temporary housing. I felt quite emotional when it was completed. I think we all did. I had a lump in my throat when I caught Tsukasa-san having a quiet moment alone inside it, and the tears arrived in full force when I found two teenagers inside, silently lying across huge floor cushions, immersed in their favourite books.

I spent much of that week racing back and forth between Ohara and Ayukawa, while trying to take care of everyone that was working on the two projects I had going on at the same time. Emily had gone home by then, and Tsukasa-san and his team were staying with me in the centre — they were lovely company. Late one night I took them to Gobanshokoen, the highest point on Oshika, where we all lay on the ground watching shooting stars.

It was great that Stephen brought his daughter Aya with him to Oshika and that they were helping to build the Ayukawa playground along with some of the locals — another lovely project that sponsors and locals could complete together. I'd ordered the playset from Playground of Hope, but discovered that parts for the swings were missing. Easily fixable, I'd thought, by someone who knew some decent knots. I was surrounded by fishermen, and thought someone was bound to be able to help, when Mr Sasaki turned up out of the blue and created the missing parts to secure the swings until the replacements arrived.

We also built a huge sandpit, filled it with toys and sand, and made a cover to protect it from curious cats. Kita-san and Nakamura-san from Shiga-ken, both chainsaw artists and long-time regular volunteers in this area, made animal character benches for the play area. Sid Lloyd from Footy Japan in Tokyo sent up lots of footballs for the kids to play with. We were on a tight deadline to get the playground itself finished though, and dragged in Tsukasa-san and his team to help with the finishing touches, which we completed under the light of our car headlamps.

The next day, the people who ran the temporary shopping street set up a barbecue, as children and parents came from all directions to see their brand new, finished playground. As the first children threw themselves all over the playset, screaming in delight, one of the local women, who had been instrumental in securing the land for the playground, burst into tears. Sometimes I wondered whether the grown ups on Oshika needed to feel cared for even more than the children did.

The principal of Oshika Junior High School was pleased to tell me that summer that the students' academic performances had really seen an improvement during the past year. He'd been so worried about them before, when students in the whole Ishinomaki area were performing worse than anywhere else in the country. He'd mentioned some software that other schools he'd worked in had used that could make a huge difference to the students' academic performances, saying that he didn't have the budget for it. So I'd contacted a few IT companies I knew, and my old friend, Tokyo entrepreneur Mike Alfant, was more than happy to fund the software, which had even made it possible for the peninsula to set up a *juku* (cram school) where the software was used. The juku teacher, Ito-sensei, was holding classes in Ohara's community centre, and joined Kucho and me in our efforts to save the centre, still scheduled for demolition, in order to preserve it as a social and learning space for the teens and young adults on Oshika. There weren't many young adults on Oshika, but it was important for the future of the peninsula that they be encouraged to stay, and that others were encouraged to move there.

Busloads of young adults descended upon Ohara for the summer festival that year, all keen to join in with the unique experience of carrying a mikoshi. To my delight, Will also visited and participated in carrying the mikoshi and in the more sedate ceremony at the shrine. I will never forget the sight of Will sitting inside the shrine that Saturday evening, with the completed kanetsukido behind him — something that he had raised over ¥2 million for — all lit up by beautiful red lanterns. I loved watching when he was called to the front of the shrine to participate in the prayer ritual, and I loved seeing him back in the centre with the Ohara boys, as he taught them a haka from his New Zealand Maori heritage. They were completely transfixed.

I took Will on a tour of the peninsula, at one point driving past Ogata-san's chaotic workshop, where I tentatively stopped to see whether the grumpy carpenter wasn't quite so grumpy and whether visitors would be welcomed. It was as though he'd been waiting there for us, because when I introduced Will as the kanetsukido's sponsor, he presented Will with the rolled up paper upon which he'd created his original design for the structure — a wonderful gift. Then he presented me with the wooden "template" he'd made for the very centre of the kanetsukido's roof, which I hadn't realized he'd attempted to design like the Union Jack flag. I was deeply touched and it stands in my living room still today.

Nick Johnston, who sponsored the school uniforms for the 2014 intake, also came to visit Oshika, and actually got to meet all the children he had helped — such a rare thing to be able to do after donating to any cause these days.

Visitors always tried to bring something up for the free shop, which I was still running, as well as trying my best to keep Mrs Sasaki stocked up on cat food to feed the increasing number of stray cats that had found their way to her after the disaster. In addition to the cat food, I also put a call out for barbecue food — English style — and put together a little party to celebrate the opening of the library. At the party, my Ohara friends sat in the beer garden before setting off fireworks as the sun went down. I will never forget Kucho-san's wife Fukumi-san — who I had never heard say anything even remotely rude — nibbling on an English sausage from the barbecue, looking me in the eye, and commenting on how big the English sausage was when compared with Japanese sausages, then winking at me before she walked off.

It was a crazy summer with my usual activities and all the guests to take care of, but, as always, I loved life on Oshika. And I slept *so* well on that trip — to the point where I was told that I talked in my sleep, something I've never done before. But to my utter delight, I was told that I spoke in *Japanese*.

I returned to the UK after that wonderful and very productive summer on Oshika to find, quite unexpectedly, that my little pickling business was very much in demand. I was soon selling over a thousand jars a month, and supplying more shops than before. And it didn't feel like it was taking a huge amount of effort — everything about the business just ran so smoothly.

I constantly felt torn between countries — loving my time in Oshika and feeling like I was doing something *meaningful* with my life; still not able to say "I live in England," but nonetheless loving becoming part of the Cirencester community, being in the same country as my mother and my nieces and nephews, and having a business that was so much easier to manage than anything I had ever done before during the almost twenty years I'd worked for myself.

A decision had been made for me though, during my previous trip — my permanent residency application had been rejected.

This *utterly devastated* me! I still considered Japan to be my home — Japan meant *everything* to me. I still had a working visa for the next few years, so it wasn't like I couldn't go back and forth as much as I liked for a while still, but I just felt so *unwanted* by a country I loved so much. I'd been in floods of tears in the immigration office, pointing out my income, the taxes I was paying in Japan, the books I had written for Japanese readers, and the numerous letters prominent people had written endorsing my application. I had been featured in the English and Japanese media so many times over so many years, with stories always focusing on the good work I had done for the international and Japanese communities alike. My pleas made absolutely no difference to the immigration official though. As soon as my current visa expired, that would be it.

While I'd submitted a document outlining my activities on Oshika, most of the media coverage I had put together for my application had been about my books or businesses. There had been quite a few pieces in the English media about my efforts since the disaster, but very little in any Japan-based media, in either English or Japanese. This was very deliberate on my part. I turned down almost every Japan-based request for an interview about my Oshika work because I didn't ever want to see any story about my projects there become a story about me when it was the stories about other people's lives that needed to be heard. I kept my network informed about what I was doing, but that was it.

So I was surprised when I found out that I was up for an award from the Japan-British Society, and when I was told that I had actually won it, I found it all quite moving. It might have been to do with the fact that I was told about the award on the day that my third niece, nine-year-old Mabel, did something that truly touched me. It was Children in Need day, and that year all British kids were instructed to go to school dressed as superheroes. Mabel had donned a T-shirt with Japanese writing on it and a pair of jeans, and decided to go as her Auntie Caroline, who "helped people." So I spent much of the day feeling rather overwhelmed and going through a lot of tissues.

The 2014 award was due to be presented by Princess Akiko of Mikasa on December 15, 2014 in Tokyo, and I decided not to go to Japan to accept it for a number of reasons. That time of year is the busiest for pickles, and my UK business was really booming, so I didn't really think I'd be able to take the time to go; I wasn't sure that it would be sensible to do two heparin injections so close together if I was literally flying in then flying out again; and the idea of spending money on a flight *just* to accept an award felt rather frivolous. The flight money I saved was for trips to Oshika, not for receiving awards.

But I hadn't counted on Mabel's influence over me …

"But Auntie Caroline, you *must* go and receive the award!"

"I can't … the pickles are so busy … I have to think of my health … I'm going in February and can't afford two flights so close together."

"*But a princess is going to give it to you!*"

And in that moment, seeing what I did with my life through Mabel's eyes, and knowing what an impact it was having on her as she grew up, made me realize that she was right. I had to go. Sometimes it's important to accept some recognition for something you really do put your heart into, even if you don't think you want it.

So after confirming with the doctor that it would be OK to inject heparin twice in such a short space of time; remembering a lovely cocktail dress I'd had tailor-made in my Tokyo days, hadn't parted with, and still fitted into; getting a generously discounted flight from Virgin; and pickling like crazy to make up for the three days I'd be away at the busiest time of year, I got on a 12-hour flight for a 24-hour stay and took another 12-hour flight straight back.

Only my dear sister-friend Emily knew I was coming to Japan — it was all supposed to be kept very quiet because the award was being presented by a member of the imperial family. I grabbed the shortest ever catch-up with Emily, then went straight to sleep in the hotel where the award ceremony was being held, setting my alarm in time for the evening's ceremony.

An hour before the ceremony I discovered that I could only just about fit into my dress. It had fit me perfectly before the flight but after the swelling that occurs after flying, my dress seemed to squeeze *everything* upward. I was horrified. Even if there were time to go shopping, I wouldn't be able to find anything suitable that would fit. So I spent the entire evening absolutely mortified at my heaving bosom, just praying that it wouldn't spill out at the dinner table when I was surrounded by these high society, mostly elderly Japanese couples or, even worse, right at Princess Akiko when I bowed to accept the award. Luckily, I made it through the evening without any mishaps.

It was an exceptional evening, and I am so glad that I went. I savoured every moment, not just for Mabel, but also for all the people who had supported my efforts during the four years since the disaster, as well as the people it was really for — my brave friends on Oshika, on whose behalf I accepted the award.

We weren't allowed to take any photographs during the event; there was an official photographer, but the photos were never made public. I did, however, ask him if I could have just one of his photos of me with Princess Akiko, not for publication, but for my niece. He very kindly sent me a beautiful photograph of me bowing deeply in front of the princess in her stunning kimono and with her beautiful smile, as she handed me the award. I had the photograph printed and framed, and presented it to Mabel with a bow just as deep as the one I had made to the princess, and thanked her for making me go.

She put that photograph next to her bed — she said it was so she could see me every night before she went to sleep.

26: A Prince

I'd met British Ambassador Tim Hitchens at the award ceremony. His wife Sara had congratulated me, and we started chatting. She immediately told me how much she had enjoyed my book — it was nice to hear that she had read it and I said that I hoped it had been helpful to her. She and her husband looked puzzled, but were both still smiling, so I continued with, "Did you learn much from it?" at which point she looked a little embarrassed and I suddenly realized that she had been referring to my book with instructions for Japanese men to help with their intimate relationships with women, and *not* my guidebook for foreign women in Japan, which is what I was talking about. Then it was my turn to be embarrassed, but I thought that I might as well stick my foot all the way in, so I asked the ambassador whether *he'd* learned much from it, to which he of course replied in a suitably diplomatic manner.

After an extremely amusing discussion about a number of the topics covered in my saucy book and discovering that Tim was also from Plymouth, I realized that he and Sara were definitely my sort of people — warm, friendly, and with a naughty sense of humour. It was a real honour to meet them. It was also a real honour to be asked whether I'd be interested in giving Prince William a tour of Oshika during his upcoming February 2015 trip to Japan.

My next trip to Oshika was coincidentally planned for the same time Prince William was visiting Japan, and I flew over in early February. I would have loved to have given him a tour of Oshika, but unfortunately, due to the extremely tight schedule that he was running under, he couldn't get as far as Oshika. But he was scheduled to visit Onagawa, which is where the northern part of Oshika meets the mainland. I was asked to go along, and to bring the Pink Ladies — Prince William wanted to meet them!

I knew this had the potential to be a good opportunity to let influential people know about what life on the peninsula was like for the people in these remote fishing communities. I also knew just how much such a meeting could lift people's spirits on Oshika. So once the details had been set and I was given permission to talk to people about it (this happened less than 72 hours before HRH was due to arrive in Onagawa), I raced around the peninsula trying to locate as many of the 73 Pink Ladies and kappa-sponsored men as possible, asking them whether they would like to see Prince William in Onagawa. I had no idea how many would show up — everyone was busy preparing for the wakame season that started that same day, and terrible weather was expected for the day Prince William was to visit the area. People prefer not to venture out on the peninsula in bad weather — future king or no future king.

But 28 of us set off on a Sunday morning, all wearing sponsored fishing outfits, most of which were pink, and all with my little Union Jack heart patches on them. We didn't need a flag to wave when we were wearing those outfits, and there was no chance of missing us. Not everybody actually worked in the fishing industry, but everybody was from Oshika, and the fishing industry is key to *everyone* who lives there. I was especially thrilled to see the head of Kujiranoshippo (Ishinomaki Shoshinkai Foundation Vocational Support Centre for the Disabled) — a facility on Oshika that sells local products and supports cognitively disabled adults — along with five of her "trainees," all so excited about the possibility of seeing Prince William. I had no idea how close we would get or whether there would be any opportunity to talk to him, and was becoming a bit stressed about the whole thing — I wanted the embassy to be happy about the turnout, and my Oshika friends to be happy about the experience. All I wanted for *myself* was the chance to tell the prince what life was really like for the people on Oshika.

And it worked out perfectly!

We positioned ourselves close to *Kibonokane* (the Bell of Hope) in the Onagawa temporary shopping centre, and had a perfect view of Prince William as he was escorted to the bell, which he dutifully rang. He was then immediately ushered over to me, as his embassy guide said, "These are the Pink Ladies."

"So what are the Pink Ladies?" Prince William asked.

I started explaining who they were, and Prince William was visibly surprised to be addressed in English, by a fellow Brit. Being the same height as my Japanese friends, and dressed in a pink fishing outfit, and with long dark hair under a hat, at first glance it would be easy to mistake me for a Japanese from Oshika. I tried to continue my explanation, but people to the right of me (not the Pink Ladies, who were very well-behaved) started pushing and shoving to get their hands out in front of him, shouting "William *oji*" ("Prince William") like they were at a gig. It was difficult to concentrate — since I had my strokes my brain doesn't really work well if people are talking all around me. Prince William must have a great ability (with years of training, I'm sure) to focus with a lot of noise going on around him, because he was very intent on talking to me, asked lots of questions, and seemed genuinely interested. I had read once that his mother had the ability to make you feel as though you were the only person in the room, and he has a similar ability — it surprised me that he genuinely seemed keen to talk for much longer than I had anticipated.

After I explained that I was with people from the nearby fishing communities, who had lost everything, and were mostly living in temporary housing, but working really hard to rebuild their lives, he asked whether they had lost their boats and all their equipment. I confirmed that they had, and then said that by providing items for the fishing communities, such as the pink fishing outfits we were all wearing, I was trying to support them, and showed him the Union Jack hearts on the outfits. I said that people from all over the world, including England, were supporting these fishing communities, but their lives were still incredibly challenging.

He then asked a few questions about me, which I wasn't prepared for (I was there because I hoped to talk about Oshika, but not really about myself), and there was still all this noise and shoving going on next to me so I couldn't concentrate and stumbled over my words quite a bit. I got as far as telling him that I used to live in Tokyo and was now based in Cirencester although spent part of each year in Tohoku, and he mentioned that he used to live near Cirencester. I told him that Japan is a beautiful and interesting country — he could have visited anywhere, but the fact that he came here really meant a lot to the people affected by the tsunami, because many of them felt so forgotten. And I thanked him.

This experience gave me a bit of insight into just how hard the embassy and their team (as well anyone else behind the scenes) has to work when putting these visits together. It is an extraordinarily impressive exercise in logistics and diplomacy. To meet diplomatic criteria for such visits, certain people have to be met with, either publicly or privately, and there are people that various decision-makers want a royal visitor to meet, and then people that a royal visitor would probably enjoy meeting. Balancing all of this in such a short amount of time is incredibly difficult. And anyone who thinks Prince William doesn't work hard has no idea what it feels like to get off a 12-hour flight, regardless of what class you've flown in (I'd flown first class several times in my Tokyo days and still ended up walking through the airport not knowing whether I should go to sleep, have breakfast, or find the nearest bar). The fact that Prince William launched straight into his busy and rigid schedule was *very* impressive.

I'm not especially into the royal family, to be honest, but I am curious in the same way I'm curious about anyone who leads an interesting life, and especially if it's a life in which the person tries to make a difference to other's lives. And Prince William's visit to Tohoku certainly made a difference to the lives of the people that I know on Oshika. He shook the hands of *all* the Pink Ladies, who were beside themselves with excitement at this. They did not stop talking about it for months, and they still talk about it now. One or another of the Pink Ladies was in the newspaper and on television, either somewhere in the footage or photos of Prince William or actually being interviewed. It generated a huge buzz on Oshika, and gave people a great boost. One 86-year-old woman who shook his hand immediately claimed to feel *years* younger.

It wasn't just the Pink Ladies who received a boost by that experience; the sponsorship received a huge boost, too, going from 73 outfits to over a hundred in a matter of weeks. One of the kappa went to a dear man who had given up all hope of ever rebuilding the hotel business he'd lost because of the lack of tourists returning to what was once such a popular destination. He decided to work in wakame instead, and his brand new kappa really encouraged him as he bravely turned his hand to a new venture.

I'd been limping while guiding the Pink Ladies all around Onagawa — on the very first day of my trip I'd done something to my left ankle. As I often do on my first morning on Oshika, I'd woken up and walked down the little hill from the centre to where everybody's homes used to be, and stood looking out over the massive black sandbags to the beautiful sea, admiring the view and breathing in the fresh air, thinking what a truly special place I was in. I still wore the same sturdy construction boots that Conny Jamieson had given me years earlier, which, like my jeans, were now covered in paint, woodstain, and goodness knows what else. They were essential attire though — the ground on Oshika was still very uneven and tiny bits of broken stones, glass, and nails were scattered all over. I spent so much time going in and out of people's homes that I rarely bothered to do the laces up, and as I stood looking out to sea, my left ankle had turned so badly that I immediately fell to the ground in agony.

    I assumed I'd only twisted it, so had carried on with my usual Oshika activities and the exciting royal visit with a bit of a limp, still maintaining my "no whinging" policy, marvelling at the weird and wonderful colours my ankle was turning, joining in with everybody laughing at my clumsiness, and thinking it would all go away soon. A week later I woke in the middle of the night, screaming in pain, and realized that I'd better go to a doctor the next day — it turned out that I had ruptured ligaments on both sides of my ankle and had three fractures, so my foot and lower leg were put in a cast for a month. I was so annoyed with myself, but very relieved that that spring's trip mainly involved planning rather than actually building anything. I was also very impressed with the plastic cube, about 8 cm square, that was taped to the bottom of my cast. It had a little cover that could be taken off when going indoors — they'd thought of everything!

    The little clinic was almost an hour away, in Ishinomaki, which meant that I got to enjoy that wonderful first view of Oshika every time I headed back to the peninsula. Every single time, without fail, I was aware of how my smile just got bigger and bigger the further I drove onto Oshika. On this trip, four years after the disaster, I was also very aware of how the road works were finally completed. Usually, the winding roads through the peninsula were made up of a series of temporary traffic lights, barriers over parts of the mountain that were in danger of collapsing or had already done so, and lots and lots of construction workers controlling the traffic, who I enjoyed seeing smile at the little Union Jack flags fluttering from my car windows. However, the roads were now safe and smooth, and had literally paved the way for the convoys of trucks that were constantly making their way on and off Oshika as the recovery and reconstruction continued.

The few permanent new buildings — wakame and oyster processing facilities built on the recently raised ports — were all related to the fishing industry. These facilities consisted of a variety of buildings with different purposes, large open spaces for manoeuvring massive amounts of wakame from the boats, and huge vats. Seeing the size of some of the equipment needed in the fishing industry gives you another perspective on the amount of debris that the tsunami washed inland and then took out to sea. And I was filled with admiration, yet again, for the people on Oshika and all their efforts in rebuilding their industry.

In many cases, including the Sasakis' situation, these were businesses that were built over forty years, if not more. Fishermen and women on Oshika rarely "retired" as such; many of them were in their seventies and still worked just as hard as the younger people. When you build a business over forty years, you invest in equipment gradually. To have all of that destroyed in a matter of minutes ... I sometimes didn't know how the older people on Oshika had the strength to rebuild. But they did, and it was taking a huge amount of money — in some cases it must have been nearly a million dollars *per business* — to rebuild the whole of something that had taken forty years or more to establish. They received some financial assistance, but the amount of money they had to find themselves was astounding.

But people there were working very hard, and their businesses were doing well. They had places where they could now work properly, and that in itself was uplifting, as many of them still didn't have places to call home.

However, there were signs of development in that area, too. Fours years on, the peninsula was scattered with patches of land that had been raised, and where the new villages were to be built. To create more habitable land, trees had been cut from the extensive forest that covered the peninsula, and earth had been loaded into trucks and driven to these new areas. Land had been raised to about three storeys high, then flattened, and was being prepared for the building that was scheduled to start on the "true" Oshika — on the south side of Shinkozumi Tunnel — by the end of 2015. On the north side of Shinkozumi Tunnel, the first homes were already going up.

Each village on the "true" Oshika was at a different stage of preparation, and relocated Fukkiura, where Mika lived, seemed to be ahead of everywhere else. A winding road led up to where this little village of just nine families was being placed — the mountain behind it had been reinforced against landslides, and each plot had been mapped out. This village — extremely isolated after the earthquake — now had an area that would be a little playground that was also specifically designed to function as a helipad in times of emergency — it had become clear during 311 that the peninsula really lacked facility for this.

Each family was being given their plot completely free of charge, but they had to fund the construction of their new homes. Mika and her husband had finished building a brand new home just before the earthquake, and were now in a position where they had to fund one all over again, which was very overwhelming. Many young people found themselves in the situation of having two mortgages to pay after the disaster — one for the house they lost and one for the house they had to build. But like everyone else, Mika and her husband work hard, and the fishing facilities that had recently been built were helping people not only to get their homes rebuilt by giving them jobs, but also by giving them a sense of purpose.

Keeping busy was important on Oshika, especially in the spring. Every year around the anniversary of the earthquake and tsunami, the media in Japan is always full of stories and images that bring back traumatic memories for the people on Oshika, and if they don't keep themselves busy, then the depression that many struggled with during the previous years can return. Bodies of family members are still missing to this day, which is understandably very difficult for many people to cope with. Flashbacks are common throughout the year, but the spring is a particularly sensitive time.

I was there for the anniversary again in 2015, and marked it in the Oshika way ... quietly and simply, alongside people that I had grown to love. No big event, no ceremonies, no speeches, no grand gestures. I knew there would be outpourings of emotion from friends in other parts of Japan (and the world) and that many people outside Tohoku found the day incredibly hard. I find the day more difficult if I'm in England, rather than on Oshika. The feelings that we have on that day are felt on Oshika all the time, every single day — it's just that the people on Oshika have learned to live with them.

Just as on previous years on March 11, people go to work as usual, but they don't go out to sea, instead working on land and at the ports. They stop sometime between 2 and 2:30 in the afternoon, and gather together with close friends and family, and stand facing the ocean, not necessarily right by it, but always looking out toward it. Just before 2:46, the loudspeaker system that runs throughout the peninsula, asks everyone to get ready to pray for one minute. And at exactly 2:46, the tsunami siren sounds for one minute, while everyone stands, praying, while facing the sea. And this time it started snowing, just as it did four years before, on the day of the disaster.

Later in the day I overheard someone say, "Tomorrow this will no longer be in the news, the volunteers will disappear, and everybody will forget about us for another year."

The news media was not popular on Oshika — I first learned the Japanese phrase for hate (*kirai*) on the peninsula when I looked it up after I kept hearing it alongside *masukomi* (mass media). Journalists would appear on the peninsula around the time of the anniversary, expecting people with whom they had no relationship to just spill their guts about the most traumatic event that had ever befallen them. You'd never see these reporters at any other time of year — and they never offered any kind of compensation or sponsorship to anyone — anything that perhaps could have helped the people that were giving them such great news stories.

So when I was approached by a Sendai newspaper that wanted to write about my award, as usual I turned it down. When Kucho found out what I had done, he told me that I should do it, and invited the journalist to come to the centre to interview me. I was a little embarrassed, but managed an entire newspaper interview in Japanese. Kucho and I hoped that this would help us in our efforts to get the local government to halt the scheduled demolition of the centre so that we could turn it into a place for the young people of Oshika.

The junior high school students were still doing well with their studies, but when asked about any challenges the school faced, the principal mentioned the music department. It had been decided by people higher up that music was not important enough to be allocated funding during challenging times, which I thought was a terrible shame. Music has so much power to heal — for both those creating it and those listening to it — and this area was still going through the healing process. Music not only has the ability to heal, but also to inspire, and in an area where traditional employment opportunities were now considerably restricted, I felt that exposing young people to as many inspirational opportunities as possible was vital to their future. I met with a representative of the school's music department, who said that all she needed was a keyboard and a set of tone chimes, which could both be sourced locally, thus supporting a local business.

Roslyn Hayman and Gilma Yamamoto of St Alban's Nursery in Tokyo had asked me almost a year earlier to look out for a project they could support, and agreed with me when I suggested that musical instruments for the junior high school students was perfect. I always appreciated the patience of those who wanted to give but were willing to wait for the right project to support — I thought it showed that they truly wanted to do what was best for people who needed help, rather than be more concerned with satisfying their *own* need to help.

The younger students on Oshika graduated from elementary school a week after the anniversary, and Kucho and I attended Ohara's ceremony, where my cast caused much unnecessary concern among the teachers and parents. It was such a beautiful way to mark the transition from elementary to junior high — much more meaningful than the chaotic leavers' assembly I remember being part of when I left primary school.

The non-graduating students, parents of graduating students, and the school staff were all seated before the special guests entered — there was the PTA representative, an Ishinomaki government representative, a Miyagi prefecture representative, the vice-principal of Oshika Junior High (where the graduating students would move on to), the heads of the villages that feed the primary school (including Kucho), and me.

Once we were all seated, the four graduating students of 2015 walked in one by one behind their teacher. Before the tsunami, students would wear kimono, but in order to ease the burden on parents, the students now wore the uniforms of their next school. Those uniforms were designed to last three years and were always a little bit big — it made me smile to see trouser legs turned up and sweaters that didn't quite fit yet. It was the third year of uniforms that I'd managed to find a sponsor for — that year the uniforms had been provided by Kspace for the second time.

There were a few elements of the ceremony that really touched me. One was when the students were presented with a certificate on the stage, which they then presented to their mothers sitting at the back of the hall. The mothers then rolled up the certificates, put a red ribbon around them, and handed them back to their children, who carried their scrolls back to their seats at the front of the hall.

Another was when every single one of the non-graduating students thanked the graduating ones for being their friends and for helping them, each mentioning something personal about their relationship. The graduating students also thanked everyone who had played a part in their education — teachers, parents, peers — and mentioned some things that were specifically important to them, as well as memories that they would carry with them. Each one promised the school community that they would do their very best at junior high, and always appreciate the opportunities that would be presented to them. It was a moving example of how the seeds of community spirit are sown — starting right there in the schools.

The singing was also very moving — there was the singing of the national anthem, which everyone participated in, a song that the four graduating students sang to everyone, and a song that the non-graduating students sang to their older friends. There was also the singing of the school song, which all the students and teachers participated in, as well as some of the other adults in the room who had attended the primary school themselves. Kucho-san, next to me, knew it well. He had attended the school himself about sixty years ago, when there were 400 students. Now there were just 23. This area had been struggling for such a long time even before the disaster.

2011 was mentioned a few times. The students expressed gratitude toward those who had helped them during the past four years, and the teachers expressed admiration for the courage with which the children had conducted themselves in overcoming various challenges. And right in the middle of the ceremony there was an earthquake that shook the gymnasium and sent every one of the children under their chairs in less than one second — I had never seen kids move so fast and so calmly.

It was a solemn ceremony, but not cold, and it was very moving. One parent spent most of the ceremony with her head bowed down, sobbing, and when the only girl out of the graduating students brought a handkerchief out from under her sweater and started bawling, that then set off her girlfriends in the year below her, which then, to Kucho's amusement, set me off, too.

Kucho and Fukumi-san took extra good care of me on that trip, with Kucho even giving me chocolates for White Day that year, which I was very touched by. I think they felt so sorry for me with my broken ankle in a cast for a whole month. I tried so hard to use the centre's shower but kept losing my balance in my attempts to keep one leg from getting wet. I worried about falling through the slowly rotting wood flooring and banging my head, imagining being found naked by the Ohara boys days later as the centre's animal inhabitants fed on my eyeballs. I had a very active imagination sometimes. Kucho kindly offered the use of their shower, which was such a relief as I could balance myself on their little stool and call Fukumi-san if I got into trouble.

Fukumi-san and Mrs Sasaki even insisted on taking care of some of my laundry, and if I agreed to that, I'd often turn up at their homes to find them outside studying my knickers as they hung them up to dry. They'd see me and start asking me questions like, "Which way round do these go?" and "How can you possibly be warm in these?" and Mrs Sasaki said that she felt sorry for my "*bebe*" (a local word used with children, to refer to female private parts). I didn't understand why until she pretended to put them on and said they didn't cover anything, asking whether the thin bit of fabric went "in the middle" of my bebe. She'd been looking at them back to front all day. Because they were from different villages, the two women rarely saw each other, but if they did, they'd immediately start discussing my underwear. Mr Sasaki thought all the underwear conversations were hilarious — he said that women's underwear in Japan was absolutely massive and somehow always ended up the same grey colour, despite their original hue.

While I knew I had second homes at Kucho's and Onodera's, my other home at the Sasakis' place had become the kind where I could literally turn up at any time of day or night, as I found out in the middle of one night on that trip. Kucho had dealt with most of the rats in the centre, but there was something else that managed to absolutely terrify me.

I love Oshika, especially Ohara, but being in that centre alone at night sometimes sent my imagination into overdrive, and I would often get the creeps. The number of volunteers had dropped off by then, four years later, so I was usually there on my own. The odd volunteer would come up from Tokyo and stay in the centre, but it didn't happen often. One volunteer arrived at 2 a.m. one night, but chose to sleep in his car. When asked why, he'd said, "I didn't know which room Caroline would be sleeping in and didn't want to open the wrong door and scare her," to which one of the Ohara boys responded, "She's not scared of anything. She's like a bloke. You should be scared of her." I *think* it was said with love.

But I did get scared sometimes. Especially one night, around midnight, when I was sleeping there alone and I heard what sounded like metal being banged against the outside wall of the centre. For an hour it slowly got closer and closer to my bedroom window, by which time I was imagining *all sorts of things*. At 1:15 a.m. I ran out of the centre, got in my car, drove over to the Sasakis in my pajamas, and crawled into what I knew was an empty bunk bed room.

The noise turned out to have been created by a *hakubishin* — a badger-like creature that was making a home below the area of the centre where I slept. I didn't like to ask what happened to it — all I know is that after I told Kucho about my scary night, the hakubishin disappeared. That's what happened to nuisance animals on Oshika. The previous summer everyone had been talking about a bear that had been spotted on the peninsula: they were laughing about how a bear could possibly have got to Oshika, suggesting it had walked across the Mangoku Bridge, which was a hilarious thought. They all made light of it, but still, I was told by everyone to take care, perhaps because they knew my tendency to wander off exploring.

In 2014 when she was here, I'd taken my niece Emily on a tour of the peninsula that included driving on the Cobalt Line road, going up to the highest points on Oshika, which provide incredible views. We came across an abandoned restaurant in the middle of a forest, and went up to it to investigate — cutlery was still on the tables and crockery lay smashed on the floor. The restaurant was on stilts — not raised very high, but high enough to be able to look underneath it, at which point I'd been overcome with a feeling I have still never been able to explain. I told my niece to get straight back to the car and drove away as fast as I could. I mentioned what happened to Kucho that afternoon, and he'd immediately said that the bear (which I'd stupidly forgotten about) would be there and that someone would be sent up with a gun. I never saw a gun on Oshika, but I heard that many people had them.

The hakubishin kept me awake that one night, and the wind — so noisy during the spring — kept me awake on other nights as it howled against the centre, making its walls bang all through the night. The daytimes were also noisy, with all the trucks constantly going back and forth along the coastal road. And there was some new construction going on that spring, which also added to the noise.

A massive sea wall was going up along the entire Oshika coastline.

The sea defence system consisted of a sea wall about six metres high with a "base" extending 30 metres out into the ocean. The road behind the sea wall, in Ohara, was to be raised two and a half metres. Taking into account the fact that the land had sunk by a metre after the earthquake, the new road would be raised to one and a half metres higher than it was before the earthquake. Its height made absolutely no sense to anyone — the tsunami was eight metres high in Ohara.

Despite it not making any sense, the process itself was quite fascinating. Existing tetrapods (those oddly shaped concrete weights you see along many shorelines, intended to defend against the impact of strong waves) would first be pulled out of the sea by huge cranes and brought onto land. Then lorries would offload tons of huge blocks of stone into the sea. When those blocks reached 30 metres from the shore, the tetrapods were to be put at the edge. The wall is to be built on top of the blocks of stone, and the road, behind it, will end up being three and a half metres lower than the wall. This wall is to go all along Ohara's seafront, and is supposed to take two years to build, with completion being around March 2017, six years after the disaster. The construction was being done section by section, from left to right as you looked out to sea, by several different companies, so that the work could be shared between several construction companies. The sea wall began where Kanta still had his little temporary restaurant that served the best fried rice I'd ever eaten — he had to move his unit further away from Ohara and nearer Kyubun, which meant that I could no longer look at the "Land for Sale" sign while I ate my lunch. The sign was still there though, and I looked at it wistfully every time I drove past, which was quite often.

When the sea wall was finished, you would not be able to see the sea *at all* from Ohara. The local people were extremely upset about the sea being hidden from view, but not for aesthetic reasons. It was for practical ones. Not being able to see the sea, and what exactly it is doing, made Ohara people feel terrified. This was a community that had lived in harmony with the sea for hundreds of years and respected its power — they wouldn't be afraid of it, as long as they could see it.

The northern part of the peninsula, the part of the peninsula that was directly facing the tsunami, was almost completely destroyed. The neighbouring towns of Yagawa and Oyagawa suffered a great difference in fatalities — Oyagawa, while losing most of its buildings, did not lose a single person, whereas Yagawa lost about a quarter of its residents. Yagawa is situated just behind an area where the land juts out, obscuring a long-range view of the sea. People on Oshika believe that this is the reason Yagawa lost so many of its residents, while nearby Oyagawa did not. So the beginning of the construction of a six-metre-high sea wall, obstructing the view, had really unsettled everyone.

While the Ohara people preferred not to have the wall at all, they had requested that the entire area be raised by six metres, so that people could walk and drive at a height where they could at least see the ocean, and know exactly what it was doing, but it was doubtful that their request would be heard. They weren't even consulted about the sea wall — yet another example of these communities not being involved in decisions that directly affect their future, and this reinforced the feeling that they had no control over their lives. Some officials had simply turned up to inform them, and the following month the building work began.

With my broken ankle, I had very little opportunity to do my own physical work, but still tried to make myself as useful as possible. I'd freed up an extra four days a month because I recently sold my last remaining publication — *Japan School News*. My pickling business, Auntie Caroline's, was becoming a great success and had the potential to be my sole source of income, so I decided to turn all my energies to that. I'd started to really enjoy spending a lot of time in a kitchen.

I cooked for the Sasakis and the few seasonal staff they'd managed to get that year — every week I prepared a meal inspired by a different country's cuisine. I had eaten at their place so many times over the years that it was a real pleasure to cook for them. I think our relationship bemused some of the out-of-town casual workers — I'd turn up, hobbling in on my crutch, shouting "zuzuhoido" (oi, wanker!) as a greeting, while Mrs Sasaki studied my knickers on her washing line. My favourite memory of that time was when I was sitting alone on the low sofa in their dining room, plastered leg resting on a stool, typing away, when a worker entered and sat down at the table after nodding at me. Mr Sasaki then entered, introducing me as his English wife, and then Mrs Sasaki, totally unaware of what Mr Sasaki had just said, introduced me as her sister. With all of us totally straight-faced, this poor worker just nodded respectfully, probably thinking that he'd heard these remote people were different and this must be the kind of thing that was meant.

My car, like most cars in Japan, was an automatic, and since I'd broken my *left* ankle, I could still drive — I was so thankful not to have any problems getting around the peninsula. I'd set up the free shop again, and was constantly putting out calls for more things that were needed; I was also still setting up mini-shops in the temporary housing communities. Boxes of clothes and household goods arrived for me every day, along with boxes of books for the library. Yuki Onodera had made a library "rule" book, in which people had to write their name and the title(s) of the book(s) they were taking home with them. Books were lent for a maximum of one week. Flicking through the rule book, I could see just how well used the library was — books had been borrowed almost every day since it opened the previous summer. And I was also told that the teenagers were using it a lot just to hang out with their friends — Kucho, Ito-sensei, and I were still trying to convince the government not to demolish the centre so we could make it into a space for the teenagers.

Lorna Nagamine from Hawaii finally visited Oshika — she had been saving her Starbucks money for years and had contributed to a number of projects, including the Koamikura sheds, the Disneyland trip, a Pink Lady, cat food for Mrs Sasaki's strays, books for the library, a barbecue set for Ohara, and countless things for the free shop. It was wonderful to be able to give her and her friend a tour of the peninsula — that kind of ongoing support had been invaluable during the four years after the disaster. Contrary to what many of us think and perhaps what the media would have us believe — help after major disasters like this is needed for *years* after the event. There are a lot of gaps left when government money runs out.

During one of my regular conversations with Kucho-san about what particular gap the village was trying to fill at that stage in the recovery, he told me about their portable AED units — there was one in the community centre and one in the temporary housing community — they were vital to this little village with so many elderly residents, and where ambulance response time was forty minutes. The units had batteries that should have been replaced four months earlier, and Kucho had given up asking the local government for support for things the locals felt they needed. He told me that each battery cost ¥20,000 and could be sourced locally, thus supporting another local business as well as this remote community. I put the word out to my network, and Jane McDonald, who works in the medical field, and Leza Lowitz, who runs Sun and Moon Yoga and herself has a heart condition, stepped forward to pay for the batteries. It was a great way to support a community with such an elderly population.

Kucho also asked whether it was possible to get some thick warm blankets to go with the futons, which would also be made by Murakami-san, and so would continue to support him as he rebuilt his business. Moko Igarashi, who had already been so supportive of Koamikura through her taiko drumming group, came forward to pay for the blankets. Murakami-san was thrilled with the new business, and drove out to the peninsula to see me, bringing along some beautiful flowers to congratulate me on the award he'd read about in the Sendai newspaper. It had turned out to be a lovely interview, which Kucho insisted that everybody read — I got the feeling that my Ohara friends were actually proud that "one of their own" had been featured in the paper.

I ended up having to keep my ankle in a cast for another week, but the time to have it removed finally arrived. The doctor on the mainland had a reputation for being rude and grumpy, but I found him very amusing, especially when he sawed into the end of my cast and proceeded to count my toes in English to check they were all still there, falling about laughing at his own joke. I walked through the waiting room, which faced straight into the genkan, where I realized that I'd forgotten to bring a shoe for my newly free foot. Acting like it was a completely normal thing to do, I removed the hospital slipper, put on just one shoe, and walked across the car park toward my car with its little flags fluttering away, with everybody staring at me, sure that this little episode would reach Ohara before I'd even got back.

I was still using a crutch, but the doctor hadn't said anything about resting my leg anymore and I was desperate to do some physical work, so as soon as I got back I grabbed some paint, called Yukio-san, and set to work repainting the bus shelter. One person after another pulled over to ask me how my ankle was and to tell me off for painting when I still had a crutch under one arm — I waved them all away, touched by their concern, but so happy to be outside and working again, even though this trip was almost over.

I often felt that every time I said goodbye to Oshika, I left a little piece of my heart behind. But I also felt that my Oshika friends would keep that piece safe until my return.

Back in Tokyo, with Andrew having moved house and lost his parking space, Tracey Northcott was now in charge of keeping my Oshika car safe in between trips. Tracey and I had been friends for ages — we were both entrepreneurs and engaged with the same networks of foreign women in Tokyo. She'd been a huge supporter of my publishing work, as well as my

Oshika work, contributing to a number of projects over the years. She used the car to support her rapidly growing holiday property business, and while we'd initially agreed to share the costs of maintaining it, Tracey always somehow insisted on paying for more than her share, which was incredibly kind.

The car was put in Tracey's name, as I'd decided to give up my resident's visa when I exited the country this time, and you had to have a resident's visa to own a car in Japan. It was a really difficult decision, but my resident's visa was no longer necessary. I no longer had a business in Japan, I had a growing business in England, and I'd been paying taxes in Japan in *full* despite all my time spent in the UK because I'd been holding on to the hope that I'd get permanent residency. It had felt like a good investment when I'd thought I would get permanent residency, but now it felt like a waste of money to keep my resident's visa.

I filled in the form that indicated I was giving up my visa, and stood in the immigration line at the airport. The closer I got to the counter, the bigger the lump in my throat got, and the more I could feel the tears welling up in my eyes. I told myself it was OK — it didn't mean I was never coming back. I'd just be on a tourist visa next time. But I was still so upset — as a self-employed person it had been such a challenge to get a visa and I had got my own visa for the *entire* time I'd lived in Japan; I had never had an employer get one for me. It was something that I had worked hard for, applied for, and got completely on my own, sponsored entirely by my own earnings for eighteen years. It was something I had done by choice. I had *chosen* Japan to be my home. And now it felt like Japan didn't want me.

I reached the front of the queue and handed in my passport with the form. The officer looked up at my tearful eyes and gently asked in English, "Are you sure?"

I nodded. She stamped my passport, and I walked through the airport, sobbing. I eventually stopped crying when I boarded the plane. I was going "home."

27: New Homes

I was still three years away from calling England "home" in 2015, but at least I had progressed from saying "I am based in the UK" to saying "I live in the UK," which felt like a huge step for me.

In addition to giving talks on Japan, I embrace any opportunity to reflect Japan and Oshika in my life in England — a beautiful obi runner is draped across my bed; a huge *kokeshi* doll given to me by Yachan's mother stands proudly on display; and there's a gorgeous kimono from Mrs Sasaki displayed on my living room wall. After seeing me return from a specialty second-hand shop in Ishinomaki with bags and bags of obi and kimono that I'd fallen in love with, Mrs Sasaki had insisted on giving me one of her own kimono as a gift. She'd once told me off for folding kimono casually, saying that they weren't like everyday clothes and had to be folded in a special way, so I was very, very careful when handling hers. She said that she had worn it to her son's wedding, it had survived the tsunami, and she wanted me to have it — I was deeply touched and hung it in my home as soon as I returned to England, where it still hangs today.

Some of the obi I'd brought back were for people in the UK who had specifically asked me to look for one for them — I delivered one to be placed across a huge dining table in a beautiful Cotswold home. It looked stunning. I later set up a little "shop" full of kimono and obi inside Cirencester Antiques Centre — an intriguing labyrinth of shops full of unique treasures. It made me happy to introduce a bit of Japan to people's homes. It wasn't an income source for me as such — whatever I sold them for would go toward buying more on my next trip, thereby regularly supporting a small business near Oshika.

My Auntie Caroline's pickling business has become my main income source, and the business just keeps growing and growing. I have stalls at markets outside Cirencester, attend trade shows and one-off market events, and hold tasting days in the increasing number of shops I supply. I *love* it when Japanese tourists come to my stall — my products don't really suit most Japanese tastes, so I don't see it as a sales opportunity, more an opportunity to speak Japanese and let them know that if they have any questions about the area, or any of the other stalls, then there's a Japanese speaker who can help them. They're always so shocked to hear a cheery "*Ohayo gozaimasu!*" ("Good morning!") in the middle of a little farmers' market in the Cotswolds, although my market friends were just as surprised when they first heard me speak Japanese. They say I come alive when I speak Japanese — I just love the chance to reconnect with Japan, and was once thrilled to meet a young man wandering around Cirencester who happened to be from Oshika.

I also love the chance to reconnect with Japan friends who had also moved to or were visiting England. Robin Maynard, another Brit who had made Tokyo his home for many years, made the effort to spend an afternoon with me in Cirencester in the summer of 2015. Robin and I had initially met years earlier at a lunch group for Brits living in Tokyo, and since retirement he had been sharing his time between the UK, Japan, and Australia. He'd sponsored some Pink Ladies and always kept an eye on my Oshika activities, looking for an opportunity to make a difference. When I'd put a call out to my network about the rapidly deteriorating 400-year-old shrine in Ohara, Robin had stepped forward, insisting that he provide the ¥3 million funding required. Both Kucho and I were completely blown away, because neither of us really expected to find someone who would be able to help with such a big project.

Robin visited me in Cirencester to talk through some details, and to tell me about his motivation for helping, something about sponsors that I am *always* interested in. Robin has a fascinating story and attitude toward philanthropy, with a history of being a quiet contributor to a variety of charitable endeavours, and those that embraced history, religion, and the spiritual are close to his heart.

Robin worked in Tokyo from the '70s until he retired, just before the tsunami, and was an active member of the British business community. For twenty-five years he attended the annual Christmas Cracker fundraiser held at the British Embassy, becoming a key sponsor of this event during its last few years. This gave him a taste of the personal satisfaction that can come from supporting charitable undertakings. Upon retirement, he found himself with spare time, and two adult children in the UK who were financially independent. The savings he had put aside for them during all those years of hard work in Tokyo were not needed. And with a reluctance to allow his earnings to later "disappear into some government black hole" in the form of inheritance tax, he decided to seek out projects in his family members' names; projects that were appealing to him personally and could be completed during his lifetime. He devised a long-term plan — a plan that would also allow him to give back to a country that had treated him well and provided thirty-two years of rewarding employment. Each project he would ultimately support had to include historical, religious, and spiritual elements.

The first project was in honour of his parents. Inside St. Mary's Church in Fryerning village in the Essex countryside there is a plaque in memory of Robin's parents. This church had a very special meaning to Robin — the cemetery is packed with his ancestors, including his parents, who were married there. Robin was baptized at St. Mary's, and he sponsored the restoration of the base of the church tower and the war memorial.

In honour of his immediate and extended family members, Robin provided funds for the refurbishment of and improvements to Kids Earth Home Tohoku, which is in Watari, south of Sendai city. This area was seriously affected by the 2011 disaster.

In honour of Robin's son and his immediate family, he became involved with "Japan400" — the 400th anniversary of the opening of diplomatic, trade, cultural, and scientific relations between Britain and Japan, which was celebrated in 2013. In 1613, King James I presented a unique telescope to the very first shogun. Over time this telescope was lost and, as part of the Japan400 celebrations, Robin sponsored a Welsh craftsperson to create one made of brass. It was presented to Shizuoka City in the presence of a direct descendant of the shogun, and is now on permanent display at Sunpu Castle.

His fourth project was dedicated to his daughter and her immediate family, and involved sponsoring the complete refurbishment of the William Adams memorial at Hirado, Nagasaki, to commemorate the 400th anniversary of

Adams's death in 2020. William Adams was the first English person to arrive in Japan, more than 400 years ago.

Robin was searching for an appropriate philanthropic endeavour to support in honour of his Japanese wife and stepson. And when he heard about the 400-year-old shrine in Ohara that was so badly in need of repair, and that was built by Date Masamune — such a significant figure in Japanese history — he felt it was the perfect project.

Robin and I had a lovely lunch in Cirencester — worlds away from the Tokyo lunches where we had seen each other in years gone by — and discussed the details that I had gathered from Kucho. The project was to start the following spring, five years after the disaster, and be completed in time for the summer festival, which Robin and his wife Midori planned to attend. We sat for hours talking about Japan, Oshika, philanthropy, and how life had changed for us both since we had last met.

I love spending time with "Tokyo people" in England, and I was delighted when one of my closest friends from Japan came to live with me for a few months. Heath is Australian and his husband Jim is American. We had been like family in Japan — they were constantly popping in to my Ebisu home, and those visits often turned into sleepovers, which would then turn into long, leisurely brunches. Heath had felt ready to leave Japan but Jim hadn't, so they were maintaining a long-distance relationship, with Heath staying with me while he kept an eye out for a suitable home for them both when Jim was ready to join him.

Jim and Heath's move to the UK made a *huge* difference to my ability to feel more at home in England. Simple things comforted us, like knowing to remove shoes before entering a home, saying *itadakimasu* before eating, referring to certain places in Tokyo without need of explanation, and not batting an eyelid if the other used a Japanese word rather than an English one because the Japanese word was more appropriate or came more naturally. Spending those months with Heath helped me grieve the loss of my life in Japan, and pushed me further along in acceptance of my new life in England. *Plus*, there was a constant flow of Japanese goodies every time Jim came to visit, which was a good thing because, unexpectedly, it turned out to be 15 months between my last trip and the next one — the longest I had ever been away from Japan since I'd moved there in 1996.

By my next trip in the summer of 2016 — five years after the disaster — my fundraising for Oshika had reached almost £150,000, just over ¥23 million. More school uniforms had been funded, as well as a steady flow of kappa for the Pink Ladies and fishermen, which I was excited about handing out on this trip.

Without a doubt though, the most exciting news that summer was that a lot of people on Oshika — including all the Ohara residents — had moved out of temporary housing and into brand new homes. There were two kinds of homes — one was paid for and owned by the individual themselves, so had been designed to their own specifications; and the other was paid for and owned by the government, which the resident rented — these houses were pretty basic. The residents were allowed to keep anything that had come with the temporary housing units, such as air conditioners, TVs, and washing machines. The units themselves were taken apart and disposed of, not used again, and the land reverted to its owner — Yachan — so that he could continue to rebuild his business.

The government-owned houses were usually lived in by people who couldn't face taking out a mortgage at their age or perhaps due to their personal circumstances. The others were owned by people who would most likely have had to take out a mortgage in order to buy them. *Both* kinds of residents may still have been paying off mortgages on the properties they lost in the tsunami — before the earthquake the vast majority of people on Oshika had owned their own homes. It was rare for anyone to be in rented accommodation. About a third of those home-owners had mortgages. The others lived in very old family homes, without any mortgage. If you lost your home in the tsunami (or it was deemed unsafe to live in even if it survived) and you had house insurance, you might have received up to 25 percent of the value of the house. And if you had a mortgage, you still had to pay it, even if you could no longer live in your home. So, before moving into their new homes, many people were paying off mortgages on properties they had lost, while living in rent-free temporary housing (residents paid only for utilities) and struggling with employment.

Out of 40 people, five residents had died in the Ohara temporary housing community during the five years they'd lived there — not all of them of old age. Sadly, Mrs Nagashima (Mrs Naughty Twinkle) passed away just a week before she was scheduled to move into her new home, but I liked to think of her as happy and at peace with her husband — they were such a sweet and loving couple that maybe a new home without him just wouldn't have been right.

With the new homes built, people now had privacy, space between them and their neighbours, more than one room to live in, and places where they could grow their own vegetables and flowers. They could move to a new stage in their healing. *But* I felt that these communities were in some ways even more fragmented than they were before. The new homes were built on higher land, further away from the sea, but also further away from the homes that had survived. Homes were built, but nothing else. There was no opportunity to take little walks to the post office, the corner shop, the grocer's, the café … those walks we take around our communities that bring about the chance encounters that lead to and often maintain friendships. I was very aware that, aside from Jim and Heath moving closer to me in England, much of what was helping me gradually feel more at home in Cirencester was seeing familiar faces when I walked into town, and those familiar faces leading to a smile, and then perhaps leading to a chat. Communities are far more than just the buildings in which people live. But the new homes were a start.

In addition to the new homes, there were some other changes. The sea wall that had been started 16 months earlier was reaching further along the left side of the Ohara shoreline and was still due for completion by the end of 2017. Those massive black sandbags were still on the right side, but now had huge grasses and weeds growing out of them — they had been there for five years by that point. The konbini was now open until 10:30 at night rather than only until 7, which was huge news on Oshika. It had been taken over by the FamilyMart chain, but was still run by the energetic Endo-san, now in her mid-80s, and still working every day.

I set up the free shop again in the container that still stood next to the konbini, and asked Osawa-san at Oshika Motors just opposite to do some work on my car. Tracey and I had agreed that we'd rather give the work to an Oshika business than a Tokyo one. Osawa-san was the only mechanic on Oshika, and his garage was up a steep hill and had a huge courtyard — he had taken care of the hundreds of people who slept there after the tsunami. He was a good man, but with a naughty side, inviting me to his village's festival but insisting I leave my car behind so he could get me drunk.

Summer was always a wonderful time to visit Oshika, with all the festivals and the fishing industry being a little quieter. The evenings were full of the sounds of people in the villages practising their musical instruments or, at least that summer, the Oshika fire department practising for a big competition that everybody was very excited about. Most of the firefighters had full-time jobs and worked for the fire department part-time or as volunteers, but they found the time to practise every single evening for a month. I'd see Kuni, Kiyotaka-kun, and Hirota-kun arrive back at Ohara, exhausted after a full day's work that had been followed by evening practice for the firefighting competition. Their hard work paid off, as the competition between all the firefighting departments in Miyagi prefecture was won by the Oshika team that summer. It gave the whole peninsula a huge boost, and I had never seen Kuni so excited.

The Sasakis were always more relaxed in the summer, so if I popped over, I didn't need to feel guilty about distracting them from their work. We'd sit around sometimes, simply enjoying each other's company, chatting about everything and nothing, and always on the same wavelength. One day Mrs Sasaki asked me what my next tattoo was going to be — a couple of years earlier I had started a series of individual kanji tattoos down my left side under my arm. Each kanji represents values I try to live by or perhaps represents some aspect of how I approach life. I always have them done individually, and every now and again I add another one. I have all my tattoos done by the same artist, Shaun Bonanos in Cheltenham, who happens to be fascinated with Japan, so we chat non-stop about the country, and when he learned about my efforts on Oshika he once refused to accept payment for one of my tattoos.

When Mrs Sasaki had asked me what kanji I was next thinking of having, I'd done a Google search for a Japanese word I had been thinking of using but still wasn't sure about. When I found the word and showed it to her, she showed me the kanji she'd written as her suggestion. It was exactly the same. Decision made. And that's why I have the kanji for "perseverance" on my left side.

It was lovely weather for giving the library and the Ohara playground a fresh coat of paint, and for my friends Andrew and Yuriko from Tokyo to visit. It was fun to have our roles reversed, with me explaining all sorts of things about food on Oshika, something they were so used to doing for me over the years when we'd gone out for dinner in Tokyo. They had given money toward that scary, exciting, and entertaining kitchen-outfitting shopping trip with Kameyama-san, so it was nice to be able to point out his house with the massive Union Jack heart painted on it that can be seen from the road.

Yuriko had found out about an "important cultural property" just around the corner from the Sasakis' place called Juichimen Kannon. Inside the building there was a three-metre high statue of the eleven-headed goddess of mercy. It was created in the 13th century, and two halves were carved out of the same tree and placed together. You cannot photograph it; to see it, you have to make an appointment with the priest of the temple, who is responsible for protecting it. It was incredible. I love the way Oshika continually surprises me.

Fukumi-san surprised me that summer with an obsession with a pimple that was rapidly growing on my face. Some things are the same wherever you go in the world I suppose, as she told me that she loved squeezing them and really wanted to get her hands on mine. I tried to take it as a loving gesture — indicative of how close we were. I had to really concentrate on getting my Japanese right though, because for some reason I kept confusing *chikubi* (nipple) with *nikibi* (pimple) and kept asking Fukumi-san whether she wanted to squeeze my nipple. Right in front of Kucho.

The work that was still going on to repair the Ohara shrine, thanks to Robin, was incredible. Kucho and I had managed to keep in regular contact throughout the whole process and, rather than waiting for me to return, tradespeople had been paid all along, throughout the job.

By this time, I had a system set up where all donations were allocated to projects before the money was sent, so sponsors sent their money directly to the manufacturer, construction company, or organization — nothing came through me. And most of the people or companies getting paid were businesses local to Oshika — I always tried to keep the money as close to the Oshika community as possible. They had done a wonderful job of repairing Ohara's shrine.

I was amazed to see that a brand new shinden had been built. The shinden is the building at the back of the shrine where the god lives and where you go to pray. The Ohara shrine's shinden is attached to the building at the front of the shrine by a little bridge. The bridge had been falling apart and was dangerous to cross, and during my previous trip, the old shinden had been covered in tarpaulin to prevent rain from pouring in and damaging the 400-year-old relics and pieces of art.

The new shinden and bridge incorporated elements of the original shrine wherever possible. The relics and art are now protected in a brand new building that is strong enough to withstand the harsh weather conditions and allows people to safely enter in order to pray. The outside of the new building is modern in appearance, but the inside is very traditional, and the timing of the construction was carefully planned so that it would be completed in time for the festival.

Robin and Midori made the effort to visit Oshika for the festival weekend, where I introduced them to Kucho and the rest of the Ohara community, and they both participated in the prayer ritual at the shrine. It was again, as it was in Will's case, a wonderful opportunity to show a sponsor just how much difference their generosity made to this very special community.

Will and Kellie were making plans to visit Oshika that summer, but unfortunately they would arrive just after I was scheduled to leave. Kellie's mother was visiting Japan, and they wanted to take her and their three children to Ohara to see the kanetsukido they had sponsored so that they could tell them the story behind it. Will and Kellie were always keen to instil in their children an understanding of and appreciation for the privilege with which they had grown up — their own childhoods had not been as privileged, and having found themselves in what they considered to be very lucky positions in adult life, they lived a life where they not only helped others at any opportunity, but also wanted to encourage their children to do the same. Kucho was thrilled at the thought of Will visiting again, and was very excited to meet Will's family. I thought it was wonderful that Will wanted to maintain the connection — his and Kellie's support had meant so much to the village.

Both Will and Robin had commented during their visits about the lack of young people in Ohara, and both would later also contribute toward school uniforms in order to support the small number of young families on the peninsula. That summer there was a new principal at Oshika Junior High School — as is common with Japanese schools, where staff regularly get moved around — and he gave me an update on the situation the young families found themselves in, five years after the disaster.

The student body was still decreasing, with less than 50 students enrolled, and 30 percent of them still lived in temporary housing. Many families had moved to Ishinomaki on the mainland, but still hoped to one day return to the peninsula. Oshika's beauty and peace was the reason many lived there in the first place, but with all the land-raising and the six-metre-high sea wall being constructed along the coastline, the entire peninsula had turned into a massive construction site. The construction work had made Oshika a noisy, "agitated" place, difficult to live in, so former residents were reluctantly remaining in Ishinomaki. Nobody on Oshika was being given much of an idea when the peninsula's reconstruction would be completed, but had resigned themselves to it taking at least another ten years ... which meant it would be fifteen years after the disaster before they *imagined* construction would be completed.

The families that remained on the peninsula worked hard. The parents of all the students had finally managed to find work, and they had enough money for general living expenses. But most of the families were living in new homes they owned themselves, rather than the government-owned houses, so had a mortgage (possibly two if they were still paying off the mortgage for the home they had lost). They were optimistic, but this situation left them with very little money for anything other than the essentials.

The principal then explained to me just what a help the school uniform sponsorship had been during the past three years, helping the parents out financially, but also helping the students emotionally and psychologically. I was quite emotional when I saw the principal and other teachers really light up when they started talking about what the uniforms meant to the students, explaining that the school uniforms actually become relevant to the students even before they start junior high.

Like children all over the world, Oshika children get excited about going to "big school" while they're still in elementary school. Junior high school is the first time for these students to ever wear a uniform — they wear casual clothes at elementary school. The Oshika students wore their uniforms for the first time at the elementary school graduation ceremony, in front of their younger schoolmates, with whom they have very special friendships. This is seen as an important rite of passage, and the uniforms are hugely symbolic. These children are taking their first steps into adulthood. They are growing up. Their lives are moving forward. The uniform sets the foundation for the future. Having attended one of these ceremonies myself, I know what an emotional moment it is for everyone concerned when those students first walk into the room wearing their uniforms.

The principal explained to me that because the students' uniforms were provided by someone who cared enough to help them, an extra element was added to their school experience that could positively affect the rest of their lives. He said that for the three years they attend junior high, every time they put on their uniforms they are reminded that other people care about them — and this was the point where my eyes started to sting. I had never really thought of the uniforms having that kind of impact on a regular basis. I was *very* moved by this realization.

My conversation with the principal was similar to the conversation that Kurosawa-san had had with me a few years earlier. I realized that because these uniforms had been given to them, the students might one day be inspired to help others in need. Stories were already circulating about young people from Oshika who had been affected by the tsunami and were now at university, volunteering their time to help others affected by flooding or earthquakes in other parts of Japan and the world. Many of these young people were determined to pay it forward and to be active contributors to their own communities, their country, and to the world in general.

On Oshika I'd often meet people from Kobe who were doing their bit to give back — they had received so much assistance after the 1995 earthquake that devastated their city. That summer I met a group of teenagers on a tour of Tohoku who were giving free taiko performances. It was the second time I had seen them, as they visited Ohara every year, but I still had to fight back tears — their performance was so overwhelming! Not only that, but they brought everything they needed with them, including refreshments for all the audience. They got the audience playing and singing with them, sat around chatting with the locals afterward, and then left. Staying less than two hours, imposing on nobody, interacting with everyone, not treating the locals like "victims" and instead treating them like normal people, and expecting nothing in return. They'd turn up, do their stuff with a massive smile, and go, leaving behind wonderful memories of a great experience. This was just the kind of thing that the Oshika Junior High principal had talked about.

Not long after my very moving conversation with the school principal, I had lunch at the little temporary sushi restaurant in Ayukawa. I liked wandering around Ayukawa and checking out the playground — children were *always* playing in it. By then it had been relocated, and the local people had managed to secure extra funding, so it had expanded quite a bit. It had become a popular place for the Oshika teenagers to hang out, even if it was originally intended for little children. I just loved seeing them enjoying it.

I regularly went to the sushi restaurant in Ayukawa, and I *thought* I knew the owner, Furuuchi-san, and his sons well. They all worked so hard, and were still living in temporary housing — it would be another year before Furuuchi-san could have a permanent home, and another year after that before he could have a permanent location for his restaurant. He had lost his wife a couple of years earlier, and poured his heart out to me at the time. On this day, he couldn't stop talking about the school uniforms, expressing his appreciation over and over again. I was surprised to find out from him that five of his grandchildren had entered Oshika Junior High since the tsunami, and every single one of them had received a school uniform. He, very emotionally, told me that this had relieved his family of a huge burden.

From Ayukawa you can take a little boat to Ajishima — the tiny island where Mr Sasaki's two sisters live, and where he had taken my niece Emily and me in the summer of 2014. Before the tsunami, Ajishima had been famous for its white sandy beach, and was usually full of tourists during the summer months — very few tourists had returned, and the island had lost a quarter of its population. Five years later, there were just 300 people living there.

One of those people was an American, Rick Mickelson, who I met on the peninsula, both of us surprised to see another foreigner fitting in so comfortably with the locals. Through chatting with Rick, who was one of the youngest people on Ajishima, I was able to find out more about this island community's needs since the disaster.

Rick told me that life on Ajishima was peaceful and relaxed, a little like life in Hawaii, Okinawa, or Jamaica. There are no convenience stores, pachinko parlours, movie theatres, traffic lights, stop signs, or even police officers. The whole island community is built on trust. People on Ajishima grow their own food, and cook for themselves — there are only a couple of small shops. The mountains are covered in green and the sea is always blue. It truly is an island paradise.

In the months immediately after the tsunami, local islanders were hired by an outside construction company responsible for removing debris and clearing the roads and docks. This really empowered the local people to be involved in the initial recovery progress and to feel in control of their future. However, since then, the islanders haven't been involved in any reconstruction, which is controlled by two major companies that don't hire local workers. They focused on rebuilding the ports and docks — clearly necessary if tourists were to return, but island life involves more than just the ports.

The local government — even if they weren't involving the locals — were at least contributing to the recovery effort on the peninsula; however, the Ajishima islanders felt that the local government didn't even know they were there. And they saw the advantages in that — they were free to be responsible for their own futures, and they had some creative ideas about how to do that. The islanders wanted to create jobs for people, support entrepreneurial visionaries, and facilitate educational experiences for children and adults alike.

Rick told me about the projects that the islanders dreamt of realizing. Their projects focused on agriculture, sustainability, and tourism: a shared kitchen space producing food for sale or export, an eco-park with a children's playground, an orchard to start up pickle- and jam-making businesses, bee hives to encourage pollination, and a farmers' market. The islanders wanted to do the work on such projects themselves, and were good at repurposing all sorts of things, but they needed help with the funding of materials and didn't know where to start.

It was quite inspiring to come across this little community of people — who were even more isolated and even more forgotten than those in the other areas on Oshika that I had worked with — because of their determination to rebuild their island on their own and the amazing ideas they had come up with. I saw a new energy in a lot of the people I met that summer, five years after the disaster, especially community leaders. When once they had seemed despondent at the lack of support from local government, they now seemed more able to take matters into their own hands. Their confidence in rebuilding their lives and in being able to actually *see* a long-term future seemed to be growing. I told Rick to leave it with me.

I met Rick right at the end of my trip — yet another wonderful summer on Oshika. I'd done lots of painting, got some new ideas for projects that needed support, and spent time with the people I loved. My dear friend Onodera-san's daughter Yuki and I had grown closer on this trip. She eventually confessed to me that she had initially found it so hard when her little village was full of volunteers and just wanted them all to go away. It was completely understandable — Ohara had been one of the few places on Oshika where volunteers could sleep after the disaster, and thousands had descended on the peninsula in the months after March 11. Of course all that support was appreciated, but Yuki's home was just on the other side of the centre's car park — she must have become exhausted from dealing with all the new people. These villages tend to have such special, unique, genuinely warm and loving atmospheres because people focus on the quality of their relationships, not the quantity. Trying to maintain relationships with lots and lots of people *is* exhausting. And sometimes you need time to identify the people who nurture your soul, rather than drain it — time you simply do not have in the immediate aftermath of a disaster.

I treasured the moments spent with Yuki; she had opened up to me about things that must have been so difficult for her to say but were so important to share, and so important for those who want to help to hear — it became clear that even *help offered* after a disaster can take a toll.

On my last night, after having dinner with Kucho and Fukumi-san, I walked through the car park back to the centre, marvelling at the clear night sky filled with a million stars. Spotting a shooting star, I stopped for a moment, then spotted another. I lay down on the ground in the car park, watching one shooting star after another, then phoned Yuki.

"Yuki, come out."

"Where are you?"

"In the car park."

"What are you doing there?"

"Looking at the stars. They're beautiful. Come out!"

So Yuki came over, giggling, and joined me on the ground. We lay there next to each other, holding hands and watching the stars shoot across the sky. Nurturing *each other's* souls.

28: New Year's

I drove back to Tokyo, surprised to find a lump in my throat at first sight of the incredible city that had been my home for fifteen years. I had thought my love affair with Tokyo was over. It seemed not though, as I kept welling up during my walk around Azabujuban and Roppongi — places I had once lived, worked, and partied. Tokyo still made me excited and I still loved it.

I ate at Yoshinoya as often as I could. Yoshinoya is a country-wide, fast-food chain, best known for its *gyudon* (thin strips of beef cooked with onions and served on top of rice). There was one in Ishinomaki, but I rarely went into the city when I was on Oshika, and there were branches *everywhere* in Tokyo; I'd developed a habit over the years since 2011 of dining at Yoshinoya as often as possible when I was there. I *loved* this cheap, tasty, and filling meal that brought back so many memories for me … eating it in Roppongi as the sun came up after dancing in '80s music club Castillo all night long, and sharing it with my mum as her first meal on her very first visit to Japan. Most of all it reminded me of when I first moved to Japan in 1996, with just a backpack and hardly any money, living on ¥1000 per day *including* train fares. But on Sundays I would splash out ¥380 and treat myself to Yoshinoya!

Just over five years after leaving Tokyo, I felt that the fact that I could smile at all the memories of my old life there — rather than look back at them wistfully — was a good sign that I was more comfortable with my new life.

I was starting to spend less time in Tokyo at the beginning and end of the Oshika trips — I wanted to spend as much time as possible with my

Oshika friends. There were a few Tokyo friends that I *always* made time for though, and one of those was Mike Alfant. He had invited me to join him and his friends at a Sunday breakfast they regularly had, saying they'd be interested in hearing about what I'd been doing on Oshika. I was pleasantly surprised to see Lowell Sheppard there — the last time I had seen him was outside the konbini on Oshika in early 2012 when, through his charity HOPE International, he had been involved in the recovery effort. It was nice to update Lowell on how Oshika was doing five years after the disaster.

I went to the breakfast without any agenda at all — Mike and I would be meeting alone later in the week so I knew we'd have a proper catch-up then; I thought he just wanted me to meet some interesting people and tell them a bit about my work on Oshika, of which he had always been supportive. And I thought when they started asking me what was needed *right now* on Oshika, they were just asking out of interest. They weren't, and by the end of that breakfast, Mike, Lowell, and their friends had pledged the ¥2 million that was required to build the Ajishima Farmers' Market and Community Kitchen. I had not expected *that* over breakfast on my first day in Tokyo.

Back in England, that summer marked 20 years since I had first set foot in Japan, and I found myself embracing my "Japanniversary" rather than feeling sad about no longer living there. I was reaching a place where I was happy living in England, having a business that allowed me to go "home" every year, and carrying Japan with me, always. My mother started making beautiful shoulder bags out of the obi that I kept bringing back from Ishinomaki, which I sold on my pickle stalls or online — and I loved giving others the chance to literally carry a bit of Japan with them, too. Mum got sick again that autumn, and I was grateful to be living in England so I could be there for her.

My Oshika projects were still moving ahead while I was in England. Shelley's school, Ohana International, had come forward to sponsor the playground on Ajishima, and the equipment arrived that winter. The islanders spent December preparing the grounds, helped by a group of volunteers from the Tohoku University Kendo Club, and everybody was looking forward to a community event where all the local children, parents, and elders would paint the wooden playset together. The islanders were inspired by the support they had received, and successfully applied to Ishinomaki City Hall to gain additional funding so that they could further develop the playground. In addition, the islanders had started renovating an old building that was to be converted into the farmers' market.

Ohana was continuing their support of the Koamikura village, and had sent money to assist with the next stage of stabilizing the shrine steps. Local people were being hired to do the work, so the money would stay in the community.

I spent the New Year's holiday in England, where I still hadn't quite worked out how to mark the transition of moving from one year to the next in a suitably Japan-inspired way. The best I could manage as a welcome to 2017 was another sunrise walk up and down Broad Ride in Cirencester Park — a lovely walk with trees on either side, at the end of which you can turn around to get a wonderful view of the parish church that Cirencester is so known for. At that time of the morning in England, when most people would have been hungover, Broad Ride was deserted. With Jim and Heath now living in their own place in Oxford, it was on occasions like New Year's Day that I would find myself feeling very isolated from Japan.

The sixth anniversary came and went that March, with the sad news in the *Japan Times* that 36,000 people were still living in temporary housing. It was definitely an improvement on the 120,000 people that were originally living in temporary housing, but six years was such a long time to still be living in quarters that were only intended to be inhabited for six months.

That summer, Robin came to visit me in Cirencester again, keen to catch up on the latest from Oshika, and keen to see whether there was anything else he might be able to do to support the little village he had so enjoyed visiting. He very generously decided to contribute a further ¥1 million to Oshika, and told me to allocate it wherever I saw fit. So I decided to split it between Ajishima, school uniforms, and Ohara. On Ajishima, the money would be used to create an orchard, so that the islanders could grow fruits, vegetables, and nuts to be sold or used to make pickles to sell and therefore encourage small business opportunities, something very dear to my heart.

In Ohara, I allocated Robin's money to the repair of the *tetsubachi* (handwashing basin) at the top of the steps to the shrine, an area that always fascinated me in every shrine I'd ever been to. I told Kucho about the sponsorship just before that year's summer festival. Knowing how much I loved being there during that week of preparations for the festival, Kucho called me a few days later from the shrine. He held up his phone so I could hear them all playing taiko, then handed the phone round so the Ohara boys could speak to me, one by one, and all the while the kanetsukido bell was ringing in the background. I couldn't wait to get back there! With my pickling business heading into its busiest season from August to December, there would be no chance of my going until after Christmas. Because of that, I decided to book a flight right after Christmas so I could be on Oshika for New Year's Eve — my first New Year's back in Japan since before the disaster.

After spending just one night in Tokyo, I arrived on Oshika in the evening of December 31, fighting off jet lag until just before midnight, when I headed up to the Ohara shrine. Onodera-san's son, Kuni, hurried by in the pouring rain, with his hood up and his hands in his pockets, barely stopping to say hello, which was very unlike him. I was soon to find out this uncharacteristic lack of social skills was because he makes it his mission, every single year, to be the first to pray at the shrine, and the first to ring the bell just after midnight.

I walked up the steps to the shrine, and was about to go in and pray, when Kuni came out full of smiles and ready with a big hug, relieved that he'd got to be the first to pray. We chatted like it had only been yesterday since we last saw each other, and not in fact a year and a half, until he suddenly stopped and ran over to the kanetsukido to ring the bell, which I'd distracted him from. The sound of that bell ringing never fails to move me, and Kuni rang it as loud as he could several times, then checked his watch to make sure he'd rung it as close to midnight as possible. He'd done it just a few minutes after midnight, so he was happy.

I prayed and rang the bell myself, and the bell continued to ring out through the village in the days that followed as, one by one, the Ohara residents, or those who were visiting, walked up the steep steps to the shrine to pray and ring the bell to mark the beginning of a new year. You can hear that bell from anywhere in the village, and a little thrill always goes through me, whether I'm up there at the shrine and feeling the sound move through the kanetsukido, or down by the sea and stopped in my tracks by the sound echoing across the land. And every time I hear it I think about Will and his family and friends, who made the kanetsukido possible. I hope they know how much their kindness is appreciated, and will continue to be appreciated by many people in the years to come.

It was my first time on Oshika during *oshogatsu* (the New Year's holiday season), so I wasn't sure what to expect. I found that most people hibernate during what is the biggest holiday in Japan. Almost all the ports were still. The boats sat at the docks, with Japanese flags and bamboo branches tied to the masts, which were swaying in the wind. The few existing shops were closed. Most businesses had shut down. Work on the massive sea wall that was by then well under construction along the entire coastline had come to a standstill, and the diggers were sitting unattended on top of it. But tourists are drawn to Oshika at this time of year.

So I did what a tourist would do, and used jet lag to my advantage by getting up at 5 a.m. on New Year's Day to drive up to Gobanshokoen to get a magnificent panoramic view from the highest point on Oshika, which I have seen many times, but this time it was to see the first sunrise of 2018. Gobanshokoen was full of people waiting for the sun to rise — some were local, but it was mostly tourists. One group of cyclists I'd passed earlier struggled and panted their way to the highest point — they'd probably come from Ishinomaki, some 40 km away.

The view was breathtaking, and the few clouds on the horizon did not spoil anybody's excitement and anticipation as the sun took its time rising behind the sacred island of Kinkasan at the tip of the peninsula. Kinkasan is the closest part of Japan to the 2011 earthquake's epicentre. It was an incredible way to welcome 2018!

After eating a noodle breakfast from a little truck at Gobanshokoen, I headed back down to Ayukawa, the main port on Oshika, which was actually bustling with little food stalls that the locals had set up. There were queues of people waiting to take the boat over to Kinkasan to explore the vast shrine complex on the first day of a new year, as well as meet the famous deer that roam wild yet are so comfortable with human visitors that they come right up to you.

I took a very small boat over to the island, intending only to walk around outside the shrines, but found myself ushered into one just as a ceremony was beginning. I've participated in many ceremonies at shrines on Oshika, but never on a shrine *island* so revered by Japanese people, and felt extremely honoured to be welcomed in, as well as mildly curious about the group of men at the front who looked suspiciously like mafia to me. Just when I thought I knew Oshika, I found myself in another world, having an experience I'd never forget.

The next day was all about Ohara. A small ceremony was held at the centre, followed by taiko drumming and a shishimai performance for visitors that included people with relatives living in Ohara or ancestors buried in the cemetery further up the hill behind Takako-sensei's house.

Taira-san, traditionally the leader of the Ohara taiko drumming, had recently had a stroke, and was still in hospital. With so few people in Ohara able to participate in taiko or shishimai, I soon joined in on one of the smaller taiko drums — they had taught me their routines years ago. After the ceremony at the centre, the visitors left and I joined the Ohara boys to drive up with the drummers and dancers to where the former temporary housing residents were now living in their new houses. We stopped at each house, took the drums off the back of a little truck, and started playing music as the shishimai team danced their way into each house and out again, sometimes just going into the genkan and back out, and sometimes going through all the rooms in the house. In the latter cases we were invited to sit down and platters of sushi and trays of beer and *sake* were presented. Having had my first beer at 11 a.m., I soon realized that this might be turning into a bit of an all-day drinking session. I was right. The New Year's drinking that I might have done in England, or even in Tokyo, was saved for this day in Ohara, rather than New Year's Eve.

At last I was in Japan for New Year's. And I loved it! More specifically, I loved New Year's on Oshika. I loved the quiet moment at midnight up at the Ohara shrine, thinking of Will and his family and friends, watching the sun rise over the peninsula, and being part of the New Year's ceremony on Kinkasan. But most of all I loved going in and out of people's houses in the little village I had come to love so much, and wishing them good fortune for the following year.

New Year's on Oshika was a reminder of why it felt important to me to continue to support people there. Maybe it was because they had a way of life that modern society was leaving behind. They were part of a tight-knit community where they took care of each other and put effort into bringing New Year's joy and luck to their neighbours, ensuring that everyone, including the elderly and those living alone, were offered love, care, and good wishes.

A few days later, I headed over to Ajishima to work on the farmers' market with Rick — while everyone else on Oshika was taking their New Year's holiday, Rick and I were keen to get to work. We cleared out the old building that was to be transformed into a farmers' market, sanded down the walls, put up some shelves, waxed the floor in the community kitchen across the street, and Rick made some fabulous display boxes. He was a genius at recycling anything and everything he found. People stopped by all day, asking what we were doing and when the market would be opening — there was never any need for PR on Oshika. Everything happened by *kuchikomi* (word of mouth).

I went to Ajishima a few times on that trip, and once discovered that the ferry back to the peninsula had been cancelled due to bad weather. I ended up spending the night in the community kitchen, which was still being renovated. I had brought absolutely nothing with me — no pajamas, toothbrush, contact lenses, or knickers. I was completely covered in dust from the work in the farmers' market building. There was no hot water. Or a toilet. *But* the brand new public toilets at the port were only a few minutes' walk away and they were *lovely*. And had heated seats. I was tempted to go and sleep on them.

The farmers' market was scheduled to be opened within a few weeks, just before my return to the UK, and, once the work on the building was done, it would need to be filled with goods to sell. The original plan was to just have fresh fruit and vegetables grown on the island available there, but this idea had since expanded in order to meet the needs of the locals on an island with very few shops, so a very small selection of "outside" products, such as milk and soy sauce, would be included.

The shop was named 808 (ya-o-ya) and Rick and his wife Michie made a beautiful sign for above the entrance, with a clock stopped at 8:08. The clock had been found discarded and hadn't worked for years. Bizarrely, when work began on the market, the clock started working again of its own accord until Rick stopped it at exactly 8:08, the time that they had planned to open the market for the first time, due to the auspicious nature of the number 8 (*hachi*), which in Japanese sounds very similar to the word for prosperity (*hanei*).

On the opening day of the farmers' market, announcements rang out on the island's loudspeaker system all morning. One by one, the islanders turned up, very excited to see what was inside, and to do some shopping at the only shop on that side of the island. Some went off to gather their friends and come back, some made more than one shopping trip, and some drove over from the other side of the island. The shop was packed for the entire time it was open, and by the time it closed, half the shelves were empty — the Ajishima Farmers' Market was a huge success!

The market also included a small clothes section, based on the free shop I had run on the peninsula every time I'd visited. This would be the first trip for me not to run the free shop next to the konbini near Ohara — the little shipping container I'd used had been removed to make way for extra parking space. On Ajishima, people had to take the ferry to Ishinomaki if they needed clothes, or rely on off-island family to mail them. Only a few young people did online shopping there, and Rick and Michie thought that having a clothing section at the market would help the island become more self-sufficient. I put a call out to my network for people to speak directly to Michie about donating clothes, as well as my regular call out for cat food for the stray cats Mrs Sasaki looked after — her herd now totalled twelve.

I was also still putting calls out for kappa for the Pink Ladies and fishermen — an ongoing need as more people returned to the fishing industry. Construction work was still going on all along the coastline, and while the hills and mountains of the peninsula were still stunningly beautiful, much of the land was still a building site. The constant disruption to everyone's lives was now taking a different kind of toll on people's spirits, and I often heard people say they were exhausted with having to *gaman* (be patient). One very emotional private conversation I had with a young lady concerned how she struggled so much with both her love for Oshika and her hate for it now — she (along with many others) hated the six-metre-high sea wall that now surrounded the peninsula, and felt that the local government didn't care. People still felt that Oshika was a lost, forgotten place.

I was still urging people not to forget Oshika and, to my delight, I'd managed to secure sponsorship for the school uniforms for another year — the 2018 intake was sponsored by the ever-generous Robin Maynard. I was invited to join the latest students who had received school uniforms — they had an English class and their teacher wanted them to practise on me. The students had to listen very carefully to my self-introduction, and take notes to see whether they had understood me correctly, and then ask questions. It took me back to more than twenty years earlier when I was an English teacher in Tokyo.

They were a very lively bunch of students, with a couple of them asking one question after another, growing more and more confident with each question. Not all of them were quite so confident though, with one girl in particular hardly saying a word until she pulled me aside at the end of the class, quietly asking whether I was the person who had brought the library to Oshika, coming alive as she told me how much she loved it and how she used it all the time. The teachers told me afterward that they were so surprised to see Kanon-chan talking to me of her own accord. It made me so happy to meet someone for whom the library meant so much.

I also met the parents of those students, and saw more than a few familiar faces in the group — people who had stopped to say hello at one point or another whenever I visited Oshika. It was nice to know that some of them had received help in the form of the school uniforms. One lady said that all three of her children had received school uniforms, and she was incredibly grateful for this support during what had been such a difficult time. I was later told that there were two other parents in the room who had three children that had each received uniforms. It was lovely to have supported people with big families when they must have been so worried about where the money for the uniforms would come from. It was those big families that held Oshika's future in their hands.

The principal privately gave me an update on how everyone was doing — all the students were now in permanent housing, which actually had some unexpected disadvantages, especially in terms of the increased financial pressure now on the parents, many of whom were paying two mortgages — one for the new house and one for the house they had lost. While the government had given *everybody* who lost their homes the option to rent and live in a new government-owned, government-built house, the rent on a property big enough to house a family was so expensive that it didn't make sense. So anyone with children didn't really have much choice except to build their own home, hence the two mortgages. It wasn't unusual for young families on Oshika to have two rather large mortgages, which is why the school uniforms, almost seven years on, were still such a huge help to the parents.

The Koamikura residents were all finally in permanent housing, although Kameyama-san still spent a lot of time in the house that he'd built on his own. I was invited to join their New Year's celebrations, and watched the young men of that village as they played taiko and danced around to entertain older residents, as well as their young wives and children. I counted seven children who looked like they had been born in the years since the tsunami, and while I recognized the fathers and the older residents, the mothers' faces were unfamiliar to me, and this was a good sign — some of the people who had been forced to leave the peninsula after the disaster were returning!

Koamikura, for the first time in almost seven years, felt full of life and hope. When I asked the new head of Koamikura — the other Kameyama-san, from the lumberyard near Kugunarihama — what the village needed at that time, he had one small request. They wanted to repair the floor of the shrine, which, underneath the mats that covered it during ceremonies, was completely falling apart. I could see by looking at the shrine that more needed to be done, but people on Oshika were, as always, modest with their requests, and would only ask for something when gently encouraged. The floor repairs would cost just ¥100,000 and they had the human resources but not the funds — Shelley and her Ohana community yet again came forward to support Koamikura in their efforts to preserve their shrine.

Kucho, Ito-sensei (the cram school teacher), and I were working on our own efforts to preserve the centre before it was scheduled for demolition in 2020 by the local government. I put together a proposal that Kucho and Ito-sensei could present, which included the ideas we had come up with for turning the centre into a youth club and learning centre. We were thinking about creating a movie room, a music room, a study space, and an indoor games room — I felt confident that between us, we would be able to find sponsors for each room, and renovate the centre bit by bit, working on the project together with the teenagers and young adults of the peninsula along the way. I had secured pledges from 26 people, who each promised to cover the monthly utility expenses until the centre was fully operational, and we had prepared answers in anticipation of every question or objection the local government could possibly have. I handed Kucho the translated document, and wished him and Ito-sensei good luck.

Although they knew they had my support, the negotiation with the local government was their domain, and it was the first time they had attempted anything like this on their own. These lovely small communities were so special in the way that they took care of each other and got along so well, which I found truly inspirational. But there were downsides to living in such small communities — people didn't naturally have an entrepreneurial spirit; they were not accustomed to creating proposals and fighting with outsiders (which is what the local government is to them) to get their voices heard and their needs met. There were few people who had the skills to move ahead with anything outside of taking care of the simple, everyday needs of their families and neighbours. This is one of the many reasons why recovery after the disaster took so long in remote communities like those on Oshika.

While people didn't have much faith in the local government, it had unexpectedly given Ohara some money so that they could temporarily move their beloved bus shelter while the ground in that area was being raised. I was there on the day it was scheduled to be moved, and watched partly with fascination, partly with dread, as a massive crane lifted the entire building from its foundations and placed it on a truck before taking it to its temporary location. It took five hours for the shelter to be moved. There were comments about how it been made in a different way to buildings made by local carpenters, so they had to try different techniques to be able to lift it from its concrete foundations. It would later be relocated to a spot along the new bus route. *And*, Kucho told me with a cheeky grin, the local government gave him far more money than was needed to move the bus shelter — he was keeping the rest aside for any projects I might want to carry out in Ohara in the years to come.

For five and a half years that shelter had provided a safe place for people to wait, or to share a coffee and look out at the beautiful view of the sea, even if they weren't going anywhere. Its comfy sofas, pictures on the walls, and cosy cushions provided a home-like environment at a time when many people there didn't have one. Its luxurious design provided many a conversation for people on and off the peninsula, right from the day we started building it when locals would pull over and ask what we were doing. It had become legendary, with tourists stopping by to take photos and, as I once heard, one Tokyo professor regularly telling his international students about a most unusual bus shelter in the middle of nowhere in Tohoku, built by a woman who came all the way from England.

And the heart building that used to be behind it had made a grieving widower smile again.

Takahashi-san hadn't joined his neighbours when they moved out of temporary housing and into the new houses in Ohara. He'd left Oshika, and moved to Higashi-Matsushima, over an hour away, but halfway between Ohara and his daughter Miyoko's home. He came back to see me on that trip. He told me that he didn't know anybody when he first moved there, but he had three friends now. He still talked to Miyoko on the phone every day, and said that his granddaughter was doing very well. He missed Yukio-san, his next-door neighbour before the tsunami, and asked me to give him some strawberries he'd brought with him but couldn't give to him personally because he wanted to get back before dark.

He apologized that the heart building was no longer there — it had been pulled down to make way for the land to be raised. I told him that it didn't matter. And then he talked and talked about how much fun it was to watch me painting all those hearts, and how he still couldn't believe that anybody would do such a thing. So many hearts. He laughed and laughed at the memories of me painting that building for him. And I remember how people said that Takahashi-san started smiling again after his building had been covered in hearts.

At ten o'clock that night Takahashi-san's daughter called me. She said that her father did not stop talking about me for one whole hour that evening. And she thanked me for still being able to make him smile.

I wasn't sad that the heart building had been pulled down; instead, I was struck by the thought that not everything had to last forever. Just as long as whatever it was — a relationship, an experience, a building, a person — it left behind happy, loving, caring, warm memories even after it was gone. I suppose that's the way things *do* last forever.

Mrs Sasaki's 65th birthday was coming up, and I was keen to help her create her own happy, warm memory on her birthday. I'd been asking her whether she wanted to do anything special and she'd been dismissing every idea I had — she was a bit grumpy because she had toothache, so she didn't want to go anywhere or do anything. So Mr Sasaki and I gave up trying to think of ideas, and instead we decided that I would get a birthday cake from her favourite patisserie on the mainland, and we would just spend a relaxing evening at home together.

Mrs Sasaki's birthday did not start well. In the early hours of the morning, Tora-chan, the first cat that Mrs Sasaki had adopted after the tsunami, then a traumatized kitten that she had nursed back to health, had passed away. In recent weeks, Tora-chan's fits had become more frequent, and we had been talking about how perhaps Tora-chan might be ready to say goodbye. Mr Sasaki buried Tora-chan in the mountain behind their home, next to their dog, which had passed away the day before the tsunami.

I didn't know that Tora-chan had died, and arrived that afternoon with a birthday cake, turning the lights off and lighting a candle on the cake before entering the room while obliviously singing "Happy Birthday." A young musician from Okinawa was visiting, and he played the shamisen for the Sasakis and two young friends who worked at a Spanish restaurant in Ishinomaki. We shared the birthday cake, and once the guests had left, Mrs Sasaki sat stroking a photo of Tora-chan while she told me what had happened that morning. We were both in tears.

After a while, Mrs Sasaki announced that she wasn't going to sit around all day crying, and that the three of us would go into Ishinomaki that night for dinner at her young friends' restaurant. Mr Sasaki and I raised our eyebrows at each other and reminded her about her tooth. But she said her tooth wasn't hurting her today and we were all going out, no matter what.

So that night we drove onto the mainland for a birthday dinner. Mrs Sasaki insisted that I sit up front while she drove, saying that Mr Sasaki was short, so he could sit in the back. She never misses an opportunity to comment on how short he is, and Mr Sasaki and I never miss an opportunity to be rude, so we both immediately commented on the size of his third leg, which, he is always claiming, is huge.

Mrs Sasaki had an ABBA CD playing in the car. She said she liked to play one song over and over again, but didn't know any of the words. So I sang "The Winner Takes It All" for her, explaining what the words meant. I told her that I knew I wasn't a very good singer, but I always tried very hard (*isshokenmei*) and didn't give up (*ganbarimasu*), which she found amusing — such Japanese words wouldn't usually be used for something as trivial as singing! We listened to more of the CD, and talked about ABBA; Mrs Sasaki was surprised to find out that they were Swedish and not American. Mr Sasaki lay asleep on the back seat and woke only for "Mamma Mia" because that was his favourite. He called them *Baba* (old woman) instead of ABBA, and laughed for ages, convinced that his joke was hilarious.

Dinner was incredible. One of the Sasakis' friends was a young woman who came to Ishinomaki as a volunteer soon after the tsunami, and had later set up the Spanish restaurant, which served delicious food and wine. I don't usually drink much on Oshika — my mind tends to be too busy thinking about what I'm working on to let itself be quiet enough to enjoy drinking. But the restaurant was warm, and beautifully designed; the staff were kind and attentive; and I was so relaxed and content to sit quietly watching the Sasakis look so, so happy, as they chatted to the three staff and two other women in their twenties who joined us for dinner. All five of them were drawn to

Ishinomaki after the tsunami, and decided to stay. One owned the restaurant, two worked for her, one was a veterinary nurse, and another worked with young children. All of them helped out with the Sasakis' wakame business on their days off. They were teasing each other about how inept they used to be at processing wakame, and Mrs Sasaki was laughing and laughing. I was lost in the moment. Lost in Mrs Sasaki's laughter. And then lost in the thoughts that her laughter brought to me.

Terrible things happen all the time. Life throws all sorts of unexpected shocks, traumas, and sadness at all of us. I hadn't been through anything like the Sasakis had, but life had thrown me a few curveballs in the past. As I watched the Sasakis with their *"shinsai-go"* friends — everything was described as pre- or post-disaster on Oshika: shinsai-mae (before the disaster) or shinsai-go (after the disaster) — I thought about the people in life that we never would have met had it not been for some horrible experience or another. And how some of those people end up having such positive impacts on our lives, bringing us so much happiness, that their ongoing presence somehow takes us further and further away from the original bad experience.

And here's an impossible question. If you had a choice to *not* go through that horrible experience, and that choice meant that you would never have met a very special person or some very special people, what would you choose? It's a *very* complicated question, and one that my Japanese wasn't good enough to be able to ask in a sensitive way. Maybe the only way to answer that question is that you have to try your utmost to come through horrible experiences with an open heart, open to the love that people want to give you when you're ready to receive it. Maybe it's the only way to move on from trauma. Yes, you still think about that horrible experience every day, and yes, you still have nightmares, but the nightmares become less frequent as daydreams of the future replace them, and the horrible memories are gradually shifted aside by beautiful new ones. And it is perhaps the new person or people around you that help that to happen.

ABBA was playing again on the long drive back home. I was singing away, and Mr Sasaki was sleeping in the back. Mrs Sasaki and I got a bit sentimental.

"Life is interesting, don't you think?" I said to Mrs Sasaki. "I'm here singing songs I knew when I was a child, driving up and down winding roads along the coast of a country on the other side of the world."

"Yes, life IS interesting, isn't it?!" she said. "It's my birthday, and this Englishwoman is here, alongside me, singing all my favourite songs."

"I wonder what zuzuhoido thinks," I said, indicating Mr Sasaki in the back.

"Probably nothing," she said. "He's fast asleep. Idiot." And we both cackled away loudly, turning the music up.

"No, no," Mr Sasaki said. "I'm awake. I'm listening to everything. And yes, life IS interesting."

29: New Normal

It was July 2019 before my next trip to Japan, a year and half after the previous one, during which time the Sasakis and I worked out how to video call each other, which we all enjoy doing. I call them with good intentions, wanting to give them my love and gentle words, but somehow, within minutes, Mr Sasaki and I always end up making innuendoes, while Mrs Sasaki rolls her eyes and tells us we're both disgusting — just like when we see each other in person!

We always compare the changes in our physical appearances since we last saw each other — over the years I've become used to my Oshika friends' constant need to comment on my weight and whether it has gone up or down since they last laid eyes on me. The Sasakis fill me in on how all the cats are doing, and we talk about our businesses, as well as whatever we've heard in the news recently about the other's country. The first time we spoke with our cameras on, I very excitedly showed them all around my house — full of Japanese memorabilia, including Mrs Sasaki's kimono hanging in my living room.

Sometimes I catch them when they're about to eat dinner, so Mrs Sasaki dishes up a bowl of rice and offers it to me, and Mr Sasaki passes me a drink. I pretend to take their offerings through our phones and we sit acting as though we're having a meal together, asking how the miso soup is, and did I want any more rice?

We always know that we're in each other's hearts — the gentle words I always plan on saying don't need to be said. And after every call, my heart is so *full* for having seen their faces.

Mrs Sasaki always demands to know when I'm coming back, but it's become not quite as easy for me to leave the UK for months at a time. I unexpectedly become a homeowner, something that was never a goal of mine, but which had become necessary if I wanted to continue my pickling business as a home-based business, and I was very keen to do that. And that business has continued to do well — by the summer of 2019 I was producing about 25,000 jars a year, and supplying 70 shops around the UK. Trips to Japan have to be carefully coordinated with the seasonal availability of ingredients for my best-selling lines, and Christmas demand. There's only a relatively small window — between March and July — when a trip to Japan can fit in. Sadly, there will be no more mushroom picking with Onodera-san in the autumn or New Year's Eves spent at the Ohara shrine while my UK business continues to do so well.

But I always promise myself, no matter what, that I'll go to Oshika every year to see what I can do to help my friends there, even if all I can do is keep their lives and stories alive through sharing them. So they're not forgotten.

I never forget Oshika when I'm in England, and do the best I can to still help from a distance.

By the summer of 2019, more school uniforms were sponsored, and more *kappa* were sent to the Pink Ladies and fishermen. Kucho and Ito-sensei were talking to the local government about our youth club idea, and the jam-makers on Ajishima had started planting trees and bushes, and ordering the equipment they needed to turn their hobbies into small businesses. The farmers' market continues its success and has become a much-needed social gathering space as well as a sales venue for local producers, and after decades of absence, honey bees have finally returned to the island, thanks to some hives sponsored by Katie Dingley, David Howenstein, Rick Weisburd, and Aya Bird (Stephen's daughter, who had also helped to build the Ayukawa playground).

I started up my talks in England about Japan and the 311 events and their aftermath again — interest in the tsunami had naturally decreased over the years and I hadn't done any school talks for a while. But in 2019 I started giving talks to Women's Institute groups in Gloucestershire and the surrounding areas. They had originally heard about me through my pickling business, so I had given pickle talks and tastings to a number of Women's Institute groups, and when they heard about my Japan connection they invited me back to talk about that, too. It was a lovely way to bring Japan back into people's thoughts that wasn't *just* about the upcoming Olympics — everybody, without fail, remembered the powerful images that filled the British news in the weeks after the tsunami. They just needed reminding sometimes that the people with whom they felt so much sympathy all those years ago were *still* recovering.

We can't really begin to imagine what the reality is for people who have suffered the kind of trauma that such a huge disaster brings with it. But I do know that it doesn't go away when the media coverage has stopped. It doesn't go away for years, if ever. There is some kind of new normal that everyone tries to come to terms with. And along with all the media coverage, the connections made in the early weeks, months, and years may well go away, too. My connection with Oshika won't go away, even if it is months or a year and a half between visits. One friend posted on Facebook on the anniversary that year, naming me as someone who had "adopted a village." But in all honesty, I think Ohara adopted me.

A huge memorial to all those lost on Oshika was erected just before the eighth anniversary, right in the middle of Ohara. It faces out to sea and was built on raised land, so it can be seen rising up in the middle of what used to be the village. It was designed so that every year on March 11 at 2:46 p.m. the sun shines through certain strategically positioned spaces within the memorial. It is engraved with the names of every single person on Oshika who died as a result of the earthquake and tsunami. It is beautifully designed and incredibly moving. You get the feeling that there is finally an appropriate place to pay respect to the local people who died.

Kucho told me that 200 people attended the unveiling of the monument on March 11, 2019 — people who still lived on Oshika as well as people who used to live there, and people who have been a part of the recovery. Many adults on Oshika talk about the importance of passing on memories of March 11 to the generations to come, and monuments like these help to heal the past as well as look to the future.

Ohara got a brand new community centre in 2019, and Kucho was very excited to tell me that I had a room there — he meant that there was a room where I could stay, like I had done in the old community centre. I had been toying with the idea of staying in a hotel somewhere on the peninsula during my next visit, but I think Kucho liked me staying in the community centre, and I didn't really have the heart to stay anywhere else. I think it made my

Ohara friends happy to know that I was near them — it certainly made me happy to be near them.

I did actually spend my first night on Oshika in a hotel on that year's visit — I could only fit in a very short trip, a matter of weeks, so I had decided to see whether I could travel from Cirencester all the way to Oshika without stopping in Tokyo, to maximize my time there. I'd never attempted such a trip before. It took 26 hours door-to-door and involved one plane, two buses, four trains (including the bullet train), and a taxi to Ohara, where I grabbed a quick coffee with Kucho and Yukio-san before crashing out, exhausted, at the Hotel New Sakai, which overlooks Kinkasan. I was so happy to be "home."

On that trip, more than eight years after the disaster, I could feel a very real sense of a future for Oshika. Much of it still looked like a building site, but there was a cleaner, fresher look amid the construction. The huge black sandbags had all gone, and the massive sea wall along the whole coastline was almost finished — it now didn't quite look like the monstrosity it did when it was first going up. Some of the new roads set higher up the hills had just opened a week before my visit.

The energy was different on that visit and I was sure it was something to do with the fact that all the temporary houses had been removed. The tiny prefabricated units that people thought they'd be living in for only six months had been scattered all over the peninsula for seven years. They represented so much negative energy, forced people to live on top of each other, and in many ways divided communities rather than bringing them together. And they were all finally gone.

The temporary shopping street in Ayukawa would soon be gone, too. A large, for Oshika, and rather impressive shopping complex was being built near the port, and it was intended to be ready for autumn occupancy. After eight years in their tiny temporary shops, the shopkeepers would finally be able to run their businesses properly and there would be space available to draw in new businesses, investors, and tourists.

The tired old shopping and housing buildings that had helped the people of Oshika through such a difficult time were all being torn down and replaced with brand new ones. The old buildings that had served a much-needed and highly valued purpose at the time, but were not considered to have a place in the new Oshika. And this included Ohara's beloved old community centre, which was still scheduled to be pulled down in 2020.

The old centre had played a vital part in the recovery process. It was one of the few community spaces that survived the tsunami, and thousands of volunteers had slept there over the years. It provided a place for meetings, social occasions, celebrations, and the distribution of donations when there wasn't anywhere else on the peninsula for such activities. But its time was coming to an end. The local government wouldn't give approval to the proposal that I had made for Kucho and Ito-sensei to present, asking for permission to renovate the centre — the demolition would be going ahead. Whereas before this would have been met with a *shoganai* ("it can't be helped") attitude, this time the local people were planning on asking the government for an investment in order to build something new on the land. I loved seeing the change in attitude among my Oshika friends.

And I loved working with them again! Kucho and Yukio-san joined me in fixing the Ohara playground fence and giving everything fresh coats of paint and woodstain, and we enjoyed reminiscing while we worked. We laughed about the crazy road trip we'd gone on to collect the cherry tree saplings, and they told me that the one we planted in the middle of the playground had blossomed for the first time that year — it was now huge. Kucho said they all missed seeing my underwear hanging out on the washing line outside the centre — a coin laundry had opened on the mainland, and I'd been using that for laundry during my last few visits.

We joined the other Ohara boys in getting the shrine and the rest of the village ready for that summer's festival, which I would sadly *just* miss that year. Thick grass had grown tall that summer, and the Ohara boys loved the chance to get their weed trimmers out — we went all around the village, including where the new houses were, tidying up *everything*. I was reminded of how much I loved the work ethic in Ohara — you work really hard and everybody just gets on with it. Nobody is "in charge." It's not necessary. You just look around and find work that needs doing. And when you've finished that job, you look around for someone who is still working and join them. Nobody works alone. And throughout the day you take lots of breaks, during which you sit and chat. Nobody gets their phones out.

During one of my last days on that trip I came across two men sitting and chatting together on their break, without mobile phones interfering with their opportunity to connect. They were sitting in front of a huge vat with steam rising out of it, and I went over to say hello and ask what they were doing, as that's what's done on Oshika.

The two men were from Ishinomaki Shoshinkai Foundation Vocational Support Centre for the Disabled, otherwise known as Kujiranoshippo. Ohara's Abe-san's wife worked there, and I knew some of the staff and "trainees," as they're referred to, from when they'd come along to meet Prince William. One of the men was a member of staff, and the other was a trainee.

The vocational centre was for cognitively disabled adults on Oshika, usually aged 30 and upward, when perhaps their families found the challenge of caring for them to be too much and required respite. I always noticed quite a lot of elderly people there, so perhaps after their parents passed away there wasn't anybody to take care of them. So they would spend their days at the support centre, and some of them spend their nights at a group home.

The vocational centre is at the back of the Seiyukan, the huge health and welfare centre opposite Hot Maru, on one of the highest points on Oshika. The Seiyukan is the place that Andrew Abbey and I visited in May 2011, where we had been quite shaken by the general energy of the building (at that point serving as an evacuation centre for 500 people) and the obvious stress that the people coordinating everything were under. Over the years, I had often popped in round the back to say hello to the people in the vocational centre, but I have never, even years later, managed to shake off the unpleasant, anxious feelings I still get when going into the building's main entrance.

It was near the back of the building where I'd seen the two men sitting in front of the vat. The wood burning below the vat was giving off a lovely aroma. They were making salt, which they sold, or added to soda, which they also sold. The staff member gave me some soda to taste. I don't have a sweet tooth and don't drink fizzy drinks but didn't want to be rude, so I tried their soda and was surprised to find it had a lovely, delicate taste and wasn't sweet and sugary at all. The vocational centre also produced seaweed, so all in all they had a good little business going, and they had the capability to send products anywhere in Japan.

I was fascinated by the process involved in making the salt — they took water from the sea around the Oshika peninsula, then boiled it for ten hours, sitting there for the entire ten hours to keep an eye on it. Ten litres of water would generate about 3 kg of salt. I don't know how they had the patience, and they admitted that it was sometimes rather dull and frustrating. But the salt was very popular and generated a lot of money for the centre, so it was important work for them to do, along with the soda and seaweed.

Even though I'd been to the centre quite a few times over the years, I didn't know their tsunami story — I *never* ask people to tell me their stories, but instead just listen if they want to talk. And I'm ashamed that my ignorance made me assume that their experience would have been similar to everyone else's, but it wasn't. Not at all.

The trainees had been learning how to make bread in the time preceding March 11, 2011, and had actually been storing it in their freezer, just in case it would be needed in any kind of emergency. They were baking as usual at the time of the earthquake, and were led outside for safety until the earthquake stopped. Soon after, people started evacuating to the Seiyukan, given that it is one of the highest points on Oshika. Eventually, 500 people arrived, and the Seiyukan became one of the biggest shelters on Oshika.

The non-disabled people slept in the Seiyukan's main halls and rooms, and the disabled people slept in their workshop, so for a while there wasn't much interaction. Most non-disabled Oshika people didn't know that there was a centre for disabled people there, and, as in many places in Japan, understanding of disabled people was limited. So initial interactions between the two groups involved a lot of misunderstandings, and some unkind comments were made during what was an extremely stressful time for everyone.

But over time, this changed. The disabled people participated alongside the non-disabled people in group meetings that were organized to determine what rules were necessary for so many people to live together as comfortably as possible in such a small place. Each group took on the same responsibilities in terms of cleaning and handing out donated supplies. And through the whole experience of sharing that small space together, the non-disabled people learned a lot about disabilities, became more understanding, and less prejudiced. And the only food that the evacuees had during the early days was the bread that had been made by the trainees — when the non-disabled people realized this, their attitude toward the disabled people become very respectful and appreciative. (Government-owned buildings that are designated as emergency shelters always have supplies of instant rice and other food items in storage, whereas privately owned buildings like the Seiyukan that become shelters through necessity do not have any food items in storage.)

Non-disabled people were prioritized when the temporary houses were built. So gradually the non-disabled people left the Seiyukan, leaving the trainees, who were still sleeping in their workshop. More than seven months after the disaster, a temporary group home for disabled people was built, which the trainees moved into. There was just one temporary group home on all of Oshika. After people on Oshika moved into their temporary housing, basic supplies were regularly delivered to all the temporary houses except for the disabled people's group home, because it wasn't automatically put on the local register. It took another two months for that to be remedied and for them to start receiving basic supplies.

People on Oshika like to pull their weight. They don't like receiving handouts, even after a huge disaster. They'd rather find work, get paid, and contribute to their community. That includes the disabled people who live there, even though they are small in number and quite separate from the non-disabled community on Oshika.

After the disaster, everyone that remained on Oshika had to look for new ways to contribute to the community, and that included the disabled residents. They took jobs that involved cleaning debris and dirt from fishing facilities that had survived the tsunami, and through that work became more connected with other people on Oshika. They actually did the work so well that they got paid more than was originally agreed on, and earned even more respect. Drawing upon skills they used when they were younger, the trainees started working in the wakame business with — guess who? — the Sasakis! Oshika was such a small place. And the work they did in processing wakame is work that they continue to do, years after the disaster.

For the disabled people on Oshika, the earthquake and tsunami experience ultimately led to them becoming an integral part of the fishing community. They are now less isolated than they were beforehand. They have more respect than before. And other people on Oshika now have a better understanding and perhaps more kindness and patience in their dealings with them. But the process of getting to that point is heartbreaking to contemplate: they were the last people on Oshika to move into temporary housing, they didn't receive basic supplies when everybody else did, and they had to deal with people's prejudice and ignorance during such a stressful time.

The newfound respect that people have for the trainees is well deserved.

30: The Tenth Year

Going into the tenth year after the tsunami, my fundraising for Oshika has reached almost £170,000 (just over ¥26 million). I never did set up a charity, but instead maintained regular contact with every single person who donated so that they knew exactly what happened to their money. That money has funded more than thirty projects to date, all led by the local communities, and in many cases sourcing materials or labour from within the local community. And I have stuck to a commitment I made many years ago, where every penny of that money would go directly to the Oshika projects and nothing would *ever* be used on expenses or administrative costs — aside from one trip that Robin Maynard very kindly insisted on paying for, I have paid for all my travel to and from Oshika, and I've made ten trips that ranged in length from two weeks to three months.

The other commitment I made many years ago was to spend time on Oshika every year, which I have also done, except in 2020 when coronavirus made travel impossible. When I'm back there, I join in with normal life, pitching in where I can, as well as doing little jobs like repainting the library or the playground — Yukio-san still ends up joining me.

The Japanese community in Oxford continue their fundraising efforts, with a major event every year and other smaller events throughout the year. Along with many other projects, they have contributed to school uniforms for four different years of incoming students at Oshika Junior High School. I've managed to secure sponsorship for those school uniforms for every single year since 2013, and sponsorship is currently pledged up to 2021. And kappa for the Pink Ladies (and brightly coloured fishermen) currently number 149. Workwear for the adults of the fishing community and school uniforms for its children are an ongoing need, and a wonderful way to remind the people of Oshika that they are not forgotten.

Through my website and Facebook page, I continue to do what I can to ensure that the people of Oshika, and Tohoku in general, are not forgotten. I also give talks to the local Women's Institute groups — I've got talks with them booked for the next couple of years.

It's now ten years on, and much of Oshika is still a construction site — noisy, dusty, and dirty — with trucks constantly driving back and forth along the coast. The land where all the villages used to be is still being raised, from Koamikura all the way to Ayukawa, which is one big construction site in itself; unrecognizable from how it looked before 311.

There's a new tourist information centre in Ayukawa called "Whale Town Oshika" that has information on the port's history, including the tsunami, as well as current guidance on things to do. After a 30-year break, Japan resumed commercial whaling in 2019, and with Ayukawa's history being so steeped in whaling, the local people hope that returning to the port's traditional industry will boost the town's economy.

Ayukawa's temporary shopping street is gone now, and the new shopping complex has opened, closer to the port. It is a big, bright, modern building, with plenty of space, and a large seating area where shoppers can relax while looking out to sea. Of course, it is wonderful that the local business owners now have a place from which to sell their wares, but to me, the new shopping centre lacks soul and character, something that Oshika was so well known for. Only the sushi shop owner, Furuuchi-san, has moved to the newly built complex — the other shop owners closed their businesses or found a way to run them from their homes, which had traditionally always been such a popular way of running any kind of shop on Oshika.

Kinkasan has suffered even more since the tsunami, with typhoons and rainstorms destroying parts of the ancient shrines and forests as well as causing landslides. While the tourist industry is very slowly returning to Oshika, it is nowhere near as busy as it was before the disaster. There used to be several boats a day going back and forth to Kinkasan; now there's just one. The island relies heavily on the tourist industry in order to maintain its sacred shrine complex and surrounding areas of natural beauty, which are now sadly neglected.

On Ajishima, almost 80 fruit and nut trees have been planted in the new orchard, and while waiting for those to bear fruit, the islanders are making jam from the more mature trees growing wild on the island. The community kitchen has been finished, and the farmers' market will be relocated to the same building, which provides even more space for future development and new projects to further contribute toward the island economy and self-sustainability. Their next project is to set up a cafe alongside the kitchen and farmers' market.

The road system around Kugunarihama is being rerouted, and a new beach is scheduled for completion by 2021. Trainees from Kujiranoshippo still work for the Sasakis during the wakame season, and continue their business of producing salt, soda, and seaweed. The FamilyMart convenience store is now open on a 24-hour basis, and Endo-san no longer runs the konbini or her egg factory; she's fully enjoying her retirement at last, although still full of energy as she nears 90 years of age.

In nearby Koamikura, a few small oyster farms are doing very well, which gives hope to the new village now set high up in the hills, overlooking where the old village was. The shrine remains on the side of the hill by the port, and Masayo and Keiko are well, still tending to their vegetable gardens near the shrine.

The massive sea wall all along the coast that was supposed to have been completed by now is still under construction, and so are the ports. The sea wall is made of very pale grey stone, which really reflects the sun, making the whole peninsula feel light and bright; although again, I feel like Oshika has lost a little of its charm with this modern construction. The locals still feel very conflicted about the wall, understanding its advantages but at the same time feeling claustrophobic because of its presence, and unsettled because their view of the sea is now blocked. People in Ohara asked for stairs to be added to their section of the wall so that they can at least feel some kind of connection with the sea. The wall's presence makes them worry more about a future tsunami — if the sea surges over the wall, they feel that the aftermath will be far worse than if there were no wall at all.

The new road, higher up in the hills, is lovely to drive on, giving beautiful views of the ocean, and passing the new villages that the former temporary housing residents were moved to. At one point the road goes right past Kameyama-san's house with the huge Union Jack heart painted on it — he did always say he wanted everybody to be able to see it from the road. Now you can't miss it!

New community centres are going up in the new villages, as are private homes. The locals are resigned to all this upheaval taking such a very long time, having got used to the barrage of noise that has been a constant part of their lives for almost ten years, and will likely continue for many more years to come. For so many years now, this beautiful peninsula has been devoid of the peace and quiet for which it was once so famous.

There is still the sense that Oshika is a forgotten place, and the locals have been left so disappointed by the lack of support and investment from the government. The feelings of neglect that the Oshika people started having *before* 311 — after Oshika's government management was transferred to Ishinomaki City in 2005 — were felt even more keenly after 311. The small number and low skill level of the construction workers who had been sent to Oshika for general maintenance of public services and facilities even before the disaster had long sent the message to the Oshika people that they were not a priority. The local government's response after 311 just emphasized it.

Despite all of Kucho's efforts to save Ohara's beloved community centre, the local government went ahead with tearing it down, just as Oshika entered its tenth year since the disaster. The centre had come to represent so much to the people of this community — after it was submerged in the tsunami, together with volunteers, the locals had repaired it themselves. The centre became such a symbol of the village's strength and resilience; it was a place from which everyone in the community had received support, both practical and spiritual.

People have needed different kinds of support during the past ten years, depending on what happened to them not just on 311, but also in the years that followed. There are people who lost everything, and people whose homes and livelihoods survived. Because people's experiences during the past ten years have been so different, tensions inevitably arose within the community.

There is just a third of the pre-disaster Ohara population left now, and about a third of those people are casual staff from China, Myanmar, Vietnam, and Indonesia — they work in the oyster and wakame industries. Ohara has continued its history of accepting people from all over the world to become part of its community. With shopping and health facilities in the area so limited, it's easy to see why elderly people follow their adult children who settle in other areas that have more facilities to offer — the stunning views and peaceful way of life that made Ohara so special just aren't the same anymore.

The peninsula's memorial in the middle of Ohara is a popular visitor spot, and the playground overlooking the memorial is always full of children — the panda is still there, still smiling. The library is still popular, and Kucho is working hard to establish it as an official bus stop location for the peninsula. He and the rest of the senior villagers are also working hard to raise funds for the shrine's roof — the tiles are gradually falling off and they are hoping to replace all the tiles with a new copper roof.

Tohoku University students still visit Ohara every year to carry the mikoshi around the village and bring some light-hearted cheer to the now mostly elderly residents.

I speak with Kucho and Fukumi-san regularly, and I'm Facebook friends with many, many people I've met on Oshika over the years, including locals and volunteers. Both Kucho and Fukumi-san are still working in a wakame factory in the next village over, where they salt boiled seaweed and package it up to fill orders to be sent all over Japan.

Abe-san — Kucho's deputy, and engineer turned farmer — and his wife are still well. Their son now works in Yachan's factory, right opposite their house, where the temporary housing used to be.

Onodera-san is still in the same house, still taking care of his wife, and still doing odd jobs here and there, which include working really hard in the wakame industry during the spring. His wife is fine, and continues singing along to the television in the evening. Kuni is his usual happy self, working hard, and still talking about the Oshika firefighters' successful performance at the regional competition from a few years ago. Yuki is still working in Watanoha, and sometimes gets a little down at having to work so hard; she looks forward to the chance to let her hair down at the festivals. She was devastated when the community centre was pulled down, and watched it alone, from outside her home, with tears in her eyes. If I'd been with her I would have cried, too.

Life is still the same for most of the other Ohara boys, who still haven't found love. Yukio is still a little up and down sometimes, and Hirota-kun, Kiyotaka-kun, and Take-chan are all busy working, but always have big smiles on their faces. Ogata-san, the grumpy carpenter, is still grumpy. And Taira-san has worked so hard at his rehabilitation after his stroke that he can now walk without support. Takako-sensei, who taught all of the Ohara boys many years ago, is now in her eighties, cheerful and active, and still doesn't stop talking.

Takahashi-buta is no longer a pig farmer. The farm in Ohara was located very close to where the new houses were built, and it was felt that the smell of the pigs would be problematic to the residents. So Takahashi-buta's boss transferred him to a farm in Ishinomaki, to a place about ninety minutes away from Ohara. He worked there until early 2020, when he changed careers entirely and became a truck driver. He says it's much better money. His new home isn't decorated with pink accessories — he finally found a girlfriend, and they now live together. He goes back to Ohara to join in with the summer and winter festivals, and to visit Yachan, and does his best to help Yachan in his efforts to find a girlfriend, too.

Yachan is still hoping to find love one day! He still works really hard managing the family business, and is keen to get a better work–life balance. The past ten years have been such a struggle for him — rebuilding his business was such a challenge, first because of radiation fears, and then later, once those fears had been allayed, he couldn't find enough people to work at his factory. He worries about Ohara's elderly and diminishing population, which makes him even more determined to find a wife soon. He'd like to do his bit in helping to increase Ohara's population.

In Fukkiura, there's a lot of effort going into increasing the village's population! Mika now has four children (the last one was born after the disaster), and there's been a sudden increase in newlyweds in the area. Mika works alongside her husband, six days a week from October to February, in the oyster industry, and in other areas of fishing during the rest of the year. Her eldest son now works alongside her. She managed to get government assistance for the mortgage on the house she built just before the tsunami, so only has to worry about the mortgage on the new house. She stays in touch with Will and Kellie, and, along with her kids, treasures the memory of the Disneyland trip. And she still loves her pink kappa!

Oshika Junior High School is sadly losing more students every year, with only 21 students enrolled on the ten-year anniversary, compared to almost 200 enrolled at the nearest junior high at Mangoku Bay in the same year. Oshika Junior High doesn't even have enough students to form proper sports teams — not many sports are currently on offer, and sports are greatly valued in the Japanese education system. About 40 percent of the students receive financial assistance from the local government for school supplies and lunches.

The disaster is referred to throughout the school year, but students, for the most part, neither remember it nor initiate personal conversations about it, although they are aware that they lost family members — it's their parents who still carry the scars. For many of the adults, I am told that it feels rather difficult to believe that it has been a decade since the disaster.

Some of the families that moved away after 311 have returned, but this has been outweighed by the number of families that left the area after their children graduated from junior high school — the entire peninsula has lost about a third of its households since before the disaster. There are currently about 1200 households on the peninsula, but this number, sadly, continues to decline.

Some of the former students at the junior high school have become committed to volunteering, and recently offered assistance to people in other parts of Japan that were badly affected by flooding and landslides. They've grown up to become young people who are determined to find ways to show their appreciation for all the help they received after March 11.

Many of the non-locals who played such a huge part in Oshika's recovery in the early years are still working in disaster relief now. Kurosawa-san spent four years on Oshika working for the Nippon Foundation, where he is still employed. Ten years after 311, he is based just outside Tokyo, where he trains firefighters and volunteers in a number of disaster response techniques that include the use of special vehicles for disaster recovery. Since leaving Oshika in 2015, he has been deployed all over Japan in response to other earthquakes, flooding, and landslides.

Hanako, Kurosawa-san's former PA, returned to Canada and used the experience she gained in Tohoku to help in other disasters, including Hurricane Sandy. She is currently taking a break from disaster relief to focus on her career as a carpenter in the events and entertainment industry, which currently involves her working on a boat. She says that her time on Oshika inspired her to dedicate part of her life to disaster relief, wherever it may be in the world, and that people like Kurosawa-san and Kucho inspired her to always treat people with unconditional love.

Kurosawa-san often works with Seiji Yoshimura, whom he had first met in 1995 after the Kobe earthquake. Seiji also continues his work throughout

Japan, arranging for the provision of equipment to disaster-struck areas, training volunteers, and coordinating community-based activities as well as organizing immediate relief and recovery where necessary.

Hiroyuki finished working for the Ishinomaki government in 2015, but continued to maintain a base on Oshika while he trained volunteers who would be sent to other parts of Japan that had been affected by natural disasters. In 2019 he began training to become a priest at Koganeyama Shrine on Kinkasan, while simultaneously working on the shrine's restoration. He is currently recovering from major surgery to relieve a spinal condition, for which there is unfortunately no cure. He plans on continuing his training at the shrine as soon as he is able.

Jamie El-Banna continued running It's Not Just Mud in Watanoha until the summer of 2014, and kept the organization going after he left Tohoku. He never returned to his old life, and instead went on to help in the aftermath of other earthquakes, typhoons, and flooding in other parts of Japan.

Robert Mangold also left his old life — giving up his work as a professional carpenter. He says that after 311 he no longer wanted to be paid for those skills. He works closely with Jamie, whom he met in Ishinomaki, and has been active in a disaster zone every year since 2011. When he isn't busy helping people in need, he helps upcoming Japanese artists by introducing their work to the Western world. He now owns an art gallery in Kyoto.

Shelley Sacks, who first introduced me to Oshika, has recently celebrated the tenth anniversary of Ohana International School in Tokyo, reflecting on how the school has grown from just six students at the time of the disaster, to over 70 now. In addition to all the support she offered Koamikura over the years, she also got involved with Santa Soul Train — a Christmas community-rebuilding project in Minamisanriku and Kesennuma, where Shelley had first volunteered in 2011.

Andrew Abbey is still living in Tokyo, where he continues to run his own business. He joined the "Knights in White Lycra" — a group of self-described unfit men (and one woman) that every year embarks on a gruelling fundraising cycling trip in Japan that covers 500 km and always ends somewhere in Tohoku. They raise millions of yen for others, and their cause is often related to 311. Prior to the disaster, Andrew was always involved in voluntary work in one way or another, and his efforts have increased ever since — he now commits to doing fifteen voluntary days per year, either with the cycling group, Place to Grow (the group that, among other things, runs Santa Soul Train), or Médecins Sans Frontières. He says that the trip he made with me brought home the direct human aspect of disasters. On his trips previous to coming to Oshika after 311, he had been delivering supplies to the Japanese army or to another official organization — literally dropping things off and driving straight back to Tokyo. Whereas when we went up to Oshika, it was the time he spent actually talking to people — especially on the night we stayed in Ohara's community centre — that made everything more personal. He admits that he has since become quite evangelical about getting other people to put time, not just money, into volunteer work.

Will and Kellie also still live in Tokyo, and still consider it a privilege to have the opportunity to live and work in such an amazing country. They also still try to give back wherever they can. In 2017, Will got involved in setting up a rugby club for children in Tokyo, starting with just 15 kids. The club now has more than 160 members. Will and Kellie will never forget Mika and her family, or Kucho and the Ohara community; learning about what the people of Oshika had to deal with made them appreciate even more just how lucky they are. They say they have nothing but admiration for the resilience, strength, and kindness of the people they met on their visit there.

Robin Maynard still shares his time between different countries, always seeking out ways he can help communities in the country that he also feels has given him so much. He is still very much involved in efforts to commemorate the 400th anniversary of the death of the first English person to set foot in Japan. And he always thinks to ask me how things are going on Oshika.

As for me, I've reached a place where I'm finally comfortable with calling England "home," although every time I visit Oshika I still find myself gazing wistfully at that "Land for Sale" sign. I occasionally toy with the idea of selling my house and business in England and moving to Oshika, but quickly remind myself of my mother's ageing years, my lack of a permanent residency visa, and the fact that I *genuinely* love living in Cirencester. It took me many, many years to come to feel this way, but I think I feel at home at last. And I'm sure a big part of it is the people I've met through doing the markets in Cirencester — people who are in many ways similar to my Oshika friends — couples often work together, and family businesses are common.

Traders work incredibly hard, make delicious food and drink, are loyal to each other, and some enjoy a rather naughty sense of humour, although I grant that mine might be among the naughtiest. I love being around them, and they, along with my customers, are always so interested in and supportive of my love for Japan — one of my much younger fellow traders actually remembers an Englishwoman who was collecting emergency supplies giving a talk about Japan when he was a school boy, many years ago!

Cirencester is about as far away from any coast as you can get in the UK, and I often think it's odd that I ended up somewhere hours away from the ocean when I love being by it so much. I live about 40 metres away from a busy major road, and the noise of the cars going by always reminds me of the swish of the sea on Oshika, which makes me smile.

My Auntie Caroline's pickling business is still based at home, and it continues to surpass my expectations in its success, having recently had a record year, with over 30,000 jars of pickles and preserves sold.

My home is Jim and Heath's second home, just like when we lived in Japan. We had thought we'd be old friends together in Japan, and never could have imagined that we'd be old friends together in England, of all places, with Jim being American, Heath being Australian, and me not at all identifying as being British all those years ago. I don't necessarily identify as being British even now, and often find myself mildly amused by elements of English culture that still remain quite unfamiliar to me.

Instead, I find myself relishing the opportunity to celebrate elements of Japanese culture. Jim and Heath come over in the spring when my Japanese cherry tree blossoms, and we celebrate *hanami* in my little garden, sitting underneath its lovely boughs with their glorious petals, eating authentic sushi from a Cotswold-based Japanese food delivery service. And in January we always have a *shinnenkai* (New Year's party), which again involves sushi, along with bottles of Asahi, and a special bottle of *sake* that Kucho will undoubtedly have given me on my most recent trip. I've even taught myself how to make Japanese breakfast for the morning after — we still have our long, leisurely brunches. They used to be English breakfasts in Japan; now they're Japanese breakfasts in England.

And I've finally found a way to celebrate New Year's in England that somehow makes me feel close to Japan on an occasion that makes me miss it so! About a half hour before midnight on New Year's Eve, I wrap up warm, and take the ten-minute walk into the middle of Cirencester. The bells of the beautiful parish church in the centre of town get louder and louder as I get closer and closer, and my smile gets bigger and bigger. I set up a picnic blanket in Abbey Grounds, right behind the church, and take out some bubbly from my little rucksack. I gaze up at the church tower in front of me, and wait for the bells to stop just before midnight. The bells eventually stop. Starting again, they chime twelve times, then continue ringing for an hour over the streets of the town I now call home, while I think of the Ohara shrine bell ringing out over a little village on the other side of the world where there are people and a place that will forever be in my heart.

On a recent call to the Sasakis they told me that I will forever be in their hearts, too. Reflecting on the ten years since the disaster, Mr Sasaki said that while his business was definitely recovering, he wasn't sure whether he would ever recover from the psychological scars that March 11 left, and the pain he still feels when he thinks about his mother, lost to the ocean. But all the people that have helped him and his wife in the years since the disaster — people from all over the world — played a huge part in their healing, and still were playing a part. Knowing they were not forgotten has meant so, so much to them.

Then Mr Sasaki asked when I'd next be visiting Oshika, and Mrs Sasaki interrupted by saying that I couldn't, because of coronavirus. At that point, the whole world was in one stage of lockdown or another, and it didn't look like I'd be visiting anytime soon. My markets had all been cancelled and many of the shops I supplied were shut — I'd probably need to dig into my Oshika travel savings for that year in order to get through the lockdown.

"Come to Oshika and set up your business here!" suggested Mr Sasaki, thrilled with the idea of my living there. It was business as usual for everyone on Oshika — coronavirus didn't seem to be bothering anyone there.

"How am I going to get there if there aren't any flights?!"

"I'll come and get you in my boat."

I couldn't stop laughing at the idea of Mr Sasaki sailing all the way to England to pick me up in his little wakame boat. He probably would do it, too! He'd tied his boats together and singlehandedly sailed through one of the biggest tsunamis in history — he'd probably see sailing to England as a pleasure cruise.

"It's actually a good time to not be making pickles — I'm working on my book about Oshika."

"Is it in English or Japanese?"

"In English, but I'll get it translated so you can read it."

Mr Sasaki asked, "But what about all the special Oshika words? Like zuzuhoido? How will you explain them?"

Mrs Sasaki tutted at her husband, "She's not writing about things like *that*!"

And I said, that actually, yes … yes I was writing about things like that. I was writing about *everything*. Everything about the times we had shared together. All the tears we had shared together — both happy and sad. About the friendship that I treasured so much. That *we* treasured. About *all* the friendship, love, and kindness I had found in — as well as attempted to offer to — everyone on Oshika.

I told them that of course something that caused *unimaginable* pain and sorrow had happened on March 11, 2011, but in the decade that followed, many beautiful things had happened, too. Becoming part of each other's lives was one of those beautiful things. The bonds that were made between so many people after 311 were wonderful, healing bonds, for *everyone*. That, along with the incredible spirit of the Tohoku people, should never be forgotten.

And as I had said to the Sasakis before, many times, I told them that I felt that Oshika was a very special place. With very special people. Who had a very special way of life. A way of life that I felt many people outside Oshika should know about. I wanted to share that, share their story, and share *our* story. And that would mean writing about *all* the moments we shared, zuzuhoido and all … if that was OK with them.

Mrs Sasaki nodded, tears rolling down her face.

And Mr Sasaki put his thumb in the air and said, "Good job, good job."

Top left: Zuzuhoido. Top right: My niece Emily working with Mrs Sasaki. Middle left: Mr Sasaki getting overexcited because he's just fixed the Ayukawa playground's swing. Middle right: Restricted to working on my laptop at the Sasakis' place because of my broken ankle. Bottom left: Mrs Sasaki on her first day back at sea. Bottom right: Emily and me on Ajishima with the Sasaki clan.

Top left: Robin and Midori on Oshika. Top right: Date Masamune's 400-year-old shrine. Middle left: The new shinden inside the shrine, sponsored by Robin. Middle: The new kanetsukido, thanks to Will and Kellie and friends. Middle right: With Katsumi-san, who despairs at my unladylike behaviour. Bottom: The Ohara boys in front, carrying the new mikoshi.

Top left: Kucho grinning as work started on the bus shelter he had so longed for. Top right: Inside the bus shelter like no other! Middle left: The bus shelter, complete with terrace, and Takahashi-san's heart-covered building. Middle right: The community library and "beer garden." Bottom: Oshika teenagers inside the library — this image still brings a tear to my eye.

Top left: The shop I set up next to the konbini — everything in it was free. Top right: Koamikura shrine, restored thanks to Shelley Sacks's network in Tokyo. Middle left: The Yagawa fishermen with their new equipment. Middle right: Volunteer Sophie Middleton, who spent weeks with me on Oshika. Bottom: The first recipients of the bright pink kappa — there's now almost 150 of them!

Top left: Commemorative stone at Koamikura shrine, acknowledging its supporters. Top right: The Thomas Keble playground in Ohara. Middle left: Katsuzo-san using his new weed trimmer for the first time. Middle right: The Disneyland trip (Will is in the top right). Bottom: Miyabi Arashi Taiko Group performing in front of the kasetsu for the Koamikura community in spring 2013.

Top left: After accepting my award from the Japan-British Society — desperately trying not to fall out of my dress. Top right: Me and my pickles at Cirencester market — how I pay for my trips to Oshika! Middle left: Looking down on Ohara as the land is being raised. Middle right: The sign that appeared in Ohara, showing the plan for the sea wall. Bottom: The Oshika memorial.

BEHIND THE STORY

I had four "companions" at various points during my many visits to Oshika since 2011. I don't mean people who joined me for the odd day, but people who spent at least a week alongside me there, living, eating, sleeping, and working just like I do. None of them spoke any Japanese, and only one had any experience of Japanese culture, and that experience was very limited. They were all entirely dependent on me during their visits.

I came to the conclusion that there is something about being on Oshika that strips away anything you might be on the outside, and reveals who you truly are on the inside. You can't rely on the distractions of modern life — television, Facebook, instant messaging, online shopping — you spend a lot of time in your own head, especially when you are surrounded by conversations of which you cannot understand a single word. Instead, you are forced to be at one and at peace with yourself, to change your focus to listening and watching instead of talking, to try to understand through looking at people's expressions and *feeling* people's emotions, rather than by processing words. Being comfortable with not being directly involved in anything that's taking place or being planned, but happy to watch and learn something, maybe about others, but also about yourself.

I know I have learned so much about myself through my visits to Oshika, and continue to do so. And I also learned so much about my four companions, and saw each of them in a new light, which gave me either a new respect for them, or made me lose any I once had.

I've written about Sophie, the Englishwoman who asked whether she could volunteer with me, and given my observations of a lot of people who had come to volunteer before her, I was reluctant to say yes, but agreed that she could come for a few days to see how she worked out. She ended up staying for weeks and epitomized everything that, to me, anyway, volunteering is about.

Then there was my niece Emily, having never so much as taken a bus outside Plymouth on her own, who travelled alone across the world to help out in this remote little peninsula and spend some time with her auntie. She was entirely out of her comfort zone, but took everything in her stride and I was so proud to have her there.

And my most recent companion surprised me by fitting in so well that it left me wondering whether there wasn't a bit of the Japanese spirit in him somewhere. His shy, quiet, reserved nature suited Oshika, but he was happy to give anything a try when asked, even if it meant being out of his comfort zone. I noticed little things, like he organized the shoes in the genkan to make it easier for people to put them on upon leaving; something that to me, was actually a big thing. He was very aware of not doing anything that might be culturally inappropriate, and was happy to follow my lead. Whereas the Japanese part of me has come from years of calling Japan home and taking on board so many of its customs, he seemed to be a natural.

I think it takes a very secure person to be comfortable on Oshika. It takes a sensitive soul, who genuinely looks to put the needs of others above their own. It takes someone who is always on the lookout for ways to make another person or other people more comfortable. It takes someone who understands the value of community spirit, and appreciates being a part of that community, if only for a short time.

Someone who understands that the kindness offered to them is not because *they* are special, but because their hosts are.

Those three companions, in bringing the right attitude to Oshika, enriched my experience there, not just in the form of the extra pair of hands they brought to various jobs, but in seeing their respect for such a very special place. During the time they shared with me there, they made my work so much easier to carry out. As did the emotional support I got from people all over the world who followed my Oshika activities through my blog and

Facebook page every time I visited. It wasn't always easy for me to be there. Far from it.

I've tried to focus this book on the challenges that the people of Oshika have faced since the disaster, and the inspiring way they have overcome them. When it comes to "my life" on Oshika, it was my aim to not dwell on any challenges that I might have faced there. It might easily be assumed that what posed the biggest difficulties to my activities on Oshika were things like my initial lack of Japanese language skills, sleepless nights tormented by an overactive imagination fuelled by the sound of unknown creatures right by my window, or working out how to process some of my own emotions while I often felt I was somehow absorbing other's emotions.

But my biggest challenges involved none of those obvious things. My biggest challenge was how some people — *non-local* people I must be clear to state — seemed to go out of their way to try to make it "difficult" for me to pursue my efforts on Oshika.

My fourth companion's behaviour on Oshika left me ashamed and embarrassed — regularly drinking to excess and greedily eating everything that was put in front of him, and behaving in the kind of self-entitled manner that I loathe, wherever I am. I had thought I knew him when I invited him to Oshika, but soon after his arrival, I realized that I never knew him at all. Not only that, but *he* didn't even know who he was. It was a challenging but enlightening experience and I was grateful to Oshika for showing me someone's true nature and inability to be sensitive toward others.

Even some members of my own family are not as sensitive and supportive as I could hope, preferring instead to drag me into whatever drama might be going on in their own lives. The very day before I was due to drive up to Oshika with all the emergency supplies I received a phone call telling me I had to get to the UK immediately to deal with a crisis — it wasn't a life or death situation but it was enough to worry me, and I remember wondering why that call couldn't have waited just three more days until my supply mission was completed. And I will never forget that when I *did* return to the UK after such a deeply moving first trip to Oshika, I was angrily told, "I don't give a shit about the Japanese." There are members of my family who have always celebrated my achievements and efforts in life, and there are some who have always resented them. It's sad, but the latter's efforts have always had more of an impact on me, and overcoming their hurtful words and actions has always been one of my life's biggest challenges, unfortunately.

If not everyone in my own family could support my activities on Oshika, then I shouldn't have been surprised that there would be total strangers that wouldn't support me either. The online criticism I received, especially in the early days, was deeply upsetting. People criticized the list of emergency supplies I was collecting, and later the things I'd accept for the free shop, and this really upset me — these were people who had never been to Tohoku and had no idea what life was like on Oshika. And I was *horrified* when I was accused online of keeping the money I was raising — nothing could have been further from the truth. I wasn't worried about what the people who had donated to my projects would think because I was in regular contact with all of them, but it upset me terribly to think that potential sponsors would be put off supporting my projects because of misinformation. I couldn't bear the thought of the Oshika people missing out just because of somebody's malicious lies.

I struggled to reconcile the nastiness I saw in the online world with the kindness I saw around me in the real world on Oshika, where people thought very, very carefully and always considered the feelings of others before they spoke.

One of the reasons I turned down all interview requests from Japan-based English-language media was because their online communities have such a reputation for being vicious. So when I reluctantly agreed to an interview about the bus shelter, I wasn't surprised when the online comments in response to the article were full of hatred and ugliness — some people will probably have a field day with this book!

I found it so difficult to see my Oshika friends struggle with the media themselves — on a number of occasions I saw media descend upon Oshika and bombard the locals with one question after another, showing no sensitivity whatsoever, taking intrusive photographs without understanding the context, and then just disappearing. I even saw people who I had thought were trying to help, suddenly turn that help into a publicity opportunity for *themselves*, not for Oshika.

And while the *local* people on Oshika welcomed me into their lives with open arms, it became apparent to me that some of the non-locals on Oshika did not like me being there at all. In some ways, I could understand why — I would descend on the peninsula, very quickly ascertain what needed doing, and find a way to do it, usually within a month. There were non-local people on Oshika who were being paid by the local government to do *exactly* that, but they weren't doing it. A non-local who moved there after 311 and was employed by the local government once said to me, "Everybody here loves you," but it was said with resentment, not kindness or encouragement. And that hurt. I would have loved to have worked with people who had access to local government funding.

I chose to not include these underlying stories in the main part of my book because they're really stories about me and my struggles, rather than stories about Oshika and its people. This may be my memoir, but it's *their* story. I also chose, for the same reason, to not include much about my personal life.

But I know that people are interested in such things, and there's always a story behind the story! In my case, Oshika was sometimes a respite from the dramatic events going on in my personal life during the past decade!

At the time the disaster took place, I was married and had a home with my then-husband in Tokyo. Ten years later, I am living with my boyfriend of three years in Cirencester. And there was another marriage in between — one from which I ran, terrified, in the middle of the night. And *that* is a whole other story.

Another book, perhaps?

The author on Oshika, Valentine's Day, 2012 © Caroline Pover

Caroline Pover was born in Devon in 1971, grew up in Plymouth, and graduated from Exeter University before moving to Tokyo in 1996, in search of adventure. She lived in Japan full-time for almost fifteen years, running a number of businesses, giving speeches, and winning numerous awards for her entrepreneurial and philanthropic endeavours.

Caroline unexpectedly ended up in the UK in the weeks after the 2011 earthquake and tsunami. She spent the following years going back and forth between Japan and England, fundraising and also managing recovery projects for the remote fishing communities on Oshika — a peninsula that was very badly affected by the tsunami. To date, she has raised almost £170,000, which has funded over thirty different projects to help these communities rebuild.

Caroline now lives in the Cotswolds, where she established Auntie Caroline's — a pickled onion and chutney business. She goes "home" to Japan every year.

This is her fifth book, and first memoir — she considers it her "love letter to Oshika."

If this story of the lives of Caroline's friends on Oshika touched your heart, please encourage others to read about the brave survivors of the tsunami by
- writing a book review on Amazon,
- recommending this book on your social media pages,
- visiting the book's Facebook page and leaving a review or comment (https://www.facebook.com/onemonthintohoku),
- asking your local media representative to review the book.

You are welcome to contact the author directly for the following purposes by emailing caroline@carolinepover.com:
- If you are a teacher who would like to include *One Month in Tohoku* in your school's curriculum.
- If you are interested in sponsoring a future project on Oshika.
- If you would like to purchase multiple copies of the paperback edition of this book for your book club.

And readers are, of course, encouraged to visit Oshika as tourists so that they can experience the beauty of the peninsula and the people for themselves, and give support to a community in its journey toward recovery.

of Navarre. — The Court of Catherine de' Medici. — The Pope Refuses the Dispensation for the Marriage. — Catherine's Proposals to Queen Elizabeth. — Warlike Preparations: Coligny's Plans. — The Court Leaves Blois for Paris. — Death of Jeanne d'Albret. — Poison Suspected 314

CHAPTER XX.

Marriage of Marguerite and Henri Deferred. — Catherine Seeks to Thwart Coligny's Plans. — Charles Flies from His Counsellors. — Catherine Opposed to War with Spain. — Elizabeth Again Pressed to Marry D'Alençon. — Arrival in Paris of Henri of Navarre. — The Betrothal. — The Dispensation Dispensed with. — "Les Noces Vermeilles." — Marguerite Declares She Never Accepted Henri. — The Admiral's Fatal Confidence in Charles IX. — Saturnalia 331

CHAPTER XXI.

Anjou a Candidate for the Crown of Poland. — The Kiss of Peace Twice Given. — Attack on the Admiral Instigated by the Guises. — The King in a Rage when Informed of It. — Charles Visits the Admiral, but Cannot Free Himself from His Mother's and Brother's Company. — The Admiral's Private Advice to Charles. — The Massacre Arranged. — A Band of Demons. — Charles Long Withstands His Infamous Mother's Arguments. — "*Par la Mort Dieu!* Give Your Orders. Let Them Die! Let None Remain to Reproach Me." . 344

CHAPTER XXII.

Arranging for the Success of the Massacre. — The Provost of Paris, Le Charron. — Catherine Regardless Even of Her Daughter's Safety. — To the Guises the Honour of Beginning the Massacre. — Alert Before Dawn. — Guilty Consciences. — The Admiral's Death Countermanded: Too Late. — Already Slain. — His Head Sent to Catherine. — Charles Like a Madman: "Kill! Kill!" — Catherine and Her "*Filles d'Honneur.*" — Rejoicings in Rome and Madrid. — Bells, Bonfires, Te Deums, and Cannon. — Medals, Pictures, and Compliments . . 357

LIST OF ILLUSTRATIONS

VOL. I.

	PAGE
MARY STUART.	*Frontispiece*
FRANÇOIS II.	10
CATHERINE DE' MEDICI	88
CHARLES IX.	124
AMBOISE PARÉ	208
GASPARD DE COLIGNY, ADMIRAL OF FRANCE	252
MARGUERITE DE VALOIS	302
HENRI, DUC DE GUISE	362

THE
LAST OF THE VALOIS

CHAPTER I.

INTRODUCTORY.

THE death of Henri II. of France — suddenly struck down in the full force of manhood, and in the midst of the brilliant festivities following the Peace of Câteau-Cambrésis and the royal betrothals and marriages, pledges of its "perpetual endurance" — was regarded by Protestants as a signal mark of Heaven's displeasure on the persecuting king. But, while the infamous compact he had entered into with the cruel and fanatical Philip II. of Spain was especially deprecated by the Reformers, Frenchmen generally, whether Catholics or Protestants, who were animated by a spark of patriotism, bowed their heads with shame and deplored the political incapacity of the sovereign who had assented to a treaty so humiliating to France, both as regarded her interests and her honour.

For at the instance of a grasping and unscrupulous favourite (the Connétable Anne de Montmorency) Henri had ceded to the Spaniard — whose military resources were at the time far inferior to his own, and his financial difficulties even more pressing — all the Italian conquests of the three preceding reigns. The Italian wars, now ended by the renunciation of all the claims of France on Italy, had continued for upwards of sixty years, causing immense expenditure to the state, and a prodigal waste of human life. But this cessation of foreign warfare was not to ensure the future tranquillity or prosperity of France. War more bitter, more bloody, more savage, was to succeed it, and lay waste and depopulate the country for the next thirty-six years — war whose object was not the conquest of territory, but the extermination of heresy.

For Philip and Henri had bound themselves to aid each other, by rigid and persistent persecution, in suppressing the efforts then making in France and elsewhere to secure liberty of conscience and freedom of religious worship.

An entire change soon ensued in the social relations of the French. Instead of going forth to fight their foes, Frenchmen now took up arms to fight among themselves, religious fanaticism as a demon suddenly seeming to possess them. The torch of discord blazed forth; the burning pile was ignited; brothers, parents, children, friends, and citizens armed against each other. The wildest and most inordinate passions inflamed and perverted men's minds. The kingdom was given up a prey to various factions, to spies, assassins, executioners, and religious strife and civil war with their attendant horrors stalked through the land.

Thus did the brilliant sixteenth century, the era of the Renaissance, so resplendent at its dawn, become for the greater part of its latter half occupied with the combat of the spirit of progress against the spirit of death — that "Demon of the South who would have stifled the independent nationalities under a counterfeit Roman Empire, and suppressed the growth of human intelligence under a counterfeit Gregory VII." (H. Martin.)

During the time that Henri lingered, hovering between life and death, the several parties in the state were actively intriguing, each to secure its succession to, or continuance in, power. The monarch's death occurred on the eleventh day, 10th July, 1559, after receiving the fatal wound at the tournament. It was the signal for the commencement of those intestine troubles and series of calamities which so long afflicted France under the last of the weak and dissolute Valois kings. Urged to crime by their iniquitous mother, Catherine de' Medici, preyed upon by a host of unworthy favourites — to support whose reckless extravagance the people were oppressed and brought to the very verge of desperation and poverty by heavy and unjust taxation — each of Catherine's unhappy sons pursued his short career of vice and bloodshed while revelling in the profligate pleasures of the depraved court over which she, as queen-mother, presided.

CHAPTER II.

Accession of François II. — The King's "Uncles." — Catherine and Diane. — The Keys of the King's Cabinet and the Crown Jewels. — Exchange of Chaumont for Chenonceaux. — François II. and Queen Mary. — The "New Opinions." — Antoine, King of Navarre, and Louis de Condé. — Antoine's Journey to Paris. — The Flying Squadron. — Antoine Threatens to Head the "Malcontents."

THE unexpected event that placed François II. — a sickly youth in his sixteenth year — on the throne of France, also raised the Duc de Guise and his brother, the Cardinal de Lorraine, to that prominent and important position in the state which by their intrigues they had already prepared for themselves in bringing about the marriage of the dauphin with their niece, Mary Stuart. This marriage, considered at the time the most favourable event that could happen for furthering the views of France on Scotland and England, and for the interests of the dauphin, became in a great measure the source of most of the troubles that followed the death of Henri, by giving a free course to the ambition of the Guises of Lorraine. That their ambitious views would be so speedily realised was, of course, far from being then foreseen. But Fortune was said to be always on the side of the Guises, playing into their hands by a timely clearing away of the obstacles that stood between them and the wealth and lucrative honours they so eagerly coveted, no matter what means must be employed to obtain them.*

Since the release from captivity and return to court of Henri's bosom friend and "good gossip," the Connétable Montmorency, the influence of the Guises had greatly waned. Consequently, they had held much aloof latterly from affairs of state, retiring to their estates in Lorraine to conceal their dissatisfaction, as well as to watch and wait for an opportunity of thwarting the views and schemes — no less rapacious than their own — of their formidable rival. To supplant him in the confidence and affections of his royal master it would have been vain to attempt. For so entirely was the weak monarch guided and governed by the constable, whose aim was to abase the Guises, as it was theirs to bring discredit on him, that Henri's opinions and decisions on all matters relating to the government of the kingdom were

---

* The Guises were six brothers, of whom the two eldest, François de Lorraine, Duc de Guise, and Charles de Lorraine, Cardinal and Archbishop of Rheims, played the most conspicuous part in the government of the kingdom. The other brothers were Claude de Lorraine, Duc d'Aumale, Louis de Lorraine, Cardinal de Guise, René de Lorraine, Marquis d'Elbeuf, and François, Grand Prieur de France, the recognised bastard of the House of Guise.

but the reflex of those of his arrogant and self-seeking favourite.

But the Guises, the Bourbons, and Montmorencys were not the only aspirants for power who in that intriguing court hastened to turn to account this critical moment of general confusion and alarm. The long pent-up hatred of Catherine de' Medici towards the Duchesse de Valentinois — Diane of Poitiers — was now, she believed, to be fully gratified. The vengeance of the slighted wife should be wreaked on the hitherto powerful and haughty favourite, to whom for many years she had been compelled submissively to yield the honours due to herself as queen. Apparently she had borne this humiliation with much meekness, though her assumed air of subjection deceived but few — perhaps not even Diane herself. The time, however, had arrived for casting aside the mask that so long had partly concealed the true feeling and character of this worthy daughter of the Medici.

No sooner did the heavily long-drawn sigh in which Henri II. breathed his last tell to those around him that the spirit had departed, than the anxious, weeping wife, watching beside him for the supreme moment that was to give her power and freedom of action, rose from her kneeling posture. Already a change had come over her. Her usually subdued manners and forced gentleness of expression — little in harmony with her true feeling, as her large, dark, restless, flashing eyes often betrayed — had wholly vanished. She now stood proud and defiant, and, as some thought, seemed to have gained in stature, as, with a queenlike air she had hitherto never dared to assume, she summoned an attendant and despatched an authoritative command to the Duchesse de Valentinois.

Diane had remained in her apartment at the Palais des Tournelles in the hope that her royal lover, who had received what proved his death-blow while wearing her colours and displaying his prowess in her presence, might yet rally, so robust was his constitution. This was not, however, the general expectation. An order to leave the palace and retire to her estates had been sent to her some few days after the tournament. But on ascertaining that it came from Catherine, and that the king still lived, and had partly recovered consciousness, she replied that "she obeyed no orders but those of her sovereign." From hour to hour those in her confidence kept her informed of Henri's condition. On the eleventh morning, on being told that Henri was rapidly sinking, and could not survive through the day, the duchess, already prepared for a sudden departure, at once left Les Tournelles and retired to her magnificent Château of Anet. Thus she avoided the mortification of being expelled from the palace by the "banker's daughter" whom she had so long patronised, compelled her husband to tolerate, and to refrain from sending back to her Florentine relatives, as both Henri and François I. had at times threatened they would do during the first ten years of her marriage.

In compliance with Catherine's demand for the restitution of the crown jewels and the keys of the king's cabinet, Diane forwarded from Anet the magnificent rings she for years had been accustomed to wear; also, with the keys of the cabinet, some pearls, diamonds, and other jewels which, although the property of the crown, were not reserved for the adornment of the queens of France, but from the time of François I. had passed, together with the monarch's favour, from mistress to mistress. They were now deposited with Catherine, who, however, was not to have the satisfaction of appearing in them at court. For the young king, acting on the suggestion of his "uncles" — the Guises had arrogated to themselves that title — ordered their delivery to the brilliant young Queen Mary.

François II., although legally of age, was of course from youth and inexperience wholly incapable of taking any important part in the government of the kingdom. He was, however, so greatly elated at becoming King of France, that his joy entirely overcame any natural grief or regret he might have been supposed to feel or express at the death of his father, or the accident that produced it. His delight was indeed so excessive that the historian Mathieu says "it had the singular effect of curing him of a fever he was suffering from when Henri died." The new king's weakly constitution, and, as most contemporary writers assert, deficiency of intelligence, together with the ascendency acquired over him by the wiles of his lively, pleasure-loving, youthful wife, placed him wholly in the power of the Guises, by whom Mary herself was guided and governed. By flattery they gained his confidence, and, having conducted him and his queen from the Palais des Tournelles to the Louvre on the announcement of Henri's death, they there in full council induced him to announce that "he desired to be assisted in governing his kingdom by the experience and counsels of his 'uncles.'" He had therefore committed the command of his armies to the Duc de Guise, and the charge of the finances to the Cardinal de Lorraine, Archbishop of Rheims.

The queen-mother soon perceived that she could not reckon on the obedience of a son so completely under the spell of his wife's fascinations. That wife was her own apt pupil. But Catherine detested her, for it was painfully evident to her that as she had bowed to the yoke of the elderly *maîtresse-en-titre*, she must again dissemble for awhile, and submit to that of a wife of seventeen.

François II.
Photo-etching from painting by Rauch.

On the former she had hoped for the satisfaction of being revenged, but here the Guises once more thwarted her. Originally they had mainly owed their elevation to the Duchesse de Valentinois, but now they were independent of her favour, needing not her good offices, and, but that these six brothers furthered each other's interests in every way, would have cared little how deeply she was humiliated. One of their number, the Duc d'Aumale, had, however, married the duchess's second daughter; consequently, he was one of her heirs. They were unwilling, therefore, that estates, which eventually, in part, if not wholly, would come into their family, should be lost to them by confiscation. A prudent attempt at conciliation had also been made by Diane's offer to Catherine of her château and domain of Chenonceaux-sur-Cher, which she had long desired to possess, and had compelled Diane to pay for, having, in her indignation at Henri's disregard of her wishes, instigated a former owner of the estate to contest her free right to it as a royal gift. Diane had greatly embellished the château and grounds, and Catherine gladly consented to accept her offer, but not exactly as a gift. She gave her in exchange for it the Château of Chaumont-sur-Loire, the advantage of the exchange being greatly on Catherine's side.

It is scarcely probable that her revengeful feelings were fully appeased by the possession of

Chenonceaux, as she was supposed to have determined on not only the humiliation, but the death of her rival. But the frustration of her hopes of governing the young king, and, as a matter of course, his kingdom, deprived her of the power of carrying out designs to which the Guises, in their own interests, gave no countenance. The Duchesse de Valentinois was therefore so leniently dealt with. She made her splendid abode of Anet her habitual residence, and retained her other estates and the immense wealth she possessed wholly unmolested. Occasionally she visited Chaumont, after its legal cession to her in December, 1559. There, architects and other artists were employed in transforming that feudal fortress into a more modern, elegant, and suitable residence for the lady of Anet.

Meanwhile political intrigue for the purpose of undermining the power of the Guises, and transferring it to herself, occupied the time and thoughts of Catherine de' Medici. The duke and the cardinal shared between them the effective power of the kingdom; but to conciliate Catherine they left her the apparent general superintendence of the government. She had, in fact, seized on that almost at the very moment of Henri's death.

The Venetian ambassador, Giovanni Michiel, says: "She had been thought timid because during the king's lifetime she had not dared to meddle in any matter of importance. But no sooner was the breath out of his body than the courage and audacity of her character were fully displayed. Disregarding the custom of the French Court, requiring a widowed Queen of France to seclude herself for forty days, she gave no time to such useless grief, but dined in public on the morrow of her husband's death, and gave audience to all who sought it. She sent to the chancellor for the great seal used by the sovereign, and began to take a hand in the direction of affairs, less like a woman than a man full of courage and well versed in the government of a state. She has not allowed," he continues, "her designs to be easily penetrated, for, like Leo X. and all his race, she is a proficient in the art of dissimulation."

Catherine, however, accompanied the king and queen, the Guises, and the Dukes of Ferrara, Savoy, and Nemours, who attended them, to the Louvre. When about to enter the carriage, as usual, before her daughter-in-law, she suddenly seemed to bethink her that she had descended a step in rank. Drawing hastily back, and turning with a dignified air towards the young queen, she said: "Madame, it is now your turn to take precedence of me." *

Besides his high office of Constable of France, Anne de Montmorency held that of grand-master of the household. This enjoined on him the duty

* Mathieu, "*Histoire de France.*"

of remaining with the body of the late king until removed from the palace for burial. Excessive grief at the untimely end of the sovereign, who alone of the court showed him either friendship or affection, also prevented him from following François and his "uncles," the queen and queen-mother to the Louvre. But ere the preparations for the royal obsequies — "surpassing in solemn splendour any that France had hitherto witnessed" — were quite ended, the constable, accompanied by his sons and nephews, snatched a moment from his duties to repair to the palace to pay his respects to the new king, and to see and advise the queen-mother.

But the Guises had taken advantage of his forced absence from the council to confirm their own power. If they stood not high in the favour of the court because of their avarice, and still more because of their success in gratifying it, they were at least not abhorred, as was the constable, for brutally insulting manners. On the contrary, they were excceedingly courteous, and were regarded by the younger nobility as models of courtly dignity and high breeding. Their reputation, too, especially that of the duke, was great among the people. Had he not saved Metz and retaken Calais, and shed fresh lustre on his arms by his humanity to the suffering soldiers of the defeated armies? Both brothers had also raised their voices in condemnation of Montmorency's ready concession to all the demands of Philip II., when the treaty of Câteau-Cambrésis was signed. Further, zealous Catholics looked to them, as the declared irreconcilable enemies of the "new opinions," to put down and effectually stamp out the "devilish heresy" now troubling the Church, also the righteous spirit of the violent and persecuting pontiff, Paul IV., as well as threatening disaster to the kingdom.

Such indeed was their credit that Catherine— in conversation with Montmorency, while the young king was learning from "his uncles" how he should receive the constable, and what he should say to him — declared that she thought it more dangerous to irritate than to raise them to power, and that it was on the whole safer to employ them in the great offices of state than to dismiss them from the court. But the constable, who had hitherto treated Catherine with much superciliousness, was now willing, in order to regain that influential position in the government which had been so audaciously, as he considered, snatched from him, to ally himself with her and the Bourbon princes for the overthrow of the Guises. He advised her, therefore, not to allow France at the beginning of the new reign to have reason to doubt of its happy and peaceful continuance. "The ardent love," he said, "which the French bore to their princes made them their willingly obedient subjects; but, on the other hand, the domination of foreigners—as were the Guises of Lorraine—was an odious and insupportable yoke to the nation. He urged her, then, to lose no time in summoning the King of Navarre—first prince of the blood—and his brothers to court; their absence being much to be regretted.

Hitherto the constable had paid assiduous court to Diane, and entered into family connections with her by marrying one of his sons to her granddaughter. Diane's day, however, was ended, and Montmorency, like the Guises, had turned his back on her. But the "Florentine banker's daughter," as he as well as Diane had sometimes called her, abhorred both her husband's favourites. She did not forget that the constable had suggested doubts of her fidelity by remarking to the king "how strange it was that none of his children at all resembled him except his natural daughter, Diane."

Yet she dissembled as usual, and, while affecting to believe, as he assured her, that her own interests were identical with those of Antoine of Navarre, resolved to accept with good grace that share in the government of the kingdom which the Guises were willing to allow her, trusting to the future, and no distant one probably, for the fuller realisation of her ambitious aims.

But the constable is summoned to the royal presence, and Catherine, as he takes leave of her, with a deferential and respectful air he had never shown her before, assures him, with a dignity and graciousness that are no less new to him, of the value she sets on his counsels, and of her sincere good-will towards him. Yet he was no more the dupe of her fair words and specious manners than she of the professed disinterestedness of his advice. They knew each other too well. He had indeed counselled the queen-mother, when Henri's recovery seemed doubtful, to send for the princes of the blood to act as a check on the Guises. But feeling assured that her longing for power would deter her from following his advice, he had taken the precaution, some days before the king's death, of secretly despatching a messenger to King Antoine urging him to set out for Paris without delay.

The young king, François II., was not yet an adept in the art of dissimulation. He received the constable very coldly, though his words were meant by the Guises to be graciously spoken while implying dismissal from court. He assured him of his great respect for his father's much-esteemed minister and friend, of his determination to continue to him the pensions and privileges granted by the late king. And, while informing him that he had conferred on his "uncles"—a startling acknowledgment of relationship to Montmorency's ears—the direction of the affairs of his kingdom, "he would still," he said, "should occasion arise, gladly listen to his opinions and advice." This was more than the constable, whose equanimity was not great, could bear from a boy whom he regarded with some contempt as a tool in the hands of the Guises. In his haughtiest manner, he replied that "he should esteem it no honour whatever to follow those whom hitherto he had preceded."

To this François was not provided with a reply, and none appears to have suggested itself to him. He remained confused and silent, and took no notice of the younger Montmorencys and Châtillons, who accompanied the constable. The latter, however, announced his retirement to Chantilly, and immediately withdrew with his sons and nephews — the whole party much displeased by the affront which they considered had been offered to the head of their family. On the other hand, the duke and the cardinal were well pleased to be relieved so easily and speedily, by his own self-banishment, of the constable's inconvenient presence in the council and at court.

For awhile he devoted himself to superintending the embellishments then in progress, and which had long employed numerous artists, at his splendid palaces of Chantilly and Écouen. At the latter, Bernard Palissy was occupied in decorating the façade with slabs and figures of enamelled earthenware, after the manner of the Château de Madrid, executed by Girolamo della

Robbia for François I. But fiery indignation and thirst for revenge did but smoulder in the breast of the imperious old soldier. Fuel, too, was added to the fire when Catherine united with the Guises in requiring Montmorency to resign his office of grand-master, as incompatible with that of Constable of France. He, however, obeyed. The survivorship had been promised to the constable's eldest son, but the king conferred the post on "his uncle," the Duc de Guise, and a marshal's baton was offered to François de Montmorency. The constable's nephew, Admiral de Coligny, was also required to resign his post as Governor of Picardy, as the Guises believed they could not count on his support. On complying with the demand, he requested that the Prince de Condé, who had married his niece, might be appointed to succeed him. But this did not answer their purpose. They were then strengthening their position by appointing as governors of provinces and commandants of strong towns those men only whom they regarded as their devoted partisans.

So nefarious were the means by which the Guise family had become enriched, and heaped up estate upon estate, that they feared to draw public attention on themselves by recommending the king to confiscate (as they were anxious to do) a large part of the constable's equally ill-gotten domains. They were, therefore, content for a time that a demand should be made for the restitution of Henri's gift of the Château of Compiègne, it being a royal fief (such was their pretext) that could not be alienated from the crown. Montmorency had been accustomed to domineer in the council of the late king with as high a hand as that with which the Guises now ruled his youthful successor and reigned over France in his name. But his haughty spirit, that ill could brook the slightest opposition, was doomed to be yet further tried by his unsuccessful attempt to ally himself, in opposing the Guises, either with Catherine de' Medici or the King of Navarre.*

Antoine was sojourning at Nérac when the constable's missive reached him. Both he and Queen Jeanne were, with much reason, greatly dissatisfied with the constable's utter neglect of their interests when peace was concluded at Câteau-Cambrésis. Upper Navarre had been wrested from the Albret family in the time of Charles V., and some arrangement had been looked for at the general peace, in recognition of the claims of Jeanne of Navarre, and for the restoration of her heritage. But Philip II. had remitted the two millions at first demanded for the constable's ransom, and he who scrupled not to sacrifice the interests of

---

* Antoine derived his title of king from his marriage with Jeanne d'Albret, Queen of Navarre. He was known previously as Antoine de Bourbon, Duc de Vendôme, and was one of the three nephews of the famous constable, Charles de Bourbon.

France in order to show his gratitude to the Spanish king, was not likely to make those of the little kingdom of Navarre an obstacle to his views.

But the husband of Jeanne d'Albret, though reputed brave in the field, was wanting in energy of character. Naturally indolent, too, and very vague in his projects, loving his ease, and caring little for any court but his own, resentment also inclined him to see in the pressing but somewhat ambiguous missive addressed to him nothing more than that his presence in Paris would in some way be advantageous to Montmorency in furthering his own interests or designs. It was, however, the duty of the princes of the blood to attend the sovereign's funeral, and to take their places in the council chamber of his youthful successor. Antoine and his brother, Prince Louis de Condé, therefore set out for Paris, the former travelling by such very easy stages that Prince Louis soon determined to pursue his journey alone.

The brothers, both in person and temperament, were the very reverse of each other. Louis was small in stature, and generally of less prepossessing appearance than Antoine, who was an exceedingly handsome man, of a commanding presence, and not a little vain of his personal advantages. But the qualities in which he was deficient were possessed by Prince Louis, who was brave, bold, and ambitious, full of energy, and fired by a restless desire for the reinstatement of his family in that high position of wealth and influence they had lost by the unfortunate revolt of Duc Charles de Bourbon, and the confiscations which followed it. Had the Prince de Condé been the elder brother, it was generally felt that the Guises would have found in him the formidable opponent which Antoine should have been, but failed to prove himself.

The roads (or, rather, no roads) of that period were not favourable for rapid travelling, but an advance of two or three leagues each day satisfied the king. At night he and his suite took up their quarters in the châteaux of the nobility that lay on their line of route. Though one of the acknowledged, if not the most ardent, of the Calvinist chiefs, the King of Navarre was well received on his journey by "moderate Catholics" as well as Protestants, and promises to support him in an effort to curb the power of the Guises were freely given. For many of the Catholic nobility began to be alarmed at the assumption of sovereign power by the Duc de Guise, while the persecuting spirit evinced by both duke and cardinal dismayed all but the most rigid and fanatical of their party.

Unduly elated by the sort of popularity that attended him on his journey, the King of Navarre entered Paris with the two or three hundred gentlemen of his retinue, expecting to create a great sensation, and proposing to do great things. But the course to be pursued for the accomplishment of these vague projects he left to the chapter of accidents to determine.

The court, at this time, was at Saint-Germain. Two gentlemen of King Antoine's suite, therefore, rode out to announce his approaching arrival. According to the etiquette of the French Court, a guard of honour, headed by an officer of the highest rank (the Duc de Guise on this occasion), should have been immediately sent forward to welcome the royal visitor and conduct him to the palace. But the Guises were resolved to retain the power they had grasped, and to share it neither with a Bourbon nor a Montmorency. No escort, then, was sent to the King of Navarre. He was merely informed that King François, the Duc de Guise, and the Cardinal de Lorraine awaited his arrival at Saint-Germain to welcome and embrace him.

But when the crestfallen prince arrived, doubts were expressed whether he could be accommodated in the royal residence; yet the principal apartment (after the sovereign's) should have been prepared for him. It was, however, occupied by the haughty duke, who cared not to cede it to him; though King Antoine probably would have offered — it being a mark of great honour and favour at that period — to share his couch with him. However, to spare him the mortification of returning to Paris to find a bed at Les Tournelles, or at the Louvre, an officer of the household gave up his sleeping quarters to him.

The boy king, François, had been taught by his "uncles," whom he regarded as nothing less than oracles, "to beware of the Bourbons" — "crafty princes," they told him, "encouragers of heresy, seeking to change the religion of the state, and watching, waiting, intriguing for a possible opportunity of seizing his 'sacred person' and laying hands on the Crown of France." The poor youth, in consequence, looked with strong suspicion on Antoine's frank and friendly manner of addressing him — assumed, it was hinted to him, as a mask to conceal the conspirator.

It was, however, rather to conceal his own mortification at the evidently studied coldness of the young king, and the absence of due respect and consideration with which he was received by the Guises and their partisans. But notwithstanding all that was done to exasperate him, he had not the courage openly to resent it, as the poorest in spirit might be supposed to have done.

The queen-mother was playing the double part so natural to her. Affecting to be ignorant of the affronts offered by the Guises to King Antoine, she received him cordially, whilst he (Catherine was quite aware of the weakest points in his generally weak character) forgot his wrongs in the society of that seductive youthful circle of facile court beauties whom, in imitation of Louise of Savoy, Catherine already was beginning to gather around her. So Antoine accompanied the court to Rheims, where François II. was crowned on the 18th September, and where, as at the funeral of the late king, the Duc de Guise arrogated to himself precedence in the order of the procession of three princes of the blood.

Great was the indignation of the old nobility at the insult offered to their natural chiefs — "*les sires du sang*" — by those "presumptuous Lorrainers." What did those acts of despotism mean by which they seemed to tread contemptuously underfoot all the ancient families of France? Was their aim usurpation, founded on the feeble state of the young king's health and the tender years of his brothers? On all sides enemies were multiplying around them, and already they were beginning to encounter the inconveniences as well as to enjoy the advantages of that uncontrolled possession of power they had so eagerly pursued. There was an urgent demand from all classes for the assembling of the States General, for the "free discussion of public grievances and the want of order in conducting the affairs of the kingdom; as well as to devise such remedies for them as should calm the present agitation of the public mind."

But this did not suit the plans and purposes of the Guises. They told the king that "such a demand from his subjects was nothing less than high treason. Were it granted, they would proceed to dictate laws to him from whom they should receive them, leaving him the mere title of king, they usurping the power." The poor languid, suffering youth, whom some historians describe as naturally of a gentle disposition, was greatly alarmed by his "uncles'" report of his subjects' rebellious projects. Their bad feeling towards him perplexed him. He knew not what he had done to excite it, or, indeed, what his people demanded of him.

"What could he do for their benefit more than he had already done?" At the instance of the duke and that holy prelate, his "uncle of Lorraine," he had solemnly announced his unalterable determination of rigorously carrying out his father's compact with Philip II. for the utter extermination of heresy. This, he was told, was his duty as Most Christian King; alike towards the Church, the sovereign pontiff, his father's memory, his promise to his brother-in-law of Spain, the welfare of his subjects, and the prosperity of his kingdom. Immediately following this announcement many persons, obnoxious to the Guises, were arrested on suspicion of heresy and imprisoned. Others were tortured, and burnt or hanged on the Place de Grève.

The Prince de Condé endeavoured to rouse his brother to take up arms — many besides the Protestants, to whom the oppressive rule of the Guises was hateful, being willing to join him — and to assert his right to the foremost place in the government. But Antoine was not to be moved by the arguments of his more fearless brother to any bolder demonstration than a threat to head the malcontents. Empty as were the threats of the King of Navarre, the Guises determined that both he and the princes of his house should quit the kingdom. The queen-mother — acting in concert with the duke and cardinal, though at the time affecting to favour the Protestants, and to give them hopes of less rigorous treatment — wrote to Philip II., setting forth that King Antoine, his brother, and other Bourbon princes, were inciting the people to demand the convocation of the States General. "Their aim," she told her son-in-law, " was to reduce her to the position of a chambermaid, and to nullify the authority of the king, her son."*

Philip replied immediately to Catherine's alarming epistle. He is said to have had at the time neither troops nor money to carry out his own secret schemes of thwarting the projects of the Guises in Scotland and England; yet he declared that "he had ready 40,000 men, whom he would willingly send to France to support the authority of his brother-in-law and his minister, should any one have the temerity to dispute it." It was, how-

* Regnier de La Planche, "*La France sous François II.*"

ever, "imperative," he said, "that those abettors of heresy, the Bourbons, should not be allowed to have any share in the government.* The King of Navarre was summoned to the council-chamber, and in his presence the Guises had the satisfaction of reading Philip's letter.

Antoine trembled. He feared that the brave words he had uttered might be responded to by a Spanish invasion of his wife's possessions in the Pyrenees. But when the Guises graciously relieved him from this embarrassment by offering him the honourable mission of conducting Elisabeth of France, the young Queen of Spain, to the frontier of his kingdom, where the Spanish envoys would be in waiting to receive her, Antoine gladly accepted, and withdrew his menace of assuming a hostile position and disputing with them his right to the possession of power.

The Duc de Guise had already honoured Prince Louis de Condé with the title of ambassador, to ratify at Brussels in the name of François II. the Treaty of Câteau-Cambrésis. This annoyed the prince greatly; and a further insult, reminding him of his indigence, was the doling out of a thousand crowns by the minister of finance (the cardinal was careful to allow little of the public money to find its way into any pocket but his own) for the expenses of this important embassy. He would have rejected it, could he have roused

* "*Règne de François II.*"

his brother to energetic action. But in vain for that purpose he delayed his departure. At last, hoping to serve the cause of reform in the country to which he was accredited, Condé set out on his journey with a retinue and equipage in accordance with the modest sum the cardinal financier awarded him. Thus Catherine and the Guises, now — in appearance at least — acting in perfect accord, were freed for a time from the troublesome presence of the Bourbons at the French Court.

CHAPTER III.

Coronation Festivities. — Tearful Adieux. — The Bridal Cortége. — Terrible Weather and Terrible Roads. — Philip's Perils by Sea. — His Grand Auto-da-fé. — Jeanne d'Albret and the Bridal Party. — The Ceremony at Roncevaux. — Grand Reception at Madrid. — A Sudden Friendship.

FOR some weeks past the Court of France had been the scene of continued revelry; the coronation of François II. occasioning these prolonged festivities. But the heroine of the *fêtes* was the youthful and brilliant Queen Mary, around whom the younger courtiers fluttered, and paid homage as to a divinity. The boy-monarch himself, who was suffering from the effects of a tertian ague, was unable to participate in the gaieties of the court further than by his presence.

Even this his physicians, with an ominous shake of the head, were unwilling to grant, and urged him to forego. But to gaze entranced on his queen as, brightly smiling, she mingled with all the fervour of youthful spirits with the throng of dancers, or glided before him, uttering as she passed some lively remark that brought momentary animation to his countenance, acted on him as the spell of an enchantress, briefly reviving his languid frame.

Dancing and mirth are, however, soon to be succeeded by tearful adieux and sorrowful partings. The Princesses Claude and Elisabeth of France, now so sprightly and happy, are indeed too young to be troubled with forebodings as to what the future may have in store for them. But willingly or not, they must bid farewell to these festive scenes, and, at an inclement period of the year, set out on long and dreary journeys to the frontiers of the respective countries, where envoys are waiting to conduct them to new homes, strange in their customs and language, and to husbands whom they have never seen, but to whom, by proxy, they are married. Claude is the bride of the reigning Duc de Lorraine, the head of the sovereign house with whom the Guises claim kindred. Elisabeth is the third wife of the "Demon of the South," Philip II. of Spain.

The Venetian ambassador, Giovanni Cappello, writing to the Senate a few months earlier, says of Catherine de' Medici's young family of four sons and three daughters, they are "all nice children." The eldest, François, he thinks "wanting in vigour both of mind and body." "He has had excellent preceptors," he says, "but shows little inclination for study." They, however, strove to teach him "never to refuse anything asked of him, in order that by constant habit he might acquire that lavish liberality deemed indispensable in royal personages." But he seems to have disappointed his preceptors, and to have adopted a contrary course until "his uncles" taught him better—at least so far as they were concerned.

In the second son, Charles, afterwards Charles IX., the ambassador appears to have taken great interest. He speaks of his "very pleasing countenance," and, as he hears, "he has a generous heart. For one so young," he says, "he shows great talent and fondness for learning, and by and by much may be looked for from this young prince, for he is a child of great promise." The third son, Henri, he mentions as having some defect of speech preventing distinct utterance, and concludes with the remark that all are indeed "too young to exhibit any certain indications of what their real characters may eventually prove to be." * Though, with the exception of the two daughters then leaving France, the unfortunate children of Henri II. developed, under the training of their infamous mother, into monsters steeped in blood and crime; yet at the period in question they seem to have been affectionate towards each other, and to have felt their first separation a heavy sorrow.

But to return to King Antoine: he, with the royal lady committed to his charge, and attended

* " Reports of Venetian Ambassadors."

by an imposing retinue, left the gay Court of
France towards the end of December. Every
arrangement was of course made for the comfort
of the young queen. Her litter and those of the
ladies accompanying her were luxuriously furnished, and when weary of that mode of travelling,
or desiring to contemplate more at ease the beauty
of the country they traversed, or to visit other
attractions on their route, well-trained *haquenées**
were provided, and experienced grooms to attend
them. But from the beginning to the end of
the journey the royal bridal party encountered the
most terrific weather—frightful whirlwinds, intense cold, heavy snow-storms, and torrents of
rain. The state of the roads, too, still further
impeded their progress. At all times hilly and
stony, they were now in some parts blocked with
ice and snow through which paths had to be cut,
and over them the queen and her maids of honour
conducted on foot, while horses and men with
difficulty dragged the litters and the baggage of
the whole party after them. Again, they would
have to wade through slushy roads along which
mountain streams had coursed, and made them
like the bed of a rivulet. But at length they
reached Bordeaux, where the Queen of Navarre
with her son — the future Henri IV., then in
his seventh year — had already arrived to greet
her goddaughter, and to accompany her on her

* Mules.

journey thence to the frontier. But at Bordeaux they rested for awhile, the bad weather continuing.

It seemed as if the Fates had determined to frustrate the intended meeting of the child-bride and her bridegroom. For no less violently than the princess was Philip opposed by the elements on his return by sea from the Netherlands to Spain to celebrate his marriage. The royal galley and nearly the whole of the flotilla convoying it were destroyed in a furious tempest when nearing the Spanish coast. Philip had a narrow escape — one of the small vessels with difficulty managing to aid him and receive him on board, when his own galley, with all the priceless jewels and rare objects of art collected at Brussels by Charles V., and which Philip was transferring to Madrid, was swallowed up by the ocean. His gratitude to God for his rescue from death he displayed on his arrival in his capital by a grand *auto-da-fé*. Nearly a hundred persons, many belonging to the first families in Spain, were then publicly burnt, the Inquisition having found them guilty of favouring the "new opinions," and Philip having made oath before that iniquitous tribunal that "he would not spare even his own son should he find him tainted with heresy" — thus justifying the epithet generally applied to him of "Demon of the South."

When news reached Paris of the perils by land encountered by the travellers, and the perils by sea by the voyagers, many superstitious but Godfearing people declared them to be signs of the marked displeasure of Heaven at the sacrifice of the young princess to the gloomy, cruel, fanatical ruler of Spain. Some three years earlier, when the five years' truce was concluded between Henri II. and Charles V., through the intervention of the Connétable Montmorency, whose private interests induced him to cling to the Spanish alliance, Elisabeth of France, then ten years of age, was betrothed to Don Carlos, a child of eleven, the grandson of Charles, and son of Philip of Spain and his first wife, Donna Maria of Portugal.

Ere five months had elapsed the five years' truce was broken, and war ensued — the Spanish army invading France and defeating the French at Saint-Quentin. In the following year, September 2, 1558, died Charles V. at his monastery of San Yuste. Two months later the death of Queen Mary of England left Philip II. a second time a widower. Not, however, a disconsolate one, as he immediately became a suitor for the hand of his wife's successor, Queen Elizabeth. The terms of the Treaty of Câteau-Cambrésis were then under consideration, and their discussion greatly prolonged, especially with reference to Calais, by the fluctuations of hope and despair agitating Philip's breast. Would England become a province of Spain, and — happy result — her heresy be trampled out in blood and flames?

Elizabeth, also anxious respecting Calais, its temporary loss or eventual restitution, seemed for awhile to waver. But soon she made it unmistakably evident that she had no mind to marry her deceased sister's husband.

Then arose the question whether it would be more desirable to complete the marriage of the affianced young couple, or to set their betrothal aside, and Philip himself take the young princess to wife. Don Carlos was said to have been weak and infirm from his birth. He was now fifteen, and his state of health gave no promise of improvement. A fall in infancy, attributed to careless nursing, was said to have so far injured him as to cause a slight contraction of the sinews of one leg. In view of these discouraging statements, it was thought that the father would be a more eligible husband for a daughter of France than the son. Philip was still in the prime of life — he was but thirty-two. But his temper was gloomy, no smile was ever seen on his countenance; his disposition was cruel, his fanaticism extreme. This, together with the excessive dulness and formality of the Spanish Court, offered but a poor promise of happiness for a lively young princess of fourteen. But, on the other hand, at once she would be elevated to the Spanish throne; while the young prince's reputed infirmities made it very doubtful that she would ever be called on to share the throne with him. This view of the

Spanish proposals prevailed, and they were in consequence readily acceded to, much to the satisfaction of the constable. The former betrothal, as so frequently happened with royal betrothals in those times, was declared null, and the new engagement (by proxy) took place with great ceremony in the presence of the king and queen and the court.

We left the young princess with the King and Queen of Navarre at Bordeaux, whence, after a brief interval of repose, they resumed their journey. While the marriage cortége continued its course on French soil, Jeanne and her husband gave precedence to the bride; but as soon as they entered their own domains they asserted their sovereign supremacy, of which the Queen of Navarre was induced to make a formal act, as a challenge to those who sought to deprive her of it. The Spanish envoys affected to consider the Navarrese frontier reached at Pignon, a small town or village near Saint-Jean-Pied-de-Port, connecting Lower with Upper Navarre, which the spoliation of 1521 had made Spanish.

But the spirited heiress of the House of Albret declined to accept a limit that would have carried with it a recognition of the fact of unjust possession as an acquired right. She drew the frontier of her kingdom at the separating line of Upper Navarre and Castile. However, this was not a convenient time for discussing her claims; so the

Spanish authorities yielded, and the bridal party passed on without stopping at Pignon.

But the elements still warred against them, the tempest so increasing in violence that it compelled them to halt at Roncevaux. In consequence, it was decided that the ceremony of delivering the bride to her husband's ambassador should take place there, at the abbey; the King and Queen of Navarre protesting that only necessity forced them to consent to this, in order to fulfil their mission. At the conclusion of these formalities, when the bride was transferred to the charge of the Duke of Alva, King Antoine made a speech, setting forth the many virtues and accomplishments of the princess. The Archbishop of Toledo should have replied to this oration by lauding in glowing terms the transcendent qualities of the royal bridegroom ; but he was so highly indignant at the conduct of the Court of France in selecting heretics to take charge of the princess, that for sole reply he turned towards Elisabeth — not deigning to notice Antoine — and said, " Listen, my daughter, to these words, and let them be engraven on thy heart : Forget thine own people and thy father's house ; " the Bishop of Burgos adding, " Then shall the king have pleasure in thy beauty, for he is thy lord." Whether he finished the Scriptural quotation, " For he is thy Lord God, and worship thou him," the chronicle and the letter of the Bishop of Limoges to François

II., February 23, 1560 (from the latter most of these particulars are derived), do not inform us. But worship of her gracious lord was probably expected of her.

After the grand *auto-da-fé*, which bore witness to Philip's zeal for the glory of God, he set out to receive his bride at a village two leagues distant from Madrid, to which city she was conducted with great pomp. A reception, attended by the grandees and ladies of the court, was held at the royal palace. All were anxious to see Philip's girl-queen. But the chilling effect of the formal etiquette of the Spanish Court formed so strong a contrast with the freedom and gaiety of the festivities in which she had so lately taken part, that the gravity, pomp, and splendour of her first grand reception seemed rather funereal to this young daughter of France.

A gleam of pleasure, however, lighted up her countenance (noticed with some curiosity by most of the company, but disapprovingly, it is said, by Philip) when Don Carlos was presented to her. It was reported that he had but recently recovered from a fever, and still was weak, but that, at his earnest request, he was allowed to attend the reception to pay his respects to the new queen. And Elisabeth received her former *fiancé* both gracefully and graciously, appearing to take an affectionate interest in him — treatment to which, it is certain, the poor youth was but little accustomed. A sudden liking for each other sprang up between these young people, who naturally looked forward to pleasant companionship in the future. These hopes were, however, destined to be crushed in the bud, as, under the circumstances, it was advisable they should be.

Marriage *fêtes* on a grand scale followed the bridal reception, and many boleros and fandangos were danced by the people in honour of their Catholic majesties' nuptials. But the programme of the court festivities, distinguished by pomp and solemnity rather than gaiety, was scarcely half completed when the young queen fell ill — her malady proving to be smallpox. It seems to have been but a slight attack, for her recovery was speedy; her beauty suffered no damage, and the interrupted *fêtes* were resumed — Spanish etiquette requiring that no part of them should be omitted.

The Bishop of Limoges, who accompanied the young queen, and remained in Spain until after her recovery, when writing to Catherine de' Medici to inform her of her daughter's restoration to health, says that "during her illness she has grown amazingly;" and, with reference to Don Carlos, he adds, "the prince had cause to be greatly delighted at her majesty's amiability and friendliness towards him, as, indeed, he has shown, and continues to show, that he was. But his visits to her cannot be frequent, for besides that opportunities for conversation are fewer in this country, and intercourse more reserved than in France, his quartan fever so exhausts him that day by day he grows weaker."

On leaving Spain, the bishop was the bearer of a letter from the Spanish queen to her mother. Probably it would not, if entrusted to other hands, have reached its destination. Evidently her elevation to the Spanish throne has not brought happiness to the lively and youthful French princess. She is oppressed by the formality and gloomy etiquette of the Spanish Court, and complains of the people about her, especially of her *maître-d'hôtel*, the Condé d' Alista, who seems to have watched her closely. He was a relative of the cruel Duke of Alva. She speaks of him as a "harsh, meddling, mischief-making man." Neither of Philip nor Carlos does she venture to speak; probably she dared not.

CHAPTER IV.

The King's Mysterious Malady. — The "Wise Men:" Their Enchantments. — Magic Scenes at Chaumont. — Ruggieri's Predictions. — Religious Persecution. — Anne Dubourg. — Appeal to the Young King. — The Gracious Concession. — The "Malcontents." — The Scotch Reformers: Their Example Followed.

SCARCELY had the king's physicians pronounced their royal patient free from the quartan fever from which he had lately been suffering, when he was attacked by a mysterious malady, against whose progress all remedies seemingly were unavailing. His complexion became livid; his face disfigured with blotches; his slight frame weaker; his spirits more drooping, and the languor consequent on his physical and mental condition greater than before. It was whispered about that some subtle Italian poison was slowly but surely undermining his constitution and bringing him to an early grave. Some there were — and the historian Mézeray seems to confirm their opinion — who thought the king's malady was leprosy, of which Louis XI. was said to have died.

Catherine de' Medici, whose position was then an exceedingly difficult one, succeeded in having her son removed to Blois, ostensibly to try the effect of change of air, but really for the greater convenience of assembling in daily consultation around the sick youth's bed the numerous soothsayers and astrologers in whose predictions she placed so much confidence. It was rumoured, and the story found credence among the ignorant and superstitious people, that the "queen-mother's wise men" had ordered as the only sure remedy for the purification of the young king's blood, vitiated from his very birth, daily baths of the blood of healthy infant children.

Though Catherine for the time being had succumbed to the Guises, her craving for power had in no way abated. To obtain it, she was believed to be capable of any crime, while as an intrigante she was regarded with distrust, alike by both the political factions then dividing the court. From the state of the king's health, it seemed likely that the ambitious hopes of the Guises would ere long be shattered, and the dormant ones of the constable revive; while on Catherine would devolve a much larger share in the government of the kingdom. It might be almost undivided sway, unless the Bourbons should act with unusual vigour and take charge of the helm of state, as a large party, both Protestant and Catholic, desired, instead of placing it — as a regency seemed imminent — in the hands of a foreigner.

Anxious to dive more deeply into the future, to

ascertain whether its aspect were menacing or favourable to her, Catherine hastened from Blois to Chaumont. There, undisturbed, she had witnessed or borne a part in many scenes of magic. There, in the lonely tower she had raised on the summit of a rock, she had often, guided by her favourite astrologer, the Florentine Cosmo Ruggieri, sought in the stars a knowledge of the projects of her enemies, and in the movements of those heavenly bodies the best mode of defeating them.

There, towards the end of December, 1559, the same astrologer awaited her in the spacious apartment or hall communicating with Catherine's private suite of rooms in the tower.* Around the walls of this room were suspended, or placed on brackets, various articles of the most heterogeneous nature — instruments of singular form, suggestive of torture; probably for goading refractory demons into revealing more fully or clearly the hidden events of the future. Also dried plants and seaweed, with numerous specimens of minerals; skins of the lion and panther; stuffed animals and birds — conspicuous amongst the latter, an owl of enormous size, with on either side a vampire bat. On the tables lay parchments, covered with geometrical lines, curves and fig-

* This was Catherine's last visit to Chaumont, the transfer of the château to the Duchesse de Valentinois being arranged to take place at the end of the month.

ures; planispheres; dial-plates; several horoscopes; scientific instruments; divining rods or magic wands; waxen figures transfixed with pins and needles — in a word, all the appliances and appurtenances of the magician and astrologer, whose art was then at the height of its glory and development.

The apartment was but dimly lighted when Catherine entered, and a mistiness at the further end added to the weird solemnity of the scene. Being seated, and having overcome the slight nervous agitation which the usually intrepid Catherine is said to have displayed on this occasion, the astrologer first showed the queen the horoscopes of her four sons, which, in obedience to her commands, he had computed, and whence it appeared that two of them were destined to a violent death. All four were to die young, and without leaving any direct successor; but stranger still, all would wear a royal crown. Apparently much affected, the queen inquired: "Are they then destined to succeed each other on the throne of France?" to which the astrologer appears to have given no precise reply — "It was not clearly set forth." The prophecy, indeed, erred in several respects, and probably, like many others, was altered after the events to correspond as nearly as it does with what actually occurred.

Catherine, however, was not quite satisfied. She wished for something more positive, therefore desired to know if magic would confirm the language of the stars and establish their decrees with more certainty. Ruggieri then led the queen in front of the magic mirror, in which she beheld a spacious hall, but expressed her disappointment on perceiving there none of her family. The magician explained that they were about to enter the hall, and that each would reign as many years as the number of times he passed around it. The first to enter was François II., the reigning king, sorrowful and dejected, who vanished so speedily that Catherine had scarcely time to recognise him ere he was gone. Her eldest son, then, was to die before a full year had elapsed!

Pale with terror, she looked again. The future Charles IX. appeared, and made thirteen turns, vanishing at about the middle of the fourteenth, the enchanted mirror at the same time becoming dimmed by a blood-stained mist. Following him came the Duc d' Anjou (Henri III.), who passed nearly fifteen times round the hall, Henri of Navarre (Henri IV.) suddenly appearing before the last turn was completed. "The Navarrese prince," says Nicolas Pasquier, "began the course with a nimble step and jovial air." Twenty full turns were made, and the twenty-first was begun, when, having completed three-fourths of it, he suddenly vanished. The Duc d' Alençon did not figure in this scene of magic; no royal crown, notwithstanding the prediction of the stars, being destined for him. Louis XIII., however, is said to have made his thirty-eight turns before the queen.

But her interest in the enchantment ended with the disappearance of the Duc d'Anjou and his Bourbon successor. By a gesture, for she was too much agitated to speak, she intimated that she cared to see no more. The magic mirror immediately became dim, and the supernatural light in the enchanted hall faded away into darkness.

Several old French writers describe this wonderful exhibition of Ruggieri's phantasmagorial skill, but they differ widely in the details given.* Brantôme ascribes it to the magician Nostradamus, in which he appears to be in error. Others also, instead of a magic mirror, substitute a magic circle, within whose limits the princes ushered in made their several rounds. The Guises, according to some accounts, were also introduced, and by their speedy disappearance the tragic end of Duc Henri de Guise was supposed to be indicated.

It has been asserted that a profound impression was made on Catherine's mind by Ruggieri's prophecy. But although constantly studying the stars herself, and seeking the aid of magicians and astrologers, in order to lift the veil concealing the future, it is certain that she accepted only so much of what she regarded as revealed to her as

* Brantôme, Nicolas Pasquier, Bayle, Felibien, the historian of Navarre, André Pavin, and others.

suited her immediate purposes. For the rest, her skilful Italian perfumers, with their subtle poisonous scents and powders, enabled her by secret means, when public ones were dangerous or impossible, to remove those obnoxious persons who were obstacles to the carrying out of her tortuous policy. Thus she believed that she could thwart or reverse the decrees of Fate when inimical to her, and turn the knowledge she had gained of them to her own advantage.

The queen-mother returned from Chaumont to Paris and Blois to find the public mind greatly agitated by the religious persecution then proceeding by order of the Guises. Not only were Protestants, but all moderate Catholics, horrified by the atrocities inflicted on unoffending persons, for whom snares were laid, and spies employed to discover whether they held what were still called the "new opinions." Madonnas were set up at the corners of the streets; images of saints also, crowned with flowers, and those who passed by these idols without saluting or bending the knee before them were beaten with sticks by men set to watch, or dragged off to prison, followed by a jeering, cursing, fanatic mob. Then they were tortured, every refinement of cruelty practised on them, and if that did not subdue them into renouncing their heretical opinions, and confessing that they had sinned against Holy Mother Church, they expiated their crime in the flames.

The execution, in December, of the sentence on the Councillor Anne Dubourg excited general indignation. For six months this upright magistrate and distinguished savant had been a close prisoner in the Bastille. He had been accused of holding heretical opinions, and did not care to deny it. His plainness of speech had so much irritated Henri II. that he signified his intention of feasting his eyes on the torture and death agonies of his victim, as soon as the close of the court festivities gave him leisure. But ere this moment for gratifying his resentment arrived, the hand of death had beckoned the monarch away. Dubourg, however, was not forgotten, but what with pompous funeral pageants, a coronation, public entries, etc., the duke and the cardinal had been fully occupied. Others accused of a like crime, less steadfast than Dubourg, had recanted, or pretended to do so, and thus escaped the gallows or the burning pile.

Many of Dubourg's friends were so sanguine as to believe that an appeal to Henri's youthful successor would result in an act of justice, as well as of clemency, wherewith to grace his coronation. But "the uncles" forbade this. François II. was reminded that he had confirmed the contract entered into between his father, the late king, and Philip II. of Spain. He replied that he would carry out his father's wishes to the letter, and thoroughly exterminate heresy from France.

Dubourg's trial was a long one, because of his several appeals to the Parliament and the various courts, both secular and ecclesiastical, against the injustice of his sentence. He had no objection to taking that course; indeed, he believed it to be his duty, in order, if possible, to enforce his rightful claim as a magistrate to be tried only by the full assembly of the Parliament, of which he was a member. But the few words, in denial of his faith, which would have saved him, no entreaties of his friends could prevail on him to utter. "He was a Christian," he said, "and was prepared to die as one." So great was Anne Dubourg's reputation, that persons of every class, not only in France but throughout Europe, were interested in his fate. The Protestant princes of Germany made a representation in his favour. Plots were organised with the view of effecting his escape from the Bastille, but resulted in nothing but a more rigorous treatment of the prisoner. Catherine de' Medici was implored by some friends to intercede for and save him; others threatened her and the kingdom with disasters innumerable if she did not prevent this martyrdom, while, as an earnest of what would follow, the President Minard, who had first denounced Dubourg as a heretic, was shot dead one evening on leaving the Palais de Justice, the murderer escaping undiscovered.

This circumstance led the Cardinal de Lorraine

to urge that the execution of Dubourg's sentence should take place without further unnecessary delay. Another motive for hastening it was the information (privately given) that the Elector Palatine was about to despatch an embassy to France, to ask of the clemency of François II. the pardon of Dubourg, whom the elector was desirous of appointing to a professorship in his University of Heidelberg. Dubourg's condemnation to death was, therefore, finally confirmed on the 22d of December. The next day, on the Place de Grève, the sentence was executed, one concession being graciously made to the earnest entreaties of friends and relatives,—instead of being thrown living into the flames, it was permitted first to strangle him. With calm heroism, the Christian martyr met his fate, and in eloquent language that touched all hearts and bedewed all eyes—even those of his craven judges—he bade adieu to both friends and foes. When the elector's ambassador arrived the deed was done, and his majesty and his "uncles" were spared the pain of refusing the elector's request.

Numerous executions followed that of Dubourg. Those of his friends who had most earnestly interposed to rescue him from death became by that act suspected persons, and the Guises, in their holy zeal, spared none on whom the shadow of suspicion rested. Hitherto the Protestants had born submissively the yoke of their persecutors.

They were now exasperated to the highest pitch by the recent acts of the Guises, and for the first time in France reprisals were contemplated. It was not the Protestants only who were dissatisfied with the rule of the duke and the cardinal. The general name of "malcontents" included many to whom the question of religion was one in which little interest was felt, but to overthrow those usurpers of the kingly power, those *soi-disant* descendants of Charlemagne, they were willing to join hands and fight for their rights side by side with, or as leaders of, those to whom liberty of conscience and freedom of religious worship were the most absorbing questions.

Those military men, mostly poor gentlemen, whose services after the signing of the Peace of Câteau-Cambrésis were no longer required by the state, had been dismissed without any settlement for the long arrears of pay then owing. Their occupation being gone and great distress ensuing, they became clamorous for the money due to them. The cardinal minister of finance was with the court at Fontainebleau. Thither, in great numbers, these needy soldiers of fortune followed him, some demanding payment, others humbly soliciting pension or place by way of compensation. His eminence was irritated beyond measure at conduct so insolent and rebellious, and to free himself from the importunities of such unwelcome visitors he had gibbets erected before the gates of Fontainebleau (as was then at times the custom, to scare seditious or threatening intruders), and a notice attached that if any of those people who came to solicit favours were found within the precincts of the palace at the expiration of twenty-four hours they would certainly be hanged. These suppliants for the cardinal's favours at once withdrew, but with the determination that he should hear from them again in another character.

The moment appeared to them exceedingly opportune for the organisation of a sort of league for the "defence of legitimate authority and for the public weal." The young king, they said, was evidently incapable of governing, and his declared majority a mere fiction. "It was desirable, therefore, for his and the people's welfare that he should be rescued from the toils of the foreign usurpation." Indignation at the arrogance of the Guises induced many of the nobility to join this adventurous band, while the recent successes of John Knox and the Scotch Covenanters against Mary of Guise, though advised and supported by her brother, inspired the French Reformers with courage to rise up against their persecutors in "defence of their religion." The introduction of the military element changed the character of the struggle for Reform. There was a vigorous awakening of the Protestants to a sense of their rights, and the doctrine inculcated by Calvin, of submission to the powers that be, no longer held them in bondage. Thus was prepared that event known as the Conspiracy of Amboise. It was then that the Calvinists, to distinguish them from the Lutherans, were first called Huguenots, a corruption of the German Eidgenossen — allies or confederates.

CHAPTER V.

The Amboise Conspiracy.—Barry de la Renaudie.—The Six Brothers of the House of Guise.—Antoine, King of Navarre.—The Plot Revealed.—Condé Joins the Court at Amboise. Nemours's Errand of Mercy.—La Renaudie's Encounter in the Forest of Château-Rénault.—Nemours Succeeds in His Mission.—Treachery.—Royal Amusements.—Condé's Challenge to Single Combat.

HE short reign of François II. was one continued period of turmoil and tragic events, of which the "Conspiracy of Amboise" may be considered the most important. In it the long pent-up discontent of political and religious factions, which for years past had distracted France, suddenly found development. The tyrannical rule of the Guises had aroused a spirit of resentment which, galling as was the yoke inflicted on the country by such rulers as François I. and Henri II., had yet been kept in check by the deep feeling of loyalty cherished by the people towards their rightful sovereigns.

Voltaire's remark that "the Conspiracy of Amboise was the first conspiracy known in France," has been repeated by most French writers who since his day have treated of the subject. Numerous instances were, however, already on record of serious court cabals, political intrigues and plots, as well as menacing risings of the populace, when taxed beyond endurance to supply the needs of prodigal, dissolute kings and their favourites. Yet a conspiracy including amongst its members men of humblest rank and of the upper and lower *bourgeoisie*, the disbanded military, many of the *petite noblesse*, also those of greater distinction (for instance, the Baron de Castelnau, of a very ancient family and of eminent learning and piety), with a prince of the blood for its head, had probably never before been known in France.

A gentleman of Perigord, named Barry de la Renaudie, undertook the organisation of the confederates, which was conducted with so much thoroughness and skill, and so much audacity yet secrecy, that in this respect the Amboise Conspiracy has been compared with that of Catilina, and the Ghibelline plot of the Pazzi of Florence. The plan of execution was decided at a general meeting convoked by La Renaudie at Nantes in the early part of February. A body of several hundred Huguenots, unarmed, was to advance on Blois on the 15th of March to present a petition to the king praying for liberty to worship God according to the rites of the reformed religion.

Five hundred cavaliers and a thousand men on foot, commanded by thirty captains, all thoroughly equipped, were to follow the above, who were to open the gates of Blois to them. The Prince de

Condé — hitherto, for concealment, designated *le prince muet* — was then to place himself at their head, and arrest the Duc de Guise and the cardinal, who were to be tried and punished according to the laws of the kingdom. The young monarch being thus freed from their usurped domination, a legitimate government, after a general consultation, was to be established. The leaders of the confederates were in correspondence with Queen Elizabeth through the English ambassador, and were largely subsidised by her "for the cause of God and religion," Reformers and dissatisfied politicians alike sharing her bounty. For though all those assembled under the banner of Reform were not Protestants, and probably had other aims than religious ones, yet equally with them they demanded a cessation of persecution and the tolerance of religious differences.

While the preparations for this daring enterprise were still proceeding, the attention of the Guises was in a measure diverted from them by the innumerable pamphlets, menacing, caustic, or derisive, with which they were overwhelmed. For their authors or printers, diligent, though generally fruitless, search was made. The printer of the famous pamphlet, "*Epître au Tigre de la France*," addressed to the cardinal, was, however, discovered and duly hanged on the Place de Grève. The vigorous language of this pamphlet appears to have made the·cardinal tremble. He was a terrible coward; but, though he had a fertile brain for the concoction of schemes and plans for his own and his family's benefit, he was fearfully alarmed when any serious resistance to them seemed probable, and his personal safety at all endangered. The duke, however, supplied what was needed in boldness and audacity. The six Guise brothers were remarkable in this respect, each possessing in a high degree some quality of mind or natural endowment wanting in the others. No wonder, then, they became so enormously wealthy, so distinguished according to their several or their united attributes, and so dangerous to the state when they began to fix their gaze on the crown, and declare themselves the lineal descendants of Charlemagne. Some intimations of what was going on could, in fact, hardly fail to reach them. They had their spies in the capital and in the provinces, ever on the alert to detect heresy or "those guilty promoters of it" who failed to denounce suspected friends or relatives. But these occasional warnings of some great movement on foot in the Vendômois (the appanage of Prince Louis de Condé) the Guises appear to have but lightly regarded.

Sir Nicholas Throckmorton, the English ambassador at the French Court, conjointly with special envoys from Elizabeth, had endeavoured to tempt King Antoine of Navarre, by promises of money and the secret support of their queen, to head an expedition against the duke and the cardinal,* who had sent French troops to Scotland to aid their sister, the Queen Regent Mary of Guise, in putting down the Protestants. For awhile she gained some advantage and seemed on the point of succeeding in her object; but assistance despatched by Elizabeth resulted in the triumph of the Covenanters.

The historian Lingard has said that Elizabeth, by encouraging the internal dissensions in France, hoped to regain possession of Calais. It was natural, however, that the English queen should resent the assumption of her title of sovereign of England and Ireland, and the quartering of her arms, by the youthful pair then on the throne of France; also that she should be willing to assist the Reformers in their attempt to obtain recognition of their right to pray to God after their own manner, as well as to free themselves from the cruel persecution of those ambitious tyrannical men who governed France in the name of its invalid boy-king. But it was soon very clear to Elizabeth's agents that King Antoine was wholly unfitted to take the lead in an enterprise requiring in its chief great energy of character, audacity, endurance, and unflinching firmness, with the power of inspiring those under his control with similar courage and daring and perfect confidence in him.

The accounts of the famous Amboise plot con-

* See "Calendar of Foreign State Papers," 1560-61.

tained in the memoirs and journals of contemporary writers are exceedingly numerous; but their discrepancies are so great — written as they are in the spirit of partisanship — that it is difficult to disentangle from them trustworthy materials for a connected narrative. However, before the time for action arrived — said to have been fixed first for the 10th of March, then for the 15th — La Renaudie appears to have crossed the Channel, either to seek an interview with Queen Elizabeth, or to consult with her ministers. He probably received, besides a supply of money, assurances of her good-will and interest in his hazardous undertaking. Beyond that, and that she was kept well informed of its progress, there would seem to have been neither aid nor interference from that quarter.

The Spanish king, who had his emissaries in every country and court in Europe, had seen with pleasure the defeat of the Scottish queen-regent and her adherents by the troops of the heretic Elizabeth. It thwarted the plans of the Guises, who desired to unite the kingdoms of France and Scotland — an arrangement entirely opposed to Philip's own views. "The death of the young Queen Mary at this time would have relieved him," as he said to his minister, Granvelle, "of much embarrassment and anxiety by depriving her uncles of all influence in Scotland." But while waiting and hoping for that desired event, he felt bound to support those zealous sons of Holy Mother Church in their efforts to exterminate the Reformers and "free the land from the damnable sin of heresy."

Two days then before the date fixed for laying the Huguenot petition before the king, the duke and the cardinal were fully informed by a Spanish agent of the serious appearance of the impending storm — he at the same time handing to them a plan of the intended confederate operations. The queen-mother also received information of a like alarming nature from, it is said, one of the confederates named Lignières, whose courage failed him as the moment for action drew near. Another account attributes the failure of this carefully organised and well-combined scheme to the imprudence of Renaudie in imparting it in confidence to a lawyer, with whom he was either on terms of friendship or had monetary transactions which, as some relate, compelled him partly to reveal his secret — the secret without a moment's loss of time being again revealed at Blois.

But whoever may have been the traitor, great was the consternation when the news of a conspiracy (whose object was declared to be the dethronement of the king, the murder of his "uncles," and the transfer of the crown to the Prince de Condé) reached the Château de Blois. The amusements of the court, but recently resumed in consequence of a slight improvement in the young king's health, were at once brought to a close, and general alarmed prevailed. The poltroon cardinal quaked in his shoes, lest his worthless body should be roasted alive, as by his intervention the flames had consumed the bodies of so many of his betters — good men and true. So great was his terror, that momentarily it is said to have acted on his brother, the duke, almost paralysing the indomitable courage of that daring soldier. But speedily recovering himself, he ordered the instant removal of king, queen, and court to the Château d' Amboise — a fortress of far greater strength than that of Blois — while he hastened secretly to assemble the king's guards, and as large a body of armed men as on the spur of the moment was possible.

At the suggestion of Catherine de' Medici, Admiral de Coligny and his brother D'Andelot were requested immediately to attend the court, "their opinion and counsel" — such was the pretext — "being desired by the duke and queen-mother." They were suspected, wrongly it apears, of being actively concerned in the conspiracy. But without any show of distrust, Coligny and D'Andelot, joined by their brother, the Cardinal Odet de Châtillon, at once obeyed the summons. By their presence at Amboise, "Catherine hoped to perplex the confederates and induce a suspicion that these military chiefs of Reform were as hostile to their project as the religious ones — Calvin,

Bèze, and others." His advice being asked, the admiral frankly declared that to exterminate the Reformers by force was now out of the question; but that if there was to be peace in France, an edict of relaxation of severity with liberty of worship must be granted. The Guises affected partly to yield to this advice, and issued a sort of amnesty, but rendered their concessions null by secret orders forbidding the release of any prisoner detained on account of his religion who was not prepared fully and publicly to recant his errors.

Though the court was transferred to Amboise, and the conspiracy divulged, it seems that the confederates might yet have attained their object, and by an audacious *coup-de-main* effected an entrance, treachery within the château aiding them. It was, nevertheless, a perilous undertaking. Yet sixty gentlemen offered themselves to accomplish it, or die in the attempt. The Prince de Condé was on his way from Orléans to Blois, when informed that the plot was divulged and the king and court transferred to Amboise. He, however, had the courage — or exceeding folly, as some of his friends thought — to continue his journey and join the royal party at the château. He was received there with great coldness; but accusation at that moment was considered premature.

La Renaudie being still absent in Paris, the chief command was held by the Baron de Castelnau-Chalone, who occupied the Château de Noizay, belonging to the Sieur de Raunay, one of the confederates. It was situated within two leagues of Amboise, on the right bank of the Loire. Thither the Duc de Guise, uncertain as to the number of the confederates assembled there, would have despatched Maréchal Vieilleville with a small party of gentlemen of the king's guard to reconnoitre and to parley with the baron. But Vieilleville, suspecting that treachery was intended, suggested that, to inspire confidence in the conspirators, a prince of the blood should be entrusted with the message of peace — a request from the king to know what they complained of, and his royal word given that in all security and without any fear for their lives the confederates might approach and lay their griefs at the foot of the throne.

The Duc de Nemours,* who, says Brantôme, was "the very flower of chivalry," was induced to accept this mission. Five hundred men were to accompany him, but unless persuasion should utterly fail, he was determined not to use force. In the morning, the king made oath to pardon the conspirators if they presented themselves respectfully before him, and Nemours in all good faith set out on his errand of mercy.

* Jacques de Savoie, the head of the younger branch of the House of Savoy, on whose ancestor François I. bestowed the Duchy of Nemours.

La Renaudie was then hastening to the relief of Castelnau, a small body of troops following. But when traversing the forest of Château-Renault, he encountered a cavalier (Regnier de la Planche, in his "Reign of François II.," says he was his cousin), a partisan of the Guises, with one or two attendants. Furiously the cavalier rushed upon him, and took aim with his pistol, but the cumbrous weapon missed fire. La Renaudie, with more effect, replied with his sword, for his adversary at the first thrust fell from his horse, and was killed as he fell by a second blow, the sword passing through his body. The servant of the slain cavalier, who seems, thus far, to have been a quiet spectator of the fight, then dismounted, and passing quickly, it is stated, behind La Renaudie, lodged the charge of his arquebuse in his back. This proved fatal, but the dying man, whose hand still grasped his sword, had yet strength enough left effectually to aim a deadly blow at his second adversary. The men who followed La Renaudie disbanded themselves on learning the death of their chief, and those who did not escape the vigilance of the king's troops, now out in all directions, were cruelly massacred. The bodies of the three combatants were removed — "two for honourable burial" — that of La Renaudie to swing on a gibbet on the bridge over the Loire, with an inscription above it, "La Renaudie, Chief of the Rebels."

When news of this *contretemps* reached the confederates, the men of whom La Renaudie was to have taken the command, and whom he had inspired with courage and a confidence of success similar to his own, were so enraged, that to avenge him they wildly rushed forth, heedless of all attempted restraint, and in open day made a desperate attack on the Château of Amboise. Though the assailants were finally repulsed, dispersed, pursued, and tracked to their hiding-places — where, as the account has it, they were "cut in pieces "— it yet appears that, could they but have subdued the thirst for vengeance until darkness concealed their movements, the attack would have been successful. It, however, caused exceeding terror to Catherine de' Medici, who affected to incline towards the conciliatory policy recommended by the admiral, and supported by the Chancellor Olivier, then at the château. The chancellor was a friend of the Baron de Castelnau, and was also strongly suspected of being "tainted" (according to the expression then in vogue) with the "new opinions."

In spite of the *espionage* both within and without the château, information was conveyed to the king that it was not against him but his ministers, the duke and the cardinal, that the confederates had taken up arms. This he repeated to them, and begged that they would retire from the court for awhile, that he might ascertain if it were truth, and also inquire what his people really wanted. "But the Guises," says La Planche, "utterly rejected this proposal," telling the feeble young king that "should they leave him, neither he nor his brothers could be sure of their lives for one hour, the House of Bourbon being bent on exterminating the royal line of Valois." And so effectually did they work on his fears, and persuade the weeping youth that their vigilance was necessary for the preservation of his crown and his life, that by a royal declaration of March 17th the Duc de Guise was named lieutenant-general of the kingdom, with powers unlimited. It was, in fact, a sort of abdication, conferring on the duke, as a right, that exercise of royal power which hitherto he had usurped.

This was a step entirely opposed to the views of the queen-mother; but to resist it would have been vain. Power seemed always to elude her grasp; but once more the opposition of their enemies had resulted in placing it more securely in the hands of the Guises. For long years Catherine had played the part of watching and waiting, but she now looked forward to a change in her favour, which she believed would at no very distant period occur. Meanwhile, regarding the Huguenots as a salutary restraint on the encroachments of the Guises, she sought to incline the court to clemency towards them. At the same time she secured for herself a certain measure of popularity amongst those who had adopted the "new opinions"—popularity which she might turn to account by and by. And, in spite of the cardinal, she did succeed in obtaining the liberation of some of the humbler members of the conspiracy, who, lagging behind on foot, had been taken prisoners. They were sent back to their homes with a testoon (5*d*.) each from Catherine for their journey.

While these things were taking place in the château, the Duc de Nemours had accomplished the object of his mission. Persuasion had succeeded with the Baron de Castelnau; who (according to the historian, De Thou) still, in preference to force, favoured the first peaceful demonstration proposed of sending a body of unarmed Huguenots to lay before the king a statement of the grievances, both religious and political, for which redress was sought. Some there were, however, who declared themselves unable to place the same reliance as their leader on the promises of their sovereign, controlled as he was by unscrupulous ministers. Nemours — who, it has been generally considered, had no part in the treachery of the Guises — replied to these objections by engaging his own word, as a man of honour and a prince of the blood, that the king's promises would be religiously performed. His assurances of good faith were accepted. The confederates assembled at Noizay then issued from the château, and, led by their chief, peacefully mingled with the soldiers and gentlemen of the prince's suite, and accompanied them to Amboise. Thus, nothing doubting, they were led as a flock of sheep to the slaughter-house.

The last of the long line of victims had passed the portcullis when the foremost ones began the ascent of the great north tower, in the upper portion of which were the royal apartments, under the guidance of the archers of the guard. Suddenly there arose one long piercing cry of indignation, reaching the ears even of the king and his ministers, when a halt was made by their conductors on the lower landing leading to the dungeons, and the confederates discovered that they had been betrayed. Nemours was still with them. He is said to have been pierced to the very soul with anguish when his eyes met the accusing and contemptuous gaze of Castelnau fixedly bent upon him. Rage in his heart, he rushed to the king's apartment, and reminded his majesty of his promises. The duke being present, he reproached him in bitterest terms, and was laughed at for his credulity in supposing that faith would be kept with rebels and heretics. Indeed, so much were both François de Guise and the cardinal elated by Nemours's success, that they exultingly told him such a triumph was quite unexpected, and scarcely could have been achieved but for the part (the infamous part) assigned him, and which, however unconsciously, he had most adroitly played.*

The Guises being now masters of the position, the slaughter of their prisoners began without loss of time. The cardinal had remarked that the ladies were growing weary of the secluded life they were leading at Amboise, and longing for the signal to return to the livelier pastimes of Blois. Gallantly, therefore, he proposed for their amusement a most unique and enlivening after-dinner recreation. The whole court attended — the king and his "uncles," the queen, the queen-mother with her young sons, Charles and Henri, and the ladies and gentlemen of the household generally. For a whole month they assembled daily at the broad open spaces or grated verandas fronting the castle windows, where they ranged themselves to assist at their ease at — and possibly, as good Catholics, to enjoy — the horrible spectacle of the unfortunate Huguenot prisoners writhing in the agony of a cruel death, or under the infliction of atrocious tortures. Water, fire, and sword were all employed in the perpetration of the unspeakable horrors devised by the ferocious imaginations of the wretches to whom the Guises entrusted the massacre of their victims.

Before the windows of the royal apartment was a broad projecting balcony, and from it a full view

---

* Brantôme represents the Duc de Nemours as a persuasive speaker and "*aussi agréable que brave.*"

of the Loire. The thoughtful cardinal, anxious that his young sovereign should have the satisfaction of watching the death-struggles of a heretic as closely as possible, ordered several, whose limbs had been dislocated on the rack, to be suspended by cords to the rails of the balcony. To add to the attractions of the river scene many of these unfortunates were tied in sacks, others attached, five or six or more together, by long iron poles passed through their bodies, and then thrown into the Loire, there to struggle and gasp out in agony, for the royal party's amusement, their few remaining minutes of life.

Headless bodies (many of the heads being placed on poles on the ramparts of the château) lay weltering in blood on the ground, while flames were consuming the rest. When from any of these poor sufferers, less heroic than others, cries of anguish proceeded, the cardinal, with an air of much satisfaction and a *benignant* smile, would draw the young king's attention to it. But when those from whom no satanic device of their tormentors could extract a word of confession, a groan, or complaint, died with fortitude, then his eminence would approach the king, his countenance full of indignation, and in a trembling, agitated voice thus address him: "Behold, sire, those shameless and enraged ruffians! even the fear of death cannot abate their pride or subdue their treasonable hopes. What, then, would they not do if your majesty were in their power?" Thus the poor youth, whose eyes are said to have been often filled with tears at the spectacle of horrors before him, when those of his young queen were dry, was led to believe that he was abhorred by his subjects, and that he owed his life to the care and vigilance of the Duc de Guise and the cardinal.

But killing and slaying went merrily on day and night both in the château and the town of Amboise — many parties of Huguenots being still at large in the neighbouring woods and villages. Respecting them the orders of the duke (who is said to have been as one drunk with blood) were not to send them to the château, but to shoot them down whenever met; for the dungeons were full, and so many dead bodies still lying about that the air was infected by them. Besides this, "the ladies were beginning to feel compassion for those rebels, and to plead for mercy." "The streets were therefore planted with avenues of gibbets, and dead bodies dangled like tapestry hung up against the walls, while down either side ran a rivulet of blood. But the daily spectacle of death at the château began to pall on the fair occupants of the balconies. The Duchesse de Guise, daughter of that very rigid Calvinist, the daughter of Louis XII., Renée de France, from the first expressed her repugnance to be present at such scenes. Sickened at the sight, she one day, addressing Catherine de' Medici, exclaimed: "Ah, madame, this blood will surely call for blood! May Heaven save your sons and mine!" Her exclamation was indeed prophetic.

The formalities of a trial and judicial sentence had been wholly dispensed with in the case of those of the confederates who were not, as the Guises considered, of a rank in life to give them any future trouble from the vengeance of relatives or friends. But with the gentlemen of noble birth captured at Noizay it was in some respects different, though the sanction of the king to their execution as rebels and heretics might seem to render the farce of a trial unnecessary. However, a tribunal was constituted, composed of the Cardinal de Lorraine, the craven-hearted Chancellor Olivier, and the grand-provost, Du Plessis de Richelieu (an ancestor of the great cardinal).

After a very summary *procès* the chiefs of the "Tumulte d'Amboise," as this plot is sometimes called, were condemned to die. Great efforts were made to save the Baron de Castelnau, whose family had given several famous captains to France. His own career also had been one of distinguished loyalty and good service to the crown. But his opposition to the tyrannical rule of the Guises was an unpardonable crime in the eyes of those despots, who urged or rather commanded the young king to close ears and heart to any appeal for mercy.

Another account * states that the king (we hear nothing of any intercession on the part of his queen) joined the queen-mother in pleading for clemency. One of the Guise brothers, the Duc d' Aumale, also added his supplications to theirs on this occasion. But "le grand Guise" was inexorable. Any entreaty coming from those three caged "suspects," the Châtillons (who were highly indignant at their detention at the château), and the more than suspected Condé, would of course be unheeded. But the presumptuous interference of the former aroused the righteous wrath of that excellent prelate, the Cardinal de Lorraine. Having ensnared his prey, he was now very bold. Forgetting in the heat of his anger the saintliness of his office, he rose from his seat and with great vehemence exclaimed: "*Par le sang Dieu!* that rebel shall die, and not a man in France, whoever he be, shall save him!" But if he would not save his head, he was at least desirous, it appears, of

---

* That of Regnier de La Planche, who, in his record of "*L'État de France sous François II.*," enters more fully into the details of the Amboise massacre than other contemporary writers. He has, however, been accused of some exaggeration. But it is very probable that, having himself openly embraced the Reformed Faith, the tragic result of the plot and the sufferings inflicted on the confederates excited deeper sympathy and greater commiseration in him than in those "untainted" with heresy. Exaggeration of the horrors that ensued seems scarcely possible, and any attempt to describe their atrocity is likely to fall far short of the actual facts — second in infamy only to the revolting deeds of the St. Bartholomew.

saving his soul by bringing him back to that true faith of which he was himself so shining an example.

The programme of that afternoon's entertainment included the execution of Castelnau, Raunay, the owner of the Château de Noizay, and the Chevalier de Mazères, the two last named being cruelly tortured before laying their heads on the block. Then followed the decapitation of Calvin's friend, the Sieur de Villemongis. This victim, before resigning himself to his fate, dipped his hands in the blood streaming from the headless bodies of his two companions, and, spreading them forth, with eyes raised towards heaven, said: "Behold, O God! this is the blood of Thy children: Thou wilt avenge it!"

A scaffold was erected, under the windows of the royal apartment, especially for the execution of these four gentlemen. But the Baron de Castelnau was the last to ascend it. The cardinal had detained him to listen to the pious exhortations that were to effect his conversion. For while condemning him as unfit to live, he still was anxious to dismiss him to another, and haply a better, world certificated by himself that his victim was worthy to find in that the mercy denied him in this. The baron, however, spoke with eloquence and dignity in defence of the faith that was in him, ably refuting the cardinal's arguments. The duke was present, and with singular brutality replied to a casual gesture of appeal from the baron that "he understood nothing of discussion and argument, his profession being that of cutting off heads, which he understood thoroughly." This fruitless colloquy ended, De Castelnau ascended the scaffold. As, with unflinching firmness, he laid his head on the block, "The justice of God," he said, "will surely overtake the Guises!"

These predictions and dying appeals to heaven, if they moved not the Guises themselves, yet were heard with fear and trembling by the men employed to execute their barbarities. On two of the council of three chosen to judge and pass sentence on the confederates of higher grade, their appeals, predictions, and reproaches also made a deep impression. The Chancellor Olivier, who had acted a very pusillanimous part, either from complaisance to the Guises, or from fear of compromising his own safety, was so much affected by the taunts of some of his friends and coreligionists, and the censure and upbraidings of others, that, conscience-stricken, he returned to his home, took to his bed, and died. The cardinal visited him when at the point of death, seeking again, excellent prelate, to bring back a wandering sheep to the fold of the faithful. But the chancellor rejected his offer to confess and absolve him. "Cardinal," he exclaimed, "you are bringing us all to perdition."

Willingly would the Guises have added a few more murders to their already long list of crimes. They thought the air of gloomy quietude assumed towards them by the Châtillons very menacing, but could not find in it a pretext strong enough for immediately arresting them. As regarded the Prince de Condé, the disclosures of several of the confederates while undergoing the torture were so strongly accusatory that an order was issued at the instance of the cardinal for the seizure of his papers. His château of Vendôme also was thoroughly ransacked, but not a line was found that could in any way be strained into proving his connection with the recent conspiracy.

The fact that he was its destined head was known to many and doubted by few, but the Guises failed to bring it home to him, while he, with great courage and audacity, demanded of the king the assembling of the princes of the blood, the chevaliers of the orders, the private council and foreign ambassadors then at Amboise, amongst whom was Sir Nicholas Throckmorton. At once they were commanded to repair to the royal audience-chamber. There, in their presence and that of the king, the queen, the queen-mother and her two young sons, the Prince de Condé "declared that whoever had informed his majesty that he was the chief and leader of a seditious band, said to have conspired against the king and the state, had lied and most unworthily accused him. On that account, setting aside his rank as prince of the blood, he would make them confess at the point of the sword that they were cowards and scoundrels, seeking themselves the subversion of the state and the crown, in the maintenance of which it was his duty to assist by a better right than his accusers." This pointed to the Guises. The prince ended by calling on those present, if among them there was any one who had accused him and was willing to maintain his accusation, there and then to declare himself.

The Duc de Guise then stepped forward, not, as was expected, to take up the gauntlet, but to announce that if any one present accepted the prince's challenge, he, as "his cousin," claimed the right of acting as his second. Astonishment was general, silence also, no adversary presenting himself. The duke then advanced towards the prince and offered his hand. But the vengeance of the Guises was but deferred. "They drew back for the present, having failed to prevail on the young king to stab his kinsmen with his own hand, after the manner of the Italian tyrants." The prince was therefore allowed to depart. He returned to Béarn to rejoin his brother, but by a very circuitous route, in order to avoid any snares that his enemies might have laid to entrap him on his journey. At the same time the Châtillons also left Amboise, expressing great dissatisfaction at the treatment they had received from the Guises. (La Planche and "*Mémoires de Condé.*")

The Amboise plot had served them, at the sacrifice of so many and valuable lives — variously stated from five to fifteen hundred — but to increase the power of the very men whose persecuting tyranny its aim had been to overthrow; Duc François de Guise now exercising that unlimited sway in the affairs of the kingdom which in former days was usurped by the mayors of the palace. Yet both duke and cardinal well knew that their enemies were less afraid of than exasperated against them, and that, instead of having secured a real victory, they had but entered on a desperate struggle, of which the result was doubtful.

CHAPTER VI.

The Court Leave Amboise. — De L'Hôpital Succeeds to the Chancellorship. — The Inquisition Opposed by Him. — Death of Marie de Guise. — Court Gaieties and Court Intrigues. — The Plan of the Tuileries. — Cellini Invited by Catherine to Paris. — Much Flattered, but Declines to Leave Florence. — The Admiral at Fontainebleau. — States General Convoked.

FRANÇOIS II. and his "uncles" were no less anxious to leave the gloomy fortress of Amboise, its blood-stained courts and infected atmosphere, than were the four suspected heretics whom they had allowed for the present to escape the fate which, if not foiled in their plans, the Guises still had in reserve for them.

The young queen and her ladies, the queen-mother, her train of fair damsels, and her two boy princes, were also well pleased when the signal was given for departure. In the brighter abodes of Saint-Germain and Fontainebleau, in mirthful *fêtes champêtres* in their parks and gardens, in the excitement of the royal hunts and the more private court festivities, which both queen and queen-mother were so fond of — rivalling each other in the lavish expense and *éclat* of their preparation —

some perhaps there were who amidst such scenes would soon forget the murderous deeds, the mental agony, the physical suffering they had recently, with but little visible emotion, witnessed.

But if the memory and mental vision of the greater number of the frail fair ones of the demoralised court of François II. and Catherine de' Medici retained but a faint impression of that sanguinary scene, the massacre of the heretics, all, doubtless, at the time would have greatly preferred a more enlivening pastime than that sombre one the cardinal so gaily prepared for them. That zealous prelate may, however, have intended, while amusing the ladies of the household, to convey a needed warning to them. For it had been whispered about that more than one, two, or three of Catherine's *filles d'honneur* had been detected assisting, in disguise at "heretic conventicles," as the meetings of the Reformers were contemptuously termed. It had even been asserted that the queen-mother herself was not free from a bias towards Reform, though it was a fact patent to all that the party to which she ever inclined was that which for the time being was in the ascendent, and at that moment the prospects of the Huguenot party had sustained a severe blow.

The Guises mistrusted the queen-mother, but as they preferred her alliance to her opposition, they yielded to her wish to recall Michel de L'Hôpital to France to succeed Olivier in the chancellorship. "This greatest and one of the most upright of the chancellors of France," as described even by the frivolous and libertine Brantôme, was a man of distinguished literary and judicial capacity. He was also an eloquent orator, a great Latinist, the elegance of his Latin verse commanding the admiration of the savants, while his just and patriotic views of government and inflexible honesty of purpose secured the respect of those who with less disinterested aims were his frequent opponents. His manners were courteous, his countenance grave but pleasing, and his general bearing dignified.

De L'Hôpital was at the court of the Duke of Savoy — who had appointed him as chancellor — when recalled to France, having, at the request of the newly married duchess (Margaret de Valois), who sincerely esteemed him and admired his great literary attainments, accompanied her and her husband to Nice. Catherine's great acuteness in discerning character, her ability to appreciate such qualities as she perceived in De L'Hôpital, and her desire to elevate such a man to the position of her guide and counsellor, would seem to speak in her favour. But Catherine de' Medici accepted from personal interest those views which in her chancellor were inspired purely by patriotism. "Strange association!" exclaims a modern historian (H. Martin), "that of a man so conscientious as De L'Hôpital with a woman so utterly destitute of all moral principle as Catherine de' Medici!"

The chancellor aimed at the pacification of the kingdom by less repressive measures against the Protestants, whom he would have ceased to persecute, and with certain limitations have conceded to them freedom of religious worship. These were the views of the party called "*Les Politiques*," consisting of moderate Catholics, including amongst them many persons of influence and distinction. Catherine also concurred in them so long as she felt persuaded that by peace alone could she reign. But when she was made to believe that the zealots of Catholicism would sacrifice her to their hatred of the Calvinists if the latter were allowed to remain unmolested without further attempt to extirpate them, then the opposing counsels of the chancellor seemed to her fraught with both danger and suspicion.

Throughout the kingdom great agitation prevailed, for the Guises proposed to follow up the defeat of the Amboise conspiracy by establishing the Inquisition in France. To their surprise, the new chancellor firmly opposed it. They knew not his character, and had expected to find in him an intelligent but docile agent to assist in the realisation of their plans. He, however, pointed out to them that the result of such a step would be a rising of both Catholics and Protestants against them, and that, as had happened in Naples and Rome, it would be difficult, if not impossible, to pacify the opponents of this measure, to whatever party or faction they belonged. Pens and pamphlets again made war on the duke and the cardinal, the fears of the latter waxing stronger as the menacing language of their foes increased in violence. This led to a royal decree—the Edict of Romorantin—a modification of the first proposal, which henceforth gave the bishops the exclusive right of taking cognisance of the crime of heresy. The Parliament murmured against such a concession to the clergy, and refused to register the edict. Forthwith a royal mandate enforced it.

Working on the fears of the young king, the cardinal obtained from him a further decree, commanding that "all houses in which heretical conventicles at any time had been held, be razed to the ground and the site never again be built on, and that all persons who had been present at those heretical assemblies be irremissibly put to death."

The sanguinary deeds which François II. had witnessed at Amboise, and the terror he had experienced of the murderous intentions—as he was taught to believe—of his rebellious and heretical subjects, had acted with most unfavourable effect on his fragile frame. Since his return to Saint-Germain, his thoughts had dwelt long and frequently on those things, and again in some mysterious way it had been whispered to him that it was not he who was the object of the people's hatred, but the Guises who were the cause of all the dissensions and troubles of the kingdom. But the poor youth was too fast bound in their coils to be released by any weak efforts of his own. He was surely, if slowly, approaching his end; his quartan fever had returned; the symptoms of his mysterious disease appeared in the blotches on his face and an abscess in his ear. Yet at times the improvement in his condition was so hopeful that his eventual recovery was deemed by his physicians probable.

In the time of François I., and to a great extent during Henri's reign, Catherine de' Medici had been accustomed to accompany those monarchs, their mistresses and their court from château to château — François I., especially, seeking in the excitement of endless changes and journeys a renewal of energy if not of health. This rambling life pleased the daughter-in-law of the " chevalier king," and she seems at that period to have found in the exercise, which these continual "goings and comings," arrivals and departures necessitated, a means of keeping within reasonable limits that tendency to *embonpoint* which later on became excessive.

A removal to Chambord for change of air and scene was now suggested by Catherine and approved by the physicians as likely to benefit the king, and cheer the spirits of the young queen — a little saddened at that moment by news of the death of her mother, Marie de Guise. This event had also its effect on the influence of the queen-regent's two brothers, by depriving them of what little remaining power they had hitherto contrived to retain in Scotland, and completing the ruin of the Catholic cause in that country. The representatives of France were, however, authorised by the duke to treat with Elizabeth and the rebel Scots — the country remaining Protestant and under English influence; its old connection with France being severed, and Mary Stuart its queen but in name.

But whatever the incident that thwarted the plans of one faction, it invariably served to elate the hopes of opposing ones — thus the queen-mother secretly rejoiced, as much as did the Huguenots openly, at the discomfiture of the Guises and the failure of their schemes in Scotland. The duke and cardinal, however, suppressed their resentment, and deferred for awhile taking vengeance on Elizabeth. With a view of regaining the ground they had lately lost and securing popularity, in the event of royal favour failing them on the young king's death, they resolved, as a preliminary to compliance with the wishes of the people for the assembling of the States General, to convoke an assembly of notables for the 20th of August at Fontainebleau.

The court then set out for the Château de Chambord — preceded by the whole of the domestic royal household and some hundreds of workmen to prepare for the court's reception the desolate apartments of that yet far from completed "wonder of the Renaissance," and accompanied by a retinue so numerous that, as the Venetian ambassador remarked — with a little exaggeration, perhaps — " it might have been mistaken for the migration of the whole of the inhabitants of some populous city."

Catherine had always been fond of Chambord. At night, ascending the loftiest of its many pinnacles, surmounted by its gigantic *fleur-de-lys*, she could study the courses of the stars; gleaning from them, as she imagined, that the future would repay her for the neglect and isolation in which her earlier years were passed. By day, accompanying the royal hunt, she would pursue the stag through the intricacies of the extensive forests that for a distance of several miles surrounded the château. Though she was short and her figure the reverse of slim, she was a skilful and daring if not a graceful horsewoman. If we may believe Brantôme, it was she who first attempted to introduce the side-saddle. But it was not so much for the greater ease and convenience she found in it when riding that she invented the mode of putting one leg on the pommel of her saddle, as for the display of the "fine *tournure* of her ankles, with their perfect-fitting silk stockings, which," he says, "she delighted in wearing."

With the same object Catherine had been fond of joining in the dance. Not the formal passing and repassing, bowing and curtseying, which preceded the more regular and stately Menuet de la Cour, and for which her *embonpoint* unfitted her to take part in with becoming dignity; but the more airy mazes of the dance introduced by the Italians, then so numerous in France, and cordially welcomed at the court festivities as a new and inspiriting pleasure. Though Queen of France, Catherine de' Medici was then a mere cipher in her own court. Her personal attractions were few, as generally supposed. But whether she really "surpassed all the ladies of the court," Diane of course included, "in the fairness of her complexion," or that "her complexion was of a dark olive tint;" whether "her features were of the 'finely chiselled' Italian type,'" or of "that grosser one distinctive of the Medici, whose short list of virtues and long one of vices she, as the last of the elder branch of that famous family, fully inherited;" whether she was "tall and dignified and her figure elegant," or "short, stout," and while still in her prime unwieldy and with no dignity at all, — "a dumpy woman," in fact, such as Byron "hated," — who shall now declare? For in this varied fashion she has been described by both the pen of the historian and the pencil of the painter.

Catherine de' Medici.
Photo-etching from painting by Clouet.

From the record of her deeds a better judgment may be formed of her character. The habit of reticence and dissimulation acquired in her girlhood concealed abilities and ambitious aspirations, which, from the time of Henri II.'s death, began to be developed in connection with duplicity, depravity, and crime of deepest dye, rendering her at once the evil genius of France and of her own sons and daughters.

The pastimes of royalty had changed but little, if at all, since François I. in 1545 held his court at Chambord. It was the chevalier king's last visit; he was then but a wreck of his former self; old before his time; the result of a career of frenetic dissipation. Like his grandson, François II. — a feeble youth but yet on the threshold of life — he went with the hope of obtaining perhaps temporary relief from the agonising pains of a fearful disease, and to shake off for awhile the melancholy that oppressed him. But both with the young man and the elderly one the hope proved vain. François I. survived his last visit to Chambord not quite two years; François II. but six months.

There was, however, no relaxation of the customary festivities on the latter occasion. To curtail them would have been like announcing to the king that his doom was sealed. Queen Mary's sorrow, too, proved fleeting as a summer cloud; so the usual round of gaieties went on with so little of variety or novelty that it is surprising the effect was not rather depressing than cheering. The tournament had gone out of favour since Montgomery's encounter with Henri II. proved fatal to that monarch. There remained then little more than the chase, the tennis-court, the dance, and the banquet; in all of which the young king strove to take a part. Perhaps the banquet was the most hurtful to him. For the prodigal expenditure on the royal table during the brief reign of the youthful François II. is said to have exceeded in lavishness that of Henri II. to no less an extent than that monarch's surpassed in extravagance the costly banquets of François I.

Catherine de' Medici had an enormous appetite, and put no restraint on gratifying it. This propensity for indulging in the so-called "pleasures of the table," her sickly son seems to have inherited, and probably it was not the least of the causes of his illness. Indeed the vicious habit of the excessive indulgence of a voracious appetite appears to have been far too general amongst the *grands seigneurs*, and even the *grandes dames* of that day. But the paucity of amusements may, in some measure, have induced both in sovereign and guests the custom of lingering long at the amply provided state banquets, and in doing something more than justice to the many rather coarse delicacies then in vogue at royal and other tables; for no engagements at concert or play, opera or ball, called them from the festive board, whether assembled at an early dinner or a later, but no less substantial, supper.

There was then no society, in fact, beyond that narrow and dissolute yet exclusive circle called the court; and dark, dingy, plague-stricken Paris, with its narrow lanes and crooked passages, its mean houses, its pestiferous Palais de Tournelles, had not yet begun to prepare for more social refinement and generally a more genial state of things. It had many years yet to wait for its Place Royale, its Place Dauphine, and other improvements, especially that of the famous Hôtel de Rambouillet, and the opening of the first *salon* — the *salon bleu* of that hôtel, to the *beau monde* of fashion and intellect — and for the *début* of the first queen of society, its celebrated marquise.

While the court was at Chambord, the queen-mother received from the architects, Philibert Delorme and Jean Bullant, the first designs for the palace of the Tuileries. She proposed to erect this palace for her own residence on ground purchased for a like object by François I. forty years before. But that monarch had so many projects of a similar kind in hand, besides many even more expensive fancies to provide for, that there was little or nothing to spare of the vast sums he lavished on his pleasures for the payment of the artists and their assistants employed on those great works. Several were therefore left unfinished, and the projected Tuileries was not in his reign, or that of his two successors, even begun. The unsettled state of the kingdom, and more particularly the emptiness of the public treasury, delayed for yet some years the laying of the first stone of the edifice. Meanwhile an order was given by Catherine for the demolition of that terrible plague-spot, the old Palais des Tournelles. But the work was so slowly accomplished, that several years elapsed ere the ground was cleared and the pestiferous sewer filled up.

There was another expensive project in whose progress she was much interested, and which the sojourn at Chambord and the temporary suspension of open persecution (though secret intrigue was actively at work amongst all parties) gave Catherine an opportunity of attending to. It was the erection of the splendid monument (which has been called "a lie in marble") to the "adored memory" of a faithless husband by — if not actually faithless — a more than indifferent wife. She strove to persuade Cellini to leave Florence in order to superintend in Paris the erection of the tomb, and to execute some portion of its sculpture. But Cellini, who in his younger and wilder days abhorred the climate of Paris and France generally — thinking that it damped his spirits and dulled his genius — was now more than ever attached to his native Florence. He had sobered down since the time that he fled so abruptly from France; had married a wife; had sons and daughters growing up around him; was in easy circumstances, and much honoured in his own country. He therefore, though professing himself much flattered by the queen-mother's proposals, yet begged to be permitted to decline them. Germain Pilon, then at the height of his fame, and whom Catherine was then employing in the changes she was making in the sculptured decorations of Chenonceaux, was chosen as Cellini's substitute. The group of the Fates is attributed to him, also that of the Graces bearing an urn, destined to contain the hearts of that devoted pair, Henri II. and Catherine de' Medici.

The month of August was well advanced. On the 20th, the "Notables" were to assemble at Fontainebleau to take into consideration the unsatisfactory state of affairs in France. Being a purely deliberative assembly controlled by no fixed rules, the Guises expected to dominate it entirely. But as it was just possible that the Bourbon princes, together with the constable, his sons and nephews, might unite and thus outweigh the influence of duke and cardinal, and dictate instead of being dictated to, they employed their leisure at Chambord in corrupting the trusted agents of King Antoine. Through them false intelligence was conveyed to Nérac, and Antoine's fears were once more aroused respecting the safety of his wife's domains. He was very assailable on this point, being fully convinced that Philip would neglect no favourable opportunity of completing the conquest of Navarre. The king and his brother, the Cardinal de Bourbon, therefore determined, most unwisely it was considered, to absent themselves from the assembly of Notables, merely sending thither an agent to act for them in concert with the constable and the admiral. This agent was arrested by order of the Guises, and of course confessed all he knew, or thought he knew, of the aims and intentions of the Bourbons and especially of the Prince de Condé. The prince was then in the South endeavouring to incite the Protestants of Dauphiny and Provence to further action, with the view of making a bold attack on Lyons.

Greatly annoyed by the conduct of the elder Bourbons in thus giving heed to timid and treacherous counsels and their own vague fears, the constable determined to convince the Guises that their manœuvres had failed to disconcert either him or his family. On the 20th of August, Anne de Montmorency, accompanied by his sons and two nephews, arrived at Fontainebleau, escorted by upwards of eight hundred cavaliers. The king and queen, the queen-mother and the ladies and gentlemen of the court, arrived at the château at nearly the same hour. Several of the principal nobility, very numerously attended, also entered the town in the course of the day, so that Fontainebleau, with its palace, its neighbouring châteaux, and dwellings of humbler pretensions, found it difficult to accommodate this great influx of distinguished visitors.

The Assembly began their deliberations on the following day, and after certain preliminaries had been discussed and settled, adjourned to the 23d, when the young king was to preside. It may be inferred from this that his few weeks' sojourn at Chambord had been at least of some temporary benefit to him. During the second *séance*, Admiral de Coligny arrived from Normandy, of which he was governor, bringing with him a petition to the king from the Reformers of that province. In it, after protesting their "unswerving fidelity to their sovereign, and their condemnation of such enterprises as that of Amboise, they proposed to prove that their doctrine was in strict conformity with the Holy Scriptures and the traditions of the primitive Church. They therefore demanded that liberty of worship with the free exercise of their religion be conceded to them." On handing the document to the young king, Coligny assured him that "in Normandy alone there were not fewer than fifty thousand persons ready to place their signatures to it, if they were permitted to assemble for that purpose."

The Duc de Guise with difficulty commanded his temper while Coligny read this plain-spoken petition, and addressed some favourable comments on it to the king. The assembly, by many signs of approval and murmurs also of disapproval, testified to the difference of feeling with which they had listened to it. Such, however, was the extreme irritation of the duke and cardinal and other members of their family, on finding that it was not unanimously condemned and rejected, that they would have attempted to close the sittings at once had not the king, who seemed to take much interest in the proceedings, requested all present to express their opinions on the subject. Catherine was present, very anxious as to the result of the discussion, but prepared to support the party, whatever its principles, that should prove itself the strongest.

Two prelates, the Archbishop of Vienne and the Bishop of Valence, declaimed in eloquent terms in favour of tolerance. The latter was influenced by views similar to those of the queen-mother. He thought the Reformers would gain the upper hand, and that speedily. Therefore he loudly condemned the dissolute lives of the Catholic clergy, and approved the austerity of the Huguenots, called on the king to summon a National Council in which the doctrines of the Reformers might be freely and fully discussed, concluding his address by a demand for the immediate assembling of the States General.*

* The Bishop of Valence was Jean de Montluc, brother of the famous Captain Blaise de Montluc, distinguished for his bravery as a soldier and his skill as a commander. But his fame was

The admiral supported the bishop's demand, and commented on the maladministration of affairs by the Guises, to which the duke replied in very harsh terms that "All the councils in the world would never prevail on him to abandon the faith of his fathers. And that if fifty thousand Huguenots were ready to sign the petition the admiral was deputed to lay before the king, his majesty could oppose it with more than a million of the true faith."

The cardinal declared that "all points of doctrine had been fully discussed and finally settled by former councils. The reform therefore of some abuses, and inquiry into a few instances of laxity of discipline which had lately occurred, could alone justify the assembling of another National Council; but on these grounds he would not oppose it." He pretended to deplore the little effect the recent "grievous executions" had produced on the heretics, and suggested that until the proposed council had concluded its sittings, the punishment of those persons who had strayed

tarnished by his exceeding cruelty, his laurels being always deeply dipped in blood. The bishop was a wily and clever diplomatist, often employed by the queen-mother. He was secretly married, and, had the Huguenot cause triumphed, as he expected, would have embraced the "reformed religion." But it did not, and the excellent bishop had no fancy for becoming a martyr. He therefore turned his back on Calvinism, and that so completely that in 1572 he was one of the most eloquent apologists of the St. Bartholomew massacre. He ended his career a worthy member of the Society of Jesus.

from the faith — but had not taken part in acts of sedition — should be suspended. Some of the clergy were not inclined to favour the cardinal's proposal.

However, after further discussion, the Guises yielded to the demand of Catholics and Protestants for the convocation of the States General. They were to assemble at Meaux on the 10th of December to discuss the long list of grievances which each of the three estates of the realm then proposed to bring forward. The National Council was convened for the 20th of January — their sittings to take place in Paris, where the impossible task was to be attempted of bringing the "new opinions" into some conformity with the doctrines of the Church of Rome, that Catholics and Protestants might refrain from murdering each other "for the glory of God," and dwell together in peace.

"Those Huguenots who would quietly wait the result of the council's deliberations would not in the interval be interfered with." Such was the promise given by both duke and cardinal; but with no intention of keeping it. It was merely a *ruse* to throw their enemies off their guard. But woe indeed unto those of a more restless spirit, who gave occasion to the myrmidons of the Guises — now more on the alert than ever to entrap them — maliciously to distort incautious words or acts into proofs of seditious intentions, whereon to manufacture false charges against them! The prisons were full of such unwary unfortunates, awaiting in damp, dark cells their miserable doom.*

* See Regnier de La Planche, De Thou, etc. La Planche was a friend and confidant of Maréchal de Montmorency. He was well informed of all that was passing relating to the above events. The Guises and Catherine were desirous of enticing him to court, to extract from him — and they would not have been scrupulous as to the means employed — the secret plans of the Montmorencys and Châtillons. But he seems to have been clever enough to baffle them.

CHAPTER VII.

The Guises and the Protestants Chiefs. — Arrest and Trial of Condé. — Proposed Assassination of King Antoine. — Plot a Failure. — Condé Condemned to Death. — Illness of François II. — His Death, December 5th, 1560. — Queen-mother's Arrangement with Antoine. — Condé Free. — The Chancellor de L'Hôpital.

T is surprising with what real or apparent zest the court resumed its customary diversions, while France was agitated to its centre by the violence of political and religious dissension, and death, in the form of a severe epidemic, was carrying off his now annual tithe of the Parisian population. The most reckless extravagance prevailed in the royal household. To support it the people were bowed down by an intolerable burden of taxation. Steeped in poverty they plotted the overthrow of their tyrants, and, further maddened by the frenzy of religious enthusiasm, both Catholics and Protestants saw in the misery that afflicted the land and the ravages of that fearful scourge, the plague, the hand of an avenging God — the former, on the heretics; the latter, on the idolatrous Church of Rome.

Huguenots and Papists were assembling their forces; waiting but the signal from their respective leaders to fly at each other's throats ; to imbue their hands in each other's blood; to march through the land, burning, devastating, laying waste all before them. Plots and counterplots were the order of the day. But the timidity of the King of Navarre again occasioned the failure of a bold and arduous enterprise prepared by the Prince de Condé against the Guises. The latter, having arrested the prince's agents and seized all the documents and private papers which, after a little pressure in the way of torture had been applied, the agents confessed were in their possession, proceeded to concoct an audacious scheme of their own — a tragic plot indeed — whose aim was the destruction of all their enemies at one fell swoop, leaving duke and cardinal masters of the field — omnipotent, in France at least.

Beyond that country the Duke of Savoy and the Italian princes promised, if aided by French troops and money, which last the French clergy were to supply, to exterminate the Vaudois of the valleys of Piedmont, and effectually, once for all, to destroy that hotbed of heresy, Geneva. Pope Paul IV. had consented to reassemble the Council of Trent, which would interdict the convening of the promised National Council, as well as the discussion of any religious question at the forthcoming meeting of the States General. The "Catholic King," the "Demon of the South," must of course have his share in this good work. He proposed to invade Navarre, and to put down any attempt of the heretical subjects of the House of Albret to rise in arms and avenge the assassination of the Bourbon princes.

Catherine de' Medici, as yet, knew not of this murderous scheme. By the advice of her chancellor she held aloof from both parties, and assumed an independent part in view of the increase of power she expected shortly to fall into her hands. Her attitude thus flattered alike the hopes of Huguenots and Catholics, while in the end it disappointed both. The Guises greatly distrusted her; but as the young queen, their niece, was no less *rusée* than the cardinal himself, who had had some part in forming her character, she was entrusted by the brothers to play the spy on the queen-mother. This was by no means an easy task, for Catherine's impenetrability was often the theme and the despair of diplomatists. She was therefore not likely to be thrown off her guard by the wiles of her young daughter-in-law, however well instructed in her part by her uncles, and the less so as Mary Stuart was greatly disliked by the queen-mother.

This feeling was shared by the ladies of the household. It may have been only feigned, as it was their interest to propitiate the queen whose influence was likely the longest to endure, and the days of Queen Mary's authority were already numbered. This they doubtless knew, for those very modest ladies began to accuse her of rarely following their example of wearing a mask. "She highly esteemed her own beauty," they said, "and never failed to avail herself of every opportunity of displaying it. Even in the religious processions she would appear with an uncovered face; her palm in her hand, and under an affected air of modesty triumphing in secret joy in eclipsing in magnificence every other *toilette*, and outshining all beauty by the radiance of her own."

The courtiers, however, the younger men especially, were less severe in their judgment of Queen Mary. They named her "Queen of the *beaux esprits*," admired her singing with the twittering accompaniment of the lute, the facility with which she wrote pleasing verses, and the piquancy of the remarks — slightly satirical — she would sometimes indulge in on the rival court of the queen-mother and her maids. At a time "when all the women," as a French writer says,* "ate with the appetite of the heroes of the 'Iliad,'" and of dishes requiring the digestion of an ostrich, Mary's table, in contrast with the queen-mother's substantial repasts, was served with extremest delicacy. The napkins were perfumed with *sachets* of flowers; the beaks and claws of game and poultry silvered or gilded; pastry, fruits, jellies, and creams arranged in fanciful or artistic forms. No sturgeons, bitterns, and peacocks, or steaming,

* Dargaud, "*Vie de Marie Stuart.*"

smoking joints, and similar horrors, requiring the fumes of scented pastilles and a liberal supply of perfumed waters to save the queen and her ladies from fainting. Nothing but *fricassées, fricandeaux, ragoûts des vols-au-vent*, and similar delicacies; all exquisitely flavoured according to recipes known only to the *chef* of the royal kitchen. The more expensive their preparation, and the greater the difficulty in procuring the ingredients, the better they were relished.

Mary ate but sparingly of these luxuries, and always to the murmur of soft music. She took but little wine, we are told, and that only of the most rare and exquisite kind and highest quality.*
To eat or drink at all, it would seem that her appetite needed coaxing and pampering; while the craving one of her royal husband, despite his feeble state of health, must surely have demanded a more substantial *régime*—the delicate kickshaws favoured at Mary's table serving but as a sort of pleasant *entr'acte* to while away the interval between the more solid and serious scenes of his dinner and supper.

The fastidiousness and general extravagance of the queen of "a poor and barbarous nation," as the French were apt to term the Scotch, did not escape the severe comment of the "banker's daughter," as Mary before Henri's death, following the discourteous example of Diane and her

* Dargaud, "*Vie de Marie Stuart.*"

partisans, was wont at times to speak of Catherine. The queen-mother, however, may have expended on the quantity of the viands beneath which her table groaned, as much as her daughter-in-law on the quality of her lighter, appetising repasts. But it is certain that as regards her *toilette* she was no less extravagant than the youthful Queen Mary. Before her widowhood she was fond of arraying her bulky figure in the richest-coloured and gold brocades, velvets, and jewelled fabrics that the looms of France and Italy could produce. Now, in imitation of her late husband's mistress, she had resolved to deplore her loss to the end of her days in flowing robes of superb black velvet, damask, or satin, embroidered in seed-pearls, or ornamented with diamonds. She had not the use of the crown jewels, which were not indeed remarkable for either their number or their value, but in both respects were far exceeded by those that were her own private property.

Queen Mary was especially fond of fancy dress, and for every *fête* was credited with the invention of some startling novelty. Sometimes she would appear in the royal tartan, in which she is said to have looked very charming — *ravissante*, as the courtiers declared. Another time she would appear in the piquant Spanish costume, veiled in the mantilla, and coquettishly fluttering her fan. Again she would charm all hearts draped as a

Grecian lady, or wearing some picturesque Italian costume. She is said to have been one of the first to use a real side-saddle, with improvements suggested by Catherine's idea of laying one leg on the pommel to display her silk stockings and the fine *tournure* of her ankles. Those fine silk stockings came from Spain, whence our Queen Elizabeth, who began about this time to wear them, received, as is very well known, her first pair as a present. Doubtless Mary Stuart was not behind the fashion in that respect, though the fact does not appear to have come down to us. Her shoes have been spoken of as wonderfully artistic productions, also her Spanish gloves richly embroidered, fringed with gold, and adorned with jewelled fastenings.

Alas! Poor Mary! With the period in question, the spring-time of her life, ended, as many have thought and written, all she ever knew of this world's happiness. Perhaps it was so. Yet to be happy would seem impossible for one so young after the deeds of blood she had witnessed, and her knowledge of the cruel persecution going on around her. But from her early training under the watchful superintendence of Catherine de' Medici and that excellent prelate, the Cardinal de Lorraine, no wonder that even from her girlish years she should have shown more hardness than tenderness of feeling, and an utter insensibility to the sufferings and sorrows of others. The Guises no doubt expected to find in her a ready and useful tool for the furtherance of their schemes, and the sustaining of their influence over the king, should he at any time display symptoms of a weariness of control. She had shown herself latterly, it was reported, less docile than they expected, and her espionage on the queen-mother does not appear to have been very vigilant or fruitful in its results.

Meanwhile, the Guises had spared neither time nor pains to secure the success of the heavy and final blow they were about to deal on the doomed heads of their adversaries. Early in September, a royal mandate, issued at the instance of the Guises, had required the attendance of the King of Navarre and the Prince de Condé at Orléans. The king replied that "if his brother's calumniators were not to be also his judges, he would without delay bring the prince to court, attended by so small a retinue that his innocence and good intentions would be at once acknowledged." It was thought advisable to lull rather than excite the fears of the timid King Antoine, consequently "assurances were conveyed to him and the prince on the part of the king, of perfect personal safety, an impartial hearing of the charge against him, and free return."

Condé would have summoned the people to arms — a summons they were well disposed to obey — and with a sufficient force to defend themselves marched boldly into Orléans. He had not, like Antoine, the fear of the "Demon of the South" ever before his eyes. Antoine, however, was much perplexed. Implicit reliance on the king's promise, or rather that of the Guises, was out of the question. Yet being reassured by his brother, the Cardinal de Bourbon, who was the bearer of the promise, that it was made in good faith, and that the feeling of the queen-mother was favourable to them, Antoine determined to set out, and with a very small escort; that, at all events, his own good faith in the matter should be perfectly clear. He had but a vague idea of the course he would take, or the attitude he would assume on arrival, but proposed to discuss the question fully on the journey northward.

Numerous were the letters and messages received *en route*, warning them of the fate awaiting them at Orléans. The Princesse de Condé, who, unlike most of the ladies of the court of that day, adored her husband, implored him to return to Béarn. The absence of one of the brothers, she thought, might be a protection to the other. She knew that against Antoine no pretext could be found for a charge of high treason, but she knew not that the Guises found him a stumbling-block to the realisation of their plans, and had decided to assassinate him. Her mother, the Dame de Roye — a sister of the Châtillons — added her supplications to her daughter's, but without avail. "The chancellor contrived secretly, by the agency of the Duchesse de Montpensier, who stood high in the favour of the queen-mother, but was much attached to the princes and inclined towards the 'new opinions,' to urge the king and the prince to change their route, march south, take up their quarters in some strong city, and call on the ancient allies of France in Germany to aid them against the Guises."

A thousand gentlemen also, well armed and equipped, met them as they entered Vienne, and in the name of the Reformers of the South offered to support them with ten thousand combatants if they would undertake to carry off the person of the king from the Lorrainers. Condé might, perhaps, have consented, but Antoine, while thanking the gentlemen for their offer, forbore to accept it. His scanty *cortège* was reassembled, the journey resumed, and in full reliance on the king's word they marched straight into the arms of their enemies. Their reception probably prepared them for what was to follow. No escort met them outside the town, and, on entering the king's apartment, he received them in that cold and sulky manner that had become almost habitual to him, from the distrust with which he was persuaded to regard all about him except his uncles and protectors, the Guises. But these protectors had so cleverly arranged their plans that the odium of the treatment they proposed to inflict on the Bourbon princes and their friends should fall alone on the young king. They refrained from being present at his interview with them. Having thoroughly taught him his lesson, they cared not to see it put in practice, withdrawing as soon as the princes entered.

Catherine, however, was present, and bade them welcome in a voice faltering with emotion, and eyes moistened by tears which she seemed scarce able to restrain from streaming forth in a torrent. She would have them infer from that crocodile demonstration that, deceived by the Guises, she had unwittingly aided them in their schemes by her assurance that the King of Navarre and his brother had nothing whatever to fear in repairing to Orléans as François requested.

"I have commanded your presence here," said the young monarch, "to hear from your own mouth the truth concerning those enterprises imputed to you against the throne and the kingdom."

Indignantly disclaiming all treasonable acts or intentions, Condé flung back on the Guises the charges brought against himself, at the same time reminding the king that he relied on his promise for his personal safety. For reply, the guards entered the royal apartment — a concerted signal being given — and Condé was arrested and imprisoned in a house that had been fortified and surrounded by cannon expressly for his reception.

The Princesse de Condé was permitted to see the king, the Guises affecting to stand aloof as unconcerned spectators of the progress of their own plot, which they were secretly straining every nerve to bring to a desired issue. But in vain the princess knelt at the feet of the royal youth and implored her husband's release. She was harshly repulsed. "Shall I not be avenged," he cried, "on the man who would have deprived me of my crown and my life!" The princess's mother was arrested, and several other persons suspected of favouring the views of the imprisoned prince.

Both the duke and the cardinal had withheld their signatures from the order for Condé's arrest, drawn up in private council and signed by the king and, with the above exception, all present. De L'Hôpital is said to have felt some hesitation at the time of signing it, but his refusal would have involved the resignation of his post, and prevented him from serving the prince more effectually, as he trusted he might be able to do, either during or after his trial.

The King of Navarre, though not placed under arrest with his brother, was treated with the greatest indignity, lodged in a mean house, deprived of the small escort that had accompanied him from Béarn, surrounded by spies, and no further liberty allowed him than to cross over— guards following—from his own lodging to the royal residence, and similarly guarded to return. His complaints of the harshness of his brother's treatment, and his appeals to the king for its relaxation, were received with much haughtiness or with extreme contempt. This course was adopted with the view of betraying him into retorting by menacing or violent language, or some imprudent act. Then, as arranged by the Guises, the king, roused to anger by his vassal's insolence, was to rise from his seat, and, with his own hand, stab him.*

Should strength or courage fail the feeble youth to do the deed, or should King Antoine, under his many temptations to resent the insults offered him, still contrive to command his temper, he was to be "invited to join the royal hunt at Chambord, and an opportunity being arranged to despatch him by an assassin's hand, his death was to be ascribed to a fatal accident." The cardinal was exceedingly elated at his own ingenuity in contriving so cleverly for the perfect carrying out of the plot without either he or his brother appearing to raise a finger to help it on. Some qualms respecting the success of their plans — though not qualms of conscience — they, however, did begin to experience. They had cast their net in the form of a royal mandate, for a large draught, but the fish they wanted were not all disposed to be drawn into it. More than one

* Regnier de La Planche.

summons reached the constable. But the arrogant Anne de Montmorency, little accustomed to obey, did not scruple to reply that "he could not then leave Chantilly," and again, "he was not well enough to take the journey to Orléans." His eldest son, the marshal, had left for Languedoc, of which province he was governor, and ruled there so royally that he was called its king, tolerating and protecting the Huguenots, though a Catholic himself, but of the moderate or the "Politique" party. The affairs of his province of course occupied him, and the second son could not do less than remain in filial attendance on his father.

Conjointly with them, the Châtillons were included in the fictitious charge of being associated with the Bourbons in plotting against the State; but the admiral alone obeyed the summons to present himself at Orléans. He knew that the King of Navarre and Prince Louis de Condé were destined by the Guises to die as traitors and heretics, and that on the same scaffold his own head was to fall. His farewell to his wife was, therefore, as both believed, a final one. He implored her to adhere with constancy to the true religion, and to suffer death rather than allow her then unborn child to be sullied at its baptism by any of the superstitions of the Papacy. Coligny's two brothers, however, were not so ready as he to lay their heads on the block for the gratification of Monsieur le Duc and his eminence, the cardinal. Odet de Châtillon retired to his episcopate, and D'Andelot at about that time made a rather romantic marriage, so might well excuse himself on the ground that "he had married a wife, and therefore could not come."

To the absentees of the family, Coligny owed his life. Such powerful relatives being yet uncaught, the Guises did not venture even closely to imprison him, but allowed him provisionally the same sort of liberty as was permitted to the King of Navarre. Meanwhile, they were hurrying on the condemnation of the Prince de Condé; and, at the same time, fearing to lose their prey, were preparing for the assassination of his brother, to whom a royal hunt was announced to take place on the 16th of November, at which he was expected to assist. But on the evening of the 15th King François, while attending Vespers, fell into a fainting fit. On reviving, he complained of intense pain from the abscess in the left ear, and passed the night in a feverish condition.

The Guises were in the greatest anxiety respecting the progress of Condé's so-called trial. Many of the usual formalities were omitted, and a novel kind of tribunal was hastily got together, consisting of the Knights of the Order of Saint Michel, two or three members of the king's private council, and the same number of peers of France. To this irregularly constituted assembly the various documents relating to his accusation, and the proofs confirmatory of the charges of high treason brought against him, were submitted, and, without further delay, sentence of death was pronounced, one only of his judges, the Vicomte de Sancerre, refusing absolutely to sign it. Nevertheless, they fixed the day for the prince's execution, the 10th of December, and a priest was sent to him, from whom of course he refused to hear what he termed the "impieties of the Roman antichrist." Further to try whether the natural clinging to life might not operate in bringing about a recantation and his submission to the Guises, one of their gentlemen was sent to ask "if there were no possible means of effecting a reconciliation between him and his cousins of Guise." He replied that "the only way he knew of agreeing with them was at the point of the sword."

Though sentence of death had been pronounced on Condé, the warrant for its execution had not yet received the necessary signature of the chancellor. He withheld it from day to day, protesting that "sufficient time had not been given to the examination of the charges brought against the prince. The tribunal commissioned to pass sentence on him had decided too hastily, and should be required to reconsider the matter." The Guises vainly sought to overcome the chancellor's objections. His object was delay. The famous surgeon, Ambroise Paré, was in attendance on the king, and kept De L'Hôpital daily informed of his condition, which, though fluctuating, gave no sure promise of improvement. He had now taken to his bed, and it was the opinion of Paré and the physicians that he could not survive many days longer.

The Guises are said to have been in a state of extremest agitation. Just as Fortune seemed to have raised them to the very pinnacle of their ambition, and to have brought all their schemes and plans to a nearly successful issue, cruel Fate had chosen that supreme moment to utterly overthrow them. Desperately they now sought the queen-mother, who was so soon to take the place they had usurped in the government. Earnestly they implored her — of course for her own and the nation's welfare — to consent to the immediate execution of both the King of Navarre and his brother. The chancellor firmly opposed it. He knew that she would not be deterred from consenting because of the criminality of the act, but he pointed out clearly to her that to consent to it would be greatly to her disadvantage.

But the Cardinal de Lorraine placed before her the flattering prospect — the Bourbons being destroyed — of wielding the sceptre of France as queen-regent with undisputed and absolute sway, he and the duke being the most devoted of her humble servants. "Catherine for a moment stood irresolute between her good and her evil genius," but the advice of the former prevailed. She thoroughly understood the character of both cardinal and chancellor, and was, besides, fully aware that, in ruling the kingdom, she had nothing to fear from the vain, weak, and indolent King of Navarre.

Instead, then, of being despatched to his doom in the forest of Chambord, or laying his head on the block at Orléans, Antoine was summoned to the dying young monarch's bedside, and thence to an interview with the queen-mother in her cabinet. She first reproached him, it appears, severely, for troubling the peace of the kingdom by joining in Condé's treasonable enterprises, then required of him the renunciation, in writing, of his claim, as first prince of the blood, to the regency, even should it be conferred on him by the States General; also a promise of reconciliation with his "cousins of Guise." On these conditions she would consent to his holding the first place, after her, in the government, would appoint him lieutenant-general of the kingdom, and, greatest boon of all, would spare his brother's life. The king had been secretly informed that, if he declined Catherine's proposals, his own doom as well as his brother's was sealed, so that she did not entirely reject the cardinal's advice, or strictly follow the chancellor's, but used both for her own advantage. The timid Antoine promised all that was exacted of him, and embraced, perhaps not very cordially, "his cousins of Guise," who on the previous day were plotting to cut his throat.*

The English ambassador, Sir Nicholas Throckmorton, writing to Queen Elizabeth on the 28th of November, says he "had stayed his despatch of the 23d because of the king's sickness, that begins now so to succeed that men doubt of his being long lasting." On the 29th, he writes again: "The constitution of the king's body is such as the physicians do say he cannot be long-lived; and thereunto he hath by his too timely and inordinate exercise now in his youth added an evil accident. Some say that if he recover this sickness, he cannot live but two years. Therefore, there is talk of the French queen's second marriage. Some say the Prince of Spain (Don Carlos); some, the Duke of Austria (Don John); others, the Earl of Arran."

November 30th: "Great lamentation at court, the king's recovery being mistrusted." "I think it not well," Sir Nicholas adds, "to let the Scots know of his danger." December 1st he writes again: "Physicians hopeful of the king. Amended, but so weak that he could not keep the feast of the Golden Fleece on St. Andrew's Day." December 3d: "King's illness supposed to be a device of the Guises, that he may hear no prisoner's supplication." This refers to the

* Henri Martin, "*Histoire de France.*"

Prince de Condé, who, however, did not supplicate, but proudly claimed his privilege as a prince of the blood to be judged only by "the king and princes, sitting in the Court of the Parliament in Paris, the Chambers also assembled." The king, whose decrees in private council were absolute, rejected his claim. Two days after, he died.

On the 6th, Throckmorton announces the event as follows: "December 5th, king died. Indisposition continued from 17th of November, growing, in the end, to a fever, together with a catarrh, or rather imposthume in the head, which purged a little by one of his ears. This brought him to a state of extreme weakness, and so spent him that at eleven of the clock in the night of the 5th he departed to God, leaving as heavy and doleful a wife, as of right she had good cause to be, who of long watching with him during his sickness, and painful diligence about him, and specially by the issue thereof, is not in best tune of her body, but without danger. The queen (Elizabeth) has good cause to thank God for so well providing for her surety and quietness by taking away the late king and his father (redoubted of all the world) considering their intentions towards her." *

Though François II. was always ailing, his death seems to have come as a surprise on the people; not an unwelcome one certainly, especially

* "Foreign State Papers" — Reign of Elizabeth, 1560.

to the Huguenots, who hoped that the influence of the chancellor would now supersede that of the Guises. But all the unpopular, arbitrary and cruel acts of the short reign of the feeble youth, who, at his death, had not by some months completed his seventeenth year, were attributed by "his uncles" solely to him, they rejecting all responsibility concerning them.

On the morning of the 6th Condé was informed of the king's death, and at the same time a messenger from the queen-mother announced that "Monsieur le Prince was free." But the prince refused to receive pardon, and to owe his life to "favour or an act of grace," without knowing who was his enemy, and by whose order he had been imprisoned. "It was the act and will of the late king." No other explanation could he obtain; but he was advised to leave Orléans, and remain in some part of his brother's domains until he received that regular and official justification of what had occurred, which his honour, it was pressed on him, exacted. This was a *ruse* of his enemies, to whom his presence in Orléans — where, instead of at Meaux, the States General were to assemble — was inconvenient. Condé departed, thus playing unconsciously into the hands of the Guises.

The constable had been kept duly informed of the state of the king's health, and a few days before his death found that he was himself well enough to leave Chantilly for Orléans. With a numerous *cortège*, he entered that city, placing his own guards at its gates, and dismissing those posted there by the Duc de Guise, who had assumed the military authority in Orléans, which, as Constable of France, belonged of right to Montmorency, who now asserted it and displaced his adversary. The Guises, however, had determined not to abandon the field to their enemies, or to relinquish an iota of the power they had usurped without a resolute effort to retain it.

The duty, therefore, which devolved on the duke, as Grand-Master of the Household, of remaining by the body of the late king and accompanying it to Saint-Denis, he failed to perform. When the poor youth ceased to live, he was of no further use or interest to his "uncles," or apparently to any one else — the princes, his "cousins of the blood," or even to his mother. She, indeed, was suspected of having released him from the prospect of protracted suffering by quietly hastening his departure from this world of sin and sorrow. No one could or would openly accuse her, and it may have been merely suspicion. Such deeds were of every-day occurrence; but it was perfectly well known that Catherine de' Medici, in her thirst for power, would flinch from no crime that enabled her to secure and retain it.

François II. was buried without any of the pomp and ceremonial customary at royal funerals;

and so hastily, also, that the almost humble *cortège* — consisting of two chamberlains, one bishop (the Bishop of Genlis, who was blind), and a score or so of the Scotch guards — reached Saint-Denis as Montmorency entered Orléans, the constable's numerous and imposing retinue passing on the road the young king's funeral carriage and its scanty following.

CHAPTER VIII.

Accession of Charles IX. — Catherine His Guardian, with the Power of Regent. — King of Navarre Lieutenant-General. — Cardinal de Lorraine Leaves for Rheims. — States General Abolish Many Abuses. — The Parliament Oppose the Reforms. — Extinction of Debts of the Crown. — States General Adjourn. — Condé's Innocence Publicly Proclaimed.

"O an imaginary majority — as contemporary writers have observed — succeeded a real minority." Charles IX. had not completed his eleventh year at the time of his accession, having been born on the 27th of June, 1550. But so great had long been the general prepossession in his favour that at Henri's death all eyes turned towards him; and had it been possible to set aside the elder brother, François, the promising boy of nine would even then have been greatly preferred to the languid youth of fifteen. The death of François II. was a welcome event to the nation, putting an end, it was hoped, to the tyrannical rule of the Guises; while the accession of Charles was greeted with pleasure as the promise to France of a great king. All who had had an opportunity of seeing much of the youthful prince, and forming an opinion of his character at that early age, seem to have been agreed in this expectation.

Giovanni Michiel, writing to the Venetian Senate, says: "The young king is tall for his age, and slight of figure; he has a pleasing countenance, with very fine eyes, like his father's. His movements and manners are easy and graceful, and he is as amiable as any child of his age can be." Another writer says: "He is of an irritable temperament, easily agitated, lively enough, but of ardent disposition and fiery imagination — capable, indeed, of much that is good, as he grows up and his fine qualities develop themselves; but also capable of much evil, according to the education he receives, and the examples set before him." "He is not robust," continues Michiel. "He eats and drinks very little, and it will be necessary to be watchful over him, and restrain the inclination he already exhibits for violent bodily exercise. He is fond of tennis, and of riding and fencing, which doubtless are suitable exercises for a prince; but at present they are beyond his strength, and when he is fatigued long repose is needed, for he enters with so much ardour into every active pursuit that the fragile frame seems to quiver under the spirit's deep emotions, and his respiration becomes difficult.

"He now takes little interest in study, but resigns himself to it to give pleasure to his mother. Being, however, but an unwilling stu-

Charles IX.
Photo-etching from painting by T. Wageman.

dent, his progress in learning is not great. War is of all subjects the one most interesting to him. The military, therefore, stand especially high in his good graces. When he was but Duc d' Orléans, and the State of Milan was spoken of as his appanage (perhaps to flatter and amuse him), he would listen with the greatest delight, and require the military men about him to promise that they would follow him to his duchy in the next expedition. But since his accession to the throne, one of his ministers, when introducing a Milanais gentleman, who came to take leave of him on his departure for the duchy, privately told the youthful monarch that it was advisable to receive this gentleman very graciously, he being a person of considerable influence in Milan. With great animation, Charles instantly replied: 'I know that well. But, as I am now a king, you should understand that I ought not publicly to speak of such matters.'

"His natural inclination for warlike themes is fostered and confirmed by his governor, M. de Sipièrre, who talks with him of nothing but battles, conquests, and the organisation of armies, as matters alone worthy the attention of a king. So that, if inclination did not impel him that way, education would train him." A device was chosen by the chancellor for this royal youth on whom such flattering hopes were built. It consisted of two pillars with the motto, "*Justice et miséricorde.*"

The States General convoked by the late king — ostensibly for inquiring into the administration of the affairs of France, and the suggestion of measures for their more satisfactory conduct in future — assembled at Orléans on the 13th of December. The death of François II. had greatly changed the face of things, and the Assembly was otherwise constituted than the Guises had intended, including amongst the deputies of the *noblesse* and the *tiers état* many "malcontents," as well as known and suspected heretics. These, the Guises, expecting to dominate the Assembly, had proposed not only to exclude as unduly elected should they refuse to sign a confession of the Catholic faith, but to send to the stake at once, without any pretence of a trial; thus, with little trouble, getting rid of a large batch of their enemies at one blow. This test of fitness to deliberate on affairs of state they still made an effort to enforce, but from the indignation it aroused were unable to do so.

The first session was in consequence opened rather clamorously. The young king was present, also the queen-mother, and the King and Queen of Navarre. The first business of the Assembly was the nomination of a regent; the next, to provide for the payment of the debts of the two preceding reigns, amounting to upwards of forty-three millions — "intrinsic value, 160,000,000 *francs*, according to the exchange rate of the *marc d'argent* of that day" (H. Martin) — and to release their youthful successor from poverty and the misery of an empty exchequer. The Chancellor de L'Hôpital opened the proceedings with an address to the three estates. His discourse was "characterised by noble sentiments, great simplicity, dignity, and eloquence." He spoke in strong terms of deprecation against religious persecution, and exhorted the Assembly to refrain from changing the name of Christians for mere party names and offensive epithets, such as Huguenots, Lutherans, and Papists. He concluded his address by asking "sympathy for the young king left in so miserable a position financially, with the accumulated debts of his father and brother to discharge, to an amount that probably had never before been laid on any orphan. He trusted that the three estates would assist the king in paying those debts, and promised that the expenses of the state should in future be reduced as much as possible."

The organisation of the government, as adopted after the death of François II., namely, that of the regency of the queen-mother, was approved by the clergy. The *noblesse* and *tiers état* preferred that of the King of Navarre, but Antoine put forward no claim, though urged by many of the nobility, and expressly enjoined by Calvin to demand his rights as prince of the blood, "the interests of the nation being endangered under the rule of a foreign woman." But Antoine kept his promise to Catherine, less, it was said, from any scruple of breaking it, than from his love of indolence. Prince Louis might have stimulated him to take a different course, but he had been cleverly induced to retire to his brother's domains in Picardy, "to await the explanations his honour demanded respecting his recent imprisonment."

The regency was, in fact, not given to any one, so much had faction, at that disastrous period, weakened the political order of the kingdom, but the personal guardianship of the king was conferred on Catherine in her maternal capacity. Having, however, fully satisfied herself that this power could not be taken from her, she feigned to have received it from the young king himself, with the approval of the three estates, on consenting to share the administration of affairs with Antoine de Bourbon, who was accordingly named lieutenant-general of the kingdom. A State Council, composed of ten of the principal nobility, was also appointed by the three estates to assist the queen-mother and her lieutenant-general by their advice in the transaction of public business. Catherine, in order to excuse herself to Philip II. for allowing the heretic King of Navarre to share the government of the kingdom with her, made it appear that she acted under restraint. But that she might be fully armed against any insidious attempt to seduce her from the true faith, she prayed her amiable son-in-law to send her a Spanish confessor.

The Duc de Guise retained his post of Grand-Master of the Household. The Cardinal de Lorraine retired to Rheims, his niece, Mary Stuart, it is supposed, accompanying him. He had expected to be the spokesman of the three estates, but the clergy alone accepted him as their orator, the two others rejecting him because of the charges they proposed to bring against him of immorality and of extensive depredations on the public purse during the time he held the office of controller of the finances. Greatly offended, he thought it dignified, as well as prudent, to withdraw from the court for awhile.

Catherine being now the first person in the realm, as well in authority as dignity, attempted to reëstablish the royal power without the aid of either Bourbons or Guises. She did not wish that her son should really be king, but that by destroying the chiefs of both parties by means of each other, she might govern alone without opposition or contradiction. In this, in a great measure, she succeeded, displaying much skill in managing affairs of state (the hereditary merit of her family). She made the appointments to offices of state and the principal benefices, dispensed favours, granted pardons, and kept possession of the great seal used by the sovereign. She spoke the last word in the Council of State, in order to give a *résumé* of the opinions of others, on which she replied, either in conformity with the deliberations of the Council or her own views and opinions. The lieutenant-general was a mere cipher on these occasions — "changeable and simple enough" (says Suriano),* "and affecting a great knowledge of affairs, but understanding them little."

She held the young king entirely under her sway, scarcely ever allowing him for an hour to be absent from her, and permitting none but herself to sleep in his chamber. Very early did this machiavellian princess begin her son's education of corruption. The violent religious and political factions which then agitated the country made it easy for her to persuade him that all about him were enemies against whom he must ever be on his guard, and that in her alone could he find fidelity. She made him an adept in dissimulation, though nature, as we may glean from contemporary witness, had endowed Charles IX. with all the qualities and even the failings most opposed to that vice. And so securely did she fix her yoke upon him from his early boyhood that, although in after years he often in his transports of rage shuddered under its galling influence, never was he able to free himself from it.

The form of government being settled, Catherine contrived to prevent the public announce-

* "Reports of Venetian Ambassadors."

ment of the King of Navarre's official appointment as lieutenant-general of the kingdom, that it might be inferred that everything, as well in the government as in the education of the princes, proceeded on her sole authority. But the attention of the nation was then wholly given to the discussions of the States General, who propounded many wise regulations for the well-being of the people, for the prosperity of commerce, for the improvement of the city of Paris and other large towns. Many reforms, both ecclesiastical and judicial, were proposed, and tolerance of the "new opinions" and freedom of religious worship also met with a favourable reception and hearing, except from the clergy.

On the 28th of July a royal mandate required the Parliament of Paris to suspend all proceedings having reference to religion, even against persons who with arms in their possession had been present at the religious assemblies, and to set at liberty all who for such causes were then imprisoned. This was followed on the 31st by the famous "Ordinance of Orléans," which in the king's name promulgated the greater part of the numerous reforms (in some instances slightly modified) demanded by the representatives of the *tiers état*. The adoption of many of these reforms was due to De L'Hôpital's earnest advocacy of them — especially those which abolished the sale of judicial offices, and forbade the judges to receive pensions, presents, or bribes in any form from accused persons whose guilt or innocence they were called upon to adjudge. The majority of the Parliament strongly resented these acts of the reforming chancellor, as they deprived the magistrates of a large part of their gains. Remonstrances on their part proving ineffectual, they revenged themselves by protesting against the public recognition of two religions in the same state, and refusing to register the decree of the 28th of January, unless a further royal decree were issued, banishing those heretics who, on being released, would not promise to live henceforth as good Catholics.

This was to render the amnesty a mere dead letter, as none of the Reformers would make the required promise. Nevertheless, the demand of the Parliament was privately complied with. Even the "Grand Ordinance," as it was termed, if not utterly rejected, seems to have remained entirely inoperative. Yet, with the exception of putting an end to the bribery and venality which had long disgraced the Parliamentary assembly, the chief reforms it enacted had often for years past been declared by the Parliament itself most urgently needed. The main cause of this opposition was, however, attributable less to disapproval of the edicts themselves than to jealousy of the States General from whom they emanated. The periodical assembling of the three estates was then very generally demanded, which the aristocratic magistracy considered threatening to the importance of the Court of the Parliament of Paris.

The two questions which to the queen-mother were of greatest interest and importance (for to gain her ends she was on all sides lavishing promises in default of money) were the replenishment of the empty exchequer and the payment of the debts of the state. They were not yet disposed of, the deputies being of opinion that the powers confided to them were not ample enough to allow them to consent to the immense sacrifices required of them by the crown. They desired, therefore, to return to their several provinces to lay before their constituents the reported condition of the state's finances, and to invite discussion upon it. An adjournment in consequence, for some months, took place on the 31st of January.

The attitude assumed by the Parliament with reference to the decree of amnesty greatly exasperated the Huguenots, and in several of the provinces the chiefs of the party had with difficulty restrained their followers from interrupting the services of the Catholic Church, even as they at their prayer-meetings had been interrupted and also ill-treated by the Papists. Conflicts had taken place in which blood had been shed; assassinations were frequent; discord was said to reign at court hand in hand with depravity. A rupture was also anticipated between the queen-mother and the lieutenant-general, when Prince Louis de

Condé should reappear to stimulate the differences known to exist in the royal circle, and to incite the Reformers to more energetic action. In full assembly the little king had declared the prince's innocence of the acts of high treason imputed to him by the Guises, authority being also given him to demand another and more ample declaration thereof in the Court of Parliament. He could not, therefore, be longer excluded from his seat in the king's private council-chamber; consequently the next meeting face to face of the intended victim and his would-be murderer was looked forward to by both factions with singular agitation and mingled hopes and fears.

The poltroon cardinal, who on his knees had implored the queen-mother to consent to the prince's execution "while yet there was time"— in other words, ere the grim tyrant Death, whose uplifted arm was about to descend on the head of her own son, had given the final blow— had fled the Court. At his Palace of Rheims, while his enormous peculations and his grossly immoral life were being exposed before the States General at Orléans, he was passing his days in the pious duties of his archiepiscopacy; reproving the backslidings of thoughtless young *abbés;* inflicting penances; exhorting the lukewarm to cultivate a more ardent zeal in the interests of Mother Church, and generally exhibiting an edifying example of the blessedness of serenity of conscience under slanderous accusations and unmerited persecution. Whether the exemplary prelate added to those duties the further one of affording at Rheims a retreat to his niece, the young queen-dowager, during the period of her mourning and retirement from the court, as some writers relate, seems doubtful.

CHAPTER IX.

Catherine's Crooked Policy. — Her "Flying Squadron." — Mary Stuart's Mourning. — Sir Nicholas Throckmorton's Letters. — Mary in Lorraine. — Her Brother, the Bishop, and Other Advisers. — Her Departure. — Charles's Deep Impressions. — Damville, Brantôme and Others Accompany Her. — Arrival in Scotland. — The Nobles Sympathise.

ART of Catherine de' Medici's wily policy for the attainment of her objects was the culpably seductive influence she brought to bear on some of the chief men of the day. It mattered little whether they were associated with her or not in the government, if likely by their popularity or position to thwart her views or to further them; or if they might be turned to account, could she ensure their support, discover their secrets, disarm or render null their resentment, as it chanced at the moment to fall in with her schemes. This she accomplished by means of the fascinations of a troop of young girls, especially trained by her for the services she required of them, in disregard of all moral principles and feminine modesty. Their number eventually reached three hundred, their courtesy title being "maids of honour," their familiar sobriquet the

"queen-mother's flying squadron," as they accompanied her (in detachments probably) on her frequent journeys, and in her endless changes of residence.

They were not, however, at the period in question, nearly so numerous a force. Great beauty of face and form, graceful manners, and an air of modesty to mask unblushing vice, good birth, much intelligence, and no troublesome scruples to lie in the way of accomplishing their gracious mistress's behests, were the necessary qualifications for the effectual discharge of their duties. To find them united in the person of one fair form was naturally very rare, so that the formation of the queen-mother's wonderful phalanx of dissolute youth and beauty necessarily demanded time, close observation, and all that keen discernment of character attributed to Catherine de' Medici, in order to discover not merely the requisite personal attractions, but with them the ductility of mind that most readily would yield to the impress of corruption.

It appears that Catherine had made some timid attempts of the kind in the lifetime of Henri II., with the view of detaching him from his allegiance to the ever fair Diane. But her success was not great, the elderly court beauty reigning supreme to the end.

When, however, the youthful and brilliant Mary Stuart became Queen of France and received the homage of the court, the courtiers, young and old — to the great scandal of the ladies — ready to fall at her feet in adoration, Catherine perceived that in this young Scotch beauty a more formidable rival than Diane had arisen. She had hastened, on Henri's death, to possess herself of the Great Seal; but the sceptre she had thought to add to it, because of the feebleness of the monarch, was grasped by the Guises, who protected their niece from insidious attempts of the queen-mother to weaken her influence with the young king. Until François died, Catherine possessed but the mere shadow of authority. But she availed herself of that shadowy power to intrigue in all directions, to flatter the Huguenots with hopes of better things, and the Catholic "malcontents" with full redress of their grievances, when she and Charles should reign.

Meanwhile, she was planning the increase of her squadron; secretly, also, seeking to undermine the favour with which many of the nobility — ladies not excepted — who were previously somewhat prejudiced against the Queen of Scots, had begun to regard her, from her affectionate and constant attendance on the young king in his illness. Catherine is said to have "mortally hated" Mary Stuart, who, doubtless, had treated her with unbecoming superciliousness. She had resolved that she should leave France, and having demanded the royal jewels, which were sent immediately by

Queen Mary to Charles IX.—who gave them into the custody of his mother—Catherine at once made it unmistakably apparent to the young widow that she had little consideration or kindness to expect from her. But that Mary did not accompany her uncle the cardinal, when, a week after the death of François, the hostile attitude of the States General induced him to repair to Rheims, is evident from the reports of Sir Nicholas Throckmorton for the information of Elizabeth and her ministers.*

"On the death of the king," he writes, "she immediately changed her lodgings" (apartment in the Louvre), "withdrew from all company, and became so solitary and exempt of worldliness, that she saw no daylight for forty days. For fifteen days she admitted to come into her chamber none save the king, his brethren, the King of Navarre, the constable, and her uncles, and four or five days after some bishops and ancient knights of the Order; but none of the younger, saving Martignes, who, having done her good service and married her chief gentlewoman, had so much favour showed him."

"The ambassadors, lastly, were admitted as they came, and all have been with her to condole, saving I, which I have forborne to do, knowing not the queen's pleasure in that behalf." The Spanish ambassador was with her longer, Throckmorton

* See "Foreign State Papers"—Reign of Elizabeth, 1560, 1561.

thought, than he should have been, "an hour," he says, "being more than necessary for the ceremony of condoling."

He adds, however, that "her wisdom and kingly modesty are so great, in that she thinketh herself not too wise, but is content to be ruled by good councils and wise men, so that by their means she could not well do amiss."

Elizabeth delayed authorising her ambassador to offer her condolences to Mary until towards the end of February. She had been much irritated by the obstinate refusal of François and Mary to renounce the title of King and Queen of England, when the Guises desired their agents, after their sister's death, to treat with Elizabeth's plenipotentiaries. Generally, Throckmorton wrote very favourably of Queen Mary. "Her ability," he says, "was not perceived while the king lived, but she now shows great wisdom and modesty, and great judgment for her years, with wise handling of herself and matters. Some who then made little account of her, now honour her for her wisdom."

There was then much speculation concerning the young dowager's second marriage. The Spanish ambassador's breach of etiquette by a too prolonged visit of condolence may have been owing to his availing himself of the opportunity of ascertaining her views respecting the suggested marriage with Don Carlos. For the English minister remarks, "The House of Guise presently bareth small rule. Their hope is in Spain." But the reports respecting Don Carlos, who was never likely to be King of Spain, were rather discouraging, and Mary said she "esteemed more the continuance of her honour, and to marry one that may uphold her greatness, than she passeth to please her fancy by taking one that is accompanied by such small benefit or alliance as thereby her estimation and fame is not increased." This also may have been announced for the purpose of damping the ardour of some members of the *haute noblesse* who were suppliants for her favour.

Sir Nicholas also reported, she "desires to return to Scotland, but at the request and suit of her subjects. Also she works that those who shall request her to come home shall promise all obedience, to whom she will assure all good favour that a prince can promise to a subject."

Notwithstanding the dissensions then disturbing the accustomed round of revelry, the young widowed queen evidently occupied more attention at court than was pleasing to the queen-mother. Much negotiation between the Princes of Lorraine and Spanish ambassador, French ministers, agents from Scotland, etc., was carried on respecting her, but its precise nature has only been suggested. As Throckmorton remarks in one of his despatches, "They will have time now to provide that the second marriage of the Queen of Scotland shall do but little harm," it may be inferred that the Spanish marriage was the subject of their conferences, from which, however, nothing satisfactory resulted.

It is, however, certain that Mary Stuart had not many real friends at the French court, and when her day of power vanished, rapidly also vanished the crowd of flatterers who erewhile had feigned to almost worship her. Even the Guises — the time of mourning, in conformity with the etiquette of the court, which Catherine had neglected, being fulfilled — counselled departure. Mary was conducted to Rheims, and afterwards retired for a while to the Convent of Saint-Pierre-les-Dames, of which her aunt, Renée de Lorraine, was abbess.

Mary's mother, who died in Edinburgh on the 11th of June, 1560, had requested on her deathbed that her heart might be sent to Lorraine. It was brought to the convent, enclosed in a silver urn, shortly before Mary's arrival. This event occasioned the renewal of her mourning and her grief. One can, indeed, well understand how forcibly the contemplation of such a relic in the unaccustomed quiet and solitude of convent life must have brought home to her feelings the lonely isolated position she was placed in by the double loss she had sustained within the past few months.

Bidding adieu to her aunt, Mary returned to Rheims, and thence (according to the historian Rapin Thoyras), "knowing that her mother-in-law did not like her, repaired to Nancy." She was visited, while at Rheims, by Martignes, De la Brosse, De L'Oysel, and the Bishop of Amiens. The latter was well acquainted with the affairs of Scotland, and knowing that she proposed shortly to return thither, thought it his duty to give her some information respecting the country she was going to govern, but of which she knew comparatively nothing, having been sent away to France when but six years old. The bishop and her friends recommended her to secure the friendship and good-will of her illegitimate brother James Stuart, the Prior of St. Andrews, attaching him to her by favours and benefits, also the Counts of Argyle and Leddington. Further, "they advised her to rely for support rather on the Protestants than the Catholics, the latter being in all respects, they assured her, inferior to the former."

Lesley (the historian, and Catholic Bishop of Scotland), who was sent to France by some of her Catholic subjects to advise with her, and who met her, it appears, while on her journey to Nancy, counselled her to pursue an entirely different course to that suggested by the Bishop of Amiens. He bade her beware of confiding in the Prior of St. Andrew's; urged her to proceed to Aberdeen, where she could put herself at the head of a body of Catholic troops, and reëstablish religion on the same footing as before the recent changes.

On the following day the prior appeared in person to pay his respects to his royal sister, whom he met in Joinville. He approved her resolve to return to Scotland, and gave her advice far more suitable in the then existing state of affairs than Lesley's. She could reign happily and tranquilly, he told her, only by following the course taken by her predecessors with the assistance of the states. Mary seems to have adopted his views, as she commissioned the prior to return to Scotland and prepare for her reception, and to authorise the states to decree whatever they considered desirable for the welfare of the people and kingdom.* Poor Mary, however, was in no haste to leave the country of her adoption for her native land. Naturally, France was far dearer to her, and the ties of family and affection which further attached her to it were wanting in Scotland. A hundred times rather would she have lived at one of the cities assigned her as dowry — Touraine or Poitou — simply as dowager, than have left the "*plaisant pays de France*" to reign over a people destitute, as she believed, of politeness or courtesy — little better, indeed, than savages. From day to day her departure was delayed. Her uncles, the Duc d'Aumale and Duc d'Elbeuf, advised her to remain; but the cardinal, who from political motives feared to offend the queen-mother, assumed an air and tone of authority, almost compelling her to leave France.

One principal reason assigned for Catherine's

* See Durgaud's "*Vie de Marie Stuart.*"

anxiety to hasten Queen Mary's departure was the fear she entertained that the beauty and accomplishments of the young dowager should some day touch the heart of the youthful sovereign. Catherine certainly extended her views very far into the future. Should the presence of this enchantress kindle, as she dreaded, a dangerous flame in Charles's heart, her motherly influence over that precocious and ardent youth would be effaced, and Catherine once more be deposed by the Queen of Scots and the Guises. Unable longer to put off the evil day, Mary returned to Paris to pay her respects to the king who had been crowned on the 15th of May while Mary was at Nancy. She accompanied him to Saint-Germain, where she took an affectionate leave of the whole court, who replied to her tender adieux, we are told, with many sighs and tears.

These tender adieux seem to have really made so deep an impression on Charles that he ever after spoke of the Scottish Queen as the most beautiful princess in the world. Some years later he could not look on her portrait in the Louvre without emotion, and, with his eyes fixed upon it, would express his regret that she left France. He for some time indulged in the hope of marrying her, often inquiring whether there would be difficulty in obtaining the needful dispensation from Rome. It was not doubted at court that had she remained he would have shared his throne with her. The cardinal, becoming aware of this, regretted the unwise haste with which he had urged her departure. His manœuvres, in consequence, gave some uneasiness to the queen-mother. It was, however, too late to retract his rash orders, and Catherine would never have consented to his bringing his niece back to France.

Mary was accompanied by the cardinal, the Duc de Guise and Duc de Nemours, and other princes of their house to Calais, where, on the 15th of August, 1561, she embarked for Scotland. She was escorted by the Grand Prior of France, the Duc d'Elbeuf, and several other noblemen, partisans of the Guises. Amongst others who made the voyage with her was Damville de Montmorency, the constable's eldest son. "This gave many people much to think of as well as to talk about." It greatly displeased the King of Navarre, who was said to have desired to repudiate his wife, Jeanne d'Albret, that he might marry Mary Stuart.

Damville had long been deeply in love with the young queen, his attentions, it was remarked, being received with unusual complaisance on her part. This gave rise to much jealousy amongst other adorers who sought her smiles with less success, and it was believed that she had a mind to make Damville her husband. He was, in fact, already married. But his wife had recently afforded him a sufficient pretext for demanding a divorce by embracing the reformed faith. Mary, it has been asserted, suggested a speedier method of removing the obstacle to their union — a groundless charge, doubtless, no incident of her life at that early period warranting such a suspicion.

Besides the revenues of her dowry, which included Épernay, Poitou, and Touraine, she received from France a pension of 20,000 *livres*. Many jewels and other valuable property also belonged to her. These the Cardinal de Lorraine advised her to leave with him for safety, as "she was about," he said, "to make a voyage, as it were, for another world." She, however, knew him too well to follow his advice, but simply replied that "as she was about to risk her life by sea, she might well venture to risk her jewels and valuables also."

Brantôme has left us an interesting account of her last adieux to that belle France she loved so much, as she sat on the deck of the vessel with strained eyes suffused with tears, striving to catch the latest glimpse of its fast receding coasts. He also accompanied her on her voyage.* On the 19th of August she landed at Leith unexpectedly, and after reposing for awhile was conducted to Edinburgh and the palace of her ancestors.

There, arrayed in the deep mourning prescribed — according to ancient usage — for the widowed queens of France, Mary Stuart received the sub-

* See Brantôme's "*Dames illustres* — Marie Stuart."

mission of the Scottish nobles. Her dress was a robe and train of rich white velvet, with sleeves of silver cloth, fitting the lower part of the arm, but full and puffed at the shoulders. Her chemisette was of fine white lace, and, covering her shoulders, she wore a veil or scarf of silver tissue and lace. Her hair lay in small frizzy curls over the temples, but was plain at the top, and tied back with white ribands. Her bonnet or cap was also of white velvet, of the pointed shape known as the Mary Stuart cap. It was placed rather backward, so as not to conceal the hair, and was edged with three rows of fine pearls. A necklace also of pearls — three rows of unequal length — encircled her throat.

Suspended from her waist by strings of pearls was a white velvet pocket or pouch, and beside it hung the small gold whistle, which the princesses and ladies of the court then used to call their attendants or pages. The pocket, as was the fashion of the time, contained the literary novelties of the day — the sonnets of Ronsard, Saint-Gelais, or other celebrity in vogue — spendidly bound, as an ornament of dress.

The interesting appearance of their young queen, her acknowledged beauty, and the perfect confidence she appeared to have in them (the cardinal had ably trained her for this scene), touched the rough Scotch barons. They could not but admire such a vision of loveliness; while by her gentle, courteous manners she succeeded, if but for awhile, in gaining their sympathy, though not exactly, as sometimes stated, "in uniting the different factions which had divided Scotland during her absence."

The rough John Knox, when referring to the youthful queen, exclaimed: "She is no woman, but some pagan goddess — a Diana or a Venus." Her return neither weakened Protestant ascendency in Scotland, nor Elizabeth's influence there.

CHAPTER X.

Condé's Return to Court. — Antoine Roused to Action. — The States of Pontoise. — Colloquy of Poissy. — The Calvinistic Minister, Théodore de Bèze. — Catherine's Letter to Pius IV. — Consternation at the Vatican. — The Legate and the General of the Jesuits. — Edict of Tolerance, January, 1562.

THE return of Prince Louis de Condé to the Court of France was speedily followed by open rupture between the King of Navarre and the Guises. For the first time the weak and vain Antoine of Bourbon was made to recognise the fact that both he and his brother had escaped, as it were by a miracle only, the death and dishonour to which the duke and the cardinal had doomed them. In a spirit of unwonted audacity, kindled at last by a sense of his own and the prince's wrongs, he attempted — in virtue of his position of lieutenant-general — to dispossess the duke of his office of Grand-Master of the Household, and succeeded in depriving him of the insignia of that post — the golden keys of the palace.

Either he or Guise, he declared, must quit the court. Catherine opposed; unwilling to place herself unreservedly in the hands of either party.

Immediately the Bourbon princes invited their friends and partisans to follow them to Paris, there to proclaim King Antoine regent of the kingdom. But just as he and Condé were about to set foot in the stirrup, the constable, his sons and nephews, and several hundred noblemen and gentlemen also proposing to mount and accompany them, the old Cardinal de Tournon urged Catherine, who affected to be in despair, to require without delay, and in the young king's name, Montmorency's immediate presence in the king's private cabinet.

As François II. was instructed by the Guises to dismiss "his father's friend" from the court, when his presence was inconvenient to them, so now the boy Charles was taught by his mother to whine out a prayer that "his father's friend" would not forsake him, as he, at his tender age, needed his counsels, therefore desired him to remain near his royal person. "Montmorency — who had no real sympathy with the views of the heretical Bourbons, Châtillons, and his moderate Catholic sons, and only on account of his feud with the Guises and the influence of his nephews had been drawn into seeming unity with this reforming party — was glad to profess himself bound to obey his sovereign's commands."*

* This is said to have been a concocted scheme between the queen-mother, the constable, and the persecuting old Cardinal de Tournon, the young king being taken into their confidence as a lesson for him in kingcraft.

This defection deprived the Bourbons of their chief authority for the step they were taking, and Antoine's courage grew rapidly lukewarm. As was foreseen, he declined, in spite of Condé's remonstrances, to pursue his project further until supported by the constable. His constant terror of rousing the ire of Philip of Spain, and of a Spanish invasion of Navarre, also damped his ardour — Jeanne, the more able ruler of her little kingdom, being then also in France. Yet the *noblesse* and *tiers état* (the States General having reassembled) were clamorous for the regency of the King of Navarre, threatening to withhold the promised subsidies if his election was opposed and the Guises retained a voice in the royal councils.

Also they approved and adopted his audacious and, as they considered, patriotic proposal to pay the debts of the crown by means of the state's resumption of the extensive domains — comprising nearly a third of the kingdom — which, together with extravagant pensions for which no services had been rendered, and the creation of useless offices for sale to the highest bidder, had been lavished with so prodigal a hand on favourites by the late king and his father. This measure, without consultation with Catherine, had been boldly suggested by Antoine, spurred on by his brother. It was especially aimed at the Guises; but it touched the constable so closely that it contributed further to alienate him from the reforming party, whose aims and heretical principles he already abhorred.

Maréchal Saint-André was another of those favourites, who, by flattering the monarch and paying court to the all-powerful Diane, had obtained the grant of nearly half a province, with governorships and other lucrative posts. The Duchesse de Valentinois herself was menaced with a demand for the restitution of those wide domains that formed a chief part of her enormous wealth, and of which the Guises looked to inherit a considerable portion.

This assumption of independent power on the part of the King of Navarre, and the support he met with from the States General, alarmed the queen-mother. At first she thought by supercilious treatment to drive him from the court, but was dissuaded by De L'Hôpital, lest the Huguenots, who were committing sad outrages in the provinces, should resent the affront by further acts of violence. "Sentence of death was suspended over the heads of all who assembled to pray or to preach according to the forms of the 'new religion.'" But the Huguenots, setting these decrees of the Parliament at defiance, now assembled openly. Persecution had not thinned their numbers, but added to them daily. This emboldened them, in those towns where they found themselves in sufficient force, to establish their prayer-meetings in some of the churches; after having broken or cleared away the "images and idols of pagan Rome" and destroyed the altars. They even disturbed the Catholic services, ridiculed the processions, and with so much impunity — though in some towns the Catholics retaliated furiously — that it seemed as if Calvin was about to triumph over Rome.

The King of Navarre took courage, and announced that "within a year he would cause the gospel to be proclaimed throughout the kingdom." But the Spanish ambassador (according to Bouillé, "*Histoire des Guises*"), requiring of Antoine confirmation or denial of this announcement, which was made, it appears, to the Danish ambassador, he privately explained it as meaning that "within a year there should be neither preaching nor prayer-meetings throughout the country." Both services were, however, then daily and publicly celebrated, with all Calvinistic rites, in the apartments of the Prince de Condé and the admiral.

The nobles of the court looked on such Calvinistic innovations as the abolition of the confessional and the suppression of abstinence in Lent with much approval. The queen-mother herself momentarily seemed disposed to follow the stream in the direction of heresy — eating meat without restraint on the fast-days, and apparently without any qualms of conscience — for which she was unsparingly attacked in many of the Catholic pulpits of Paris. Notwithstanding, the Bishop of

Valence (Montluc) was permitted to preach at Fontainebleau before the queen, the king, and the whole court, on the necessity of praying to God and singing psalms in French, and having the Scriptures translated into that language that the people might read and understand them. Some indirect allusions, also, he ventured to make to the undue authority usurped by the Pope, and concluded his sermon, as he began it, without an invocation to any saint. One, at least, among the congregation was scandalised beyond measure, and hesitated not to express in the rough and arrogant manner habitual to him "his horror that doctrines so subversive of all authority should have been uttered in the presence of the youthful monarch. For himself, he had had more than enough of the preaching of Bishop Montluc, whom he hoped never again to see or to hear."

This indignant personage was the Connétable de Montmorency, and mainly from the effect produced on him by the bishop's sermon resulted the political alliance of the constable, the Duc de Guise, and the Maréchal Saint-André, named by their adversaries the "Triumvirate." But Montmorency did not readily join them. His resentment towards the Duc de Guise was too strong to be easily surmounted. It required the most earnest entreaties and persuasions of political partisans; many appeals to his loyalty; his fidelity to the royal house; and lastly, but by no means the least effective, the prayers of his ancient friend Diane and his fanatical Catholic wife, to overcome his reluctance and the efforts of his nephews and sons to retain him on the Bourbon side. But conquered at last, the triumviri sealed and sanctified their pact by receiving the communion together at the chapel of the lower court of Fontainebleau on Easter Sunday.

This alliance was displeasing to Catherine, who, to make the balance of power more equal, ranged herself once more on the side of the Bourbons and Châtillons. She had completely won over the weak and vacillating King of Navarre; first by granting the royal letters she had hitherto withheld, proclaiming him lieutenant-general of the kingdom, which office he contentedly accepted in lieu of the regency. The perfect intelligence existing between the queen-mother and the Bourbons was also publicly announced. But to retain the ever-fluctuating Antoine in close allegiance to her — the "Triumvirate" desiring to seduce him from her by means similar to her own — Catherine selected one of the most fascinating of her swarm of beauties, a Mademoiselle Du Rouet, who soon obtained complete ascendency over him.

The efforts of the Chancellor de L'Hôpital to modify the severe and cruel edicts of the Parliament against the Protestants, before their final registration, were incessant. His constant advocacy of tolerance and conciliatory measures probably had some effect in bending the queen-mother's views in the same merciful direction, especially as both she and her agent, the Bishop of Valence, believed for awhile that Reform was destined to triumph. But with what object, it may be asked (for it can scarcely be supposed that so accomplished an *intrigante* questioned without an object), did she inquire of the Duc de Guise, when Charles was crowned at Rheims, "whether if she and the king should embrace the new religion"—which she was careful to add they had no intention of doing—he and his party would refuse obedience to them. The duke curtly replied "Yes."*

The wiles of the "flying squadron" would scarcely have harmonised with Calvinistic austerity. But if Protestantism had been destined to obtain the upper hand and become the religion of the state, she would doubtless then have readily adopted the "new opinions" to retain, if possible, her position. The queen's letter to the Pope (Pius IV.) would seem to be intended as the first step towards it. This "semi-Protestant epistle," said to have been the joint production of Catherine and Bishop Montluc, was despatched to Rome some two or three weeks before the assembling of the Catholic clergy and Protestant ministers to take part in the religious discussion known as the "Colloquy of Poissy."

* See Bouillé's "*Histoire des Guises*."

With reference to this colloquy, previously announced as a national council, Catherine informs his holiness that "the dissentients have become so formidable both by their numbers and their power and influence that it is no longer possible to exterminate them. The friends of Catholic unity," she goes on to state, "would wish that those among them who are not Anabaptists, or persons of dissolute life, should be received into the communion of the Church, or at least, with that end in view, should on points of difference be argued with in a conciliatory spirit. That the occasion would seem to be opportune, in order to prevent further defections amongst the faithful, to remove the images from the altars and the sanctuary; to abolish the ceremonial added to the sacrament of baptism; to reëstablish the collective communion, in both kinds, with the abolition of private masses." The suppression of the "*fête* of the Saint-Sacrament" she also recommends, and suggests the desirability of "singing the psalms in French." The reading of this missive stirred the Vatican to its centre. "Heresy!" was the general exclamation. Nor was consternation at all abated by the queen-mother's assurances that "no attack on the holy father's authority or any change of doctrine should be permitted at the projected colloquy."

In the interval that occurred between the despatch of the above letter to the Pope and the assembling of the ecclesiastics at Poissy, a section of the States General — the States of Pontoise — commenced their sittings at Saint-Germain, where the court was then residing. Amongst the deputies of the *noblesse* and the *tiers état* were many political "malcontents" and many ardent Protestants, all apparently animated by violent hostility to the Guises, the Pope, and the Spanish king. Towards the queen-mother, also, they assumed an attitude rather alarming, calling upon her to resign the regency in favour of the King of Navarre, of whom, with the rest of the princes of the blood, they were stanch partisans, in opposition to "the foreign princes, the Lorrainers." So determined were they to have King Antoine to reign over them, that only at his own entreaty, conjointly with that of Coligny, were they prevailed on to allow the arrangement already agreed on respecting his share in the government to continue unaltered. "There was," says the historian, H. Martin, "an audacious grandeur in the views of the *tiers état*, of the States of Pontoise, in which the *noblesse* largely participated."

The deputies of the clergy did not attend, being wholly opposed to the reform of the abuses insisted on by the two lay orders, whose propositions seem to have been no less judicious than patriotic. The "Grand Ordinance of Orléans," which all the efforts of De L'Hôpital had failed to induce the Parliament of Paris to register, the king's private council, at the demand of the States, now imperatively required that assembly duly to record and give effect to. The debts of the state were provided for, without too heavily bearing on the people — the clergy, *noblesse* and *tiers état* contributing in due proportion. Very numerous were the reforms proposed, both in favour of toleration of religious differences and freedom of worship, as well as the more impartial administration of the law, the abolition of many undue privileges of the clergy, and generally for the welfare of the kingdom and all classes of the king's subjects.

The two cardinals, Tournon and Lorraine, should have been present during the sittings of the States, but when about to take their seats, finding they were placed below the princes of the blood, they left the Assembly in great indignation, in order "that the red hat might not humble itself before the fleurs-de-lys." As though divining the troubles likely to ensue, should the frail health of Catherine's three sons place the legitimate succession to the throne in jeopardy, the States passed an edict confirming the Salic law.

Great was the terror of the clergy when it was announced that the Colloquy of Poissy, whose professed object was to reconcile theological differences, if possible, and bring the two religions into accord, would open its proceedings on the 9th of September. All was agitation amongst the doctors of the Sorbonne, who implored the queen "not to expose the youthful ears of the king to the taint and poison of heresy." Trepidation prevailed at the Vatican, at the Escurial, and amongst the holy brethren of the Inquisition. To invite the Huguenot preachers of heresy to discuss their profane doctrines in all security with the bishops of the Church was so monstrous a scandal, that unless proposed as a snare, with the view of destroying them all at one fell swoop, Rome and Spain, by a united effort, must at once put an end to it.

Catherine's heretical letter had raised exasperation against her to its highest pitch. An energetic part was attributed to her in this supposed concerted plan to favour the "new religion" and its introduction at court, in opposition to the Church. To counteract this, a double embassy arrived in Paris — the Pope's legate being Cardinal Ferrara (a son of Lucrezia Borgia), charged by his holiness to oppose the opening of the colloquy, and, further, with the secret mission of inducing the King of Navarre to return to the fold of the faithful. The Spanish envoy — Iago Lainez, the general of the Jesuits, and successor of Ignacio y Loyola — was a far less insinuating and courtly personage. They found Catherine and the youthful monarch at Saint-Germain, in the midst of a court mainly composed of heretics. The Calvinistic form of worship was also established in full freedom in the royal château, Condé and the King and Queen of Navarre being resident there.

The reception accorded to the envoys was rather discouraging than cordial, and the legate and the inquisitor soon discovered that the edict of July, enacting banishment or death to all Huguenots who did not live after the manner of good Catholics, was not only condemned at court, but everywhere was practically null. The legate, when he appeared in public, was compelled to dispense with the attendance of his cross-bearer, being followed by a mocking crowd of people — servants, for the most part, of the Huguenot courtiers — whenever he ventured to show himself with the insignia of his dignity borne before him.

The Duc de Guise was absent, but the Cardinal de Lorraine had encouraged rather than opposed the opening of the colloquy. Two discussions had already taken place when the envoys arrived. This surprised both the legate and Lainez. It seemed to throw some doubt even on the cardinal's orthodoxy. His motive, however, was to take advantage of the widening of the breach which he foresaw would ensue from this theological discussion, and the intestine feuds it would lead to — making it necessary to call in the aid of Spain, with whose troops, and if possible the funds also of the "Demon of the South," he hoped to stamp out and exterminate this "evergrowing and damnable heresy." So, on the date fixed, the famous conference was opened in the grand refectory of the Benedictine Monastery of Poissy — a short address being spoken in a feeble childish voice by the young king.

Besides the king, Catherine brought with her her second son, the Duc d' Orléans (Henri III.). The King and Queen of Navarre, the Bourbon princes, and the members of the private council were also present. The chancellor explained the object of the conference, and in impressive and eloquent terms "exhorted the assembly to conduct the discussion in a serious but conciliatory spirit;" at the same time enjoining the cardinals, archbishops, bishops, doctors of the Sorbonne, and delegates from various chapters, to the number of a hundred or more, to welcome the ministers of the "new religion with gentleness and cordiality, as baptised Christians like themselves." Even this short address excited some irritation, as suspiciously favourable to the heretics.

There were present many who trembled with rage when the learned and eloquent Théodore de Bèze rose to address the assembly, as the spokesman of his coreligionists. He was considered, after Calvin, the head of the "new religion," and was usually referred to as "Calvin's lieutenant." But indignation, which at the first prevailed mainly because this chief of the heretics had been received with favour at court, and was the guest of King Antoine, soon subsided into approval as he proceeded with calmness, eloquence, moderation, and courtesy, to explain the points of difference and agreement between the Catholics and Reformers.

So ably did he tone down the repellent severity of Calvin's extreme doctrines, that he was listened to with quiet attention until he came to speak of the Eucharist. He then emphatically declared that "far as highest heaven was separated from earth, so far was Jesus Christ corporally separated from the consecrated elements of bread and wine; His body and blood being spiritually and by faith alone partaken of." Then were heard murmurs, loud and deep, and the old Cardinal de Tournon, turning towards the royal party, his feeble, tottering frame quivering with passionate anger, said that, "saving his majesty's presence, he and his colleagues would have risen to put an end to the abominable language and horrible blasphemies which had just been uttered." Amidst great confusion and excitement the assembly at once broke up.

The old cardinal advised that the colloquy should there and then come to an end. The Cardinal de Lorraine desired to prolong it. He had not yet confuted Théodore de Bèze, and was anxious to show his ability in making the worse appear the better cause. It was arranged, therefore, that he should reply on two points — the authority of the Church, and the Eucharist. After much discussion and much subtle argument on both sides in defence of their several opinions and articles of faith, the dispute ended, as foreseen, in the aggravation of hostile feelings and the widening of the breach already existing between the two religions. After a few more sittings the colloquy was eventually brought to a close — first by the Cardinal de Tournon's exhortation to the young king to believe no other doctrine than that he had heard from the lips of the Cardinal de Lorraine, and to immediately purge his kingdom of all those persons who refused to subscribe to it ; secondly, by a vituperative address of the Jesuit general, in which he spoke of the Reformers as "serpents, foxes, wolves, and monkeys, who aped Rome at Geneva." The question in discussion, he said, concerned neither women, children, nor military men, and should be referred to the Council of Trent.

But Catherine and her chancellor, who still inclined her — perplexed though she was — to a policy of peace and tolerance, requested Théodore de Bèze, Pierre Martyr (Pietro Vermiglio), and other "gospel ministers," to remain in France for awhile. If it was not possible to bring the two religions into any sort of agreement, it might be practicable, they thought, so to frame an edict of pacification sufficiently satisfactory to both parties to enable the two religions to exist peaceably side by side. The beneficent efforts of De L'Hôpital resulted in the issue of the Edict of Tolerance of January, 1562, approved by the government, and allowing the Huguenots to assemble for worship with their families privately in their own houses, and publicly outside the walls of towns. The Calvinist ministers readily accepted it, promising for their people strict compliance with all its conditions. But the fanatical priests by their ravings in the pulpit roused the people to frenzy, and the edict, intended as a message of peace, proved but the signal for bloodshed.

CHAPTER XI.

The Cardinal Ferrara.— Antoine's Conversion.— His Promised Rewards.— His Treatment of Jeanne d'Albret.— Her Heart Henceforth Closed to Love.— Guise Urged to Return to Paris. — Massacre of Vassy.— Catherine and Charles at Monceaux. — Count Flying from Château to Château. — Guise Enters Paris in Great State.— Antoine and De Bèze.

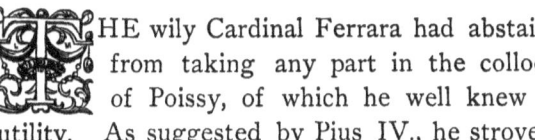HE wily Cardinal Ferrara had abstained from taking any part in the colloquy of Poissy, of which he well knew the futility. As suggested by Pius IV., he strove to do the Church more effective service by depriving the Huguenot cause of one who in name at least was its principal leader. The vain, imprudent, and inconstant Antoine de Bourbon was not, in a religious point of view, a conquest that so accomplished an intriguer as the grandson of Alexander VI. would have been proud of. But Antoine being the representative of "an heretical faction which it was desirable for the peace of the world to exterminate," his defection, it was believed, would deal it a crushing blow which, if it did not slay, at least for a time would paralyze, while sterner measures for finally stamping it out were preparing.

But (as Giovanni Michiel reports) the King of Navarre was not a man on whom the Huguenots greatly relied. He had accepted all the rites of the Reformers of Geneva, but more with a view, as was generally surmised, of being chief of a party, than from zeal for the "new religion." "He discourses well," continues the ambassador, "is courteous to all, without ceremony or affectation. His manners are frank and thoroughly French; his liberality so great that he is always in debt, and by those two qualities — affability and open-handedness — he has gained the general good opinion; of the nobility especially, who, for the most part, greatly like him. He is very willing to undertake any proposed great enterprises, but is considered wanting in firmness and strength of principle to carry them out."

The Italian cardinal was too wary to startle the King of Navarre by any reference to a change of religion until he had won his confidence. He was insinuating and deferential, which Antoine in his vanity regarded as a tribute this distinguished prelate was anxious to pay to his loftiness of character and general merits. By degrees the cardinal's well-timed allusions to the Prince de Condé's ability and activity, and his apparent influence with his party, excited Antoine's jealousy and produced a coldness between the brothers.

The Cardinal de Lorraine now came to the legate's assistance, and Antoine was reminded, rather reproachfully, that but for the difference in religion, how much more prominent, how much more suited to his rank than that of the leader of a band of heretics, was the position he might have held — of course as a defender of the venerable pontiff and Holy Mother Church, who desired only the peaceful return of her erring children, whom she longed once more to gather into her maternal bosom. He had, they told him, but to leave the paths of error, into which a too easy compliance with the mistaken views of his wife had seduced him. They even promised, as an inducement to recant and to forsake his party, absolution without the infliction of any penance, and, as a further reward, the hand of the young Queen of Scotland. Her beauty and seductive graces of mind and person they greatly vaunted, in order more closely to ensnare poor Antoine, whose weaknesses they knew, and who, they perceived, was lending a willing ear to their solicitations.

Besides sharing the Scottish throne with Mary, they hinted at the probability of the crown of France, at no distant period, descending to him, Catherine's sons being all of sickly constitution. While he, robust of frame and in the prime of life, having thrown aside his "new opinions," might govern France for many years. There was even a third crown they could venture to promise him — that of England. The Cardinal de Ferrara, being the holy father's legate, could in the name of his holiness assure him of his willingness to fulminate a bull of excommunication against the heretic Elizabeth, and to adjudge her kingdom to Mary Stuart and the King of Navarre after their marriage.

To the luxurious, ease-loving Antoine de Bourbon this was a very pleasing prospect; yet he was inclined to think it too far away in the distance to be realised within a reasonable time. Something nearer at hand, it was perceived, would fascinate him still more. It was now the Jesuit's turn to speak. He was able to promise that Philip II., in exchange for Lower Navarre, would consent to cede to him the island of Sardinia. A glowing description was given of the beauties of this island — "it was a perfect scene of enchantment." Antoine was in ecstasies. What a dream of love and idleness his imagination conjured up! Shared, too, not with Mary of Scotland or the heretic Queen Jeanne, but with one of Catherine's captivating belles.

The enchanting isle possessed the further advantage of nearness to the continent of Africa, where, it was suggested, "should ambition prompt him to extend his views of territorial acquisition beyond his isle of beauty, he might found an empire no less vast than flourishing." But, said his tempters, "Your majesty must reflect on the advantages offered, and compare them with the disadvantages resigned. Above all, let not Queen Jeanne know anything of this project, which assuredly she would oppose."

But when Antoine reflected that the first step towards the realisation of the flattering proposals laid before him was his repudiation of Jeanne, he hesitated. The more he contemplated this act, the more his conscience pricked him. Jeanne d'Albret had been a devoted wife, and, as was not often the case in royal marriages, when giving him her hand, and with it a share in the government of her little kingdom, she gave him also her heart. He knew her worth, and had not ceased to admire her, though he had yielded to the fascinations of the facile beauties thrown in his way.* At all events, Antoine would try to bring Jeanne over to his views, and to persuade her to enter with him into the fold of the Shepherd of Rome.

As a precaution, probably, against any wavering on his own part, when he came to discuss with Jeanne their renunciation of the "new opinions," he privately despatched a member of his household to make his submission to Pius IV. A messenger was also sent off to the Duc de Guise, recommending his speedy return to Paris — the moment, it appears, being favourable for the adoption of

---

* Calvin had recently written a very severe letter to the King of Navarre, in which, while disapproving of much of his conduct at the French Court, he especially reproved him for his "*folles amours*" (H. Martin).

any measures for the putting down of heresy that he (the duke) might suggest, and which the now Catholic lieutenant-general would deem it his duty to enforce.

The duke, on a recent occasion, replied to an appeal to spare the life of a pious, learned, and eloquent man, but a heretic, "that his trade was cutting off heads, not arguing" (to which he might well have added, "heads far worthier to remain on their shoulders than was his own"). He had quitted Paris in disgust on the issuing of the Edict of Tolerance of the 3d of January, leaving his brother, the cardinal, whose trade was arguing and discussing, to aid in the conversion of the King of Navarre. The queen-mother, with her children and the court, had also fled from the capital to seek refuge at her country house of Monceaux from the storm impending over her. The chancellor accompanied, if not in disgust, yet in despair that the work of peace in which he had induced the queen to concur had but hastened the catastrophe it was his aim to avert — organised civil war.

From every Catholic pulpit in the kingdom, with but two or three rare and honourable exceptions, the priests, disgracing the name of Christians, appealed to the people in language the most violent to aid in the extermination of the heretics. Not alone on the heads of the Reformers did they invoke fearful curses and calamities, but on those

Catholics, also, who, if any of "the accursed sect" fell on their way, should listen to the inner voice of humanity pleading for mercy, or sparing from death man, woman, or child.

Would they secure the favour of God? (What profanation of that great name! Should not they rather have said Satan?) They must denounce, betray, hand over to the executioner (even those nearest and dearest to them, would they not risk their own souls), and, if need be, do a murderous deed themselves — "a deed so pleasing in the sight of heaven that absolution was not needed."

Not all the authority, influence, and entreaties of Théodore de Bèze, Pierre Martyr, and other chief Protestant ministers — who still, at the request of the queen-mother and the chancellor, deferred for awhile their departure from Paris — could wholly restrain the Huguenot people from attempting to retaliate by interrupting the service of the mass, as their own services were daily interrupted, for, when exercising their newly-acquired right of assembling together for prayer and preaching, their opponents were in the habit of bursting in upon them with yells, hootings, and throwing of stones, compelling the breaking up of the meeting.

Calvin's doctrine was to offer no resistance to the authority of the powers that be, but passive obedience to it could not long be yielded by ardent men under such unceasing persecution. A deep and terrible vengeance was near at hand, and surely the blood of its victims should be on those who provoked it. This, then, was the favourable moment for the "Grand Guise" to resume his congenial calling — so, at least, thought the contemptible King of Navarre.

Antoine's efforts to win over Jeanne to follow his example and renounce her religion were doomed to utter failure. She expressed herself astonished at his culpable duplicity, knowing that his opinions had undergone no real change. She reproached him for his unworthy conduct towards his brother and his friends, the Châtillons, as well as for his newly-formed alliance with his own and their great enemies. (Antoine would have arrested Coligny and his brother, had Catherine been willing; but his zeal in the new cause he had embraced was checked by the chancellor, rather than encouraged by Catherine.) Greatly irritated at hearing from Jeanne what he knew to be the truth respecting himself, he complained to the Cardinal de Lorraine of her obstinate adherence to her heretical opinions. The worthy prelate advised him to arrest his wife in the very midst of the court.

But Antoine recoiled from so bold a step. Jeanne was a queen in her own right, and, besides, had not obtruded her opinions on the court. He was aware, also, that she was greatly respected for her modesty, and many virtues then rare in the Court of France, and that any violence of the kind proposed would bring forward many friends to resist it.

He preferred, therefore, to resort to stratagem. He would order her to leave the court and repair to his Duchy of Vendôme, despatching an agent to arrest her on her journey. He refused her the companionship of her son, then in his ninth year, as he intended, he said, to bring him up in the true religion.* But Jeanne, before her departure, availed herself of an opportunity of conversing seriously with the youthful Henri of Navarre. She urged on him, as her most earnest wish, never to attend mass, assuring him that if he obeyed not that wish she would disinherit him, and never allow him to regard her as his mother.

Friends had not failed privately to inform Jeanne of her husband's base intentions. Consequently, soon after leaving Paris, she changed her route, and while Antoine's and the cardinal's myrmidons thought to surprise her at Vendôme, she entered Châtellerault, where she was received with all honour by the Marquis de Caumont de la Force. There she was taken ill, having greatly suffered in mind from the excitement of the journey, the feeling of danger barely escaped, and the shock she experienced on discovering how mean and base was the man she had been accustomed to confide in. Yet courage did not

* Mathieu's "*Histoire de France.*"

fail her, and after some few days of rest she was able to continue her journey to Nérac, where she had a very fine château. She was accompanied by her little daughter Catherine, then in her third year.

On leaving her host of Châtellerault, she said: "I have closed my heart to the love I once felt for my husband, to open it henceforth wholly to my duty to my people and the affairs, civil and religious, of my domains." * A certain severity of character not hitherto remarked in Jeanne d'Albret is said to have developed itself from the time of this separation from her husband, and her loss of respect for, and confidence in, him. She and Antoine met no more. Yet troubles and persecution were still reserved for her. Antoine, however, was quite consoled for the loss of his wife in the society of the fascinating Mademoiselle Du Rouet de la Baraudière—*en attendant* their departure for the enchanting Isle of Sardinia.

François de Guise was in Alsace when King Antoine's message reached him. He was visiting the Duke of Wurtemberg, who was connected with his family by marriage, and through whose influence he hoped to prevent the German Protestant princes from affording aid to the French Reformers in the civil war now imminent. To secure his aims he, and, at an earlier period,

---

* Mathieu's "*Histoire de France*," and Mademoiselle Vauvillier's "*Vie de Jeanne d'Albret.*"

the cardinal also, had not scrupled to declare that they approved the Lutheran doctrines and shared in the duke's belief in them. "Never," François de Guise assured him, "had he caused any man to be put to death for his religious opinions. Those who had suffered — calling themselves Reformers — were but dangerous political intriguers who had used the 'new religion' as a cloak for their schemes."

With but little delay the Duc de Guise responded in person to the lieutenant-general's message. On his way to Paris, however, he had the satisfaction of achieving a triumph over the "accursed Huguenot," as well as of showing his contempt for the Edict of Tolerance, issued by the authority of the queen-mother and the Chancellor of France.

As he and his troop of horsemen were entering Vassy — a small town in the province of Champagne — the Huguenot population happened to be assembled for worship outside the walls — according to the terms of the edict. Their modest temple was a barn, and they were singing psalms — in French, too, to add to the heinousness of their crime. These unwelcome sounds startled the pious ears of the duke, who, galloping forward with his armed escort, attacked the worshippers in the barn. They naturally endeavoured to defend themselves, and strove to barricade the entrance. But unprepared for attack, and much less for an armed one, their efforts at resistance proved powerless. Thus (on the authority of De Bèze) between two and three hundred men, women, and children were either mercilessly slaughtered or badly wounded; victims to the savage fury of the "Grand Guise" and his infamous myrmidons. The life of the Protestant minister was spared, but for a time only; he and the provost of the town — guilty of obeying the injunctions of the royal edict — were carried prisoners to Paris as trophies to grace the hero's triumph. The carnage is said to have lasted more than an hour — "in the barn, on the roof, and in the street."

The queen-mother, being informed that Antoine had sent for Guise to Paris, was advised to summon the latter in the king's name to repair to her court at Monceaux. This was in order to avert the conflict likely to ensue there between the duke and the Prince de Condé, who, at the head of an armed band, was protecting the Protestants of the capital from annoyance or attack when assembled for prayer. But Guise, who had set at naught the royal edict, now treated the royal summons with similar disrespect, and a few days after entered Paris with all the pomp and circumstance of a monarch returning to his kingdom with laurel-bound brows to receive the homage of his subjects. Besides his own retinue of several hundred footmen and horsemen, he was accompanied by the constable and Saint-André, and a squadron of cavalry. At the gate of Saint-Denis the provost and officers of the municipality waited in grand state to receive him, and he was joined on entering Paris by the King of Navarre and the Spanish ambassador, "suitably attended." The Catholic people, urged on by their priests, by whom the massacre of Vassy was applauded with savage joy, welcomed him with frantic cries of "Vive Guise!" the messenger "sent of God for the destruction of the heretics and the glory of His name."

Very different was the feeling of the Protestants towards this heaven-sent murderer. Scarcely could they be restrained from laying violent hands on him, while "the Prince de Condé, Théodore de Bèze, and other Protestant chiefs sought the king and queen-mother at Mélun, whither they had fled in alarm from Monceaux." The ministers demanded justice on the violators of the Edict of January; and in the name of the Reformers generally, Condé supported the demand by offering the queen a force of fifty thousand men. The King of Navarre, however, in the excess of his new-found zeal, inveighed against the action of his brother, and declared that "whoever touched the tip of the finger of his 'brother of Guise' would touch the whole of his body."

Very rough indeed was his treatment of his former friend, De Bèze, whose proceedings "in furthering the spread of heresy" he strongly condemned. De Bèze's reply to this foolish prince is well known. "Sire," he said, after quietly listening to Antoine's angry reproofs and his justification of the murderous zeal displayed by Guise and his companions — attacked, as he asserted, by the Protestants — " Sire, it is true that the part of the Church of God is to endure blows rather than to inflict them ; but you must remember that it is an anvil that has already worn out many hammers."

CHAPTER XII.

Catherine Perplexed. — Massacre of Sens. — Frightful Retaliation. — Churches Sacked. — The Admiral's Wife. — Attack on Rouen. — Antoine Wounded. — Jeanne d'Albret. — Her Anxiety Respecting Her Son. — Returns to Her Own Dominions.

PERHAPS at no period of the reigns of her three sons, during which she held the helm of government, was Catherine de' Medici more perplexed what course to pursue than at the present critical conjuncture. The uncontrolled authority she so much coveted, and looked to possess on Charles's accession, still eluded her grasp. Influenced by De L'Hôpital, so far since her possession of power, she seems to have really endeavoured to secure peace, and to have supported the Reformers; but only because being herself troubled by no scruples, religious or moral, they appeared to her likely to become a great power in the state. But now, through the audacity of the Duc de Guise and his colleagues in the "Triumvirate," conjointly with their new friend — the convert Antoine — a real Catholic government was constituted in Paris, outside the royal one.

Antoine was very anxious to parade his zeal — walking proudly beside his "brother of Guise" in the procession of the "*Pâques fleuries*" (Palm Sunday), a sort of solemn review of the whole Catholic party then in the capital. The *débutant* was also supported by the Spanish ambassador, who addressed him respectfully as King of Navarre — a title that Philip II. had hitherto persistently refused him. He had now no claim to it whatever. The Navarrese, on hearing of his treatment of their queen, to whom they were loyally devoted, had declared that "henceforth they would neither acknowledge him as their sovereign, nor pay him any obedience." The Spaniard, then, should rather have addressed him as his majesty of Sardinia.

The queen-mother's anxiety daily increasing, she fled from Monceaux to Mélun, that she might be within reach of Orléans, whither the Bishop of Valence and other friends of Reform urged her with her sons to seek refuge. The chancellor also advised her — seeing that war was inevitable — to write to the Prince de Condé, placing herself and her children under his protection. This she did, at the same time authorising him to take up arms. Scarcely, however, had she arrived at Mélun, when a deputation from Paris, headed by the provost, was announced, praying her to return thither with the king. Her answer probably was evasive; for as soon as the Parisians left she departed from Mélun for Fontainebleau, there to await the arrival of Condé.

But the prince, who from inferiority of numbers was unable to hold Paris against the forces of the "Triumvirate," was yet unwilling to abandon the city to his enemies. This occasioned delay. However, his brother, the Cardinal de Bourbon — lately appointed by the queen provisional Governor of Paris — consented, though by no means sharing the prince's opinions, to order both him and the Duc de Guise, with their followers, to quit the capital. Condé, breaking up his camp, obeyed; but the duke, while affecting to obey, contrived to be compelled to disobey. The military pomp he displayed in preparing for his pretended departure attracted a large number of the excited populace, who "would not" — as they loudly vociferated — "let their 'Grand Guise' leave them." Condé, who, it appears, was expected to proceed immediately to Fontainebleau "to protect the sons and their mother," merely despatched thither one of his gentlemen to inquire what were the queen-mother's wishes. As possession of the king would have fully compensated for the evacuation of the capital, Condé is supposed to have thus neglected a great opportunity of increasing the prestige of his party, of which his enemies failed not to take advantage.

For while the prince was pursuing his journey with all speed to Meaux, where the Protestant nobility were assembled, the King of Navarre — grown very bold since serving under the orders of the "Triumvirate" — made his appearance at Fontainebleau. He was accompanied by his colleagues, who put him forward as spokesman, they remaining with their troops in the vicinity of the château; his part in the government being to make promises and proposals for which the "Triumvirate" cared not to be responsible. The renegade lieutenant-general urged the queen and her sons to accompany him at once to Paris to avoid the dangers that would surely ensue from their falling into the hands of the rebel Huguenots. Undismayed by his representations, and encouraged by the chancellor, she resisted for several days.

An alarming report of Condé's movements reaching them, determined Guise and the constable to waste no more time in persuasion, and Antoine accordingly informed the queen (who seems to have omitted at this crisis to call in the aid of her invincible "flying squadron") that "he and his friends had resolved on removing the king and his brothers from Fontainebleau, to prevent their being kidnapped. With her liberty, however, they would not presume to interfere. She might accompany them or remain at Fontainebleau, or elsewhere, as she pleased." Catherine de' Medici, as usual, bowed before the breeze. The court returned to Mélun. On the following day they moved on to Vincennes, and thence once more to the Louvre — a strong-armed escort closely surrounding them. The youthful Charles IX., alarmed by these rapid changes, hurried journeys, the serious countenances of those about him, and the closeness with which he was guarded, wept bitterly, and refused to be comforted; being under the impression that the King of Navarre and the Duc de Guise were carrying him off to prison.

A report that "the sons and their mother" had been forcibly brought from Fontainebleau, and were held captive at the Louvre by the chiefs of the Catholic faction, was quickly spread through the country. Practically, it was so; but a proclamation, purporting to be issued by royal command, speedily contradicted it.

To Coligny's unwillingness to strike the first blow in this civil war, which he foresaw would be long and terrible, the delay in Condé's movements has been attributed. The admiral was a man of far more serious character than the prince. Brantôme says of the latter: "He was more ambitious than religious, and more a man of pleasure than an ambitious one." Whether it was so or not, he was undoubtedly a man of great courage; zealous for reform, and true to the cause he had espoused. The admiral was not less zealous, but more prudent and cautious. He perceived the disadvantages the Reformers would be under from their want of means, and the smallness of their forces for carrying on war successfully. The calamity this rising in arms would bring on his family, his friends, and the country, filled him with agony. He had also honourable and patriotic scruples to the Reformers being the first to call foreign soldiers into France to aid them. He therefore retired to his château of Châtillon-sur-Loing, and would probably have wholly refrained from joining the Huguenot army, but for his wife's reproaches and entreaties.

Her zeal bordered on fanaticism. "The blood of those," she said, "whom he had made no effort to save from death, would be on his head;" and when he proposed a short delay for reflection on her part of what she and her family would have to suffer, she exclaimed that she would be a witness against him at the Judgment of God, if he allowed the further guilt of causing the death of those who were slain in the interval to rest upon him. He had absolutely refused to yield to the solicitations of his brothers. But his wife's earnest appeals conquered. His resolve was taken, his preparations speedily made, and bidding adieu to the "valiant Charlotte Laval," mounted his horse, and at the head of two thousand noble cavaliers rapidly joined the prince at Meaux, then in the possession of the Protestants.

In deference to Coligny, it was determined that the pacificatory mediation of the German princes should alone be sought, and the Swiss Protestant cantons requested to prevent the Catholic ones from sending soldiers to the "usurpers of royal power," unless similar aid was granted to the Protestant churches of France. The assistance of Elizabeth of England was desired rather in money than in men. But her ambassador, Throckmorton, took a very busy if a secret part in these religious troubles ; and if Elizabeth seemed at times to grow lukewarm, Sir Nicholas did not fail to make it his business to infuse a little more ardour into her sentiments, and to urge her to more active sympathy.

The Protestant chiefs formed themselves into an association under Condé, swearing "before God and His holy angels" to remain united until the king attained his majority. To make it evident that they were friends of the crown, they adopted as a rallying sign, after the manner of the old French loyalists, the white scarf, which, from the time of Charles VII., had been the royal colour of France. The Catholic chiefs, by a similar association, followed their example ; but instead of the white scarf, they assumed the red one of Spain, with which they decorated the young king and his brothers. Many of the Catholic nobility took great objection to this investiture of the king and princes with what they termed the "insignia of the vassalage of France to Spain," as determined by the Treaty of Câteau-Cambrésis. So serious was the displeasure they evinced, that the red scarf was modified by an embroidered white cross.

The smouldering flames of civil war, so long with difficulty repressed from bursting forth with full fury, at last resisted all further efforts to stifle them. A massacre, more atrocious than even that of Vassy, excited the Huguenot people to the highest pitch of frenzy. Scenes of carnage too horrible to depict had taken place at Sens, the archbishopric of Cardinal de Guise, a younger brother of the duke. Again an unoffending people assembled for worship were set upon by a mob of howling demons, and a hundred or more of men, women, and children savagely murdered, and their bodies thrown into the Yonne.

Hitherto, the Huguenots, though committing some inexcusable (as well as excusable) ravages, by way of revenging the persistent persecution with which their enemies pursued them, had generally displayed a spirit of moderation compared with the Catholics. It has been remarked that, while the rage of the latter was usually shown in savage and atrocious murder, that of the former was far less implacable towards men than against things — statues, images of saints, and the monuments, as they termed them, of idolatry.

It was important to the cause of Reform that its leaders should restrain their people within the bounds of legitimate defence. But on the present occasion they were powerless. The people were bent on "avenging God and annihilating all traces of the idolatrous worship of the Papists." The Huguenots were masters of Orléans, and Catholics and Protestants had mutually consented to refrain from interfering with each other's mode of worship. But now in their mad fury the Huguenots, heedless of their promise, burst into the cathedral, destroyed the altars, broke the statues, burnt the finely carved woodwork of the screen and pulpits; tore down the pictures, profaned the tombs, and thoroughly sacked the fine old edifice, growing, as it seemed, drunk with the delirium of their own excesses. Entreaties, commands, on the part of Coligny, De Bèze, and Condé, were alike futile to stay the hands of the devastators.

Nor were the cathedral and churches of Orléans the only sacred buildings desecrated by the infuriated Huguenots. It seemed as though "the blast of some infernal trumpet had sounded through the land and awakened the spirit of destruction." The work of hundreds of years was destroyed in the space of a day — sometimes in a few hours. The towns which had fallen into the hands of the Huguenots — Rouen, Poitiers, Cléry, Caen, Lyons, Bourges — suffered equally with Orléans in the destruction of all they possessed of the more or less splendid products of human genius. Calvin wrote to De Bèze to express his indignation at what he perhaps too mildly designated the "indiscreet zeal" of the Reformers.

But especially he condemned those Calvinist ministers who at Lyons had "allowed themselves to be drawn into taking part, and even directing the fanatical people, in this work of destruction."

The splendid choir in the church of Saint-Jean de Lyons was utterly demolished. It appears to have been a most superb work of the Middle Ages, constructed of marble, with columns of jasper and porphyry, and decorated with groups of figures representing scenes from the historical books of the Old Testament. The tombs of kings, queens, saints, and other celebrated personages were rifled, and their remains treated with the utmost indignity, burnt, or thrown into the rivers. Some had rested in their graves undisturbed for hundreds of years — William the Conqueror and his queen Matilda, for instance, in the two churches they built at Caen; Richard Cœur de Lion at Rouen, and that of Rollon the pirate king, and first Duke of Normandy, A.D. 931.

At Cléry they destroyed the copper statue of Louis XI., dragged him from his tomb, and burnt his bones with those of his daughter Jeanne. At Orléans they even threw down and battered the statue of Joan d' Arc; burnt the heart of their last youthful sovereign, François II., and destroyed the silver urn in which it was deposited in the cathedral of the town in which he died. Before one name only — the revered one of Cardinal Georges d'Amboise, Louis XII.'s great minister —

did they pause in their sacrilegious work of destruction. He who had enriched Rouen — his archbishopric — with so many *chefs-d'œuvre* of architecture, had generally improved the town with a view to the greater comfort and well-being of the people, and had been munificent in acts of charity, might well command their respect. It could hardly be admiration of his magnificent tomb that made them stop short in their ferocious acts of vandalism. Yet in the midst of the desolation around it, the cardinal's mausoleum remained untouched, as also some other fine specimens of the sculptor's art especially associated with his name.

This furious iconoclastic onslaught had a most unfavourable effect on the cause of Reform. Many friends were lost to it, while the Catholic people athirst for blood cried aloud for vengeance. At the call of the Parliament the peasantry rose *en masse;* the women like furies marching with the men "to murder the destroyers of their churches." Fearful massacres ensued, and tortures the most horrible were inflicted to prolong the sufferings of their victims. Three men, rivals in their unpitying cruelty, Maréchal Tavannes, Blaise de Montluc, and the Duc de Montpensier, were scouring the country, "butchering whole garrisons, filling the wells with the bodies of the slain, and turning the trees into gibbets."

The Protestant chief, the Baron des Adretz,

was as merciless as his adversaries, and as cruel in his reprisals when opportunity offered. These atrocities continued for months, varied by frequent skirmishes. Every town became a stronghold, and its streets fields of battle.

But both Protestant and Catholic chiefs were preparing for more regular warfare. The Triumvirate had not scrupled to seek the aid of foreign troops, and Philip II. — hoping to succeed where his father had failed, in getting possession of Burgundy or other province of France — promised a *corps d'armée* of 36,000 men. Catherine, who had recovered a part of her influence in the government, was alarmed at her son-in-law's liberality. The nobility and the *bourgeoisie* being also opposed to this Spanish invasion, the Catholic king was immediately informed that money was more needed than soldiers. He therefore reduced the 36,000 to 3,000; but no money was forthcoming — Philip's coffers, notwithstanding his many wide domains, being as empty as those of France. The German Protestant princes, in spite of the Guises' professed Lutheran proclivities, sent troops to the assistance of the French Reformers; while Elizabeth, driving a hard bargain with Condé for the possession of Havre (which the pressing needs of the moment eventually compelled him to accept), promised 3,000 men and 100,000 gold crowns.

The two opposing armies, headed by the two

brothers — Coligny serving under Condé — took the field in June. The "Triumvirate" accompanied King Antoine, but to him the chief command was assigned. Taking advantage of the share in the government which Guise and his colleagues, accused of usurping royal authority, were compelled to yield the queen-mother, she once more assumed the part of mediatrix. Hastening to the Catholic camp at Beaugency, she proposed, as suggested by the chancellor, to grant an amnesty, with liberty of conscience, but not of worship; the King of Navarre insisting — Catherine, it is supposed, being unable to act in opposition to him — that "the toleration" of two religions in the same state was too monstrous a proposal for the Government to lend an ear to.

Another attempt at negotiation also failed, the advantages offered being rendered almost null by the stringent conditions attached to them. The King of Navarre, "who had neither heart nor head," is said to have shown exceeding harshness and want of feeling when discussing his proposals with the friends and nearest relatives, with whom, until very recently, he was united in amity and affection, and was the acknowledged leader of their party and their cause. These fruitless negotiations were followed by a raid on the Protestants who still remained in Paris. Some sixty or seventy of them, together with a few persons who were guilty of the humanity of sheltering or not denouncing them, were slaughtered, and their bodies thrown into that blood-stained river, the Seine.

The Protestant army marched towards Normandy, where many reverses were sustained, and several towns lost. Condé, fearing that Rouen also would fall into the enemy's hands, determined — Coligny consenting, though with heartfelt sorrow — to accept Elizabeth's offer. The treaty was signed at Hampton Court on the 20th of September. The 3,000 soldiers who were to form the English garrison of Havre were the first despatched by the prudent Elizabeth. The second 3,000 were delayed by contrary winds and boisterous weather. Before there arrival, Rouen was besieged by the Catholic, lately become the Royal, army — the young king and the queen-mother having been brought to the camp to give authority by their presence to the proceedings of the "Triumvirate."

The convent of Mont-Sainte-Catherine was taken by surprise and two murderous assaults on the 13th and 14th of October sufficed to make a breach in the ancient walls of Rouen. Some few days after, in spite of the vigorous resistance of the Protestant citizens, to the number of 4,000, together with 1,000 soldiers, the Catholics forcibly entered, and the wealthy city of Rouen, then the second in the kingdom, was given up to sack and pillage. To save the lives of the people, and also to save the city, De L'Hôpital induced Guise to propose an amnesty and other conciliatory measures. They were at once rejected. No promises of Guise or the queen-mother could be relied on. Horrors unspeakable ensued, and amongst the heaps of slain lay the bodies of many women who had fallen with arms in their hands.

On the morning of the second attack a ball from an arquebuse wounded the King of Navarre in the shoulder. As the surgeons did not succeed in extracting it, inflammation soon set in, and rapidly increased. But Antoine, who did not consider himself in danger, expressed a wish to enter Rouen by the breach, carried in his bed by Swiss soldiers, and preceded by drums and trumpets. His wound, however, proved fatal, and three weeks after the taking of Rouen he died, aged forty-two. Nearly the whole of that time he passed in arranging with Mademoiselle Du Rouet their mode of life in their bower of bliss at Sardinia; the planting of their orange and myrtle groves; their sails on summer seas, and their rambles on the banks of crystal-clear rivers flowing over golden sands.

Catherine de' Medici, on hearing that the King of Navarre was not likely to recover, went to visit him.

"How do you pass your time?" she inquired. "Have you no one to read good books to you?"

"Madame," he replied, "the greater part of the people about me are Huguenots."

"They are none the less your servants," she answered.

As soon as Catherine took leave of him, he ordered his attendant to place him on a small low bed near the fireplace, and to tell the Huguenot minister, Bézières, to come to him. On entering the king's chamber, he was told to take the Bible and read the Book of Job. The king listened attentively, his hands clasped, his eyes raised towards heaven. Several Catholics were present.

"I know," he said, "you will publish it about that the King of Navarre repented, and died a Huguenot. But do not trouble yourselves about what I am. Be content with knowing that I die in the faith of the Confession of Augsbourg. But should I perchance recover, I will cause the gospel to be again preached throughout France."

Antoine appears to have been regretted by none but the wife he was so unjustly anxious to repudiate. Jeanne alone said a prayer for him. Catholics and Protestants alike rejected him. When he found that life was indeed fast ebbing away, he dictated a very touching letter to Jeanne, concluding with much good advice, and many wise counsels, which he should rather have taken to heart and observed as a rule of life himself.* Jeanne's anxiety was now the education of her son. She thought, with the great Huguenot captain, La Noue, that "it was impossible a man

* Mathieu's "*Histoire de France.*"

should be crowned with honour in his latter years if he had not been taught in the springtime of life to walk in the paths of virtue."

To shield him from the baneful influence of a shameless court, where the grossest debauchery incurred no ignominy, and treason and perfidy no dishonour, she desired, and earnestly impressed it on his preceptors, that he should be brought up in the practice of piety; that he should be made acquainted with the duties of his station, and regard it as rigorously incumbent on him to fulfil them; that he should be sincere and truthful, and the enemy of all dissimulation and craft (*feintise et cautèle*). It was her wish that he should be forewarned against all that could give him false ideas of men, of things, and his times; that the great models of antiquity should be constantly placed before his mind, in order to kindle in him a noble emulation, and to preserve him from pride. Finally, this noble Calvinist lady concluded the scheme she drew up for the education of young Henri of Navarre, with the recommendation to his preceptor not to neglect the arts that give pleasure and variety to life, which she would have his pupil cultivate in leisure hours.

Jeanne was not, however, so sanguine as to believe that her son would be trained up in the way he should go under the eye of Catherine de' Medici, who gave no heed to the morals and conduct of her own children. Besides, a prediction of the time assigned the Crown of France to the youthful Béarnais. This might prove a source of danger to him. The Queen of Navarre therefore repaired to Paris as soon as a temporary suspension of arms permitted; for Jeanne had given shelter and support to the Huguenots to the full extent of her power. Very courteously she requested young Charles, whose majority (thirteen years and a day) had been recently proclaimed at Rouen, to allow her son to return with her to Béarn. He immediately assented, and Jeanne — fearing that the queen-mother, who, it appears, was not consulted by the precocious young sovereign, would find some pretext for detaining Prince Henri, and bringing him up at the French Court as the betrothed of Marguerite de Valois — at once prepared for her departure.

Serious troubles had arisen in her absence, from the acts and intrigues of Philip II., who, as she learned on leaving Paris, had publicly protested against her suppression of Catholicism in Béarn, and the support she gave to the enemies of Rome. By bribes and promises he had seduced from their allegiance many of her subjects in Lower Navarre. The object of Philip and his allies, the Guises, was, through the treachery of trusted dependents, to get possession of Jeanne and her children; to deliver over the former to the tender mercies of the Spanish Inquisition; to shut up Henri and Catherine in separate fortresses; to invade Navarre, and to offer Béarn to Charles IX. for annexation to France. Preparations were rapidly going forward for carrying out this scheme when, it is said, the young Queen of Spain became Jeanne's protectress.* (" *Vie de Catherine de Bourbon* " — Mdme. d'Armaèlle.)

The valiant Queen of Navarre was, however, nothing daunted. Instead of seeking refuge, as advised, at Nérac, she adopted defensive measures, visited the fortresses of Béarn, and, with her accustomed firmness when danger threatened, carried the inspection of her frontiers to the very borders of Spain. She then leisurely retreated to the Château-fort of Navarre, with her ladies and her children, prepared to stand a siege. She also wrote to the Court of France, requiring that justice be done to her. The wily Catherine de' Medici, however, was too much intent on recovering the position in the government, of which recent events had in a great measure deprived her, to trouble herself about justice, and, besides, far too prudent to quarrel with her son-in-law of Spain for the sake of the Queen of Navarre.

The plot being discovered, and the plotters supposed to be baffled, danger apparently ceased to

---

* This is perhaps doubtful, as Philip was not accustomed to be moved to show mercy to heretics from whatever quarter the appeal might come, and in the instance in question even less so than usual.

exist. But the pious zeal of the Court of Rome and the "Demon of the South" was not so readily baffled, and an unusual and striking act of authority was resolved on. Eight or ten French prelates, convicted or suspected of heresy, were, together with the Queen of Navarre, cited to appear at Rome before the supreme tribunal of the Holy Inquisition, within six months from the 20th of September, 1563. Failing to do so, Jeanne d'Albret would forfeit her kingdom with any other possessions she laid claim to; and this without prejudice to other and graver punishments, which by her heretical acts she may have incurred. The stake awaited poor Jeanne. Once more she appealed to Charles IX. and the queen-mother. This produced a vigorous protestation from the Court of France to Pius IV. in the name of the royal dignity, the Gallican liberties, and the king's suzerainty over the domains of the House of Albret. As it did not suit the Pope's interests to oppose at that moment the views of the Court of France, he quietly allowed the proceedings against Jeanne and the prelates to drop without further notice.

Jeanne, with her little court, then left the gloomy walls of the sombre old fortress to resume her usually calm and quiet course of life at Nérac, and to devote herself to the superintendence of Catherine's education. The Baronne de Trignonville was the little princess's head governess — a

Protestant lady of great learning and severely moral life. But Catherine was not brought up in solitude. Jeanne thought it too dreary, and a check on the natural flow of youthful spirits. The baronne's daughter and other children of the Navarrese nobility were therefore the companions of Catherine's studies and amusements.

CHAPTER XIII.

Battle of Dreux. — Montmorency and Condé Prisoners. — Guise's proposed Attack on Orléans. — His Assassination. — The Peace of Amboise. — Condé and the Flying Squadron. — Princesse de Condé dies of Grief. — Mademoiselle de Limeuil. — The Maréchale Saint-André. — Catherine's Reign now begins.

HE fall of Rouen was followed by the submission of Caen, Dieppe, and nearly the whole of Normandy. But again the hopes of the Protestants revived when D'Andelot reached Orléans with 3,000 German cavalry, a corps of 4,000 infantry, and promises of further aid. Though ill, and suffering from a quartan fever, which compelled him to use a litter, he safely conducted these men from the banks of the Rhine — very ably avoiding an encounter with a body of Catholic troops sent to oppose his passage. Thus reinforced, Condé and Coligny left Orléans and encamped under the walls of Paris. This audacity created great alarm in the capital, and a good deal of brisk skirmishing ensued before the boulevards of the Faubourg Saint-Victor. The Protestant chiefs, however, had no expectation of becoming masters of Paris. They had

merely replied by an act of defiance to a decree of the Parliament condemning to death "Coligny and his associates."

Ten days after, they decamped and marched towards Normandy to effect a junction with the English troops, and to receive the promised gold florins. Their German auxiliaries were already demanding their pay, and, as was customary with them, threatening to desert when their services were most needed. No time was lost by the "Triumvirate" in following up the Huguenot army, which they overtook at Dreux, where was fought the first regular battle of the first religious war. The Connétable Montmorency, who held the chief command of the Catholic army, was wounded and taken prisoner. A reserve under the command of the Duc de Guise then attacked the corps headed by the Prince de Condé, who, with desperate but imprudent valour mingling with his men in the fight, fell into the enemy's hands, his horse being shot under him.

Of the two small armies opposed to each other (18,000 Catholics, and about 16,000 Protestants), between six and seven thousand were left dead or wounded on the field. Coligny's corps retreated in good order, Guise being unable to pursue; yet the Catholics claimed the victory. It was, indeed, a very barren one, though the Huguenot chief was captured, as the constable was also a prisoner, his youngest son and Saint-André, his second in command, killed, and nearly the whole of their cavalry destroyed. Some fugitives from the Catholic army reported the Huguenots victorious, and both Montmorency and Saint-André slain. This was welcome news to the queen-mother, who on hearing it quietly remarked, "We must now pray to God in French." But when a more correct report arrived, she, with equal composure, ordered bonfires to be lighted, and a Te Deum to be sung in the churches.

Though Condé and Guise were mortal enemies, yet the duke did not omit that singular customary act of courtesy towards the captive prince, of inviting him to share his couch. The constable was conducted with a strong escort to Orléans, the Protestant headquarters, where he was received and treated with all due graciousness by the Princesse de Condé, who was his niece. But the absence of the prince, of course, prevented that chiefest mark of distinction — the offer of half a bed — being conferred on him. On the day after the battle, Queen Elizabeth's ambassador, Sir Nicholas Throckmorton, was taken prisoner while following the retreating Protestant army. Luckily, he did not carry the gold florins with him. They would have been as acceptable to the needy Catholics to pay their Spanish and Swiss allies, as to the Protestants to satisfy their clamorous German friends.

The Duc de Guise, having received from the

queen-mother letters patent appointing him commandant-general of the king's forces during the absence of the constable, at once entered upon the realisation of an extensive plan he had conceived for the termination of the civil war. The first act of the sanguinary drama was an immediate attack on Orléans, and a massacre, of course, to follow. The prince and the admiral being absent, terror reigned in the city, for it was generally reported that Guise, in rivalry of Montluc, had "determined to slay not only every man, woman and child, but to extend his murderous onslaught even to the animals, to raze the city to the ground, and sow salt on its ruins."

The Huguenot infantry was lodged in the faubourg of Portereau, and there Guise began his attack. French and Germans, commanded by D'Andelot, made a valorous resistance; but their German allies (great cowards those mercenary soldiers appear to have been in those days) abandoned them, and fled for refuge to the city. Eight or nine hundred men were slain, taken prisoners, tortured, or drowned. This satisfied the bloodthirsty Guise for a first attempt.

Hatred, the most intense, a burning desire for vengeance, had glowed fiercely in many Huguenot hearts since the massacre of Vassy. Even the detested cardinal, "the tiger of France," seemed to be less an object of their implacable hate than the tyrant duke, the instigator of that butchery.

Many projects were suggested for "ridding the earth of this tyrant. Death, anywhere and by any means; but death on the battle-field was too honourable an end for him."

A young gentleman of Angoumois, Poltrot de Méré, a relative of that Renaudie who took so prominent a part in the Amboise plot, and whose dead body was gibbeted by the duke's orders, had sworn that "the tyrant should die by no other hand than his." He was believed to be rather boastful than zealous. Coligny employed him as a spy, in which capacity he had already served the Protestant commander at Lyons. Availing himself of a certain facility this gave him for accomplishing his purpose, Poltrot sought the Catholic camp. Representing himself as a repentant rebel, as several others who had treacherously deserted the Protestant cause had done, he was well received by Guise.

The duke was hastening on his preparations for attacking Orléans from the isles of the Loire, and expecting an easy conquest. For not only were the Huguenots feeble in forces to resist him, but a terrible epidemic was raging, and had already taken off from eight to ten thousand of the inhabitants. Poltrot, when about to do the dastardly deed he had resolved on, seems to have been assailed by doubts of its righteousness in the sight of heaven, or, perhaps, by fears of the consequences of it to himself. But the favourable moment had arrived. It was the 18th of February, and the attack from the isles was to begin on the morrow. The duke, accompanied by two gentlemen only, had ridden out to inspect the advanced posts. In the brief dusky twilight of a February evening he was returning to the Château de Corney to welcome his wife, whom an unwonted anxiety had brought thither to be near the scene of his defeat or victory.

Poltrot, meanwhile, alighting from his horse, and throwing himself on his knees, fervently supplicated God to turn his mind from doing this deed, if it were displeasing in His sight. If not, then he implored Him for strength, courage, and constancy to carry out his purpose to the end. No change of mind coming over him, Poltrot believed himself acting under Divine inspiration, and stealthily following his victim until within six or seven paces of him, he took aim with his pistol, the cumbrous weapon being charged with three balls. The whole charge lodged in the duke's armpit, and he fell forward on his horse's neck, while his assassin, putting spurs to his horse, fled with all speed across the woods and marshes of La Sologne.

The duke was conveyed to the Château de Corney. The surgeons were speedily in attendance; but the famous Ambroise Paré, the most skilful surgeon of the time, was not so successful in his present operation for the extraction of the balls, as some years before he had been with that terrible wound in the face that had gained the duke the sobriquet of "Le Balafré." As Catherine hastened with the young king to the camp on hearing that Guise was assassinated, it may be inferred that it was she who proposed, when his case was declared to be beyond surgical aid, that the methods of the occult sciences should be resorted to, and the cure of his wounds be attempted by incantations and charms. The duke, however, "objected to recourse being had to enchantments which God had forbidden."

"Le Grand Guise," as he was then called, ended his blood-stained career on Ash Wednesday, the 24th of February, aged forty-four. He was a dauntless soldier and an able general; but he was cruel and rapacious in the extreme, a persecutor of the Reformers, and oppressor of the people generally. He and his brother, the infamous Cardinal de Lorraine, by their joint depredations on the public purse, had brought the kingdom to the very verge of ruin. Of course his end was edifyingly pious and Christian-like. He exculpated himself from any blameworthy share in the massacre of Vassy, to the satisfaction of, at least, the courtly priest who confessed and absolved him.* He advised Catherine to make peace, which hitherto he had done all in his power to oppose and prevent. He gave excellent counsels

* "*Mémoires de Castelnau.*"

Amboise Paré.
Photo-etching from painting in "L'École de Méde-cine" at Paris.

to his eldest son, suggesting moderation in his views, disregard of the world's pleasures, and generally urged him to follow a course of life of which he had failed to set him any example.

Catherine de' Medici, though affecting grief, and shedding an abundance of those crocodile tears she had always near her eyes ready to flow forth as occasion required, as also she had the name of God always on her lips, yet rejoiced greatly in heart at this unexpected breaking up of the "Triumvirate." Now she was about to reign — to reign uncontrolled. But a few days since, that devoutedly wished-for consummation of her hopes seemed further away than ever. The stars in their courses must surely have fought for her, when "le Grand Guise," the great obstacle in her path to power, was suddenly removed. This Poltrot de Méré, against whom her anger seemed boundless, and on whom every species of horrible torture was to be inflicted, she would have willingly set on a pedestal and worshipped for his deed of noble daring, and the immense service he had done her.

In the fullness of her heart she promised all sympathy, consideration, and ample provision for the widow and sons of the man who had been heaping up wealth, and appropriating estate upon estate, with or without the consent of his sovereign, for the last twenty years. At the moment the hand of a fanatic laid him low, a decisive victory over the fever-stricken Orléanists would have thrown into his hands power great as that formerly wielded by the ancient mayors of the palace. Catherine would have received the law from him, and he would have governed the king and reigned in his stead in spite of her. She knew that, and in heartfelt thankfulness for his removal she decreed him an almost royal funeral. In military pomp, perhaps, more than royal — for Guise was very popular with the army; which had sacked, and pillaged, and, sanctioned by their brilliant leader, committed every possible enormity. Naturally, then, those soldier savages regretted "the Grand Guise," and followed him to his grave with bowed heads and saddened hearts.

The unfortunate Poltrot de Méré having lost his way in the woods in attempting to regain the Huguenot camp during the night, concealed himself in the daytime in a farmhouse, where he was discovered and arrested. Under the horrible torture of portions of his flesh being nipped off with red-hot pincers, he confessed to anything and everything his tormentors suggested or desired. He accused first the admiral of having for months incited him to assassinate Guise and other chiefs of the Catholic party. He then said that Théodore de Bèze and D'Andelot had urged him to do the deed, a varying statement being elicited each time the torture was applied to the wretched man. His agonising slow death was at last accomplished by quartering and burning. Such horrors make the blood run cold and deaden one's sympathies, whether practised by Catholics or Protestants.

Coligny, De Bèze, and other officers and ministers accused by De Méré, absolutely denied, in a memoir addressed to the queen-mother, all complicity in the assassin's deed. But Coligny acknowledged that the death of Guise appeared to him to be the most fortunate event that could have happened for France, for the churches of God, and for himself and his party. "He had many times," he said, "informed the Cardinal de Lorraine and the Duchesse de Guise that plots were on foot to take the duke's life. But since it had come to his knowledge on trustworthy authority that the duke himself had planned the assassination of the Prince de Condé, and of himself and his brother D'Andelot, he frankly avowed, while declaring on his word of honour that he had never counselled or incited any one to take the duke's life, he yet had not thought it his duty to dissuade any person from doing so. Coligny recommended the queen to keep Poltrot in prison until peace was signed, when he might be confronted with those whom he accused. But Catherine preferred to put him out of the way at once, that an accusation which could neither be proved nor refuted might rest on Coligny to his disadvantage.

Catherine now became anxious to negotiate a

peace, Coligny — whose influence with his party she imagined would suffer from her attempt to disparage him as a man of honour — having left Orlèans and succeeded in rapidly reëstablishing, to her great chagrin, the Huguenot cause in Normandy. The 300,000 gold florins had safely reached him, and with them he had completely reorganised and reinforced his army. The Catholic and Protestant chiefs being both prisoners, a preliminary conference took place between the queen and the Princesse de Condé, and France seemed threatened with another "Ladies' Peace." For when Condé and Montmorency were conducted to one of the isles of the Loire to continue the discussion opened by the ladies, the old constable displayed such extreme irritation, obstinacy, and even more than his usual brutality of speech and manners, that Condé's indignation was greatly aroused, and a *duel-à-mort* seemed a more likely result of their conference than a treaty of peace.

De L'Hôpital was then directed to draw up the terms of pacification she was disposed to offer the prince, while privately she informed Montmorency that peace *must* be concluded, and that there need be but little scrutiny of the terms, as it could be broken whenever occasion required. Montmorency, having given full vent to his spleen, became more tractable. He was very weary, too, of his imprisonment; more so, probably, than Condé — the *ennui* of captivity in the prince's case having been rendered more supportable by the amiability of the queen-mother in assigning him a companion — one of the fascinating belles of the "flying squadron." By this sort of diplomacy Catherine for awhile subdued Prince Louis, not sinking him to quite so low a level as his brother, King Antoine, but sufficiently deep and long enough to suit her temporary projects.

Setting aside the advice of the Protestant military chiefs, and disregarding the remonstrances of the ministers of religion, he signed the Treaty of Amboise without waiting for the approval of the admiral, who, on returning to Orléans four days after, joined his associates in the camp and the pastors of the church in most thoroughly condemning it. Condé was especially blamed, and Calvin in his indignation did not scruple to apply some very harsh and uncomplimentary epithets to him. Liberty of conscience was generally granted by this treaty; and freedom of worship was conceded to the *noblesse*, but in their own dwellings, and for their families only. To the *bourgeoisie* that privilege was forbidden; but in certain towns in their possession they were allowed to continue the form of worship "called reformed," while the poorer class could only meet for prayer at certain intervals, and under still more stringent restrictions.

A sort of amnesty was granted, and Condé and his followers were declared "the king's good and loyal subjects; his majesty accounting them to have acted for good ends, and with the intention of doing him service." The treaty was published in the form of an edict. The refractory Parliament, as usual, refused to register it. The chancellor in the king's name insisted, and after some further delay his command was obeyed, the whole of the members appearing in mourning robes. Zealous Catholics refused to recognise a peace with the Huguenots who had slain "the Grand Guise," on any conditions, and resisted the order to disarm — the Protestants of course also declining — unless the Catholics set the example. It soon became evident that this peace which the chancellor — and the chancellor only — was so sanguine as to believe would prove the foundation of a system of tolerance was destined to be really nothing more than a short truce.

The Duchesse de Guise with her four sons, all in deepest mourning, appeared continually in Paris, agitating and exciting the people by their unceasing demand for vengeance on Coligny, whom they denounced as the murderer of the head of the House of Guise. The duchess had probably forgotten her own prophetic words at Amboise, when, sick with the sight of blood flowing in torrents by command of the sanguinary monster whose death she now deplored and sought to have avenged, "Madame," she exclaimed, turning towards the queen-mother, "this blood will surely call for blood. May heaven spare your sons and mine!"

The just judgment of God which she then invoked and, by her words, seemed to foresee, had, in strict retributive justice, first fallen on the chief promoter of that terribly tragic scene.

The Peace of Amboise was, however, celebrated by Catherine de' Medici by one of those brilliant *fêtes* she was fond of giving at Chenonceaux for the purposes of seduction, and to which she invited those whom she was most desirous of chaining to the car of her ambition. There, she exhibited before her dazzled guests her whole swarm of corrupt loveliness, who, arrayed in scanty drapery of transparent gossamer, and with their hair falling loosely around them, served at table, in the presence of the youthful king and his young brothers — "displaying their charms with more art and complaisance than the most severe modesty took pains to conceal them."

By these lascivious means the queen-mother often succeeded in dominating for awhile those who had most defied and laughed at her efforts; by the same arts she had been working on Condé, and hoped to succeed with him as she had succeeded with Antoine. Her object was to read his mind and thoughts, and to seduce him from the Protestant cause by promises of place and power. Condé ventured to put in a claim to succeed the King of Navarre in the lieutenant-generalship of the kingdom. But Catherine had no intention of giving herself another master; she therefore merely reminded him that he had an elder brother, the Cardinal de Bourbon.

The beauty of Isabelle de Limeuil seemed greatly to attract the prince's notice. Catherine observing this — though aware of the Princesse de Condé's devoted attachment to her husband, and that she was then suffering in health from the fatigue, anxiety, and excitement she had undergone in accompanying the Huguenot army — forthwith instructed De Limeuil in the course she was to pursue in order to captivate the prince and extract from him a statement of his secret intentions respecting his party; Coligny and Condé being at that moment less cordial in their relations than usual, with regard to their difference of opinion concerning the treaty of Amboise. Isabelle, constantly thrown in his way, became the frequent companion of those hours of idleness enforced on him by his captivity.

But this captivity ended, Condé showed no eagerness for quitting the court and rejoining his party. Mademoiselle de Limeuil had not only kindled a flame almost as ardent in the breast of Condé as that Mademoiselle Du Rouet had excited in the susceptible bosom of the King of Navarre; but, unlike that more prudent damsel, she had allowed her own heart to be taken captive. Catherine de' Medici by no means contemplated such a result to the intrigue she herself had originated and encouraged. She was, or feigned to be, exceedingly irritated, the "invincible flying squadron" being trained to subdue, not to be subdued. Worse than all, this erring member of the queen-mother's forces had discovered no secrets. Condé had made no political statement, and mademoiselle apparently had sought none. Neither had she urged on him the advantage he would find in a change of religion. Without delay the queen-mother ignominiously expelled her from court, and shut her up in a convent in Burgundy, "there," as Catherine remarked, "to bury her grief and her shame."

Conde's infidelity so deeply distressed his wife, and so seriously increased her illness, that she shortly after died. Catherine then lost no time in suggesting as her successor the widow of Maréchal Saint-André, whose husband was killed at the Battle of Dreux; not exactly perhaps by Condé's own hand, but at all events by the troop he commanded after the marshal was taken prisoner. He, however, had no mind to marry her, though the immense wealth left by Saint-André made his widow and daughter two of the richest matches in France. The daughter was betrothed to the young Duc Henri de Guise. But the widow, in order to dazzle Condé by the vastness of the riches a marriage with her would place at his command, scrupled not to poison her daughter; such, at least, was the popular cry. She offered him as a present her estate of Saint-Valery, and was prepared to make the entire sacrifice of her wealth to him. He, however, remained inflexible.

The deceased marshal was a man to whom vice and crime were unstintingly attributed, and it would seem that he had a wife quite worthy of him; but her wealth, and her crime to increase it, failed to secure a prince of the blood for her second husband.

Neither pencil nor pen has depicted Prince Louis de Condé as a handsome or fascinating man. Yet it was his misfortune to be much pursued by the ladies. Of wealth he possessed very little; but he was a prince of the blood; it was just possible that he might one day wear the crown, at which he was already supposed to aim; and if he was not overburdened with prudence, he was certainly full of courage, and by far the most estimable of the three brothers.

When Isabelle de la Touche de Limeuil heard that the prince was a widower, she, too, cherished hopes of becoming his wife; for she was of a distinguished family, distantly related to the younger branch of the Bourbons. Doubtless, convent life, if not very strict in those days, was a dull affair to a young lady partly brought up at the voluptuous Court of Catherine de' Medici. Her unhappiness and her penitence were brought under the notice of the queen by friends and relatives, who earnestly entreated her restoration to favour. After some real or affected hesitation on Catherine's part, the fair Isabelle was permitted to leave her convent. But not that she might marry Condé. A husband was provided for her — an Italian gentleman of the queen's suite. Should she refuse him, the only alternative was her return to the convent.

The proposed marriage was utterly repugnant to the feelings of the fair penitent; but when she reflected on the matter, convent life seemed more so. She therefore yielded with the best grace she could under the circumstances. She, however, did not allow the husband she was compelled to accept to forget that she was of higher lineage than he. This he seems generally to have meekly acknowledged. But one day when more forcibly than usual she was impressing on him her great condescension in marrying him, he replied: "Really, madame, I think I have made a greater sacrifice in this matter than you have." She was startled at his presumption. "Have not I," he said, "sacrificed my honour to enable you to retain yours?" (Mathieu, "*Histoire de France.*")

CHAPTER XIV.

Coligny Accused of Assassinating Guise.—Siege and Capitulation of Havre.—A Royal Tour in the Provinces.—A Change of Tactics.—Catherine Decides for the Catholic Cause.—The First Stone of the Tuileries.—Piety and Pleasure the Order of the Day.—The Queen of Spain at Bayonne.—Grand Festivities.—The Salmon and the Frogs.—Double Marriage Proposed.

VERY embarrassing to Catherine de' Medici and her counsellors were the consequences of the death of the Duc de Guise and the trial of Poltrot de Méré; the barbarous punishment of that obscure fanatic not satisfying the duke's family. Popular excitement was kept alive by their frequent mourning processions in Paris, and their unceasing demand for justice on the man (Coligny being undertood but never named) who had caused the murder of the hero of their house. To increase the agitation and general bad feeling existing between Catholics and Protestants, the latter were loud in praise of the deed which the Guise family sought to avenge — exalting the assassin as the "liberator of the people of God, to whom, for his righteous zeal, the martyr's crown was due."

After the signing of the Treaty of Amboise,

Coligny retired to Châtillon-sur-Loing to pass some time with his family. He then announced to the queen his intention to repair in the course of a week to Saint-Germain, where the court was residing. The Guises and their partisans determined to give him battle, even if it were in the grounds of the château. The admiral was already well on his way, escorted by five hundred gentlemen. Catherine — greatly alarmed at the prospect of an encounter which, from the exasperation of feeling on both sides, would probably have been a very sanguinary affray — entreated Condé to set out with all speed to meet the admiral and request him to defer his visit to the court for awhile.

The prince obeyed. The next day he returned, accompanied by D'Andelot. The private council being assembled, the prince then declared that "notwithstanding that the edict of peace should cover all acts committed during the continuance of hostilities, the admiral would yet consent to the course demanded — the trial taking place before impartial judges ; and provided also that his adversaries would consent to the same judicial measures being taken in respect to the criminal attempts imputed to them." The prince added that, apart from these judicial proceedings, he should consider any attacks on the admiral as directed towards himself. Maréchal de Montmorency, in his own and his father's name, made a similar declaration.

The constable was by no means better disposed towards the cause of Reform. But he had listened to overtures of reconciliation with his nephews because of the extreme resentment he felt towards the queen-mother. To quiet the Guises, Catherine had promised that the young Duc Henri should succeed to his father's post of Grand-Master of the Household, instead of restoring it to the constable, as he had expected, "the late king having unjustly taken it from him to confer it on his uncle." To appease his wrath, Catherine now gave him the Duchy of Châtellerault. The private council then forbade both parties to offer any sort of offence towards each other, and deferred the judicial proceedings until they had obeyed the royal command to lay down their arms.

As the late peace seemed to have irritated men's minds, and created new troubles, rather than to have smoothed away differences and restored contentment, it occurred to De L'Hôpital, who was so sincerely anxious to secure tolerance for the Huguenots, and a true religious peace for France, that the recovery of Havre offered a favourable means of drawing Catholics and Protestants together in friendly union in furtherance of the same patriotic aim. He therefore suggested the siege of that town by the troops of both parties, united under the command of the constable, and urged Catherine to make an appeal to the patriotism of both the Catholic and Protestant chiefs. In moving terms, and with tear-suffused eyes, "she prayed them to set aside their quarrels, at least so long as the foreigner held a footing in the land." Condé and a large part of the Huguenot army at once hastened to join the constable's forces, while to inspire the waverers with a spirit of loyalty, the queen-mother, with the king, the young princes, and the ladies and gentlemen of the court, took up her residence at Fécamp.

There were, however, many who steadfastly adhered to their English ally, and even fought in the ranks of the English troops. Coligny refrained from taking any part in the siege. He had at the outset of the civil war been utterly opposed to seeking foreign aid, and bringing foreign troops into France. But as it had eventually been done, their opponents setting them the example, and the aid then asked been granted, he thought it neither right nor politic to break engagements which, he too plainly foresaw, must at no distant period be renewed.

Havre was, however, soon restored to the French. A long resistance had been looked for after Elizabeth's refusal to receive in exchange for it the money she had advanced to Condé and a renewal of the Treaty of 1559, promising the restitution of Calais to the English in 1569. There was a garrison of between six and seven hundred men in Havre under the orders of the Earl of Warwick, who offered but a feeble resistance to the assailants. For a terrible epidemic prevailed amongst the troops, and there was a want of provisions and pure water — the French having succeeded in cutting off the sources whence supplies were obtained. The siege, or merely the preparations for a siege, were scarcely completed when the English commander capitulated (28th of July.) The next day a large fleet, bringing a reinforcement of troops and a supply of provisions, anchored in the roadstead. But this relief came too late, and a few days after the fleet returned to England with the remnant of the fever-stricken garrison which had escaped death. War had been declared on the part of France; but Elizabeth forbore to continue it. Peace was proclaimed in the following year, 120,000 gold crowns being paid for Calais, though 500,000 was the sum stipulated by treaty in case of the failure of the French to restore it to England.

General rejoicing, bonfires, Te Deums, and the queen-mother's usual sybaritic entertainments followed the exit of the foreigner. De L'Hôpital, and possibly Catherine, believed that the flames of discord, if not utterly extinguished between Catholic and Protestant by their combined feat of arms, were stifled, at least, for a time. The court was at Meulan, where the young king hunted daily, Catherine and the court accompanying him. Charles IX. already began to display those strange outbursts of apparently motiveless anger, and that inclination — as if seeking by such means to suppress it — for violent bodily exertion, which so sorely tried and so early exhausted his naturally delicate frame. Except the queen-mother, who liked the wild sport — as her efforts to keep the king always in sight necessitated great exertion, which she fancied kept down her ever-increasing obesity — few really cared to join in what seemed to be a mere wild goose chase in pursuit of the flying, frantic young king. Happily, probably, would it have been for him and for France, had he, after his majority was declared, possessed the moral courage to shake off by degrees that horrible mother's galling yoke, which even from childhood, when he came to the throne, seemed so heavily to oppress him, and transformed him, as he grew up, from a youth of great promise, to a madman and a murderer.

In the midst of these courtly rejoicings, there arrived at Meulan a solemn procession requiring an audience of the king. It consisted of the mother, the widow, the four sons, and the four brothers of the late Duc de Guise. A very numerous *cortège* accompanied them, all wearing deepest mourning. "They desired the king's permission to proceed at once with the inquiry into that most treacherous and inhuman murder of the head of their house." Of the Châtillon brothers, Odet, the cardinal, only was with the court. Coligny again was not directly charged by name, though indirectly the crime was attributed to him alone. The cardinal therefore suggested, and Catherine consented, that the Grand Council, instead of the Parliament of Paris, should be required to take cognisance of the proceedings, as more likely to give an unbiassed judgment than that assembly of magistrates, so strongly prejudiced against the Huguenots and Reform.

The Guise family rejected as partial, or incompetent, more than half the members of the Grand Council, and Coligny objected to nearly all the rest. There remained, therefore, but the king and one or two of the councillors to decide the important question of Coligny's guilt or innocence. The decision, however, really rested with the queen-mother, who determined on letting it remain for the present undecided — an edict of January, 1564, announcing that judgment was deferred for three years, in order that a moment more opportune than the present might occur for inquiry into the facts of the case.

No sooner was one dispute settled in those troublous times than another arose, bringing with it further dissension, persecution, and hostile feelings. A grand embassy, comprising representatives from the Pope, the King of Spain, the German Emperor, and the Duke of Savoy, arrived in Paris at the time of the issuing of the above edict. The object was to prevail on the king to accept and to enforce in France the decrees of the Council of Trent. This council, after eighteen years of existence, had brought its proceedings to a close by a series of anathemas on the opinions of the Huguenots relative to the existence of purgatory, the setting up of images, the worship of saints, of the Sacrament of the Lord's Supper, of divorce, the marriage of priests, and many other matters, all of which they solemnly cursed, and declared contrary to the doctrines of the Roman Catholic Church, and punishable by death. Other questions, more immediately concerning the Catholics, were introduced into the list of decrees, and an exhortation added, urging on the king the revocation of the absolution (or amnesty) granted to the heretics by the Treaty of Amboise — also the speedy punishment of the well-known murderer of the Duc de Guise.

The boy-king, who, under the able tutelage of the queen-mother, was growing up an adept in the art of dissembling, gave the evasive reply — neither consenting nor refusing — as Catherine had taught him. But privately, the Cardinal de Lorraine — who had returned with the embassy from Rome — urged her most earnestly to command the acceptance of the decrees of the council. As earnestly De L'Hôpital opposed it, thus drawing on himself the anger of the cardinal, who accused him of holding heretical opinions, and of ingratitude to the House of Guise (his father had been secretary to the cardinal's grandmother); but the chancellor replied that debts of gratitude were not to be repaid at the expense of the king and the state. The Parliament of Paris agreed with the chancellor, which was a rather unusual event, and refused to register the decrees. They considered several of them as "a derogation of the king's rights, and of the liberties of the Gallican Church." They, however, yielded with regard to the revocation of the amnesty or "absolution," which greatly exasperated the Huguenots, but was received with much favour by the Catholics.

Meanwhile, the cardinal attempted a reconciliation between the Prince de Condé and the Guise family, in order to detach him if possible from Coligny and the Protestant cause. Mary of Scotland was again the bribe offered for the renunciation of heresy, and, as in the case of the King of Navarre, the dazzling prospect of three crowns was dangled temptingly before him. But they were temptations that had lost the charm of novelty, and their possible realisation had become more distant than ever. Condé, like his brother Antoine, preferred to amuse himself amongst the queen's bevy of beauties ; but unlike him, he forsook not the Huguenot faith or party.

In the midst of all the troubles and intrigues, political and religious, that afflicted France, the chancellor was unwearying in his efforts for the encouragement of commerce, and the repression of that ruinously lavish expenditure and luxury which prevailed in the royal household, and had thoroughly exhausted the resources of the State. He had successfully introduced several judicial reforms, and he was now of opinion that the young king should visit the several provinces of his kingdom, believing that it would be productive of much benefit both to the youthful sovereign and to his people. He therefore suggested such a course to the queen, and persuaded himself that the sight of those terrible results of civil war — the ravages that had been committed in various towns and cities — would impress Charles with a desire to preserve peace and unity amongst all classes of his subjects.

Catherine appeared to enter very readily into the chancellor's views. She was exceedingly fond of change of place and scene, and perhaps an interval of comparative quiet after the strife and turmoil amidst which she had so long lived was a pleasant prospect to her. For political objects she was also desirous of seeing her daughter, the Queen of Spain, and of consulting the Duke of Alva, Philip's confidant. The proposed journey from province to province would afford her the opportunity of a meeting at Bayonne, and would also enable her to see and judge for herself in what force the Protestants really were in the various provinces of the kingdom. Doubtless in Catherine's brain there then floated some project, as yet immature, of a Huguenot extermination; not, at that time, by violent or sudden means, but, as she flattered herself, by more subtle arts and gradual extinction.

Towards the end of March the court left Fontainebleau to make the tour of France, a numerous *cortège* and large detachment of the "flying squadron" accompanying. Previous to her departure, the queen-mother laid the first stone of her palace of the Tuileries; the building of which was begun in the month of May following, after the plans (preserved by Ducerceau) of Philibert Delorme and Jean Bullant.

According to the programme arranged for the due ordering of the royal progress, the tour was to be accomplished by very short journeys of from two to six leagues.* Long intervals of rest were to follow, to be spent in feasting and *fêtes*, sanctified by religious ceremonies and prayers. The religious part of the programme was added because of Catherine's recent determination, after much wavering, to place herself and her sons at the head of the Catholic party. She now felt convinced that the Catholics were destined to be triumphant, the peasantry and the mass of the people in the towns being with them. A change in the education of her sons was therefore imperative, and was observed by the Huguenots with some alarm.

Hitherto, the royal children, wholly unchecked, had sung the Huguenot psalms and hymns, to the

* See Abel Jouan's "*Voyage de Charles IX.*," etc.

great scandal of the Catholics. At the dissolute revels at Chenonceaux they had masqueraded in priests' vestments; tossed their rosaries and Catholic books of devotion into the fire; spoken contemptuously of the "Papists;" and eaten freely of meat in Lent and on the customary fast-days. The court had followed their and the queen-mother's example as she seemed to desire, while many believed that no fasting, no confession, and the singing of psalms and hymns in French were the chief doctrines of "the people of the religion," as the Reformers were frequently called. But a change of tactics was now needed, and henceforth the king and the rest of her children were to omit none of the external practices of devotion — the same indifference to principles and absence of moral training still continuing. For the same reason, before setting out on the projected tour, " Catherine required that the ladies and gentlemen of the court — under penalty of being expelled for disobedience — should confess, and receive the Sacrament at Easter."

Escorted by ten companies of infantry, commanded by Maréchal Strozzi, the royal travellers first halted at Champagne, passing on thence to Troyes, where they remained a month. The inhabitants were all very eager to see the youthful monarch, the rest of the young royal family, and their gracious Florentine mother — a further interest being given to this visit by the signing at

Troyes, on the 12th of April, of a peace between the Queen of England and the King of France. Continuing their journey, Charles and his mother visited the Duchesse de Lorraine, Catherine's eldest daughter; Charles acting as sponsor to his sister's infant son.

On their road to Lyons they were met at the gates of Dijon by Catherine's formerly devoted friend, Maréchal Gaspard de Tavannes—a brave and able general, a most zealous Catholic and cruel persecutor of the Huguenots. On accosting the king, he laid his hand on his heart and said: "This is yours;" then placing it on his sword, he continued, "and with this I am able to serve you."

At Lyons, at Orléans, and other towns which had been the Huguenots' principal cities of refuge, Catherine ordered the construction of strong citadels; appointing as governors men opposed to the cause of Reform. An edict was also issued forbidding the Reformers the exercise of religious worship in any city or town where the king might be sojourning. Pius IV., to whom Catherine communicated her plan for the gradual extinction of Calvinism, by a temporising system which she explained to him, is said to have been far from disapproving it, though he would have preferred some scheme more swift and sure in its operation.

The winter of 1564 and 1565 was one of unusual severity throughout France. "So intense was its rigour that it was considered one of the chief calamities of the epoch." The sufferings of the people were very great; but neither this widespread misery nor the political and religious contests, resulting in frequent assassinations, general disquiet, and the prospect of fresh hostilities, interrupted the round of *fêtes*, banquets, and balls with which the "good towns" welcomed their young sovereign, and the *élite* were in return entertained. Charles seems to have been more than once indisposed from excessive feasting and fêting. Into all those "good towns" he made his public entry with the queen-mother. Generally he was saluted with frantic cries of "*Vive la messe!*" The city guilds passed in procession before him. Children were named after the king, queen, and madame. Te Deums were sung from morn till eve, and piety and pleasure marched on hand-in-hand.

But Catherine had expressed a desire to see her daughter, the Queen of Spain. Her son-in-law, the king, she would have preferred to see, alone, but hoped that at all events he would accompany the queen. He did not, but consented that Isabelle (as Elisabeth was called in Spain) should visit her mother, accompanied and guarded by his second self, the Duke of Alva, and other Spanish grandees, as spies on the young queen. Elisabeth was well trained before leaving Spain by Philip himself in the part she was to play; and she seems to have done her best, as attested by Alva, to secure the approval of her amiable lord and master. On the 12th of June, 1565, Charles IX., Catherine de' Medici, and the court arrived at Saint-Jean-de-Luz, and left the next day to receive the Queen of Spain on the extreme frontier of France, near Fontarabia. The young king was escorted by the detachment of troops under Strozzi, and a company of light cavalry.

A bower, or tent of foliage, was erected in a field on the banks of the river Bidassoa, and a splendid collation of "Mayonnaise hams, beeves' tongues, Bologna sausages, pâtés, fruit, salads, preserves, and a large supply of good wine awaited there her majesty's arrival." She, however, dined at Irun, and after dinner descended the mountain, escorted to the river's brink by 300 mounted archers of the Spanish king's guard and an ensign's company of infantry. The queen-mother then crossed the river on a bridge of boats and embraced her daughter, afterwards conducting her to the king, who, with his court, was waiting to receive her in a boat moored in mid-stream, as he might not set foot on Spanish ground. Having landed on the French bank of the river, the royal party entered the verdant bower to refresh themselves. "They remained there an hour — trumpets, hautbois, and tambourines joyously celebrating the happy event of the queen's arrival."

On the journey to Bayonne the Queen of Spain

rode between her mother and brothers. On the 15th of June she and her retinue, and Charles IX. and his court and military escort—forming a grand procession—made their public entry into Bayonne in the evening, by torchlight. During the seventeen days the young queen remained at Bayonne, *fêtes*, tournaments, jousts, combats of three hours' duration, plays, balls, banquets, succeeded each other in one unceasing round; while bonfires and illuminations lighted up the town during the semi-darkness of the short midsummer nights.*

Notwithstanding that "the hopes of Christendom ran high concerning the result of the Spanish visit," the great circumspection observed on both sides not to commit themselves to the adoption of any suggestion in particular, together with their mutual distrust, prevented any definite scheme for the wholesale extermination of heresy being positively agreed to. To seize the leaders of the faction and cut off their heads seemed to be the method that found most favour. "The head of one salmon is worth more than the heads of ten thousand frogs," said the Duke of Alva, rather impatiently, in reply to the queen-mother's plan of gradual extinction.

A boy of eleven was amusing himself within hearing. He was struck by the duke's remark on the relative value of the heads of salmon and

* Abel Jouan's "*Voyage de Charles IX.*"

frogs, and repeated it to his mother. The boy was Henri of Navarre. Jeanne d'Albret with her children had joined the court at Bayonne; for the Spanish interview concerned her also. Unwisely following the example of more powerful sovereigns who had refused liberty of worship to the Reformers, she, *en revanche*, had forbidden the Catholic form of worship in her domains. She now consented to remove that prohibition; the peace of her little kingdom being threatened, and Spanish interference certain.

Whether from fear of her cruel, fanatical husband, or that from her residence in the gloomy, formal, and priestridden Court of Spain, Elisabeth had really adopted the bigoted views of Philip and the people about her, she supported the proposals which Alva made in the king's name with a sort of feverish energy, and joined him in urging on her mother the immediate dismissal of De L'Hôpital, "the abettor and protector of evil-doers." But Catherine absolutely refused; though she had secretly abandoned the chancellor's policy, while leaving him at full liberty to effect judicial and civil reforms. On the whole, nothing was concluded at Bayonne. Each party desired to deceive the other — Philip and Catherine having secret and separate aims which neither he nor she cared to disclose.

A double marriage was proposed by the queen-mother between her daughter Marguerite and

Don Carlos; and the Duc d' Anjou (Henri III.) and the Princess of Portugal, or other relative of the King of Spain. The young queen replied that the Catholic king was not then disposed to marry his son. In Alva's account of these interviews, he refers with praise to the "great earnestness and consummate prudence" displayed by the young queen in her replies to her mother in support of Philip's views. The queen-mother herself was surprised at her daughter's warm advocacy of them; but she was generally supposed to be under the influence of fear of failure in the part imposed on her.

On the departure of the Spanish Queen, Charles made her a present of a white mule, on whose trappings, ornamented with gold and precious stones, he is said to have spent 400,000 ducats — disregarding the ruined state of the finances and the poverty of the people; from whose pockets were extracted all the cost of that vain pageantry which preceded and followed, for another seventeen days, the Spaniards' departure. Catherine crossed the river with her daughter and slept at Irun. Elisabeth desired to recross it in the morning with her mother; but Spanish etiquette forbade it. Before leaving Bayonne a hundred or more people, who had journeyed long distances for the purpose of being thus cured of their maladies, were touched by Charles for the king's evil (Abel Jouan).

The royal party then reëntered the interior of Gascony, passing through the domains of Jeanne d'Albret, who accompanied the Court on their leisurely journey towards the Loire. Along this route the fearful ravages of the civil war were but too plainly visible — devastated churches, ruined convents, broken statues, open tombs. The young king, scarcely controlling his rage, pointed out to Jeanne d'Albret this fearful desecration of sacred things — his gestures, his exclamations, showing the deep hatred then kindled in him towards the Huguenots; a feeling very different from that with which De L'Hôpital hoped they would impress him.

This tour of the French provinces had taken, so far, nearly two years to accomplish, ending in the month of December with the arrival of the court at Moulins, where the princes of the blood, the knights of the Order, dignitaries of the Church, and other great personages were, by command of the king, to assemble in council early in January, 1566.

CHAPTER XV.

The Court at Moulins. — The Reconciliation and "Kiss of Peace." — The New Year. — Horrors in the Netherlands. — Surprise and Arrest of Condé and Coligny Projected. — Hasty Departure of the Court. — Charles in a Rage at Flying before His Subjects. — A Long Ride; Charles Weary and Hungry. — Battle of Saint-Denis, November, 1567. — Death of Montmorency.

THE Christmas of 1565 and the New Year, 1st of January, 1566, were celebrated by Charles IX., Catherine de' Medici, and the French Court, at the splendid Château de Moulins.* There, forty-four years before, the celebrated but unfortunate constable, Duc Charles de Bourbon, first prince of the blood, so magnificently entertained François I. and his court, that the jealousy of that monarch and the cupidity of his mother, Louise of Savoy, were greatly excited — the grandeur of the duke's

---

* It had been customary to begin the year at Easter, which, being a movable feast, had frequently occasioned much confusion and inconvenience. The chancellor therefore proposed, and the suggestion, generally adopted, was also approved by the Parliament of Paris, that "henceforth in all judicial acts the year should begin on the 1st of January, as was formerly the custom of the Romans."

abode, and the royal state in which he lived, far surpassing that of the sovereign. At this princely château (confiscated after the duke's revolt) the Guises, the Châtillons, the Montmorencys, and the greater part of the princes and grand seigneurs of the kingdom were commanded to attend. The three years to which the decision respecting Coligny's imputed complicity in the assassination of Duc François de Guise was deferred had not yet quite elapsed. But in view of what was in her mind with reference to the Huguenots, Catherine thought it well to settle that question at once.

During the period that royalty was making the tour of France, the Protestants lost their spiritual chief, John Calvin (24th of May, 1564) — a loss which Catherine imagined would occasion a large falling off in the number of adherents to the doctrines of the austere "Pope of Geneva," as Calvin was frequently called. The more zealous Catholics rejoiced extravagantly at his death, while Protestants mourned him deeply. Still they were not left as sheep without a shepherd. The learned and pious Théodore de Bèze worthily succeeded Calvin, maintaining his doctrines with equal firmness, while less repellently stern in his manners. Calvin was in his fifty-sixth year, and had long been a great sufferer from a complication of painful maladies — so much so, that death would seem to have been an almost welcome release from a living martyrdom. " To be united in Christ and inflexible towards the enemies of Christ" was his dying injunction to his followers.

Besides the accusation against Coligny, another question had been deferred for settlement by the council of grandees assembled at Moulins. A conflict — at that time threatening great disturbance in the capital — had taken place in Paris in the preceding year, between Maréchal François de Montmorency, the constable's eldest son, who was Governor of Paris, and the Cardinal de Lorraine. The cardinal, always terribly alarmed at the possibility of harm befalling his sacred person, had become, since his brother's assassination, more nervously timid than ever. Consequently, he sought from Catherine authority to surround himself, when travelling, with an arn ed escort; but haughtily refused to exhibit the document granting this permission, when required to do so by the governor. The latter, therefore, determined not to allow an open infringement of the recent royal order prohibiting any of his majesty's subjects from passing through the kingdom armed.

The cardinal, disregarding the marshal's announcement, proposed not merely to secure himself from danger, but, accompanied by his nephew and a numerous armed *cortège*, to make a sort of public entry into Paris, after his rather prolonged absence from the kingdom. At the gate of Saint-Denis the provost was stationed with a company of gendarmes, who required the cardinal's pass. He deigned no reply, and his escort, equally indifferent to the provost's command to lay down their pikes and arquebuses, passed after my lord cardinal through the gate. A body of cavalry, headed by Montmorency, was drawn up near the Marché des Innocents. The cardinal and his escort were again commanded to halt; but as they were not disposed to obey, the marshal's troops, armed with heavy horse-pistols, fired on the "Lorrainers." Probably this was intended only to frighten the rebel cardinal, as no one was killed or wounded.

That timorous prelate was, indeed, very much frightened. The sound of the first pistol-shot made him leap from his horse and rush into the nearest house, dragging his nephew after him; the youth indignantly resisting. In this hiding-place he remained until nightfall. His escort wisely dispersed, with as little delay as possible, and the cardinal, with the young duke and but two or three attendants, entered Paris quietly, shunning observation, instead, as he had proposed, with colours flying and beat of drum. He had expected to create a great sensation in Paris, and to revive the excitement caused by the late duke's death. Also to rekindle enthusiasm for the House of Guise by parading the young Duc Henri (a handsome youth of fifteen) before the admiring eyes of the Parisian people. Finally, as Maréchal de Montmorency favoured the cause of Reform, the cardinal hoped to make his duty, as governor, of maintaining peace in Paris, more arduous than it already was, by the additional strife and hatred he expected to stir up between Catholics and Protestants.

Full of gall and wormwood, having just returned from anathematising at the Council of Trent, the cardinal addressed a memorial to the king, complaining of the outrage and indignity put upon him by the Governor of Paris. His brother, the Duc d'Aumale, also wrote to the most violent of the Catholic chiefs, asking their assistance in avenging the much-insulted cardinal. Montmorency, on his part, called in the aid of Coligny and his partisans. But when this affair came to the queen-mother's knowledge, she immediately forbade both the Guises and the Châtilions to enter Paris, and required that no further steps should be taken in this dispute until the assembling of the Grand Council at Moulins.

All who were summoned to attend were now assembled. The "flying squadron" was there in full force; while to put everybody in good temper, and, with the assistance of the squadron, to inspire all present with the inclination to assent to whatever she proposed, Catherine opened the proceedings by giving a splendid *fête*. It does not appear to have greatly subdued the hearts of the Catholics, or seduced the Calvinists, who were thus compelled to attend a reunion which the austerity of their doctrines led them to regard as a species of temptation of the devil.

The reconciliation of the marshal and the cardinal was not readily brought about. The former was obstinately bent on refusing to utter words of peace. Catherine was compelled to persuade the constable — though he was rarely in a conciliatory mood, and far from it on the present occasion — to undertake the bringing of his son to listen to reason, which was to assure the cardinal that "in what he had done there was no intention on his part of offering any personal offence. He had acted solely from the sense of a necessity of doing his duty." This was all that the constable by threatening to disinherit his son could extract from him. The cardinal was more amenable to Catherine's persuasion. He professed himself satisfied, being anxious to secure the queen-mother's favour now she was independent of him.

The council having pronounced this quarrel amicably settled, judgment was next to be given in the Guise and Coligny affair. The admiral now "solemnly swore that he had been neither the author of the assassination of the Duc de Guise, nor an accomplice in it, and that he challenged to single combat whoever sustained the contrary." The council, after a short consultation, were unanimously of opinion that no grounds existed for the charges brought against the admiral. The king forthwith declared him innocent, and enjoined both parties to live henceforth in peace and amity.

The duke's widow had married again, and was now Duchesse de Nemours. She and the cardinal promised to obey the king's injunction, and gave the admiral the kiss of peace. The young duke, however, was absent, and the Duc d'Aumale purposely delayed his arrival that he might not be present at the reconciliation. He openly protested against the decision of the council, and displayed such violent animosity towards the Châtillons, even in the presence of the king and court, that both parties were requested to leave Moulins. The duke was accused of having authorised an attempt to assassinate Coligny and D'Andelot; and the young Duc de Guise, who had just completed his sixteenth year, afterwards declared that as he was not present he did not consider the promises of his mother and uncle binding on him. Thus ended the Grand Council of Moulins. Peace and good-will were proclaimed, but hatred and resentment rankled in every heart.

Jeanne d'Albret and her children had accompanied the court from Bayonne to Moulins. But finding that the queen-mother's new orders, strictly prohibiting within the residence of the court the singing of psalms in French, or any other practices of the Calvinist form of worship, extended even to her, she speedily withdrew from the royal residence and returned, with her son and daughter, to Gascony and Béarn.

Charles and his mother did not greatly prolong their stay at Moulins after the departure of the dissatisfied disputants. Catherine brought their sojourn to an end, as she began it, with a very grand and very expensive *fête*. That it should be expensive was always to her the chief attraction of any court festivity; but how the expense was to be provided for she cared not at all.

On the 1st of May, 1566, Charles IX., after an absence of two years and two months, returned to Paris, and, with his mother, dined in the Faubourg Saint-Honoré at Madame du Perrin's (Pierre de L'Éstoile). Charles was now within a few weeks of completing his sixteenth year; he had grown considerably during his tour, and in general appearance was much improved. But his irascibility of temper had become more noticeable then before, and there was a restlessness in his manner, a sort of ill-suppressed exasperation, that noisy amusements and violent exercise alone relieved. But in his milder moods he displayed a fondness for music, and poetical talent that did not fall below Ronsard's; while later on he developed some skill in metal-chasing.

But a new element of discord was introduced about this time into unhappy France. The Jesuits, through the intervention of some influential chiefs of the Catholic faction, succeeded, against the strenuous efforts of the chancellor, the opposition of the University, the ancient religious orders and the municipal body, in obtaining from the Parliament — itself opposed to them — "provisional authority" for continuing their course of teaching in Paris. For as a community of teachers only, not as a new religious order, were they recognised by the ecclesiastical synod of Poissy.

What was provisional, of course, soon became perpetual. They established themselves in all the great towns of France, and as they were more learned and more dignified than the clergy of that period were generally, their success was rapid, and their importance daily increased throughout Europe. As preachers, their earnestness and eloquence were employed to arouse the bad feeling of the Catholic people against the Huguenots, teaching that "faith need not be kept with them, and that to put them to death was an act agreeable to God." One of their famous orators, Edmond Auger, was the instigator of many sanguinary attacks on the Protestants. Very singularly, after one of these conflicts in which several of their number were slain, Auger, who had fallen into their hands, was saved from being hanged, by a Protestant minister who, deeply moved by his eloquence, interceded for him.*

Horrible cruelties were then being perpetrated by order of Philip II. on the people of the

* The "Preachers of the League," C. Labitte.

Netherlands, and, as if to abet and encourage the monstrous horrors which suggested themselves to that demon's mind, a Pope of congenially demoniacal spirit had succeeded (December, 1565) to the papal throne — vacant by the death of Paul IV. Pius V., or Saint Pius — for he was afterwards canonised — was a man into whose soul not one single feeble ray of pity or human feeling of any kind had ever entered. Michel Ghislieri, the exterminating genius of the Inquisition, had passed from the office of Grand Inquisitor to fill the chair of Saint Peter. His pontificate of six and a half years was one long reign of terror, one long *auto-da-fé*, in which many of Italy's greatest men perished by his order.

This saintly pontiff was desirous of uniting with that zealous Christian, the Catholic king, in urging on Catherine de' Medici the adoption of a more vigorous course for purging France from heresy than that slow and ineffectual system she habitually followed, of alternate delay, concession, and dissimulation. He is said to have trembled with rage when referring to it, and especially to her endeavours to keep on terms with the "apostate cardinal," Odet de Châtillon. To remedy in some degree the woes of the kingdom, he would have thrust the Inquisition on France; but Catholics as well as Protestants were resolutely determined not to submit to it. Its introduction at this time into the Netherlands, by order of Philip II., occasioned the rising *en masse* of the Protestant population, who, following the example of their French coreligionists, desecrated the churches, broke the statues, defaced the pictures of saints, and established their own form of worship in the greater part of the cities. But their triumph was of short duration, and terrible vengeance was soon to follow.

The "Christian prince and avenger of God," as Philip dared to call himself, delayed not to despatch the merciless Duke of Alva with a body of troops to "exterminate" the Flemings and the Dutch. "The extermination of the people and the laying waste of the country he preferred, he said, to allowing any obstacle to his absolute will henceforth to exist in that rebel State." His wishes were carried out *con amore* by his able lieutenant and his myrmidons. Horrors unspeakable were perpetrated; tortures inflicted that make the blood curdle but to think of, and which must surely have been suggested to these monsters in human shape by the satanic influence of the very spirit of evil.

If not exactly through France, yet close as possible to its frontiers, marched the exterminating hosts of the "Demon of the South." The French Protestants were greatly agitated, and their alarm was shared by the Reformers throughout Europe. They no longer doubted that Catherine, conjointly with Philip and the Pope, had concocted a similar plan for the extinction of the Huguenots in France. So wide-spread was this opinion that several of the German princes sent a united embassy to France to entreat the king, in the name of the long-existing friendship between the two countries, to extend tolerance towards his Huguenot subjects, and to enforce the observance of the edict of pacification.

Charles received the German envoys very discourteously. Scarcely restraining his passionate anger, he replied that he was "fully disposed to respect the ancient friendly feeling between France and Germany, if the princes would not in future intermeddle in his affairs, as he certainly would not in theirs." Equally harsh in tone, and disrespectful in manner, was his conversation with the admiral, when complaining to him of the ill-treatment and many unprovoked attacks the Protestants were receiving at the hands of some Catholic fanatics, urged on by their priests.

Charles was now seventeen, yet without his mother's approval he dared not exercise any act of sovereignty. Appeals to him were futile, as he keenly felt — expending his rancour in the irritability of his replies. He yearned for freedom, and seemed to incline towards the counsels of the chancellor; but courage failed him to break the chain with which his hated and hating mother held him in bondage. Her strong will completely dominated his weak one, while his rage was vented in impotent acts of fury. Shortly before the arrival of the Germany embassy, Catherine, in the king's name, had asked the hand of a daughter of the German Emperor, Maximilian II. She desired his alliance as a counterpoise to the pressure put upon her by Philip II. and Pius V. respecting the Protestants, whom she would have preferred to exterminate after her own more subtle system, and without *autos-da-fé*.

Maximilian II. was a prince of a very tolerant spirit and estimable character. He greatly favoured his Lutheran subjects, and political reasons alone are said to have deterred him from declaring himself of their faith. He declined, however, to entertain the king's proposal, unless restitution was made to the empire of Metz, Toul, and Verdun. Catherine had previously — disregarding the disparity of their years — suggested to Elizabeth of England a marriage with Charles, or with his brother, the Duc d'Anjou; for the latter she was exceedingly anxious to secure a throne, with or without a wife to share it, and had promised the fanatical Philip to coöperate zealously with him in "avenging God," if he would cede the Duchy of Milan to her second son.

Meanwhile it transpired that Catherine was secretly making great efforts to borrow money and to raise troops. Six thousand Swiss had already entered France, and were advancing by forced marches to the centre of the kingdom — it being given out that these six thousand Swiss were to form a corps of observation on the frontier of Picardy. As these preparations were not directed against Spain, they indicated some sinister intentions on Catherine's part towards the Reformers. Urged by Philip and the Pope, she had resolved on aiming a blow at heresy that should strike terror into the hearts of the Huguenots. She was, in fact, about to follow the example of the Duke of Alva, who, in the Netherlands, as his first act of authority, had arrested Count Egmont and Count Horn, and brought them before his "tribunal of blood."

The two chiefs of the French Protestant party were secretly informed of this design by De L'Hôpital, as supposed. Condé was to be condemned to perpetual imprisonment, Coligny to death. Hitherto they had restrained the Huguenots, though with difficulty, from again taking up arms. All France was, indeed, in a state of ferment. Murders and dastardly attacks by night on the Protestants were committed with impunity, while similar offences on their part, whatever the provocation, were punished with cruel rigour.

Now, however, it had become evident that action in self-defence was a necessity. Coligny therefore proposed the bold plan of calling on the Protestants to rise *en masse;* to attack and destroy the Swiss before they could join the royal troops; to arrest the Cardinal de Lorraine; to

Gaspard de Coligny, Admiral of France.
Photo-etching from an old print.

seize the person of the king, his mother and brothers, and to govern in the name of Charles IX. The Protestant nobility of the northern provinces were to assemble at Rosay, in Brie, and to begin the attack on the 29th of September.

The queen-mother, the king, and the court were amusing themselves at the queen's Château of Monceaux, while awaiting the news of the surprise and capture of the Protestant prey. But when, instead of that welcome intelligence, Catherine's messengers informed her that large bodies of armed Huguenot cavaliers were arriving in Brie from various parts, she took alarm, and with the king and the court fled in all haste to Meaux. Thence, courier after courier was despatched requiring the Swiss to hasten on to Meaux. Opinions were divided as to the best course to pursue. Should the queen-mother and the king remain at Meaux and negotiate, or, with their escort — eight or nine hundred unarmed gentlemen — and surrounded by the 6,000 Swiss, endeavour to reach Paris as quickly as possible?

The constable and the chancellor were for remaining; the cardinal and Duc de Nemours for departure. Catherine took the advice of the latter, and the Swiss having arrived late in the evening of the 26th, at four on the following morning the royal party, escort and guards, set out on their journey, Charles — in a very irritable mood at the idea of flying before his subjects — taking command of the Swiss, sword in hand. As the full force of the Huguenots had not yet assembled, Condè and Coligny, at the head of only 500 armed cavaliers, could not hope to break through a body of troops 6,000 strong. Some skirmishing, however, occurred with the royal troops, which induced the constable to recommend a change of route — in case Protestant reinforcements should arrive and endanger the king's safety — leaving the Swiss with him to oppose the pursuit of the Huguenots.

The king and the queen-mother assented. It was nightfall ere they arrived in Paris, Charles as usual in a rage; his ride of fifteen hours was a longer one than even he cared to take. "He was exceedingly weary," we are told, "also very hungry" (Pierre de L'Estoile). Catherine had energy enough for anything; but how the ladies generally, on their mules or in their litters, bore the fatigue and necessarily the attendant terror of flying before an enemy, the chroniclers do not say.

The cardinal was less fortunate than the royal party. He had recommended to them the more dangerous course; but it was not in his nature to adopt it himself. He quietly trotted off to Rheims, expecting to reach his archbishopric without molestation or adventures. He, however, narrowly escaped falling into the hands of a party of Huguenots on their march to join the prince and the admiral. His Spanish mule bore him swiftly out of danger; his attendants as swiftly followed, and there was no attempt at pursuit. For he left his baggage behind him, containing a costly service of plate, with which the Huguenots went on their way perfectly satisfied, and probably rejoicing.

Arrived at Rheims, his eminence lost no time in laying a statement of his trials and his losses before the King of Spain. He prayed him to send the Duke of Alva and his troops into France, and craved his powerful protection for himself and the House of Guise. The members of that house he assured him were all devoted to him, and "when Catherine de' Medici's sickly sons had died off — of which there seemed a not distant prospect — would aid him in setting at naught the Salic law, and, in the name of his wife Elisabeth, claiming the throne of France."

But the Protestant chiefs, being reinforced, speedily followed the royalists; and, with the intention of blockading Paris, directed their partisans to rendezvous under the walls of the city. Their headquarters were at Saint-Denis — the prince taking the precaution of closing the abbey to prevent its desecration. Several towns were occupied with the view of interrupting the arrival of supplies by the Upper and Lower Seine, the Marne, and the Yonne. Great was the outcry of the Parisians at the prospect of a dearth of provisions, while Catherine, amazed at the energy and audacity of the Protestant chiefs, was induced, at the suggestion of the chancellor, in which the constable concurred, to attempt negotiation.

It was rather a short truce than a peace that Catherine desired, to last until she could obtain the aid she sought from Spain. But the Protestants demanded liberty of worship throughout the kingdom, and, equally with the Catholics, admission to offices in the government. Catherine refused. A stormy scene appears to have occurred in the Huguenot camp between the constable and his nephew Odet, the "apostate cardinal," whom, for the first time, he then saw in cuirass and helmet, armed *cap-à-pie*.

War being inevitable, the queen-mother urgently demanded of the Duke of Alva, of the Pope, of the city of Paris, and of the clergy, aid and support in troops and money. Forced loans were raised, and the crown diamonds and rubies pledged to Italian bankers for 200,000 gold crowns. The Protestants applied for similar assistance to the Germans. On the 10th of November, the constable, commanding-in-chief, attacked the Huguenot army late in the day. Both sides fought with savage valour. Five times the constable was wounded, when a Scotchman, said to have been Robert Stuart, rode up and shot him in the loins, piercing his cuirass. He was borne from the field of battle by his sons, who commanded under him.

Fighting was then resumed with greater energy by the Protestants, and intenser fury by the Catholics. Condé's horse being wounded, the prince determined to retreat on Saint-Denis, and darkness coming on put an end to the carnage. The victory was not a decisive one, but both sides claimed it as such. The Huguenots, being reinforced, offered battle to their adversaries on the following day. The Catholic chiefs did not accept the challenge. They were assembled round the death-bed of the constable, who died the next day (12th of November).* His funeral was of royal grandeur, and as a grand spectacle the Parisians flocked to gaze on it. But the constable, harsh in manners, brutal in character, had never, while living, awakened any sympathy in the people, and none regretted him now dead.

Catherine affected to grieve while inwardly rejoicing at the removal out of her path of the last of the "Triumvirate;" the last of those powerful subjects who had contested her right to the supreme authority she sought to usurp, and had allowed her but a small share of it. Now, she was wholly free — the uncontrolled sovereign of France. Henceforth, she was determined that only men — men chiefly of her own nation — who owed wealth and power to her alone should participate in the government with her.

---

* Anne de Montmorency was seventy-five years of age. He had been unfortunate as a commander, having lost more battles than he had won. His reputation, both as a statesman and a general, is said to have been greater than his merits.

As her last mark of respect to the constable, Catherine caused his heart to be enclosed in the urn containing that of Henri II. This urn — borne by the Graces, and, as already observed, one of Germain Pilon's finest groups — was originally designed by her to contain her own heart in the vacant place now ceded to that of Anne de Montmorency.

CHAPTER XVI.

Anjou Lieutenant-General. — Siege of Chartres. — Jean Casimer and the German Troops. — Catherine's Treachery. — Warned by Tavannes. — Fording the Loire. — Jeanne d'Albret and Her Son. — Odet de Châtillon and Elizabeth of England. — De L'Hôpital's Retirement. — Don Carlos and Elisabeth of France.

ATHERINE DE' MEDICI was fond of vaunting the fancied virtues of her second son, Henri, Duc d'Anjou. His youthful courage, martial ardour, great ambition, intense devotion, and remarkable docility of character, were habitually set forth as if to mark the strong contrast between him and the impetuous, irascible Charles and his uncertain moods of temper. Her training and her treatment of her children do indeed give warrant to the generally accredited statement that she had no affection for any of them, except this son; and that, so far as she was capable of any tenderness of feeling, "she loved him — as the viper loves the most venomous of her brood" (Henri Martin).

Catherine had great hopes of Anjou. In him she looked forward to giving France a true Italian prince — a despotic tyrant — after the model depicted by Machiavelli, as understood by her, and such as the Borgia and Medici families had sometimes inflicted on Italy. The constable's death furnished her with an opportunity she hastened to seize of placing Henri, then sixteen, at the head of the armies of France. The vacant post of constable was not to be filled up. "It put into the hands of a subject," as she duly impressed on Charles, "too large a share of power in the government." But the lieutenant-generalship of the kingdom — an office that involved the command-in-chief of the armies — was to be revived and conferred on Anjou.

The young king was disposed to head his army himself. But his mother, and the Italians she was continually introducing to prominent posts in the government, urged on him that it was inconsistent with his dignity as sovereign to conduct in person an army to chastise rebels. Charles abhorred his brother, and this feeling Henri fully reciprocated. But he yielded to the advice, or rather the commands of the queen-mother, though not with a very good grace. Instantly he set off for Chambord to expend his rage in hunting — pursuing the wild boar with a sort of mad energy almost realising the fury of the wild huntsman, who, according to the legend, hunted nightly in those forests, with "a pack of demon hounds in full cry." Charles would blow his hunting-horn with such force that his eyes would seem ready to start from their sockets, and would slay whatever animals he came across with a ferocious eagerness and savage joy.

To Chambord Catherine pursued this wayward, excitable son, who occasioned her so much disquietude, and inspired her with so much antipathy. She was always in dread of his eluding her grasp and acting in direct opposition to her. But her clutch on him was so firm that, however he may have desired to shake himself free, he was incapable of sustained effort long enough to accomplish it.

The Huguenot army was not sufficiently strong to subdue Paris by famine; it therefore decamped, hoping to join a detachment of 11,000 cavalry and infantry sent by the Calvinist Elector Palatine, under the command of his son, Jean Casimer. The weather was terrible in its severity, and the march of the Huguenots through Champagne was no less dangerous than laborious. They were without resources, without stores, or strongholds, and were compelled to levy contributions on the villages and small towns they passed through. An army double their number, well provided and equipped, was following them but at a few leagues' distance; an army, reinforced by Philip, the Pope, and the Swiss, which might well have overwhelmed them and accomplished its mission of extermination. Its commander-in-chief was the Duc d'Anjou, with the able and experienced general,

Maréchal Tavannes, as his guide and counsellor. Notwithstanding, a want of discipline prevailed in the ranks of this motley assemblage of nations.

Maréchal Tavannes could not certainly be accused of such weakness as a leaning towards mercy's side, nor could too large a share of humane feeling be imputed to Maréchal de Cossé-Gonnor, who commanded the French division. Yet it appears that the latter, joined by other French officers, expressed some repugnance to slaughtering his countrymen — "in arms only for the defence of liberty and life." As the French troops and their officers were alike generally influenced throughout this struggle by fanatic zeal rather than by humanity and a spirit of tolerance, it may be that the slaughter of their countrymen was objected to on this occasion because not wholly confided to them.

The presence of Spanish troops in France was an abomination to the French, and the interference of the Pope and his Italian troop was no less so, however Catherine and her court might have sought or desired their aid. But whatever the cause, dissension reigned in the royal camp, and the authority of the young lieutenant-general was too little respected to restore discipline. The Huguenots, meanwhile, were plodding on their weary way — effecting their junction with Jean Casimer in Lorraine before the royalist armies could overtake them. While besieging Chartres, they received the gratifying intelligence that the important maritime city of La Rochelle had declared for the cause of Reform — thus assuring them, in the west, a stronghold of the first order.

Catherine now divided her time, to the admiration of the Venetian ambassadors, between the court and the camp. She had her scouts abroad, who diligently kept her informed of the proceedings of both armies.* As soon as she heard that harmony did not prevail in the councils of the lieutenant-general, and that Fortune was favouring the Huguenots, she set out immediately for the royalist headquarters. A suspension of arms was agreed on, while an envoy with proposals of peace was despatched to the Protestant camp. This was her usual proceeding when any success attended the Protestant arms. She now offered to abolish all restrictions on their freedom of worship enacted since the Treaty of Amboise, and to advance the sum due to their German auxiliaries.

After some hesitation — knowing how worthless were these treaties of peace — the Huguenots authorised Odet de Châtillon, the diplomatist of their party, to accept her proposals. They wanted to reorganise their army, to give it some needed rest; and they wanted money also. Silver shrines and silver statues, as well as the gold plate and other treasures of the despoiled churches, had been melted down and converted into coin. But the

* Gironamo Lippomano, "Reports of Venetian Ambassadors."

needs of the army, and the stern demands of their mercenary allies for prompt payment of their claims, soon emptied the military coffers. An edict of peace was therefore published on the 23d of March, at Longjumeau. It was a temporary relief to the much-harassed army, but was regarded with fear and distrust by the Huguenot people.

This peace, however, excited the highest indignation of the Catholic king and the Pope. The latter had sent a corps of Italians, equipped and paid by himself, and, further, on the strength of Catherine's promises to outvie in zeal even the Spanish king, had contributed 10,000 ounces of gold towards an exterminating war against the heretics of France. To Philip a peace apparently so advantageous to the Huguenots was exceedingly inopportune. It seemed as though Catherine had really designed by it to join with other nations in holding up both king and Pope to universal execration.

The infamous Inquisition had just declared the whole population — "peoples, orders and estates " — of the Netherlands guilty of heresy, apostasy, and *lèse-majesté*, and condemned them to death — the one part for having "openly rebelled against God and the king;" the other, "for not having repressed the rebellion." This murder on a grand scale was then being carried out by the sanguinary Duke of Alva. All who could make their escape fled from the blood-stained territory of the "Demon of the South;" some to Germany to prepare for vengeance; others — chiefly merchants and manufacturers — to England.

Catherine had some difficulty in appeasing her allies. Her confidential agents were despatched with assurances that her plans were unchanged, but had been unexpectedly deferred by some necessary changes in the command of the army. That she was anxious to follow the counsels and example of Alva was soon made evident. The forced peace of Longjumeau was really nothing more than the cessation of open war for a secret one of murder, robbery, and assassination. France was in a more disastrous condition than ever. The kingdom was ravaged from one end to the other, and neither Catholic nor Protestant, priest nor merchant, artisan nor peasant, could rest in safety beneath his own roof. The land was left untilled, or where any attempt was made at cultivation, it was done with arms ready to hand.

"When the vintage is finished," said the peasantry of the wine-growing districts, "we will fall on these heretics in such force, that in a short time there will be an end of them." "But if the king should interfere to prevent it, what then?" "He shall go into a convent," was the reply, "and another be put in his place." This other was Anjou, who had gained amongst the populace a high reputation for sanctity. He was to be seen walking barefoot in all the religious processions, mumbling prayers and counting his beads, while privately, though so young, his life was of exceeding depravity.

In the midst of all the strife and turmoil of civil war, and the desperate condition of the finances, Catherine yet found both time and — thanks to the Pope's gold ounces — means to devote to the building of a new palace. The Tuileries, for some unexplained reason — though a handsome structure and nearly completed — did not find favour in her eyes as a residence. The new palace, of which the façade was designed by herself, was somewhat smaller than the Tuileries. It was constructed by Jean Bullant, and had an elegant chapel attached to it; also a stone column of the Doric Order, eighty-five feet in height, designed and erected by Bullant in 1571.*

There Catherine with her mathematicians and astrologers nightly studied the course of the stars — her appeals to the heavenly bodies at that stormy sanguinary period being even more frequent than usual. For she sought to learn from their movements the most favourable moment for the accomplishment of that stupendous crime on

* Catherine's magnificent hôtel — whose site was that of the present Halle au Blé and the surrounding streets which branch from it — was taken down in 1749. The stone column alone was left standing. The palace was then called the Hôtel de Soissons, from having belonged to Charles de Bourbon, Vicomte de Soissons, the romantic lover of Catherine de Bourbon, sister of Henri of Navarre.

which she had long pondered, and which was probably first suggested by Philip's deeds of blood in the Netherlands and the satanic counsels of Pius V. Sometimes she wavered; not from repugnance to the deed, but from dread of failure, should the stars not be propitious. Then she made treaties and truces to gain time, to allay any suspicions, and to invite the confidence of her intended victims.

The two inhuman monsters of Spain and Rome could not understand her hesitation, and never wholly trusted her, notwithstanding her asseverations that she would prove herself their worthy colleague. Yet they urged her on — so piously anxious were they to free France from heresy — and incited her to keep in the strait path of Christian duty, and kill and slay for the honour of God and the holy Catholic Church.

In spite, however, of the efforts of the Chancellor de L'Hôpital, who addressed a memorial to the king — explaining in eloquent and forcible terms the necessity of maintaining peace for the welfare of his people and for securing returning prosperity to France — the third religious war was resolved on, and at the instigation of Pius V. He had consented to an application of the court for permission to alienate certain Church property to the extent of 50,000 gold crowns of revenue, "on condition that the amount raised should be expended on the extermination of heretics." The chancellor energetically opposed the publication of an Act couched in such terms, and several members of the council joining him, the holy Father was requested to modify the wording of his Bull. To this Catherine also consented, while freely availing herself of the permission to raise the money and of employing it, or such small portion as she thought fit to spare, in the manner indicated. She merely desired to allay any fears the terms of the Bull might excite in the Huguenots; lest their alarm might prevent her from renewing the attempt she had concerted with her favourite Italian, Birago, and the Cardinal de Lorraine, of surprising and arresting the prince and the admiral at the château of the former at Noyers.

Maréchal Tavannes, who had formerly been one of Catherine's admirers, and on whom she thoroughly relied, was commissioned to do the deed. From no friendly feeling to the Huguenot chiefs, he, however, contrived that letters should fall into their hands giving them timely notice of their danger. He thought there was a chance of failure, and that he might become the victim of the plot, and did not choose to incur the risk, even for Catherine, of being made responsible for violating the peace supposed to be still unbroken.

As soon as the news reached the château that troops were on their way to Noyers to arrest them, Condé, with his wife and children,* the admiral

* He had married recently his second wife, a daughter of the House of Orléans Longueville.

(then a widower) and his sons, with other Protestant chiefs and ministers, and a large party of their followers, immediately left Noyers. They were hotly pursued by the royalists, but reached the banks of the Loire before them. The river from recent heavy rains was already much swollen. But a friend from the adjacent Protestant town of Sancerre pointed out a spot where it was still easily fordable. Condé led the way, carrying his youngest son before him, and singing the 114th Psalm, "When Israel came out of Egypt," in which all joined as they waded across, and before nightfall safely reached the opposite bank. The whole party then knelt down and solemnly thanked God for their rescue.

A miracle similar to that of which they sang seemed to them to have been wrought in their favour. For at daylight on the following morning, when the royalist troops reached the Loire, the banks of the river were flooded, and the swollen stream was rushing impetuously onward in a foaming torrent. To ford it was impossible. Tavannes' mission was therefore brought to an end. He and his troops had but to retrace their steps, while the Huguenots, uninterrupted, moved onward to La Rochelle, the general rendezvous.

Not expecting the sudden attack devised by Catherine and her counsellors, the chiefs of the Protestant party were then rather widely dispersed. D'Andelot was in Brittany, but soon after appeared at La Rochelle with a corps of 4,000 men; his wife remaining at Noyers. Mdme. d'Andelot was a *grande dame* of Lorraine, who had fallen in love with her husband for his heroism; and, proud to share with him the dangers and hardships of civil war, had married him in defiance of all the attempts of her family to prevent her. The "apostate cardinal," who had also married a wife, was looking after the vintage on his estate at Beauvoisis. Not being able to reach La Rochelle, he contrived to pass over to England. As diplomacy was more his forte than fighting, he is said to have done his party far greater service in his interviews with Queen Elizabeth than he would have done in the camp.

She showed him much more consideration than she was accustomed generally to do towards the foreign Protestants who sought refuge in England. She had frequent and long conversations with him, and although she rather preferred to discourse on *belles lettres* than on public affairs, yet she often yielded to his arguments and adopted his opinions.

When war was resumed she sent money, cannon, and ammunition to the French Protestants, and supported them much more effectually while he remained with her as their envoy than she had done before, or did afterwards. She liked to read his despatches, and greatly admired the clearness, the elegance, the smoothness and fluency of his style.*

* Varillas, " *Vie de Charles IX.*"

The intrepid Jeanne of Navarre, who, with her son, was also to have been entrapped, left Nérac with a corps of four or five thousand Gascons and Béarnais, and succeeded in evading the pitiless Blaise de Montluc and his murderous band, who had orders to waylay the queen, and send her and the young Prince of Béarn to the court; but Jeanne, with the prince and her troops, reached La Rochelle in safety. Having made up her mind to be saved or to perish with the "cause of Reform," she, on arrival, presented young Henri to the Rochellois, and having armed him herself (he was then but fifteen), gave him to his uncle, the Prince de Condé, as his companion-in-arms.

Catherine de' Medici and her counsellors were disappointed and enraged beyond measure at the failure of their deep-laid scheme. The desired prey had not been entrapped, nor any person of importance seized. "There had been treachery somewhere," to which remark the Cardinal de Lorraine suggestively murmured, "The chancellor." He also called the queen-mother's attention to the king's growing regard for De L'Hôpital, the deference he had observed him lately evince in the council to any advice or opinions that came from him, and his apparent regret that they were not adopted. His eminence ventured to recommend precaution.

But Catherine had already determined on the chancellor's dismissal. She had used his integrity and uprightness of character to veil her own deceitful and tortuous policy. She now needed him no longer, for she had adopted the sanguinary counsels of Philip and the Pope, and was resolved to follow Alva in his blood-stained path. The chancellor, with his unceasing arguments for mercy, tolerance, and peace, did but importune her. But they might yet have their effect on Charles, in whom there still lingered some traces of a natural feeling towards a less evil course than that in which she had assiduously striven to train him. She dreaded, therefore, that, in one of those sudden impulses to which he was prone, the young king, influenced by the chancellor's precepts, might openly resist her and effectually free himself from her oppressive domination.

She resolved to ward off this threatened blow, first coming to an open rupture with the chancellor. The first effect of this step on the king was angry surprise, but Catherine insinuated that she had discovered him to be a Huguenot in disguise, a friend and abbettor of rebels, whom he had warned to escape, and thus saved for a time from their well-merited doom. Catherine appears never to have suspected treachery in her former lover, Tavannes. It is his son who tells the story, as editor of his father's memoirs.

On this occasion, Charles certainly displayed less of the great intelligence many writers have credited him with than excessive weakness. He is said to have received the chancellor at his next interview with haughty coldness, and to have listened to the counsels he gave him on the then lamentable state of affairs, not, as hitherto, with a willing ear, but in a resentful, disdainful manner, that seemed to bid him trouble him no further. Perceiving that his efforts to serve unhappy France and her king must henceforth be unavailing, De L'Hôpital, without waiting for a formal dismissal, voluntarily retired to his modest home near Épernay, with his wife and family.* He had not enriched himself, as was the custom of the time, by inroads on the public purse, but was in such straitened circumstances that, when on his death-bed, Charles sent him word that he would provide for his family. "Honour, patriotism, and humanity," writes the French historian, H. Martin, "may be said to have been driven from the court with him."

Whilst Catherine was preparing to reveal herself in all the hideousness of her true character, and striving to convince both Pius and Philip that she was ready to dye her hands in heretic blood as deeply as their own had been, the death of her eldest daughter, the Queen of Spain, was announced. The young queen had just attained her

*In the memorial written by De L'Hôpital shortly before his death (March 15, 1573), he says of the young king, "He had no power whatever, and dared not speak his mind, or give utterance to his real thoughts."

twenty-third year, and was said to have died in childbirth on the 3rd of October — probably by foul means. For a terrible tragedy had doubtless taken place in Spain in the course of that year, Don Carlos, Philip's son, having also died, according to the date given, towards the end of July, very mysteriously, in prison.

Philip was believed to have put both the queen and his son to death from jealousy. A very sad but romantic story was founded on that event, and more reasons still exist for accepting it as true than for its rejection. That the ordinary feelings of humanity had ever stood between Philip II. and the perpetration of any crime, however terrible its nature, it would be difficult to credit. Don Carlos is represented, with evident exaggeration, to have been passionate, impetuous, unruly, and, as he grew up, scarcely caring to conceal his contempt for the monkish rule that prevailed in Spain — declaring that, when he came to the throne, he would speedily change that — or to disguise his aversion to his fanatical, bloodthirsty father. The cruelties inflicted on the Netherlanders, he stigmatised as revolting, and strove to communicate with the envoys with a view of escaping to Flanders.

He is said to have been violent in temper even to ferocity; but he may well have been maddened to fury, if detained against his will amidst such scenes as those with which Philip and the satanical tribunal of the Inquisition delighted to "honour God." The suspected heretical views of the Spanish prince having developed into certainty as he attained manhood, Philip hesitated no longer. After conferring with the Supreme Tribunal of the Inquisition, he, one evening in January, accompanied by two or three of the Inquisitor's myrmidons, entered the prince's apartment, and with his own hand arrested him. Carlos was transferred to a prison, and Philip officially announced his son's arrest to the papal nuncio. He further stated that "he had preferred the honour of God and the preservation of the Catholic religion to his own flesh and blood, and that, in order to obey God, he had sacrificed his only son."

Nothing further is positively known concerning his fate — whether he was at once put to death in pursuance of a sentence of the Inquisition, or was allowed to linger on until the end of July, when it was announced that he had died of a malignant fever, the result of the excesses of a dissolute life. On the faith of some inexplicit and doubtful documents, it has been attempted to show that nature prevailed even in the breast of so unnatural a monster as Philip II. of Spain — that he did not actually with his own hand slay his son; but so far relented as to allow him to drag out a few months of grief and despair in a horrible dungeon.

The more generally accredited story is the more probable one — that he had formed an unfortunate attachment for the *fiancée* of his boyhood, whom political arrangements afterwards gave him for a stepmother. The attachment, unhappily, became mutual. That there was an eager desire on the part of this boy and girl of fifteen and fourteen to see each other on the arrival of the latter in Spain is evident from the letter of the Bishop of Limoges to Catherine de' Medici, giving the particulars of the young queen's first reception and her meeting with Don Carlos.* It was certainly ominous of what afterwards occurred, and seems at the time to have been so regarded. He appears then to have been gentle in manners, and rather delicate in health. That he should, as he advanced towards manhood, have become "passionate, impetuous, unruly, subject to fits of anger, and have conceived an aversion for his father," is thus easily explained.

But objection has been taken to there having been any reciprocity of affection on the part of the young queen, because of the energy with which, on her visit to Bayonne, she supported the views of Philip, as explained by the Duke of Alva to Catherine. Her "energy" was described as "feverish anxiety lest she should fail to play the part assigned her to the satisfaction of the duke, who watched her every word and action. It was evident that this girl of eighteen had not become a

* See letter of Bishop of Limoges, pp. 40 and 41 of this volume.

fanatic, but that she was under the influence of fear. Philip himself, when writing to Granvelle concerning the Bayonne conference, says that "Catherine proposed a marriage, but that the Queen of Spain replied evasively as he had commanded her."

But whether she was poisoned, as at the time supposed, or died a natural death — death, doubtless, was welcomed, both by the unhappy young queen and the unfortunate Don Carlos, as a desirable release from the power of a despotic and unsympathising tyrant.

CHAPTER XVII.

Battle of Jarnac.— Death of Condé. — Anjou's Delight; the Te Deum.— Henri of Navarre; the Oath and the Medal. —Death of D'Andelot; Poison Suspected.— Fifty Thousand Crowns for Coligny, Dead or Alive.— Victory or Death; Money or Battle.— Battle of Moncontour.— Coligny Wounded. — Peace of Saint-Germain, 8th of August, 1570.

CATHERINE DE' MEDICI never permitted useless grief to interfere with the pursuit of her projects. As on the death of her husband, and again when her eldest son died, so now, she indulged in no vain regrets on the death of her daughter — suddenly cut off in the bloom of youth, and under circumstances which she well knew to be more than suspicious. She was far more intent on fulfilling the promise she had given to Philip and the Pope of exterminating a large part of her son's subjects. "All edicts of tolerance," she assured the Spanish tyrant, "were to be immediately revoked. All ministers of the religion called Reformed were to quit the kingdom within fifteen days; also, within the same period, all persons holding any office in the government who professed the same heretical opinions — the exercise of any religion but that of the

Roman Catholic being henceforth punishable with death. An oath of fidelity to Catholicism was henceforth to be also required of all the members of the various Parliaments, the universities, and other public establishments in France."

Philip and the saintly Pius were at last persuaded that they might now place some trust in the promises of this hitherto double-dealing *intrigante*. "For nothing remained," she told them, "but to combine the military operations in France and the Netherlands."

The edicts were duly published at the end of September, and in reply to them the Huguenots rose *en masse*. One long cry of fury and despair echoed through the land. The chiefs of the party were unable to restrain the rage of the soldiers. Onward they rushed in ever-increasing numbers and like a devouring torrent, ravaging and destroying all that lay in their way; from province to province, from the Rhone to the Charente. For though the edicts were published, the Catholic army was not ready to march and enforce them. The Huguenots, who were always expecting to be attacked, may be said to have constantly lived with their arms ready to hand. They therefore were speedily prepared, and, for the three weeks during which they were unopposed, conquered all before them.

Unhappily, they committed terrible **excesses** — pillaging and devastating the churches; freely selling church property, without asking leave of the Pope, of course, in revenge for the pontiff's permission to Charles IX. to alienate Church revenues to raise funds for exterminating the Huguenots. But worse far than that, many lives were sacrificed to the blind fury of revenge. Certainly the Huguenots were sometimes the aggressors; but so persistently were they persecuted, that although it may be matter for regret, yet it can scarcely cause surprise that they did not always abstain from rendering evil for evil. Perhaps throughout the whole of the civil war, neither Catholic nor Protestant, in his most maddening thirst for vengeance, committed atrocities at all approaching in horror the deeds of the Duc de Montpensier and his brutal band. Inspired by the example of their savage leader, they seemed to glory in their career of blood and crime.*

The two armies, however, met almost face to face on the 16th of November in the neighbourhood of Poitiers, but without coming to an engagement. The Catholic army was commanded by the able but brutal Maréchal Tavannes, but nominally by the Duc d'Anjou; for whom Catherine was desirous of building up a great military reputation

---

* The Huguenots on their march towards Saumur took the Château de Champigny, the splendid residence of the Duc de Montpensier. The duke was absent, but his confessor, a Cordelier monk, who shared in the infamous deeds of his penitent, was seized and hanged (Brantôme).

at the expense of the generals who were supposed to command under him. The winter of 1568 and 1569 was one of extremest severity; so much so, that the two armies were so thoroughly benumbed and unnerved by the intensity of the frost, that courage failed them to begin the attack. The hoar-frost (*verglas*) is said to have had so severe an effect on the soldiers' arms and legs, that they snapped and broke when a skirmish was attempted. Consequently, the generals on both sides determined to put their troops into winter quarters.

The interval was employed by the Huguenots in endeavouring to obtain additional resources for carrying on the ensuing campaign. Queen Elizabeth, at the solicitation of her "good sister," the Queen of Navarre, sent 100,000 gold angelots,* and some ammunition. Jeanne herself authorised the sale of Church lands in those towns of her domains where the Huguenots were established. The privateers of La Rochelle, who pillaged all vessels of Roman Catholic nations, faithfully contributed the tithe of their booty—amounting to a large sum—in aid of the Protestant cause, while Protestant Germany promised to send a considerable force to its assistance.

Want of discipline in the Huguenot nobility appears to have greatly embarrassed the leader of

* An ancient English gold coin of the value of about five shillings.

the Protestant forces. He was therefore compelled, on the resumption of hostilities in the spring, to accept battle at a great disadvantage in the vicinity of Jarnac. On the morning of the 13th of March, as Condé was hastening to the admiral's assistance—though wounded in the arm on the previous evening—he was kicked on the leg by the Duc de Longueville's horse, and with such violence that it was broken. Rejecting all advice and persuasion to allow his troop to remove him to his tent, he exclaimed: "Nobles of France! The long-desired moment has arrived. Remember in what a condition Louis de Bourbon enters the combat for Christ and his country!"*

He then charged the Catholics with so much impetuosity, that at first he overthrew all before him. But he was speedily surrounded by a mass of gendarmerie and thrown from his horse, which, wounded and dying, fell partly upon him. More than two-thirds of the small troop accompanying Condé were killed in the attempt to defend their prince; the rest, for the most part, were wounded or taken prisoners. Being released from the pressure of his horse, Condé, who was unable to rise, delivered his gauntlet to a gentleman of the royalist army. Scarcely, however, had he done so than the captain of Anjou's Swiss guards, recognising the prince, rushed up behind him, and com-

* The device on his standard was "*Doux le péril pour Christ et le pays.*"

mitted the dastardly deed of shooting him in the back of his head. His death was instantaneous.

The Duc d'Anjou, it is asserted, suggested this act to several of his favourites in the camp, desiring them to be diligent in seeking the opportunity and availing themselves of it. It fell to the lot of the Swiss, Montesquiou, to gratify the great general's wish.* Anjou was returning from the performance of his morning devotions, and receiving the sacrament, before looking on the battle well out of harm's way, when the pious youth had the satisfaction of seeing the dead body of his heroic relative stretched on the ground before him, and of "knowing from that event that God had favoured his arms."

An ass was brought by his direction, and the body thrown across it, to be thus ignominiously carried into Jarnac for the amusement of the duke and his favourites, and for the derision of all good Catholics. The prince's brother-in-law, the Duc de Longueville, however, protested against this indignity, and, after some hesitation, Condé's remains were delivered to him to be sent to Vendôme for burial.

To celebrate this "manifest interposition of heaven" on behalf of her gallant son, Catherine de' Medici, despite the king's anger at Anjou being thus honoured, ordered a Te Deum to be sung in every church in the kingdom. Madrid,

* Brantôme.

Rome and Brussels followed her example; and, as a further act of thanksgiving, the queen-mother gave one of her sumptuous *festins* at the Louvre, in the Hall of the Caryatides — then Salle des Gardes, or des cent Suisses — with scenic representations, in which the band of dissolute women, always in close attendance upon her, appeared in full force. So great was Anjou's joy at Condé's death that he was about to order the building of a chapel on the spot where the Swiss assassinated him; but an officer of his troop, Carnavalet, his former governor, dissuaded him from thus openly avowing himself the instigator of the deed.

The death of their leader naturally occasioned some confusion, as well as deep regret, in the ranks of the Protestant army. But the cavalry only had taken part in the combat of Jarnac, and were quickly rallied by D'Andelot and Coligny, who, two days after, effectually repulsed the attack of the royalists on Cognac. Jeanne d'Albret, who was at Saintes with her son and her nephew, hastened to Tonnay-Charente, where, after an affecting address to the troops — her own emotion causing a deep impression — she presented to them the two youths of sixteen and seventeen (Henri of Navarre and Henri of Condé) as the heirs and avengers of the assassinated prince. Before this army they took the solemn oath never to abandon the Huguenot cause. The men repeated it after them, and proclaimed with enthusiasm Henri of Navarre their chief, the effective command of the army devolving of course on Coligny.

To commemorate this event a gold medal was struck by Jeanne's command. It bore her own effigy and her son's, with the noble motto, "*Pax certa, victoria integra, mors honesta.*" Her devotion to "the cause" was testified by raising a loan for its service on the security of her jewels, and the alienation of a portion of her estates for the same object, "preferring" (writes D'Aubigné) "liberty of conscience to wealth, grandeur, or even life itself."

Notwithstanding Tavannes's energy and military skill, and the reinforcements daily expected from the Pope and the Duke of Alva, the royalist army — often repulsed with great vigour by the Protestants — achieved but very partial success.

They were unable to take any of the heretic towns on the Charente. But this appears to have been chiefly due to court intrigues. Charles IX. was outrageously jealous of his brother. He exhibited also intense resentment towards the queen-mother, who was using every means to secure popularity for her favourite son amongst the more influential of the chiefs of the Catholic party. The king, in fact, refused to send the heavy cannon required for siege operations, thus preventing the royalist army from profiting by any advantages it had gained. Discord, as usual, reigned in the camp, and both officers and men were enraged at having to beat a retreat to avoid being enclosed between Coligny's army and the German troops marching to join him.

The king was secretly encouraged in his opposition to the queen-mother and Anjou by the intriguing Cardinal de Lorraine. The cardinal, while plotting with Catherine to carry out the views of Spain and Rome against heresy, was actuated by a feeling of jealousy similar to the king's towards Anjou, on account of the young Duc de Guise, whom the cardinal desired should take the late duke's place as the head of the Catholic party, but who, as he considered, did not hold a sufficiently prominent command in the army.

The saddening intelligence of the death of the valorous D'Andelot, at Saintes on the 27th of May, threw a heavy gloom over Coligny and his army. After the admiral, D'Andelot was the most eminent man of the Protestant party. He was much beloved by his troops, and was in every sense a great loss, both to them and the cause of Reform. Another misfortune befell them in the death of the commander of the German cavalry, the Duc de Deuxponts, on the 14th of June, the day following his junction with the Protestant army. Both these deaths were attributed to poison. But D'Andelot had been out of health for some time; while the sufferings and privations undergone by both generals during the extraordinary severity of the preceding winter, together with the fatigue of long marches harassed by their enemies, and the general anxiety occasioned by this prolonged civil war, have been thought reasons sufficient to account for their death without the aid of poison.

Yet Catherine had become very anxious to secure the chiefs of the party, whether by poison, pistol, sword, or imprisonment. A cowardly attempt to poison Coligny, by seducing one of his attendants to administer some potent potion to him, was discovered shortly after, and the miscreant hanged. On the 12th of September, on raising the siege of Poitiers, Coligny learned that a decree of the Parliament of Paris condemned him as "chief of the rebellion against the king and state," to be hanged on the Place de Grève, and his body afterwards exposed on a gibbet at Montfaucon. Against his brothers, their families, and the valiant Count Montgomery, and others, a similar decree was issued. The sentences were executed in effigy, and, at the king's or queen-mother's request, a reward of 50,000 gold crowns was offered for Coligny, dead or alive.

During the short period of repose that Coligny felt compelled to grant his weary troops, a reinforcement from the Pope and the Duke of Florence of another 6,000 Italians joined the royalist army. Their commander, the Conte de Santa Fiore, was especially charged by his holiness to "kill on the spot every heretic who fell into his or his soldiers' hands; to give no quarter; to let not one escape." Though barbarous enough, it appears that the count did not carry out the monstrous orders he had received, so literally as would have found favour with the holy pontiff; for he is said to have spared more than one of the Protestant leaders, and amongst them the great Huguenot captain, La Noue.*

This reinforcement, together with 3,000 or 4,000 troops of various nations, sent by the Duke of Alva, enabled the royalists at once to take the field. The chief command was now divided between Maréchals Tavannes and Biron, who, with

---

* At the same time Pius wrote to the queen-mother to stimulate her zeal in the murderous work he had so much at heart:

"In no manner, and under no pretence, must the enemies of God be spared. No considerations of human respect, either for persons or things, should lead you to entertain the thought of sparing the enemies of God, who have never spared either God or you. It is only by the utter extermination of these heretics that the king will be able to restore the ancient religion to that noble nation" (France). "We are informed that some persons are striving to get a certain number of prisoners pardoned. But you must use every effort to prevent that, and to make sure that those flagitious scoundrels are given up to receive the punishment so justly their due."

To the inhuman Duke of Alva—who, in 1568, beheaded Counts Egmont and Horn with twenty others of the chief nobility of Flanders, and condemned hundreds daily, at his "tribunal of blood," to tortures and deaths the most horrible he could devise—the saintly Pope wrote (accompanying his letter with the present of a helmet and sword, blessed by himself): "Continue, dear son, to pile up those praiseworthy deeds as steps which will conduct you to life eternal."

25,000 fresh troops, pitched their tents within a league of the Huguenots. Coligny, with a force of but 18,000 men, ill provided, worn and weary, would have willingly avoided the battle until joined by an expected corps of German cavalry, which the Prince of Orange had gone in disguise to conduct to him. But the impatience of the Huguenot nobility, weary of so much suffering and fatigue, would not allow him. "Victory or death!" they exclaimed; while the mercenary German troops, dissatisfied that their arrears of pay were not yet forthcoming, replied with no less energy, "Money or battle!"

The two young princes were also eager for the combat. But Coligny impressed on these youths that they were reserved for the support of "the cause" in the future; then giving them an escort of 4,000 cavalry, he sent them to Parthenay, whence, from some hilly ground, they could see the battle. From the impetuosity of one part of his troops, and the indiscipline and mutinous disposition of the rest, Coligny was prevented from choosing the most advantageous spot for receiving the enemy's attack. After a long cannonade the battle began at three in the afternoon of the 3rd of October in the plain of Assay, near Moncontour. Desperate valour was displayed on both sides.

But when the Comte de Nassau repulsed the cavalry charge of the young Duc de Guise and dispersed his troops, Henri of Navarre, who from the heights of Parthenay perceived this, was with difficulty restrained from rushing down with his 4,000 cavalry, and attacking the *corps de bataille*. "Ah!" he exclaimed, "then we lose the battle, as we give the enemy time to reconnoitre and receive succour." It appears he was right, and that the royalist army would have been beaten if the prince's corps had at that moment charged the enemy. Great expectations were founded on this circumstance of his military capacity (J. Servan, "*Guerres des Français*").

Coligny was aimed at and wounded in the cheek by the Rhingrave in command of a corps of German Catholic cavalry. Coligny replied with more effect, for the Rhingrave was killed on the spot. But he was near being killed by the Rhingrave's troops, who were surrounding him, when Wolfrad de Mansfeld rode up and released him from his perilous position. Mansfeld was then attacked himself, and in the skirmish that followed the Margrave of Baden, commander of the royalist Germans, was killed. Coligny was conveyed to his tent for the dressing of his wound. The issue of the battle was, as he had foreseen, a defeat for the Huguenots. According to D'Aubigné, they lost near 15,000 men at the battle of Moncontour, the royalist army only 500. The disproportion is so great that there would seem to be some error in the statement. Coligny's whole army is said to have amounted but to about 18,000 men, of whom 4,000 were detached as an escort for the young princes.

This small detachment of cavalry excepted, the Huguenot army must have been annihilated. The queen-mother and the court certainly believed the Protestant cause ruined, and again Te Deums, and pæans in honour of the young victor, resounded through the land. The blessing of Pius V., with the addition of a consecrated helmet and sword, was also conveyed to him, and he was admonished "not to grow faint or weary in well-doing." Charles could bear this triumph of his hated brother no longer. Secretly encouraged by the cardinal, he resolved to repair to the camp. Neither persuasion nor remonstrance availed to detain him. Thither he was speedily followed by Catherine, accompanied by the cardinal, who was playing a double part, caring neither for Catherine nor Charles, but anxious only that the prestige so lately attaching to the House of Guise should, with all its pretensions to military rule and its eye on the throne, revive in his nephew. The youthful valour of this brilliant young duke — then in his nineteenth year — he feared to see obscured by the false *éclat* bestowed on a worthless scion of the degenerate House of Valois.

Notwithstanding the defeat of Moncontour and the magnitude of the Huguenot losses, Coligny without delay assembled the wreck of his army, and revived the failing courage of his men by his firmness, hopefulness, and energy. On the morrow of the battle letters were already written, and trusted envoys despatched to their Protestant confederates of England, Scotland, Denmark, Germany, and Switzerland, to inform them that "hope survived defeat," and requesting aid as soon as possible. Garrisons were placed in the towns on the Charente, and Coligny and the young princes, leaving Jeanne d'Albret at Rochelle, took the route of Quercy to join Montgomery, who had beaten the Catholics of Gascony.

Neither these measures nor the diligence with which they were accomplished would, it appears, have saved the Huguenots, but for the dissension in the enemy's camp. "Tavannes and his most experienced captains suggested that Coligny and the princes should immediately be pursued, even into Gascony, where, reduced to seek refuge in some fortress, they might be besieged, and the war terminated at one blow." But the king had written to Anjou that nothing was to be attempted until he arrived. In the contemplated final dispersion of the Protestant army, Charles was resolved that his brother should not defraud him of a share of the laurels of victory, stained though they might be with the blood of his subjects.

Charles quickly made his appearance in the camp, and the council of war assembled. Tavannes's proposals were at once rejected. The marshal was known to have long been one of Catherine's devotees, and though his advice in a military sense might be good, yet if followed, the credit of it would redound on her favourite son; so Charles immediately vetoed it. The Montmorencys had opposed Tavannes, which seemed to give sanction to the young king's act. Their motive, however, was sympathy with "the cause," as moderate Catholics, and a desire that the admiral, their near relative, should not be too hardly pressed. Tavannes, greatly offended, required to be relieved of his command, and returned to his estates in Burgundy.

The military council then decided that, before pursuing Coligny and the princes, the fortresses on the Charente occupied by the Huguenots should be recovered, and their garrisons, of course, massacred. This, it was supposed, would be easily and speedily accomplished. The siege of Saint-Jean-d'Angely was the first attempted; but the small garrison, instead of surrendering at discretion, made so vigorous and determined a resistance that the royalist army was detained for upwards of six weeks under the walls of the town; and had lost between five and six thousand men before the garrison, exhausted by fatigue and suffering, and wanting ammunition, would listen to any terms of capitulation.

Winter had then set in with some rigour; an epidemic prevailed amongst the troops; many of the Germans deserted, and as no more laurels were likely to be gathered by seeking further conquests that year, the army separated, and the king, with the queen-mother and the Duc d'Anjou, returned to Blois. Attempts at negotiation were made in the month of January. But the king would not grant the demands of the Protestants, and the concessions he offered were rejected by Coligny and the Queen of Navarre, to whom Catherine sent an envoy.

Maréchal Biron was also despatched in the spring by Charles IX. to Languedoc, where the admiral had arrived with the young princes and some small reinforcements to his army. The marshal was the bearer of letters from the king, the queen-mother, and Anjou, couched in the most friendly and conciliatory terms. But Coligny was not then disposed to be ensnared by the protestations and fine promises of those who had so lately set a price on his head, had hanged him in effigy, and sought his death by poison and dagger. He courteously acknowledged the missives of that amiable trio, but did not suspend his march.

He was aware that the king and queen-mother were at the end of their resources; that the immense sums received as gifts from the clergy and the large towns, the loans Catherine had effected, and the considerable amount derived from the sale of Church property, which had been sold at a very high rate, had been spent, not only on the army, but to a great extent squandered by Catherine herself. For *fêtes*, balls, banquets, and bonfires went on unceasingly, in celebration of some skirmish and massacre on a small scale, in default of success in a regular battle to triumph over.

The court then exhibited in its habits and manners a singular *mélange* of gallantry and bloodthirstiness, voluptuousness and ferocity; strange contradictions, which then threatened to become national characteristics. It was, indeed, one of the queen-mother's aims to seduce by this courtly depravity and licentious freedom of manners, those weaker brethren amongst the Huguenot nobility to whom the severe austerity of life enjoined by Calvin's doctrines rendered existence an almost cheerless burden.

There have been few such noble examples of Calvinism as that displayed in the character and acts of the Protestant martyr, Coligny. He was without fanaticism, was humane, tolerant, and patriotic, yet firm in the faith he had adopted. Doubtless his influence was generally felt by the Calvinists, and served to restrain many from abandoning "the cause." The small army he commanded at the period now in question was kept together only by their confidence in him. Yet many fell away from him when early in April he halted at Nîmas, and there communicated to his companions-in-arms the project he had formed of carrying the war into the neighbourhood of

Paris, to disquiet the Parisians, and compel the court to make peace. A wild and hazardous scheme it appeared to them, and few were found to approve it.

But Coligny explained that their numbers would be increased by rallying the Reformers in every province they passed through, and the facility of joining the troops promised by the German princes become greater the nearer they approached the North. But it seemed to the Reformers of the South too adventurous an expedition, and not more than 5,000 were inspired by his heroism to share its perils with him; but naturally they were those whose audacity would be likely to contribute to its success. The Huguenots had no artillery, but all were mounted, and set out on their daring and hazardous campaign in high spirits.

Catherine, informed by some of her emissaries of Coligny's project, despatched, as it would seem, on her own authority, a corps of 12,000 men under Maréchal de Cossé-Gonnor to exterminate Coligny and his troop, even to the last man ("*Guerres des Français*," J. Servan). On arriving at Saint-Étienne, Coligny was taken suddenly and dangerously ill. Consternation spread amongst his followers; but fortunately for them (if not for him, considering what a fate he was reserved for) that famous remedy for all maladies at that period —bleeding—was in his case efficacious. Weak and weary, he was scarcely able to do more than give the young commanders the necessary instructions for repulsing the royalists encountered at Arnay-le-Duc.

The nature of the ground was favourable for the advantageous disposal of his small force, and here occurred Henri of Navarre's first exploit of arms. As it was a successful one, it was regarded as of fortunate augury.* Having completely repulsed their assailants, Coligny with his troop passed on so rapidly that Cossé, encumbered with heavy artillery, could not keep up with him. On reaching the Protestant town of Sancerre, the admiral despatched a messenger to the king with proposals of peace. The moment was well chosen; for the Protestants had beaten the Catholics in several provinces. All the towns between Les Sables-d'Olonne and the Gironde had fallen into their power, and La Noue had taken Sainte-Gemme and Fontenay. At the siege of the latter town his arm was shattered by a ball from an arquebuse. Jeanne d'Albret is said to have held it during its amputation.

Catherine was perplexed and disquieted by the change in the prospects of the heretics. She suspected Cossé of having purposely allowed Coligny to escape. The king was less docile of late, and in his hatred of Anjou continued to thwart all her projects for the great successes of her favourite

* Henri was fond of referring to it when in after years he succeeded to the throne.

son. The zealous Catholics, whose chief she intended he should be, rejected him for the young Duc de Guise. The Montmorencys sought the recall of De L'Hôpital; the Protestants expressed a similar wish. But that she resolved should never be; and Charles was also unwilling to make that concession, so thoroughly had the queen-mother imbued him with the idea that the chancellor was a Huguenot in disguise and a friend of the rebels.

With that exception he had no objection to peace, and as Catherine needed time more effectually to reconstruct her plots for heretic extermination, peace was signed at Saint-Germain on the 8th of August, on terms very favourable to the Protestants. Some few days after, the effigy of the admiral, which had dangled for several months on Montfaucon, was quietly removed in the night, and the gibbet taken down. It was Coligny's hope that this treaty would be honourably carried out, and that the country would have rest to recover from the ravages inflicted on it by civil war. "But Catherine's sentiments were of an entirely opposite character, and treason was already in her heart at the moment when, with her full concurrence in all its stipulations, her son signed the treaty of peace" (H. Martin).

CHAPTER XVIII.

Peace Disapproved by Philip and Pius V. — Marguerite and Duc de Guise. — Anjou Refuses to Marry Queen Elizabeth. — Philip's Fourth Wife. — Charles Marries Elizabeth of Austria. — Marguerite's Hand Refused by Sebastian of Portugal. — The Bourbon Marriage Resolved on.— Biron Sent to Queen of Navarre to Offer Marguerite to Henri. — Coligny Invited by Charles IX. to Château de Blois. — Sets out from La Rochelle, against Advice of Friends.

WHEN rumours reached Rome and Madrid that projects for the renewal of peace were again entertained by the Court of France, the righteous spirits of Philip II. and Pius V. were exasperated exceedingly. Again the Florentine *intrigante* had deceived and disappointed them, and at the very moment, too, that his holiness thought so favourable for launching his anathemas and bulls of excommunication against the heretic Queen of England. But a few months previously he had issued his harmless bull of deposition in favour of Mary Stuart— harmless to Elizabeth, but doubtless tending to increase the rigour of the unfortunate Scottish queen's captivity.

But for the perversity of the queen-mother in giving her sanction to this "infamous proposal of peace," Pius had intended to incite the Catholics to further acts of rebellion both in Scotland and Ireland. In the hope, however, that the calamitous peace might yet perchance be averted, Pius, in virulent language, addressed letters to the queen-mother and her two sons: "Know ye not," he wrote, "that between Satan and the sons of light there can be no fellowship? It should therefore be held as certain that between Catholics and heretics there can be no agreement or composition, unless it be one of dissimulation and pretence."

This rebuke was accompanied by an offer from Philip of nine thousand troops, if reinforcements were needed to put down those "scoundrels." (Philip and the Pope were both fond of applying the epithet "scoundrels" (*scélérats*) to the Huguenots. Yet surely no two individuals ever deserved it more than themselves.) Philip's offer was declined. "Articles of peace were signed before its arrival;" but Catherine could console the Spanish tyrant and the persecuting Pope with the promise that the consummation which they, and no less she, so devoutly desired was but deferred, and was even almost assured by this peace. She is said to have insinuated at Rome and Madrid that the peace of Saint-Germain would prove more murderous to "those of the religion" than a war. The Huguenots generally put little faith in its possible duration, though it was guaranteed by assigning to them for two years the four strong places they held on the Charente.

Coligny, however, was more hopeful, and with the two young Bourbon princes and the principal Huguenot nobility — after conducting their German allies to the frontier — rapidly crossed the kingdom to join Jeanne d'Albret and the little Princesse Catherine at La Rochelle, to await there in security the conclusion of the peace negotiations. The cessation of the long-continued state of anarchy in France gratified most of the moderate Catholics; but the fanatical zealots of Rouen and Orange, at the suggestion of their priests — taking "the rise and overflowing of some of the rivers of France at that time as an expression of the anger of God at this peace" — fell suddenly on the Protestants and savagely massacred them.

Hitherto such murderous attacks, though frequent, were never inquired into, or any one concerned in them arrested. On the present occasion a different course was pursued, and the perpetrators of these outrages severely punished. This inspired confidence in the more sanguine of the Huguenot party. The court, too, was said to be peacefully occupied with matrimonial negotiations, which, however, seemed likely to end in revenge and resentment. Even before the peace was signed, the Montmorencys, in the interests of tolerance, suggested the marriage of Madame

Marguerite, Catherine's youngest daughter, with Prince Henri of Navarre.

Twelve years before, when Henri, a bright little boy of five, was taken to Amiens by his father, King Antoine, Henri II. was much pleased with him, and asked him if he would be his son. To which, in the Gascon patois, he replied:

"*Quet es lo seigne pay.*"

"Will you then be my son-in-law?" said the king.

"*O bé,*" he answered.

No betrothal had ever taken place, yet, until events arose that seemed to put their marriage out of the question, Henry and Marguerite were regarded as destined for each other. Jeanne was said rather to incline to the idea of marrying her son to Elizabeth of England, notwithstanding the disparity of age.

It had been for some months understood that Marguerite was to marry the young Duc de Guise, the handsomest and most brilliant cavalier of the French Court. "She had given him her heart." Such, at least, was the joke of "the squadron;" and Marguerite, then eighteen, beautiful, accomplished, and *spirituelle*, had inspired the duke, they laughingly said, with love as ardent as her own. He was probably the first of her rather long list of lovers. To the dismay of the brilliant young couple, the audacity of Guise in pretending to the hand of the princess suddenly put Charles

Marguerite de Valois.
Photo-etching from an old print.

IX. into one of his fits of rage. He ordered that Guise should be shot when attending the royal hunt; but, warned by a friend, the young duke escaped. Catherine also expressed her deep indignation at the conduct of both Marguerite and Guise, though she had hitherto made her daughter the lure by which she sought to gain the duke over to her interests.

Anjou, however, was the most violent of the three. Guise so entirely eclipsed him in military capacity, in popularity, and personal advantages, that, in the excitement of jealousy and hate, he vowed he would "put a dagger in his heart." The prudent young duke, following the counsels of his worthy uncle, the Cardinal of Lorraine, at once smoothed the ruffled feelings of the royal trio by assenting to a marriage with Catherine de Clèves, the young widow of the Prince dè Portien. Guise was at once restored to favour. The ambitious projects attributed to him were, in a measure, disavowed by this alliance voluntarily contracted; while there was the further advantage that, sheltered by it, Marguerite, without any shock to the courtly morality of that day, could still retain her lover.

She, however, decidedly expressed her aversion to a marriage with Henri of Navarre. It was not yet formally decided to propose it to Queen Jeanne. Catherine was awaiting the result of the offer she had made of Marguerite's hand to Sebastian, the young King of Portugal. He declined the proffered honour; such a marriage being highly displeasing to Philip II., Catherine having some vague pretensions to the Crown of Portugal, which she thought by its means to strengthen.

Charles, too, was seeking a matrimonial alliance, being for the second time a suitor for the hand of the Archduchess Elizabeth, younger daughter of the Emperor Maximilian II. The emperor, after a lengthened negotiation, consented to give his daughter to Charles, and without again demanding, as one of its conditions, the restitution of the three bishoprics to the empire. To the fact of Charles and Catherine having this marriage in view may be ascribed the unusual steps taken to punish the perpetrators of the outrages of Rouen and Orange. To have allowed such murderous attacks to pass unnoticed would have been unfavourable to Charles's suit, in the eyes of so humane a prince as Maximilian II., whose alliance Catherine hoped to turn to political account by using it as a means of securing that of the Protestant princes in the event of new wars against the "*seditious* Calvinist chiefs." For that difference of religious belief or persecution for heresy was the cause of them, Catherine, at all events, affected to ignore.

The marriage of Philip II. to his niece, and fourth wife, the Archduchess Eléonore, the elder sister of the Archduchess Elizabeth, took place a month or two earlier than that of Charles and his bride. The queen-mother had been careful to inform herself of the character of this young princess, who was of a very gentle, amiable temper, and, compared with the effrontery of the women who chiefly composed the court of Catherine de' Medici, her manners were pronounced "very retiring." A second Mary Stuart, ruling her husband, interfering in public affairs, and assuming to lead the court, would not have suited the queen-mother. Charles, too, was not so likely to be transformed into a doting husband as poor François II. He had already his mistress, Marie Touchet, to whom he was much attached, and "le petit Charles," who in later years proved himself worthy to have been a legitimate scion, instead of a bastard offshoot, of the degenerate race of Valois, had already come into the world.

The marriage of Charles IX. and the Archduchess Elizabeth was celebrated with great magnificence on the 26th of November, at Mezières, whither the bride was conducted by the archbishop, Elector of Trèves, Chancellor of the Empire. The winter was setting in with its accustomed severity; great distress prevailed throughout the country. The people complained of the ever-increasing burden of taxes, and the treasury was said to be empty. Yet all sorts of expedients — and chiefly the old ones of creating titles of nobility, inventing new offices, and selling them to the highest bidder — were resorted to for funds to defray the expense of the unprecedented pomp of this royal wedding. The princes and the most distinguished of the Huguenot nobility were invited to share in the marriage festivities; but they begged respectfully to decline, thinking themselves safer in the stronghold of La Rochelle. Coligny, however, wrote to assure the queen-mother that "the past was entirely forgotten, and to place his services at the king's disposal."

Once more the recall of De L'Hôpital was suggested; but Catherine was inflexible, and the chancellor himself did not greatly desire it. At one time he had hopes that Charles might be saved from the domination of his mother. But that vain hope was ended. Since the chancellor's departure, she had surrounded her son with Italians — Birago, who succeeded De L'Hôpital; Gondi (created by Charles Comte de Retz); Davila, her secretary; and others of similar character — men who owed everything to her, and faithfully carried out her views, while availing themselves to the full of the opportunities she gave them of enriching themselves at the expense of the state. The chancellor would have found Charles more excitable and violent than ever, yet occasionally sinking for hours and even days into a state of languor or deep melancholy. He had a worn, weary appearance, too, unusual in so young a man. The name of God was always on his lips; but only to give more emphasis to the frightful oaths with which he was accustomed, in common with the young nobility of the period, to preface almost every sentence he uttered. It was the fashion thus to proclaim their orthodoxy — profane swearing being forbidden to the Calvinists.

An embassy from the German Protestant princes met Charles, on his return from the frontier, to congratulate him on his marriage and the reëstablishment of religious peace in France. An address, in the name of the princes represented, was read to the king, earnestly recommending the continuance of tolerance. Charles responded more courteously than was his custom, and took immediate steps for entering into a defensive treaty with the Protestant states of Germany.

Another negotiation was also on foot, in the success of which Charles, in his desire to get rid of the presence of his brother, was greatly interested, and Catherine also, from anxiety to find a crown for her favourite Anjou — this was the young duke's proposal for the hand of Queen Elizabeth. But the proposal was Catherine's rather than Anjou's; for while the agents of the Court of France were urging for a favourable reply, Anjou announced to his mother that he would not marry Elizabeth on any conditions whatever. This perversity on the part of the usually docile Anjou perplexed the queen-mother. La Mothe-Fénelon was then French ambassador in England. He had but just before informed the English queen how greatly this alliance was desired by the Court of France, when a private letter from Catherine made known to him the young duke's resolve to reject the position of "husband of a queen who conferred on him neither title nor power."

But Anjou, urged by his favourite Lignerolles, gave as his chief objection, the "reports he had frequently heard to her dishonour."* "She was very sorry," Catherine said, "but trusted that means might be found of making the younger brother, the Duc d'Alençon, acceptable to the queen. This was a rather delicate commission for the ambassador, as, respecting Anjou, the initiative was said to have indirectly been taken by Elizabeth herself, at the suggestion, in the previous year, of Odet de Châtillon, the "apostate cardinal," and the Vidame de Chartres, who had sought refuge in England in 1568, both of whom were well received by the queen.

De Châtillon was returning to France, in February, 1571, after an absence of three years in England — charged by the queen to confer with Coligny on the subject — while letters respecting this matrimonial negotiation were passing between Catherine de' Medici and the French ambassador. At Southampton, when about to embark, Odet de Châtillon was taken suddenly ill, and died almost

* This refers to her supposed relations with Dudley, Earl of Leicester.

immediately. He was poisoned by his servant, who, being afterwards arrested as a spy, confessed the deed, and declared that he was instigated to it by the queen-mother. Lignerolles, of whom she had said "he should repent of the advice he had given Anjou," was also assassinated shortly after in open day, by five or six men wearing masks. No one doubted by whom they were employed. Such assassinations were frequent in Paris, the victims being, for the most part, those who had opposed, or were in some way obstacles to, the carrying out of the queen-mother's schemes.

The Pope and Philip II. were decidedly averse to the marriage with the excommunicated heretic queen. To tempt Anjou to reject it they offered him either the command of the fleet which the Pope, conjointly with Spain and Venice, had armed against the Turks, or the direction of the descent on Ireland, with the hand of Mary Stuart, who was to be divorced by Pius V. if they succeeded in effecting her release. But Charles, in a great rage, forbade his brother to accept either command, and Catherine immediately wrote to the French ambassador that the Duc d'Anjou, notwithstanding some religious scruples, yet was exceedingly desirous of securing the honour of Elizabeth's hand.

The ambassador probably refrained from informing the queen of her young suitor's change of mind. It, however, effected none in hers, and no further negotiation on the subject seems to have taken place as regarded Anjou, with whom she had refused to enter into any public engagement respecting "the free exercise of the Catholic religion in his chapel." The Bourbon alliance was now formally proposed by the court; the hand of the Princesse Marguerite being offered by the king to the Queen of Navarre for her son Prince Henri, and Maréchal Biron sent to La Rochelle as the negotiator.

Count Louis of Nassau, who was then with the Huguenots, was at the same time desired to repair to the court, secretly and in disguise, to confer privately with the king and queen-mother. He had solicited the aid of Charles IX. for the unhappy Netherlanders, 18,000 of whom the Duke of Alva had already put to death, and was still adding to their number; still "piling up," as Pius V. had urged, to make of their bodies a ladder by which to reach heaven. Nothing could exceed the misery which the wretched Philip and his worthy lieutenant had inflicted on the people, the desolation and ruin they had brought on the country.

After a twelvemonth of carnage he at length deigned to grant to the remnant of the population an amnesty, from the benefit of which all were excluded who had ever acted or spoken in favour of public rights or liberties. The publication of this gracious edict, which was to be proclaimed in the name of the Pope and the Spanish king by Alva — seated on a lofty throne in the centre of the great square of Antwerp — was still deferred. Blood enough had not yet been shed to satisfy these sanguinary monsters. The commerce of the country was also to be ruined by a tax of the tenth part of the price of every object sold. This impost on the various manufactures and products of the country could not be supported. A cry of alarm and despair arose among the people, and all who were able fled to France or England, but chiefly to the latter country, because of their religion. The historian, De Thou, names several partly abandoned English cities — Norwich, Colchester, Sandwich, Southampton, etc. — that were repeopled by the Flemings and Dutch, and owed their future prosperity to the manufactories of various kinds they then established there.

To stay the stream of emigration Alva racked his satanic brain for new and even more terrible tortures, and crueller modes of death. To serve perhaps as a warning to the more timid, he set up in the citadel a statue of himself "crushing the demon Rebellion under his feet." It was cast from the cannon he had taken from "the rebels" at Gemmingen.

It was scarcely sympathy that Louis of Nassau expected from Charles IX. and Catherine de' Medici, who were little less cruel and sanguinary than the agent of Philip II. and Pius V., whose infamy and crime they were waiting but for a favourable opportunity of rivalling. Yet Charles appears to have listened with deep attention to the sad tale of the people's wrongs and sufferings. It was, however, to his ambitious views that the appeal was especially addressed — the great advantages that would ensue to France should she decide on protecting the unfortunate Netherlanders, and aiding them to throw off the yoke of Spain. Charles seemed to be vividly impressed in favour of this project — so much so that he bade the prince be "of good hope," adding that he desired to hear the opinion and have the advice of Admiral de Coligny on the subject.

A letter inviting him to repair to the court for that purpose was sent off to La Rochelle, where it occasioned considerable agitation, and was regarded by most of the Huguenots as a mere device of the queen-mother to ensnare their leader. The perfidy of her character forbade any confidence being placed in her, while she had trained her sons, they said, to "heed neither law nor gospel." Madame de Coligny also expressed great fear lest by complying with the king's command the admiral's life should be endangered.* Charles, however, author-

* Coligny had lately remarried, under circumstances as romantic as the marriage of D'Andelot. A noble lady of Savoy had fallen in love with the admiral's great renown, and "desired," as she said, "to become the Martia of this new Cato." The Duke of Savoy, the suzerain of the "Dame d'Entremonts"— such was her title — forbade her to leave her domains. She, how-

ised him to surround himself with an armed escort for his personal safety. He therefore ceded, hoping to prevent the renewal of civil war, which in the highest degree was repugnant to him.

He might, he knew, be risking his life in the attempt to avert it, but, at all events, he would make the attempt. He believed that further intestine strife could only be averted by a foreign war, which would give employment to those restless, turbulent spirits, both Catholic and Protestant, to whom the warfare of the last ten years had made war a need. Coligny, though not too sanguine of success, yet trusted that he might be able to bring the king to consent to this war, by showing him that his true interests were involved in it; thus — such, at least, was Coligny's noble wish — would their fellow Protestants of the Low Countries be released from the tyranny they now groaned under, and France be indemnified for the troubles of the past by the increase of her territory and her power.

ever, escaped from Savoy, and married Coligny at La Rochelle, March, 1571 (H. Martin).

CHAPTER XIX.

Coligny's Reception at Blois by Charles IX. — Catherine Jealous of Coligny's Influence. — Jeanne d'Albret Visits the French Court. — Jeanne's Letter to Her Son, Henri of Navarre. — The Court of Catherine de' Medici. — The Pope Refuses the Dispensation for the Marriage. — Catherine's Proposals to Queen Elizabeth. — Warlike Preparations: Coligny's Plans. — The Court Leaves Blois for Paris. — Death of Jeanne d'Albret. — Poison Suspected.

CHARLES and the queen-mother, on learning that Coligny was about to leave La Rochelle, at once announced the departure of the court for Blois. Their new attitude towards the Reformers was made evident to all by the courteous information forwarded to the admiral that the king would advance thus far to meet him and spare him the fatigue of half his journey. Coligny arrived at Blois on the 19th of September. On approaching the king, in the humble attitude customary at that period, his majesty graciously raised him, pressed his hand, embraced him three times, and kissed him on both cheeks. "My father," he said, laughingly, "now we have got you, you will not escape from us again" (D'Aubigné).

Though no sinister interpretation was put on the words at the time, yet the manner of the admiral's reception seemed to those chiefs of "the Reform" who remained with the Bourbons at La Rochelle, to be an exaggerated affectation of friendliness on the part of the king, which increased rather than allayed their fears and suspicions. They, however, thought that the fact of his having avengers at hand, should any treachery be attempted, might serve to lessen his danger. But as no signs of any danger appeared, they were gradually lulled into confidence.

Charles appeared thoroughly fascinated by Coligny's grand designs, the desire to realise them increasing as they were more and more fully explained to him. "France," the admiral told him, "should have the Scheldt for her frontier; Flanders and the Walloon and Belgian provinces, speaking the French language, should be reunited to the crown. Independence should be given to Brabant and Holland under the protectorate of the princes of Nassau, a portion of Zealand being reserved for England. The French navy should be, he proposed, powerfully organised, and Spain attacked not only in the Netherlands but in America, where the possession of the new world should be disputed with her." *

---

* This latter part of his scheme was a favourite one with the admiral. In 1555 he endeavoured to found a colony in Brazil. " Five or six years later three or four small vessels were sent by

No schemes on foot in the French Court, however secretly carried on, were unknown to Philip II. He had his emissaries even in the king's council-chamber and the queen-mother's private cabinet. Therefore, not long after Coligny's arrival, the Spanish ambassador Alava, in Philip's name, threatened Charles IX. with war if the Huguenot intrigue was not brought to an end. The king replied that "Spain might do what she pleased; for he feared her not." Catherine, more prudent, complained to Philip of his ambassador, who, she said, "invented false rumours, and generally, by his officiousness, gave much annoyance at court." Philip knew better. But he recalled his ambassador, replacing him by one no less intriguing and officious.

Coligny was much gratified by the ardour with which the king appeared to enter into his views. It exceeded his expectations. The Montmorency or "politique" party also approved them, and even Catherine was almost persuaded by her relative Strozzi—who looked for a prominent command in the Flanders expedition—to give them more

---

his direction to discover a fitting spot for a French settlement. They sailed along the coast and ascended some of the rivers of Florida, Georgia, and Carolina, then unoccupied by Europeans. As soon as the Peace of Saint-Germain was signed, Coligny again turned his thoughts towards colonisation, and but a few weeks before leaving La Rochelle he despatched from that port a small squadron to reconnoitre the Antilles and prepare for an attack on that archipelago" (H. Martin).

than a tacit assent by an open expression of her approbation. But it was not the scheme for the aggrandisement of France — though she desired not war with Spain — that displeased her, but the growing influence which the man who proposed it appeared to be gaining over the king.

Charles IX. at this time was probably playing no dissembling part under his fiendish mother's directions. As he had formerly shown respect for the Chancellor de L'Hôpital and deference to his advice and opinions, so now the honest, upright, and sensible counsels of an honourable man like Coligny produced the same effect on him. For Charles was not, like his brother, the Duc d'Anjou, naturally vicious. His mother was his evil genius. Yet his better nature was not wholly extinct. Some flickering gleams of it did at rare intervals still appear, and under judicious and friendly guidance he might possibly even then have triumphed over that perversion of his moral senses by which the queen-mother had gained the mastery over him.

That the Parisian people might be witnesses of the honour now paid to the admiral, Charles entered his capital on December the 16th, with a numerous retinue, the new favourite riding on his right. This distinction conferred on the "chief of the heretics" was far from meeting with general approval. The exasperation of feeling that existed in both factions was as yet very slightly toned down, and much distrust prevailed. Coligny was then about to return to his domain of Châtillon-sur-Loing. His château had been sacked and pillaged during the civil war; the king, therefore, as some compensation for the loss sustained, made him a present of 100,000 *livres*, for (as Brantôme says) "M. l'Amiral was poor for a man of his rank and station, having valued honour more than riches."

The negotiation respecting the Bourbon marriage was continued through the winter. Coligny had been charged to present to the king the Queen of Navarre's letter of thanks for the honour he had done her by the offer of his sister's hand to her son. But so strong was her repugnance to the match, so great her fears that Henri might be led to renounce his religious profession, that Jeanne, though six months had elapsed, had not yet been persuaded by the assurances of the king's sincerity in his advances towards the Reformers, and the triumph which, through this marriage, the Huguenot gentlemen believed would accrue to "the cause," to visit the court with her son. She foresaw in this alliance the destruction of those plans of conduct she had formed for the young prince, the evil influence of the queen-mother, and the seductions of her surroundings.

At last, after much hesitation, she yielded to Coligny's entreaties, and, with the ladies and gentlemen of her court, left the Château of Pau early in February, 1572. The Princesse Catherine, then in her twelfth year, accompanied the queen; but the young prince, to whom his mother revealed all her anxieties, remained at Béarn. They were received at Tours on the 4th of March by Charles and the queen-mother with every appearance and expression of friendship and welcome. Jeanne was sumptuously lodged at Blois, and the next day the Princesse Catherine writes to her brother:

"Monsieu—— j'ay veu Madame (Marguerite) que j'ay troué fort belle et eussé bien désiré que vous l'eussié veue, ie luy ai bien parlé pour vous qu'elle vous tinst en sa bonne grace ce qu'elle m'a promis et m'a fait bien bon chère et m'a donné un bau petit chien que jeme bien."

The young princess was much admired at the Valois Court, and was pronounced charming. At all events, she charmed as a novelty by the quaint plainness of her Huguenot style of dress, so different from the voluminous finery in which young girls of high station were then usually arrayed, even at Catherine's age. There was much *naïveté*, too, in her manners and mode of speech, and she had a graceful bearing, a bright, lively countenance, a joyous temper like her brother, and already was almost as quick at repartee as he. It may have been found judicious to admire the queen's interesting young daughter. It was a sort of mild flattery wherewith to smooth over the many proposals and concessions that were to be laid before the Queen of Navarre relating to the marriage of her son, and to which, against her better judgment, consent at last was wrung from her.

On the 8th of March, she writes to Henri from Blois, complaining of the obstacles she has to surmount; of the intrigues to which she is exposed; of the trickery she has to baffle.

"I have to negotiate this matter," she says, "in a quite different manner from that I had expected and was promised, no opportunity being given me of speaking to the king or madame, but to the queen-mother only, who treats me with treachery and deceit. Madame, indeed, I never see, except in that very improper place, the queen-mother's apartments, whence she stirs not, and where, without being heard by some of the ladies in attendance, who never think of withdrawing, I cannot speak to her.

"Seeing then, my son, that no advance was made, that there was no desire to conduct matters in due order, but simply a design to force me to precipitate them, I several times spoke on the subject to the queen-mother. She did but jest, and laugh at me, and immediately told every one something altogether contrary to what I had said to her, so that my friends blamed me. And when I said, 'Madame, such and such things were not spoken by me, but by yourself,' she contradicted, and said, 'There's a fine tale,' and laughed in my face, so that it may truly be said my patience passes that of the Griseldas."

Jeanne's character being honest, open, and confiding, she could not comprehend the machiavelian genius of Catherine de' Medici. She at last succeeded in having some conversation with Marguerite, whom she describes as

"handsome, discreet, and docile, but brought up amidst the most cursed (*maudite*) and corrupt society that ever existed;" and she makes no exceptions. "I meet with none," she says, "who are free from its influence. Your cousin, the marquise (the recently married wife of the young Prince de Condé), is so much changed by it that there is no longer any appearance of religion in her, except that she goes not to mass; but, idolatry excepted, she does as the Papists do."

Marguerite acknowledged to the Queen of Navarre that "she had but little mind towards the match, but on the ground of her religion"—to which, contrary to what Jeanne had been assured, she declared she was greatly attached. In another letter to Henri, the queen says:

"As I write privately the bearer will tell you what kind of life the king leads, putting no restraint on himself whatever. It is a great pity. I would not for all the world that you should come here to reside; for you could never escape the contagion except through the great Grace of God. My wish, should you be married, is that you and your wife should retire from this scene of corruption, which, indeed, I had believed to be great, but find it far worse than I had imagined. It is not the men who make love here to the women, but the women to the men."

The hideous fashions of the period, both those of the men and the women, were also displeasing to the Queen of Navarre. She would have persuaded Marguerite to give up the habit of excessive patching and painting, then in vogue, which spoiled her complexion, and instead of heightening, as she considered, diminished her beauty. Nor could she see grace or elegance in increasing the size of that part of the body naturally larger than the rest, by spreading the dress over the "vertugadin" eight or ten feet in a circle around her. Reform in the fashions of the day was certainly needed. But the preaching of Jeanne d'Albret as a reformer of court costume, though it may have afforded amusement to the belles of Catherine's squadron, certainly made no converts.

At length, after much hesitation, and less of her own free will than to satisfy the urgent entreaties of her Huguenot advisers — amongst whom was Coligny, so fully assured was he of the king's sincerity — Jeanne gave her consent to this inauspicious marriage. It was her wish that it should be celebrated at Blois, and according to the rites of the reformed religion. To the proposal of mass and the Catholic ceremony she would not listen. But the queen-mother was bent on its performance in Paris. Charles was also of her opinion that the capital of France was the proper place for the marriage of its kings' daughters. On that point Jeanne then ceded, though she knew that the Parisians cherished the deepest hate towards the Huguenots. Catherine also knew that well, and hence, it was afterwards believed, she determined that the marriage should take place there. Doubtless, also, the compromise respecting the ceremonial was acceded to because of the exasperation it would cause amongst the Catholics of the capital.

But although the marriage treaty was signed on the 11th of April, no dispensation from the Pope had arrived. Pius V. had already sent his nephew, the Cardinal Alessandrino, to Paris to induce the king to abandon the idea of marrying his sister to a heretic; at the same time absolutely refusing to grant the dispensation required on account of their relationship as cousins.

The king, replying to the Queen of Navarre's remark, which probably expressed her wish, that "it would be very long indeed, she believed, before it was obtained, because of the religious difference," said: "Not so, dear aunt, for I honour you more than the Pope, and fear him less than I love my sister. I am not a Huguenot, neither am I a blockhead; but if M. le Pape plays the fool too long (*fait trop la bête*), I will take Margot by the hand, and will publicly lead her to the Huguenot temple to marry Henri."

Pius continued inflexible, though Charles is said to have sent him word that "this marriage afforded him the only means he had of revenging himself on his enemies." If he did so, the Pope of course understood that the wholesale murder he had so long recommended was about to be perpetrated. Heaven, however, as he would have said, did not permit him to see and rejoice over the accomplishment of this good deed. For on the 1st of May the persecuting Pius V. departed this life; whether for a better or more congenial one, who shall declare? Pius was succeeded, to the great disappointment of the Cardinal de Lorraine, by Cardinal Buoncompagno, who took the name of Gregory XIII. The new Pope was less absolute than his predecessor in his refusal of the dispensation. Certain conditions were proposed by him, which, being agreed to, he was willing to yield. Negotiation on the subject then commenced.

On the 29th of April a defensive alliance was concluded between France and England. The queen-mother apparently thought this a favourable opportunity for renewing proposals of marriage to Elizabeth — no longer on the part of Anjou, but of her youngest son, the Duc d'Alençon, a boy of sixteen — Elizabeth being then thirty-eight. This royal youth raised no scruples on the score of religion. He required no private chapel or staff of priests. On the contrary, his religious sympathies inclined towards heresy. Nothing came of this proposal at that time, for it was accompanied by a preposterous request from Catherine, in the interests of her favourite son, "that Elizabeth should consent to the marriage of Anjou with her captive, the Scottish Queen Mary, whom she should also declare her heir.*

* Yet at the time of his death Pius V. and Philip II. were plotting to put Mary on the English throne, after marrying her to

But Elizabeth did not wholly reject this third boy-husband offered by Catherine de' Medici to the English queen during the last three or four years. She was then somewhat incensed at the ungallant conduct of Anjou. Later on, however, she amused herself at the expense of this gay-tempered, valiant, and adventurous prince, now partly accepting his proffered hand — now declining it — and again raising his hopes but to damp them. His interests did not allow him to be deterred by her years from playing the lover, and Elizabeth, herself so open to flattery, probably saw little to object to in that respect. Her ambassador had insinuated that she looked scarcely older than the prince, and that there was "more beauty in her majesty's little finger than in the whole body of any lady he had seen at the French Court."*

The Papal Court was slow in its decision concerning the heretic marriage, for Gregory's proposals were not well received by Jeanne; but meanwhile, great preparations, military and naval, were making at Bordeaux, Brouage, and Normandy, and a numerous corps of Protestants was forming at Poitiers at the king's expense. Coligny had retired during the king's *grandes chasses* to Châtillon to spend some time with his family, who

---

the Duke of Norfolk, and imprisoning Elizabeth, or, better still, putting her to death.

* "Foreign State Papers" — "Correspondence of English Ambassadors," 1572.

urged him not to return to the court. Not only his wife and children on their knees entreated him, but friends and partisans of "the cause" warned him not to put faith in Charles IX. They reminded him of the Catholic maxim that "faith ought not to be kept with heretics," of the perversity of the queen-mother, the detestable education she had given her sons, of Charles's horrible cruelty and mad delight in slaughtering beast and bathing his hands in their blood — a fitting preparation for the slaughter of human beings.

But Coligny declared that "he would rather be dragged dead through the streets of Paris than witness the renewal of the horrors of civil war." He departed then for the court. Charles had urged his speedy return; he could not live without his "good father." He would have, he said, Margot's marriage no longer delayed, and the court, in consequence, towards the end of May repaired to Paris.

The bridegroom was still at Béarn. Jeanne so feared the evil influence which the depraved morals and manners of the court might probably have on her son, that she was anxious he should defer his arrival until the date was fixed for the ceremony actually to take place. She expressed a fear of falling ill, so much had the anxiety and annoyance she had undergone affected her. To add to her troubles, her daughter Catherine had been attacked by pleurisy, and reduced to a state of such extreme weakness by the copious bleedings then in vogue, that months of repose would be needed, she said, for her restoration. (Catherine's constitution, it appears, was permanently affected by this weakening system.) They, however, decided on following the court to Paris, and on the 4th of June, in solemn silence, the Queen of Navarre, her friends, and a small escort entered the capital. The secret influence of the Guises was already felt, and the people received the ally — as they were told — of the heretic Elizabeth of England, and the Protestants of Germany, with a sort of hostile curiosity. She preferred instead of the Louvre, as a residence, the Hôtel de Condé, offered to her by her relative. Her anxiety respecting the marriage had produced a feverish energy, to which great languor now succeeded, and a depressed state of feeling she was unable to surmount. Preparations were making for the marriage, and by a great effort she strove to appear the gracious, eloquent, brilliant, and enlightened person she naturally was (Mademoiselle Vauvilliers).

Accompanied by Maréchal Montmorency, the queen visited the ateliers of the artists and the armourers of renown, and made many purchases of jewels and other presents for the bride, her friends, and her children; deeming it right not to be sparing of expense on this occasion, for her son's sake. Seeing the magnificence of the preparations then making by the court, she sent orders to Béarn for the due equipment of the numerous *cortège* destined to attend the prince. The high-spirited Jeanne d'Albret, notwithstanding her general adherence to Huguenot ideas of simplicity, would not allow Prince Henri of Navarre to be wholly eclipsed by the splendour of his bride.

It was while visiting the various establishments of Paris that the queen entered the laboratory of Catherine de' Medici's perfumer, and purchased a pair of perfumed gloves, said to have been prepared with some subtle but odorous poison. On the morrow she was attacked by violent pains in the head. The king's physicians were instantly sent to her, but on the following morning, the 9th of June, she died — but five days after her arrival in Paris.

It was long generally believed that Jeanne d'Albret was the victim of one of the poisoning secrets of the Borgia and Medici. But although it has been urged that she suffered from an affection of the chest, the symptoms of which were aggravated by the fatigue and mental anxiety she had undergone respecting her son's marriage — to which she had been urged by Huguenot partisans to consent, though she could not give it her approval — it has never been clearly proved that the unscrupulous Catherine de' Medici, through her no less unscrupulous agents, had not some hand in the Queen of Navarre's death. Her body was opened and (according to Palma-Cayet) her head also, and no trace of poison, of course, was discovered. The court physicians declared that her death was caused by an abscess on the lungs. But Catherine's Italian secretary, Davila, who has been at such pains to exalt her crimes into traits of the great genius and elevation of mind with which he credits her, says of Jeanne d'Albret's death, "It was the first thunder-peal announcing the tempest then preparing against the Huguenots."

The unexpected death of the Huguenot queen did certainly spread consternation as of the fall of a thunderbolt amongst the Reformers. "Sublime in the hour of death as in the many perils that already had menaced her life, her only regret was leaving her children; the destiny of her daughter especially occupying her thoughts. She entreated Coligny and the Cardinal de Bourbon, who with the Prince of Nassau were hastily summoned to receive her last wishes, to supply the place of parents to both Henri and Catherine — the pledges of her dearest affections and of her bitterest regrets." *

Jeanne d'Albret was buried with as much of the ceremonial customary at royal funerals as the austere simplicity of the religion she had adopted would permit. She lay in state for five days in a

* Mademoiselle Vauvilliers.

room draped with black. Her dress was of white satin embroidered in silver, and a royal mantle of violet velvet was thrown over her. "The bed she lay on," writes Marguerite de Valois, "was her ordinary one, and the curtains were open; but there were no wax lights, no priests, no cross, and no holy water." The public walked slowly through the gloomy apartment, bowing reverently as they passed the body. A sentiment of profound pity arose in the hearts of all who could momentarily contemplate the now rigid features of the valiant and noble lady, whose counsels had so often troubled the projects of her adversaries.

CHAPTER XX.

Marriage of Marguerite and Henri Deferred. — Catherine Seeks to Thwart Coligny's Plans. — Charles Flies from His Counsellors. — Catherine Opposed to War with Spain. — Elizabeth Again Pressed to Marry D'Alençon. — Arrival in Paris of Henri of Navarre. — The Betrothal. — The Dispensation Dispensed with. — "Les Noces Vermeilles." — Marguerite Declares She Never Accepted Henri. — The Admiral's Fatal Confidence in Charles IX. — Saturnalia.

THE marriage of Marguerite and Henri of Béarn — now King of Navarre — was delayed for two months by the death of Jeanne d'Albret. It was even supposed by the more zealous of the Huguenot party that it would not take place at all, and that Coligny's relations with Charles IX. would either come to an end, or be greatly modified by the suspicious circumstances that surrounded Jeanne's sudden and mysterious death. But this did not appear to be the admiral's view of the subject. Suspecting no foul play, he accepted undoubtingly the declaration of the physicians as to the true cause of death, just as he believed, as a man of honor, that the king was acting towards him in good faith respecting the projected war against Spain. He rejected, therefore, the suggestions pressed upon him to refrain

from following up the plans agreed on between Charles IX. and himself.

It was, indeed, too late to draw back. Louis de Nassau and the valiant La Noue — "the Bayard of the Huguenots" — had taken Valenciennes and Mons, entering those cities to the cry of "France and Liberty!" It was now for Charles to keep his word, and ready enough he was, it appears, to draw the sword. But Catherine, opposed to war with Spain and jealous of Coligny, would not let him. She succeeded also in preventing orders being sent for the sailing of the fleet from La Rochelle. At the same time she and Anjou informed the Duke of Alva of the object of these warlike preparations, and the Cardinal de Lorraine conveyed similar intelligence to Philip II.

France at this period has been compared to a vessel buffeted by contrary winds. The helm of the state was certainly in very unskilful hands. But having proceeded thus far on a hazardous course, a council was held to determine what further steps should be taken.* Anjou and the queen-mother attended this council, with their sworn allies, the Italian chancellor, Birago, and the ferocious Maréchal Tavannes. But while opinions for and against this Spanish war were being debated, news arrived

---

* The memorial presented to the king by Coligny on this occasion was prepared by a young Huguenot gentleman, Du Plessis-Mornay, who afterwards became famous as the diplomatist and friend of Henri of Navarre and the Huguenot party.

that Alva, reinforced, had retaken Valenciennes and was besieging Mons, the "military operations being supplemented by the enchantments and divinations of soothsayers and astrologers" ("*Lettres de Morillon à Granvelle*"); and further, that the second corps of Catholic and Protestant volunteers from Picardy, which the Huguenot captain, Genlis, was marching with to relieve Mons, had been surprised *en route* and defeated. The greater part of this corps had been put to death as heretics, and Genlis, their captain, taken prisoner, thrown into a dungeon, and strangled.

Catherine and Anjou rejoiced in this result of their treachery. This check had also, for their purpose, the further advantage of inducing those who were before undecided to protest against the war. Coligny remained firm, and Charles seemed still to cling to his view of the question, giving him authority to raise another corps of volunteers, notwithstanding that further news from Flanders reported that in Genlis's baggage a letter from Charles IX. was found, fully proving that the King of France had aided and connived at the rebellion of the princes of Nassau.

The king was pressed to disavow his complicity with the Nassaus by some striking act that should appease the resentment of Philip II. He, however, did not, and, to free himself from the distracting importunity of both parties, he fled to Brie for some days of violent hunting. But the queen-mother would not let him escape so easily. She followed him with all haste to reproach him with his ingratitude to a mother who had sacrificed herself for him, and whose enemies he now preferred to her. She therefore humbly requested permission to retire, with her son Anjou, to her own country and family. A torrent of tears followed the request of the heartbroken mother. But Charles had seen this torrent flow so often and so readily that it affected him not. If she and Anjou had really decamped without troubling him, he would have been only too glad. Such scenes, however, put him into a frenzy of passion, and to be free from them he promised anything she asked of him. He would follow her counsels, he now told her, after his rage at being pursued had spent itself; and Catherine, but partly consoled and scarcely assured that she had regained her authority over him, returned to Paris with murderous thoughts in her heart towards Coligny.

But when Charles, after an absence of some days, again met the admiral in Paris, his influence once more seemed likely to supercede that of the queen-mother. After his promises to her, Charles dared not declare war openly; but his anti-Spanish policy revived; the armaments were continued, and all that now was wanting to engage in war against Spain was that the German princes and the Queen of England should come to a decision on the proposal of France to make their alliance with her offensive as well as defensive. Several months had elapsed since the proposal was made; but distrust of Charles and the queen-mother had occasioned this hesitancy in acceding to it. Elizabeth also was scarely willing to take the initiative, as Charles desired, and declare war against Philip.

But Catherine was far more anxious that Elizabeth should decide to accept the Duc d'Alençon for her husband. This marriage was continually forced on her attention. The good qualities of the young gentleman's head and heart were lauded in glowing terms; but, alas! little could be said in favour of his personal advantages, on which Elizabeth seems to have laid some stress. In that respect, he was the least favoured of Catherine's children. He was short, and inclined, like his mother, to obesity, and unfortunately the ravages of that fearful disease, the smallpox, had made him (not to say hideous; it is an unpleasant term) sublimely ugly. He, however, bore his misfortune gracefully, and as the disease had at that period many victims, the disfigurement was not so remarkable.

The queen-mother had hoped to celebrate this marriage with the excommunicated heretic queen at the same time as Marguerite's with the King of Navarre. But Elizabeth had decided neither on the political nor matrimonial alliance when, on the 12th or 13th of August, Marguerite's heretic bridegroom made his entry into Paris with his cousin, Prince Henri of Condé, and attended by eight hundred Huguenot gentlemen. All were in deep mourning. Amongst the spectators the same ominous silence prevailed as when, but two months past, Queen Jeanne and her modest *cortège* arrived in the capital. But the young king had a jovial air; he rode well, and bore himself gallantly, the few Huguenots who greeted him gazing on him with pride and pleasure.

Certainly he was not handsome, but the expression of his countenance was pleasing. His eyes were lively and penetrating, and shaded by thick black eyebrows. His hair was black and wavy; his nose aquiline and rather too long for beauty; while of beard he, as yet, had little to speak of, being then but in his nineteenth year. But he was "altogether a goodly prince," and as "at the French Court all who were not lame or humpbacked were accounted handsome," Henri of Navarre, who was neither, though he could not contest the palm of manly beauty with Duc Henri of Guise, might have advantageously been compared with many of the beaux chevaliers of the Court of Charles IX.

The betrothal of Marguerite and Henri took place at the Louvre on the 17th in the presence of the court and a brilliant assemblage of the principal Catholic and Huguenot nobility. The Duc de

Guise and his brothers were present, and Charles, considering the occasion favourable for a reconciliation, insisted on the duke giving his hand to the admiral, who, on his part, repeated his denial of any complicity in the assassination of the late duke, and proposed to sign a solemn declaration to that effect. The duke, in deference to the king probably, appeared satisfied, but his feeling towards Coligny and burning desire for vengeance, as the event proved, remained unchanged.

No dispensation had been sent from Rome. The four conditions: 1st, that Henri should make profession of the Catholic faith before the king; 2nd, that he should reëstablish the Catholic faith in his own domains; 3rd, that he should himself make the request to his holiness for the necessary dispensation for his marriage; and 4th, that the marriage should be solemnised in the church, without any variation from the customary ceremonial, were not agreed to. Charles urgently pressed the Pope to renounce these four conditions, assuring him, rather suspiciously, that he asked it "in the interests of religion," and praying him to take it in good part should he be constrained, notwithstanding his refusal to yield, at once to celebrate the marriage.*

The Cardinal de Bourbon was to officiate at this ceremony, but was not prepared to do so without the authority of Rome. "The cardinal," according

* "*Histoire des Ducs de Guise*," *par* M. de Bouillé.

to Geronimo Lippomano, "was one of the most zealous Catholics in France," yet withal it appears a man of narrow views and little intelligence — rather a simpleton, in fact. It seemed then likely that, after all the grand preparations were made for it, there was to be no marriage at all. The king, however, undertook to convince the cardinal that his objections were not valid. The dispensation truly had not yet arrived, but "it was granted," he told him, "and on its way to Paris." Putting faith in the king's word, the cardinal promised compliance with his wish, and on the 18th these strange nuptials, these "Noces Vermeilles," destined to be sealed with blood, took place. "They were celebrated," as Marguerite herself informs us, "with a triumph and magnificence that none other had hitherto been."

The King of Navarre, the princes of his house, and his eight hundred gentlemen, had discarded their mourning for the occasion, and appeared in the glittering gala costume in vogue at that extravagant period. The royal bridegroom wore a state mantle of black velvet, embroidered in gold; doublet and trunk-hose of light brown and white silk, with jets and trimmings in gold; pantalon of white silk with gold embroidery, and black velvet hat with a white plume. His sword-belt and sheath were black; the hilt of the sword gold. His shoes, and gold-fringed gloves also, were white, much ornamented with seed-pearls and gold. The

Order of Saint-Michel, surrounded with precious stones, completed the young king's costume. Charles IX. and his courtiers were similarly attired, but surpassed the Huguenots in the number and magnificence of their jewels.

The bride herself was "arrayed," as she says, "*á la royale*," wearing a "circlet, stomacher, and corset of spotted ermine, or minever. The dress itself was of cloth of silver embroidered with pearls, and opening over a richly jewelled satin petticoat — pearls and diamonds also bordering the long Venetian sleeves of the under robe. The crown jewels of France were worn by her for this occasion. Her mantle was of blue velvet embroidered in gold, the train four ells in length, and borne by three princesses." But this train of four ells was but a small affair compared with that worn by Elizabeth of Austria on her marriage with Charles IX. "Its length," says Marguerite, "was twenty ells, and, being heavily embroidered in gold, required eight ladies of the court to assist the four princesses who were selected to bear it."

From the residence of the Archbishop of Paris to the great portal of the "Temple of Notre Dame" (D'Aubigné), a high platform was erected, from which, descending by a lower one, the nave of the temple was entered. These platforms were protected from the pressure of the crowd by barricades covered, like the platforms, with cloth of gold. The bride was conducted from the archbishop's house by Charles IX., the queen-mother, the princes of the blood, also those of Lorraine and the great officers of the crown. On the opposite side walked the King of Navarre with his two cousins, the admiral, the Comte de La Rochefoucauld, and other nobles and gentlemen. The two processions arrived together at the entrance of "the Temple," where the Cardinal de Bourbon was waiting to receive them, and where, according to a ceremonial and form of words already supplied to him, and which satisfied neither party, Marguerite and Henri were married. The bride with her relatives and their retinue then entered "the Temple" to hear mass, the bridegroom meanwhile retiring to the courtyard of the bishop's house, while the rest of the Reformers promenaded the cloisters and nave (D'Aubigné). Mass being ended, Maréchal de Montmorency reassembled the party, and the cardinal then gave the nuptial benediction. It was remarked by several persons of the company (according to Davila), that when the cardinal asked Marguerite if she would take the King of Navarre for her husband, she gave no reply. Charles, noticing this, laid his hand on her head, and compelled her to bend it in assent. "But," continues Davila, "both before and after the ceremony, she declared — whenever she could venture to speak freely — that she never would consent or had consented to renounce the Duc de Guise, to whom her faith was previously engaged, or to take as her husband one of the duke's chief enemies."

The pledge of alliance between Catholic and Protestants was now supposed to be solemnly given to the Reformers. Coligny, therefore, lost no time in urging on the king no further delay in taking those steps already resolved on against Spain. But Charles laughingly excused himself for setting aside all thoughts of war at a time when the propitious nuptials, now happily concluded, called for a brief space of mirthful rejoicing. Though about to share in the pastimes and festive doings prepared to celebrate the auspicious event, "the admiral might rest assured," he said, "that he would not leave Paris before he had fully satisfied him." The admiral, under a sort of infatuation, as it would seem, continued to place full confidence in Charles, a flattering mark of which he gave him in the surrender, some months before the time had expired, of the four strong cities assigned for two years to the Huguenots, as guarantees, on the signing of the Treaty of Saint-Germain.

Some festivity on the occasion of a royal marriage was certainly expected by the court, if not by the more rigid Huguenots. The admiral accordingly reconciled himself to the delay of a few days of gaiety. In the interval, Elizabeth might make up her mind. She had asked for the restitution of Calais as the price of her alliance, but Coligny resisted that demand. Flushing, he said, was more advantageous to her, and the suggestion was not unfavourably received.

The festivities prepared under the direction of the Duc d'Anjou in honour of his sister's marriage were of a kind that fully exemplify the excessive depravity of the Court of France under Catherine de' Medici and the last of the Valois kings. They were no less singular than revolting. Strange scenes of debauchery, masquerades, and divertissements which one shrinks from describing, and in which the court "squadron" of dissolute women figured prominently. "In one of the allegorical divertissements, paradise and the infernal regions were represented, with a party of knights-errant defending the entry of the former against another party who, finally defeated, were drawn away by devils and cast into the flames of the latter place." This was understood to be the fate reserved for the heretics at the hands of the faithful.

Charles IX., his brothers, and the Guises, the young King of Navarre, the Bourbon princes, and some of the younger Huguenot nobility, were the principal performers, together with "the squadron," in these saturnalia. The elder and more austere Reformers were both grieved and disgusted. It was well, perhaps, that poor Jeanne d'Albret was spared the pain of witnessing how easily her cherished son was led astray, as she feared he would be, in the midst of the gross seductions of the dissolute Court of France. The queen-mother observed him narrowly, and clearly perceived that he had inherited much of the weakness of his father's character. But that he had other qualities which in some measure counterbalanced that weakness, she apparently did not then suspect, as she for some time thought but contemptibly of her heretic son-in-law.

CHAPTER XXI.

Anjou a Candidate for the Crown of Poland.—The Kiss of Peace Twice Given.—Attack on the Admiral Instigated by the Guises.—The King in a Rage when Informed of It.—Charles Visits the Admiral, but Cannot Free Himself from His Mother's and Brother's Company.—The Admiral's Private Advice to Charles.—The Massacre Arranged.—A Band of Demons.—Charles Long Withstands His Infamous Mother's Arguments.—"*Par la Mort Dieu!* Give Your Orders. Let Them Die! Let None Remain to Reproach Me."

THE boisterous joyousness with which Charles had taken part in those strange festivities, though consistent with the fitful moods of his violent and impulsive character, was yet partly due to the hope he then had of being quickly freed from the hated presence of Anjou. Sigismund Augustus, King of Poland, had lately died, and Catherine, ever on the watch to secure a throne for her best beloved, despatched, on the 17th of August, Montluc, Bishop of Valence, to Cracow to support, conjointly with another of her secret agents, Gaspard de Schomberg, the candidature of the Duc d'Anjou; to secure whose election they were to be "sparing neither of flattery, promises, nor bribes."

The bishop had formerly favoured the cause of Reform, when, like Catherine, he thought it likely to gain the upper hand in France. He had since returned to his allegiance to Rome — in outward seeming at least. He, however, still retained a certain interest in the success of "the cause," which induced him before setting out on his Polish mission to warn the Comte de La Rochefoucauld, and some other Huguenot gentlemen, that they would do well to return to their homes, or to seek refuge in their strong cities, for mischief was plotting, and great danger menacing them. Little attention was given to this warning, or to other secret intimations to be on their guard, for the admiral's confidence in the king acted as a check to any doubts his partisans might otherwise have entertained.

But the four days' saturnalia being ended, Catherine, to her intense consternation, perceived that the king's inclination towards Coligny was not only not abated, but that the private conferences concerning the war in Flanders were to be renewed. Her terrible anxiety was shared by Anjou, who saw that his brother's aversion to him was increasing daily. He relates that, "on one occasion when he entered his apartment, so furiously was Charles pacing to and fro, and so fiercely did he glare on him, at the same time placing his hand on his dagger, that he quickly slipped out of the room while Charles's back was turned, fearing that he meant to kill him."*

* "*Discours de Henri III.*" — Mathieu's "*Histoire de France.*"

Further intrigue appeared to the queen-mother to be useless. She had not regained her influence by the weeping scene at the Château de Montpipeau, and of the disgrace of the admiral by any act emanating from the king, there was now apparently no hope. She would hesitate no longer to free herself from this hated rival; and the course suggested to her by Alva during the visit to Bayonne in 1564, in the remark that "one salmon's head was worth more than the heads of twenty thousand frogs," probably arose in her mind. During the eight years that had elapsed the same suggestion, in other words, had been often urged on her. Twice she had tried to put it into effect, and had failed. But just as the fortunes of the Huguenots during that interval had fluctuated between success and defeat, so had Alva's suggestion to deprive them of their leaders recurred to her, been rejected, and again recalled.

It was now to be put into practice with a better chance of success; for the victims were caged, and in former attempts they had first to be caught. But now, as before, though Catherine was to profit by the "*crimes utiles*" she incited or hired others to commit, she would not take on herself the responsibility and the odium of them. In this instance she determined to lay them on the shoulders of the Guises. The Duchesse de Nemours accordingly was secretly sent for by Catherine and Anjou. They knew that her hatred of Coligny was implacable; that notwithstanding that the farce of reconciliation had twice taken place before the king, and the " kiss of peace " had twice been given, her belief that the admiral had assassinated her former husband, and her desire for revenge, remained strong as ever.

With her usual calmness, Catherine told the duchess that she placed in her hands the vengeance she had so long and so earnestly desired. It was believed that she had a double motive in selecting the Guises to do this deed of blood for her. " The Huguenots, she doubted not, would rise in arms to avenge the murder of their chief, and would attack the Guises even in their hôtel. The duke's partisans and the Catholic Parisian populace would hasten to defend him, and Huguenot and Politique in the heat of this savage conflict would slay each other. The former would be overpowered by numbers; the Lorrainers exhausted by their victory — the butchery ending in the massacre also of the Guises by the royal guards — leaving Catherine mistress of the field."

Such was the sanguinary programme attributed to her and accepted as true by contemporary writers — De Thou and others.* But whether or not, events did not follow exactly in the order proposed or expected. The young Duc de Guise,

---

* De Thou was the director of the commission appointed by Charles IX. to inquire into the attack on Coligny, and to discover and punish its authors.

in the prospect of vengeance, exhibited a sort of furious joy, a mad paroxysm of delight worthy of Charles IX. Under its influence he would have had his mother take up the arquebuse, and with her own hand, "in, as he said, the very midst of the court," fire the shot intended to pierce the admiral's heart, and kill him on the spot. But she suggested less publicity, and that a surer hand than a woman's, though strengthened by revenge, should be employed to assassinate the assassin. Maurevert was then summoned — a man whose business it was to do such deeds for hire, and who shrank from no atrocity. He had already been charged by the court to take the admiral's life, failing which, with unusual brutality even for those bloodthirsty times, he had murdered one of his officers.

This wretch was put into a house belonging to the duchess, to watch from behind a curtain for the admiral, who was accustomed to pass that way on returning from the Louvre to his own residence. The assassin took his aim from the window, his practised hand rarely failing to strike a vital part. But the admiral happened to be reading as he slowly passed along, and the position of his hands prevented the shot taking the direction intended. The ball struck the forefinger of the right hand and entered the lower part of the left arm. Thus disabled, the admiral was assisted to his hôtel, whence he sent to inform the king of what had happened, that he might judge of the manner in which the Guises kept their promises of peace and amity.

Meanwhile, the admiral's people had forced the door of the house whence the attack proceeded. The arquebuse they found, but the arquebusier had fled. A swift horse from the stables of the Duc de Guise had been waiting for him at the back of the building. He was pursued; but having had considerably the start of his pursuers, and all trace of him being soon lost, the pursuit was given up.

Charles was playing at tennis with the Duc de Guise and the admiral's son-in-law, Teligny, when news of the attempted assassination reached him. He heard it at first with a sort of stupor; then, changing to violent anger, he dashed his racket on the ground with such force that it was broken, and exclaiming, "Am I then never to know peace?" went hastily to his apartment, while Guise slunk off in silence. The King of Navarre and his cousin of Condé were quickly at Coligny's bedside. He was attended by the famous surgeon, Ambroise Paré, who amputated his finger, and afterwards extracted the ball from his arm. "With quietude and a little patience," he told the princes, "the admiral would do very well" — the ball not being poisoned, as at first supposed.

Believing that their lives were not safe in Paris, they sought the king's permission to leave the capital. He begged them not to stir, and with one of his customary oaths, emphasised by a violent blow on the table, swore that he would make such an example of the assassin and his accomplices that it should not be soon forgotten in France. He then sent a detachment of his guards to protect Coligny's house, and seemed even more angry and more grieved than were the princes themselves. "It is I who am wounded!" he continually exclaimed; to which Catherine, who never allowed him to be a minute alone, rejoined, "It is all France!" artfully adding, "Soon we shall have these desperadoes attacking the king in his bed." A message from Coligny was soon after received, praying the king to come to him, as he had many things of importance to tell him. Charles at once complied, but could not escape from the companionship of his mother and brother.

Arrived at the admiral's bedside, the king was profuse in expressions of concern for the injuries he had received. "To you, my father," he said, "the pain of the wounds — to me the insult and outrage." Catherine affected to be greatly moved, and vehemently inveighed against the "dastardly assassins." But Coligny, as though on his deathbed, appealed to Heaven in witness of the sincerity of his attachment and fidelity to the king and the state. He blamed Charles for neglecting the great opportunity Providence had given him of extending his dominions, and protested against the treason of those persons who betrayed the secrets of the king's private council to the Duke of Alva. He then requested to speak to the king alone. Charles signified to his mother, his brother, and the courtiers, his wish that they should withdraw. This was agony to Catherine and Anjou; but the former, though she could not prevent this secret conference, determined that it should be but of short duration. Affecting anxiety for Coligny, she rose, and approaching the king, said aloud that it was "unkind and even dangerous to make M. l'Amiral talk so much. Such exertion might produce fever, which should be particularly guarded against." The king hesitated, and glanced furiously at her and his brother; but Catherine did not flinch. She succeeded in leading him away.

On returning to the Louvre, the queen-mother and Anjou pressed the king to tell them what Coligny had said to him. At first he gave no reply to their repeated inquiries, but in an angry tone muttered his usual oaths. As they ceased not to torment him with questions, he at last burst forth: "*Par le sang Dieu!* what the admiral told me is true! You two," he raved at them, "have artfully drawn into your own hands all power, and the whole management of the affairs of state. Your power and your authority may some day become very prejudicial to me as well as to my kingdom. I should beware of it, he said, and keep a watchful eye on you! As you wish to know, that is what the admiral told me, as my faithful servant, which he is; for, *par le sang Dieu!* what he said is true!" Catherine and her son listened to Charles's words with so much consternation that Anjou says ("*Discours de Henri III.*") "they were unable to decide that day what course it would be best to pursue, so put off its consideration until the morrow."

The reports of the commission respecting the attack on the admiral greatly compromised the Guises. The king, in consequence, ordered the arrest of some members of their household, and threatened the duke himself, at the same time conferring many marks of his favour on the Protestants. In the afternoon the duke and his uncle D'Aumale sought an interview with the king to request permission to retire from the court, as their presence there appeared to be no longer agreeable to his majesty. Charles replied abruptly, "They might go wherever they pleased; but that he should be able to find them if it were proved that they had any hand in the attempt on the admiral." But the Guises retired from the court no further than their own hôtel.

The night of the 22nd passed off quietly. The Huguenots had taken some precautions against an attack, but on the following one they failed to do so, relying on the protection of the king's guards and the Swiss guards of the King of Navarre.

Charles had desired the two Bourbon princes to bring their friends to the Louvre, where he also offered to lodge the Huguenot nobility in the suite of the admiral.

Meanwhile, the Florentine Jezebel assembled her trusty counsellors at the Tuileries — Birago, the Piedmontese chancellor; Gondi, the Florentine, employed by Catherine to corrupt her son; the Duc de Nevers, of the Mantuan family Gonzaga; and the ferocious Tavannes, a Frenchman and marshal of France; the rest, Italian assassins. Amongst them they arranged the plan for the massacre — to begin, of course, with the admiral. But Catherine dared not strike Coligny unless the king was implicated in the act. The council therefore adjourned, to reassemble at the Louvre, in order to bring over the half-mad king to their views, by working on his fears by false reports of the designs of Coligny and the principal Huguenots then in Paris. "It was she," Catherine tells her son, "who sought the admiral's life; but it was that she might save his. She has begun the work; it remains with him to finish it."

"Surrounded by this band of demons, of whom the worst was his mother," Charles (as stated by Anjou) resisted their murderous arguments for more than an hour and a half. "The Huguenots were arming," the queen-mother told him, "but not in his service; rather to deprive him of all authority and to obtain complete mastery over him. The loyal Catholics were determined to put an end to these traitorous projects, and, if the king was not on their side, to elect a captain-general, and under him to attack the pretended Reformers." Charles scowled fiercely at his brother. He quite understood that he was the threatened captain-general, and Catherine well knew the exciting effect it would have on him. "Paris is already under arms," she said. The king, with a sudden start, inquired, "How is that? I forbade them to arm in the *quartiers*." "But they are armed," she replied, curtly. "One man only," she continued, "is the cause of all these troubles. He deceives the king, and, under the pretence of extending his dominions, urges on the state to its ruin. Let the king remember the conspiracy of Amboise; let him recall to mind Meaux, when he fled before his revolted subjects to Paris." That long and rapid ride from Meaux to Paris in 1569, to escape falling into the hands of the Huguenot troops, was always a vexatious subject to touch upon with Charles.

"The Huguenots," Catherine went on, "will cry for vengeance on the Guises, who, to exonerate themselves, will denounce your mother and brother as the authors of the attack; and if the king does not finish the work, both he and we are lost." Charles, pacing the room in a frenzy, declared, with many oaths, that "he would not have a hand laid on the admiral." Then, sinking into gloom and despondency, he prayed his mother and her agents " to find some other mode of ensuring safety." "There was no other way," they told him; "the death of the admiral and his chief captains alone could ensure it." Strangely enough, the Comte de Retz (Gondi) — who had taken a principal part in the arrangement for the massacre — declared, to the great surprise of his associates in crime, that " what was proposed was dishonourable both to the king and the nation, and would lead to a series of calamities of which neither they nor their children would see the end."

"Too late! — too late!" was the vehement response. "The Guises will denounce the king as well as his mother and brother, and war will be inevitable. Better far to gain a certain battle in the streets of Paris than to risk one in the open field." De Retz made no reply, and Charles, reclining in a chair, exhausted and panting for breath (he was then suffering from incipient consumption), had given no heed to his governor's remarks. Had he noticed and supported them, he might have been saved from his fearful crime by the very man who had been specially engaged to work his moral ruin.

Catherine, however, had not spoken her last word. "Sire," she asked, " do you refuse?" No answer. "Grant me and your brother, then, permission to take leave of you — to depart." Charles trembled with suppressed rage, but uttered no word. Again she spoke, "Sire, is it fear of the Huguenots that makes you refuse?" Starting up in a fury, he exclaimed, "*Par la mort Dieu!* since you are resolved that the admiral shall die, let it be so; but also every Huguenot in France, that none may remain to reproach me afterwards with his death. *Par la mort Dieu!* give your orders promptly;" and he rushed like a madman from the room.

All, then, were to be murdered. So Catherine and her assassins had already determined, the two young Bourbons excepted. They were to be spared, lest by their death the Guises should become too powerful.

CHAPTER XXII.

Arranging for the Success of the Massacre. — The Provost of Paris, Le Charron. — Catherine Regardless Even of Her Daughter's Safety. — To the Guises the Honour of Beginning the Massacre. — Alert Before Dawn. — Guilty Consciences. — The Admiral's Death Countermanded: Too Late. — Already Slain. — His Head Sent to Catherine. — Charles Like a Madman: "Kill! Kill!" — Catherine and Her "*Filles d'Honneur.*" — Rejoicings in Rome and Madrid. — Bells, Bonfires, Te Deums, and Cannon. — Medals, Pictures, and Compliments.

ON the evening, Anjou and his mother were joined by the Ducs de Guise and D' Aumale, Tavannes and the rest, for the purpose of assigning the murderers their *quartiers*, and arranging for the full and successful execution of their plot. Le Charron, provost of the merchants and chief of the municipality of Paris, was sent for, and the king — who apparently had now reconciled himself to the commission of the crime which, as M. Henri Martin says, "was to be his damnation in history" — gave him orders to have the city artillery ready that night to be moved to any part of the town that might be directed, and to station detachments of the militia, armed, in all the squares and open parts of the capital. When at last Le Charron comprehended what was required of him, he protested against it as horrible, and declared that his conscience forbade him to take part in such a crime. He was threatened with hanging, but was allowed to go his way. The orders he received he detained, so that the regular authorities of the Hôtel de Ville did not participate in the slaughter.

That Le Charron would not obey appears to have been expected, and measures were therefore taken to secure the aid of some less fastidious agent, to rouse as many "good Catholics" as possible in those parts of the capital to which the municipal authority did not extend. They were to be informed that the king had resolved to exterminate, in Paris and throughout the kingdom, the seditious faction which had already taken up arms against him, and had now reassembled in Paris to organise a fresh conspiracy. The bell of the clock-tower of the Palais de Justice, at break of day, would give the signal for these "good Catholics" to come forth and slay; each one having, as a sign of recognition, a white cross in his hat, that the faithful might not perchance be slain with the heretics. Towards midnight the king's regiment of guards, 1,200 strong, and a corps of Swiss Catholics were placed under arms, inside and around the Louvre, also round the admiral's hôtel, and in some parts of the neighbouring streets.

The Queen of Navarre, who has given so

graphic a description of the occurrences in her apartment, and her participation in the dangers of that night of horrors, was unaware of what was about to take place. Solely intent on the success of her sanguinary plot, Catherine cared not to save her daughter from the probable vengeance of any Huguenot who might escape from the general slaughter. Some hints of the tragedy in preparation had been given to the Duchesse de Lorraine, who, therefore, endeavoured that night to detain her sister in her own or the queen-mother's apartment. Catherine angrily forbade it. "You are deliberately sacrificing her," remonstrated the duchess. "Whatever may happen," replied this anxious mother, "she must go, lest any suspicions should arise"—amongst the Bourbons, of course, and their friends in the Louvre.

To the Guises was accorded the gratifying honour of beginning the massacre at dawn of day, August the 24th, the festival of Saint-Bartholomew. How great then their exultation, inspired by the fact that the first victim was to be the man in whose blood they had so long ardently yearned to slake their thirst for vengeance. In their eagerness to begin the carnival of murder, they were probably on the alert before dawn. For a few minutes before the first faint flush of day appeared in the east, those three great criminals, the king, his mother, and brother, repaired to the upper part of the grand gate of the

Louvre, thence to witness the beginning of the general slaughter, when, suddenly, the report of a pistol startled them. But for the stillness of the hour, and the deed of blood that had brought them there, it would have passed unnoticed. It now struck terror, as of a solemn warning, into the guilty consciences of those three associates in crime. Trembling with fear lest their plot was discovered, and dreading the consequences that might ensue from it to themselves, a messenger was instantly despatched in the king's name to the Duc de Guise, prohibiting him from making any hostile attack on the admiral. This order obeyed, would have put an end, it appears, to the whole of the sanguinary proceedings of that terrible day. But the messenger returned with the announcement that the order had arrived too late, and the queen and her sons, having recovered from their fright, "resolved to let matters take their course." *

Guise, with his uncle, D'Aumale, and the bastard of Angoulême — natural son of Henri II. —

* "*Discours de Henri III.*" This discourse, or recital, was dictated by the Duc d'Anjou, when King of Poland, to his principal physician, Miron, while suffering from sleeplessness and anxiety of mind occasioned by the vexation he felt at the affronts he met with from the German princes, who, because of the part he had played in the Saint-Bartholomew massacre, received him with extreme coldness on his journey to Cracow. It is generally regarded as authentic by French writers. It differs on several points from other narratives, which indeed one would expect it to do.

together with a whole band of assassins, led by a man named Bœsme, was already in the courtyard of the admiral's hôtel. At first the noise was attributed to some encounter between the Huguenots and Guise's partisans, but when the admiral became aware that it was an attack on him, "he requested the Calvinist minister, who was with him, to say a prayer." "He had long been quite disposed to die," he said, "and now commended his soul to his Saviour." Bœsme, at that moment, rushed into the room. The French guards closed round him. "Are you the admiral?" asked Bœsme. "I am, young man," he replied. "Do whatever you choose, for you have no power of yourself to make my life shorter than God has ordained it." Muttering one of the horrid oaths of that period, Bœsme thrust his spear into the admiral's breast. The rest of the band then advanced, and also plunged their spears into him, aided in their murderous work by the guards, whom the king, but two days before, had placed there for the admiral's protection. He now fell at their feet covered with wounds.*

"Bœsme," called the duke from the courtyard (he had not dared to face Coligny himself) — "Bœsme, have not you finished?" "The deed is

---

*Some accounts relate that the admiral defended himself with his sword, and afterwards with the bed-clothes, which must be an error, as on the previous day he had undergone two operations which would prevent him from using his sword with either hand.

done, and well done," answered Bœsme. "Then throw him out, that we may look at him." Out of the window the dying man was instantly thrown. He fell on his face; but the vile bastard kicked him over and wiped away the blood that hid his features, "that he might recognise him," he said. Guise, equally vile, also stooped and peered into his face, then spurned him with a kick. An Italian servant of the Guises cut off his head and sent it to the queen-mother, who ordered it to be embalmed and forwarded to the Pope. (It was never known whether this present safely reached his holiness.) The populace, who with yells of frantic joy assisted at this scene of blood, took up the headless corpse and dragged it through the streets, finally hanging it by the feet on a gibbet at Montfaucon.

Teligny, the admiral's son-in-law, and some other Huguenot nobles and gentlemen, thinking to escape by the roof of the admiral's hôtel, were hunted down and shot by the king's guards, who also fired on the Swiss Protestant troops who escorted the King of Navarre. All those whom the king had lodged in the Louvre were surprised in their beds, and killed before they could, in their bewilderment, attempt defence. The streets were now full of infuriate people, who were told that the Huguenots had risen in the night and attacked the king in the Louvre; that they had killed several of his guards and refused quarter. To

Henri, Duc de Guise.
Engraved by W. Wellstood.

avenge this attack, as they fancied, cruelties the most barbarous were inflicted on the helpless and unoffending. Passionate rage, vengeance, frenzy, fanaticism, presided at the horrible scenes that at every step met the eye on that fatal day. Maddened by excitement, the people rushed through the city, breathing only murder. Doors were forced in, houses pillaged, and the inhabitants killed — private hate availing itself of this opportunity of taking vengeance. The dead and the dying lay together in the streets, old men, women, and children — some of them the victims of a barbarous zeal, others of the cupidity of those who slew only the more effectually to rob. The robberies on the 24th and following days produced a large sum in money, besides jewelry and plate, the king, it was asserted, not disdaining to take his share of the booty.

Catherine and Anjou continually drew the king to the window, that there might be no doubt of his approval of the massacre. He, indeed, seemed to glory in the butchery that was going on around him; to be jealous of being deprived of the merit of so magnanimous a deed. "Kill! kill!" he cried, as he leaned from the window, and raved that "all was done by his order." Yet sometimes he seemed stupefied by this excess of carnage; again he was furious, levelling his carbine at every Huguenot he recognised, but the range of this weapon appears to have been too limited, happily, to do much mischief.

The King of Navarre and Prince de Condé were, by his order, brought before him, with the gentlemen of their suite. The latter he presently disposed of. "Send those scoundrels below!" he cried. No sooner had they left the room than the king's guards fell upon them, one or two only escaping with life. To the young princes he declared that, henceforth, he would tolerate in France no religion but his own, offering them the choice of "*Messe, mort, ou la Bastille.*" Henri of Navarre prayed the king "not to force his conscience." The Prince de Condé rejected the mass, but left death or the Bastille to the king's decision. Charles, however, gave them three days to consider the matter; but with the threat of death hanging over them should they refuse to abjure.

Although the greater part of the leaders and the chief men of the Huguenot cause were slain, yet a remnant escaped the "net of death," and lived for vengeance. They were those who either had not accepted the "king's proffered hospitality," or, for want of room at the admiral's hôtel, were lodged on the opposite bank of the river, in the Faubourg Saint-Germain-les-Prés. Awakened by the strange uproar and confusion of sounds that burst forth in Paris on the signal for the massacre being given — the howls, the yells, and hootings of the frenzied mob, mingled with the frequent reports of the arquebuse and pistol — they imagined that some serious riot had occurred, probably between Huguenot and Catholic. Hastily assembling, to aid, if needed, their own and the king's party, they proposed to cross the river, but found all the boats removed. Two or three bleeding corpses floated by them, and descending the Seine were several boats filled with the king's guards and led by Guise and his party, who fired on them as they advanced.

Comprehending from these acts and previous warnings that serious danger threatened them, they mounted their horses and fled. Guise and other massacrers prepared to follow; but the precautions taken to enclose in their net as many victims as possible, served others to effect their escape. The city gates had been locked, and for the Porte de Bussy, opening on the faubourg, the wrong keys were sent to Guise, causing a delay, which, though every exertion was used, rendered his and "the bastard's" pursuit useless. Charles, from the window of his apartment, was a witness of this scene. Stamping with rage and uttering a series of curses and horrible oaths, he cried in accents of agony, "*Ah! mort Dieu!* they fly, they escape!" But a scene then passing under his eyes, in the front of the Louvre just below him, must have soothed him in his then insane state of mind. Hundreds of his subjects who could not escape their doom — bleeding corpses, of which it was necessary to clear the streets — were being thrown into the Seine, leaving, as the stream carried them away, long streaks of blood behind them.*

On the morning of the 25th, Catherine and her "maids of honour," with the courtiers in attendance, went down to the entrance of the Louvre to examine the pile of dead and yet bleeding bodies, raised up as a trophy before the grand portail. "The maids," with their dishevelled hair and scanty attire, as they jested and gibed, and laughed at the revolting jokes of the queen-mother and courtiers, on the nakedness of some of the bodies and the clothing of others, seemed to represent the Furies, or Bacchanals drunk with the vapour of blood, instead of the juice of the grape.

The number of victims on the 24th and two following days in Paris has been variously estimated from two thousand to four or five thousand, and with the slaughter in the several provinces from twenty to thirty thousand. The anniversary of the Saint-Bartholomew was ordered by Charles to be "celebrated in perpetuity by a procession in Paris, and thanksgiving to God for saving the king and the state." A "jubilee extraordinary" took place on the 28th, at which Charles would have had the King of Navarre and Prince de Condé attend. But neither by persuasion nor menaces could he prevail on them to appear, or to follow afterwards in the procession. On the same day

* Brantôme says: "*Charles y prit grand plaisr.*"

the king's declaration was issued, professing "to make known the real cause and occasion of the death of the admiral and his accomplices."

A few days after, the chief officer of the Mint presented the king with two medals " commemorative of his victory." On one Charles was represented seated on his throne; beneath his feet was a heap of dead bodies. In one hand he bore the sceptre, in the other a sword and the palm of victory. The legend was *Virtus in rebelles.* On the reverse, laurel and olive branches surrounded the arms of France, with the device chosen for the king on his accession by De L'Hôpital, but accommodated to the occasion, *Pietas excitavit Justitiam*, instead of *Pietate et Justitiâ.* The other medal bore the king's effigy, with the legend in French, "*Charles IX., dompteur des rebelles,*" 24th August, 1572.

But while the massacre of the Huguenots was still going on in the provinces, and even in Paris, where it was found more difficult to stop it than Catherine expected, the news of that unparalleled crime spread through Europe. In the Protestant states it was received with one general cry of horror. The humane and tolerant Emperor Maximilian II. is said to have wept bitterly on hearing of the savage brutality of his son-in-law. Italy and Spain, on the contrary, burst forth into songs of joy and gladness, and the "Demon of the South" "laughed for the first time in his life."

No expressions could he find sufficiently strong, ardent, and full of meaning, to convey to his "most Christian majesty" his profound admiration of so holy a deed. The conduct of the queen-mother also excited his high approval; nor did he exclude Anjou and the Guises from their share in his commendations, but pronounced their efforts in the service of God and the Church most praiseworthy. He then bade them all "continue in well-doing," offering his aid to Catherine and her son for the completion of their great work. He feigned, too, to believe all that Catherine told him of the king's pretended hostility to Spain in order to more effectually deceive the Huguenots.

As regarded Rome, not even "Saint-Pius" himself could have displayed more enthusiasm than did Gregory XIII. on receiving intelligence of this deed of blood. Every street in Rome was ablaze with bonfires; bells rang out joyously; the cannon of San-Angelo thundered forth in the face of heaven the infamous act that was called "the good news." Gregory and his cardinals, with the ambassadors and a swarm of priests, went in procession from church to church, concluding with a mass of thanksgiving to God for the double victory of the Church, over the Turks at Lepanto and the heretics in Paris. The Cardinal de Lorraine was beside himself with joy, as well may be imagined from the fact that, in his enthusiasm, he — who so loved to put money in his purse, but so disliked to take any out of it — actually gave a thousand crowns to the messenger who brought him the news of that "glorious work" in which his nephew and brother had so greatly distinguished themselves. He overwhelmed the king, queen-mother, and Anjou with congratulatory compliments. "They had achieved on that great day of extermination more than he had ever dared hope to see, or even pray for."

"May it please Heaven to send the Poles a truly Catholic king," prayed Gregory, "for they are a nation proud and haughty rather than submissive." This was a message for Anjou. Further, in celebration of the great event, the pontiff ordered of the painter Vasari that horrible picture of the massacre of the Huguenots, for the adornment of the Vatican, and from the inscription — *Pontifex Colignii necem probat* — one must infer for his own glorification also. A medal, too, was struck, having on one side the effigy of Gregory XIII.; on the other, the exterminating angel slaying the Huguenots, and around it *Hugonotorum strages*. Venice was not behindhand in congratulatory addresses, and the Pope sent a legate expressly to offer his felicitations to the court; also to suggest the establishment in Paris, at this favourable moment, of the holy Inquisition, and to propose a marriage between the Duc d'Anjou and an infanta of Spain.

But the king and queen-mother began to be

much embarrassed by these extravagant compliments and felicitations, and, in order to avoid receiving the congratulations of the legate, absented themselves from Paris on his arrival. So cold and distrustful was the attitude of the rest of Europe towards them, that they were compelled to request their admiring friends to be more moderate in their praises, and less demonstrative in their enthusiasm, as they were desirous of assigning to the events of "that great day" a political rather than a religious motive.

END OF VOL. I.

www.ingramcontent.com/pod-product-compliance
Lightning Source LLC
Chambersburg PA
CBHW030214170426
43201CB00006B/82